Windows® Graphics Programming

Windows® Graphics Programming

Julio Sanchez

Maria P. Canton

IDG Books Worldwide, Inc.
An International Data Group Company

Foster City, CA ◆ Chicago, IL ◆ Indianapolis, IN ◆ New York, NY

IDG BOOKS WORLDWIDE

Windows® Graphics Programming

Published by
M&T Books
an imprint of IDG Books Worldwide, Inc.
An International Data Group Company
919 E. Hillsdale Blvd., Suite 400
Foster City, CA 94404
www.idgbooks.com (IDG Books Worldwide Web site)

ISBN: 0-7645-3251-0

Printed in the United States of America

10 9 8 7 6 5 4 3 2 1

1B/QW/QW/ZZ/FC

Distributed in the United States by IDG Books Worldwide, Inc.

Distributed by CDG Books Canada Inc. for Canada; by Transworld Publishers Limited in the United Kingdom; by IDG Norge Books for Norway; by IDG Sweden Books for Sweden; by Woodslane Pty. Ltd. for Australia; by Woodslane (NZ) Ltd. for New Zealand; by TransQuest Publishers Pte Ltd. for Singapore, Malaysia, Thailand, Indonesia, and Hong Kong; by ICG Muse, Inc. for Japan; by Norma Comunicaciones S.A. for Colombia; by Intersoft for South Africa; by Le Monde en Tique for France; by International Thomson Publishing for Germany, Austria and Switzerland; by Distribuidora Cuspide for Argentina; by Livraria Cultura for Brazil; by Ediciones ZETA S.C.R. Ltda. for Peru; by WS Computer Publishing Corporation, Inc., for the Philippines; by Contemporanea de Ediciones for Venezuela; by Express Computer Distributors for the Caribbean and West Indies; by Micronesia Media Distributor, Inc. for Micronesia; by Grupo Editorial Norma S.A. for Guatemala; by Chips Computadoras S.A. de C.V. for Mexico; by Editorial Norma de Panama S.A. for Panama; by American Bookshops for Finland. Authorized Sales Agent: Anthony Rudkin Associates for the Middle East and North Africa.

For general information on IDG Books Worldwide's books in the U.S., please call our Consumer Customer Service department at 800-762-2974. For reseller information, including discounts and premium sales, please call our Reseller Customer Service department at 800-434-3422.

For information on where to purchase IDG Books Worldwide's books outside the U.S., please contact our International Sales department at 317-596-5530 or fax 317-596-5692.

For consumer information on foreign language translations, please contact our Customer Service department at 800-434-3422, fax 317-596-5692, or e-mail rights@idgbooks.com.

For information on licensing foreign or domestic rights, please phone +1-650-655-3109.

For sales inquiries and special prices for bulk quantities, please contact our Sales department at 650-655-3200 or write to the address above.

For information on using IDG Books Worldwide's books in the classroom or for ordering examination copies, please contact our Educational Sales department at 800-434-2086 or fax 317-596-5499.

For press review copies, author interviews, or other publicity information, please contact our Public Relations department at 650-655-3000 or fax 650-655-3299.

For authorization to photocopy items for corporate, personal, or educational use, please contact Copyright Clearance Center, 222 Rosewood Drive, Danvers, MA 01923, or fax 978-750-4470.

Library of Congress Cataloging-in-Publication Data
Sanchez, Julio, [DATE]
Windows graphics programming / Julio Sanchez, Maria P. Canton.
p. cm.
ISBN 0-7645-3251-0
1. Computer graphics. 2. Microsoft Windows (Computer file)
I. Canton, Maria P. II. Title
T385.S2493 1999
006.6'8684--dc21

99-23531
CIP

ABOUT IDG BOOKS WORLDWIDE

Welcome to the world of IDG Books Worldwide.

IDG Books Worldwide, Inc., is a subsidiary of International Data Group, the world's largest publisher of computer-related information and the leading global provider of information services on information technology. IDG was founded more than 30 years ago by Patrick J. McGovern and now employs more than 9,000 people worldwide. IDG publishes more than 290 computer publications in over 75 countries. More than 90 million people read one or more IDG publications each month.

Launched in 1990, IDG Books Worldwide is today the #1 publisher of best-selling computer books in the United States. We are proud to have received eight awards from the Computer Press Association in recognition of editorial excellence and three from Computer Currents' First Annual Readers' Choice Awards. Our best-selling *...For Dummies®* series has more than 50 million copies in print with translations in 31 languages. IDG Books Worldwide, through a joint venture with IDG's Hi-Tech Beijing, became the first U.S. publisher to publish a computer book in the People's Republic of China. In record time, IDG Books Worldwide has become the first choice for millions of readers around the world who want to learn how to better manage their businesses.

Our mission is simple: Every one of our books is designed to bring extra value and skill-building instructions to the reader. Our books are written by experts who understand and care about our readers. The knowledge base of our editorial staff comes from years of experience in publishing, education, and journalism — experience we use to produce books to carry us into the new millennium. In short, we care about books, so we attract the best people. We devote special attention to details such as audience, interior design, use of icons, and illustrations. And because we use an efficient process of authoring, editing, and desktop publishing our books electronically, we can spend more time ensuring superior content and less time on the technicalities of making books.

You can count on our commitment to deliver high-quality books at competitive prices on topics you want to read about. At IDG Books Worldwide, we continue in the IDG tradition of delivering quality for more than 30 years. You'll find no better book on a subject than one from IDG Books Worldwide.

IDG BOOKS WORLDWIDE

John Kilcullen
Chairman and CEO
IDG Books Worldwide, Inc.

Steven Berkowitz
President and Publisher
IDG Books Worldwide, Inc.

VIII WINNER — *Eighth Annual Computer Press Awards 1992*

IX WINNER — *Ninth Annual Computer Press Awards 1993*

COMPUTER CURRENTS 1995 READERS' CHOICE 1995

X WINNER — *Tenth Annual Computer Press Awards 1994*

XI WINNER — *Eleventh Annual Computer Press Awards 1995*

IDG is the world's leading IT media, research and exposition company. Founded in 1964, IDG had 1997 revenues of $2.05 billion and has more than 9,000 employees worldwide. IDG offers the widest range of media options that reach IT buyers in 75 countries representing 95% of worldwide IT spending. IDG's diverse product and services portfolio spans six key areas including print publishing, online publishing, expositions and conferences, market research, education and training, and global marketing services. More than 90 million people read one or more of IDG's 290 magazines and newspapers, including IDG's leading global brands — Computerworld, PC World, Network World, Macworld and the Channel World family of publications. IDG Books Worldwide is one of the fastest-growing computer book publishers in the world, with more than 700 titles in 36 languages. The "...For Dummies®" series alone has more than 50 million copies in print. IDG offers online users the largest network of technology-specific Web sites around the world through IDG.net (http://www.idg.net), which comprises more than 225 targeted Web sites in 55 countries worldwide. International Data Corporation (IDC) is the world's largest provider of information technology data, analysis and consulting, with research centers in over 41 countries and more than 400 research analysts worldwide. IDG World Expo is a leading producer of more than 168 globally branded conferences and expositions in 35 countries including E3 (Electronic Entertainment Expo), Macworld Expo, ComNet, Windows World Expo, ICE (Internet Commerce Expo), Agenda, DEMO, and Spotlight. IDG's training subsidiary, ExecuTrain, is the world's largest computer training company, with more than 230 locations worldwide and 785 training courses. IDG Marketing Services helps industry-leading IT companies build international brand recognition by developing global integrated marketing programs via IDG's print, online and exposition products worldwide. Further information about the company can be found at www.idg.com. 1/24/99

Credits

ACQUISITIONS EDITOR
John Osborn

DEVELOPMENT EDITORS
Matthew E. Lusher
Doug Lloyd
Robert Kern, TIPS Technical Publishing, Inc.

TECHNICAL EDITOR
Richard Wright

COPY EDITOR
Amy Eoff

PRODUCTION
IDG Books Worldwide Production

PROOFREADING AND INDEXING
York Production Services

COVER DESIGN
© mike parsons design

About the Authors

Julio Sanchez is an associate professor of Computer Science at Minnesota State University, Mankato. He is the author of numerous books on computer programming. His books have been translated into Chinese, Japanese, and Korean.

Maria P. Canton is the executive vice president of Skipanon Software-Associates, a software development and consulting firm. She teaches at Minnesota State University, Mankato, and is the author of several computer books.

Preface

This book is about Windows programming and Windows graphics using C++. It assumes that you have a basic understanding of C or C++, but it does not require knowledge of object-oriented topics nor of Windows programming. We have used C++ instead of plain C because some Windows functions are easier to code in C++. In fact, the first five chapters of the book are an introduction to Windows programming at the API level. They provide the necessary information and skills for developing Windows graphics applications. In summary: this book is for you if you have a basic knowledge of C or C++ and want to learn how to develop Windows graphics programs.

About This Book

The book covers Windows 95, 98, and NT 4, not NT 5 (Windows 2000), which at the time of this writing had not yet been released to the public. We concentrate on the graphics programming mainstream; therefore, the emphasis is on Windows 95 and Windows 98. Exclusive features of Windows NT are sometimes mentioned, but not covered in detail.

We approach Windows programming at its most basic level, that is, using the Windows Application Programming Interface (API). This book does not discuss the Microsoft Foundation Class Library (MFC) or other wrapper functions that are furnished as part of commercial development environments. Microsoft's MFC is an object-oriented framework that encapsulates many of the functions in the API. It is intended for use in conjunction with Developer's Studio App Wizard, which facilitates the creation of a program skeleton for a Windows application. In spite of these conveniences, most Windows programs that require even moderate levels of performance are developed and coded at the API level. One reason is that MFC introduces an unnecessary overhead that slows down execution and limits the program's functionality, limitations that are particularly intolerable in graphics programming. Another objection to using wrapper libraries is that the additional interface requirements, instead of facilitating development, just get in the way. A third reason that programmers mention for not using the class libraries is that programs created with them tend to look like each other, as well as like a standard Windows product. Most developers want their graphics programs to have a certain uniqueness that sets them apart from the group.

Although we do not use wrapper functions, we do rely heavily on other tools from the development environment. The Visual C++ package includes resource editors for creating menus, dialog boxes, icons, bitmaps, and other standard program components. We take advantage of these development facilities since there are no advantages to hand-coding these program elements.

The development environment used in the book is Visual C++ versions 5 and 6 – either one works well. Because we do not use the Foundation Class Library, most of the code can easily be ported to other systems. Users of products such as Borland C++ Builder will find few problems in moving our code and projects into these environments.

In Parts III and IV we discuss graphics programming using some of the components of Microsoft's DirectX Software Development Kit. This environment, originally intended for developing computer games, makes it possible to achieve high-performance graphics by allowing direct access to video memory and to the hardware features of the video card. Practically every graphics application can benefit from these enhanced facilities. DirectX 6.1, the current version of the SDK, is the one discussed in the book. The DirectX 6.1 SDK is furnished in the book's CD-ROM.

The Sample Programs

The suitability of code listings in computer books has always been a controversial topic. At one extreme are books with little or no code listings, or with short code snippets that are missing so many details that they are useless as programming samples. At the other extreme are books that list entire programs, often repeating the same functions and routines. As programmers, we appreciate the value of a code sample that compiles and runs as described. In many cases this is all we need to solve the problem at hand. At the same time, it is wasteful to relist the same code over and over again. Our approach is to reference the specific processing routines and code fragments that are necessary for illustrating the point at hand. Program listing are found in the CD-ROM.

We are often troubled by examples that are unnecessarily complicated: it is as if the authors are trying to impress and baffle us with their coding skills. We think that each example should be the simplest possible illustration of the problem being discussed, without being trivial. When the coding gets too complicated it becomes difficult to follow and we often give up in frustration. We have tried to maintain a middle-ground approach throughout the text.

The book's CD-ROM contains all of the programs, projects, and templates discussed in the book. Each project is located in its own directory and contains all of the files necessary for recreating the samples using Visual C++ versions 5 or 6. The executables were created using the Debug configuration of Developer Studio, although there are a few cases in which the Release configuration is also provided. The authors or the publisher make no copyright claims regarding the code listings, which you are free to copy, edit, or reuse in any way you see fit.

Technical Level

One of the most difficult questions regarding a book's contents is whether it is elementary, intermediate, or advanced. In the first place, the terms are relative. A programmer struggling with the fundamentals of a language may consider a particular book to be advanced, while this same book may be quite basic to someone who has already learned the elementary material. Another issue to consider is that most books do not sustain the same technical level throughout their contents. In writing a tutorial we often start with the most elementary topics, move on to intermediate ones, and conclude with the more advanced issues. Allowing for this uncertainty, we think that this book should be classified as intermediate because this is the level that is most often sustained; notwithstanding the fact that the first chapters in the book serve as an elementary tutorial, and the chapters at the end of the book contain some topics that could be considered rather advanced.

Portability Issues in Graphics Programming

The use of some graphics products, such as DirectX, often introduces a certain level of device dependency. The literature about these products sometimes exaggerates the importance of maintaining universal software compatibility with all Windows machines. It is true that in the case of applications intended for a mass market the vendor usually strives to make the product compatible with as many systems as possible, even if in marginal machines, performance or graphics quality is not optimal. But many Windows graphics programs are high-tech products, developed for specialty markets. In this case a certain degree of device-dependency is not only tolerable, but even expected. A typical case is a high-end computer-assisted design (CAD) program, which typically requires specific system, video, and data-input hardware. Furthermore, many graphics applications are furnished as dedicated workstations, in which the vendor supplies both the hardware and the software components. In such cases the developer need not be overly concerned with some loss of portability in order to ensure the necessary quality or performance of a software product.

Acknowledgments

It has often been said, in many different ways, that producing a book is a collective effort. This is particularly true of a technical book. Starting with the refinement of the original ideas for the book's plan, and ending with the last grammatical detail, it takes many minds and much hard work to bring a book project to fruition. In the case of *Windows Graphics Programming*, we have been very fortunate to have the support of many talented and dedicated collaborators. John Osborn, Senior Acquisitions Editor, has been an invaluable support by providing many ideas of his own and serving as a sounding board for ours. Matt Lusher, Senior Development Editor, directed the book's production and supervised the editing process. Robert Kern, of TIPS Technical Publishing, was in charge of the developmental and technical editing. Doug Loyd was the Developmental Editor and Richard S. Wright Jr. of Starstone Software Systems, Inc. was the Technical Editor. The book owes much to their expertise. Amy Eoff did the copyediting. We are very grateful to all of them.

Contents at a Glance

Contents

Part II API Graphics

Part I

Windows API Programming: Getting Down to the New Metal

CHAPTER 1:
Computer Graphics and Its Applications

CHAPTER 2:
Event-driven Programming

CHAPTER 3:
API Programming

CHAPTER 4:
Application Support Services

CHAPTER 5:
Graphics Support Services

Chapter 1

Computer Graphics and Its Applications

IN THIS CHAPTER

- The graphics language and pictorial perception
- Overview of graphics technology
- Image properties
- The human element in a graphics system
- Esthetics and computer graphics
- Graphics applications

THIS FIRST CHAPTER discusses the art, science, and technology of computer graphics. It was designed to serve a triple purpose. First, to provide background information about graphics technology; second, to present the major fields of application of computer graphics; third, to ignite your imagination regarding the possibilities of cutting-edge graphics topics such as simulations, artificial life, virtual reality, and fractals.

This chapter begins with a discussion about how our minds are able to extract information from a picture, and how we are sometimes able to think visually. Next, we consider the graphics properties of an image and how these properties are measured. The human element is also an important factor in computer graphics: how and what we see must be taken into consideration when creating graphics images. Since most graphics must be visually pleasant, we discuss composition, shape, depth perception, light, color, and other topics that relate to the aesthetics of computer graphics. The chapter concludes with a brief description of the most important and popular fields of application.

Aside from basic terminology and technical concepts, the content of this chapter is not linked to the rest of the book. It is designed to serve as background information, as a reference, and to help you design more effective graphics imagery. If you are anxious to get into the programming, you can skip this chapter without affecting your ability to understand the rest of the book.

The Language of Graphics

An interesting capability of the human mind is its power to extract the fundamental elements of a thought or idea and to condense them into a pictorial representation. In other words, to make a sketch, a drawing, or a picture. Also admirable is the mind's ability to infer an idea from an image. A common road sign found in many rural highways of the United States is the symbol of a jumping deer (see Figure 1-1). To most of us this image conveys several messages: that there are deer in the area, that these animals may cross the roadway, and that care should be taken to avoid a possible collision. It would be very difficult to compose a textual message that transmitted this amount of information in a manner as forceful and as condensed as this graphic symbol. Additionally, graphics convey a message to drivers without relying on their ability to understand any one single language.

Figure 1-1: A simple picture effectively conveys a message.

Pictures were used by our cave-dwelling ancestors as a means of conveying information. It has been speculated that written languages originated in pictures of familiar objects, and evolved with the simplification of these graphic symbols. In Egyptian hieroglyphics many of the original objects are still recognizable. In the modern world, these pictorial origins are evident in the characters of oriental languages.

Pictorial Perception

The individual gains awareness of the surrounding world through a process called *perception*. For centuries philosophers have debated about the physical mechanisms and the mental transformations that take place during this acquisition and exchange of information. Such investigations concern the psychological processes of creating and interpreting words, pictures, and models as substitutes for reality. The most important vehicle for this form of secondhand perception is language: languages are so important in our culture that a substantial part of our education is spent in learning them. However, pictures and symbols are also often used as a means of acquiring and transmitting information. Pictorial representations are the most effective method of conveying a message. However, we do not receive formal training for the creation and interpretation of pictures and symbols. Instead, we rely mostly on intuition to help us use graphic symbols, and we hope that we understand the intended message.

A historical explanation of the mechanism of perception is based on the assumption that ideas exist and can be transmitted. According to this theory, symbols carry ideas intrinsically. But this intuitive explanation of perception introduces concepts as mysterious as those that it tries to explain. A more satisfactory definition, originally proposed by James J. Gibson, describes the symbol as a surrogate stimulus produced by another individual. According to Gibson, by nature, humans are inclined to make surrogates, which can take the form of vocal sounds, body mimicry, drawings, paintings, writings, sculptures, models, or even musical sounds.

It is likely that the most important consequence of using such symbols is that they allow another person to comprehend events and objects perceived by the symbol-maker. But it is interesting to note that the symbol-making process also involves self-stimulation. The speaker hears and is gratified by his or her own voice, artists find pleasure in their own drawings, paintings, or sculptures, writers in their verse or prose, and composers in their own music. The symbol-maker is also a symbol-perceiver, and often is not a very good judge of the worth or value of his or her own symbols.

Visual Thinking

Charles W. Morris points out in his book, *Signs, Language and Behaviors* (see bibliography) that the circular response in the symbol-maker and perceiver explains how a vocal sound is converted into a symbol and how the cycle of symbol creation and perception takes place even in the absence of other persons, and even in the absence of stimulating objects. In children, this stage of development can be identified with the beginning of the thinking stage. Because this circular pattern can exist with nonverbal symbols, it is reasonable to assume that the process of thinking can take place in terms of graphic images, as well as in words or other purely intellectual symbols.

Visual thinking can be demonstrated by describing two possible mental paths for calculating the time of day. For example, if at ten minutes to 11:00 you are told to calculate the time one-half hour later, you can proceed arithmetically, as follows:

11' 50" + 30" = 11' 80" = 11' + 1' + (80" - 60") = 12' 20"

Or you can visualize the face of the clock and mentally divide it in half, as shown in Figure 1-2.

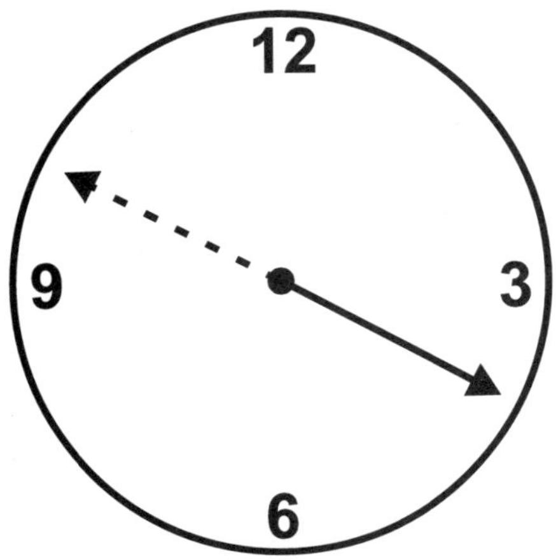

Figure 1-2: Visual thinking on a clock face

In the preceding examples, one solution is obtained by performing arithmetic calculations, probably with little reference to external images. In the other you used a mental image of a clock's face to arrive at the solution. Some people find that the digital clock is not as satisfactory a timepiece as the conventional dial-faced clocks, because the digital clock does not reflect our visual image of time.

But visual images are not available to match every intellectual concept. The more abstract a concept, the harder it is to find an image that corresponds to it. The word *animal*, for example, includes so many species with dissimilar appearances and characteristics that it is impossible to find a valid graphic symbol that includes all of them. A number in the millions is also hard to visualize in terms of individual units. Yet, we can visualize the concept of the animal kingdom and of millions of dollars in our minds. This has led some Western authors to the conclusion that thinking takes place independently of perceptual experience, which is to say that thinking happens in terms of words and numbers alone.

During the 18th, 19th, and even part of the 20th century, perceptual experience was often considered sensual and even sinful. Visual images were thought to serve no other purpose than to distract the senses. Mathematics books used in universities during that period contained very few drawings and illustrations. At that time, mathematicians thought that sketches and drawings should be used sparingly to illustrate specific points, and that mathematical truths and demonstrations had to be grasped conceptually.

Today, we are much more aware of the importance of pictures in the generation and communication of thoughts. We encourage our children to represent their ideas pictorially. It is no longer considered undignified to include sketches and drawings in a book on calculus. But we are still far from understanding the part that graphic images play in our mental processes. We know we have an inborn capacity to express ourselves graphically, but, for lack of understanding, we rely mostly on instinct and intuition for the creation of these images. The impressionist painters were among the greatest graphics experimenters of all time. Their discoveries have changed most of our aesthetic and perceptual conceptions.

Graphics Technology

Oscilloscopes are laboratory instruments that use a cathode ray tube (CRT) for graphic display. The oscilloscope performs manipulations and calculations of the input signal to display the graph of the electric or electronic wave on a fluorescent screen. In this sense, the oscilloscope is a graphic machine, but its major contribution to computer graphics was its demonstration of the feasibility of using the CRT for displaying electronically generated images.

An interactive graphic system is one in which the user can create or modify the graphic images displayed on the CRT. The first interactive computer graphic devices were developed in the 1950s for military use. The Sage tactical air defense system was a multi-user graphics system that employed feedback signals generated by light pens. A *light pen* is an input device that allows the entering of information into a system through the computer screen or a separate photosensitive surface. In the early 1960s, Ivan Sutherland and his associates at the Lincoln Laboratory of the Massachusetts Institute of Technology developed a graphic system named SKETCHPAD for the TX-2 computer. SKETCHPAD uses a light-pen input for interactive graphics. Many of the principles and operations of SKETCHPAD became standards for future graphic systems.

In the following sections we present a general overview of computer graphics hardware. Some of the devices and systems described are of historical interest. In such cases, the presentation is brief. Other descriptions actually correspond to graphic systems currently in use.

Primary Graphic Hardware

Graphic devices have become greatly diversified in the last decade. Plotters, dot-matrix, ink-jet, and laser printers; light pens, digitizer tablets, pointing devices, and several types of CRT video screens are all considered graphics hardware. It is possible to distinguish between primary and secondary graphics devices. *Primary devices* are those that take part in the creation and display of the original image. Included in this group are the CRT, the graphics-control devices, and in some systems, the memory area dedicated to the graphic function. The secondary graphics devices are typically used for input and output; and include for example, the keyboard, mouse, digitizer tablet, and printers and plotters.

The technologies most used for CRT displays can be grouped as follows:

- Storage-tube display
- Vector-refresh display
- Raster-scan display

The Storage-tube Display

From a hardware point of view, the storage tube display is the simplest CRT display. The tube is coated with a specially formulated phosphor that, when struck by an electron beam remains fluorescent for up to one hour. This enables the cathode ray tube to serve both as a display and as a storage device, hence the name storage tube. The entire display can be erased by flooding the tube with a voltage that turns the phosphor to its dark state. Because of this mode of operation, specific screen areas or lines cannot be individually erased, which makes animation practically impossible on these systems.

Another disadvantage of the storage-tube display system is that to make a change in a displayed element, the entire image must be redrawn. In addition, the contrast is low and the system has no color capabilities. Consequently, interaction with a storage-tube system is slower and more difficult than with the other types of CRTs. Therefore, in spite of its inherent simplicity, the long-persistence or storage-tube displays are seldom used in modern graphic systems and never in microcomputer graphics.

Vector-refresh Displays

In contrast with storage tube displays, the vector-refresh display uses a short-persistence phosphor that must be reactivated 30 to 50 times per second. Figure 1-3 shows the operation of a simplified vector-refresh CRT.

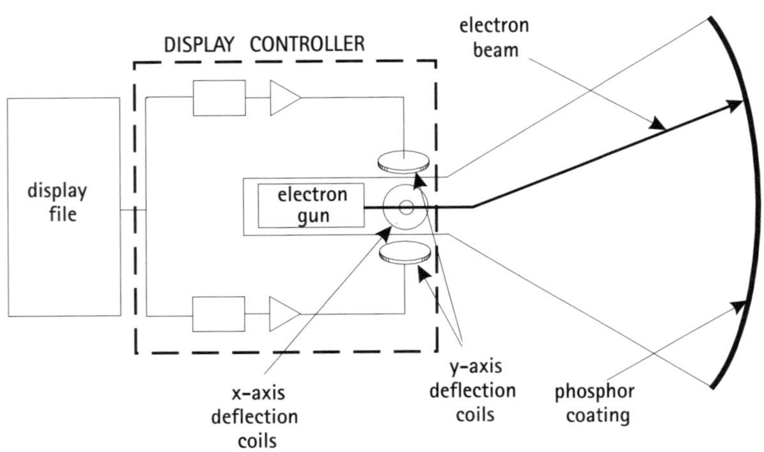

Figure 1-3: Diagram of a CRT display system

In addition to the cathode ray tube, a vector-refresh system requires a *display file* and a *display controller.* The display file is a memory area that holds the instructions for drawing the graphics objects. The display controller reads this information from the display file and transforms it into instructions for the electronic components of the CRT.

Vector-refresh displays offer the following advantages over storage-tube displays: selective erasure of screen elements, a high degree of interaction with the operator, and the capability for transforming images by translating, scaling, or rotating them. The main disadvantages of the vector-refresh CRT are its high cost and its limited color capabilities.

Raster-scan Displays

Until the late sixties, the only graphics display devices available were the expensive storage-tube and vector-refresh CRTs. Since then, important advances have taken place in television technology that made the use of mass-produced components as display devices feasible for computer systems. The pioneer research along these lines was made by Conrac Corporation. This company took advantage of the methods of image refreshing used in television receivers, as well as other television standards, equipment, and concepts, to develop a new computer image-processing technology known as *raster-scan graphics.*

Figure 1-4 shows the path followed by the electron beam of a raster-scan display. The scanning cycle takes place 50 to 70 times per second. At the start of each horizontal line the controller turns on the electron beam. The beam is turned off during the horizontal and vertical retrace cycles.

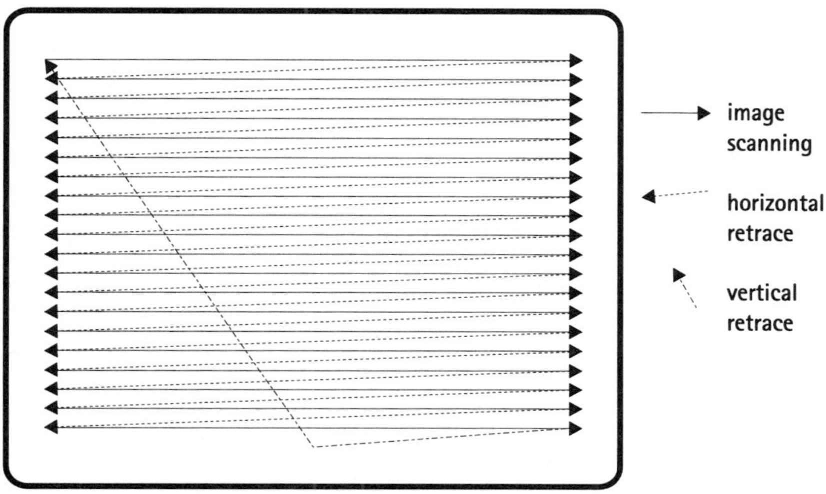

Figure 1-4: Raster path of the electron beam

The display surface of a raster-scan CRT is physically divided into a pattern of individual dots, generally called *pixels*. This word is derived from the words *picture* and *element*. An area of RAM is usually reserved to record the state of each individual screen pixel. The simplest storage scheme corresponds to a black-and-white display system. In such a case, each pixel requires a single bit in the screen memory area. If the memory bit is set, the display scanner lights the corresponding pixel. If the memory bit is cleared, the pixel is left dark. The area of memory reserved for the screen display is frequently called the *frame buffer* or the *video buffer*, and the entire video system is said to be *memory mapped*. Figure 1-5 shows the basic elements of a memory-mapped, black-and-white display.

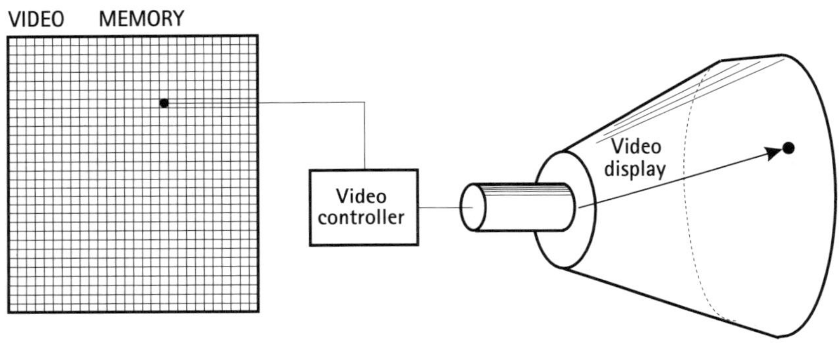

Figure 1-5: A memory-mapped, black-and-white video system

A more complicated scheme is required for memory-mapped systems with color displays. In this case, the CRT is equipped with several electron guns; one for each color that is used in activating the pixels. In the following description, we assume a color display with a red, a green, and a blue component, usually called an *RGB system*. Three separate memory maps are required for storing the state of each individual pixel. Memory map R reflects the state of the red component in the pixel. Memory maps G and B hold the state of the green and blue components respectively. If the R, G, and B bits for a certain pixel are on, all three color guns are used in activating the pixel, which is white. If only the R and G bits are on, the pixel is illuminated by the red and green guns and its resulting color is yellow. Table 1-1 shows the possible color combinations with red, green, and blue lights.

Table 1-1 COLOR COMBINATION WITH RED, GREEN AND BLUE LIGHTS

Number	Red	Green	Blue	Color
1	0	0	0	Black

Number	Red	Green	Blue	Color
2	1	0	0	Red
3	0	1	0	Green
4	0	0	1	Blue
5	1	1	0	Yellow
6	1	0	1	Magenta
7	0	1	1	Cyan
8	1	1	1	White

All the graphics hardware systems used in personal computers are of the memory-mapped, raster-scan type. The advantages of raster-scan displays are the low cost, color capabilities, and the rapid interaction with the user or operator. The main disadvantage is a consequence of the physical structure of the display: lines that are not vertical, horizontal, or at exactly 45 degrees exhibit a staircase effect, technically known as *aliasing*. Figure 1-6 shows this effect on pixel-structured CRTs.

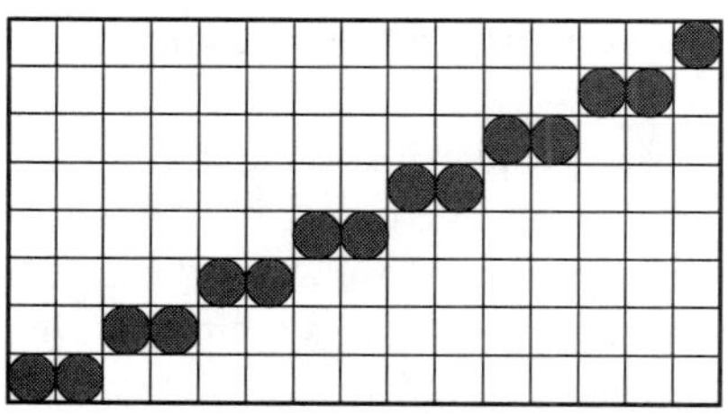

Figure 1-6: Staircase effect on a pixel grid

The raster-scan CRT is also limited in its animation capabilities. Two factors contribute to this problem: one, in raster-scan displays all the screen pixels must be updated with each image change; two, to ensure smoothness, the successive images that create the illusion of motion must be flashed on the screen at a fast rate. These constraints place a large processing load on the display system; only sophisticated hardware is capable of performing these changes fast enough to achieve satisfactory results.

Image Properties

The ideal computer graphics system displays a full-color, 3-D image, with very high resolution, animated in a lifelike fashion. Present day technology is still far from this ideal.

The purpose of the computer graphic image is to create a surrogate of reality that conveys visual information. The surrogate is usually a light pattern displayed on a CRT monitor. Some of the characteristics of this image can be scientifically measured, or at least, evaluated objectively. Other features cannot be so readily analyzed, because the human element in the perception of the graphic image introduces factors that are not easily measured. Aesthetic considerations, for instance, can help decide that a certain graphic image "looks better" than another one. At the same time, an eyestrain headache can annul many technological virtues.

Brightness and Contrast

Luminance is the light intensity per unit area reflected or emitted by a surface. The human eye perceives objects by detecting differences in color values or levels of luminance. Increasing the brightness of an object also increases the acuity with which it is perceived. However, its visibility or legibility is more dependent on contrast than on the absolute values of color or brightness.

The angular visual acuity of an average observer is estimated to sustain an arc of approximately one minute. This means that, while viewing a CRT display at a typical distance of 18 inches, the average observer can resolve an object that measures five one-thousands of an inch across. Note that an 8-inch wide display, like the ones used in many conventional computer video systems, can have as many as 1600 pixels per row.

Acuity falls rapidly with decreased luminance levels and with reduced contrast. This is the reason why ambient light, reflected off the surface of a CRT, decreases legibility. Another peculiarity of human vision is the decreasing ability of the eye to perceive luminance differences or contrasts as the absolute brightness increases. This accounts for the fact that absolute luminance values between object and background are less important to visual perception than the relative luminance, or contrast.

Color

Approximately three-fourths of the light-perceiving cells in the human eye are color-blind. This helps explain why luminance and contrast are more important to visual perception than color. Nevertheless, it is generally accepted that color capability is a valuable enhancement in a computer graphic system. This opinion is probably based on the popular belief that color photography, cinematography, and television are preferred over the black-and-white versions.

Resolution

In a raster-scan CRT the resolution of the display surface is determined by the total number of separately addressable pixels contained per unit area. The simplest way to express resolution is in pixels-per-inch. For example, a CRT with eight-inch rows containing a total of 640 pixels has a horizontal resolution of 80 pixels per inch. By the same token, a CRT measuring six inches vertically and containing a total of 480 pixels per column has a vertical resolution of 80 pixels per inch.

If the vertical and the horizontal resolutions of a CRT are equal, as in the previous case, the pixel structure forms a symmetrical grid. However, if the vertical and horizontal resolutions are different, the pixel grid is asymmetrical. It is easy to see that a symmetrical pixel grid facilitates plotting on the screen surface. The programmer can treat a symmetrical screen as if it were quadrille graphing paper. Figure 1-7 shows symmetrical and asymmetrical screen grid patterns.

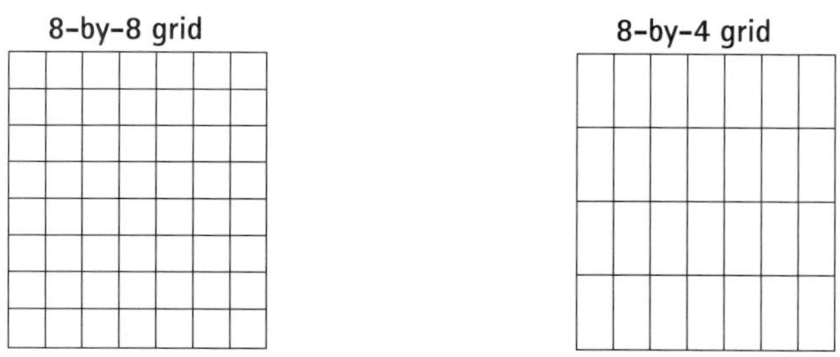

Figure 1-7: Symmetrical and asymmetrical screen grids

Aspect Ratio

The aspect ratio of a CRT display is the relation between the horizontal and vertical dimensions. For example, the CRT mentioned in the previous paragraph, measuring eight inches horizontally and six inches vertically is said to have a 4:3 aspect ratio. An eight inch by eight inch display has a 1:1 aspect ratio. Figure 1.8 shows a CRT with a 4:3 aspect ratio.

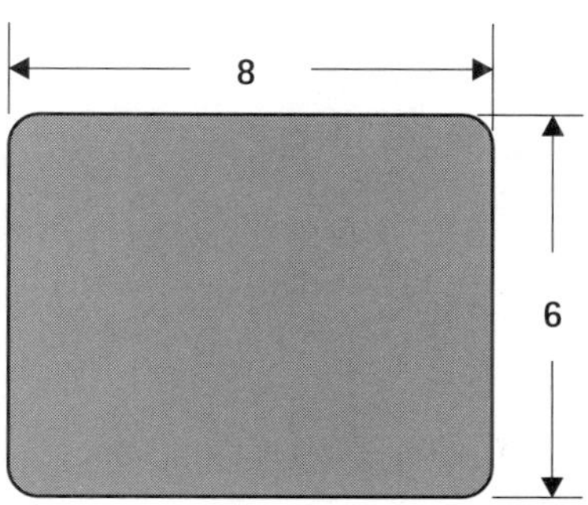

Figure 1-8: CRT with 4:3 aspect ratio

Access to the Display Elements

In a conventional graphics system, each pixel must be accessed every time that the screen image is changed. A simple and direct way for controlling a pixel array is to have a signal source connected to each pixel. But considering that a display of 640 by 480 pixels contains 307,200 individual elements, you can see that the number of circuits required for directly accessing each element results in an excessively complicated network.

Multiplexing and Time-sharing

The word *multiplexing* is used to describe the process by which a single facility is able to handle more than one operation. The best known multiplexing technique is *time-sharing*, also called *time-division multiplexing* or TDM. In time-sharing, the system assigns a time period, called a *time slot* or *time slice*, to several sharing components or devices. A familiar case of multiplexing is a network server and several terminals. Here, the computer's operating system schedules the resources to each workstation or terminal for very short time periods. The sequence of time slots occurs so rapidly that the user is not aware that the system is being shared with other users.

The method called *scan addressing*, developed by television technology and used in the raster-scan CRT, provides a practical way of dramatically reducing the circuitry required for CRT operation. Scan addressing is a multiplexing technique based on time-sharing. In Figures 1-3 and 1-4, you saw how an electron beam can be deflected along the *x*- and *y*-axes so that the entire pattern of phosphor dots is scanned in a raster-like fashion. In this case, a single signal from the electron gun is time-shared by all the elements on the CRT surface. The *x* and *y* deflector signals provide the scan-addressing function, directing the electron beam to the desired pixel. The 307,200 addressing lines that would be required for controlling the individual pixels on a 640 by 480 display are reduced to three lines: the on/off electron gun control, the *x*-axis deflection, and the *y*-axis deflection.

Memory Mapping

The basic idea behind a memory-mapped display system regards the storing, in memory, the information that determines whether a certain pixel is to be turned on or off during the scan cycle. In a monochrome memory-mapped display, each pixel is represented by a memory bit, as shown in Figure 1-5. If the memory bit is on, or set, the corresponding pixel is illuminated by the CRT controller. If the bit is off, or reset, the corresponding pixel is dark. In mapping the CRT surface to memory, the pixel in the upper-left corner of the display corresponds to the lowest numbered memory address; numbering progresses horizontally along the same row and then vertically to successive rows.

> **NOTE:** Other graphics systems use other mapping schemes for pixel rows and columns, but all PC video graphics devices have the lowest numbered pixel at the upper-left corner.

In displaying alphanumeric characters, it is possible to construct a compact storage scheme by placing ASCII, ANSI, and other codes that represent characters, in display memory, instead of the bit patterns. In this case, the code is a reference to the bit pattern stored elsewhere. The practical result is a substantial simplification of the programming necessary for character display. Another advantage is a reduction in the portion of user memory devoted to video functions.

This method for manipulating, storing, and displaying alphanumeric characters relies on the operation of a device often called a *character generator*. It is the character generator that translates the code into the address of the dot pattern for the character and presents this pattern to the CRT controller. The main disadvantage of pure alphanumeric displays is that the individual screen dots cannot be controlled; therefore, the graphic function is limited to the use of specially encoded symbols.

The Human Element

The ultimate purpose of a graphics representation is to communicate visual information to a human observer. The output of the graphic machine is conditioned by the input of the human machine. For example, raster-scan multiplexing is possible because the human eye responds slowly to changes in the luminance level, and the rapid flashing of each screen dot cannot be perceived by the human eye. The techniques for avoiding flicker and the advantages of higher resolution and of colored and animated screen images, are all directly related to the process of visual perception and to the physiology and psychology of human eyesight.

Eyesight is taken for granted. Few of us will ever take time to investigate how the process of seeing takes place in our vision organs and inside our minds. For decades we have accepted the explanation that the human eye works like a camera; that it has a lens and a light-sensitive film called the *retina* composed of tiny light-sensitive units. According to this theory, the lens forms an image that stimulates the light cells on the retina and these sensations are transmitted through the optic nerve to the brain cells that specialize in vision. This theory postulates that, somewhere inside the brain, a group of cells performs the functions of an inner screen where the image of the outside world is somehow projected.

Although this theory is intuitively appealing and easy to understand, it has recently been found lacking. The explanation that human vision is a photographic process fails to account for many assumptions, interpretations, and illusions that we know are part of the seeing process. Understanding how the mind extracts information from a scene and how it reaches conclusions from a retinal image has baffled philosophers and scientists for centuries.

Consider how many different forms and versions of the same symbol the mind is capable of interpreting correctly. For example, we can easily identify the number 4 in different styles, sizes, and fonts. The eye-mind complex has no problem immediately associating the mental symbol of 4 with any of one of hundreds of handwritten and printed variants of the Arabic numeral. Yet, it is very difficult to list the specific characteristics that make the symbol for the number 4 recognizable to a human observer. How can we describe 4 in terms of line segments and angles so that the description satisfies all the possible representations?

The Vision Machine

The computer graphics designer, as well as the graphics programmer, often requires an understanding of the physiology and psychology of human vision. For example, the phenomenon of visual retention determines how fast an animation must flash successive images to achieve an illusion of natural movement. The eye's perception of color and light contrasts can help devise ways to strengthen a portion of a display. Knowledge of voluntary and reflex movements of the eyeball can be used in designing a graphics terminal that does not fatigue the user's eyes too excessively.

Figure 1-9 is a cross section of the human eye. The *cornea* serves as a hard, transparent, protective shield. The chamber behind the cornea contains a fluid called the *aqueous humor.* This fluid supplies nutrients to the lens, carries away the waste products and maintains pressure within the eyeball. The *iris* contains muscles that make it act as a diaphragm. When the light level decreases, the iris opens and vice versa, in an effort to maintain constant brightness of the image formed on the retina. Information from the retinal image is transported to the brain through the optic nerve.

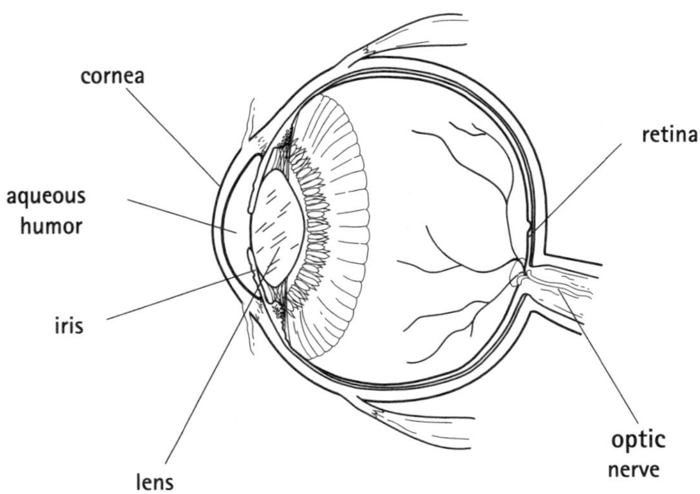

Figure 1-9: The human eye

Visual Accommodation

The human eye focuses on objects at varying distances by changing the refractive power of the lens; that is, the lens thickens or thins according to the viewing distance. In addition, to see objects closer than 20 feet, the two eyes must converge by turning inward. Finally, to perceive objects at close range, the eye must also constrict. The entire process is known as accommodation. A child's eyes can adapt to clearly see objects three inches away, but the accommodating power of the eye decreases with age. For this reason, the comfortable minimum viewing distance for an adult is considered to be 16 to 20 inches.

Eye Movements

Six different muscles control the movement of each eyeball. The origin of an eye movement can be voluntary or reflex, but involuntary actions are sometimes part of an eye movement of voluntary origin. For example, when the eyes scan a stationary image, like this page of text, eye movement takes place in small jerks called *saccades.* Each saccade lasts from 1/25 to 1/50 of a second and the pause between them lasts approximately 1/4 of a second. On the other hand, while watching a moving object the eyes move smoothly, except if the object exceeds an angular speed of 30 degrees per second, in which case the eyes automatically revert to the saccade movement mode.

A visual image can cause an involuntary eye movement by several different reflex mechanisms. For example, the eye automatically focuses on a bright object against a dark background and follows a moving object against a fixed background. Commercial advertisements take advantage of these reflex movements to catch and direct our attention, such as animated billboards with bright moving objects.

Retention

Images of objects that no longer exist in the real world can persist for a brief period of time in our visual organs. This physiological phenomenon is called *retention.* Although the biological mechanisms of retention are not fully understood, it is known that visual retention involves the chemistry and the structure of the cells and neurons in the retina.

Cinematography creates the illusion of continuous movement by consecutively flashing images at a rate of 24 per second. Because of visual retention, our brains merge the images together with no perception of the individual flashes. This happens because the previous image is still retained in our vision organs when the next one is projected. Raster-scan technology is also based on image retention. It is this retention that determines the frequency with which image scanning must be maintained to avoid flicker. The determination of this rate, called the *critical flicker frequency,* involves the careful experimental evaluation of the span of visual retention under specific conditions.

Some types of computer animation rely on frame-by-frame projections of successive images to create the illusion of movement. Frequently, the animation programmer must take visual retention into consideration to ensure a smooth screen movement. Failure to do so causes the bumpy effects observed in the more primitive computer-animated graphics.

Acuity

Visual acuity is the angular distance at which two individual lines will appear to our eyes as a single line. Acuity varies considerably among different individuals; it is ultimately a physiological limitation of the human eye determined by the physical separation of the cone cells in the retina. This keenness of human vision is usually estimated to be from one-half to one minute of an arc. If we approximate the tangent of 1 minute as 0.0003, we can derive a simple formula for determining the visual definition (d) at a given distance (D):

$$d = 0.0003 * D$$

If the average viewing distance for a computer monitor is 18 inches, then the visual acuity at this distance is as follows:

$$d = 0.0003 * 18 = 0.0054$$

= approximately 5-thousandths of an inch.

The limits of visual acuity determine that we perceive many individual colored dots as a continuous shade. This is used in halftone printing and in computer displays. The graphic designer, or the programmer of a raster-scan system, sometimes take advantage of the limitations of visual keenness by creating figures and curves that are actually composed of small, straight line segments that appear to flow together smoothly and naturally.

Field of Vision

Visual acuity is concentrated at the point where our vision is focused. The cone- and rod-shaped cells of the retina that actually perceive the optical image formed by the crystalline lens are denser in the central area, called the *fovea*; they become less dense further from this area. In fact, the sole outcome of peripheral vision is to call our attention to movements or light sources on which the eye must focus.

Although the exact angle of comfortable human visual acuity cannot be exactly determined, in the field of computer graphics we can assume that objectionable discomfort begins at angles of about 30 degrees. At a viewing distance of 18 inches, an angle of 30 degrees sustains a screen size of 9.6 inches. For this reason, screens more than 9.6 inches wide or high theoretically exceed the comfortable field of vision at normal distance. Today, however, it is common to see systems with screens larger than 10 inches across.

Eye Fatigue

The human eye evolved over millions of years basically as an instrument for daytime, outdoor vision. It is only in the last few centuries that we have started making extraordinary demands on our vision. Continuous, close-range observation of fine detail is probably the most difficult task that our eyes can confront. Many eyestrain headaches bear witness to this fact. Close-range observation demands constant tension in all of the muscles used for distance adjustments and eye fatigue naturally results from this muscular tension.

Eye fatigue cannot be permanently prevented: any muscle that is held constantly tense eventually tires. Yet, there are some circumstances that are known to accelerate the onset of this condition:

- Low-image resolution
- Flicker
- Excessive closeness or separation
- Incorrect horizontal or vertical viewing angles
- Crowded screen designs or clashing color combinations

In computer terminals and graphic CRTs, some of the most common user errors that tend to promote eye fatigue are the following:

- Wearing bifocal lenses while using a screen that is placed high enough to force a permanent, upward tilt of the head
- Ambient light reflecting on the CRT surface

The science of *ergonomics* proposes to adapt working conditions to the physical and psychological requirements of the worker. An ergonomically designed computer workstation requires consideration of all the conditions that tend to produce eye fatigue. Sometimes, the solution to eye fatigue obtained from staring at a CRT transcends ergonomics and becomes a matter of common sense. For example, many CRT workstations require constant observation of the screen for the detection of critical or dangerous circumstances. In most of these cases, it is preferable to implement an audible signal to warn the operators of danger and thus relieve them of considerable visual and mental strain.

The Hypnotic Effect

The stereotypical hypnotist is often depicted swinging a pocket watch, or some other bright object, in front of the subject's eyes. The physiological reason for this sometimes comic typification is that a synchronously repeated movement is visually tiresome, and therefore, induces boredom and sleep. Many popular remedies for insomnia, such as counting sheep, are based on this hypnotic property of monotonous repetition. Yet, computer-display technologists and computer graphic designers often forget these elementary facts. A flashing object, so often used in displays to signal the active screen position, has many of the hypnotic properties of the swinging watch. For this reason, in spite of its convenience, the use of a flashing object should always be questioned by the graphic program designer, especially when it can be replaced with a more imaginative symbol or call the user's attention by means of color or luminosity contrasts.

Composition and Eye Fatigue

The graphic program designer can often relieve the visual fatigue of the user or operator by avoiding dullness and boredom in the display's appearance. The designer should aim at uncluttered screens that make it easy for the eye to find the center of attention and use color combinations that are contrasting, but not clashing.

The Aesthetic Element

The computer graphics designer is a maker of visual images, much like a painter or a photographer. The fruits of their labor should go beyond the strict functionality of displaying the information on the screen, because communication through graphic images is, or should be, art.

Graphic art is described as the exaltation of personal communication through visual images by the refinement of techniques, and by following aesthetic principles. This definition includes both creative and commercial graphics art, as well as the work of artists who create their own techniques or discover new aesthetic effects. But the purpose of graphic creation does not enter into the definition, since it can range from the purely sensual to the totally utilitarian.

Composition and Graphic Beauty

Almost intuitively we think of "beautiful" as that which gives pleasure to our minds or our senses. Some philosophers state that we delight in objects that approximate our ideal, but the fact is that aestheticians have debated for generations on the theory of beauty and of our psychological response to beauty; they have found little ground for agreement. Even the words that we commonly use to describe beauty – beautiful, pretty, lovely, handsome, comely, fair, and good-looking, to mention but a few – are difficult to differentiate and explain.

Nevertheless, it can be stated that within certain cultural bounds, we frequently find consensus regarding what is visually pleasant or beautiful. Allowing for personal variations, individuals of similar culture share a sense of artistic taste. What is more, many authors seem to believe that aesthetic judgments are based in both innate and acquired elements of artistic tastes; human visual perception detects an interplay of tensions inherent to the graphics object, independent of cultural conditioning. This means that there are some intrinsic characteristics that make a graphics object pleasurable or not pleasurable to look at. Graphics composition is the discipline that studies these innate characteristics.

An interesting effect of cultural conditioning on graphic composition is related to the reading habits of our Western culture. We start reading at the top-left corner of a page and scan each line left-to-right and the page top-to-bottom. This explains the fact that we will scan a rectangular field of small graphic objects starting at the top-left corner and proceed horizontally, as if we were reading text. The graphic designer should be aware of this pattern, but also of the fact that this method of reading is not followed by individuals who read in other languages.

Balance and Weight

In physics, balance is described as a state where the prevalent forces compensate each other. An example of balance is two forces of equal strength pulling the same object in opposite directions. Aesthetically, balance is related to a sense of physical equilibrium that makes us assign an imaginary fulcrum, or center of gravity, to a graphic representation. Figure 1-10 shows several cases of aesthetic balance.

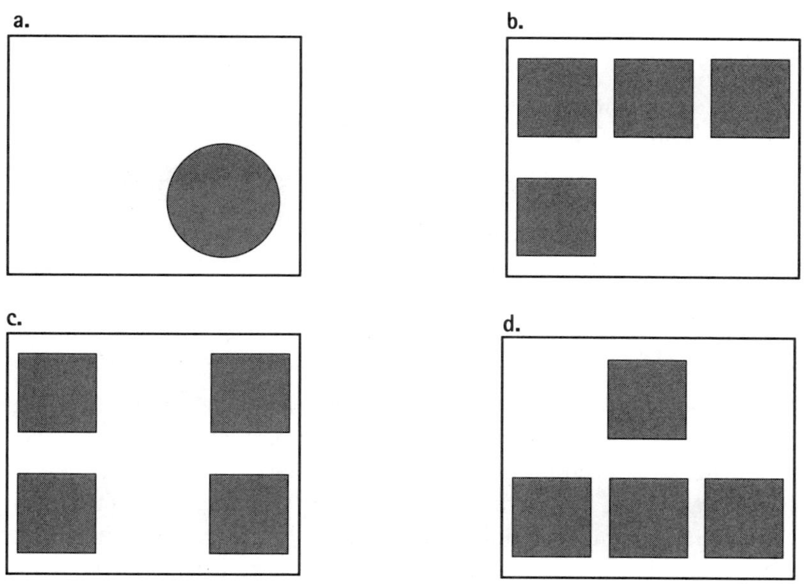

Figure 1-10: Visual balance

Image *a* in Figure 1-10 is a circular disk enclosed in a square frame. At first glance, we can detect that this figure is graphically unbalanced. The position of the disk inside the frame creates an uncomfortable tension. You can feel the urge to reach into the drawing and move the disk to the center of the frame. Image *b* in Figure 1-10 shows four small squares placed inside a rectangular frame. This type of graphic configuration is commonly used in screen menu blocks. In this case, the unpleasant arrangement results from placing the screen blocks consecutively without regard to the final pattern.

Images *c* and *d* in Figure 1-10 depict two different ways of balancing the squares. Although both arrangements appear satisfactory, there are subtle differences between them. For instance, the arrangement of image *c* assigns equal value to all four squares, while image *d* emphasizes the square on the top line. The triangular arrangement in image *d* appears more interesting and stable, while the symmetrical pattern of image c can be considered dull.

In the physical world, the force of gravity exerts a downward pull on all material objects. It seems that we mentally extend this phenomenon to the world of graphic figures. In fact, physical and graphical weight are so similar that physical principles, like that of the lever, can also be applied in the determination of graphic balance. The principle of the graphic lever can be stated as follows: The action of a graphic element on the balance of a figure increases as the element moves farther away from the center of the figure. In general, the weight of a graphic element is influenced by many factors, such as:

- The element's location in the figure
- The element's size
- The element's color; warm colors appear heavier than cool ones; black is heavier than white
- The element's intrinsic interest, which increases its apparent weight
- The element's shape; simple geometrical figures, a circle for example, appear heavier than irregular ones.

Shape and Form

Experimental findings from recent research have forced a total turnaround in the classical interpretation of the mental processes of shape perception. Psychologists had assumed that the generalization process that takes place in the recognition of similar figures requires a high intellectual ability. It came as a surprise to investigators that both chimpanzees and rats could easily identify boxes that contained food and that were marked with any of the symbols shown in Figure 1-11. Even when the triangles were made larger or smaller, turned on the side, or colored, the animals could still recognize the marked boxes. This discovery seems to prove that primary data obtained by visual perception is not the product of intellectual abstraction but an elementary and intuitive process. The two-year-old child perceives the image of a cat in one or two picture books and intuitively learns to identify "catness" in new images, even if they remotely resemble the ones previously seen.

Figure 1-11: Similar triangles used in shape perception research

We are still a long way from fully understanding how the mental patterns that represent cat or triangle are formed in the brain. But it does appear that visual perception is, in fact, a creative activity of the mind, and that our eyes do more than register an objective image of the outside world. Seeing involves thinking.

Shape is the characteristic of an object as determined by its boundaries. A sailboat is perceived to have a different shape when viewed from the side than from the front. But, as we have seen, our concept of shape is not exclusively determined by the retinal image of the object; it is the result of accumulated visual experiences of similar objects. Each new visual experience adds information to our perceptual image of the object.

Form is the graphic configuration of an object considered apart from its more elementary properties of shape and color; although, on occasion, shape and form seem to merge into the same aesthetic property. This happens with very simple figures, like the line drawing of a triangle. It is pure semantics if we state that the object has triangular shape, and no specific form, or if we state that it is triangular in form. It is sometimes helpful in grasping the concept of form to list those attributes to which it is related. You can say that form is related to spatial orientation, to size or scale, to the dimensions of depiction, to artistic style or school, and to levels of abstraction. All these attributes are evidently unrelated to the object's shape.

Figure and Background

Shapes can be distinguished in two-dimensional space, but three-dimensional space extends the freedom of our visual imagery to its maximum. Eventually, technology will make available machines capable of real three-dimensional representation, but it is hard to predict if this hardware will ever become as prevalent as computer displays. In many applications, two-dimensional representation of objects will probably continue to be preferred over three-dimensional ones. For instance, the use of solid patterns as a guide in manufacturing, instead of conventional blueprint drawings commonly used, probably creates more inconveniences than advantages.

In two-dimensional representations we must regularly distinguish between objects that are seen as figures and objects that are seen as background. A number of conditions have been identified that tend to make us consider a plane image to be a figure. Figure 1-12 shows some of the elements that determine whether an object is perceived as a figure or as background. For example, a surrounded object is usually perceived as a figure, and so are smaller objects drawn over larger ones, as can be seen in images *a* and *b* in Figure 1-12. A surrounded object appears to be denser than the background. By using graphic manipulations we can enhance or diminish this effect, as shown in images *c* and *d*. We also tend to assume that the lower part of a figure carries more weight than the top part; therefore, if two fields are divided horizontally, the lower one is perceived as figure, as in the case of image *e* in Figure 1-12. This phenomenon probably results from our repeated observation of landscapes, where the trees, rocks, houses, and mountains normally occupy the lower half of the picture while the clouds and sky take up the upper part. Finally, we can observe that symmetry and convexity tend to be interpreted as figure and asymmetry and concavity as background. The banisters in image *f* in Figure 1-12 demonstrate this effect.

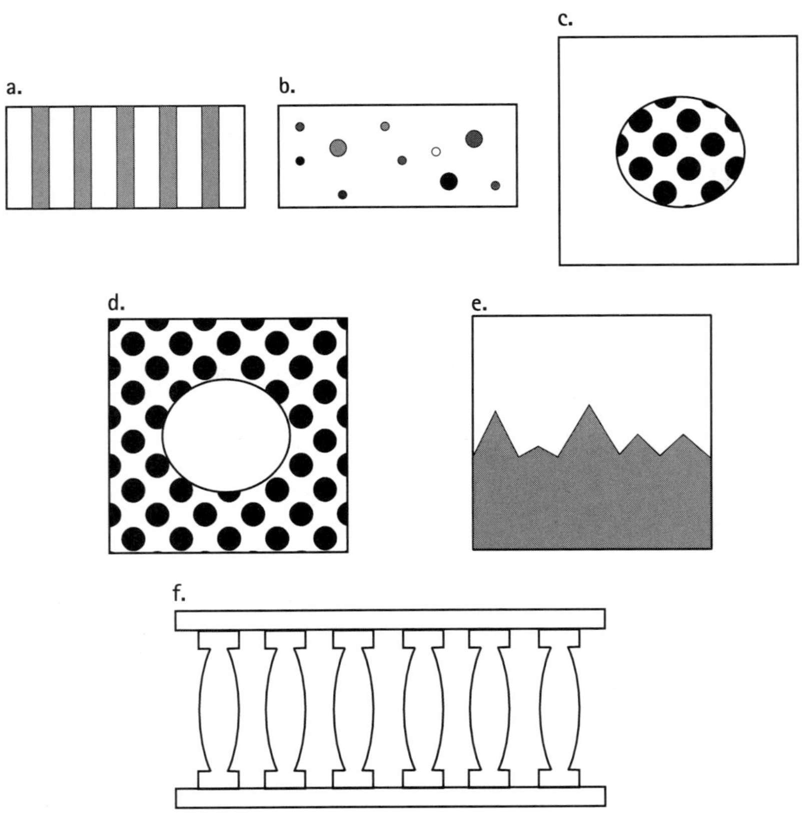

Figure 1-12: Identification of figure and background

Space and Depth Perception

There is more to depth perception than the mental processing of a flat retinal image. The simple experiment of observing a complex object at close range, like a vase of flowers, first with both eyes and then with one eye covered, demonstrates how depth perception is enhanced by binocular vision. This phenomenon, called *stereopsis*, depends on the brain's interpretation of the tension in the muscles that make the eyes converge and also on the retinal images produced by the difference in the viewpoints of the eyes. The effect is sometimes called *binocular disparity*. As the distance to the object decreases, the muscular tension increases, and so does the image disparity, enhancing stereopsis. By the same token, when the distance increases, the muscular tension decreases and the visual images tend to become identical. When observing an object 20 feet away, both eyes are parallel. With no muscular tension, depth perception is solely determined by image disparity. At an 80-foot distance, stereopsis rapidly diminishes.

Once the basic principles of binocular vision are understood, it is not difficult to imagine a device to simulate depth perception by offering each eye a different image on a flat surface. The first such machine, named a *stereoscope*, was invented by Sir Charles Wheatstone in 1833. Most of us have had the opportunity to use some form of stereoscope and to admire the realism in the illusion of depth induced by this device. A stereoscope is built so that the user's eyes are optically or mechanically isolated from each other.

Most stereoscopes use an optical component named a *prism-cum-lens* to slightly bend the images coming to each eye so that they appear to be one. Alternatively, we can produce separate stereoscopic images by printing, projecting, or displaying the images in different colors and providing the user with correspondingly colored lenses for each eye. This method is called *anaglyphic stereoscopy;* the individual color-coded images are called *anaglyphs*. The greatest advantage of the anaglyphic stereoscope is that the 3-D effect can be produced with a single image and that the viewing device is quite simple. Anaglyphic stereoscopy was successfully used in 3-D motion pictures during the 1950s and 1960s, and is compatible with computerized color graphic systems. Its greatest drawback is that the user is forced to wear color lenses; without them, not only is the 3-D effect lost, but the image becomes distorted.

A more recently developed technology for simulating depth on a flat medium is *holography*. This method uses a split laser beam to detect and record the different interference patterns on a photographic film. The image can later be reconstructed by reflecting light on this film.

At the present state-of-the-art in computer graphics, the question of representing solid images usually refers not to stereoscopy or holography, but to the depiction of 3-D objects on a flat medium using the principles of graphic composition. Considering that our perception of depth is a consequence of the processing by our minds of a two-dimensional image formed on the retina, this simple trickery is not only plausible, but physiologically valid. Part IV of this book is devoted to 3-D graphics.

Techniques for enhancing our depth perception are based on creating an unambiguous pattern that we can relate to our visual experiences in a 3-D world. Figure 1-13 shows several effects that are used in simulated depth perception. The simplest graphic condition that enhances our depth perception occurs when two or more graphic objects overlap each other. Image *a* shows two overlapping rectangles. It is easy for our vision to judge which of these rectangles is closest to us, since there are no graphic ambiguities. On the other hand, the rectangles of image *b* also overlap, but they present an ambiguous view of their spatial positions. The effect created by overlapping figures is always one of visual tension, which can be irritating if there are spatial ambiguities or contradictions in them.

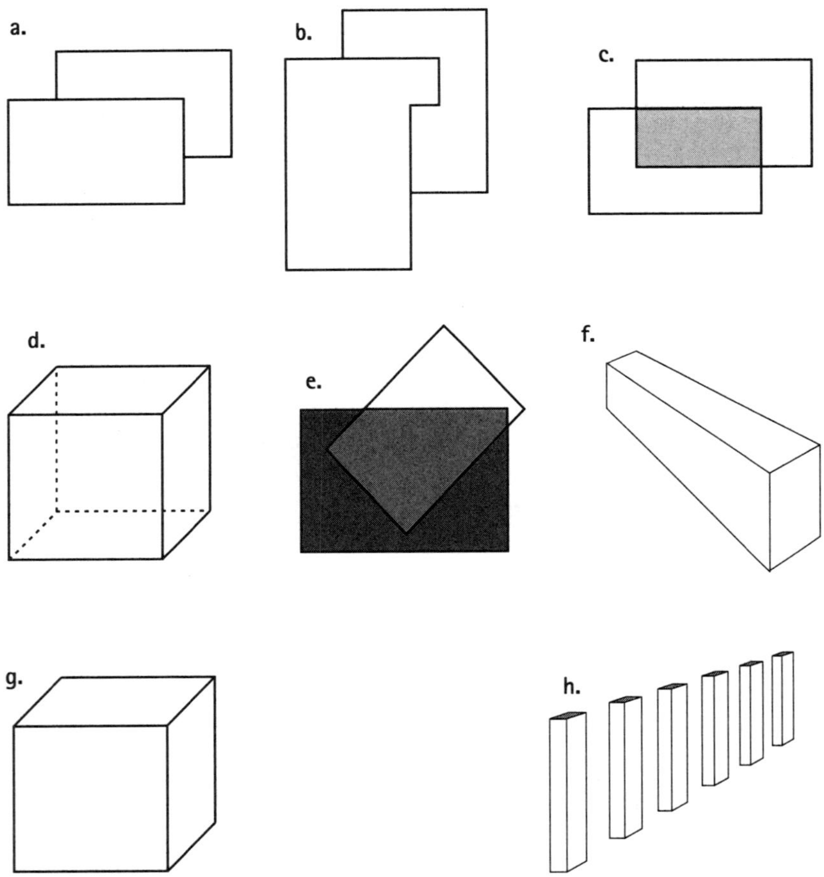

Figure 1-13: Simulation of depth

The visual perception of depth created by overlapping can sometimes be enhanced by using graphic means to simulate transparency. The gray area in image *c* of Figure 1-13 achieves this. Our eyes interpret the figure as composed of two rectangles, one of which is transparent. In image *d* the same effect is obtained using dashed lines to represent the hidden edges of a cube. Solid colors or shades of gray can also create the illusion of transparency if they are combined in a plausible manner. If the shapes shown in image *e*, Figure 1-13, are made of dark-gray, white, and light-gray colored paper, they are interpreted by the human eye as two overlapping, transparent, white and dark-gray rectangles. The visual illusion takes place because the light-gray area is read by the eye as a portion of the white rectangle when viewed through a dark-gray, transparent medium (or vice versa). Plausibility is ensured because light-gray is rendered by a mixture of the dark-gray and white. If a nonplausible color or shade is used for the overlapping area, the transparency effect is lost.

The art of perspective drawing deals with the graphic manipulations required to foster the illusion of depth. Geometrically speaking, a photograph is a perspective rendering, more or less perfect, according to the sophistication of the optical and mechanical means used in producing it, and to the photographer's skills in applying the laws of perspective. Image *f* in Figure 1-13, shows a rectangular solid drawn in perspective. Alteration of the rectangular planes is the key to the realism of a perspective rendering.

It is interesting to note that the human mind accepts the cube shown in image *g* of Figure 1-13 as a valid rendering of a solid object. Yet this figure is impossible, from a perspective viewpoint; for if we are able to see one face of a cube as a perfect square, then all other faces would be completely hidden from view. The reasons for the subjective validity of such an optically incorrect rendering is psychological; the cube derives from a square; therefore, a square face is psychologically consistent. Because depth perception in this representation is wholly dependent on the obliqueness of the lateral lines, this depiction is called an *oblique projection*. Obliqueness creates an illusion of depth because it represents a gradual change in the coordinates of each point. This gradual increase or decrease of a graphic attribute is called a *gradient*. Gradients greatly enhance the illusion of depth. A commonly used graphic gradient is the convergence of railroad tracks. Image *h* represents a gradient in the form of a series of fence posts. The depth effect is further enhanced by gradually decreasing the size of the posts and the spacing between them.

Light and Color

Although we cannot be certain that we all react to color sensations in the same way, undoubtedly color adds a new and enlivening dimension to our visual universe. In fact, it is the illumination or color of a surface that allows our vision to define its boundary and shape. Therefore, we can say that the visual appearance of an object is mostly determined by its brightness and color. Even a thin line in an ink drawing becomes visible because of its color contrast with the white surface of the paper.

In physics, we learn that white light can be created with a balanced mixture of the light of any three colors. In practice, the colors red, green, and blue, the primary colors, are used as a theoretical basis of color vision and color reproduction. Technically, it is possible to create white light by blending just two colors. The color that must be blended with a primary color to form white is called the *complement* of that primary color. Figure 1-14 shows the primary and the complementary colors.

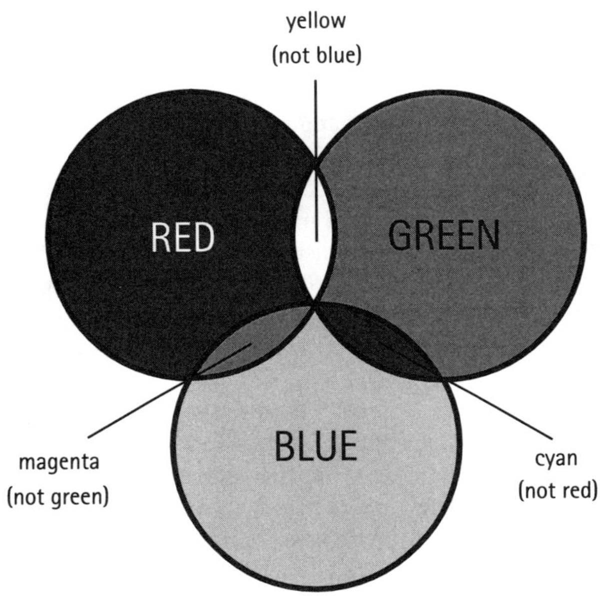

Figure 1-14: Primary and complementary colors

The complementary colors can also be described as white light minus a primary color. White light without the red primary (not red) gives a shade of blue-green known as *cyan*; not green gives a mixture of red and blue called *magenta*; and not blue gives *yellow*, which is a mixture of red and green light. Additive color reproduction uses light of the primary colors to generate all the colors of the spectrum. Color CRT displays use additive color blending. Subtractive methods are based on dyes that absorb the undesirable, complementary colors. A cyan-colored filter, for example, absorbs the green and blue components of white light. Subtractive mixing is used in color photography and color printing.

In addition to its red, green, and blue light components, a color can also be described by three characteristics that can be precisely determined. They are hue, intensity, and saturation, sometimes collectively called *HIS*. The hue is described as *the color of a color* and can be measured by its dominant wavelength. The intensity of a color is its brightness, which is measured in units of luminance, or *nits*. The saturation of a color is its *purity*. If the color contains no white diluent, it is said to be fully saturated. Color signals used in television are encoded in HIS.

Text Characters

The Phoenicians modified and condensed Egyptian hieroglyphics into an alphabet of 22 letters that was later adopted by the Greeks. The Greek letters evolved into an Eastern and a Western type. The Western Greek alphabet served as a base for the Latin alphabet, also of 22 letters. All modern western European languages used the letters of the Latin alphabet and added a few to represent their unique vowels and consonants.

Before the invention of the printing press, letters were drawn by hand, each writer adding his or her own embellishments. This changed in the 15th century with the advent of mechanical printing machines that used manufactured letters. Nevertheless, the printers and type-makers also followed national and personal preferences in the selection and design of letter styles. The original German printers adopted a design based on the hand-drawn characters used by English writers. This style is appropriately named *Old English*. In Italy and other South European countries, the most popular type style was inspired by the letters in Roman inscriptions, drawn with a wide tipped pen in a manner that made the vertical traces wider than the horizontal ones. This letter style is called *roman*.

Letter styles that use wide downward strokes and thin connecting strokes, like the roman letters previously described, are named *serif* letters, while letters of uniform thickness are classified as *sans serif*. Serif letters have greater contrast and are, therefore, more readable. Most magazines, newspapers and books are printed with serif type styles. Sans serif letters are used in technical applications and for some graphic effects that take advantage of their strong appearance. An assortment of letters of the same style and size is called a *font*. Figure 1-15 shows several common typefaces.

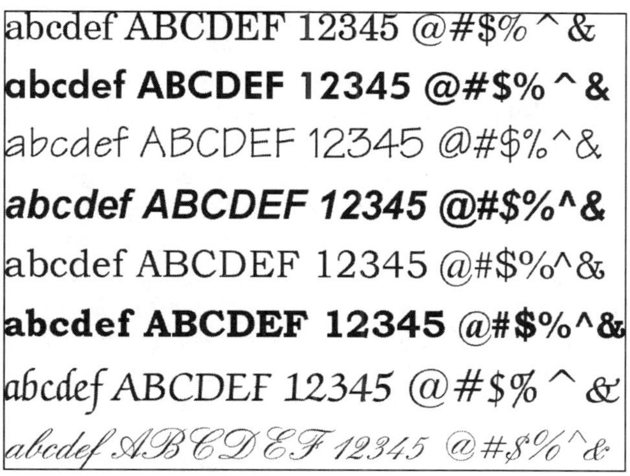

Figure 1-15: Examples of typefaces

To the graphics designer and programmer, text is just another graphics object. Text characters can be filled, outlined, stretched, made transparent, overlaid on other objects, and otherwise manipulated. Character graphics is sometimes considered a specialty field, much like vector and bitmapped graphics. In this book, we often discuss graphics operations on text characters.

Applications of Computer Graphics

The applications of computer graphics seem to grow without bounds, to the point that it would be easier to list the fields that do not employ graphics than to list those that do. The limitations in applying computer graphics seem to be related more to economics and technology, than to intrinsic factors. It is difficult to find a sphere of computing that does not profit from graphics in one way or another. This is true not only in regards to applications; graphics operating systems have become the norm, rather than the exception. A few years ago you could purchase a personal computer that had no graphics capabilities, and many users did. Who would consider this option today? The PC has evolved into a powerful graphics machine. To a programmer or program designer, graphics are no longer an option, nor can graphics programming be considered a specialty that you can learn or not. In today's technology, graphics is the reality of computing.

Engineering and Technology

The term "engineering" encompasses many disciplines, including architecture, mechanical, civil, electrical, and many others. Virtually every field of engineering finds applications for computer graphics. The most generally applicable technology is *computer-aided design.* (CAD) systems have replaced the drafting board and the T-square in the design of components for civil, electrical, mechanical, and electronic systems. A few years ago, a CAD system required a mainframe or minicomputer with high-resolution displays and other dedicated hardware. Similar capabilities can be had today with off-the-shelf PC hardware and software.

CAD systems do more than generate conventional engineering drawings. Libraries of standard objects and shapes can be stored and reused. For example, a system used in mechanical engineering can store nut-and-bolt designs, which can be resized and used as needed. The same applies to other frequently used components and standard shapes. The use of color adds a visual dimension to computer-generated engineering drawings, a feature that is usually considered too costly and difficult to do manually. Plotters and printers generate high-quality hard copy of drawings, rapidly and efficiently. Three-dimensional CAD systems store and manipulate solid views of graphics objects and automatically generate perspective views and projections. Wire-frame and solid modeling techniques allow the visualization of real-world objects and contours. CAD systems can also have expertise in a particular field. This "knowledge" can be used to check the correctness and integrity of a design.

Computer graphics are used to predict and model system behavior. Simulation techniques enable the creation of virtual representations of practically any engineered system, be it mechanical, electrical, or chemical. Mathematical equations are used to manipulate 3-D representations to predict their behavior over a period of *simulated* time. Graphics images, sometimes color-coded, are used to display movement, and to show stress points or other dynamic features which, without this technique, would have been left to the imagination.

In architecture and civil engineering, graphics systems find many applications. Architects use 3-D modeling for the display of the interior and exterior of buildings. A graphics technique known as *ray tracing* allows the creation of solid models that show lighting, shading, and mirroring effects.

Geographic Information Systems (GIS) use computers to manipulate and store geographic, cartographic, and other social data that can be used in the analysis of phenomena where geographical location is an important factor. Usually, the amount of data manipulated in a GIS is much larger than can be handled manually. Much of this data is graphics imagery in the form of maps and charts. GIS systems display their results graphically. Geographic Information Systems are used in land use and land management, agriculture, forestry, wildlife management, archeology, and geology.

Remote sensing refers to the collection of data at a distance, usually through satellites and other spacecrafts. Most natural resource-mapping done today uses this technology. As the resolution of remotely-sensed imagery increases, and their cost decreases, many more practical uses will be found for this technology. We (the authors) have recently finished a book titled *Space Image Processing* (see bibliography) which describes the computer processing and graphics manipulation of spaceborne imagery.

Automation and robotics also find extensive use for computer graphics. Computer Numerical Control (CNC) and Computer Assisted Manufacturing (CAM) systems are usually implemented in a computer graphics environment.

Art and Design

Artists use computer graphics as an experimental platform, and some as a final medium. While it is debatable whether computer-generated images can be considered fine art, there is no doubt that graphics technology is one of the most powerful tools for commercial graphics and for product design. As CAD systems have replaced the drafting board, draw-and-paint programs have replaced the commercial artist's sketchpad. The commercial artist uses a drawing program to produce any desired effect with great ease and speed, and to experiment and fine-tune the design. Computer-generated images can be stretched, scaled, rotated, filled with colors, skewed, mirrored, resized, extruded, contoured, and manipulated in many other ways. Photo-editing applications allow scanning and transforming bitmapped images, which can later be vectorized and loaded into a drawing program or incorporated into a design as bitmaps.

Another specialty field in which computer graphics has achieved great success is in digital composition and typesetting. So-called desktop-publishing programs allow the creation of originals for publication, from a brochure or a newsletter to a complete book. The traditional methods were based on "mechanicals" on which the compositor glued strips of text and images to form pages. The pages were later photographed and the printing plates manufactured from the resulting negatives. Today, composition is done electronically. Text and images are merged in digital form. The resulting page can be transferred into a digital typesetter or used to produce the printing plates directly. The entire process is based on computer graphics.

Business and Data Visualization

In recent years, we have witnessed data explosion. In many cases, more data is generated than there are people to process it. Imagine a day in the near future in which 15 remote-sensing satellites orbit the earth, each one of them transmitting an image every 15 minutes, of an area that covers 150 square miles. The resulting acquisition rate of an image per minute is likely to create processing and storage problems, but perhaps the greatest challenge will be to find ways of using this information. How many experts will be required just to look at these images? In recent years there have been two or three remote-sensing satellites acquiring Earth images and it is estimated that no more than ten percent of these images have ever been analyzed. Along this same line, businesses are discovering that they accumulate and store more data than can be used. *Data mining* and *data warehousing* are techniques developed to find some useful nugget of information in these enormous repositories of raw data.

Digital methods of data and image processing, together with computer graphics, provide our only hope of ever catching up with this mountain of unprocessed data. A business graph is used to compress and make available a large amount of information, in a form that can be used in the decision-making process. Computers are required to sort and manipulate the data and to generate these graphs. The field of image processing is providing methods for operating on image data. Science and technology is being developed to allow computers to "look at" imagery and obtain useful information. If we cannot dedicate a sufficient number of human experts to look at a daily heap of satellite imagery, perhaps we will be able to train computers to perform this task.

Command and control systems used in the distribution and management of electricity, water, and gas, in the scheduling of railways and aircraft, and in military applications, are based on automated data processing and on graphics representations. At the factory level, these systems are sometimes called *process controls*. In both small and large systems, graphics displays are required to help operators and experts visualize the enormous amount of information that must be considered in the decision-making process. For example, the pilot of a modern-day commercial aircraft can obtain, at a glance, considerable information about the airplane and its components from a graphic depiction on a video display. This same information was much more difficult to grasp and process when it originated in a dozen or more analog instruments.

In business, computer graphics often serves to enhance the presentation of statistical data. In this context, the graphics environment and computer animation serve to make the presentation more interesting. For example, the evolution of a product from the raw materials to its finished form, the growth of a real estate development from a few houses to a small city, or the graphic depiction of a statistical trend. Business graphics serve to make more convincing presentations of products or services offered to a client, as a training tool for company personnel, or as an alternative representation of statistical data. As a selling tool, computer graphics techniques can make a company's product or service more interesting by adding to an otherwise dull and boring description of properties and features.

Simulation and Training

Natural or man-made objects and environments can be represented in computer graphics. We use optical planetariums to teach astronomy in an environment that does not require more costly optical instruments and that is independent of the weather and other meteorological conditions. Computer graphics systems can simulate a planetarium or many other natural environments used in education and training. Other natural phenomena cannot be easily reproduced in a physical or optical laboratory. For example, the transformation of mass according to the theory of relativity would be practically impossible to reproduce physically. However, we can use a graphics system to simulate physical entities or to represent complex scientific phenomena such as nuclear and chemical reactions, hydraulic flow, physiological systems and organs, or structures under load.

One such type of computer-assisted device, sometimes called a *simulator*, finds practical and economic use in experimentation and instruction. Astronauts training for a lunar landing practiced in simulators of the landing module and the mother ship. Airplane pilots often train in computer-assisted simulators that can safely reproduce unusual or dangerous flying conditions. These devices are all based in computer graphics.

Games and Entertainment

Since the introduction of Pac Man in the 1980s, computer games have played an important role in the entertainment field. More recently we have seen an increase in popularity of dedicated computer-controlled systems and user-interaction devices, such as those developed by Nintendo™, Sega™, and GameBoy™.

In microcomputers – CD-ROM, digital audio, software, and specialized user-interaction devices – have been combined in an environment called *multimedia*. The quality of the animated imagery and sound effects that can be obtained in a present-day multimedia computer compete with those in dedicated systems. The realism of many applications has achieved such a degree of refinement that moral and ethical issues are being raised about the use of sexually explicit or violent applications.

In the past three or four years, computer games have gone through a remarkable revival. The availability of more powerful graphics systems and of faster processors, as well as the ingenuity and talent of the developers, has brought about an unpredicted increase in the popularity of this field. Computer games are one of the leading sellers in today's software marketplace, with sales supported by an extensive subculture of passionate followers. Electronic games are always at the cutting edge of computer graphics and animation. A game succeeds or fails according to its performance. It is in this field where the graphics envelope is pushed to the extreme. DirectDraw and 3-D graphics technologies, which are the subjects of Parts III and IV of this book, relate very closely to computer games.

Artificial Life

A new discipline of computer science, named *artificial life*, or *ALife*, has evolved around the computer modeling of biosystems. ALife is based on biology, robotics, and artificial intelligence. The results are digital entities that resemble self-reproducing and self-organizing biological life forms. Computer viruses, of the harmful and benign forms, are examples of artificial life.

The core notion of Alife is the *cellular automaton*. The idea was first considered by John von Neumann (Professor at the Institute for Advanced Studies and Research at Princeton University), who describes it as a theoretical model of a parallel computing device which is subject to various restrictions to make possible the formal investigation of its various computing powers. The model is reminiscent of a living organism since it is based on an interconnection of identical cells, each of which behaves like a finite-state machine. Each unit computes an output based on input received from cells that are said to form its *neighborhood*. It is also possible for a cell to receive input from an external source.

Computer graphics are usually required in the implementation of cellular automata. Each clock cycle is an iteration update of the automata system, viewed graphically on the computer screen. The resulting changes in the system give rise to an image set that simulates an animated entity. In general, the notion of artificial life is naturally associated with biological forms capable of self-reproduction and self-organization. These actions imply changes that can be graphically represented. In the same way that we associate natural life with movement and action, artificial life often requires the depiction of transformations and movements by means of computer graphics and animation.

Virtual Reality

Developments in technology have made possible a new level of user interaction with a computing machine, called *virtual reality*, or VR. It consists of a computer system, a viewing device (typically in the form of *VR goggles* or *head-mounted display*), and one or more input devices that allow the user to interact with the graphics system.

Virtual reality creates a digital universe in which the user is more or less immersed, according to the level of isolation from the surrounding environment. This digital universe has been named *cyberspace*, a term coined by science fiction writer William Gibson in his 1984 book *Neuromancer*. Possible applications of VR technology range from pure entertainment to practical industrial controls. You can put on VR goggles to travel to the planet Mars and walk on its surface, to control a complex robot used in industry or manufacturing, or to go on a date with a virtual friend. Other possible applications include scientific and medical research, art, music, electronic games, CAD, information management, engineering, education, and surgery.

Computer graphics are required in virtual reality as part of the feedback mechanism. In a typical VR system, the goggles take the place of the video display. Graphics programmers use their art to present to the user a convincing image of the virtual environment created by the system. For example, when the system detects a left-hand movement of the user's head, the video image displayed on the VR goggles is smoothly panned to the left to make objects that were previously outside the field of view, visible. If the virtual universe includes entities that move, then the system must reflect this action on the virtual environment. Thus, a VR representation of the Jurassic period requires that images of dinosaurs move in predetermined or random fashion, perhaps interacting with the user.

Technology has not yet achieved the level of refinement, or the image-processing power, necessary for creating a realistic virtual environment on the personal computer. It is not yet possible to manipulate many virtual entities that are simultaneously animated according to the user's interaction with the system, or to predefined or random factors. This is the future, and the future is close at hand.

Fractal Graphics

Natural surfaces are highly irregular; they do not follow predictable geometrical patterns. Such is the case with coastlines, islands, rivers, snowflakes, and galaxies. For this reason, many natural objects cannot be satisfactorily represented by means of polygons or smooth curves, since the resulting image is too regular and contrived. However, it is possible to realistically represent some types of natural objects by means of a mathematical entity called a *fractal*.

The word fractal was derived from *fractional dimensions*. It is best visualized by means of a structure called a *triadic Koch curve*. The evolution of the Koch curve starts with a straight line of length 1. The middle third of this line (1/3 fraction) is replaced by two lines of the same length that form a 60 degree angle. The result is a curve that is more rugged than the original one. This second order curve can be transformed into a curve of the third order by repeating the same process with each of its four segments. The evolution of a Koch curve to the third order is shown in Figure 1-16.

Figure 1-16: Fractal based on a triadic Koch curve

In Figure 1-16, the length of the curve increases in relation to the number of straight-line segments that it contains. This means that the second order Koch curve has a greater length than the first order curve. By the same token, the third order curve has a greater length that the second order one. By continuing the process to infinity, the length of the curve also increases to infinity. In other words, the curve cannot be measured in one dimension. On the other hand, the Koch curve cannot be measured in two dimensions, since, by definition, its area is always 0. This leads to the conclusion that the curve must have a dimension that is greater than one and less than two, which is the fractional dimension, or fractal. The term "fractal" was coined by Benoit Mandelbrot in his book *The Fractal Geometry of Nature* (see bibliography).

One interesting feature of fractals is that they can be generated by computers following what is called a *production rule.* In Figure 1-16 you can see the production rule for a triadic Koch curve. Other fractals, such as the popular Mandelbrot set and the many Julia sets, have their own unique production rules. The Koch curve exhibits a feature known as *self-similarity.* This means that parts of the curves are similar to the whole curve. Natural objects, on the other hand, rarely exhibit self-similarity, although they do show what is called *statistical self-similarity.* In using fractal curves to simulate natural objects, it is necessary to introduce a random factor that eliminates the curve's self-similarity property. The result can be compared to the image formed in a kaleidoscope, in which the random placement of the colored glass fragments ensures a unique picture with every change.

Computer graphics are used to show the progression in the approximation of random fractals in a computer system. A truly random fractal has an infinitely complex shape; therefore, it cannot actually exist as a visible object. The introduction of a random element in the creation of the fractal curve ensures that the result is unpredictably different every time the fractal is approximated. The imagery that results from the generation of a random fractal graphic approximation is quite interesting from both an artistic and a mathematical viewpoint.

Summary

In this first chapter we have covered several core computer graphics topics that should be familiar to every graphics programmer. Pictorial perception and visual thinking explain how our minds interpret and use graphics imagery. The section on graphics technology covers the fundamentals of computer graphics hardware and its operation. The section on image properties discusses the brightness, color, resolution, and aspect ratio of graphics imagery and also explains how display elements are accessed in a multitasking operating system. The human element section is about the eye and its properties. A graphics designer or programmer must be aware of how the human seeing machine operates. The section on aesthetics refers to the beauty of graphics and how it is achieved through composition, balance, shape, space, light, color, and text. The chapter concludes with a short presentation of the applications of computer graphics – in engineering, art, design, business, simulations, games, artificial life, virtual reality, and fractals.

You have now acquired a basic level of computer graphics information. With this background information, you can begin to learn how graphics programming operates in Windows, which is explained throughout the rest of this book.

Chapter 2

Event-driven Programming

IN THIS CHAPTER

- Evolution and architecture of graphical operating systems
- Programming models
- Windows program files
- Dynamic linking
- Windows programming fundamentals
- A program's visual elements
- Programming style and templates

THIS CHAPTER DEALS with the principles of Windows programming. If you have already developed Windows applications in C or C++, you may want to glance lightly over the contents of this chapter, or skip it altogether. It is intended mostly for programmers who have never worked in the Windows environment. In this chapter, we explain the differences between a DOS and a Windows program and provide a model, called *event-driven programming*, that is suitable for graphics and multitasking applications. We also describe the fundamental components of a Windows program, its file structure, and visual features.

Graphical Operating Systems

The operating systems used in the first generation of digital computers required that the user toggle a series of binary switches, each one with an attached light, to enter data into the machine. In these systems, the bootstrap sequence consisted of a predefined sequence of switch-toggling and button-pressing actions that the operator memorized and executed in a ritual-like fashion. To handle one of these machines, you had to belong to a select class of binary-speaking, hexadecimal-minded experts who devoted most of their lives to deciphering the arcane mysteries of hardware and software.

Evolution

In the years that followed, several inventions and adaptations simplified computer input and output. IBM Corporation developed punched cards for its business machines and adapted this technology to its first line of computers. Teletype machines (called TTYs) were invented for use in the communications industry, but were soon adapted for use as computer devices. With the TTY, the typewriter keyboard found its way into computing. Next came the use of cathode ray tubes, used in televisions, as a way of displaying text without having to print it on paper. An added bonus was that the CRT could also be used to display pictures.

Other devices followed suit. Some have become standard elements of the technology while others have disappeared. They include the lightpen, the touch screen, the graphic tablet, the joystick, and the mouse. The common element in all of these devices is that they allow the user to visually interact with the machine. The idea for a visually interactive interface came from Allan Kay's work at the Xerox Palo Alto Research Center in the early 1970s. Dr. Kay was attempting to design a computer that could be used by preschool children who were too young to read or to type commands in text form. A possible approach was to use small screen objects, called *icons*, that represented a familiar thing. A mechanical device (the mouse) enabled users to move these objects around on the screen and to interact with the system. Interactive graphics and the graphical user interface were the result.

Steve Jobs, one of the founders of Apple Computer, visited Xerox PARC and saw the mouse and the graphical user interface. He immediately concluded that interactively controlling a computer was the way of the future. Back at Apple, Jobs started the development of an operating system that supported graphical, mouse-controlled, icon-based, user interaction. After an unsuccessful try with the Lisa, Apple released the Macintosh. Not too long thereafter, Microsoft delivered a graphical operating system for the PC, called Windows.

Windows Versions

Many realized the advantages of a more reasonable and physical interaction with a computing machine. It took many years, however, for the actual implementation of this idea in an effective operating system that would be preferred by the majority of users. Douglas Engelbart demonstrated a viable mouse interface in 1968, but it took fifteen years for the mouse to become a standard computer component. To implement a graphical user interface (GUI) it was necessary to have, not only a pointing device that worked, but also a graphics-capable video terminal. In addition, the software would have to provide a set of graphics services in a device-independent manner.

In the PC world, the evolution of hardware and software components into a graphical operating system took approximately one decade. The first versions were rather crude and achieved little popular acceptance. It was not until Windows 95 that Microsoft's graphical operating system for the PC became the standard. Table 2-1 lists the different versions of Microsoft Windows and their fundamental characteristics.

TABLE 2-1 VERSIONS OF MICROSOFT WINDOWS

Version	Release Date	Features
1.01	November 1985	Original version of Microsoft Windows
		Tiled display
		No multitasking
		640K limit
2.0	November 1987	Overlapping windows
		Appearance and interaction consistent with IBM's OS/2 Presentation Manager
/386	December 1987	Virtual 86 mode or the 386 CPU
3.0	May 1990	Three-dimensional look of icons and buttons
		Proportionally spaced type
		Extended memory on 80286
3.1	April 1992	Easier installation and configuration
		Common dialog boxes
		Drag-and-drop file operations
		Scalable fonts
		32-bit operation
		Network support in Windows for Workgroups
NT 3.1	August 1993	Network support
		Preemptive multitasking
		New graphics capabilities
		Improved security
		Multiprocessor support
		Minimum of 16MB RAM
		Limited DOS support

Continued

TABLE 2-1 VERSIONS OF MICROSOFT WINDOWS *(Continued)*

Version	Release Date	Features
NT Advanced Server	July 1993	Server optimization
		Client/server database support
NT Server 3.5	September 1994	Minor enhancements and bug fixes
Windows 95	August 1995	16/32-bit hybrid environment
		Subset of Win32 API
		Minimum of 4MB RAM
		Preemptive multitasking and multithreading
		Less address space protection than NT
		New program manager
		NT-like graphics capabilities
		Plug-and-play hardware installation
NT 4.0	August 1996	NT 4.0 API
		Greater stability than Windows 95
Windows 98	June 1998	32-bit file allocation
		Integrated browser
		Bug fixes

In the beginning, the development of a graphical operating system for the PC was a joint effort between Microsoft and IBM. But soon, the two companies had major strategic and tactical differences. IBM's efforts resulted in a product called Operating System/2, or OS/2. It seemed that Windows and OS/2 would share the PC operating system market. However, for reasons unrelated to its technical merits, OS/2 quickly lost ground to Windows. Although OS/2 Warp version 4.0 is still on the market, its present market share is so small that it is frequently ignored.

Text-based and Graphical Programs

To a programmer, DOS and Windows are in different worlds. DOS programs have complete and unrestricted access to the machine's hardware. When the code gains control it can do whatever it pleases. Its only limitations are the hardware capabilities and the programmer's skills. Although the designers of DOS-like operating systems often list rules that *well-behaved* programs should follow, there is no way of enforcing these rules. Intentionally or by error a DOS program can raise havoc with the system by deleting files from storage and even attempting to physically destroy a hardware device. Each DOS application has total control over all system resources. It can allocate all memory to itself, set whatever video mode is convenient, control the printer and the communications lines, and manage the mouse and the keyboard. Resources need not be shared because the operating system is dormant while an application is in the foreground. In this environment, it is rare that more than one application executes simultaneously.

The programmer developing a DOS graphics application can count on little help from the operating system. Originally, a few attempts were made at providing some elementary graphics support services at the BIOS level. Most of them never worked well or else had extremely bad performance. For example, the original BIOS interface had services for reading and setting a screen pixel in a mode-independent fashion. But these functions were so badly implemented and executed so slowly that they have not been used in practice. For these reasons, a DOS program must initialize the graphics modes and devices, and control them by implementing all the necessary device drivers and primitive functions in program code. Implementing a graphical user interface for an individual application is a monumental task. Saying that the DOS graphics programmer has total control over the machine resources but little assistance from the operating system summarizes the situation.

Windows applications, on the other hand, must share resources between themselves and with the operating system. Memory, CPU, display hardware, communications lines and devices, mouse, keyboard, and disk storage are all shared. Each program operates in its private address space and has limited access to other memory areas. Code cannot access the hardware devices directly but must to do so through operating system services called the Application Program Interface (API). As we will shortly see, this mechanism ensures that all programs are well behaved.

Windows and DOS graphics programming are quite different. Because all resources are shared, Windows must control access to all devices and resources, including memory, the video system, communications devices, and input and output components. Figure 2-1 shows how DOS and Windows programs access system resources.

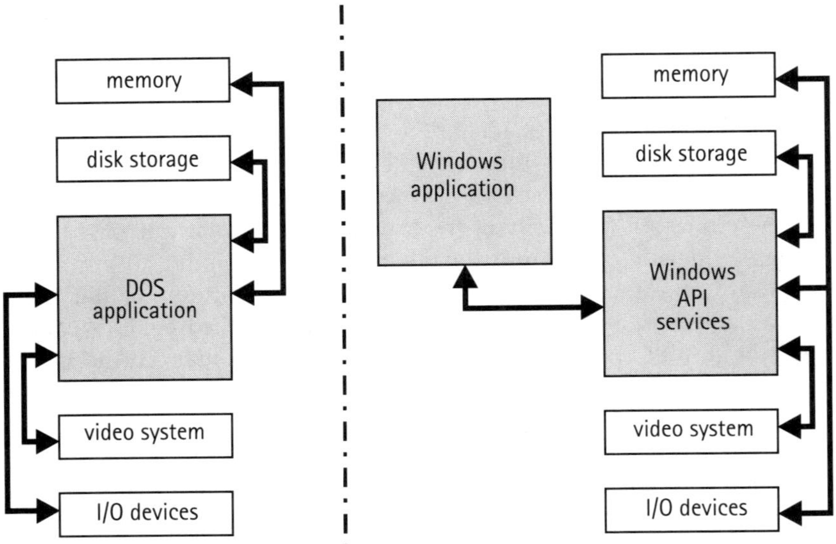

Figure 2-1: DOS and Windows applications access system resources differently.

Graphics Services

Windows is a graphical operating system; therefore, a Windows application is a graphics program. Because Windows applications use a graphical user interface, and because an application's access to resources must be controlled, Windows is forced to provide a host of graphics services to applications. In a protected-mode environment, applications cannot access memory or devices directly. If an application attempts to do so, the CPU notifies the operating system (Windows in this case) which proceeds first to halt and eventually to destroy the offending program. The general rule under Windows is *Behave or you will be destroyed.* The Windows graphics programmer has no direct control over the machine resources, but the operating system provides services that allow supervised access.

Programming Models

The nature of the operating system environment determines the programming models. In DOS, a program is "the god of the machine." The running code has unrestricted access and control. It executes on its own strengths, implements its own functionality, and calls the operating system only to request a specific service. It shares the machine with no other program. Therefore, the programming model for a DOS program is a set of sequential instructions and program constructs. Control does not return to the operating system until the application terminates. This form of interaction between the application and the operating system gives rise to the *sequential programming model.*

The *conceptual model* for a Windows program is quite different. In the Windows program, the code has no direct access to devices and resources and must share the machine with other applications and with the operating system itself. True multitasking implies the power of the OS to preempt (turn off, switch off) a thread or application. Non-preemptive multitasking (as in Windows 3.*x*) is unreliable and dangerous. In Windows 3.*x*, the OS has little control over applications, and threads have no real share of CPU time. The current versions of Windows implement preemptive multitasking so the operating system can switch the foreground (CPU access) from one application to another. If an application misbehaves, Windows can simply turn it off. Therefore, it is the operating system that is "the god of the machine," not the running program.

Event-driven Programs

To accommodate the mode of interaction between an application and the system code, a new programming model is necessary. The model is sometimes called *event-driven programming.* In event-driven programming, synchronization between the operating system and the application is in the form of program events. For example, when the user changes the size of an application's window (a user event), the operating system takes the appropriate action and then notifies the application code (a system event). The application, in turn, may decide to take its own action to update its display area, or it may decide not to take any action at all. In either case, it returns control to the operating system. The event-driven model, although simple and effective, can appear odd to a programmer used to working in DOS. In the case of a Windows program, the application's code is no longer a sequential set of instructions, but a series of blocks of code that execute when the corresponding message is received.

The event-driven model is implemented by means of messages passed among the participants. In this example, we can say that in response to the user's window-resizing event, the mouse device sent a message to the operating system, which in turn, sent a message to the application. These messages, however, are not like the interrupts so often used in DOS programming. DOS interrupts can run concurrently; that is, a new interrupt can take place before the previous one has concluded. On the other hand, Windows messages are queued and must wait in line until their turn for processing arrives.

DOS programmers have to change their mindset when working in Windows. Figure 2-2 shows two models of programming: the sequential model in a DOS program and the event-driven model in a Windows program. In DOS, the application receives control at load time and retains it during its entire life span. In a Windows program, a user-input event sends a message to the operating system. The operating system takes the appropriate action and sends a message to the corresponding application. The application looks at the message and decides if an action is required or if the message should be ignored. In either case, it returns control to Windows. At termination time, the application sends a message to Windows requesting to be ended.

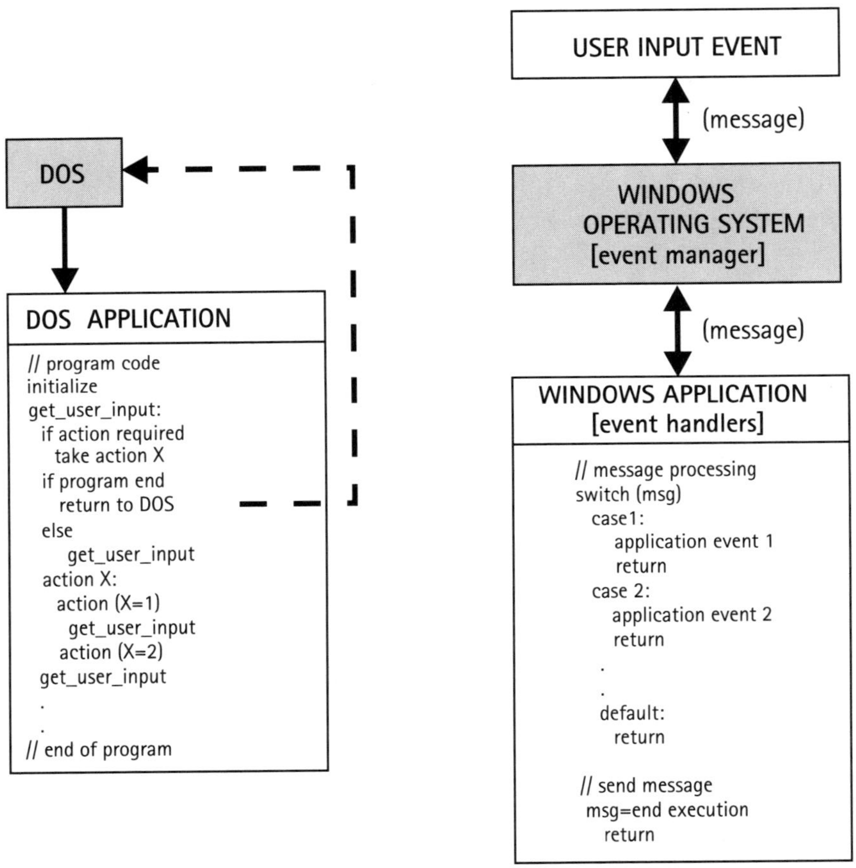

Figure 2-2: Comparing DOS (sequential) and Windows (event-driven) programming models

The Event Manager

The principal difference between sequential and event-driven programs is that one is active and the other one is passive. Event-driven code need not provide loops to monitor user input because Windows performs this function. The application stays dormant until it is notified by the operating system that an event has taken place. It is the operating system code that must monitor the hardware devices to detect actions that must be handled by the code. This function is called *event management*, and Windows is the *event manager*.

It is the event manager's responsibility to detect events and to make sure that applications that must react to the events are promptly notified. This is usually called an *event-dispatch* operation. The event manager monitors hardware devices that can generate events, such as the keyboard and the mouse. The software routine that checks for action on the event-generating devices is sometimes called the *event loop*.

The Event Handler

In the event-driven model, the application is the *event handler*. Its function is to wait for an event to occur and then perform the corresponding action. The event handler does not monitor event-generating devices directly, and often does not provide the first level response to an event. It simply performs the action or actions within its responsibilities and returns control to the event manager.

DOS graphics programmers may feel relieved by the fact that all the complications of the device interface are performed at the system level. In this sense, event-driven programs are easier to code because the "dirty work" is done by the operating system.

Event Types

Events can be grouped into several types, although the classification is not very rigorous. Often one event can be placed into more than one group according to our own definitions. Three general groups, however, can be delimited without much overlap:

- System events
- Control events
- Program events

One event often triggers another one of the same or a different type. For example, a system-generated event can generate a control event. Or a program event can be the cause of a system event, which, in turn, generates another system event, and so forth. This interaction between events creates an *event chain*, and it is this interconnection between related events that sometimes makes it difficult to pinpoint a particular event type.

System Events

This group consists of events that originate in the operating system software. For example, if the user presses the left mouse button while the cursor is inside the client area, Windows sends a `WM_LBUTTONDOWN` message to the application. This message indicates to the application code that a certain action has taken place (or is about to take place) to which, perhaps, the program should respond. Many other system-generated events are possible, including a user typing on the keyboard, selecting a menu item, moving the mouse cursor, dragging an object with the mouse, resizing a window, or operating a scroll bar control.

Control Events

Control events relate to graphics control objects, which are very abundant in the Windows environment. Among them are buttons, list boxes, combo boxes, scroll bars, up/down controls, and many others. A control event takes place when user interaction with a control requires a reaction from the operating system or the application. In this case, the control *sends a message* to the operating system. If necessary, the operating system can then generate an event to notify the application of the user's action.

Much of the programming required to implement a user interface consists of responding to control events. The reason is that Windows programs have available many standard controls. Programmers usually find it more convenient to use one of these canned components than to create a customized one. Windows controls are discussed in greater detail later in this chapter.

Program Events

In Figure 2-3 you can see that the termination of a Windows application requires that the program code send the corresponding message to the operating system. In this case, the application originates an event in the form of a request to terminate execution. This type of event is called a *programmer-created* or *program event.*

Event Modeling

A program event is generated when the application code sends a message to the operating system requiring a service or action. However, program events rarely occur at the origin of the event chain. For example, the program event that requests program termination often originates in a control event in which the user indicated a desire to end the program. Figure 2-3 shows the event chain that takes place when a user clicks on the close button on a Window's title bar.In Figure 2-3, the message sent by the operating system to the application is labeled `WM_DESTROY`. This is one of many standard messages used by Windows. The `WM_DESTROY` message indicates to an application that the operating system has already destroyed the window, and the message is therefore received after the fact. Another Windows message named `WM_CLOSE` is sent to an application to notify it that it is time to clean up and terminate. `WM_CLOSE` is a sort of warning; Figure 2-3 is actually a rough sketch of a process, which actually entails several other steps.

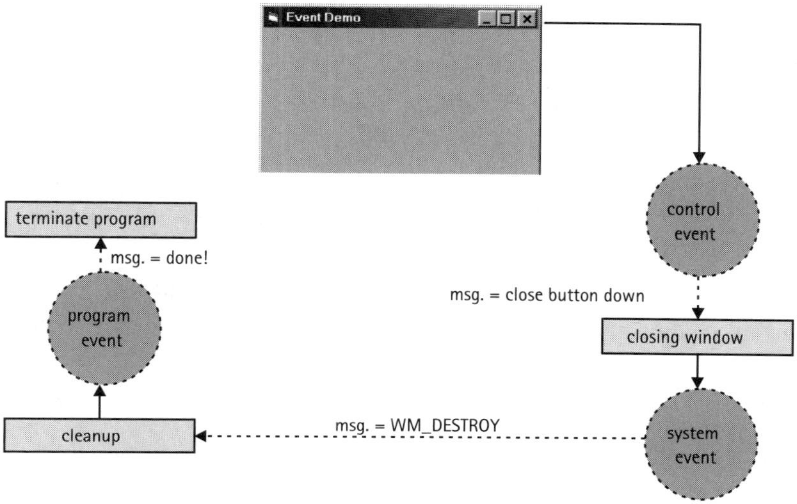

Figure 2-3: An event chain occurs when the user clicks the Close button.

The Windows messaging system that results from event generation and handling mechanisms can get quite complicated. The programmer or program designer often needs to create a model of an event chain. Several modeling tools have been developed for the purpose of graphically depicting processes and data. Data flow and entity-relationship diagrams are well-known tools used by program designers. However, these conventional tools are not well suited to modeling event-driven systems. Several authors have introduced variations of the data-flow diagrams that are better suited for representing systems in which events take place in real time. In Figure 2-3 we have used symbols from conventional data-flow diagrams and from the Ward and Mellor extensions to model an event chain. More elaborate and detailed representations could include symbols for data stores, control stores, and for processes.

File Structure of a Windows Program

In addition to adopting an event-driven programming model in replacement of the conventional sequential model, the Windows programmer also needs to become familiar with the file structure of a Windows application. Many DOS programs have simple file structures. In many cases, the only files external to the source are the various include files listed in the program header. Internally, the DOS compiler sets the necessary linker options, references the corresponding libraries, and creates the executable file. The process is almost completely transparent to the programmer. Windows compilers are also designed to automatically manage much of the complications of program generation; however, Windows programs usually require more files than their DOS counterparts. Several of these files have no equivalent in DOS systems.

Source Files

The source files in Windows are of the same type as in DOS programming. In both cases, they contain the language statements and constructs of a C or C++ program. Specific filename extensions are associated with different source file types: .C, .CPP, and .H. The .C extension depicts a program in C. The presence of this extension usually indicates that the program is coded in straight C; therefore, it does not include any keywords and constructs that are part of C++. The .CPP extension indicates a source file that can contain C++-specific keywords and constructs. The .H extension corresponds to a header file, usually referenced at the beginning of a program by means of the `#include` statement.

Library Files

C and C++ are small languages: they do not provide functions for performing input and output operations. For this reason, most useful programs coded in C or C++ require support libraries to provide the functionalities that are not part of the language. Most DOS programs, and virtually all Windows programs, require the support of library functions.

Library files differ from source files. All the program files containing source code are merged at compile time. Library functions are incorporated at link time, although the internal mechanisms of C and C++ development systems sometimes prevent us from noticing the difference. What often happens is that an `#include` statement in a source file references a header file, which in turn, contains references to other sources or to object code in a library. These references are usually made by means of the `extern` declarator, which serves to indicate that a variable or function has external linkage. Figure 2-4 shows the different source, object, and library files that can be part of a C or C++ program.

Resource Files

Windows programs have access to data items stored within the executable file, or in a library file, called *resources*. Although resources are data, and though they are often associated with the program's .EXE file, they are unique. In the first place, resources cannot be modified at run time. They are actually read-only files and are not directly accessible to program code. Furthermore, resources do not reside in the program's data area. At load time, program resources are usually left on a disk file until they are needed. Typical resources are icons, cursors, dialog boxes, menus, bitmaps, and character strings.

The current generation of software tools for developing Windows applications, such as Microsoft Visual C++ and Borland C++, contain special tools for working with resources. In the Microsoft system there are several specialized resource editors. The initial screen of a resource-editing interface is shown in Figure 2-5. The resource-editing tools in the Borland software are part of what is called the *Resource Workshop*.

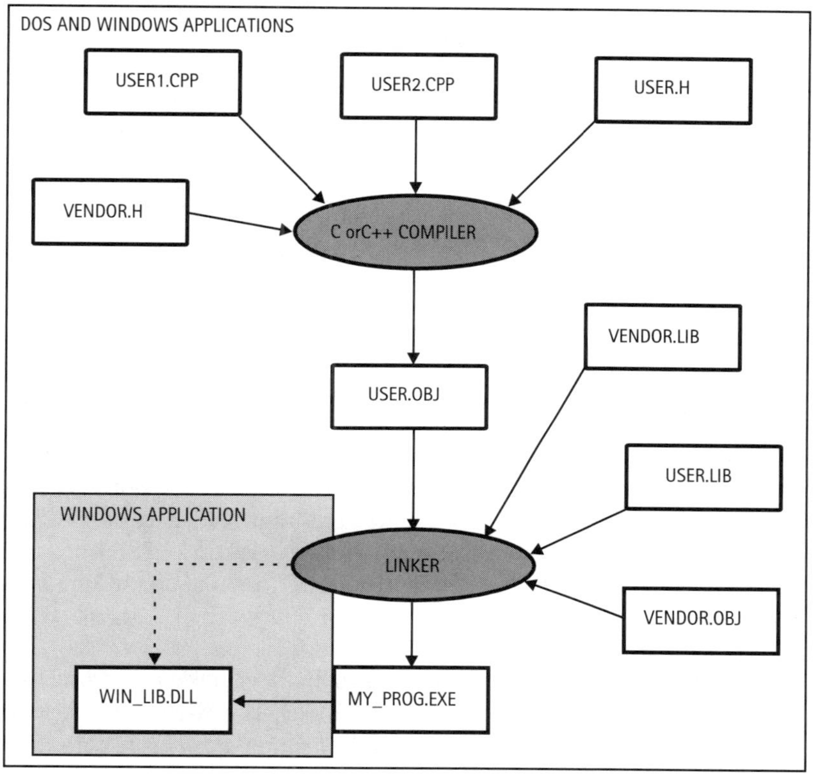

Figure 2-4: A C or C++ program can contain source, object, and library files from various sources.

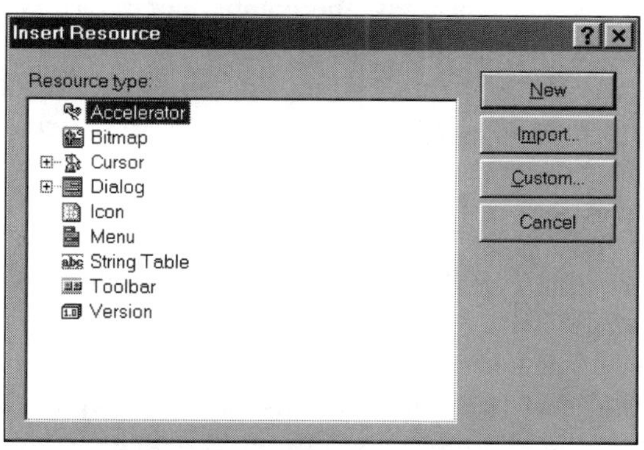

Figure 2-5: The initial screen of Microsoft Visual C++ Resource Editor

Resources, which have no equivalent in DOS programming, provide the following several advantages to Windows applications:

- User interface components are isolated from the rest of the code.
- Applications can be modified without changing the resources.
- Data can be shared among applications by reusing the same resources.
- Graphical elements in the user interface can be created easily.
- Graphical elements in the user interface can be modified without changing the application code.

Several special file types are used by Windows to manage resources. The resource script file (extension .RC) is an ASCII text file from which the binary resources are created. Resource script files can be created manually by the programmer or they can be automatically generated by the resource facilities in the development environment. The Resource Compiler program, which is part of the development system, produces binary resource files (extension .RES) from the ASCII script files (extension .RC). In Microsoft Visual C++, the command line version of the Resource Compiler is named RC.EXE; in Borland C++ it is named BRCC.EXE or BRCC32.EXE.

Before Windows 95, the Resource Compiler also had the task of adding the binary resources to the executable file created by the linker. The Microsoft linker for Windows 95, furnished with Visual C++, can directly manipulate files in both .OBJ and .RES formats.

Make Files

During the evolution of software-development systems, the component programs became increasingly more powerful. Consequently, the number of switches, options, and modes that could be selected in compilers, linkers, and other tools also grew rapidly. It became progressively more difficult for the programmer to remember and enter all of these options every time a project had to be compiled or updated. Various forms of so-called *make* programs and utilities were developed to remedy this situation. By means of a make program the programmer would record all of the switches and options in a text file and the make utility would automatically apply them in a particular project.

In DOS programming, the simplest implementation of a make utility is a batch file. An additional refinement is a program that reads the switches and options selected in the development environment, and applies them to the assembler, compiler, linker, or other software tools. In most environments, the use of the make program is optional. However, in the Windows platform the options and controls are so intricate that most programmers would not consider entering them manually.

All major Windows C and C++ development systems for the PC have a make utility. In Microsoft's Visual C++, it is named NMAKE.EXE. In the Borland system, it is called MAKE.EXE. The text file for either system has the extension .MAK. Make files consist of instructions in ASCII-text format. They can be created manually or generated automatically by the development environment. The make programs can be entered from the command line or they can be activated from inside the development environment, usually by selecting a specific menu option. The method that we follow in this book takes advantage of the Visual C++ Development Environment to automatically compile and link the program sources. Therefore, no specific make file is necessary.

Object Files

The compiler program generates a file called an object file, which has the extension .OBJ. The Microsoft Visual C++ development system uses the Common Object File Format (COFF) specification, which originated in the UNIX operating system. The Microsoft version of COFF adds additional header data to make the format compatible with DOS and with 16-bit versions of Windows.

The compilers in Windows development systems have many different switches, options, and modes of operation selectable by the user. In Visual C++, the compiler options are selected through the Settings command of the Build menu. The Project Settings dialog box contains a C/C++ tab, which activates the compiler switches and controls, as shown in Figure 2-6.Once the C/C++ tab is active in the Project Settings, a drop-down list box labeled Category is displayed. When the Category box is expanded (see Figure 2-6), eight options appear. Selecting any one of these options activates a dialog box with a new set of selectable choices. The Warning Level and Optimizations drop down list boxes are also shown in Figure 2-6. The compiler warning level determines the severity of warnings for which the compiler generates a message. Optimizations consist of four predefined modes: default, disable, maximize speed, and minimize size. In addition, an entry labeled Customize (not shown in Figure 2-6) is also in the list box. Selecting this option activates another list box of customized optimizations when the Optimizations option is selected in the Category list box.

Mastering all of the compiler options and switches requires considerable experience with the development environment. Most programmers use the default settings and make modifications to these settings only when necessary. However, graphics applications such as computer games or display-intensive programs often need to obtain the maximum possible performance from the machine and the software. In this case, the programmer should be able to handle the project settings to maximize critical performance elements. In this book, we often describe manipulations of the project settings options to perform customizations or to improve code performance.

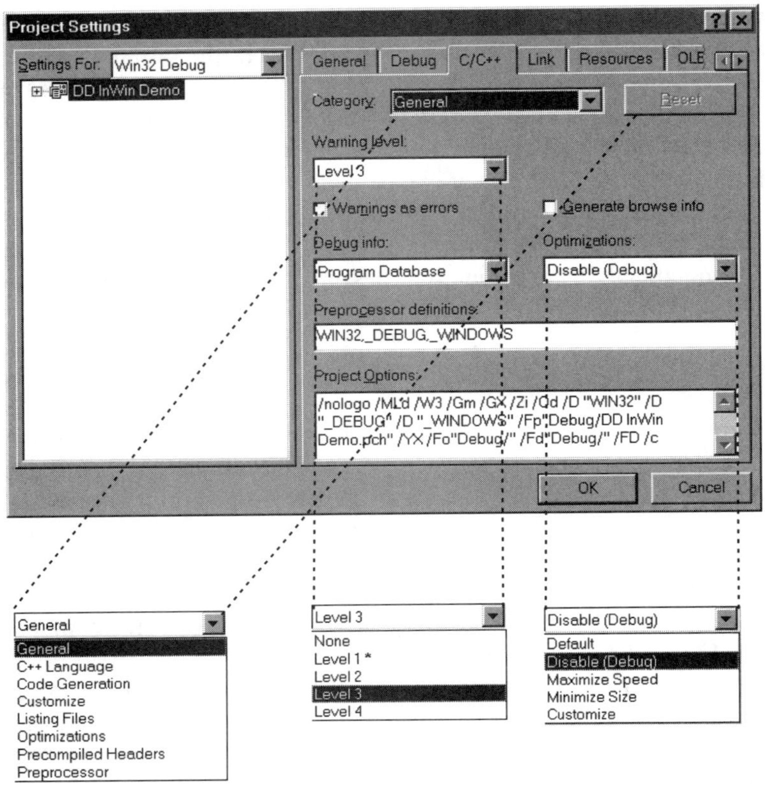

Figure 2-6: In Microsoft Visual C++ the compiler options are selected by clicking the C/C++ tab in the Project Settings dialog box.

Executable Files

In both DOS and Windows, the executable file is generated by a linker program. The link command can be entered manually from the command line, through a batch file or make program, or it can be entered automatically by the development environment. In Windows 95 systems, the link operation takes an object file generated by the compiler or assembler (extension .OBJ), the library files generated by a library manager (extension .LIB), files in Common Object File Format (extension .COFF), and the binary resource files created by the resource compiler (extension .RES), and creates an executable file with the extension .EXE. In addition, the Microsoft linker automatically converts 32-bit Object Module Format (.OMF) files into COFF. The output of the linker can also be a dynamic link library (extension .DLL).

The linker is the tool that generates the executable file. However, the Windows development environments can activate the linker functions indirectly. In Microsoft Visual C++, the CL program can be used to compile source files, or to compile and then link object files into executables. Make files can also reference the linker operation. In Borland C++, the default mode is that the compiler automatically calls the linker, so an explicit link command is not required unless the default mode of operation has been changed. Additionally, most command-line linkers can read special response files that store the switches, options, and filenames normally entered by the user. In the Borland system, a file called a *configuration file* is used for the linker options, and a linker response file serves to enter both options and filenames.

As in the case of the compiler, a considerable number of switches and options can be selected at link time. In Visual C++, the linker options are activated through the Settings command of the Build menu. The Project Settings dialog box contains a Link tab, as shown in Figure 2-7.

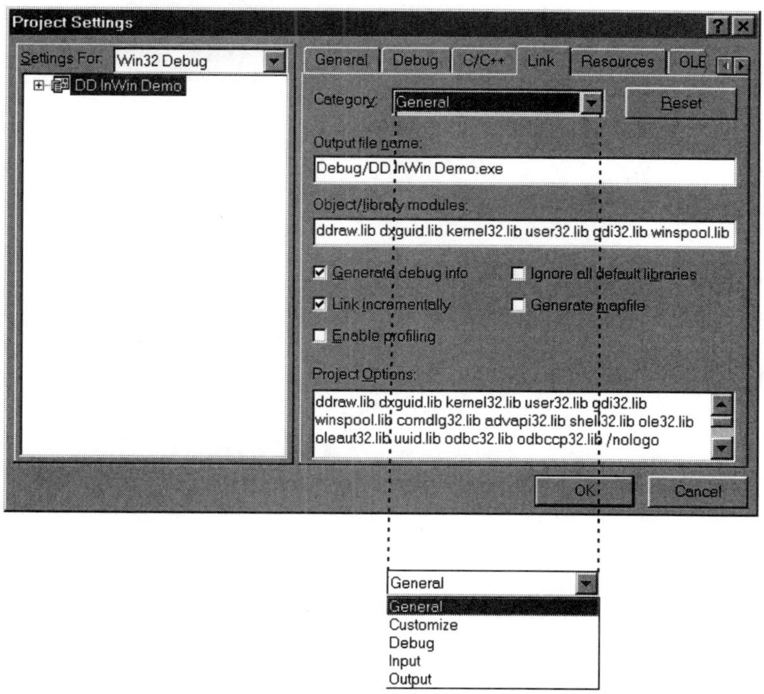

Figure 2-7: In Microsoft Visual C++, the linker options are selected by clicking the Link tab in the Project Settings dialog box.

When the Link tab is active in the Project Settings, a drop-down list box labeled Category is displayed. Five options appear when the Category box is expanded (see Figure 2-7). Selecting any one of these options activates a dialog box with a new set of selectable choices. Table 2-2 lists the options related to each of the entries in the Category box as they relate to the linker command-line options.

TABLE 2-2 LINK OPTIONS IN THE PROJECT SETTINGS DIALOG BOX

Project Setting	Command-Line Switch Screens	Default State
General Category		
Output File Name	/OUT:filename	NONE
Object	/Library Modules filename on command line	NONE
Generate Debug Info		/DEBUGON
Link Incrementally	/INCREMENTAL:{YES|NO}	ON
Enable Profiling	/PROFILE	OFF
Ignore All Default		
Libraries	/NODEFAULTLIB	OFF
Generate Mapfile	/MAP	OFF
Customize Category		
Use Program Database	/PDB:filename	ON
Link Incrementally	/INCREMENTAL:{YES|NO}	YES
Program Database Name	/PDB:filename	NONE
Output File Name	/OUT:filename	NONE
Force File Output	/FORCE	OFF
Print Progress Messages	/VERBOSE	OFF
Suppress Startup Banner	/NOLOGO	ON
Debug Category		
Mapfile Name	/MAP:filename	NONE
Generate Mapfile	/MAP	OFF
Generate Debug Info	/DEBUG	OFF
Microsoft Format	/DEBUGTYPE:CV	OFF
COFF Format	/DEBUGTYPE:COFF	OFF
Both Formats	/DEBUGTYPE:BOTH	OFF

Project Setting	Command-Line Switch Screens	Default State
Input Category		
Object	/Library Modules filename on command line	NONE
Ignore Libraries	/NODEFAULTLIB:library	OFF
Ignore All Default		
Libraries	/NODEFAULTLIB	OFF
Force Symbol		
References	/INCLUDE:symbol	NONE
MS-DOS Stub File Name	/STUB:filename	NONE
Output Category		
Base Address	/BASE:address	NONE
Entry-Point Symbol	/ENTRY:function	NONE
Stack Allocations	/STACK:reserve,commit	NONE
Version Information	/VERSION:major.minor	NONE
Common Options		
/nologo/subsystem: windows/machine:|386		

Learning how to use all the linker switches and options requires a mastery of the development system as well as an intimate knowledge of the Windows operating system. Most programmers change the default linker options only when absolutely necessary, but this attitude often results in the sacrifice of functionality and performance. In this book, we often change linker options to accommodate the high performance requirements of graphics applications.

Dynamic Linking

One of the unique characteristics of Windows is dynamic linking. In DOS, the linker operates statically: it takes one or more object and library files and merges them into an executable which physically includes all the code in both the sources and the library modules (see Figure 2-4). Windows programs use conventional libraries and source files at link time, but they also use a special type of file called a *dynamic-link library* or DLL. In dynamic linking, the library files are referenced at link time, but the code is not physically incorporated into the executable. When the program runs, the required run-time libraries are loaded into memory and the references are resolved.

Dynamic-link libraries are binary files that have functions that can be shared by several applications. In addition to sharing code between applications, DLLs can be used to break up an application into separate components that are more manageable and easier to upgrade. Dynamic linking has the following advantages:

- Several processes can share the same code, thus saving memory space and reducing access time.
- DLLs can be modified and upgraded independently of the applications that use them. Programs that use static libraries must be recompiled when the libraries are modified. This mechanism can be effectively used to provide after-sale support for a program.
- DLLs can be accessed from different programming languages or environments as long as the application follows the calling conventions.

There are also disadvantages associated with DLLs. One of them is that the code is not self-contained because it depends on the DLL's files being present on the target system. If a process that uses load-time dynamic linking references a DLL that is not available on the host machine, Windows immediately terminates the program. In the case of applications that depend on run-time dynamic linking, the program is not terminated if the DLL is not loaded, but the functionality associated with the missing DLL is not available to the code.

Dynamic link libraries are stored in different formats and associated with various filename extensions. In Windows 95, the standard extension is .DLL but files with the extension .EXE, .DRV, .FON, and others can also perform as dynamic-link libraries. The system-level DLL files, such as KERNEL32.DLL, USER32.DLL, and GDI32.DLL, are found in the WIN95\SYSTEM directory. Files with the extension .DLL are loaded automatically by Windows. Others must be explicitly loaded by the program module using the `LoadLibary()` or `LoadLibaryEx()` API functions.

In addition to DLLs, the two following types of libraries and their associated files are used in Windows programming:

- **Object libraries** (extension .LIB) contain object code that is added to the application at link time. Object libraries are used in static linking. The standard C libraries named LIBC.LIB and LIBCMT.LIB are in this group.
- **Import libraries** (extension .LIB) are a special form of an object library that contains no code. Import libraries provide information to the linker regarding dynamic-link libraries. Access to the dynamic-link library GDI32.DLL can be gained by means of the import library named GDI32.LIB.

Characteristics of Windows Programming

Experienced and talented DOS programmers are often intimidated by their first encounter with a Windows program. Windows programming has been described as weird, convoluted, and awkward. Popular computer culture considers Windows programmers the priests of some arcane and mysterious cult that's access requires extraordinary talents and years' of knowledge. Those initiated into this "rocket science of programming," and the companies that make millions of dollars selling products that reputedly "help simplify Windows programming," sometimes demonstrate a vested interest in preserving these myths.

In fact, Windows general programming is not more difficult than DOS programming, although at first Windows programs appear more complicated. Regarding graphics, Windows programs are much easier to design and code than their DOS counterparts. Windows is a graphics environment and it contains a multitude of services, canned routines, and coding aids not available in DOS. Anyone who has ever implemented a graphical user interface for a DOS application will greatly appreciate the graphics facilities in Windows.

In their book "The C Programming Language" (published by Prentice-Hall in 1978), Kernighan and Ritchie, list the code for a short program that displays the message "hello, world!" on the screen. This program has since been known as the *Hello World program*, and many other authors of programming books have followed their lead. The C++ version of the Hello World program is as follows:

```
#include <iostream.h>
void main() {
  cout << "\nHello, World!";
}
```

In a text-based operating system, such as DOS or UNIX, the Hello World program is quite simple. The message is displayed at the current position of the text cursor, with whatever attributes are active. It assumes that the video system is a "glass teletype" that scrolls automatically when the text reaches the end of the screen. This text-based paradigm has no provisions for graphical user interfaces or for multitasking.

A Windows program that performs these same functions must deal with many other levels of complexity. In the first place, it must coexist and share resources with the operating system and with other applications. Earlier in this chapter, we discussed the model of an event-driven program which is necessary in this case. In addition, a Windows application is a graphics-based, not a text-based program. Finally, the program executes as a window that can be overlapped, overlaid, minimized, maximized, one to which keyboard and mouse input can be given or withdrawn, and with many other functions. As can be expected, the code is lengthier, although it is relatively simple considering the functionality achieved. The following is a listing for a Windows 95 version of the Hello World program:

```
/*******************************************************
   WIN_HELLO.CPP - Displays the message "Hello World from
   Windows 95!" in the client area.
*******************************************************/
#include <windows.h>
LRESULT CALLBACK WndProc (HWND, UINT, WPARAM, LPARAM) ;
// WinMain()
int WINAPI WinMain (HINSTANCE hInstance, HINSTANCE
                    hPrevInstance, PSTR szCmdLine,
                    int iCmdShow)
{
  static char szAppName[] = "WinHello" ;
  HWND         hwnd ;
  MSG          msg ;
  // Defining a structure of type WNDCLASSEX
  WNDCLASSEX  wndclass ;
  wndclass.cbSize        = sizeof (wndclass) ;
  wndclass.style         = CS_HREDRAW | CS_VREDRAW ;
  wndclass.lpfnWndProc   = WndProc ;
  wndclass.cbClsExtra    = 0 ;
  wndclass.cbWndExtra    = 0 ;
  wndclass.hInstance     = hInstance ;
  wndclass.hIcon         = LoadIcon (NULL, IDI_APPLICATION) ;
  wndclass.hCursor       = LoadCursor (NULL, IDC_ARROW) ;
  wndclass.hbrBackground = (HBRUSH) GetStockObject
                           (WHITE_BRUSH) ;
  wndclass.lpszMenuName  = NULL ;
  wndclass.lpszClassName = szAppName ;
  wndclass.hIconSm       = LoadIcon (NULL, IDI_APPLICATION) ;
  // Registering the structure wmdclass
  RegisterClassEx (&wndclass) ;
  // CreateWindow()
  hwnd = CreateWindow (szAppName,
        "WIN_HELLO Program",       // window caption
         WS_OVERLAPPEDWINDOW,      // window style
         CW_USEDEFAULT,            // initial x position
         CW_USEDEFAULT,            // initial y position
         500,                      // initial x size
         300,                      // initial y size
```

```
          NULL,                       // parent window handle
          NULL,                       // window menu handle
          hInstance,                  // program instance handle
          NULL) ;                        // creation parameters
  ShowWindow (hwnd, iCmdShow) ;
  UpdateWindow (hwnd) ;
  // Message loop
      while (GetMessage (&msg, NULL, 0, 0))
          {
          TranslateMessage (&msg) ;
          DispatchMessage (&msg) ;
          }
     return msg.wParam ;
}
// Window procedure
LRESULT CALLBACK WndProc (HWND hwnd, UINT iMsg, WPARAM wParam,
                          LPARAM lParam)
{
     HDC         hdc ;
     PAINTSTRUCT ps ;
     RECT        rect ;
     switch (iMsg)
          {
          case WM_PAINT :
               hdc = BeginPaint (hwnd, &ps) ;
               GetClientRect (hwnd, &rect) ;
               DrawText (hdc, "Hello World from Windows 95!",
                         -1, &rect, DT_SINGLELINE | DT_CENTER |
                         DT_VCENTER) ;
               EndPaint (hwnd, &ps) ;
               return 0 ;
          case WM_DESTROY :
               PostQuitMessage (0) ;
               return 0 ;
          }
     return DefWindowProc (hwnd, iMsg, wParam, lParam) ;
}
```

Figure 2-8 shows the result of the WIN_HELLO program.

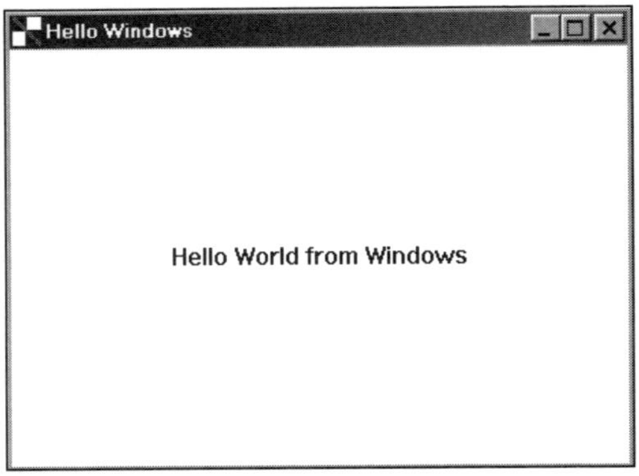

Figure 2-8: The result of the WIN_HELLO program

Naming Conventions

A programmer used to working in a non-Windows environment will immediately notice that a Windows program has certain unfamiliar elements. One of them is the unusual names assigned to variables. For example, in the WIN_HELLO program, we find the following line:

```
static char szAppName[] = "WinHello" ;
```

If you are a C or C++ programmer the statement itself is quite familiar: it is the declaration and initialization of a static array of type char. What may strike you as unusual is the array name `szAppName` This name, which is later used in the `CreateWindows()` function, follows the conventions recommended by Microsoft for variable names. Reputedly, this naming style originated with a Microsoft programmer of Hungarian descent named Charles Simonyi, and is, in his honor, called *Hungarian notation.*

In Hungarian notation the variable name provides a way for identifying the data type. In `szAppName`, the prefix `sz` stands for *s*tring terminated in *z*ero. The word or words that follow the prefix describe the variable contents, in this case the *app*lication *name*. Table 2-3 lists the standard variable name prefixes recommended by Microsoft.

Table 2-3 STANDARD PREFIXES RECOMMENDED BY MICROSOFT

Prefix	Data Type	Interpretation
b/f	BOOL	zero = false, non-zero = true (f stands for flag)

Prefix	Data Type	Interpretation
by	BYTE	8-bit unsigned integer
ch	CHAR	single ASCII character
cx/cy	INT	count of *x* values and count of *y* values
d	DOUBLE	IEEE double precision real
dw	DWORD	32-bit integer
h	HANDLE	32-bit unsigned integer handle
hwnd	HWND	handle to a Window
i	INT	16-bit integer value
l	LONG	32-bit unsigned integer value
lp/np	FAR*	32-bit far pointer
n	SHORT	16-bit unsigned integer value
p	pointer	any pointer, usually far
pt	POINT	32-bit coordinates, labeled x and y, packed in a structure
rgb	RGB	red, green, and blue values packed in 32-bits as follows: 00BB GGRR
x/y	INT	x-coordinate and y-coordinate
s	array of char	string
sz	array of char	string terminated in zero
w	WORD	16-bit unsigned integer

The merits of Hungarian notation are passionately debated. Those who support it claim that it helps avoid data-type mismatch errors because the variable name itself describes the data type. The detractors say that linking the name and the data type forces the programmer to alter the name whenever the data type is changed, which can lead to unnecessary program editing. Also, Microsoft itself does not follow Hungarian notation consistently because in many cases this style leads to confusion.

Perhaps the most noted source of confusion caused by Hungarian notation is the `wParam` passed to the Windows procedure (see WinProc in the WIN_HELLO program listing). In this case, `wParam` indicates a word according to the naming convention, but when the Win32 API was developed, `wParam` was changed to a 32-bit unsigned integer. For consistency with older code, the Windows documentation still refers to it as `wParam`, which is confusing and inconsistent, to say the least.

In principle, we agree that Hungarian notation creates more problems than it solves. However, deviating from it only makes things worse because Microsoft has officially adopted it in Windows and in the Visual C++ documentation. In this book, we use Hungarian notation in the sample programs and the code listing, especially when referring to Windows data types and structures. In our own variables we use it rather loosely, and only for the sake of simplicity and uniformity.

Regarding Function names, there is less reason for debate. Microsoft suggests that programmers use a verb-noun model that describes what the function does and what it operates on: like, for example, the Windows API functions `BeginPaint()`, `GetClientRect()`, `DrawText()`, and `EndPaint()` referenced in the WIN_HELLO program listed earlier in this chapter. The function name begins with a capital letter and so does every other word in the function name. The underscore is not used as a separator. Because this style is familiar to most C and C++ programmers, we need not adopt a different one for our own functions.

Numeric Constants

The Windows header files define many numeric constants that can be a source of bewilderment to the uninitiated. For example, in the WIN_HELLO program listed previously, we find the upper-case identifiers `CS_HREDRAW`, `CS_VREDRAW`, `WS_OVERLAPPEDWINDOW`, and `CW_USEDEFAULT`, among others. These, and many other identifiers, serve as placeholders for numeric constants. The rationale is that symbolic names are more significant than numeric values, and that they can be changed transparently to the code and the documentation. Table 2-4 lists the meaning of some common prefixes used for numeric constants. Many others not listed here are also used by Windows functions.

TABLE 2-4 SOME COMMON WINDOWS PREFIXES FOR NUMERIC CONSTANTS

Prefix	Type
BS	button style
CBS	combo-box style
CS	class style
CW	create window related
DT	draw text related
DS	dialog box style
ES	edit class style
IDI	ID number of an icon

Prefix	Type
IDC	ID number of a cursor
LBS	list-box style
SBS	scroll-bar style
SS	static class style
WS	window style
WM	window message

Windows Handles

In the context of Windows programming, a handle is a token that represents an item, object, or resource. For example, consider the following line in the WIN_HELLO program:

```
hwnd = CreateWindow (szAppName, ...
```

This is a call to the `CreateWindows()` function, which returns a value assigned to the variable `hwnd`. In turn, `hwnd` is defined as a variable of the type `HWND`, as discussed earlier in the code listing, as follows:

```
HWND          hwnd ;
```

In this case, the value returned by the `CreateWindow()` call is a handle to a window of the type `HWND` as defined in the windows.h header file. After a handle has been obtained it can be used to reference the object or data item that it represents. For example, later in the listing of the WIN_HELLO program we see that the handle to the program's window serves to obtain system information. The call

```
GetClientRect (hwnd, &rect) ;
```

passes the handle to the Windows API function to retrieve the coordinates of the Windows client area, which are stored by the function in the structure variable named rect. In addition, Windows uses this same handle to identify a particular window to your program. If your application has several windows open simultaneously, it can tell to which of them the message refers, by examining the handle.

Many DOS programmers first learned about handles in relation to disk files. DOS has little use for handles other than for disk files and standard devices. Windows handles, on the other hand, refer to many types of objects and resources in the environment, including handles to windows, to strings, to icons, to menus, to cursors, to instances of a program, to graphical objects (including pens, brushes, fonts, and bitmaps), to dynamically allocated memory, to regions, and to color palettes. Table 2-5 lists some of the handles used frequently in Windows programming.

TABLE 2-5 COMMON WINDOWS HANDLE TYPES

Handle Identifier	Refers To
HACCEL	an accelerator
HBITMAP	a bitmap
HBRUSH	a brush
HCURSOR	a cursor
HDC	a device context
HFONT	a font
HICON	an icon
HINSTANCE	a program instance
HKEY	a registry key
HMENU	a menu
HPALETTE	a GDI palette
HPEN	a GDI pen
HRGN	a GDI region
HWND	a Window

Visual Elements of a Windows Program

Visually, a Windows application has a characteristic appearance that makes it different from a typical text-based program, and even from other programs in graphics, multitasking environments. Most of the elements that make a Windows program different are the components of the main window and the input/output controls used in implementing the graphical user interface.

The Main Window

Although it is possible for a Windows program to execute without output to the display device, most Windows applications will have a main window. The main window is a program's principal means of input and output and its only access to the screen. In Visual Basic, the main window is called the form. Figure 2-9 shows the basic components of a program's main window.

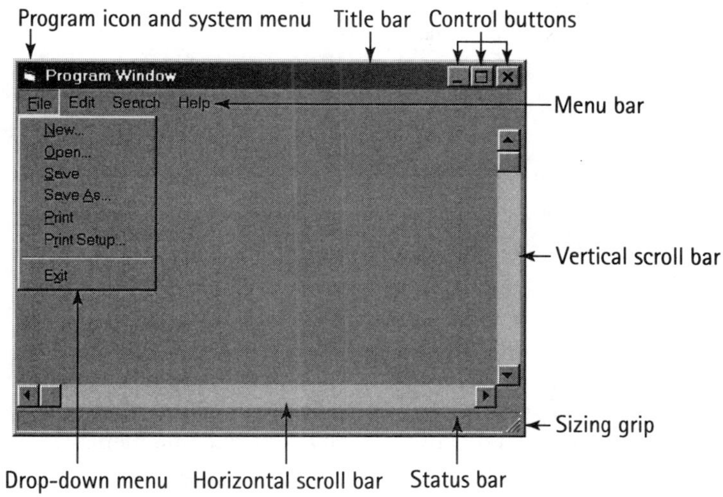

Figure 2-9: The basic graphic components of a program window

Some of the elements of the window in Figure 2-9 are present in all program windows, others must be present but can be configured in different ways, and a third group is optional. The following are the fundamental building blocks of a program window:

- The main window display has a title bar, although the caption can be left blank.
- The control buttons to the right of the title bar are used to minimize, maximize, and close the program window. The programmer can select which of these control buttons are displayed.
- The icon on the left side of the title bar activates the system menu. Programs can use the Windows default icons or one of their own.
- The menu bar is optional. A typical menu bar contains one or more drop-down menus. Each drop-down menu lists commands you can activate by a mouse click or by using the Alt key and the underlined letter code. Menu commands that expand into submenus are indicated by a small

triangle. Ellipses following the menu item indicate that additional input is required for the menu item.

- The program main window, as well as many input/output controls, can have vertical or horizontal scroll bars. Windows notifies the application of user's action on the scroll bars, but the application must provide the required processing.
- Windows programs can have a status bar at the bottom of the screen that can contain a single text display area (like the one in Figure 2-9), or be divided into multiple areas. The status bar, as its name indicates, serves to display messages that inform the user about the program's status. A status bar includes sizing grips on the right-hand side, which are used to change the window's size.
- The screen zone assigned to each program window is called the client area. The dimensions and graphics attributes of the client area can be obtained from the operating system using the window's handle.

Controls

The window in Figure 2-9 contains several controls: the buttons on the title bar, the menu items and commands, the sizing grip, the scroll bars, and the button that activates the system menu. These are just a few of the many control components available in Windows. These graphical components used in implementing input/output operations are generically called *controls.* Some controls have been around since the original Windows operating system; others were added with the various versions and revisions; still others are furnished as add-on or third-party products.

Controls are classified in two groups: *predefined controls* and *common controls.* The differences between them are mostly related to the message type used to communicate with the application and to historical considerations. Programmers can create their own customized controls and provide processing routines to operate them. In this section we refer to standard controls that are part of Windows; these include: buttons, checkboxes, edit boxes, list boxes, combo boxes, scroll bars, dialog boxes, toolbars, ToolTips, status bars, tree views and tree lists, progress bars, up/down controls, trackbars, and many others. Figure 2-10 shows some controls frequently used by Windows applications.

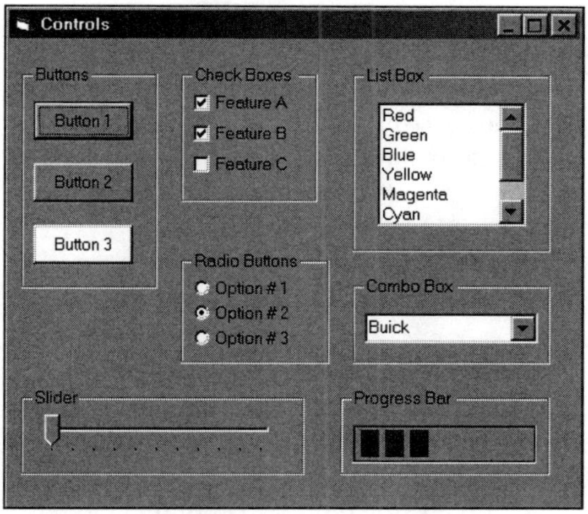

Figure 2-10: Controls frequently used by Windows applications

Other Visual Components

In addition to the input/output controls such as those shown in Figure 2-10, Windows applications have a rich selection of additional program elements available. Every Windows user is familiar with dialog boxes, list and tree views of files, tab controls, toolbars and ToolTips, and property sheets. Controls are discussed in Chapter 5. Wizards are used to assist the user in executing complex tasks. Much of Windows programming involves learning how to implement these canned program components in your own code and how to adapt them to perform the tasks that your program requires.

Programming Style

Books have been written on styles of coding, most of them not very useful to the working programmer. Furthermore, to discuss style may seem like a contradiction in itself. If style is the distinctive originality that identifies an individual, then we should let it be the result of each person's personality and not try to influence it by our opinions and recommendations. In part this is true, however, in the context of Windows programming a bad coding style easily leads to programs that are undecipherable and to the proverbial "spaghetti code."

As we mentioned earlier in this chapter, Windows programming is not difficult or profound, but many Windows programs end up being extremely complicated. Well-organized and commented sources let you quickly find the fundamental routines and grasp the basics of the processing operations. A good style promotes the organization of the code into execution blocks and the use of comments to describe the mechanism by which the program accomplishes its basic purposes. On the other hand, program comments should not be used to explain the fundamentals of a programming language nor trivial or obvious manipulations. Sometimes we see a line of code that contains several flaws, for example:

```
int var1, var2 = 22;    // Creating and initializing
                        // variables
```

In this line, we can spot several style problems. In the first place, modern programming techniques advise that each variable be declared separately. Multiple declarations and initializations are possible in C and C++, but the code is clearer if you devote a single text line to each variable. Another flaw in the sample line is that the variable names are not indicative of their function in the program. Finally, the comment is useless because any C programmer knows that the statement is a variable declaration.

Commented Headers

One way to make sure that the necessary information is included in the source is to use a predesigned comment block. Software companies often furnish their programmers with standard headers to attach to all source files. These headers serve to remind the programmer of all the items of information that should be included with each source file. The following can be used as a checklist for information that may be included in the program's commented header block:

- Developer's copyright notice
- Program name
- Programmer's name and other personal information
- Name of the source file
- List of related sources, program modules, and support files, including libraries, DLLs, and required add-ons
- Description of the development system and resources
- Program hardware and software requirements
- Program update chronology listing dates and modifications
- Program test history and bug fixes

The following is the commented header used by our own software company:

```
//*************************************************************
//*************************************************************
//                       PROGNAME.CPP
//     Copyright (c) 199? by Skipanon Software Associates
//                    ALL RIGHTS RESERVED
//*************************************************************
//*************************************************************
// Date:                            Coded by:
// Filename:                        Module name:
//                                  Source file:
// Description:
//
//*************************************************************
// Libraries and software support:
//
//*************************************************************
// Development environment:
//
//*************************************************************
// System requirements:
//
//*************************************************************
// Start date:
// Update history:
//           DATE               MODIFICATION
//
//*************************************************************
// Test history:
//  TEST PROTOCOL          DATE       TEST RESULTS
//
//*************************************************************
// Programmer comments:
//
//
//*************************************************************
//*************************************************************
```

Assertions Notation

During the past few years, there has been a movement in the programming community that favors more formal methods of program specifications. It is claimed that programs specified mathematically can be easily tested for consistency, thus avoiding many design problems and defects. Furthermore, the belief is that formal specifications will eventually lead to automated coding, that is, to machines that can write programs without the intervention of a human programmer.

The jury is still out regarding the practical viability of formal methods of program specification, but most programmers agree that it is a good idea to reduce the ambiguity and inconsistency in the coding. A semiformal method of specifications called *assertions notation* has been progressively gaining favor. It consists of a specific style of comments inserted into the code to define the state of computation. The following sections describe the types of assertion that serve as comment headers:

ASSERT

The ASSERT comment header describes the state of computation at a particular point in the code. The idea is to state what is certainly known about variables and other program objects so that this information can be used in designing and testing the code that follows.

Special symbols and terms are associated with the ASSERT header. The term Assigned represents variables and constants initialized to a value. The symbol && represents logical AND, while the symbol || represents logical OR regarding the terms of the assertion. The symbol == serves to document a specific value and the symbol ?? indicates that the value is unknown or undeterminable at the time. Finally, the symbol ->, or the word `Implies`, represents logical implication. The programmer is also free to use other symbols and terms from mathematics, logic, or from the project's specific context, as long as they are clear and consistent.

INV

The INV comment header represents a loop invariant. It describes a state of computation at a certain point within a loop. The intention of the loop invariant is to document the fundamental tasks to be performed by the loop. Because the invariant is inserted inside the loop body, its assertion must be true before the body executes, during every loop iteration, and immediately after the loop body has executed for the last time. Loop invariants are also used in code-optimization techniques.

PRE AND POST

The **PRE** and **POST** comment headers are associated with functions. They establish the conditions expected at the function's entry and exit points. The **PRE:** assertion describes the elements (usually variables and constants) that must be supplied by the caller. The **POST:** assertion describes the state of computation at the moment the function concludes its execution. Taken together, they represent the terms of a contract between caller and function. If the caller ensures that the **PRE:** assertion is true at call time, then the function guarantees that the **POST:** assertion is satisfied at return time.

FCTVAL

The **FCTVAL** assertion represents the value returned by a function. In C, this value is associated with the function name. Therefore, it should not be used to represent variables modified by the function.

Programming Templates

For reasons explained in the Introduction, the programming in this book is based on using the Windows API directly. We do not address programming with the Foundation Class Library that is part of Microsoft's Visual C++ package. One objection often made to API-level programming for Windows is coding complications. In the program named WIN_HELLO, listed previously in this chapter, you saw that the code for a simple *Hello World* program in Windows can be quite elaborate.

One way in which to reduce the difficulties of Windows programming is by means of code templates that provide a standard framework of operations. A further simplification is by means of "wrappers" that allow the accessing of API services indirectly, thus avoiding some coding difficulties. Development environments such as the MFC, Visual Basic, Power Builder, and Delphi are based on these two simplifications, although implemented differently in each language.

Our approach precludes the use of "wrappers" for accessing API services; however, it is possible to simplify direct API-level programming by means of source code templates. A template is a program, or a part of a program, from which all the "specifics" have been removed. The template method is reminiscent of how a sculptor uses a wood-and-wire frame to build a statue by adding and manipulating the modeling clay. In the case of sculpture, the frame has a body, a head, arms, and legs – but no sex, age, or clothing. The same frame could be used to build a statue of a naked caveman or that of a fully dressed lady in the court of Louis XIV.

The programming version of the sculptor's wood-and-wire frame is a coding template. If we take the idea of a standard header block and add to it the generic portions of the WIN_HELLO program, we come up with the following source code template for a Windows program:

```
//*********************************************************
//*********************************************************
//  TEMPL01.CPP
//  Copyright (c) 199? by
//  ALL RIGHTS RESERVED
//*********************************************************
//*********************************************************
// Date:                            Coded by:
// Filename:                        Module name:
//                                  Source file:
// Program description:
```

```
//
//***************************************************************
// Libraries and software support:
//
//***************************************************************
// Development environment:
//
//***************************************************************
// System requirements:
//
//***************************************************************
// Start date:
// Update history:
//           DATE            MODIFICATION
//
//***************************************************************
// Test history:
//  TEST PROTOCOL           DATE        TEST RESULTS
//
//***************************************************************
// Programmer comments:
//
//
//***************************************************************
//***************************************************************
#include <windows.h>
// Predeclaration of the Windows Procedure
LRESULT CALLBACK WndProc (HWND, UINT, WPARAM, LPARAM) ;
//****************************
//        WinMain
//****************************
int WINAPI WinMain (HINSTANCE hInstance, HINSTANCE hPrevInstance,
                    PSTR szCmdLine, int iCmdShow)
{
     static char szAppName[] = "AppName" ; // Application name
     HWND        hwnd ;
     MSG         msg ;
     // Defining a structure of type WNDCLASSEX
     WNDCLASSEX  wndclass ;
     wndclass.cbSize        = sizeof (wndclass) ;
     wndclass.style         = CS_HREDRAW | CS_VREDRAW ;
     wndclass.lpfnWndProc   = WndProc ;
     wndclass.cbClsExtra    = 0 ;
     wndclass.cbWndExtra    = 0 ;
     wndclass.hInstance     = hInstance ;
```

```
     wndclass.hIcon          = LoadIcon (NULL,IDI_APPLICATION);
wndclass.hCursor        = LoadCursor (NULL, IDC_ARROW) ;
     wndclass.hbrBackground = (HBRUSH) GetStockObject
                              (WHITE_BRUSH) ;
     wndclass.lpszMenuName  = NULL ;
     wndclass.lpszClassName = szAppName ;
     wndclass.hIconSm       = LoadIcon (NULL,IDI_APPLICATION);

     // Registering the structure wmdclass
     RegisterClassEx (&wndclass) ;
     // CreateWindow()
     hwnd = CreateWindow (szAppName,
           "Window Caption",          // window caption
            WS_OVERLAPPEDWINDOW,      // window style
            CW_USEDEFAULT,            // initial x position
            CW_USEDEFAULT,            // initial y position
            CW_USEDEFAULT,            // initial x size
            CW_USEDEFAULT,            // initial y size
            NULL,                     // parent window handle
            NULL,                     // window menu handle
            hInstance,                // program instance
// handle
            NULL) ;                   // creation parameters
     ShowWindow (hwnd, iCmdShow) ;
     UpdateWindow (hwnd) ;
     // Message loop
     while (GetMessage (&msg, NULL, 0, 0))
          {
          TranslateMessage (&msg) ;
          DispatchMessage (&msg) ;
          }
     return msg.wParam ;
}
//***************************
//    Windows Procedure
//***************************
LRESULT CALLBACK WndProc (HWND hwnd, UINT iMsg, WPARAM wParam,
LPARAM lParam)
{
     HDC         hdc ;
     PAINTSTRUCT ps ;
     RECT        rect ;
     switch (iMsg)
          {
     // Windows message processing
```

```
          case WM_PAINT :
               hdc = BeginPaint (hwnd, &ps) ;
               GetClientRect (hwnd, &rect) ;
          // Initial display operations here
               EndPaint (hwnd, &ps) ;
               return 0 ;
          // End of program execution
          case WM_DESTROY :
               PostQuitMessage (0) ;
               return 0 ;
          }
     return DefWindowProc (hwnd, iMsg, wParam, lParam) ;
}
```

You can use this template as a frame on which to build a Windows application. Remember that a programming template is not a sample program, just as a sculptor's frame is not a statue. Some templates may compile while others may not. Each template contains instructions regarding its use. Typically, the programmer removes these notes when they are no longer necessary. The directory \TEMPLATES in the book's CD-ROM contains the electronic source for all of the templates listed in the text.

Summary

In this chapter we introduced Windows programming and provided a model that is compatible with graphical applications that execute in a multitasking environment. This model, called event-driven programming, is based on a message-passing mechanism by which the operating system and the applications communicate. We compared DOS and Windows programs and pointed out the differences and similarities. We also considered the file structure of a Windows program and analyzed its different components, such as source, library, resource, make, object, and executable files. Dynamic-link libraries were described and we discussed the use of DLLs in Windows programming.

Windows applications have unique characteristics. We pointed out some of the more original features: Windows naming conventions, numeric constants, and Windows handles. Windows programs are also visually different because a typical Windows application has a graphics window and interactive controls. Finally, we addressed the issue of the styles suitable for Windows programming, and mentioned a style of program comments called *assertions notation,* which appears to be gaining favor. Programming templates were described as a means of simplifying the coding effort.

In Chapter 3, you get to the nitty-gritty of Windows programming, using the background and models established in this chapter.

Chapter 3

API Programming

IN THIS CHAPTER

- Creating a Windows program
- Dissecting a Windows Program
- The WinMain() Function
- The Window Procedure
- Message Processing
- Creating the first Windows program

THIS CHAPTER INTRODUCES API programming in Windows. It is intended for programmers who have worked at the Foundation Class Library level or who have no Windows experience.

There is no doubt that Windows programming is complicated. No matter where we start, or how we approach it, the discussion soon gets into the details of many options, modes, switches, and alternatives. Well over one thousand API services exist, many of which take a dozen or more parameters. The event-driven mechanism at the heart of a Windows program often becomes extremely complex; system and application code may have to exchange eight or ten messages to accomplish a simple task. The fact that the Windows environment is powerful and sophisticated seems to imply that the programming is difficult, sometimes tortuous. The only viable approach is to jump right in and face the complications one at a time.

In the context of this book, we create Windows programs in a visual environment. Although we don't use class libraries or other wrappers, we take advantage of the editing and code-generating facilities provided by Developer Studio. The process of fabricating a program requires not only knowledge of the language constructs that go into it, but also skills in using the development environment. For example, to create a program icon for an application you need to know about the API services used in defining and loading the icon, but you also need to have skills in activating and using the icon editor that is part of Developer Studio. Furthermore, once the icon graphics have been stored in a file, you need to follow a series of steps that make this resource available to the program.

The following topics are covered in Chapter 3:

- Preliminary Steps
- Creating a Project from the Template
- Dissecting a Windows Program
- The WinMain() Function
- The Window Procedure
- The WinHello Program
- Creating a Program Resource
- WinHello Program Listing

Preliminary Steps

In the discussion that follows, we assume that you have installed one of the supported software development products. This text is compatible with Microsoft Visual C++ Version 5, but the programs and exercises have also been tested with Version 4 and with the prerelease of Version 6. Appendix B contains information about the use of the Borland C++ line of products. The following section describes the steps in creating a new project in Microsoft Developer Studio, inserting a source-code template into the project, modifying and saving the template with a new name, and compiling the resulting file into a Windows executable.

Creating a Project from a Template

Once Visual C++ is installed, Developer Studio is started by double-clicking on the program icon on the desktop, or selecting it from the Microsoft Visual C++ program group. The initial Developer Studio screen varies with the program version, the Windows configuration, the options selected when Developer Studio was last executed, and the project currently under development.

> Visual C++ Version 5.0 introduced the notion of a *project workspace*, or simply a workspace, as a container for several related projects. In version 5 the extension .mdp, used previously for project files, was changed to .dsw, which now refers to a workspace. The dialog boxes for creating workspaces, projects, and files were also changed. The workspace/project structure and the basic interface are also used in Visual C++ Version 6.0. The descriptions that follow refer to Visual C++ Version 5.0 and later.

The following paragraphs are a walk through the process of creating a project from a template file. At this point in the book you have not yet learned Windows programming; therefore, the walk-through consists of using Developer Studio. Later in this chapter you will learn about the different parts of a Windows program and develop a "Hello Windows" application that actually does something. We call this first project *Do Nothing Demo*, for lack of a better name. The project files are found in the Do Nothing Demo project folder in the book's CD-ROM.

A project is located in a workspace, which can include several projects. Both a project and workspace can be located in the same folder or subfolder or in different ones, and can have the same or different names. In the examples and demonstration programs used in this book we use the same folder for the project and the workspace. The result of this approach is that the workspace disappears as a separate entity, simplifying the creation process.

A new project is started by selecting the New command from the Developer Studio File menu. When the New dialog box is displayed, click on the Project tab option and select a project type from the displayed list. In this case our project is Win32 Application. Make sure that the project location entry corresponds to the desired drive and folder. If not, click the button to the right of the location text box and select another one. Next, enter a project name in the corresponding text box in the upper-right corner of the form. The name of the project is the same one used by Development Studio to create a project folder. In this example we create a project named *Do Nothing Demo* which is located in a folder named CPP_PROJECTS. You can use these same names or create ones of your own. Note that as you type the project name it is added to the path shown in the location text box. At this point the New dialog box appears as shown in Figure 3-1.

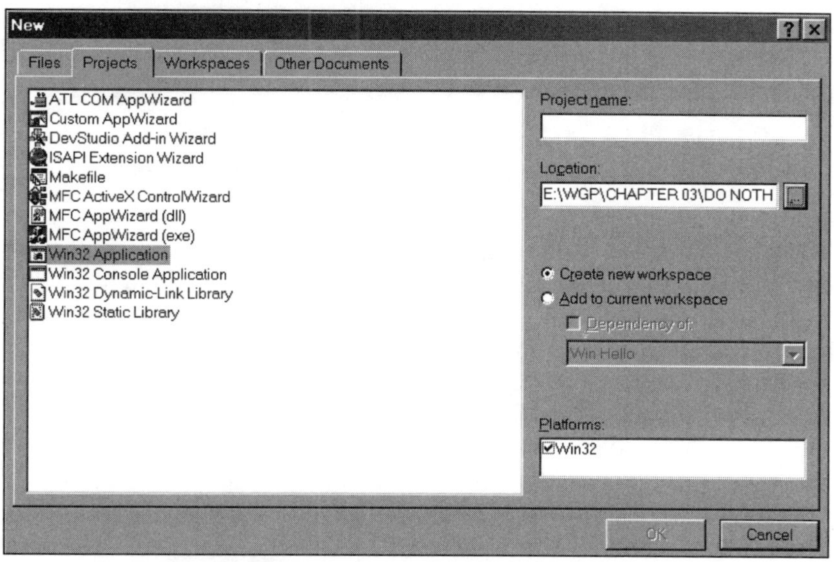

Figure 3-1: Developer Studio dialog screen for the New command in the File menu

Make sure that the radio button labeled "Create new workspace" is selected so that clicking the OK button on the dialog box creates both the project and the workspace. At this point, you have created a project, as well as a workspace of the same name, but no program files are yet in it. How you proceed from here depends on whether you are using another source file as a base or template, or starting from scratch.

If you wish to start a source file from scratch, click on Developer Studio Project menu and select the "Add To Project" and New commands. This action displays the same dialog box as when creating a project, but now the Files tab is open. In the case of a source file, select the C++ Source File option from the displayed list and type a file name in the corresponding text box. The dialog appears as shown in Figure 3-2.

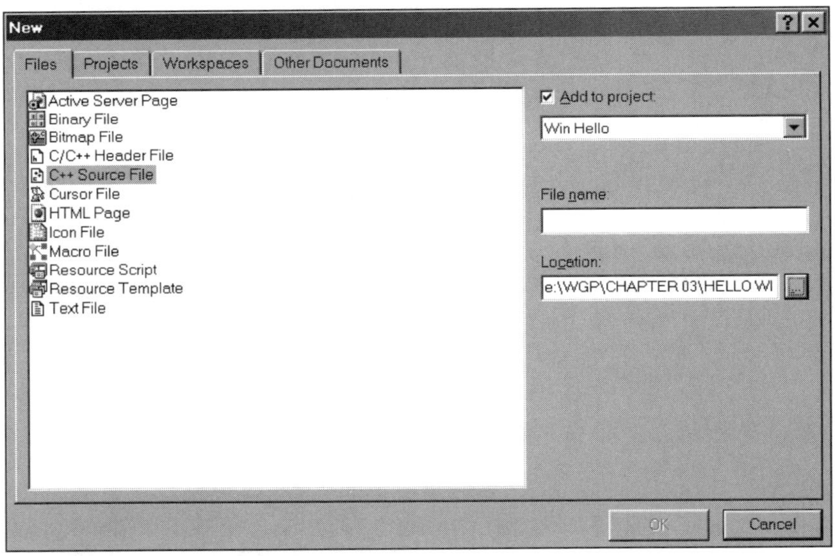

Figure 3-2: Developer Studio dialog screen for creating a new source file

The development method we use in this book is based on using source code templates. To use a template as a base, or another source file, you have to follow a different series of steps. Assuming you have created a project, the next step is to select and load the program template or source file. We use the template named Templ01.cpp listed in Chapter 1. If you have installed the book's CD-ROM on your system, the template file is located in the path WGP/Templates. If you have not installed the CD-ROM you can copy the program file Templ01.cpp from the CD-ROM into your project folder.

To load the source file into your current project, open Developer Studio Project menu and select the "Add To Project" item and then the Files commands. This action displays an "Insert Files into Project" dialog box. Use the buttons to the right of the Look In text box to navigate into the desired drive and folder until the desired file is selected. Figure 3-3 shows the file Templ01.cpp highlighted and ready for insertion into the project.

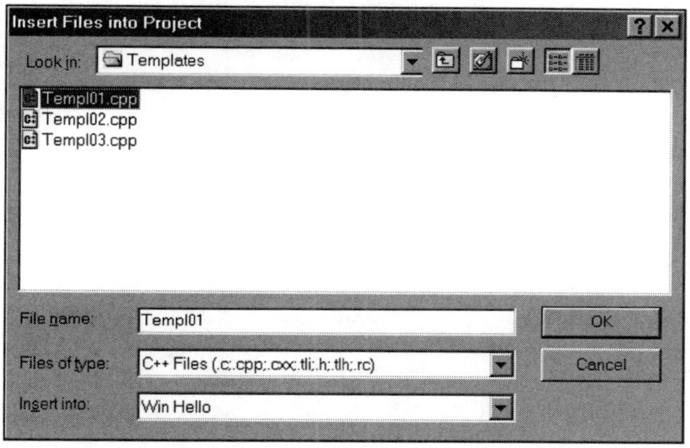

Figure 3-3: Developer Studio dialog screen for inserting an existing source file into a project

When using a template file to start a new project you must be careful not to destroy or change the original source. The template file is usually renamed once it is inserted into the project. It is possible to insert a template file in a project, rename it, delete it from the project, and then reinsert the renamed file. However, it is easier to rename a copy of the template file before it is inserted into the project. The following sequence of operations are used to do this:

1. Select the Open command from the File menu. Navigate through the directory structure to locate the file to be used as a template. In this case the file Templ01.cpp is located in WGP/Templates folder.
2. With the cursor still in the Developer Studio editor pane, open the File menu and select the Save As command. Navigate through the directory structure again until you reach the CPP_PROJECTS\Do Nothing Demo folder. Save the file using the name Do_nothing.cpp.
3. Select Add To Project→Files from the Project menu. Locate the file named Do_nothing.cpp in the "Insert Files into Project" dialog box, select it, and click the OK button.

The file Do_nothing.cpp now appears in the Do Nothing Demo file list in the Developer Studio workspace pane. It is also displayed in the Editor window.

The Developer Studio main screen is configurable by the user. Furthermore, the size of its display areas is determined by the system resolution. For this reason, it is impossible to depict a Developer Studio screen display that matches the one that every user will see. In the illustrations and screen dumps throughout this book we have used a resolution of 1152 by 854 pixels in 16-bit color with large fonts. However, our screen format may not exactly match yours. Figure 3-4 shows a full screen display of Developer Studio with the file Do_nothing.cpp loaded in the Editor area.

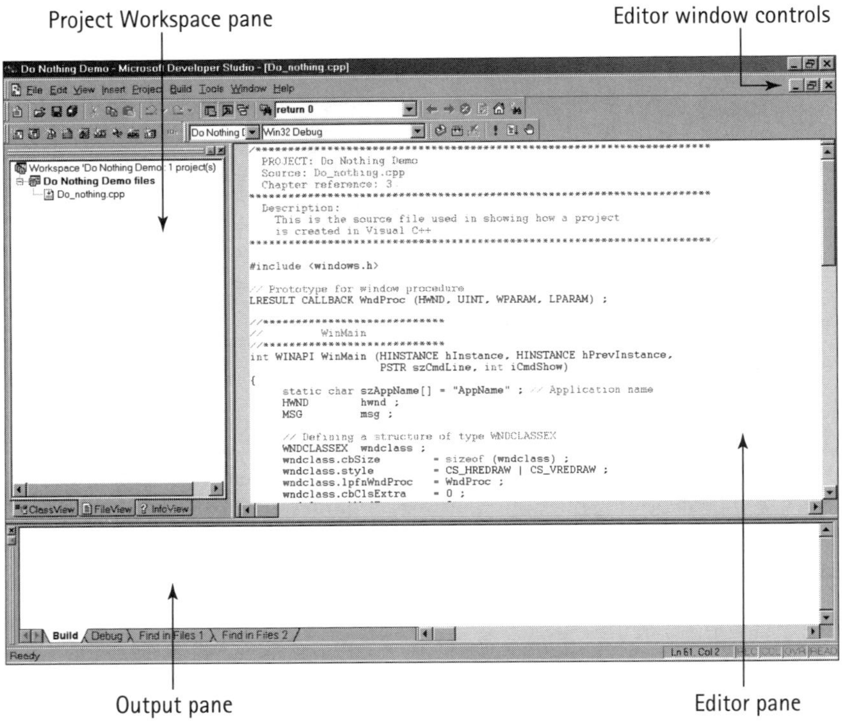

Figure 3-4: Developer Studio main screen showing the Project Workspace, Editor, and Output panes

The Project Workspace pane of Developer Studio was introduced in Version 4.0. It has four possible views: Class View, File View, Info View, and Resource View. The Resource View is not visible in Figure 3-4. To display the source file in the Editor pane, you must first select File View tab and double-click the Do_nothing .cpp filename.

At this point, you can proceed to develop the new project using the renamed template file as the main source. The first step is to make sure that the development software is working correctly. To do so, open the Developer Studio Build menu and select the Rebuild All command. Developer Studio compiles and builds your program, which is at this stage, nothing more than the renamed template file. The results are shown in the Output area. If compilation and linking took place without error, reopen the Build menu and select the "Execute Do_nothing.exe" command button. If everything is in order, a "Do nothing" program executes in your system.

Now click the Save command on the File menu to make sure that all project files are saved on your hard drive.

Dissecting a Windows Program

The template file Templ01.cpp, which we used and renamed in the previous example, is a bare-bones Windows program with no functionality except to display a window on the screen. Before proceeding to edit this template into a useful program, you should become acquainted with its fundamental elements. In this section, we take apart the template file Templ01.cpp for a detailed look into each of its components. The program contains two fundamental components: `WinMain()` and the Window procedure.

WinMain()

All Windows GUI applications must have a `WinMain()` function. `WinMain()` is to a Windows GUI program what `main()` is to a DOS application. It is usually said that `WinMain()` is the program's entry point, but this is not exactly true. C/C++ compilers generate a startup code that calls `WinMain()`, so it is the startup code and not `WinMain()` that is actually called by Windows. The `WinMain()` header line reads as follows:

```
'|---------- Return type
'|     |-------- One of the standard calling conventions
'|     |              defined in windows.h
'|     |       |---- Function name
'|     |       |
'|     |       |      [ parameter list ...               ]
-- ---- ----  --------------------------
int WINAPI WinMain (HINSTANCE hInstance, HINSTANCE
                    hPrevInstance, PSTR szCmdLine,
                    int iCmdShow) {
```

`WINAPI` is a macro defined in the windows.h header file that translates the function call to the appropriate calling convention. Recall that calling conventions refer to how the function arguments are placed in the stack at call time, and if the caller or the called routine is responsible for restoring stack integrity after the call. Microsoft Basic, FORTRAN, and Pascal push the parameters onto the stack in the same order in which they are declared. In these languages the stack must be restored by the caller. In C and C++, the parameters are pushed in reverse order, and the stack is restored automatically after the call returns. For historical reasons (and to take advantage of the hardware features of the Intel processors) Windows requires the Pascal calling convention. In previous versions of Windows, the calling convention for `WinMain()` was `PASCAL` or `FAR PASCAL`. You can still replace `WINAPI` for `FAR PASCAL` and the program will compile and link correctly, but the use of the `WINAPI` macro makes your program more portable.

Parameters

Most often parameters are passed to `WinMain()` by Windows, but some can be passed by whatever program executes your application. Your code can inspect these parameters to obtain information about the conditions in which the program executes. Four parameters are passed to `WinMain()`:

- `HINSTANCE` is a handle-type identifier. The variable `hInstance` is an integer that identifies the instance of the program. Consider that in a multitasking environment there can be several copies (instances) of the same program running simultaneously. Windows sets this value and passes it to your code. Your program needs to access this parameter to enter it in the `WNDCLASSEX` structure, and also when calling the `CreateWindow()` function. Because the handle to the instance is required outside `WinMain()` by many functions of the Windows API, the template file stores it in a public variable, named `pInstance`. In general, the use of public variables is undesirable in Windows programming, but this case is one of the valid exceptions to the rule.
- The variable `hPrevInstance` is also of type `HINSTANCE`. This parameter is included in the call for compatibility with previous versions of Windows, which used a single copy of the code to run more than one program instance. In 16-bit Windows, the first instance had a special role in the management of resources. Therefore, an application needed to know if it was the first instance. `hPrevInstance` held the handle of the previous instance. In Windows 95/98/NT this parameter is unused and its value is set to NULL.
- `PSTR szCmdLine` is a pointer to a string that contains the command tail entered by the user when the program is executed. It works only when the program name is entered from the DOS command line or from the Run dialog box. For this reason, it is rarely used by code.
- The `int iCmdShow` parameter determines how the window is to be initially displayed. The program that executes your application (normally Windows) assigns a value to this parameter, as shown in Table 3-1.

TABLE 3-1 WINMAIN() DISPLAY MODE PARAMETERS

Value	Meaning
SW_HIDE	Hides the window and activates another window.
SW_MINIMIZE	Minimizes the specified window and activates the top-level window in the system's list.
SW_RESTORE	Activates and displays a window. If the window is minimized or maximized, Windows restores it to its original size and position (same as SW_SHOWNORMAL).
SW_SHOW	Activates a window and displays it in its current size and position.
SW_SHOWMAXIMIZED	Activates a window and displays it as a maximized window.
SW_SHOWMINIMIZED	Activates a window and displays it as an icon.
SW_SHOWMINNOACTIVE	Displays a window as an icon. The active window remains active.
SW_SHOWNA	Displays a window in its current state. The active window remains active.
SW_SHOWNOACTIVATE	Displays a window in its most recent size and position. The active window remains active.
SW_SHOWNORMAL	Activates and displays a window. If the window is minimized or maximized, Windows restores it to its original size and position (same as SW_RESTORE).

Data Variables

The program file Templ01.cpp defines several variables. One of them, the handle to the program's main window, is defined globally. The other ones are local to WinMain() or the window procedure. The variable defined globally is:

```
HWND          hwnd ;
```

HWND is a 16-bit unsigned integer that serves as a handle to a window. The variable hwnd refers to the actual program window. The variable is initialized when we make the call to CreateWindow() service, described later in this section.

The variables defined in WinMain() are as follows:

```
static char szClassName[] = "MainClass" ; // Class name
MSG         msg ;
```

szClassName[] is an array of char that shows the application's class name. In the template it is given the name MainClass, which you can replace for a more meaningful one. The application class name must be the same one used in the WNDCLASSEX structure.

MSG is a message-type structure of which msg is a variable. The MSG structure is defined in the Windows header files as follows:

```
typedef struct tagMSG {      // msg
    HWND   hwnd;      // Handle to window receiving message
    UINT   message;   // message number
    WPARAM wParam;    // Context-dependent additional
                      // information
    LPARAM lParam;    // about the message
    DWORD  time;      // Time at which message was posted
    POINT  pt;        // Cursor position when message was
                      // posted
} MSG;
```

The comments to the structure members show that the variable holds information important to the executing code. The values of the message variable are reloaded every time a new message is received.

WNDCLASSEX Structure

This structure is defined in the Windows header files, as follows:

```
typedef struct tagWNDCLASSEX {
UINT        cbSize ;
UINT        style ;
WNDPROC     lpfnWndProc ;
int         cbClsExtra ;
int         cbWndExtra ;
HINSTANCE   hInstance ;
HICON       hIcon ;
HCURSOR     hCursor ;
HBRUSH      hbrBackground ;
LPCSTR      lpszMenuName ;
```

```
LPCSTR      lpszClassName ;
HICON       hIconSm ;
} WNDCLASSEX;
```

The `WNDCLASSEX` structure contains window class information. It is used with the `RegisterClassEx()` and `GetClassInfoEx()` functions. The structure is similar to the `WNDCLASS` structure used in 16-bit Windows. The difference between the two structures is that `WNDCLASSEX` has a `cbSize` member, which specifies the size of the structure, and the `hIconSm` member, which contains a handle to a small icon associated with the window class. In the template file Templ01.cpp the structure is declared and the variable initialized as follows:

```
// Defining a structure of type WNDCLASSEX
WNDCLASSEX  wndclass ;
wndclass.cbSize        = sizeof (WNDCLASSEX) ;
wndclass.style         = CS_HREDRAW | CS_VREDRAW ;
wndclass.lpfnWndProc   = WndProc ;
wndclass.cbClsExtra    = 0 ;
wndclass.cbWndExtra    = 0 ;
wndclass.hInstance     = hInstance ;
wndclass.hIcon         = LoadIcon (NULL, IDI_APPLICATION) ;
wndclass.hCursor       = LoadCursor (NULL, IDC_ARROW) ;
wndclass.hbrBackground = (HBRUSH) GetStockObject
                         (WHITE_BRUSH) ;
wndclass.lpszMenuName  = NULL ;
wndclass.lpszClassName = szClassName ;
wndclass.hIconSm       = LoadIcon (NULL, IDI_APPLICATION) ;
```

The window class is a template that defines the characteristics of a particular window, such as the type of cursor and the background color. The class also specifies the address of the window procedure that carries out the work for the window. The structure variables define the window class, as follows:

`cbSize` specifies the size, in bytes, of the structure. The member is set using the `sizeof` operator in the statement:

```
sizeof(WNDCLASSEX);
```

The structure member `style` specifies the class style or styles. Two or more styles can be combined by means of the C bitwise OR (|) operator. This member can be any combination of the values in Table 3-2.

Table 3-2 SUMMARY OF WINDOW CLASS STYLES

Symbolic Constant	Action
`CS_BYTEALIGNCLIENT`	Aligns the window's client area on the byte boundary (in the *x* direction) to enhance performance during drawing operations. This style affects the width of the window and its horizontal position on the display.
`CS_BYTEALIGNWINDOW`	Aligns a window on a byte boundary (in the *x* direction) to enhance performance during operations that involve moving or sizing the window. This style affects the width of the window and its horizontal position on the display.
`CS_CLASSDC`	Allocates one device context to be shared by all windows in the class. Window classes are process specific; therefore, different threads can create windows of the same class.
`CS_DBLCLKS`	Sends double-click messages to the window procedure when the user double-clicks the mouse while the cursor is within a window belonging to the class.
`CS_GLOBALCLASS`	Allows an application to create a window of the class regardless of the value of the `hInstance` parameter passed to the `CreateWindowEx()` function. If you do not specify this style, the `hInstance` parameter passed to `CreateWindowEx()` function must be the same as the one passed to the `RegisterClass()` function.
`CS_HREDRAW`	Redraws the entire window if a movement or size adjustment changes the width of the client area.
`CS_NOCLOSE`	Disables the Close command on the System menu.
`CS_OWNDC`	Allocates a unique device context for each window in the class.
`CS_PARENTDC`	Specifies that child windows inherit their parent window's device context. Specifying `CS_PARENTDC` enhances an application's performance.
`CS_SAVEBITS`	Saves, as a bitmap, the portion of the screen image obscured by a window. Windows uses the saved bitmap to recreate the screen image when the window is removed. This style is useful for small windows (such as menus or dialog boxes) displayed briefly and then removed before other screen activity takes place.
`CS_VREDRAW`	Redraws the entire window if a movement or size adjustment changes the height of the client area.

Of the styles listed in Table 3-2, the styles `CS_HREDRAW` and `CS_VREDRAW` are the ones most commonly used. They can be ORed to produce a window automatically redrawn if it is resized vertically or horizontally, as implemented in the Templ01.cpp code.

> NOTE: Microsoft uses semi-standard prefixes to identify Windows variables. The most common of these are listed in Table 2-3, but it is impossible to include all of them because no established standard exists that is systematically followed. Sometimes the programmer has to guess the meaning of a particular prefix combination. For example, `lpfn` could be a long pointer to a function, and `hbr` the handle to a brush.

`lpfnWndProc` is a pointer to the window procedure, described later in this chapter. In the template Templ01.cpp it is initialized to the name of the Window procedure, as follows:

```
wndclass.lpfnWndProc     = WndProc;
```

`cbClsExtra` is a count of the number of extra bytes to be allocated following the window-class structure. The operating system initializes the bytes to zero. In the template this member is set to zero.

`cbWndExtra` is a count of the number of extra bytes to allocate following the window instance. The operating system initializes the bytes to zero. In the template this member is set to zero.

`hInstance` is a handle to the instance of the window procedure.

`hIcon` is a handle to the class icon. If this member is NULL, an application must draw an icon whenever the user minimizes the application's window. In the template this member is initialized by calling the `LoadIcon()` function.

`hCursor` is a handle to the class cursor. If this member is NULL, an application must explicitly set the cursor shape whenever the mouse moves into the application's window. In the template this member is initialized by calling the `LoadCursor()` function.

`hbrBackground` is a background brush. This member can be a handle to the physical brush to be used for painting the background, or it can be a color value. If it is a color value, then it must be one of the standard system colors listed in Table 3-3.

TABLE 3-3 COMMON WINDOWS STANDARD SYSTEM COLORS

Symbolic Constant	Meaning
COLOR_ACTIVEBORDER	Border color of the active window
COLOR_ACTIVECAPTION	Caption color of the active window
COLOR_APPWORKSPACE	Window background of MDI clients
COLOR_BACKGROUND	Desktop color
COLOR_BTNFACE	Face color for buttons
COLOR_BTNSHADOW	Shadow color for buttons
COLOR_BTNTEXT	Text color on buttons
COLOR_CAPTIONTEXT	Text color for captions, size boxes, and scroll-bar arrow boxes
COLOR_GRAYTEXT	Color for disabled text
COLOR_HIGHLIGHT	Color of a selected item
COLOR_HIGHLIGHTTEXT	Text color of a selected item
COLOR_INACTIVEBORDER	Border color of inactive window
COLOR_INACTIVECAPTION	Caption color of an inactive window
COLOR_MENU	Background color of a menu
COLOR_MENUTEXT	Text color of a menu
COLOR_SCROLLBAR	Color of a scroll bar's gray area
COLOR_WINDOW	Background color of a window
COLOR_WINDOWFRAME	Frame color of a window
COLOR_WINDOWTEXT	Text color of a window

When this member is NULL, an application must paint its own background whenever it is required to paint its client area. In the template this member is initialized by calling the `GetStockObject()` function.

`lpszMenuName` is a pointer to a null-terminated character string that specifies the resource name of the class menu, as it appears in the resource file. If you use an integer to identify the menu, then you must use the `MAKEINTRESOURCE` macro. If this member is NULL, the windows belonging to this class have no default menu, as is the case in the template file.

lpszClassName is a pointer to a null-terminated string or it is an atom. If this parameter is an atom, it must be a global atom created by a previous call to the GlobalAddAtom() function. The atom, a 16-bit value, must be in the low-order word of lpszClassName; the high-order word must be zero. If lpszClassName is a string, it specifies the window class name. In Templ01.cpp this member is set to the szClassName[] array.

In Windows 95/98 hIconSm is a handle to a small icon that is associated with the window class. This is the icon shown in dialog boxes that list filenames and shown by Windows Explorer. A Windows 95/98 application can use a predefined icon in this case, using the LoadIcon() function with the same parameters as for the hIcon member. In Windows NT this member is not used and should be set to NULL. Windows 95/98 applications that set the small icon to NULL still have the default small icon displayed on the task bar.

In most cases it is better to create both the large and the small icon than to let Windows create the small one from the large bitmap. Later in this chapter we describe how to create both icons as a program resource and how to make these resources available to the application.

Loading Icons: LoadIcon() versus LoadImage()

Contrary to what has sometimes been stated, the LoadIcon() function cannot be used to load both large and small icons from the same resource. For example, if the icon resource is named IDI_ICON1, and we proceed as follows:

```
wndclass.hicon      = LoadIcon (hInstance,
                      MAKEINTRESOURCE(IDI_ICON1);
.
.
.
wndclass.hiconSm  = LoadIcon (hInstance,
                    MAKEINTRESOURCE(IDI_ICON1);
```

The result is that the large icon is loaded from the resource file, but not the small one. This happens even if the resource file contains both images. Instead, you must use the LoadImage() function, as follows:

```
wndclass.hIcon        = LoadImage(hInstance,
                        MAKEINTRESOURCE(IDI_ICON1),
                        IMAGE_ICON,        // Type
                        32, 32,            // Pixel size
                        LR_DEFAULTCOLOR) ;
.
.
```

Continued

Loading Icons: LoadIcon() versus LoadImage() *(Continued)*

```
.
wndclass.hIconSm      = LoadImage(hInstance,
                        MAKEINTRESOURCE(IDI_ICON1),
                        IMAGE_ICON,         // Type
                        16, 16,             // Pixel size
                        LR_DEFAULTCOLOR) ;
```

Now both the large and the small icon resources are loaded correctly and are used as required.

Registering the Windows Class

Once your code has declared the `WNDCLASSEX` structure and initialized its member variables, it has defined a window class that encompasses all the structure attributes. The most important ones are the window style (`wndclass.style`), the pointer to the Window procedure (`wndclass.lpfnWndProc`), and the window class name (`wndclass. lpszClassName`). The `RegisterClassEx()` function serves to notify Windows of the existence of a particular window class, as defined in the `WNDCLASSEX` structure variable. The address of operator serves to reference the location of the specific structure variable, as shown in the following statement:

```
RegisterClassEx (&wndclass) ;
```

The `RegisterClassEx()` function returns an atom (16-bit integer). This value is non-zero if the class is successfully registered. Code should check for a successful registration because you cannot create a window otherwise. The following construct ensures that execution does not proceed if the function fails.

```
if(!RegisterClassEx (&wndclass))
  return(0);
```

This coding style is the one used in the template Templ01.cpp.

Creating the Window

A window class is a general classification. Other data must be provided at the time the actual window is created. The `CreateWindowEx()` function receives the additional information as parameters. `CreateWindowEx()` is a Windows 95 version of the `CreateWindow()` function. The only difference between them is that the new version supports an extended window style passed as its first parameter.

The CreateWindowEx() function is rich in arguments, many of which apply only to special windows styles. For example, buttons, combo boxes, list boxes, edit boxes, and static controls can all be created with a CreateWindowEx() call. At this time, we refer only to the most important function parameters that relate to the program's main window.

In the file Templ01.cpp the call to CreateWindowEx() is coded as follows:

```
hwnd = CreateWindowEx (
       WS_EX_LEFT,            // left aligned (default)
       szClassName,           // pointer to class name
       "Window Caption",      // window caption (title bar)
       WS_OVERLAPPEDWINDOW,   // window style
       CW_USEDEFAULT,         // initial x position
       CW_USEDEFAULT,         // initial y position
       CW_USEDEFAULT,         // initial x size
       CW_USEDEFAULT,         // initial y size
       NULL,                  // parent window handle
       NULL,                  // window menu handle
       hInstance,             // program instance handle
       NULL) ;                // creation parameters
```

The first parameter passed to the CreateWindowEx() function is the extended window style introduced in the Win32 API. The one used in the file Templ01.cpp, WS_EX_LEFT, acts as a placeholder for others that you may want to select because it is actually the default value. Table 3-4 lists some of the most common extended styles.

TABLE 3-4 COMMON WINDOWS EXTENDED STYLES

Symbolic Constant	Meaning
WS_EX_ACCEPTFILES	The window created with this style accepts drag-drop files.
WS_EX_APPWINDOW	A top-level window is forced onto the application task bar when the window is minimized.
WS_EX_CLIENTEDGE	Window has a border with a sunken edge.
WS_EX_CONTEXTHELP	The title bar includes a question mark. When the user clicks the question mark, the cursor changes to a question mark with a pointer. If the user then clicks a child window, it receives a WM_HELP message.

Continued

ABLE 3-4 COMMON WINDOWS EXTENDED STYLES *(Continued)*

Symbolic Constant	Meaning
WS_EX_CONTROLPARENT	Allows the user to navigate among the child windows of the window by using the Tab key.
WS_EX_DLGMODALFRAME	Window that has a double border. Optionally the window can be created with a title bar by specifying the WS _CAPTION style in the dwStyle parameter.
WS_EX_LEFT	Window has generic "left-aligned" properties. This is the default.
WS_EX_MDICHILD	Creates an MDI child window.
WS_EX_NOPARENTNOTIFY	Specifies that a child window created with this style does not send the WM_PARENTNOTIFY message to its parent window when it is created or destroyed.
WS_EX_OVERLAPPEDWINDOW	Combines the WS_EX_CLIENTEDGE and WS_EX _WINDOWEDGE styles.
WS_EX_PALETTEWINDOW	Combines the WS_EX_WINDOWEDGE, WS_EX _TOOLWINDOW, and WS_EX_TOPMOST styles.
WS_EX_RIGHTSCROLLBAR	Specifies that the vertical scroll bar (if present) is to the right of the client area. This is the default.
WS_EX_STATICEDGE	Creates a window with a three-dimensional border style intended to be used for items that do not accept user input.
WS_EX_TOOLWINDOW	Creates a tool window. This type of window is intended to be used as a floating toolbar.
WS_EX_TOPMOST	Creates a window that is placed above all windows except the topmost one and that stays above them, even when the window is deactivated.
WS_EX_TRANSPARENT	Creates a transparent window. That is, any windows beneath it are not obscured by it.
WS_EX_WINDOWEDGE	Specifies a window that has a border with a raised edge.

The second parameter passed to the CreateWindowEx() function call is either a pointer to a string with the name of the window type, a string enclosed in double quotation marks, or a predefined name for a control class.

In the template file, szClassName is a pointer to the string defined at the start of WinMain(), with the text "MainClass." You can edit this string in your own applications so that the class name is more meaningful. For example, if you are coding an editor program you may rename the application class as "TextEdClass." However, this is merely a name used by Windows to associate a window with its class; it is not displayed as a caption or used otherwise.

Control classes can also be used as a window class name. These classes are the symbolic constants BUTTON, COMBO BOX Combo box, EDIT, LIST BOX List box, MDI-CLIENT, SCROLL BAR Scroll bar, and STATIC Control classes are discussed in Chapter 5.

The third parameter can be a pointer to a string or a string enclosed in double quotation marks entered directly as a parameter. In either case, this string is used as the caption to the program window and is displayed in the program's title bar. Often this caption coincides with the name of the program. You should edit this string to suit your own program.

The fourth parameter is the window style. Over 25 styles are defined as symbolic constants. The most-used ones are listed in Table 3-5.

TABLE 3-5 COMMON WINDOW STYLES

Symbolic Constant	Meaning
WS_BORDER	Specifies a window with a thin-line border.
WS_CAPTION	Specifies a window with a title bar (includes the WS_BORDER style).
WS_CHILD	Creates a child window. This style cannot be used with the WS_POPUP style.
WS_CLIPCHILDREN	Excludes the area occupied by child windows when drawing occurs within the parent window.
WS_CLIPSIBLINGS	Clips child windows relative to each other. When a particular child window receives a WM_PAINT message, this style clips all other overlapping child windows out of the region of the child window to be updated. If WS_CLIPSIBLINGS is not specified and child windows overlap, it is possible to draw within the client area of a neighboring child window.
WS_DISABLED	Specifies that the window is initially disabled. A disabled window cannot receive input from the user.
WS_DLGFRAME	Specifies a window with a border of a style typically used with dialog boxes. The window does not have a title bar.
WS_HSCROLL	Specifies a window with a horizontal scroll bar.

Continued

TABLE 3-5 COMMON WINDOW STYLES *(Continued)*

Symbolic Constant	Meaning
WS_ICONIC	Specifies that the window is initially minimized. Same as the WS_MINIMIZE style.
WS_MAXIMIZE	Specifies that the window is initially maximized.
WS_MAXIMIZEBOX	Specifies a window with a Maximize button. Cannot be combined with the WS_EX_CONTEXTHELP style.
WS_MINIMIZE	Specifies a window that is initially minimized. Same as the WS_ICONIC style.
WS_MINIMIZEBOX	Specifies a window with a Minimize button. Cannot be combined with the WS_EX_CONTEXTHELP style.
WS_OVERLAPPED	Specifies an overlapped window with a title bar and a border.
WS_OVERLAPPEDWINDOW	Specifies an overlapped window with the WS_OVERLAPPED, WS_CAPTION, WS_SYSMENU, WS_THICKFRAME, WS_MINIMIZEBOX, and WS_MAXIMIZEBOX styles. Same as the WS_TILEDWINDOW style.
WS_POPUP	Specifies a pop-up window. Cannot be used with the WS_CHILD style.
WS_POPUPWINDOW	Specifies a pop-up window with WS_BORDER, WS_POPUP, and WS_SYSMENU styles. The WS_CAPTION and WS_POPUPWINDOW styles must be combined to make the System menu visible.
WS_SIZEBOX	Specifies a window with a sizing border. Same as the WS_THICKFRAME style.
WS_SYSMENU	Specifies a window with a System-menu box in its title bar. The WS_CAPTION style must also be specified.
WS_TILED	Specifies an overlapped window with a title bar and a border. Same as the WS_OVERLAPPED style.
WS_TILEDWINDOW	Specifies an overlapped window with the WS_OVERLAPPED, WS_CAPTION, WS_SYSMENU, WS_THICKFRAME, WS_MINIMIZEBOX, and WS_MAXIMIZEBOX styles. Same as the WS_OVERLAPPEDWINDOW style.
WS_VISIBLE	Specifies a window that is initially visible.
WS_VSCROLL	Specifies a window that has a vertical scroll bar.

The style defined in the template file Templ01.ccp is WS_OVERLAPPEDWINDOW. This style creates a window that has the styles WS_OVERLAPPED, WS_CAPTION, WS_SYSMENU, WS_THICKFRAME, WS_MINIMIZEBOX, and WS_MAXIMIZEBOX. It is the most common style of window.

The fifth parameter to the CreateWindowEx() service defines the initial horizontal position of the window. The value CS_USERDEFAULT (0x80000000) determines the use of the default position. The template file uses the same CS_USERDEFAULT symbolic constant for the *y* position, and the windows *x* and *y* size. These are parameters six, seven, and eight of the CreateWindowEx() function.

Parameters nine and ten are set to NULL because this window has no parent and no default menu.

The eleventh parameter, hInstance, is the handle to the instance that was passed to WinMain() by Windows.

The last entry, called the creation parameters, can be used to pass data to a program. A CREATESTRUCT-type structure serves to store the initialization parameters passed to the window procedure of an application. The data can include an instance handle, a new menu, the window's size and location, the style, the window's name and class name, and the extended style. Because no creation parameters are passed, the field is set to NULL.

The CreateWindowEx() function returns a handle to the window of type HWND. The template file Templ01.cpp stores this handle in a global variable named hwnd. The reason for this is that many functions in the Windows API require this handle. By storing it in a global variable we make it visible throughout the code.

If CreateWindowsEx() fails, it returns NULL. Code in WinMain() can test for this error condition with the statement:

```
if(!hwnd)
  return(0);
```

We do not use this test in the template file Templ01.cpp because it is usually not necessary. If WinMain() fails, you may use the debugger to inspect the value of hwnd after CreateWindowEx() to make sure that a valid handle was returned.

Displaying the Window

CreateWindowEx() creates the window internally but does not display it. To display the window your code must call two other functions: ShowWindow() and UpdateWindow(). ShowWindow() sets the window's show state and UpdateWindow() updates the window's client area. In the case of the program's main window, ShowWindow() must be called once, using as a parameter the iCmdShow value passed by Windows to WinMain(). In the template file the call is coded as follows:

```
ShowWindow (hwnd, iCmdShow) ;
```

The first parameter to `ShowWindow()` is the handle to the window returned by `CreateWindowEx()`. The second parameter is the window's display-mode parameter, which determines how the window must be initially displayed. The display-mode parameters are listed in Table 3-1, but in this first call to `ShowWindow()` you must use the value received by `WinMain()`.

`UpdateWindow()` actually instructs the window to paint itself by sending a `WM_PAINT` message to the window procedure. The processing of the `WM_PAINT` message is described later in this chapter. The actual code in the template file is as follows:

```
UpdateWindow (hwnd) ;
```

If all has gone well, at this point your program is displayed on the screen. It is now time to implement the message-passing mechanisms that are at the heart of event-driven programming.

The Message Loop

In Chapter 2 we discussed the event-driven characteristic of Windows programming and how it is implemented by passing messages between the participants. Because there can be no guarantee that messages are processed faster than they originate, Windows maintains two message queues. The first type of queue, called the *system queue*, serves to store messages that originate in hardware devices, such as the keyboard and the mouse. In addition, every thread of execution has its own *message queue*. The message handling mechanism can be described with a simplified example: when a keyboard event occurs, the device driver software places a message in the system queue. Windows uses information about the input focus to decide which thread should handle the message. It then moves the message from the system queue into the corresponding thread queue.

A simple block of code, called the *message loop*, removes a message from the thread queue and dispatches it to the function or routine that must handle it. When a special message is received, the message loop terminates, and so does the thread. The message loop in Templ01.cpp is coded as follows:

```
while (GetMessage (&msg, NULL, 0, 0))
    {
    TranslateMessage (&msg) ;
    DispatchMessage (&msg) ;
    }
  return msg.wParam ;
```

The `while` statement calls the function `GetMessage()`. The first parameter to `GetMessage()` is a variable of the structure type `MSG`, described previously and reproduced in Appendix A. The structure variable is filled with information about the message in the queue, if one exists. If no message is waiting in the queue, Windows suspends the application and assigns its time slice to other threads of execution. In an event-driven environment, programs act only in response to events. No event, no message, no action.

The second parameter to `GetMessage()` is the handle to a window from which to retrieve a message. Most applications set this parameter to NULL, which signals that all messages for windows that belong to the application making the call should be retrieved. The third and the fourth parameters to `GetMessage()` are the lowest and the highest message numbers to be retrieved. Threads that only retrieve messages within a particular range can use these parameters as a filter. When the special value 0 is assigned to both of these parameters (as is the case in our message loop) then no filtering is performed and all messages are passed to the application.

There are two functions inside the message loop. `TranslateMessage()` is a keyboard-processing function that converts keystrokes into characters. The characters are then posted to the message queue. If the message is not a keystroke that needs translation, then no special action is taken. The `DispatchMessage()` function sends the message to the window procedure, where it is further processed and either acted upon, or ignored. The window procedure is discussed in the following section. `GetMessage()` returns 0 when a message labeled `WM_QUIT` is received. This signals the end of the message loop; at this point execution returns from `WinMain()`, and the application terminates.

The Window Procedure

At this moment in a program's execution the window class has been registered, the window has been created and displayed, and all messages are being routed to your code. The *window procedure*, sometimes called the window function, is where you write code to handle the messages received from the message loop. It is in the window procedure that you respond to the events that pertain to your program.

Every window must have a window procedure. Although the name `WinProc()` is commonly used, you can use any other name for the window procedure provided that it appears in the procedure header, the prototype, in the corresponding entry of the `WNDCLASSEX` structure, and that it does not conflict with another name in your application. Also, a Windows program can have more than one window procedure. The program's main window is usually registered in `WinMain()`, but others can be registered elsewhere in an application. Here again, each window procedure corresponds to a window class, and has its own `WNDCLASSEX` structure, as well as a unique name.

In the template, the window procedure is coded as follows:

```
'   |————————————— Return type, equivalent to a long
'   |        |———————— Same as FAR PASCAL calling
'   |        |                  convention. Use in Windows and
'   |        |                  dialog procedures
'   |        |          |——-- Procedure name
```

```
'  |        |         |      [ parameter list ...              ]
___- ____ ___-  _____________________-

LRESULT CALLBACK WndProc (HWND hwnd, UINT iMsg, WPARAM wParam,
                          LPARAM lParam) {
```

The window procedure is of callback type. The CALLBACK symbol was first introduced in Windows 3.1 and is equivalent to FAR PASCAL, and also to WINAPI, because all of them currently correspond to the __stdcall calling convention. Although it is possible to substitute __stdcall for CALLBACK in the function header, it is not advisable because this could compromise the application's portability to other platforms or to future versions of the operating system.

The return value of a window procedure is of type LRESULT, which is a 32-bit integer. The actual value depends on the message, but it is rarely used by application code. However, a few messages for which the window procedure is expected to return a specific value exist. It is a good idea to check the Windows documentation when in doubt.

Window Procedure Parameters

The four parameters to the window procedure are the first four fields in the MSG structure. The MSG structure is discussed earlier in this chapter and listed in Appendix A. Because Windows calls the window procedure, the parameters are provided by the operating system at call time, as follows:

- hwnd is the handle to the window receiving the message. This is the same handle returned by CreateWindow().
- iMsg is a 32-bit unsigned integer (UINT) that identifies each particular message. The constants for the various messages are defined in the Windows header files. They all start with the letters WM_, which stand for *window message*.
- wParam and lParam are called the message parameters. They provide additional information about the message. Both values are specific to each message.

The last two members of the message structure, which correspond to the message's time of posting and cursor position, are not passed to the window procedure. However, application code can use the functions GetMessageTime() and GetMessagePos() to retrieve these values.

Window Procedure Variables

The implementation of the window procedure in Templ01.cpp starts by declaring a scalar of type HDC and two structure variables of type HWND and MSG respectively. The variables are as follows:

hdc is a handle to the device context. A device context is a data structure maintained by Windows that is used to define the graphics objects and their attributes, as well as their associated graphics modes. Devices such as the video display, printers, and plotters, must be accessed through a handle to their device contexts, which is obtained from Windows. The device context is discussed in detail in Chapter 4.

ps is a PAINTSTRUCT variable. This structure is defined by Windows as follows:

```
typedef struct tagPAINTSTRUCT {
  HDC    hdc;           // identifies display device
  BOOL   fErase;        // not-zero if background must be
                        // erased
  RECT   rcPaint;       // Rectangle structure in which
                        // painting is requested
  BOOL   fRestore;      // RESERVED
  BOOL   fIncUpdate;    // RESERVED
  BYTE   rgbReserved[32]; // RESERVED
} PAINTSTRUCT;
```

The structure contains information used by the application to paint its own client area.

rect is a RECT structure variable. The RECT structure is also defined by Windows as follows:

```
typdef struct _RECT {
  LONG   left;     // x coordinate of upper-left corner
  LONG   top;      // y of upper-left corner
  LONG   right;    // x coordinate of bottom-right corner
  LONG   bottom;   // y of bottom-right
} RECT;
```

The RECT structure serves to define the corners of a rectangle, in this case of the application's display area, which is also called the *client area.*

Message Processing

The window procedure receives and processes messages. A message can originate as follows:

- Some messages are dispatched by WinMain(). In this group are the messages placed in the thread's message queue by the DispatchMessage() function in the message loop. Messages handled in this manner are referred to as queued messages. Queued messages originate in keystrokes, mouse movements, mouse-button clicks, the system timer, and in orders to redraw the window.

◆ All other messages come directly from Windows. These are called nonqueued messages.

The window procedure examines each message, queue or nonqueued, and either takes action or passes the message back for default processing. In the template file Templ01.cpp the message processing skeleton is coded as follows:

```
switch (iMsg) {
// Window message processing
     // Preliminary operations
     case WM_CREATE:
          return (0);
     // Redraw window
     case WM_PAINT :
          hdc = BeginPaint (hwnd, &ps) ;
          GetClientRect (hwnd, &rect) ;
     // Initial display operations here
          EndPaint (hwnd, &ps) ;
          return 0 ;
     // End of program execution
     case WM_DESTROY :
          PostQuitMessage (0) ;
          return 0 ;
     }
return DefWindowProc (hwnd, iMsg, wParam, lParam) ;
```

Messages are identified by uppercase symbolic constants that start with the characters WM_ (window message). Over 200 message constants are defined in Windows. Three messages are processed in the template file: `WM_CREATE`, `WM_PAINT` and `WM_DESTROY`.

When the Window procedure processes a message it must return 0. If it does not process a particular message, then the function `DefWindowsProc()` is called to provide a default action.

WM_CREATE Message Processing

The `WM_CREATE` message is sent to an application as a result of the `CreateWindowEx()` function in `WinMain()`. This message gives the application a chance to perform preliminary initialization, such as displaying a greeting screen, or playing a sound file. In the template, the `WM_CREATE` processing routine does nothing. It serves as a placeholder where the programmer can insert the appropriate code.

WM_PAINT Message Processing

The WM_PAINT message informs the program that all or part of the client window must be repainted. This happens when the user minimizes, overlaps, or resizes the client window area. Recall that the style of the program's main window is defined in the template with the statement:

```
wndclass.style     = CS_HREDRAW | CS_VREDRAW ;
```

This style determines that the screen is redrawn if it is resized vertically or horizontally.

In WM_PAINT, processing begins with the BeginPaint() function. BeginPaint() serves to prepare the window for a paint operation by filling a variable of type PAINTSTRUCT, previously discussed. The call to BeginPaint() requires the hwnd variable, which is the handle to the window to be painted, and a variable ps, of a structure of type PAINTSTRUCT, which is filled by the call. During BeginPaint() Windows erases the background using the currently defined brush.

The call to GetClientRect() requires two parameters. The first one is the handle to the window (hwnd), which is passed to the window procedure as a parameter. In the template file this value is also stored in a public variable. The second parameter is the address of a structure variable of type RECT, where Windows places the coordinates of the rectangle that defines the client area. The left and top values are always set to zero.

Processing ends with EndPaint(). EndPaint() notifies Windows that the paint operation has concluded. The parameters passed to EndPaint() are the same ones passed to BeginPaint(): the handle to the window and the address of the structure variable of type PAINTSTRUCT.

WM_DESTROY Message Processing

The WM_DESTROY message is received by the window procedure when the user takes an action to destroy the window, usually clicking the Close button or selecting the Close or Exit commands from the File or the System menus. The standard processing performed in WM_DESTROY is:

```
PostQuitMessage (0) ;
```

The PostQuitMessage() function inserts a WM_QUIT message in the message queue, thus terminating the GetMessage loop and ending the program.

The Default Window Procedure

The code in the template file contains a return statement for each of the messages that it handles. For example:

```
case WM_PAINT :
     hdc = BeginPaint (hwnd, &ps) ;
     GetClientRect (hwnd, &rect) ;
// Initial display operations here
     EndPaint (hwnd, &ps) ;
     return 0 ;
```

The last statement in this routine returns a value of 0 to Windows. The Windows documentation states that 0 must be returned when an application processes the WM_PAINT message. Some Windows messages, but not many, require a return value other than zero.

Many of the messages received from Windows, or retrieved from the message queue, are of no interest to your application. In this case, code must provide a default action for those messages that it does not handle. Windows contains a function, named DefWindowProc(), that ensures this default action. DefWindowProc() provides specific processing for those messages that require it, thus implementing a default behavior. For those messages that can be ignored, DefWindowProc() returns zero. Your application uses the return value of DefWindowProc() as its own return value from the window procedure. This action is coded as follows in the template file:

```
return DefWindowProc (hwnd, iMsg, wParam, lParam) ;
```

The parameters passed to DefWindowProc() are the same message parameters received by your window procedure from the operating system.

Creating the WinHello Program

In the first walk-through, at the beginning of this chapter, we used the template file Templ01.cpp to create a new project, which we named *Do Nothing Demo*. Do Nothing Demo resulted in a do-nothing program because no modifications were made to the template file at that time. In the present walk-through we proceed to make modifications to the template file to create a Windows program different from the template. This project, which we named *Hello Windows*, is a Windows version of the classic "Hello World" program mentioned in the preceding chapter.

We first create a new project and use the template file Templ01.cpp as the source code base for it. To do so we must follow all the steps in the first walk-through, except that we now name the project *Hello Windows* and the name template file Templ01.cpp is copied and renamed WinHello.cpp. After you have finished all the steps in the walk-through you will have a project named Hello Windows and the source file named WinHello.cpp listed in the Project Workspace and displayed in the Editor window. After the source file is renamed, you should edit the header block to reflect the file's new name and the program's purpose. Figure 3-5 shows the Developer Studio screen at this point.

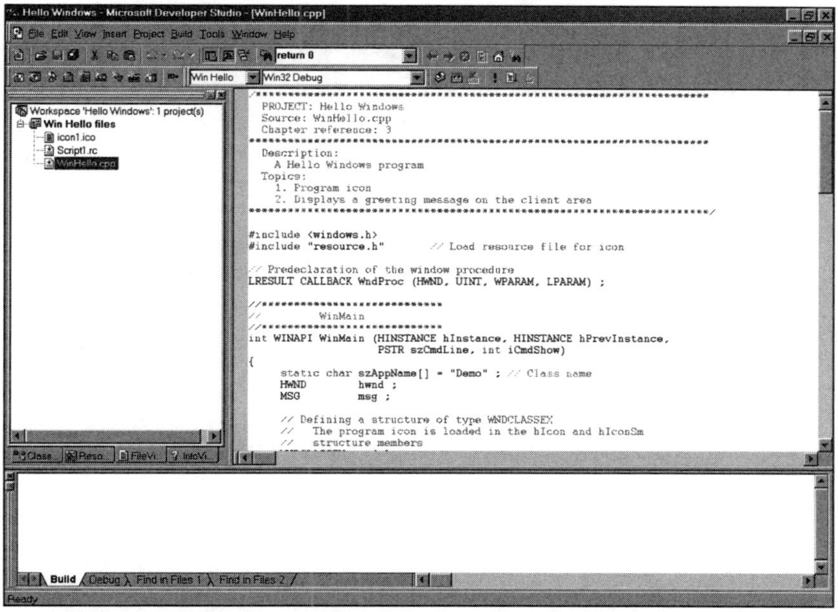

Figure 3-5: Developer Studio main screen showing the Hello Windows project and source file

The project Hello Windows, which we are about to code, has the following features:

- The caption displayed on the program title bar is changed to "Hello Windows."
- When the program executes it displays a greeting message on the center of its client area.
- The program now contains a customized icon. A small version of the icon is displayed in the title bar and a larger one is used when the program's executable is represented by a shortcut on the Windows desktop.

Once you have created the project named Hello Windows and included in it the source file WinHello.cpp, you are ready to start making modifications to the source and inserting new elements into the project.

Modifying the Program Caption

The first modification that we make to the source is to change the caption displayed on the title bar when the program executes. This requires editing the third parameter passed to the `CreateWindowsEx()` function in `WinMain()`. The parameter now reads "Hello Windows." Throughout this book we use the project's name, or a variation of it, as the title-bar caption. The reason for this is to make it easy to find the project files from a screen dump of the executable.

Displaying Text in the Client Area

The second modification requires entering a call to the `DrawText()` API function in the case `WM_PAINT` processing routine. The routine now is:

```
case WM_PAINT :
     hdc = BeginPaint (hwnd, &ps) ;
     GetClientRect (hwnd, &rect) ;
     // Display message in the client area
        DrawText (hdc,
                 "Hello World from Windows",
                 -1,
                 &rect,
                 DT_SINGLELINE | DT_CENTER | DT_VCENTER);
      EndPaint (hwnd, &ps) ;
      return 0 ;
```

The call to `DrawText()` requires five parameters. When calls require several parameters, we can improve the readability of the source by devoting a separate text line to each parameter, or to several associated parameters, as in the previous listing.

The first parameter to `DrawText()` is the handle to the device context. This value was returned by the call to `BeginPaint()`, described previously in this chapter.

The second parameter to `DrawText()` points to the string to be displayed. The string can also be enclosed in double quotation marks, as in the previous listing.

The third parameter is -1 if the string defined in the second parameter terminates in NULL. If not, then the third parameter is the count of the number of characters in the string.

The fourth parameter is the address of a structure of type `RECT` that contains the logical coordinates of the area in which the string is to be displayed. The call to `GetClientRect()`, made in the `WM_PAINT` message intercept, filled the members of the `rect` structure variable. Chapter 4 explains text formatting in greater detail.

The fifth parameter consists of the text formatting options. Table 3-6 lists the most-used of these controls.

Table 3-6 SYMBOLIC CONSTANTS USED IN DRAWTEXT() FUNCTION

Value	Meaning
DT_BOTTOM	Bottom-justifies text. Must be combined with DT_SINGLELINE.
DT_CALCRECT	Determines the width and height of the rectangle. If multiple lines of text exist, DrawText() uses the width of the rectangle in the RECT structure variable supplied in the call and extends the base of the rectangle to bound the last line of text. If only one line of text exists, DrawText() modifies the right side of the rectangle so that text is not drawn.
DT_CENTER	Centers text horizontally.
DT_EXPANDTABS	Expands tab characters. The default number of characters per tab is eight.
DT_EXTERNALLEADING	Includes the font external leading in line height. Normally, it is not included.
DT_LEFT	Aligns text to the left.
DT_NOCLIP	Draws without clipping. The function executes somewhat faster when DT_NOCLIP is used.
DT_NOPREFIX	Causes DrawText() to interpret the control character & as a command to underscore the character that follows. The control characters && print a single &. By specifying DT_NOPREFIX, this processing is turned off.
DT_RIGHT	Aligns text to the right.
DT_SINGLELINE	Displays text on a single line only. Carriage returns and linefeeds are ignored.
DT_TOP	Top-justifies text (single line only).
DT_VCENTER	Centers text vertically (single line only).
DT_WORDBREAK	Breaks words. Lines are automatically broken between words if a word extends past the edge of the rectangle specified by the lpRect parameter. A carriage return-linefeed sequence also breaks the line.

Creating a Program Resource

The last customization that you have to perform on the template file is the creation of two customized icons, which are associated with the program window. The icons correspond to the `hIcon` and `hIconSm` members of the `WNDCLASSEX` structure described previously and listed in Appendix A. `hIcon` is the window's standard icon. Its default size is 32 by 32 pixels, although Windows automatically resizes this icon as required. The standard icon is used on the Windows desktop when a shortcut is created and in some file-listing modes of utilities like Windows Explorer. The small icon is 16 by 16 pixels, which makes it one-fourth the size of the large one. This is the icon shown in dialog boxes that list filenames, and shown by Windows Explorer and in the program's title bar. Windows NT uses a scaled version of the standard icon when a smaller one is required.

An icon is a resource. Resources and resource files were discussed in Chapter 2. Briefly recapping: a resource is stored in a read-only, binary data file that the application can access by means of a handle. We introduce icons at this time because other program resources such as cursors, menus, dialog boxes, bitmaps, and fonts are handled similarly. The icons that we create in this walk-through are considered an application-defined resource.

The most convenient way of creating and using resources is to take advantage of the facilities in the development environment. Visual C++ provides several resource editors, and Developer Studio facilitates the creation and manipulation of the support files required for using resources. Graphics programmers often want to retain the highest possible control over their code; however, the use of these facilities in creating and managing resources does not compromise this principle. The files created by the development environment are both visible and editable. As you gain confidence and knowledge about them, you can progressively take over some or all of the operations performed by the development software. In this book we sometimes let the development environment generate one or more of the program files and then proceed to edit them so that they better suit our purpose.

The convenience of using the automated functions of the development environment is made evident by the fact that a simple resource often requires several software elements. For example, a program icon requires the following components:

- A bitmap that graphically encodes the icon. If the operating system and the application support the small icon, then two bitmaps are required.
- A script file (also called a resource definition file) which lists all the resources in the application and may describe some of them in detail. The resource script can also reference other files and may include comments and preprocessor directives. The resource compiler (RC.EXE) compiles the script file into a binary file with the extension .RES. This binary file is referenced at link time. The resource file has the extension .RC.

- The script file uses a resource header file, with the default filename resource.h, which contains preprocessor directives related to the resources used by the application. The application must reference this file with an `#include` statement.

Creating the Icon Bitmap

Developer Studio provides support for the following resources: dialog boxes, menus, cursors, icons, bitmaps, toolbars, accelerators, string tables, and version controls. Each resource has either a graphics editor or a wizard that helps create the resource. In this discussion we refer to both of them as a resource editor.

Select the Resource command from the Insert menu to activate resource editors. At this time Developer Studio displays a dialog box with an entry for each type of resource. Alternatively, you can access the resource editors faster by displaying the Resource toolbar. In Visual C++ 4 and later versions, this is accomplished by selecting the Toolbars command from the View menu, and then selecting the checkbox for the Resource option. In Version 5 and 6 select the Customize command from the Tools menu, open the Toolbars tab in the Customize dialog box and select the checkbox for the Resource option. The Graphics and Colors boxes should also be checked to display the normal controls in the resource editors. The resulting toolbar is identical in both cases. When the Resource toolbar is displayed, you can drag it into the toolbar area or to any other convenient screen location. The Insert Resource dialog screen and the resource toolbar are shown in Figure 3-6.

You can activate the Icon editor either by selecting the Icon option in the Resource dialog box or by clicking the appropriate button on the toolbar. The Icon editor is simple to use and works well in most cases. It allows creating the bitmap for several sizes of icons. Although the interface to the Icon editor is simple, it is also powerful and flexible. You should experiment with the Icon editor, as well as with the other resource editors, until you have mastered all their options and modes. Figure 3-7 shows the Icon editor in Developer Studio.

The toolbar on the right of the icon editor is similar to the one used in the Windows Paint utility and in other popular graphics programs. Several tools that allow drawing lines exist – curves, and geometrical figures in outline or filled form. Also, there is a palette box from which colors for foreground and background can be selected.

Developer Studio makes possible the creation of a large and a small icon in the same resource. To request the small icon, click on the "New Device Image" button and then select the 16 by 16 icon. The two icons, 32 by 32 pixels and 16 by 16 pixels, can be developed alternatively by selecting one of them in the "Open Device Image" scroll box in the Icon editor. Windows automatically uses the large and the small icon as required.

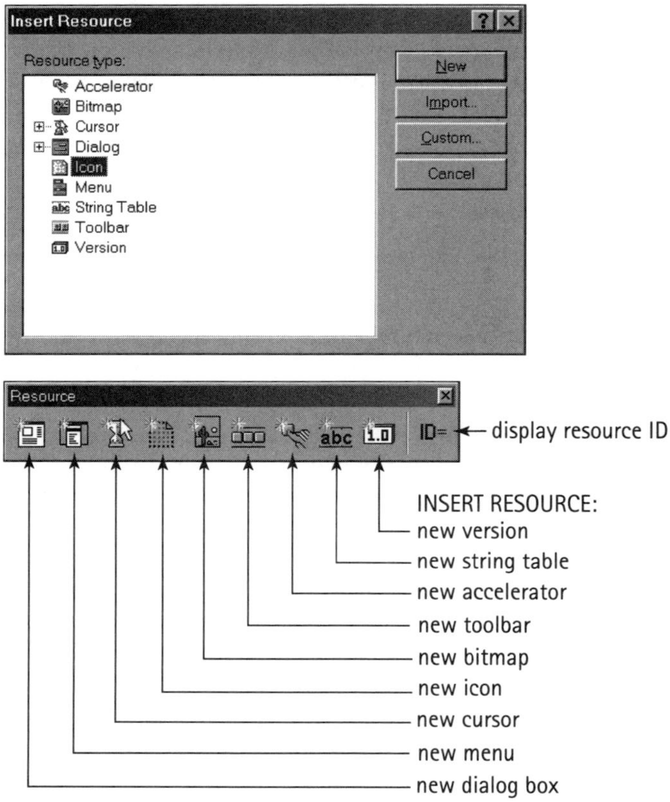

Figure 3-6: Developer Studio Insert Resource dialog screen and toolbar

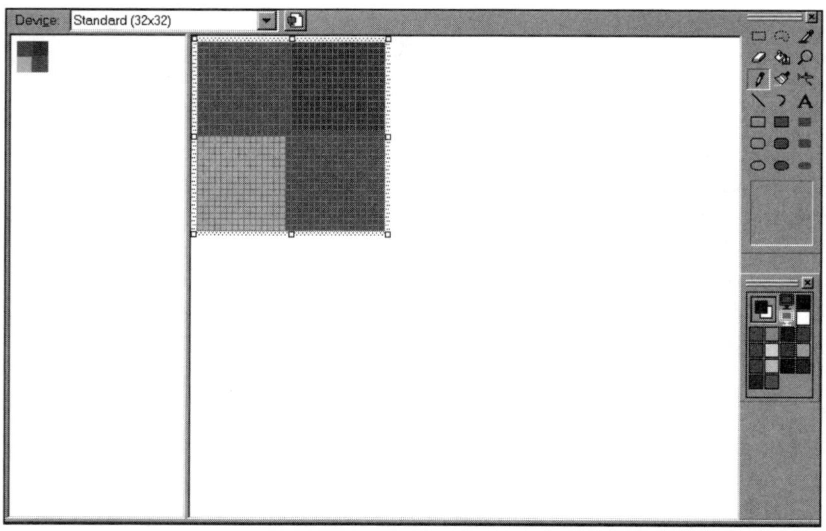

Figure 3-7: The Developer Studio icon editor allows creating an icon resource

In the WinHello program the `WNDCLASSEX` structure is edited to support user-created large and small icons, as follows:

```
//   The program icon is loaded in the hIcon and hIconSm
//   structure members
WNDCLASSEX  wndclass ;
wndclass.hIcon          = LoadImage(hInstance,
                          MAKEINTRESOURCE(IDI_ICON1),
                          IMAGE_ICON,        // Type
                          32, 32,            // Pixel size
                          LR_DEFAULTCOLOR) ;
.
.
.
wndclass.hIconSm        = LoadImage(hInstance,
                          MAKEINTRESOURCE(IDI_ICON1),
                          IMAGE_ICON,         // Type
                          16, 16,             // Pixel size
                          LR_DEFAULTCOLOR) ;
```

The `MAKEINTRESOURCE` macro serves to convert an integer value into a resource. Although resources can also be referenced by their string names, Microsoft recommends the use of the integer value. The name of the icon resource, `IDI_ICON1`, can be obtained from the resource script file. However, an easier way of finding the resource name is to click the Resource Symbols button on the Resource toolbar (labeled ID=) or select the Resource Symbols command in the View menu. Either the symbolic name or the numerical value for the icon resource shown on the Resource Symbols screen can also be used in the `MAKEINTRESOURCE` macro.

In the process of creating an icon bitmap, Developer Studio also creates a new script file, or adds the information to an existing one. However, when working outside the MFC, you must manually insert the script file into the project. Do so by selecting the "Add to Project" command from the Project menu and then selecting the Files option. In the "Insert Files into Project" dialog box, select the script file, which in this case is the one named Script1.rc, and then click the OK button. The script file now appears on the Source Files list in the Files View window of the Project Workspace.

In addition to the script file, Developer Studio also creates a header file for resources. The default name of this file is *resource.h*. For resources to be available to the code you must enter an `#include` statement in the main source file, as follows:

```
#include "resource.h"
```

Notice that the double quotation marks surrounding the filename indicate that it is in the current folder.

At this point, all that is left to do is compile the resources and the source files, and link the program into an executable. Do so by selecting the Rebuild All command from the Build menu. Figure 3-8 shows the screen display of the WinHello program.

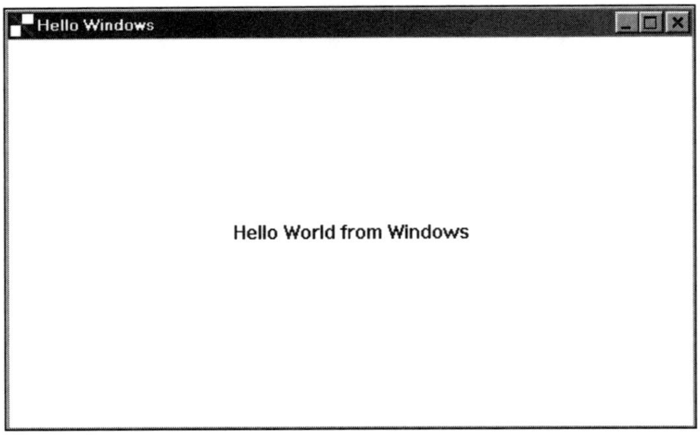

Figure 3-8: Screen dump of the WinHello Program

The following is a listing of the WinHello program. We have excluded the header block to economize space.

```
//  WinHello.cpp
#include <windows.h>
#include "resource.h"          // Load resource file
// Storage for program instance
HINSTANCE    pInstance;
// Predeclaration of the Window Procedure
LRESULT CALLBACK WndProc (HWND, UINT, WPARAM, LPARAM) ;
//****************************
//         WinMain
//****************************
int WINAPI WinMain (HINSTANCE hInstance, HINSTANCE
                    hPrevInstance, PSTR szCmdLine,
                    int iCmdShow) {
     static char szClassName[] = "MainClass" ; // Class name
     HWND        hwnd ;
     MSG         msg ;
     // Defining a structure of type WNDCLASSEX
     //   The program icon is loaded in the hIcon and hIconSm
```

```
//   structure members
WNDCLASSEX  wndclass ;
wndclass.cbSize        = sizeof (wndclass) ;
wndclass.style         = CS_HREDRAW | CS_VREDRAW ;
wndclass.lpfnWndProc   = WndProc ;
wndclass.cbClsExtra    = 0 ;
wndclass.cbWndExtra    = 0 ;
wndclass.hInstance     = hInstance ;
wndclass.hIcon         = LoadImage(hInstance,
                         MAKEINTRESOURCE(IDI_ICON1),
                         IMAGE_ICON,       // Type
                         32, 32,           // Pixel size
                         LR_DEFAULTCOLOR) ;
wndclass.hCursor       = LoadCursor (NULL, IDC_ARROW) ;
wndclass.hbrBackground = (HBRUSH) GetStockObject
                         (WHITE_BRUSH) ;
wndclass.lpszMenuName  = NULL ;
wndclass.lpszClassName = szClassName ;
wndclass.hIconSm       = LoadImage(hInstance,
                         MAKEINTRESOURCE(IDI_ICON1),
                         IMAGE_ICON,        // Type
                         16, 16,            // Pixel size
                         LR_DEFAULTCOLOR) ;
// Store program instance
pInstance = hInstance;
// Registering the structure wmdclass
RegisterClassEx (&wndclass) ;
// CreateWindow()
hwnd = CreateWindowEx (
    WS_EX_LEFT,                // Left aligned (default)
    szClassName,               // pointer to class name
      "WinHello Program",      // window caption
       WS_OVERLAPPEDWINDOW,    // window style
       CW_USEDEFAULT,          // initial x position
       CW_USEDEFAULT,          // initial y position
       CW_USEDEFAULT,          // initial x size
       CW_USEDEFAULT,          // initial y size
       NULL,                   // parent window handle
       NULL,                   // window menu handle
       hInstance,              // program instance
       NULL) ;                 // creation parameters
ShowWindow (hwnd, iCmdShow) ;
```

```
     UpdateWindow (hwnd) ;
     // Message loop
     while (GetMessage (&msg, NULL, 0, 0))
          {
          TranslateMessage (&msg) ;
          DispatchMessage (&msg) ;
          }
     return msg.wParam ;
}
//****************************
//    Window Procedure
//****************************
LRESULT CALLBACK WndProc (HWND hwnd, UINT iMsg, WPARAM wParam,
                          LPARAM lParam) {
     HDC         hdc ;
     PAINTSTRUCT ps ;
     RECT        rect ;
     switch (iMsg)
          {
     // Windows message processing
      case WM_CREATE:
               return 0;
         case WM_PAINT :
               hdc = BeginPaint (hwnd, &ps) ;
               GetClientRect (hwnd, &rect) ;
      // Display message in the client area
       DrawText (hdc,
            "Hello World from Windows",
             -1,
            &rect,
            T_SINGLELINE | DT_CENTER | DT_VCENTER);
        EndPaint (hwnd, &ps) ;
        return 0 ;
      // End of program execution
        case WM_DESTROY :
            PostQuitMessage (0) ;
             return 0 ;
          }
     return DefWindowProc (hwnd, iMsg, wParam, lParam) ;
}
```

Summary

The purpose of this chapter is to familiarize you with the Developer Studio environment so that you can create a simple project using the program templates furnished in the book's CD-ROM. The chapter includes two walk-throughs: in the first one you created a do-nothing program by just inserting the template file into a project. In the second walk-through you edited the template file to create an actual Windows program, with its own icons, and which displays a message on its client area.

Now that you are familiar with the development environment, you can start learning the details of Windows API programming. Chapter 4 discusses general-purpose services and functions, such as text display and keyboard operations. Chapter 5 deals with mouse programming and with graphics program elements, such as menus, controls, and toolbars.

Chapter 4

Application Support Services

IN THIS CHAPTER

- Text Operations
- Mapping Modes
- Graphics with text
- Input
- The caret and caret processing

IN THIS CHAPTER we discuss the part of Windows programming not conventionally considered part of computer graphics, mainly text display and keyboard input operations. However, Windows is a graphics environment; all Windows programming is, in a sense, graphics programming. A natural line of demarcation between graphics and non-graphics services does not exist in the GDI. Text can be considered a graphics resource because displaying and manipulating text characters is not different than any other graphics object.

Furthermore, there is a practical reason for discussing text programming and other basic application support services at this point: it serves as an introduction into Windows application development. Understanding text and keyboard programming requires knowledge of the fundamental concepts of Windows programming. These are the *client area*, the *Windows coordinate system*, the *display context*, and the *mapping mode*, which are also central elements of Windows graphics programming.

Text Display in Windows

Computer systems, including the PC, have historically differentiated between text and graphics. The original notion was that programs could either execute in textual form, by displaying messages composed of alphabetical and numeric characters, or they could use pictures and images to convey information. When the VGA (Video Graphics Array) video standard was released in 1987, it defined both text and graphics modes, with entirely different features and programming. Even in Windows, which is a graphics environment by design, there is a distinction between *console-based* applications and *graphics-based* applications. In console-based applications, Windows refers to a *Console User Interface*, or CUI, and in graphics-based applications, to a *Graphics User Interface*, or GUI. When you select the New command in the Developer Studio File menu, the Projects tab contains an option for creating a Win32 Console Application. But in the real world, a Windows console-based application is a rarity.

In fact, in the Windows environment, the distinction between text and graphics programs is not clear. The text-related functions in the API, which number more than twenty, are actually part of the GDI (*Graphics Device Interface*). Text is a graphics resource. This gives rise to the contradiction that a console application has no access to most of Windows text services.

In this section, we consider Windows text operations to be related to GUI programming. Console-based applications are so rarely used in Windows programming that they can be safely ignored for the purposes of developing graphics-based applications. Although text is actually a graphics element in a Windows program, in most of our minds, text and graphics continue to be different creatures. Furthermore, text manipulations and programming provide an introduction to topics related to client-area access and control.

Client Area

The part of the window on which a program can draw is called the *client area*. The client area does not include the title bar, the sizing border, nor any of the optional elements such as the menu, toolbar, status bar, and scroll bars. The client area is the part of the program window that you access to convey information to the user and on which your application displays child windows and program controls.

DOS programmers own the device, whether working on graphics or on text modes. Once a DOS text program has set a video mode, it knows how many characters can be displayed in each text line, and how many text lines fit on the screen. By the same token, a DOS graphics program knows how many pixel rows and columns are in its domain. Some Windows programs use a fixed-size window, but in most cases, a Windows application cannot make assumptions regarding the size of its client area. Normally, the user is free to resize the screen vertically, horizontally, or in both directions simultaneously. There is practically no limit to how small it can be made, and it can be as large as the entire Windows application area. Writing code that can reasonably accommodate the material displayed to any size of the client area is one of the challenges of Windows programming.

Device and Display Contexts

In Chapter 3 we encountered the notion of a device context, described as a Windows data structure that stores information about a particular display device, such as the video display or a printer. All Windows functions that access the GDI require a handle to the device context as a parameter. The device context is the link between your application, the GDI, and the device-dependent driver that executes the graphics command on the installed hardware. Figure 4-1 is a schematic diagram of this relationship.

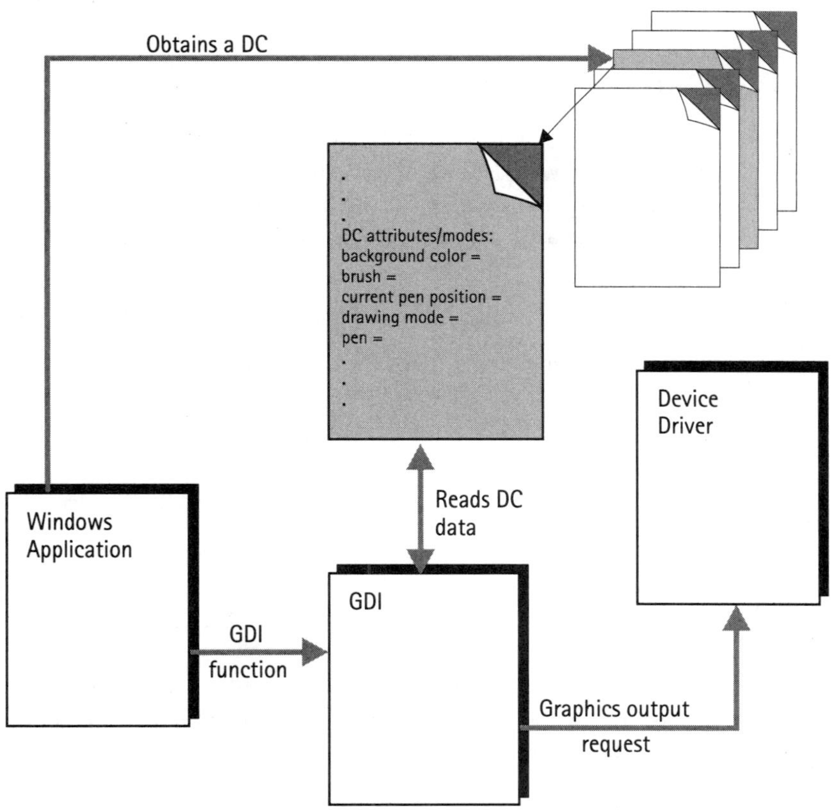

Figure 4-1: Relationship among the device context, the application, the GDI, and the device driver

In Figure 4-1 we see that the Windows application uses one of several available operations to obtain a device context. The call to `BeginPaint()`, used in TEMPL01.CPP and in the WinHello program listed in Chapter 3, returns the handle to the device context. `BeginPaint()` is the conventional way of obtaining the handle to the device context in a `WM_PAINT` handler. The `GetDC()` function is often used to obtain the handle to the device context outside `WM_PAINT`. In either case, from now on, a particular device context-data structure is associated with the application.

Once a device context has been obtained, GDI calls examine the device context attributes to determine how to perform a drawing operation. In Figure 4-1 we see some DC attributes: the background color, the brush, and the current position of the drawing pen. Many attributes are associated with a common display context. For example, the default stock pen is defined as BLACK_PEN in the device context. If this stock pen is not changed, the GDI uses it in all drawing operations. The application can, however, change the stock pen in the device context to NULL_PEN or WHITE_PEN by calling `SelectPen()`.

The Display Context

The video display is a device that requires careful handling in a multitasking environment. Several applications, as well as the system itself, usually share the display device. The notions of child and parent windows, client and non-client areas, desktop windows, and of applications area, all relate to this topic. The *display context* is a special device context for a display device.

The principal difference between a device context and the display context is that a device context allows access to the entire device, while the display context limits access to the output area of its associated window. A display context usually refers to one of the following areas:

- The window's client area
- The window's entire surface, including the non-client area
- The entire desktop surface

Application output is usually limited to the client area; therefore, this is the default display context.

Since the display context is a specialization of the term *device context*, it is correct to refer to the display context as a device context. The reverse, however, is not always true. For example, the printer device context is not a display context. In Chapter 3 we referred to the display context as a device context, which is acceptable. Windows documentation does not always use these terms rigorously. This has been the cause of some misunderstanding. The fact that Windows documentation sometimes uses the term *display device context* as equivalent to *display context* has added to the confusion.

Display Context Types

According to the application's needs, four possible classes of display contexts exist: *common DC*, *single DC*, *private DC*, and *parent DC*. The type of display context for a window is defined in the WNDCLASSEX structure. During the call to RegisterClassEx() we establish the type of display context for the windows class. This is determined by the value entered in the wndclass.style member of WNDCLASSEX.

Table 3-2 shows three constants that refer to the display context types: CS_OWNDC, CS_CLASSDC, and CS_PARENTDC. When no display type constant is entered in the wndclass.style, then the display context type is common, which is the default. In the case of a common display context, Windows resets all attributes to the default values each time the handle is retrieved. This requires the application to reset each attribute that is different from the default settings.

The class display context is enabled with the CS_CLASSDC constant at the time of registering the window class. In this case, Windows initializes the display context attributes once, for all windows of the class. When the display context is retrieved, Windows resets the device origin and the clipping region, but not the other attributes. All windows of this class obtain the same attributes with the handle to the display context. One disadvantage of a class display context is that if one window makes changes to the display context, these changes remain in effect for all subsequent windows that use it.

Entering the CS_PARENTDC constant in the WNDCLASSEX structure enables the parent display context. In this case, Windows creates a common display context and sets its clipping region to the same as that of the parent. The result is that a child window can draw to its parent's client area. The most common use of a parent display context is in drawing controls inside dialog boxes. Round-off errors that result from calculating the bounding box for dialog boxes sometimes cause controls to be clipped at display time. Using a parent display context solves this problem.

The private display context is associated with a window when the CS_OWNDC constant is used in the wndclass.style member of WNDCLASSEX. At registration time, each window created from the class is given a private display context. Because each window has its own display context permanently associated, it need be retrieved only once. All attributes assigned to a private display context are retained until they are explicitly changed. In some types of applications the use of a private display context minimizes coding and improves performance.

Applications that often make changes to the client area, as is the case with many graphics programs, can often profit from a private display context. To accomplish this, several changes have to be made to the TEMPL01.CPP program file. In the first place, an OR operation must be performed between the CS_OWNDC constant and the other values in the wndclass.style member of WNDCLASSEX, as follows:

```
// Defining a structure of type WNDCLASSEX
  WNDCLASSEX  wndclass ;
  wndclass.cbSize        = sizeof (wndclass) ;
  wndclass.style         = CS_HREDRAW | CS_VREDRAW | CS_OWNDC;
     .
     .
     .
```

The remaining changes take place in the Windows procedure. In the first place, you must declare a variable of type `HDC`. This variable must have static scope so that its value is preserved between reentries of the window procedure. The display context can be obtained during `WM_CREATE` processing, which executes at the time the window is created. This is possible because the display context is private. In this case, you can use the `GetDC()` function to obtain the handle to the display context, as in the following code fragment:

```
LRESULT CALLBACK WndProc (HWND hwnd, UINT iMsg, WPARAM wParam,
                          LPARAM lParam) {
     // Local variables
     PAINTSTRUCT         ps ;
     RECT                rect ;
     static HDC          hdc;       // Handle to private DC

     switch (iMsg)
         {
     // Windows message processing
          case WM_CREATE:
               hdc = GetDC(hwnd);      // Obtain handle to
                                       // private DC
               return 0;
     .
     .
     .
```

The private display context is available during `WM_PAINT` message intercept, and need not be retrieved during each iteration. Therefore, the return value from `BeginPaint()` can be discarded and the `EndPaint()` function becomes unnecessary, as in the following code fragment:

```
case WM_PAINT :
     BeginPaint (hwnd, &ps) ;
     GetClientRect (hwnd, &rect) ;
     // Display message in the client area
     DrawText (hdc,
               "Demo program using a private DC",
               -1,
               &rect,
                DT_SINGLELINE | DT_CENTER | DT_VCENTER);
     return 0 ;
        .
        .
        .
```

The project named *Private DC Demo* on the book's CD-ROM contains the full source for a private DC demonstration. You can use the source file TEMPL02.CPP as a template for creating applications that use a private display context.

Window Display Context

Applications sometimes wish to draw not only on the client area, but also elsewhere in the window. Normally, areas such as the title bar, menus, status bar, and scroll bars are inaccessible to code that uses one of the display context types previously mentioned. You can, however, retrieve a window-level display context. In this case, the display context's origin is not at the top-left corner of the client area, but at the top-left corner of the window. The `GetWindowDC()` function serves to obtain the handle to the window-level display context and the `ReleaseDC()` function to release it. In general, drawing outside the client area should be avoided; it can create problems in the application and in Windows.

Mapping Modes

One of the most important attributes of the display context is the *mapping mode* because it affects practically all drawing operations. The mapping mode is actually the algorithm that defines how logical units of measurement are translated into physical units. For you to understand mapping modes, we must start by explaining logical and device coordinates.

The programmer specifies GDI operations in terms of logical coordinates, or logical units. The GDI sends commands to the device driver in physical units, also called device coordinates. The mapping mode defines the logical units and establishes the methods for translating them into device coordinates. This translation can be described as a mapping operation. In regards to the display device, as well as in most printers, device coordinates are expressed in pixels. Logical coordinates depend on the selected mapping mode. Windows defines six fixed-size mapping modes, as shown in Table 4-1.

TABLE 4-1 WINDOWS FIXED-SIZE MAPPING MODES

Mapping Mode	Logical Units	x-axis	y-axis
MM_TEXT	pixel	right	down
MM_LOWMETRIC	0.1 mm	right	up
MM_HIGHMETRIC	0.01 mm	right	up

Continued

TABLE 4-1 WINDOWS FIXED-SIZE MAPPING MODES *(Continued)*

Mapping Mode	Logical Units	x-axis	y-axis
MM_LOENGLISH	0.01 inch	right	up
MM_HIENGLISH	0.001 inch	right	up
MM_TWIPS	1/1440 inch	right	up

Two other mapping modes, not listed in Table 4-1, are MM_ANISOTROPIC and MM_ISOTROPIC. These modes can be used for shrinking and expanding graphics by manipulating the coordinate system. These two scalable mapping modes, useful for powerful graphics manipulation, are discussed in Chapter 6.

The default-mapping mode, MM_TEXT, is also the most used one. In MM_TEXT, the logical coordinates coincide with the device coordinates. Programmers who learned graphics in the DOS environment usually feel comfortable with this mapping mode. Note that the name MM_TEXT refers to how we normally read text in Western languages: from left to right, and top to bottom. The name is unrelated to text display.

The selection of a mapping mode depends on the needs and purpose of the application. Two of the mapping modes, MM_LOMETRIC and MM_HIMETRIC, are based on the metric system (millimeters). MM_LOENGLISH and MM_HIENGLISH are based on the English system of measurement (inches). MM_TWIPS is based on a unit of measurement used in typography called the *twip*, which is equivalent to 1/20th of a point, or 1/1440 of an inch. An application that deals with architectural or technical drawings, in which dimensions are usually in inches or millimeters, can use one of the mapping modes based on metric or English units of measurement. A graphics-design program, or a desktop publishing application, would probably use the MM_TWIPS mapping mode.

The SetMapMode() function serves to change the mapping mode in the device context. One of the parameters in the call is the handle to the device context; the other parameter is one of the predefined mapping mode constants. For example, to change the mapping mode to LO_METRIC, you would code:

```
static int      oldMapMode;
     .
     .
     .
oldMapMode = SetMapMode (hdc, LO_METRIC);
```

The function returns the previous mapping mode, which can be stored in an integer variable. Later on, the original mapping mode can be restored as follows:

```
SetMapMode (hdc, oldMapMode);
```

`SetMapMode()` returns zero if the function call fails.

Screen, Client Area, and Window Coordinates

Windows uses several coordinate systems. The basic unit of measurement is the pixel, also called a *device unit*. Horizontal values increase from left to right and vertical values from top to bottom. The origin of the coordinate system is the top-left corner of the drawing surface. Three different *extents* are used in relation to the device area: *screen*, *client area*, and *window* coordinate systems.

The screen coordinate system refers to the entire display area. This coordinate system is used when location and size information refer to the entire video display. The call to `CreateWindowEx()`, in the program WINHELLO.CPP and most of the template files, uses the symbolic constant `CW_USEDEFAULT`. This constant lets Windows select a position and size for the program's window. Alternatively, we could have specified the window's location and size in device units. For example, the following call to `CreateWindowEx()` locates the window at 20 by 20 pixels from the screen's upper-left corner and forces a dimension of 400 by 500 pixels:

```
// CreateWindow()
hwnd = CreateWindowEx (
       WS_EX_LEFT,                  // Left aligned (default)
       szClassName,                 // pointer to class name
       "WinHello Program",          // window caption
       WS_OVERLAPPEDWINDOW,         // window style
       20,                          // initial x position
       20,                          // initial y position
       400,                         // initial x size
       500,                         // initial y size
       NULL,                        // parent window handle
       NULL,                        // window menu handle
       hInstance,                   // program instance handle
       NULL) ;                      // creation parameters
```

Other Windows functions, such as those that return the mouse cursor position, the location of a message box, or the location and size of the windows rectangle, also use screen coordinates.

Client-area coordinates are relative to the upper-left corner of the client area, not to the video display. The default unit of measurement is the pixel. The function `ClientToScreen()` can be used to obtain the screen coordinates of a point in the client area. `ScreenToClient()` obtains the client area coordinates of a point defined by its screen coordinates. In either function, the *x* and *y* coordinates are passed and returned in a structure of type `POINT` (see Appendix A for more information).

Window coordinates refer to the top-left corner of the window itself, not to the client area. Applications that use the window display context, mentioned earlier in this chapter, use Windows coordinates instead of client-area coordinates.

Viewport and Window

The terms *viewport* and *window,* when used in relation to logical and device coordinates, can be the source of some confusion. In the first place, Windows documentation uses the term *viewport* in a way that does not coincide with its most accepted meaning. In graphics terminology, a viewport is a specific screen area set aside for a particular graphics function. In this sense, the notion of a viewport implies a region within the application's window.

In Windows, the viewport is often equated with the client area, the screen area, or the application area, according to the bounds of the device context. The one characteristic element of the viewport is that it is expressed in device units, which are pixels. The window, on the other hand, is expressed in terms of logical coordinates. Therefore, the unit of measurement of a window can be inches, millimeters, twips, or pixels in the six fixed-sized mapping modes, or one defined by the application in the two scalable mapping modes.

Regarding viewports and windows, two specific boundaries must be considered: the origin and the extent. The *origin* refers to the location of the window or viewport, and the *extent* to its width and height. The origin of a window and a viewport can be set to different values in any of the mapping modes. Function calls to set the window and the viewport extent are ignored when any one of the six fixed-sized mapping modes is selected in the device context. However, in the two scalable mapping modes, MM_ISOTROPIC and MM_ANISOTROPIC, both the origin and the extent of the viewport and the window can be set separately.

A source of confusion is that both the viewport and the window coincide in the default mapping mode (`MM_TEXT`). In the fixed-size mapping modes, the extent of the viewport and the window cannot be changed, as mentioned in the preceding paragraph. This should not be interpreted to mean that they have the same value. Actually, the measurement in units of length of the viewport and the window extent is meaningless. It is the ratio between the extent that is useful. For example, if the viewport extent is 20 units and the window extent is 10 units, then the ratio of viewport to window extent is of 20/10, or 2. This value is used as a multiplier when converting between window and device coordinates. Other factors that must be taken into account in these conversions are the location of the point, the origin of the viewport, and the origin of the window. Figure 4-2 is a simplified, schematic representation of the concepts of viewport and window.

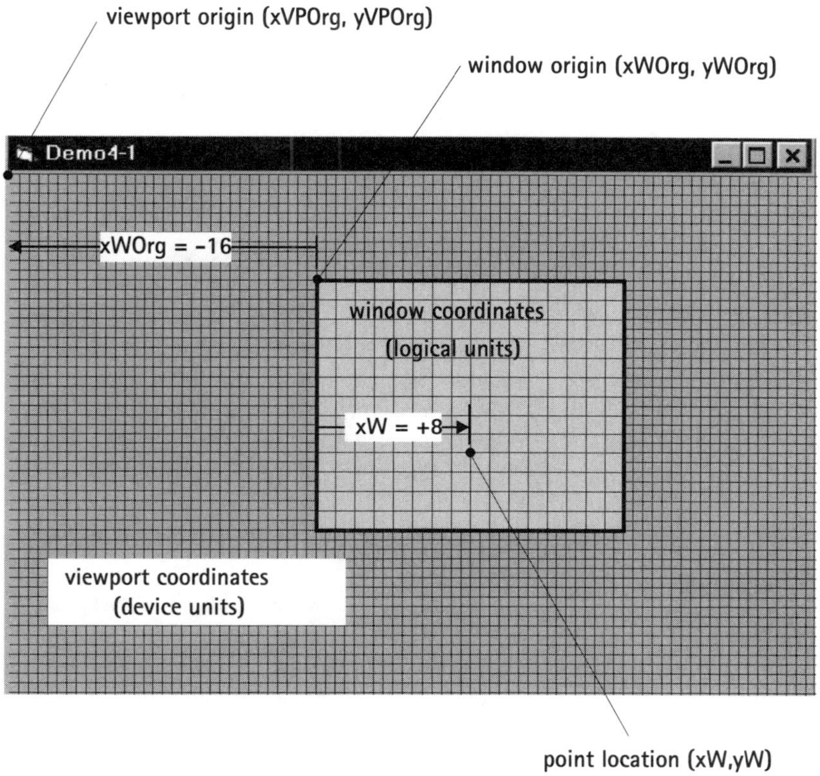

CONVERSION FORMULAS: (allmappingmodes)

xVP = (xW-xWOrg) x (xVPExt/xWExt) + xVPOrg
yVP = (yW-yWOrg) x (yVPExt/yWExt) + yVPOrg

xW = (xVP-xVPOrg) x (xWExt/xVPExt) + xWOrg
yW = (yVP-yVPOrg) x (yWExt/yVPExt) + yWOrg

Figure 4-2: Relationship between viewport and window coordinates

In Figure 4-2, the dimension of the logical units is twice that of the device units, in both axes. Therefore, the ratio between the window extension and the device extension (xVPExt / xWExt and yVPExt / yWExt) equals 2. The point located at *x*W, *y*W is at window coordinates *x*W = 8, *y*W = 9, as shown in the illustration. To convert to device coordinates, we apply the corresponding formulas. In calculating the *x*-axis viewport coordinate of the point *x*W, *y*W, we proceed as follows:

xVP = (xW - xWOrg) x (xVPExt / xWExt) + xVPOrg
xVP = (8 -(- 16)) x 2 + 0
xVP = 48

This means that in the example in Figure 4-2, the point at window coordinates $x = 8$, $y = 9$, located in a window whose origin has been displaced 16 logical units on the x-axis, and 5.5 logical units in the y-axis, is mapped to viewport coordinates xVP = 48, yVP = 25. Note that the sample calculations do not include the y-coordinate.

Programming Text Operations

Text operations in console-based applications are usually a simple task. The text characters are displayed using whatever font is selected at the system level, and at the screen line and column where the cursor is currently positioned. In an analogy with the old Teletype machines, this form of text output programming is said to be based on the model of a "glass TTY." But even when the program takes control of the display area, the matter of text output is no more complicated than selecting a screen line and a column position.

In graphics programming, and particularly in Windows graphics, the coding of text operations often becomes a major task, to the point that Windows text programming is considered a specialty field. In this sense, it is possible to speak of bitmapped graphics, of vector graphics, and of text graphics. Developing a GDI-based text-processing application, such as a Windows word-processing or desktop publishing program, involves a great amount of technical complexity. In addition to programming skills, it requires extensive knowledge of typography, digital composition, and graphics arts. At present, we are concerned with text graphics in a non-specialized context. That is, text display is one of the functions that is normally necessary in implementing a Windows application. But even in this more general sense, text programming in Windows is not without some complications.

Typefaces and Fonts

A collection of characters of the same design is called a *typeface*. Courier, Times Roman, and Helvetica are typefaces. Courier is a monospaced typeface that originated in typewriter technology. The characters in the Courier typeface all have the same width. Times Roman is a typeface developed in the 19th century by an English newspaper for the purpose of making small type readable when printed on newspaper stock. Times Roman uses short, horizontal lines of a different thickness. To some, these elements resemble hooks; for which the typeface is called *serif* (hook, in French). On the other hand, the characters in the Helvetica typeface have the same thickness; therefore, it is called a sans-serif typeface (without hooks).

Times Roman and Helvetica are proportionally spaced fonts; that is, each character is designed to have an ideal width. In a proportionally spaced font, the letter "w" is wider than the letter "i." In Windows, proportionally spaced fonts are sometimes called *variable pitch* fonts. They are more pleasant and easier to read than monospaced fonts, but digits displayed in proportionally spaced fonts do not align in columns. Figure 4-3 shows text in Courier, Times Roman, and Helvetica typefaces.

These lines are in *Courier* typeface.
All characters have the same width.

These lines are in *Times Roman* typeface.
Times Roman is a serif typeface of
great readability.

These lines are in *Helvetica* typeface.
Helvetica is a sans-serif typeface
often used for display type.

Figure 4-3: Text in Courier, Times Roman, and Helvetica typefaces

A group of related typefaces is called a *typeface family*; for example, Helvetica Bold and Helvetica Oblique are typeface families. A *font* is a collection of characters of the same typeface and size. In this sense you can speak of the Times Roman 12-point font. *Type style* is a term used somewhat loosely in reference to specific attributes applied to characters in a font. Boldface (dark), roman (straight up), and italics (slanted towards the right) are common type styles.

Historically, Windows fonts have been of three different types: *raster*, *vector*, and *TrueType*. Raster fonts are stored as bitmaps. Vector fonts, sometimes called stroke fonts, consist of a set of drawing orders required to produce each letter. TrueType fonts, introduced in Windows 95, are similar to PostScript fonts. They are defined as lines and curves, can be scaled to any size, and rotated at will. TrueType fonts are more versatile and have the same appearance on the screen as when printed. TrueType fonts also ensure portability between applications. Programmers working in Windows 95 and NT deal mostly with TrueType fonts.

For reasons related to copyright and trademark laws, some Windows fonts have names that differ from the traditional typefaces. For example, Times New Roman is the Windows equivalent of Times Roman, and the Helvetica typeface is closely approximated by the Windows versions named Arial, Swiss, and Switzerland.

The default Windows font is named the *system font*. In current versions of Windows, the system font is a proportionally spaced font. It is also a raster font, therefore, the characters are defined as individual bitmaps. Figure 4-4 is a screen dump of a Windows program that demonstrates the screen appearance of the various non-TrueType fonts.

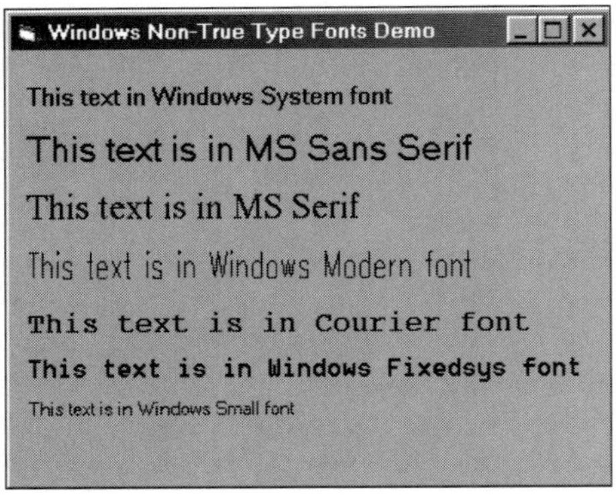

Figure 4-4: Screen display of Windows non-TrueType fonts

Text Formatting

In order to display text in a graphics, multitasking environment (one in which the screen can be resized at any time), code must be able to obtain character sizes at run time. For example, to display several lines of text you must know the height of the characters so that the lines are shown at a reasonable vertical distance from each other. By the same token, you also need to know the width of each character, as well as the width of the client area, to handle the end of each text line.

The `GetTextMetrics()` function provides information about the font currently selected in the display context. `GetTextMetrics()` requires two parameters: the handle to the device context and the address of a structure variable of type `TEXTMETRICS`. Table 4-2 lists the members of the `TEXTMETRIC` structure:

TABLE 4-2 THE TEXTMETRIC STRUCTURE

Type	Member	Contents
`LONG`	`tmHeight`	Character height (ascent + descent)
`LONG`	`tmAscent`	Height above the baseline
`LONG`	`tmDescent`	Height below the baseline
`LONG`	`tmInternalLeading`	Internal leading
`LONG`	`tmExternalLeading`	External leading
`LONG`	`tmAveCharWidth`	Width of the lowercase letter "x"
`LONG`	`tmMaxCharWidth`	Width of widest letter in font

Type	Member	Contents
LONG	tmWeight	Font weight
LONG	tmOverhang	Extra width per string added to some synthesized fonts
LONG	tmDigitizedAspectX	Device horizontal aspect
LONG	tmDigitizedAspectY	Device vertical aspect. The ratio of tmDigitizedAspectX / tmDigitizedAspecty members is the aspect ratio of the device for which the font was designed.
BCHAR	tmFirstChar	First character in the font
BCHAR	tmLastChar	Last character in the font
BCHAR	tmDefaultChar	Character used as a substitute for those not implemented in the font
BCHAR	tmBreakChar	Character used as a word break in text justification
BYTE	tmItalic	Nonzero if font is italic
BYTE	tmUnderlined	Nonzero if font is underlined
BYTE	tmStruckOut	Nonzero if font is strikeout
BYTE	tmPitchAndFamily	Contains information about the font family in the four low-order bits of the following constants:

Constant	Bit	Meaning
TMPF_FIXED PITCH	0	fixed pitch font
TMPF_VECTOR	1	vector font
TMPF_TRUETYPE	2	TrueType font
TMPF_DEVICE	3	device font

Type	Member	Contents
BYTE	tmCharSet	Specifies the font's character set

NOTE: In printing and display technology, the *baseline* is an imaginary horizontal line that aligns the base of the characters, excluding descenders. The term *leading* (pronounced "led-ing") refers to the space between lines of type, usually measured from the baseline of one line to the baseline of the next.

Figure 4-5 shows the vertical character dimensions represented by the corresponding members of the TEXTMETRIC structure.

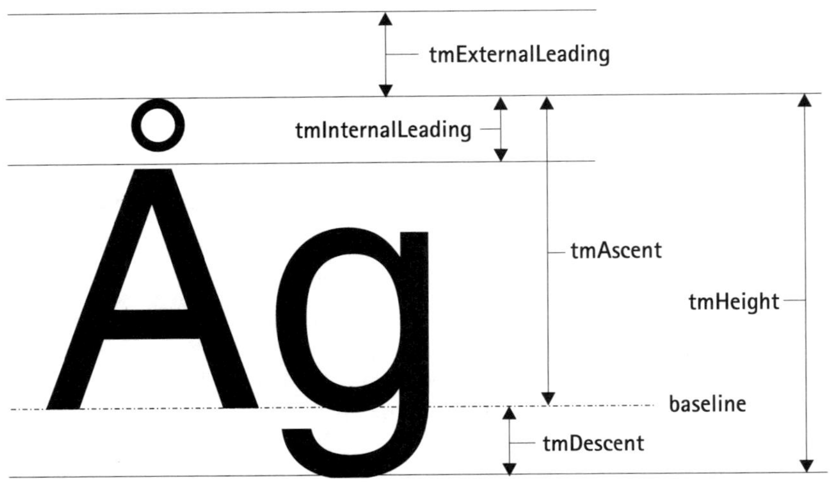

Figure 4-5: Vertical character dimensions as encoded in the various members of the TEXTMETRIC structure

The font installed in the device context determines text-metric values. For this reason, where and how an application obtains data about text dimensions depend on the font and on how the device context is handled. An application that uses the system font, and no other, need only obtain text-metric values once in each session. Because the system font does not change during a Windows session, these values are valid throughout the program's lifetime. However, if an application changes device contexts or fonts during execution, then the text-metric values may also change.

In the simplest case, a text-processing application can obtain text-metric data while processing the WM_CREATE message. Usually, the minimal data required for basic text manipulations is the character height and width. The height is calculated by adding the values in the tmHeight and tmExternalLeading members of the TEXTMETRIC structure for the current display context (see Figure 4-5). The width of the lowercase characters can be obtained from the tmAveCharWidth member.

The calculation of the average width of uppercase characters is somewhat more complicated. If the font currently selected in the display context is monospaced (fixed pitch, in Windows terminology), then the width of the uppercase characters is the same as the lowercase ones. However, if the current font is proportionally spaced (sometimes called a variable pitch font in Windows), then you can obtain an approximation of the width of the uppercase characters by calculating 150 percent of the width of the lowercase ones. We have seen that the tmPitchAndFamily member of TEXTMETRIC has the low-order bit set if the font is monospaced. We can logically AND this value with a binary 1 to test if the font is monospaced. Assuming that a TEXTMETRIC structure variable is named tm, and that the width of the lowercase characters is stored in an integer variable named cxChar, the code would look as follows:

```
int cxCaps;    // Storage for width of uppercase characters

if(tm.tmPitchAndFamily & 0x1)
   cxCaps = (3 * cxChar) / 2;   // 150 percent
else
   cxCaps = cxChar;             // 100 percent
```

More compact coding results from using the ? operator, as follows:

```
cxCaps = (tm.tmPitchAndFamily & 1 ? 3 : 2) * cxChar / 2;
```

The values can be stored in static variables for future use. The following code fragment shows the usual processing in this case:

```
static int cxChar;    // Storage for lowercase character width
static int cxCaps;    // Storage for uppercase character width
static int cyChar;    // Storage for character height plus
                      // leading
   .
   .
   .
   case WM_CREATE :
     hdc = GetDC (hwnd) ;
     GetTextMetrics (hdc, &tm) ;

     cxChar = tm.tmAveCharWidth ;
     cxCaps = (tm.tmPitchAndFamily & 1 ? 3 : 2) * cxChar / 2;
     cyChar = tm.tmHeight + tm.tmExternalLeading ;

     ReleaseDC (hwnd, hdc) ;
     return 0 ;
```

In addition to information about text dimensions, text-processing applications also need to know the size of the client area. The problem in this case is that in most applications, the size of the client area can change at any time. If the window was created with the style WM_HREDRAW and WM_VREDRAW, a WM_SIZE message is sent to the Windows procedure whenever the client-area size changes vertically or horizontally. A WM_PAINT message automatically follows. The application can intercept the WM_SIZE message and store, in a static variable, the vertical and horizontal dimensions of the client area. The size of the client area can be retrieved from these variables whenever you need to redraw to the window. Traditionally, the variables named cxClient and cyClient are used to store these values. The low word of the lParam value, passed to the Windows procedure during WM_SIZE, contains the width of the client area, and the high word contains the height. The code can look as follows:

```
static int cxClient;     // client area width
static int cyClient;     // client area height
.
.
.
case WM_SIZE:
  cxClient = LOWORD (lParam);
  cyClient = HIWORD (lParam);
  return 0;
```

Paragraph Formatting

We are now familiar with much of the logic needed for text formatting at the paragraph level. First, we can determine the character dimensions by calling the GetTextMetric() and then reading the corresponding members of a TEXTMETRIC structure. Second, we can obtain the size of the client area during WM_SIZE processing by means of the high- and low-word of the lParam argument. This information is sufficient for performing an exact calculation on a monospaced font. In the case of a proportionally spaced font, we are forced to deal in approximations, because what we have obtained is the average width of lower-case characters and an estimate of the width of the upper-case ones.

GetTextExtentPoint32(), a function that has suffered several transformations in the various versions of Windows, computes the exact width and height of a character string. The function takes as a parameter the handle to the device context because the string size calculated is based on the currently installed font. Other parameters are the address of the string, its length in characters, and the address of a structure of type SIZE where information is returned to the caller. The SIZE structure (see Appendix A) contains only two members: one for the x dimension and another one for the y dimension. The value returned by GetTextExtentPoint32() is in logical units.

Putting it all together, suppose you have a rather long string, one that requires more than one screen line, stored in a static or public array, and you want to display this string breaking the screen lines only at the end of words. Because in Windows the length of each line in the client area can be changed at any time by the user, the code would have to dynamically adjust for this fact. Placing the processing in a WM_PAINT message handler ensures that the display is updated when the client area changes in size. This also requires that we intercept the WM_SIZE message to recalculate the size of the client area, as discussed previously. The processing logic in WM_PAINT could be as follows:

1. Step through the string, pausing at each space, and calculate the string length using GetTextExtentPoint32(). Keep count of the number of characters to the previous space, or at the beginning of the text string in the case of the first word.
2. If the length of the string is larger than can fit in the client area, then backtrack to the previous space and display the string to that point. Reset the string pointer so that the new string starts at the last character displayed. Continue at step 1.
3. If the end of the string has been reached, display the string starting at the last space and exit the routine.

The actual implementation requires a few other processing details. For example, you may want to leave a margin of a couple of characters on the left and right sides of the display area. In addition, the code would need to manipulate pointers and counters to keep track of the string positions and the number of characters to the previous space. One possible algorithm is reminiscent of the classic case of a circular buffer with two pointers: one to the buffer head and another one to the tail. Figure 4-6 graphically shows the code elements in one of many possible implementations.

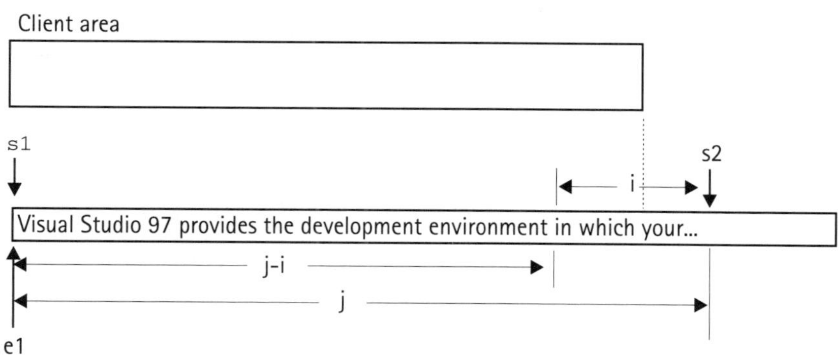

Figure 4-6: Processing operations in displaying multiple text lines

In Figure 4-6, the pointer that signals the start of the string is designated with the letter *s* and the one for the end of the string with the letter *e*. *s1* and *e1* are the starting positions for both pointers. The variable *i* is a counter that holds the number of characters since the preceding space, and *j* holds the number of characters in the current substring. The code steps along the string looking for spaces. At each space, it measures the length of the string and compares it to the horizontal dimension of the client area. When the *s* pointer reaches location *s2*, the substring is longer than the display space available in the client area. The variable *i* then serves to reset the pointer to the preceding space and to decrement the *j* counter. The sub-string is displayed starting at *e1*, for a character count of *j*. Pointers and counters are then reset to the new sub-string and processing continues until the end of the string is found.

A demonstration program named TEX1_DEMO is located on the book's CD-ROM. The message to be displayed is stored in a public string, as follows:

```
// Public string for text display demonstration
char TextMsg[] = {"Visual Studio 97 provides the development "
"environment in which your programming and Web site "
"development packages run. This integrated set of tools runs"
  .
  .
  .
"spreadsheet programs." };
```

The processing operations, located in the Windows procedure, are coded as follows:

```
LRESULT CALLBACK WndProc (HWND hwnd, UINT iMsg, WPARAM wParam,
                              LPARAM lParam) {
 static int  cxChar, cxCaps, cyChar ;// Character dimensions
 static int  cxClient, cyClient;  // Client area parameters
     HDC         hdc ;            // handle to device context
     int j;                       // Offset into string
     int i;                       // characters since last
                                  // space
     char *startptr, *endptr;     // String pointers
     int cyScreen;                // Screen row holder

 // Structures
     PAINTSTRUCT ps;
     TEXTMETRIC  tm;
     SIZE        textsize; // Test string size

 switch (iMsg)
         {
      case WM_CREATE :
           hdc = GetDC (hwnd) ;
           GetTextMetrics (hdc, &tm) ;

           // Calculate and store character dimensions
           cxChar = tm.tmAveCharWidth ;
           cxCaps = ((tm.tmPitchAndFamily & 1) ? 3 : 2) *\
```

```
                cxChar / 2 ;
          cyChar = tm.tmHeight + tm.tmExternalLeading ;

          ReleaseDC (hwnd, hdc) ;
          return 0 ;

     case WM_SIZE:
          // Determine and store size of client area
          cxClient = LOWORD(lParam);
          cyClient = HIWORD(lParam);
          return 0;

     case WM_PAINT :
          hdc = BeginPaint (hwnd, &ps) ;

          // Initialize variables
          cyScreen = cyChar;        // screen row counter
          startptr = TextMsg;       // start position pointer
          endptr = TextMsg;         // end position pointer
          j = 0;                    // length of string
          i = 0;                    // characters since last
                                    // space

          // Text line display loop
          // INVARIANT:
          //        i = characters since last space
          //        j = length of current string
          // startptr = pointer to substring start
          //   endptr = pointer to substring end

          while(*startptr) {
            if(*startptr == 0x20){     // if character is
                                       // space
              GetTextExtentPoint32 (hdc, endptr, j,\
                                    &textsize);

     // ASSERT:
     //       textsize.cx is the current length of the
     //       string
     //       cxClient is the abscissa of the client area
     //       (both in logical units)
     // Test for line overflow condition. If so, adjust
     // substring to preceding space and display
        if(cxClient - (2 * cxChar) < textsize.cx) {
```

```
            j = j - i;
            startptr = startptr - i;
            TextOut (hdc, cxChar, cyScreen, endptr, j);
            cyScreen = cyScreen + cyChar;
            endptr = startptr;
            j = 0;
            }
      // End of space character processing.
      // Reset chars-to-previous-space counter, whether
      // or not string was displayed
            i = 0;
             }
      // End of processing for any text character
      // Update substring pointer and counters
           startptr++;
           j++;
           i++;
           }
      // End of while loop
      // Display last text substring
           j = j - i;
           TextOut (hdc, cxChar, cyScreen, endptr, j);
           EndPaint (hwnd, &ps);
           return 0 ;

      case WM_DESTROY :
            PostQuitMessage (0) ;
            return 0 ;
      }
    return DefWindowProc (hwnd, iMsg, wParam, lParam) ;
  }
```

Figure 4-7 shows two screen dumps of the TEX1_DEMO program in the *Text Demo No 1* project folder. The first one shows the text line as originally displayed in our system. The second one shows them after the client area has been resized.

Before resizing

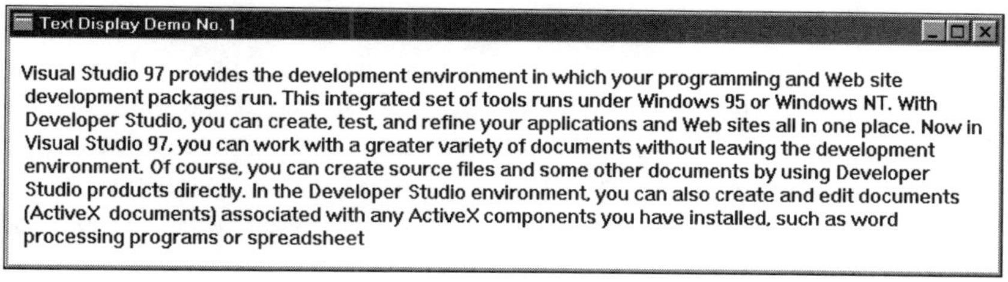

After resizing

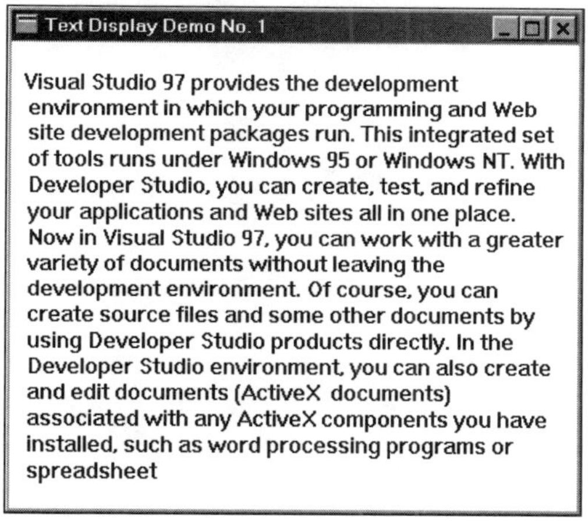

Figure 4-7: Two screen dumps of the TEX1_DEMO program

The TEX1_DEMO program uses a variable (j) to store the total size of the substring (see Figure 4-6). In C++ it is valid to subtract two pointers to determine the number of elements between them. The code in the TEX1_DEMO program could have calculated the number of elements in the substring by performing pointer subtraction.

The DrawText() Function

Another useful text display function in the Windows API is DrawText(). This function is of a higher level than TextOut() and, in many cases, text display operations are easier to implement with DrawText(). DrawText() uses a rectangular screen area that defines where the text is to be displayed. In addition, it recognizes some control characters embedded in the text string as well as a rather extensive collection of format controls, which are represented by predefined constants. The following are the general forms for TextOut() and DrawText():

```
BOOL TextOut(
       HDC hdc,            // 1
       int nXStart,        // 2
       int nYStart,        // 3
       LPCTSTR lpString,   // 4
       int cbString        // 5
       );
int DrawText(
       HDC hDC,            // 1
       LPCTSTR lpString,   // 2
       int nCount,         // 3
       LPRECT lpRect,      // 4
       UINT uFormat        // 5
      );
```

In both cases, hdc is the handle to the device context and lpString is a pointer to the string to be displayed. In TextOut() the second and third parameters (xXstart and nYStart) are the logical coordinates of the start point in the client area, and the last parameter is the string length. In DrawText() the third parameter (nCount) is the string length in characters. If this parameter is set to -1, then Windows assumes that the string is zero-terminated. The positioning of the string in DrawText() is by means of a rectangle structure (type RECT) described in Chapter 3 and listed in Appendix A. This structure contains four members; two for the rectangle's top-left coordinates, and two for its bottom-right coordinates. The values are in logical units. The last parameter (uFormat) is any combination of 19 format strings defined by the constants listed in Table 4-3.

TABLE 4-3 STRING FORMATTING CONSTANTS IN DRAWTEXT() FUNCTION

Symbolic Constant	Meaning
DT_BOTTOM	Specifies bottom-justified text. Must be combined with DT_SINGLELINE.

Symbolic Constant	Meaning
DT_CALCRECT	Returns width and height of the rectangle. In the case of multiple text lines, DrawText() uses the width of the rectangle pointed to by lpRect and extends its base to enclose the last line of text. In the case of a single text line, then DrawText() modifies the right side of the rectangle so that it encloses the last character. In either case, DrawText() returns the height of the formatted text, but does not draw the text.
DT_CENTER	Text is centered horizontally.
DT_EXPANDTABS	Expands tab characters. The default number of characters per tab is eight.
DT_EXTERNALLEADING	Includes the font's external leading in the line height. Normally, external leading is not included in the height of a line of text.
DT_LEFT	Specifies text aligned flush-left.
DT_NOCLIP	Draws without clipping. This improves performance.
DT_NOPREFIX	Turns off processing of prefix characters. Normally, DrawText() interprets the ampersand (&) mnemonic-prefix character as an order to underscore the character that follows. The double ampersands (&&) is an order to print a single ampersand symbol. This function is turned off by DT_NOPREFIX.
DT_RIGHT	Specifies text aligned flush-right.
DT_SINGLELINE	Specifies single line only. Carriage returns and linefeeds are ignored.
DT_TABSTOP	Sets tab stops. The high-order byte of nFormat is the number of characters for each tab. The default number of characters per tab is eight.
DT_TOP	Specifies top-justified text (single line only).
DT_VCENTER	Specifies vertically centered text (single line only).
DT_WORDBREAK	Enables word-breaking. Lines are automatically broken between words if a word would extend past the edge of the rectangle specified by lpRect. A carriage return (\n) or linefeed code (\r) also breaks the line.

The program TEX2_DEMO, located in the *Text Demo No 2* project folder on the book's CD-ROM, is a demonstration of text display using the `DrawText()` function. Following are excerpts from the program code:

```
LRESULT CALLBACK WndProc (HWND hwnd, UINT iMsg, WPARAM wParam,
                          LPARAM lParam) {

 static int  cxChar, cyChar ;       // Character dimensions
 static int  cxClient, cyClient;    // Client area parameters
 HDC      hdc ;                     // handle to device context

 // Structures
 PAINTSTRUCT ps;
 TEXTMETRIC  tm;
 RECT        textRect;

 switch (iMsg) {
    case WM_CREATE :
         hdc = GetDC (hwnd) ;
         GetTextMetrics (hdc, &tm) ;

         // Calculate and store character dimensions
         cxChar = tm.tmAveCharWidth ;
         cyChar = tm.tmHeight + tm.tmExternalLeading ;

         ReleaseDC (hwnd, hdc) ;
         return 0 ;

    case WM_SIZE:
         // Determine and store size of client area
         cxClient = LOWORD(lParam);
         cyClient = HIWORD(lParam);
         return 0;

    case WM_PAINT :
         hdc = BeginPaint (hwnd, &ps) ;

         // Initialize variables
           SetRect (&textRect,        // address of structure
                    2 * cxChar,               // x for start
                    cyChar,                   // y for start
                    cxClient -(2 * cxChar), // x for end
                    cyClient);                // y for end

         // Call display function using left-aligned and
```

```
            //wordbreak controls
            DrawText( hdc, TextStr, -1, &textRect,
                      DT_LEFT | DT_WORDBREAK);

            EndPaint (hwnd, &ps);
            return 0 ;

       case WM_DESTROY :
            PostQuitMessage (0) ;
            return 0 ;
     }

   return DefWindowProc (hwnd, iMsg, wParam, lParam) ;
}
```

Text Graphics

Comparing the listed processing operations with those used in the TEX1_DEMO program (discussed previously in this chapter) you can see that the processing required to achieve the same functionality is simpler using `DrawText()` than `TextOut()`. This observation, however, should not mislead you into thinking that `DrawText()` should always be preferred. The interpretation of the reference point at which the text string is displayed when using `TextOut()` depends on the text-alignment mode set in the device context. The `GetTextAlign()` and `SetTextAlign()` functions can be used to retrieve and change the 11 text-alignment flags. This feature of `TextOut()` (and its newer version `TextOutExt()`) allow the programmer to change the alignment of the text-bounding rectangle and even to change the reading order to conform to the Hebrew and Arabic languages.

Windows NT and Windows 95 GDI supports the notion of paths. Paths are discussed in detail in Chapter 7. For the moment, we define a path, rather imprecisely, as the outline produced by drawing a set of graphical objects. One powerful feature of `TextOut()`, which is not available with `DrawText()`, is that when it is used with a TrueType font, the system generates a path for each character and its bounding box. This can be used to display text transparently inside other graphics objects, to display character outlines (called stroked text), and to fill the text characters with other graphics objects. The resulting effects are often powerful. Figure 4-8, later in this chapter, shows the use of paths in creating special text effects.

Selecting a Font

The one limitation of text display on paths is that the font must be TrueType. Therefore, before getting into fancy text graphics, you must be able to select a TrueType font into the device context. Font manipulations in Windows are based on the notion of a *logical font*. A logical font is a description of a font by means of its characteristics. Windows uses this description to select the best-matching font among those available.

Two API functions enable the creation of a logical font. `CreateFont()` requires a long series of parameters that are used to describe the font characteristics. `CreateFontIndirect()` uses a structure in which the font characteristics are stored. Applications that use a single font are probably better off using `CreateFont()`, while programs that change fonts during execution usually prefer `CreateFontIndirect()`. Note that the item list used in the description of a logical font is the same in both functions. Therefore, storing font data in structure variables is an advantage only if the structure can be reused. The description that follows refers to the parameters used in the call to `CreateFont()`, which are identical to the ones used in the structure passed by `CreateFontIndirect()`.

The `CreateFont()` function has one of the longest parameter lists in the Windows API: 14 in all. Its general form is as follows:

```
HFONT CreateFont( nHeight, nWidth, nEscapement, int nOrientation,
                  fnWeight, fdwItalic, fdwUnderline, fdwStrikeOut,
                  fdwCharSet, fdwOutputPrecision, fdwClipPrecision,
                  fdwQuality, fdwPitchAndFamily,
LPCTSTR lpszFace);
HFONT CreateFont(
        int nHeight,                    // 1
        int nWidth,                     // 2
        int nEscapement,                // 3
        int nOrientation,               // 4
        int fnWeight,                   // 5
        fdwItalic,                      // 6
        DWORD fdwUnderline,             // 7
        DWORD fdwStrikeOut,             // 8
        DWORD fdwCharSet,               // 9
        DWORD fdwOutputPrecision,       // 10
        DWORD fdwClipPrecision,         // 11
        DWORD fdwQuality,               // 12
        DWORD fdwPitchAndFamily,        // 13
        LPCTSTR lpszFace                // 14
        );
```

Following are brief descriptions of the function parameters.

- `nHeight (int)` specifies the character height in logical units. The value does not include the internal leading, so it is not equal to the `tmHeight` value in the TEXTMETRIC structure. Also note that the character height does not correspond to the point size of a font. If the MM_TEXT mapping mode is selected in the device context, it is possible to convert the font's point size into device units by means of the following formula:

```
hHeight = (point_size * pixels_per_inch) / 72
```

- The pixels per inch can be obtained by reading the LOGPIXELSY index in the device context, which can be obtained by the call to `GetDeviceCaps()`. For example, to obtain the height in logical units of a 50-point font we can use the following expression:

```
50 * GetDeviceCaps (hdc, LOGPIXELSY) / 72
```

- `nWidth (int)` specifies the logical width of the font characters. If set to zero, the Windows font mapper uses the width that best matches the font height.
- `nEscapement (int)` specifies the angle between an escapement vector, defined to be parallel to the baseline of the text line, and the drawn characters. A value of 900 (90 degrees) specifies characters that go upward from the baseline. Usually this parameter is set to zero.
- `nOrientation (int)` defines the angle, in tenths of a degree, between the character's base line and the *x*-axis of the device. In Windows NT the value of the character's escapement and orientation angles can be different. In Windows 95 they must be the same.
- `fnWeight (int)` specifies the font weight. The constants listed in Table 4-4 are defined for convenience.

TABLE 4-4 CHARACTER WEIGHT CONSTANTS

Weight	Constant
FW_DONTCARE	= 0
FW_THIN	= 100
FW_EXTRALIGHT	= 200
FW_ULTRALIGHT	= 200
FW_LIGHT	= 300
FW_NORMAL	= 400
FW_REGULAR	= 400

Continued

TABLE 4-4 CHARACTER WEIGHT CONSTANTS *(Continued)*

Weight	Constant
FW_MEDIUM	= 500
FW_SEMIBOLD	= 600
FW_DEMIBOLD	= 600
FW_BOLD	= 700
FW_EXTRABOLD	= 800
FW_ULTRABOLD	= 800
FW_HEAVY	= 900
FW_BLACK	= 900

`fdwItalic (DWORD)` is set to 1 if font is italic.
`fdwUnderline (DWORD)` is set to 1 if font is underlined.
`fdwStrikeOut (DWORD)` is set to 1 if font is strikeout.
`fdwCharSet (DWORD)` defines the font's character set. The following are predefined character set constants:

ANSI_CHARSET

DEFAULT_CHARSET

SYMBOL_CHARSET

SHIFTJIS_CHARSET

GB2312_CHARSET

HANGEUL_CHARSET

CHINESEBIG5_CHARSET

OEM_CHARSET

Windows 95 only:

JOHAB_CHARSET

HEBREW_CHARSET

ARABIC_CHARSET

GREEK_CHARSET

TURKISH_CHARSET

THAI_CHARSET

EASTEUROPE_CHARSET

RUSSIAN_CHARSET

MAC_CHARSET

BALTIC_CHARSET

The `DEFAULT_CHARSET` constant allows the name and size of a font to fully describe it. If the font does not exist, another character set can be substituted. For this reason, this field should be used carefully. A specific character set should always be defined to ensure consistent results.

`fdwOutputPrecision (DWORD)` determines how closely the font must match the values entered in the fields that define its height, width, escapement, orientation, pitch, and font type. Table 4-5 lists the constants associated with this parameter.

TABLE 4-5 OUTPUT PRECISION PREDEFINED CONSTANTS

Value	Meaning
`OUT_CHARACTER_PRECIS`	Not used.
`OUT_DEFAULT_PRECIS`	Specifies the default font mapper behavior.
`OUT_DEVICE_PRECIS`	Instructs the font mapper to choose a Device font when the system contains multiple fonts with the same name.
`OUT_OUTLINE_PRECIS`	Windows NT: This value instructs the font mapper to choose from TrueType and other outline-based fonts. Not used in Windows 95.
`OUT_RASTER_PRECIS`	Instructs the font mapper to choose a raster font when the system contains multiple fonts with the same name.
`OUT_STRING_PRECIS`	This value is not used by the font mapper, but it is returned when raster fonts are enumerated.
`OUT_STROKE_PRECIS`	Windows NT: This value is not used by the font mapper, but it is returned when TrueType, other outline-based fonts, and vector fonts are enumerated. Windows 95: This value serves to map vector fonts, and is returned when TrueType or vector fonts are enumerated.

Continued

TABLE 4-5 OUTPUT PRECISION PREDEFINED CONSTANTS *(Continued)*

Value	Meaning
OUT_TT_ONLY_PRECIS	Instructs the font mapper to choose from only TrueType fonts. If no TrueType fonts are installed in the system, the font mapper returns to default behavior.
OUT_TT_PRECIS	Instructs the font mapper to choose a TrueType font when the system contains multiple fonts with the same name.

If more than one font with a specified name exists, you can use the OUT_DEVICE_PRECIS, OUT_RASTER_PRECIS, and OUT_TT_PRECIS constants to control which one is chosen by the font mapper. For example, if there is a font named *Symbol* in raster and TrueType form, specifying OUT_TT_PRECIS forces the font mapper to choose the TrueType version. OUT_TT_ONLY_PRECIS forces the font mapper to choose a TrueType font, even if it must substitute one with another name.

fdwClipPrecision (DWORD) specifies the clipping precision. This refers to how to clip characters located partially outside the clipping region. The constants in Table 4-6 are recognized by the call.

TABLE 4-6 CLIPPING PRECISION PREDEFINED CONSTANTS

Value	Meaning
CLIP_DEFAULT_PRECIS	Default clipping behavior.
CLIP_CHARACTER_PRECIS	Not used.
CLIP_STROKE_PRECIS	Not used by the font mapper, but is returned when raster, vector, or TrueType fonts are enumerated. Windows NT: For compatibility, this value is always returned when enumerating fonts.
CLIP_MASK	Not used.
CLIP_EMBEDDED	Specify this flag to use an embedded read-only font.
CLIP_LH_ANGLES	The rotation for all fonts depends on whether the orientation of the coordinate system is left- or right-handed. If not used, device fonts always rotate counterclockwise.
CLIP_TT_ALWAYS	Not used.

fdwQuality (DWORD) specifies the output quality. This value defines how carefully GDI must attempt to match the logical font attributes to those of an actual physical font. The constants in Table 4-7 are recognized by CreateFont().

TABLE 4-7 OUTPUT PRECISION PREDEFINED CONSTANTS

Value	Meaning
DEFAULT_QUALITY	Appearance of the font does not matter.
DRAFT_QUALITY	Appearance of the font is less important than when the PROOF_QUALITY value is used.
PROOF_QUALITY	Character quality of the font is more important than exact matching of the logical-font attributes. When PROOF_QUALITY is used, the quality of the font is high and no distortion of appearance is visible.

fdwPitchAndFamily (DWORD) defines the pitch and the family of the font. The two low-order bits specify the pitch, and the four high-order bits specify the family. The two bit fields usually use a logical OR for this parameter. Table 4-8 lists the symbolic constants recognized by CreateFont() for the font pitch and the family values.

TABLE 4-8 PITCH AND FAMILY PREDEFINED CONSTANTS

Type	Value	Meaning
Pitch		
	DEFAULT_PITCH	
	FIXED_PITCH	
	VARIABLE_PITCH	
Family		
	FF_DECORATIVE	Novelty fonts (such as Old English).
	FF_DONTCARE	Don't care or don't know.

Continued

TABLE 4-8 PITCH AND FAMILY PREDEFINED CONSTANTS *(Continued)*

Type	Value	Meaning
Family		
	FF_MODERN	Fonts with constant stroke width, with or without serifs, such as Pica, Elite, and Courier New.
	FF_ROMAN	Fonts with variable stroke width and with serifs, such as MS Serif.
	FF_SCRIPT	Fonts designed to look like handwriting, such as Script and Cursive.
	FF_SWISS	Fonts with variable stroke width and without serifs, such as MS Sans Serif.

`lpszFace (LPCTSTR)` points to a null-terminated string that contains the name of the font's typeface. Alternatively, the typeface name can be entered directly inside double quotation marks. If the requested typeface is not available in the system, the font mapper substitutes with an approximate one. If NULL is entered in this field, a default typeface is used. Example typefaces are *Palatino*, *Times New Roman*, and *Arial*. The following code fragment shows a call to the `CreateFont()` API for a 50-point, normal weight, high-quality, italic font using the Times New Roman typeface.

```
HFONT      hFont;       // handle to a font
    // Create a logical font
    hFont = CreateFont (
        50 * GetDeviceCaps (hdc, LOGPIXELSY) / 72, //height
        0,                             // width
        0,                             // escapement angle
        0,                             // orientation angle
        FW_NORMAL,                     // weight
        1,                             // italics
        0,                             // not underlined
        0,                             // not strikeout
        DEFAULT_CHARSET,               // character set
        OUT_DEFAULT_PRECIS,            // precision
        CLIP_DEFAULT_PRECIS,           // clipping precision
        PROOF_QUALITY,                 // quality
        DEFAULT_PITCH | FF_DONTCARE,   // pitch and family
```

```
        "Times New Roman");          // typeface name

    // Select font into the display context
    SelectObject (hdc, hFont);
```

Drawing with Text

Once a TrueType font is selected in the display context, you can execute several manipulations that treat text characters as graphics objects. One of them is related to the notion of a path, introduced in Windows NT and also supported by Windows 95. A path is the outline generated by one or more graphics objects drawn between the `BeginPath()` and `EndPath()` functions. Paths are related to regions and to clipping. These topics are covered in detail in Chapter 7.

The `TextOut()` function has a unique property among the text display functions: it generates a path. For this to work, a TrueType font must first be selected into the display context. Path drawing operations are not immediately displayed on the screen but are stored internally. Windows provides no handles to paths, and only one path for each display context exists. Three functions are available to display graphics in a path: `StrokePath()` shows the path outline, `FillPath()` fills and displays the path's interior, and `StrokeAndFillPath()` performs both functions. You may question the need for a `FillAndStrokePath()` function since it seems that you could use `StrokePath()` and `FillPath()` consecutively to obtain the same effect. This is not the case. All three path-drawing APIs automatically destroy the path. Therefore, if two of these functions are called consecutively, the second one has no effect.

The path itself has a background mix mode, which is delimited by the rectangle that contains the graphics functions in the path. The background mix mode is a display context attribute that affects the display of text, as well as the output of hatched brushes and nonsolid pens. Code can set the background mix mode to transparent by means of the `SetBkMode()` function. This isolates the text from the background. The program TEX3_DEMO, located in the *Text Demo No 3* folder on the book's CD-ROM, is a demonstration of text display inside paths. One of the text lines is stroked and the other one is stroked and filled. The program first creates a logical font and then selects it into the display context. Processing is as follows:

```
case WM_PAINT :
    hdc = BeginPaint (hwnd, &ps) ;
    .
    .
    .
    // Start a path for stroked text
    // Set background mix to TRANSPARENT mode
    BeginPath (hdc);
```

```
SetBkMode(hdc, TRANSPARENT);        // background mix
TextOut(hdc, 20, 20, "This Text is STROKED", 20);
EndPath(hdc);
// Create a custom black pen, 2 pixels wide
aPen = CreatePen(PS_SOLID, 2, 0);
SelectObject(hdc, aPen);            // select it into DC
StrokePath (hdc);                   // Stroke the path

// Second path for stroked and filled text
BeginPath (hdc);
SetBkMode(hdc, TRANSPARENT);
TextOut(hdc, 20, 110, "Stroked and Filled", 18);
EndPath(hdc);
// Get and select a stock pen and brush
aPen = GetStockObject(BLACK_PEN);
aBrush = GetStockObject(LTGRAY_BRUSH);
SelectObject(hdc, aPen);
SelectObject(hdc, aBrush);
StrokeAndFillPath (hdc);           // Stroke and fill path

// Clean-up and end WM_PAINT processing
DeleteObject(hFont);
EndPaint (hwnd, &ps);
```

Figure 4-8 is a screen dump of the TEXTDEM3 program.

Figure 4-8: Screen dump of the TEXTDEM3 program

Keyboard Input

Since the first days of computing, typing on a typewriter-like keyboard has been an effective way of interacting with the system. Although typical Windows programs rely heavily on the mouse device, the keyboard is still the most common way to enter text characters.

The mechanisms by which Windows monitors and handles keyboard input are based on its message-driven architecture. When the user presses or releases a key, the low-level driver generates an interrupt to inform Windows of this action. Windows then retrieves the keystroke from a hardware register, stores it in the system message queue, and proceeds to examine it. The action taken by the operating system depends on the type of keystroke, and on which application currently holds the keyboard foreground, called the *input focus*. The keystroke is dispatched to the corresponding application by means of a message to its Windows procedure.

The particular way by which Windows handles keystrokes is determined by its multitasking nature. At any given time, several programs can be executing simultaneously, and any one of these programs can have more than one thread of execution. One of the possible results of a keystroke (or a keystroke sequence) is to change the thread that holds the input focus, perhaps to a different application. This is the reason why Windows cannot directly send keyboard input to any specific thread.

It is the message loop in the `WinMain()` function of an application that retrieves keyboard messages from the system queue. In fact, all system messages are posted to the application's message queue. The process makes the following assumptions: first, that the thread's queue is empty; second, that the thread holds the input focus; and third, that a keystroke is available at the system level. In effect, it is the application that asks Windows for keystrokes; Windows does not send unsolicited keystroke data.

The abundance of keyboard functions and keyboard messages makes it appear that Windows keyboard programming is difficult or complicated. The fact is that applications do not need to process all keyboard messages, and hardly ever do so. Two messages, `WM_CHAR` and `WM_KEYDOWN`, usually provide code with all the necessary data regarding user keyboard input. Many keystrokes can be ignored because Windows generates other more easily handled messages. For example, applications can usually disregard the fact that the user selected a menu item by means of a keystroke because Windows sends a message to the application as if the menu item had been selected by a mouse click. If the application code contains processing for menu selection by mouse clicks, then the equivalent keyboard action is handled automatically.

Input Focus

The application that holds the input focus is the one that gets notified of the user's keystrokes. A user can visually tell which window has the input focus since it is the one whose title bar is highlighted. This applies to the parent window as well as to child windows, such as an input or dialog box. The application can tell if a window has the input focus by calling the `GetFocus()` function, which returns the handle to the window with the input focus.

The Windows message `WM_SETFOCUS` is sent to the window at the time that it receives the input focus, and `WM_KILLFOCUS` at the time it loses it. Applications can intercept these messages to take notice of any change in the input focus. However, these messages are mere notifications; application code cannot intercept these messages to prevent losing the input focus.

Keyboard data is available to code holding the input focus at two levels. The lower level, usually called keystroke data, contains raw information about the key being pressed. Keystroke data allows code to determine whether the keystroke message was generated by the user pressing a key or by releasing it, and whether the keystroke resulted from a normal press-and-release action or from the key being held down (called typematic action). Higher-level keyboard data relates to the character code associated with the key. An application can intercept low-level or character-level keystroke messages generated by Windows.

Keystroke Processing

Four Windows messages inform application code of keystroke data: `WM_KEYDOWN`, `WM_SYSKEYDOWN`, `WM_KEYUP`, and `WM_SYSKEYUP`. The keydown-type messages are generated when a key is pressed, sometimes called the *make action*. The keyup-type messages are generated when a key is released, called the *break action*. Applications usually ignore the keyup-type message. The "sys-type" messages – `WM_SYSKEYDOWN` and `WM_SYSKEYUP` – relate to system keys. A system keystroke is one generated while the Alt key is held down.

When any one of these four messages takes place, Windows puts the keystroke data in the `lParam` and `wParam` passed to the window procedure. The `lParam` contains bit-coded information about the keystroke, as shown in Table 4-9.

TABLE 4-9 BIT AND BIT FIELDS IN THE LPARAM OF A KEYSTROKE MESSAGE

Bits	Meaning
0-15	Repeat count field. The value is the number of times the keystroke is repeated as a result of the user holding down the key (typematic action).
16-23	OEM scan code. The value depends on the original equipment manufacturer.
24	Extended key. Bit is set when the key pressed is one duplicated in the IBM Enhanced 101- and 102-key keyboards, such as the right-hand ALT and CTRL keys, the / and Enter keys on the numeric keypad, or the Insert, Delete, Home, PageUp, PageDown, and End keys.
25–28	Reserved.
29	Context code. Bit is set if the Alt key is down while the key is pressed. Bit is clear if the `WM_SYSKEYDOWN` message is posted to the active window because no window has the keyboard focus.

Bits	Meaning
30	Previous key state. Key is set if the key is down before the message is sent. Bit is clear if the key is up. This key allows code to determine if the keystroke resulted from a make or break action.
31	Transition state. Always 0 for a `WM_SYSKEYDOWN` message.

The `wParam` contains the virtual-key code, which is a hardware-independent value that identifies each key. Windows uses the virtual-key codes instead of the device-dependent scan code. Typically, the virtual-key codes are processed when the application needs to recognize keys that have no associated ASCII value, such as the control keys. Table 4-10 lists some of the most-used virtual-key codes.

TABLE 4-10 SOME USEFUL VIRTUAL-KEY CODES

Symbolic Name	Hex Value	Key
VK_CANCEL	0x01	Ctrl + Break
VK_BACK	0x08	Backspace
VK_TAB	0x09	Tab
VK_RETURN	0x0D	Enter
VK_SHIFT	0x10	Shift
VK_CONTROL	0x11	Ctrl
VK_MENU	0x12	Alt
VK_PAUSE	0x13	Pause
VK_CAPITAL	0x14	Caps Lock
VK_ESCAPE	0x1B	Esc
VK_SPACE	0x20	Spacebar
VK_PRIOR	0x21	Page Up
VK_NEXT	0x22	Page Down
VK_END	0x23	End

Continued

Table 4-10 SOME USEFUL VIRTUAL-KEY CODES *(Continued)*

Symbolic Name	Hex Value	Key
VK_HOME	0x24	Home
VK_LEFT	0x25	Left arrow
VK_UP	0x26	Up arrow
VK_RIGHT	0x27	Right arrow
VK_DOWN	0x28	Down arrow
VK_SNAPSHOT	0x2C	Print Screen
VK_INSERT	0x2D	Insert
VK_DELETE	0x2E	Delete
VK_MULTIPLY	0x6A	Numeric keypad *
VK_ADD	0x6B	Numeric keypad +
VK_SUBTRACT	0x6D	Numeric keypad -
VK_DIVIDE	0x6F	Numeric keypad /
VK_F1..VK_F12	0x70..0x7B	F1 .. F12

NOTE: Originally, the "w" in `wParam` stood for "word," since in 16-bit Windows the `wParam` was a word-size value. The Win32 API expanded the `wParam` from 16 to 32 bits. However, in the case of the virtual-key character codes, the `wParam` is defined as an *int* type. Code can typecast the `wParam` as follows:

```
int       aKeystroke;
char      aCharacter;
.
.
aKeystroke = (int) wParam;
aCharacter = (char) wParam;
```

Simple keystroke processing can be implemented by intercepting `WM_KEYDOWN`. Occasionally, an application needs to know when a system-level message is generated. In this case, code can intercept `WM_SYSKEYDOWN`. The first operation performed in a typical `WM_KEYDOWN` or `WM_SYSKEYDOWN` handler is to store in local variables the lParam, the wParam, or both. In the case of the wParam code can cast the 32-bit value into an *int* or a *char* type as necessary (see the preceding Note).

Processing the keystroke usually consists of performing bitwise operations to isolate the required bits or bit fields. For example, to determine if the extended key flag is set, code can logically AND with a mask in which bit 24 is set and then test for a non-zero result, as shown in the following code fragment:

```
unsigned long     keycode;
.
.
WM_KEYDOWN:
    keycode = lParam;             // store lParam
    if(keycode & 0x01000000) {   // test bit 24
    // ASSERT:
    //   key pressed is extended key
```

Processing the virtual-key code, which is passed to your intercept routine in the lParam, consists of comparing its value with the key or keys that you wish to detect. For example, to know if the key pressed was the Backspace, you can proceed as shown in the following code fragment:

```
int     virtkey;
.
.
WM_KEYDOWN:
    virtkey = (int) lParam;       // cast and store lParam
    if(virtkey == VK_BACK) {      // test for Backspace
    // ASSERT:
    //   Backspace key pressed
```

Determining Key States

An application can determine the state of any virtual-key by means of the GetKeyState() service. The function's general form is as follows:

```
SHORT GetKeyState(
              int nVirtKey   // 1
);
```

GetKeyState() returns a SHORT integer with the high-order bit set if the key is down and the low-order bit set if it is toggled. Toggle keys are those that have a keyboard LED to indicate their state: Num Lock, Caps Lock, and Scroll Lock. The LED for the corresponding key is lit when it is toggled and unlit otherwise. Some virtual-key constants can be used as the nVirtKey parameter of GetKeyState(). Table 4-11 lists the virtual-keys.

Table 4-11 VIRTUAL-KEYS USED IN GETKEYSTATE()

Constant	Key	Returns
VK_SHIFT	Shift	State of left or right Shift keys
VK_CONTROL	Ctrl	State of left or right Ctrl keys
VK_MENU	Alt	State of left or right Alt keys
VK_LSHIFT	Shift	State of left Shift key
VK_RSHIFT	Shift	State of right Shift key
VK_LCONTROL	Ctrl	State of left Ctrl key
VK_RCONTROL	Ctrl	State of right Ctrl key
VK_LMENU	Alt	State of left Alt key
VK_RMENU	Alt	State of right Alt key

The following statement is a test for the left Shift key pressed.

```
if(GetKeyState(VK_LSHIFT) < 0) {
// ASSERT:
//        Left shift key is pressed
```

NOTE

In testing for the high-bit set condition returned by GetKeyState(), you may be tempted to bitwise AND with a binary mask, as follows:

```
if(0x8000 & (GetKeyState(VK_SHIFT))) {
```

Although, in many cases, such operations produce the expected results, its success depends on the size of a data type, which compromises portability. In effect, if GetKeyState() returns a 16-bit integer, then the mask 0x8000 effectively tests the high-order bit. If the value returned is stored in 32 bits, however, then the mask must have the value 0x80000000. Because any signed integer with the high-bit set represents a negative number, it is possible to test the bit condition as follows:

```
if(GetKeyState(VK_SHIFT) < 0) {
```

This test does not depend on the operand's bit size.

Character Code Processing

Applications often deal with keyboard input as character codes. It is possible to obtain the character code from the virtual-key code since it is encoded in the `wParam` of the `WM_KEYDOWN`, `WM_SYSKEYDOWN`, `WM_KEYUP`, and `WM_SYSKEYUP` messages. The codes for the alphanumeric keys are not listed in Table 4-10; however, there is also a virtual-key code for each one. The virtual-key codes for the numeric keys 0 to 9 are VK_0 to VK_9, and the ones for the alphabetic characters A through Z are VK_A through VK_Z.

This type of processing has complications. For example, the virtual-key code for the alphabetic characters does not specify if the character is in upper- or lowercase. Therefore, the application would have to call `GetKeyState()` to determine if the <Shift> key was down or the Caps Lock key toggled when the character key was pressed. Furthermore, the virtual-key codes for some character keys, such as: ;, =, +, <, are not defined in the windows header files. Applications must use the numeric values assigned to these keys or define their own symbolic constants.

Fortunately, character-code processing in Windows is much easier. The `TranslateMessage()` function converts the virtual-key code for each character into its ANSI (or Unicode) equivalent and posts it in the thread's message queue. `TranslateMessage()` is usually included in the program's message loop. After `TranslateMessage()`, the message is retrieved from the queue, typically by `GetMessage()` or `PeekMessage()`. The final result is that an application can intercept `WM_CHAR`, `WM_DEADCHAR`, `WM_SYSCHAR`, and `WM_SYSDEADCHAR` to obtain the ANSI character codes that correspond to the virtual-key of a `WM_KEYDOWN` message.

Dead-type character messages refer to the diacritical characters used in some foreign-language keyboards. These are marks added to characters to distinguish them from other ones, such as the acute accent (á) or the circumflex (â). In English-language processing, `WM_DEADCHAR` and `WM_SYSDEADCHAR` are usually ignored.

The `WM_SYSCHAR` message corresponds to the virtual-key that results from `WM_SYSKEYDOWN`. `WM_SYSCHAR` is posted when a character key is pressed while the Alt key is held down. Because Windows also sends the message that corresponds to a mouse click on the system item, applications often ignore `WM_SYSCHAR`.

This leaves us with `WM_CHAR` for general-purpose character processing. When the WM_CHAR message is sent to your Windows procedure, the `lParam` is the same as for `WM_KEYDOWN`. However, the `wParam` contains the ANSI code for the character, instead of the virtual-key code. This ANSI code, which is approximately equivalent to the ASCII code, can be directly handled and displayed without additional manipulations. Processing reads as follows:

```
char      aChar;           // storage for character
.
.
case WM_CHAR:
   aChar = (char) wParam;
```

```
// ASSERT:
//     aChar holds ANSI character code
```

Keyboard Demonstration Program

The program KBR_DEMO.CCP, located in the *Keyboard Demo* folder on the book's CD-ROM, is a demonstration of the keyboard processing routines described previously. The program uses a private device context; therefore, the font is selected once, during `WM_CREATE` processing. KBR_DEMO uses a typewriter-like, TrueType font, named Courier. Courier is a monospaced font (all characters are the same width). This makes possible the use of standard character symbols to produce a graph of the bitmaps. Figure 4-9 is a screen dump of the KBR_DEMO program.

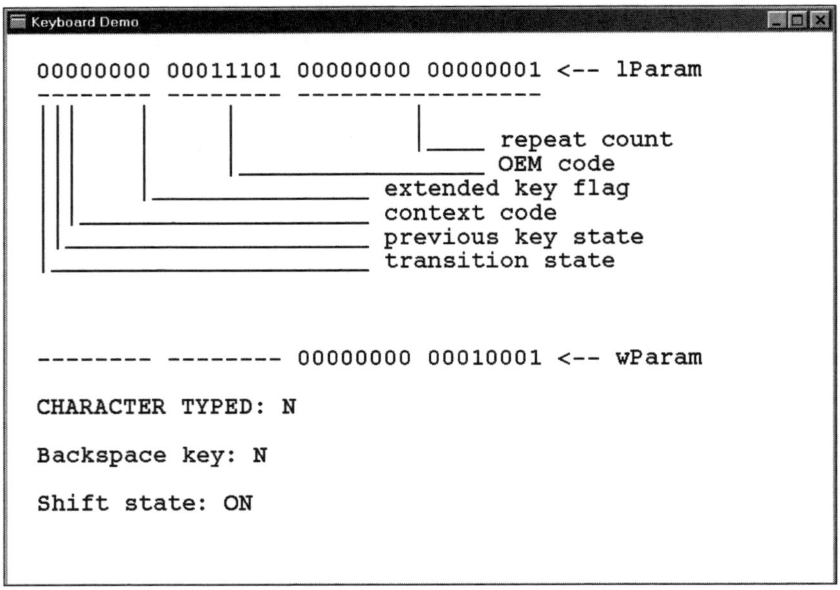

Figure 4-9: Screen dump of the KBR_DEMO program

Figure 4-9 shows the case in which the user has typed the Alt key. Note that the `wParam` value 00010010 is equivalent to 0x12, which is the virtual-key code for the Alt key (see Table 4-10). The critical processing in the KBD_DEMO program is as follows:

```
LRESULT CALLBACK WndProc (HWND hwnd, UINT iMsg, WPARAM wParam,
                          LPARAM lParam) {

    static int  cxChar, cyChar ;     // Character dimensions
```

```
static int  cxClient, cyClient;  // Client area parameters
static HDC       hdc ;            // handle to private DC
unsigned long    keycode;         // storage for keystroke
unsigned long    keymask;         // bit mask
unsigned int     virtkey;         // virtual-key
int              i, j;            // counters
char             aChar;           // character code

// Structures
PAINTSTRUCT ps;
TEXTMETRIC  tm;
RECT        textRect;             // RECT-type
HFONT       hFont;
.
.
.
case WM_PAINT :
    // Processing consists of displaying the text messages
    BeginPaint (hwnd, &ps) ;
     // Initialize rectangle structure
     SetRect (&textRect,           // address of structure
        2 * cxChar,                // x for start
        cyChar,                    // y for start
        cxClient -(2 * cxChar),    // x for end
        cyClient);                 // y for end
     // Display multi-line text string
     DrawText( hdc, TextStr0, -1, &textRect,
        DT_LEFT | DT_WORDBREAK);

     // Display second text string
     SetRect (&textRect,           // address of structure
        2 * cxChar,                // x for start
        13 * cyChar,               // y for start
        cxClient -(2 * cxChar),    // x for end
        cyClient);                 // y for end
     // Display text string
        DrawText( hdc, TextStr1, -1, &textRect,
        DT_LEFT | DT_WORDBREAK);
        .
        .
        .
        EndPaint (hwnd, &ps);
        return 0 ;
```

```
// Character code processing
case WM_CHAR:
     aChar = (char) wParam;
     // Test for control codes and replace with space
     if (aChar < 0x30)
        aChar = 0x20;

     // Test for shift key pressed
     if(GetKeyState (VK_SHIFT) < 0) {
        i = 0;          // counter
        j = 13;         // string offset
        for(i = 0; i < 3; i++){
           TextStr4[j] = StrON[i];
           j++;
        }
      }
      else {
        i = 0;          // counter
        j = 13;         // string offset
        for(i = 0; i < 3; i++){
           TextStr4[j] = StrOFF[i];
           j++;
        }
      }

    TextStr2[17] = aChar;
    return 0;

// Scan code and keystroke data processing
// Display space if a system key
case WM_SYSKEYDOWN:
     TextStr2[17] = 0x20;

case WM_KEYDOWN:
// Store bits for lParam in TextStr0[]
   keycode = lParam;    // get 32-bit keycode value
   i = 0;               // counter for keystroke bits
   j = 0;               // offset into string
   keymask = 0x80000000;// bitmask

   for (i = 0; i < 32; i++) {
     // Test for separators and skip
     if(i == 8 || i == 16 || i == 24) {
        TextStr0[j] = 0x20;
        j++;
```

```
        }
       // Test for 1 and 0 bits and display digits
       if(keycode & keymask)
          TextStr0[j] = '1';
       else
          TextStr0[j] = '0';
       keymask = keymask > 1;
       j++;
       }

// Store bits for wParam in TextStr1[]
   keycode = wParam;    // get 32-bit keycode value
   i = 0;               // counter for keystroke bits
   j = 18;              // initial offset into string
   keymask = 0x8000;    // bitmask

   // 16-bit loop
     for (i = 0; i < 16; i++) {
       // Test for separators and skip
       if(i == 8) {
          TextStr1[j] = 0x20;
          j++;
       }
     // Test for 1 and 0 bits and display digits
       if(keycode & keymask)
          TextStr1[j] = '1';
       else
          TextStr1[j] = '0';
          keymask = keymask > 1;
          j++;
       }

// Test for Backspace key pressed
virtkey = (unsigned int) wParam;
      if (virtkey == VK_BACK)
         TextStr3[15] = 'Y';
       else
         TextStr3[15] = 'N';

// Force WM_PAINT message
InvalidateRect(NULL, NULL, TRUE);
return 0;
.
.
.
```

The Caret

In the MS DOS environment, the graphic character used to mark the screen position where typed characters are displayed is called the cursor. The standard DOS cursor is a small, horizontal bar that flashes on the screen to call the user's attention to the point of text insertion. In Windows, the *cursor* is an icon that marks the screen position associated with mouse-like pointing. Windows applications signal the location where keyboard input is to take place by means of a flashing, vertical bar called the *caret*.

In order to avoid confusion and ambiguity, Windows displays a single caret. The system caret, which is a shared resource, is a bitmap that can be customized by the application. The window with the input focus can request the caret to be displayed in its client area, or in a child window.

Caret Processing

Code can intercept the `WM_SETFOCUS` message to display the caret. `WM_KILLFOCUS` notifies the application that it has lost focus and that it should therefore destroy the caret. Caret display and processing in `WM_SETFOCUS` usually starts by calling `CreateCaret()`. The function's general form is as follows:

```
    BOOL CreateCaret(hwnd, hBitmap, nWidth, nHeight);
BOOL CreateCaret(
            HWND hWnd,          // 1
            HBITMAP hBitmap,    // 2
            int nWidth,         // 3
            int nHeight         // 4
            );
```

The first parameter is the handle to the window that owns the caret. The second one is an optional handle to a bitmap. If this parameter is NULL then a solid caret is displayed. If it is (HBITMAP) 1, then the caret is gray. If it is a handle to a bitmap, the other parameters are ignored and the caret takes the form of the bitmap. The last two parameters define the caret's width and height, in logical units. Applications often determine the width and height of the caret in terms of character dimensions.

`CreateCaret()` defines the caret shape and size but does not set its screen position, nor does it display it. To set the caret's screen position you use the `SetCaretPos()` function, which takes two parameters, the first one for the caret's x-coordinate and the second one for the y-coordinate. The caret is displayed on the screen using `ShowCaret()`, whose only argument is the handle to the window.

Applications that use the caret usually intercept `WM_KILLFOCUS`. This ensures that they are notified when the window loses the keyboard focus, at which time the caret must be hidden and destroyed. The `HideCaret()` function takes care of the first action. Its only parameter is the handle to the window that owns the caret. `DestroyCaret()`, which takes no parameters, destroys the caret, erases it from the screen, and breaks the association between the caret and the window.

Applications that use the caret to signal the point of input often display the characters typed by the user. But since the caret is a graphics object, it must be erased from the screen before the character is displayed. Otherwise the caret symbol itself, or parts of it, may pollute the screen. A program that processes the `WM_CHAR` message to handle user input usually starts by hiding the caret; then the code processes the input character, and finally, resets the caret position and redisplays it.

Caret Demonstration Program

The CAR_DEMO program, located in the *Caret Demo* folder on the book's CD-ROM, is a demonstration of caret processing during text input. The program displays an entry form and uses the caret to signal the current input position. When the code detects the Enter key, it moves to the next line in the entry form. The Backspace key can be used to edit the input. When Backspace is pressed, the previous character is erased and the caret position is updated. Program logic keeps track of the start location of each input line so that the user cannot backspace past this point. The Esc key erases the caret and ends input. Note that because user input is not stored by the program, the text is lost if the screen is resized or if the application looses the input focus. Figure 4-10 is a screen dump of the CAR_DEMO program.

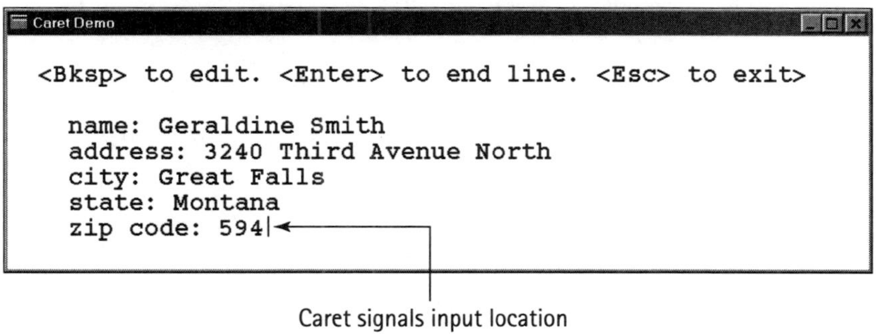

Figure 4-10: Screen dump of the CAR_DEMO program

Figure 4-10 shows execution of the CAR_DEMO program. The following are excerpts of the program's processing:

```
LRESULT CALLBACK WndProc (HWND hwnd, UINT iMsg, WPARAM wParam,
                          LPARAM lParam) {
 static int  cxChar, cyChar ;    // character dimensions
 static int  cxClient, cyClient; // client area parameters
 static int  xCaret, yCaret;     // caret position
```

```
static int  xLimit;               // left limit of line
static int  formEnd = 0;          // 1 if Esc key pressed
static int  lineNum = 1;          // input line
static HDC  hdc ;                 // handle to private DC
char        aChar;                // storage for character code

// Structures
PAINTSTRUCT ps;
TEXTMETRIC  tm;
RECT        textRect;
HFONT       hFont;

switch (iMsg) {

    case WM_CREATE :
         .
         .
         .
        // Calculate and store character dimensions
        cxChar = tm.tmAveCharWidth ;
        cyChar = tm.tmHeight + tm.tmExternalLeading ;
        // Store size of client area
        cxClient = LOWORD(lParam);
        cyClient = HIWORD(lParam);
        // Store initial caret position
        xCaret = xLimit = 10;
        yCaret = 3;
        return 0 ;
        .
        .
        .
     case WM_PAINT :
          BeginPaint (hwnd, &ps) ;
          // Initialize rectangle structure
          SetRect (&textRect,         // address of structure
                   2 * cxChar,                // x for start
                   cyChar,                    // y for start
                   cxClient -(2 * cxChar),    // x for end
                   cyClient);                 // y for end
          // Display multi-line text string
          DrawText( hdc, TextStr1, -1, &textRect,
                    DT_LEFT | DT_WORDBREAK);

          EndPaint (hwnd, &ps);
```

```
 return 0 ;


// Character input processing
case WM_CHAR:

HideCaret(hwnd);
aChar = (char) wParam;

switch (wParam) {   // wParam holds virtual-key code
case '\r':          // Enter key pressed
     yCaret++;
     aChar = 0x20;
// cascaded tests set x caret location in new line
     if(yCaret == 4)    // in address: line
        xCaret = xLimit = 13;

     if(yCaret == 5)    // in city: line
        xCaret = xLimit = 10;

     if(yCaret == 6)    // in state: line
        xCaret = xLimit = 11;

     if(yCaret == 7)    // in zip code: line
        xCaret = xLimit = 14;

     if(yCaret > 7) {     // Enter key ignored on
                          // last line
        yCaret—;
}
break;

case '\b':          // Backspace key pressed
  if (xCaret > xLimit) {
     aChar = 0x20;        // Replace with space
     xCaret—;
     // Display the blank character
     TextOut (hdc, xCaret * cxChar, yCaret * cyChar,
              &aChar, 1);
       }
    break;

case 0x1b:       // Esc key processing
    formEnd = 1;
```

```
            // Destroy the caret
            HideCaret(hwnd);
            DestroyCaret();
            break;

     default:
        // Display the character if Esc not pressed
        if(formEnd == 0) {
            TextOut (hdc, xCaret * cxChar, yCaret * cyChar,
            &aChar, 1);
              xCaret++;
           }
      break;
    }
     if(formEnd == 0) {
          SetCaretPos(xCaret * cxChar, yCaret * cyChar);
          ShowCaret(hwnd);
    }
    return 0;

  case WM_SETFOCUS:
        if(formEnd == 0) {
            CreateCaret (hwnd, NULL, cxChar / 4, cyChar);
            SetCaretPos(xCaret * cxChar, yCaret * cyChar);
            ShowCaret(hwnd);
        }
        return 0;

  case WM_KILLFOCUS:
        // Destroy the caret
        HideCaret(hwnd);
        DestroyCaret();
        return 0;
```

Summary

In this chapter you have learned about Windows programming in general and about non-graphics application support services that are part of the Windows API. These notions were introduced in the context of text display, keyboard input, and caret manipulations. To understand all this, you also had to become familiar with some basic concepts of Windows programming, such as the display context, the Windows coordinate system, the mapping modes, and the client area.

Some of the demonstration programs in this chapter could be modified into small, but useful utilities. The TEX1_DEMO program manipulates text character and client-area parameters to adjust a paragraph to the window size. The program logic shows the fundamentals of programming in an event-driven environment. In this case, the application interacts with the environment and adjusts its display to any change in the size of the client area. In this demonstration, you saw how application code reacts to user- and system-level events and gained insight into the Windows message passing mechanism.

The keyboard demonstration program, KBD_DEMO, and the caret demonstration, CAR_DEMO, show how to input keyboard data, manipulate the caret, and monitor special keystrokes for processing. By putting together the text display and keyboard operations you have acquired all the elements necessary for developing a simple text-editor application. You may want to attempt such a program as an exercise. In Chapter 5 we move into graphics-related support services such as programming the mouse and displaying controls and dialog boxes.

Chapter 5

Graphics Support Services

IN THIS CHAPTER

- Mouse programming
- Programming window styles and controls
- Creating menus
- The dialog box
- Programming common controls

THIS CHAPTER DEALS with several topics that are closely related to Windows graphics. We start with mouse programming, then discuss window styles, child windows, menus, dialog boxes, and the new common controls.

Some of the most important information in this chapter regards programming the Windows user interface. The Windows user interface is a graphical one, therefore the material covered in this chapter is very closely related to the book's title. Many of the built-in controls are also graphical components, such as status bars, toolbars, ToolTips, trackbars, up/down controls, and many others. The discussion also includes general-purpose controls such as message boxes, text boxes, combo boxes, as well as the most-used of the common controls. All of these components are required to build a modern Windows program; it is difficult to imagine an application that does not contain most of these elements.

Mouse Programming

The use of a mouse as an input device dates back to the work at Xerox PARC, which pioneered the ideas of a graphical user interface. Since mouse and GUI have been interrelated since their original conception, one would assume that a graphical operating system, such as Windows, would require the presence of a mouse device. This is not the case. Windows documentation still considers the mouse an option and recommends that applications provide alternate keyboard controls for all mouse-driven operations; not often an easy task, and sometimes even an impossible one.

During program development, you can make sure that a mouse is available and operational by means of the `GetSystemMetrics()` function, shown as follows:

```
assert (GetSystemMetrics(SM_MOUSEPRESENT));
```

In this case, the `assert` macro displays a message box if a mouse is not present or not operational. The developer can then choose to ignore the message, debug the code, or abort execution. In the release version of a program that requires a mouse you can use the `abort` macro to break execution. For example:

```
if (!GetSystemMetrics(SM_MOUSEPRESENT))
   abort();
```

Typically, before the program aborts, a message indicating the reason for program termination is displayed. The implementation of message boxes is discussed later in this chapter. Alternatively, an application can call `PostQuitMessage()`. This indicates to Windows that a thread has made a termination request and it posts a `WM_QUIT` message. `PostQuitMessage()` has an exit code parameter that is returned to Windows, but current versions of the operating system make no use of this value. The objection to using `PostQuitMessage()` for abnormal terminations is that execution ends abruptly, without notification of cause or reason. In this case the program should display a message box informing the user of the cause of program termination.

Windows supports other devices such as pens, touch screens, joysticks, and drawing tablets, which are all considered mouse input. The mouse itself can have up to three buttons, labeled *left*, *middle*, and *right* buttons. A one-button mouse is an anachronism and the three-button version is usually associated with specialized systems. The most common one is the two-button mouse, in which the left button is used for clicking, double-clicking, and dragging operations, and the right button activates context-sensitive program options.

An application can tell how many buttons are installed in the mouse by testing the `SM_CMOUSEBUTTONS` with the `GetSystemMetrics()` function. If the application requires a certain number of buttons, then the `assert` or `abort` macros can be used, as previously shown. For example, a program that requires a three-button mouse could test for this condition as follows:

```
assert (GetSystemMetrics(SM_CMOUSEBOUTTONS) == 3);
```

If the three-button mouse is required in the release version of the program, then the code could read as follows:

```
if(GetSystemMetrics(SM_CMOUSEBUTTONS) != 3))
   abort();
```

The assert macro is intended to be used in debugging. If the condition is false, the macro shows information about the error and displays a message box with three options: abort, debug, and ignore. Assert has no effect on the release version of the program; it is as if the statement containing assert had been commented out of the code. For this reason conditions that must be evaluated during execution of the release version of a program should not be part of an assert statement.

The abort macro can be used to stop execution in either version. Abort provides no information about the cause of program termination.

Programs that use the assert macro must include the file assert.h. VERIFY and other debugging macros are available when coding with the Foundation Class Library, but they are not implemented in ANSI C.

Mouse Messages

There are 22 mouse messages currently implemented in the Windows API. Ten of these messages refer to mouse action in the client area, and ten to mouse action in the nonclient area. Of the remaining two messages, WM_NCHITTEST takes place when the mouse is moved either over the client or the nonclient area. It is this message that generates all the other ones. WM_MOUSEACTIVATE takes place when a mouse button is pressed over an inactive window, an event that is usually ignored by applications.

The abundance of Windows messages should not lead you to think that mouse processing is difficult. Most applications do all of their mouse processing by intercepting two or three of these messages. Table 5-1 lists the mouse messages most frequently handled by applications.

Table 5-1 MOST FREQUENTLY USED CLIENT-AREA MOUSE MESSAGES

Mouse message	Description
WM_LBUTTONDOWN	Left button pressed
WM_LBUTTONUP	Left button released
WM_RBUTTONDOWN	Right button pressed
WM_RBUTTONUP	Right button released
WM_RBUTTONDBLCLK	Right button double-clicked
WM_LBUTTONDBLCLK	Left button double-clicked
WM_MOUSEMOVE	Mouse moved into client area

In Table 5-1 we have listed only client-area mouse messages because nonclient area messages are usually handled by the default windows procedure.

Mouse processing is similar to keyboard processing, although mouse messages do not require that the window have the input focus. Once your application gains control in a mouse message handler, it can proceed to implement whatever action is required. However, there are some differences between keyboard messages and mouse messages. To Windows, keyboard input is always given maximum attention. The operating system tries to ensure that keyboard input is always preserved. Mouse messages, on the other hand, are expendable. For example, the `WM_MOUSEMOVE` message, which signals that the mouse cursor is over the application's client area, is not sent while the mouse is over every single pixel of the client area. The actual rate depends on the mouse hardware and on the processing speed. Therefore, it is possible, given a small enough client area and a slow enough message rate, that code may not be notified of a mouse movement action over its domain. Mouse programming must take this possibility into account.

In client-area mouse messages, the `wParam` indicates which, if any, keyboard or mouse key was held down while the mouse action took place. Windows defines five symbolic constants to represent the three mouse keys and the keyboard Ctrl and Shift keys. These constants are listed in Table 5-2.

TABLE 5-2 VIRTUAL KEY CONSTANTS FOR CLIENT ARE MOUSE MESSAGES

Constant	Originating Condition
MK_CONTROL	Ctrl key is down.
MK_LBUTTON	Left mouse button is down.
MK_MBUTTON	Middle mouse button is down.
MK_RBUTTON	Right mouse button is down.
MK_SHIFT	Shift key is down.

Code can determine if one of the keys was held down by ANDing with the corresponding constant. For example, the following fragment can be used to determine if the Ctrl key was held down at the time that the left mouse button was clicked in the client area:

```
case WM_LBUTTONDOWN:
  if(wParam & MK_CONTROL) {
  // ASSERT:
  //   Left mouse button clicked and <Ctrl> key down
```

The predefined constants represent individual bits in the operand; therefore, you must be careful not attempt to equate the wParam with any one of the constants. For example, the MK_LBUTTON constant is always true in the WM_LBUTTONDOWN intercept. For this reason the following test always fails:

```
case WM_LBUTTONDOWN:
  if(wParam == MK_CONTROL) {
```

On the other hand, you can determine if two or more keys were held down by performing a bitwise OR of the predefined constants before ANDing with the wParam. For example, the following expression can be used to tell if either the Ctrl keys or the Shift keys were held down while the left mouse button was clicked:

```
if(wParam & (MK_CONTROL | MK_SHIFT)) {
   // ASSERT:
   //    Either the <Ctrl> or the <Shift> key was held down
   //    when the mouse action occurred
To test if both the <Ctrl> and the <Shift> keys were down when the
mouse action occurred, you can code as follows:
if((wParam & MK_CONTROL) && (wParam & MKSHIFT)) {
   // ASSERT:
   //    The <Ctrl> and <Shift> key were both down when the
   //    mouse action occurred
```

Cursor Location

Applications often need to know the screen position of the mouse. In the case of the client-area messages, the lParam encodes the horizontal and vertical position of the mouse cursor when the action takes place. The high-order word of the lParam contains the vertical mouse position and the low-order word the horizontal position. Code can use the LOWORD and HIWORD macros to obtain the value in logical units. For example:

```
int     cursorX, cursorY;     // Storage for coordinates
 .
 .
 .
case WM_MOUSEMOVE:
     cursorX = LOWORD(lParam)
     cursorY = HIWORD(lParam);
     // ASSERT:
     //   Variables now hold x and y cursor coordinates
```

Double-click Processing

Handling mouse double-clicks requires additional processing as well as some forethought. In the first place, mouse double-click messages are sent only to windows that were created with the CS_DBLCLKS style. The CS_DBLCLKS style is described in Table 3-2. The structure of type WNDCLASSES for a windows that it to receive mouse double-clicks can be defined as follows:

```
// Defining a structure of type WNDCLASSEX
   WNDCLASSEX  wndclass ;
   wndclass.cbSize     = sizeof (WNDCLASSEX) ;
   wndclass.style      = CS_HREDRAW | CS_VREDRAW |
                         CS_DBLCLKS;
   .
   .
   .
```

Three client-area mouse messages are related to the double-click action, one for each mouse button. If the window class includes the CS-DBLCLKS type, then client-area double-click messages take place. WM_LBUTTONDBLCLK intercepts double-clicks for the left mouse button, WM_RBUTTONDBLCLK for the right mouse button, and WM_MBUTTONDBLCLK for the center button.

The double-click notification occurs when a mouse button is clicked twice within a predefined time interval. Selecting the Mouse Properties option in the Windows Control Panel sets the double-click speed. The SetDoubleClickTime() function can also be used to change the double-click interval from within an application, although it is not a good idea to do this without user participation. The default double-click time is 500 msec (one-half second). In addition, the two actions of a double-click must occur within a rectangular area defined by Windows, according to the display resolution. If the mouse has moved outside of this rectangle between the first and the second clicks, then the action is not reported as a double-click. The parameters for the double-click rectangle can be retrieved with the GetSystemMetrics() function, using the predefined constant SM_CXDOUBLECLK for the x-coordinate, and SM_CYDOUBLECLK for the y-coordinate.

A double-click intercept receives control on the second click, because at the time of the first click it is impossible to know if a second one is to follow. Therefore, if the code intercepts normal mouse clicks, it also receives notification on the first click of a double-click action. For this reason, programs are usually designed so that the action taken as a result of a double-click is a continuation of the one taken on a single click. For example, selecting an application file in Windows Explorer by means of a single mouse click has the effect of highlighting the filename. If the user double-clicks, the file is executed. In this case the double-click action complements the single-click one. Although it is possible to implement double-click processing without this constraint, the programming for this is more complicated and the user interface becomes sluggish.

Capturing the Mouse

The mouse programming logic discussed so far covers most of the conventional programming required for handling mouse action inside the active window. By intercepting the client-area messages, not the nonclient area ones, we avoid being notified of actions that usually, do not concern our code. However, there are common mouse operations that cannot be implemented by processing client-area messages only. For example, a Windows user installs a program icon on the desktop by right-clicking on the icon and then dragging it outside of the program group window. When the right mouse button is released, Windows displays a menu box that includes options to move or copy the program item, to create a shortcut, or to cancel the operation. In this case, the action requires crossing the boundary of the active window. Therefore, client-area messages cease as soon as this boundary is reached.

Another case is a drawing program that uses a mouse-dragging operation to display a rectangular outline. The rectangle starts at the point where the button is clicked, and ends at the point where the button is released. But what happens if the user crosses over the client-area boundary before releasing the mouse button? In such a case the application is not notified of the button-release action since it occurs outside the client area. Furthermore, if the drawing action is performed during the `WM_MOUSEMOVE` intercept, the messages also stop being sent to the applications windows procedure as soon as the client-area boundary is crossed. It would be a dangerous assumption to implement this function assuming that the user never crosses the boundary of the program's client area.

Problems such as these are solved by capturing the mouse, which is done by the `SetCapture()` function. The only parameter to `SetCapture()` is the handle of the capturing window. Once the mouse is captured, all mouse actions are assumed to take place in the client area, and the corresponding message intercepts in the application code are notified. The most obvious result of a mouse capture is that the client-area message handlers are active for mouse actions that take place outside the client area. Only one window can capture the mouse, and it must be the active one, also called the foreground window. While the mouse is captured, all system keyboard functions are disabled. The mouse capture ends with the call to `ReleaseCapture()`. `GetCapture()` returns the handle to the window that has captured the mouse, or NULL if the mouse capture fails.

Applications should capture the mouse whenever there is a possibility, even a remote one, of the user crossing the boundary of the client area during mouse processing. Implementing a simple drag-and-drop operation usually requires capturing the mouse. Mouse operations that take place between windows, whether they be child windows or not, also require capturing the mouse. Multitasking operations are limited during mouse capture. Therefore, it is important that the capture is released as soon as it is no longer necessary.

The Cursor

The screen image that corresponds to the mouse device is called the cursor. Windows provides 13 built-in cursors from which an application can select. In addition, you can create your own customized cursor and use it instead of a standard one. There are over 20 Windows functions that relate to cursor operations; however, even programs that manipulate cursor images hardly ever use more than a couple of them. Figure 5-1 shows the Windows built-in cursors and their corresponding symbolic names.

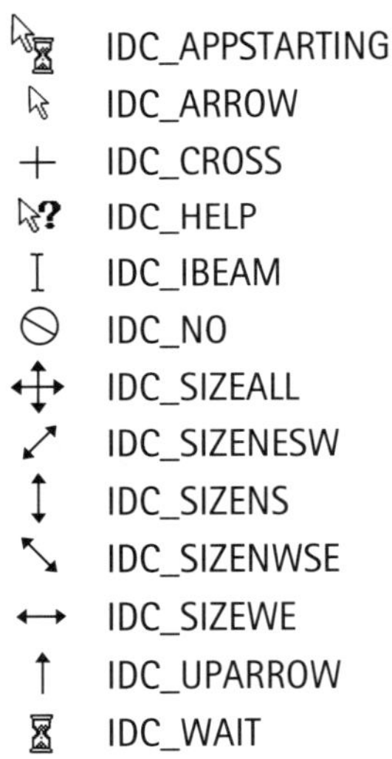

Figure 5-1: Windows built-in cursors and their symbolic names

Code that manipulates cursor images must be aware of Windows cursor-handling operations. A mouse-related message not yet discussed is `WM_SETCURSOR`. This message is sent to your window procedure, and to the default window procedure, whenever a noncaptured mouse moves over the client area, or when its buttons are pressed or released. In the `WM_SETCURSOR` message, the `wParam` holds the handle to the window receiving the message. The low-order word of `lParam` is a code that enables the determination of where the action takes place, usually called the *hit code*. The high-order word of the `lParam` holds the identifier of the mouse message that triggered `WM_SETCURSOR`.

One of the reasons for `WM_SETCURSOR` is to give applications a chance to change the cursor; also for a parent window to manipulate the cursor of a child window. The problem is that Windows has a mind of its own regarding the cursor. If your application ignores the WM_SETCURSOR message, the default window procedure receives the message anyway. If Windows determines (from the hit code) that the cursor has moved over the client area of a window, then the default window procedure sets the cursor to the class cursor defined in the hCursor member of the WNDCLASSEX structure in WinMain(). If the cursor is in a nonclient area, then Windows sets it to the standard arrow shape.

What all of this means to your application code is that if you ignore the WM_SETCURSOR message, and don't take other special provisions, Windows continuously changes the cursor according to its own purposes, probably interfering with your own manipulations. The simplest solution is to intercept WM_SETCURSOR and return a nonzero value. In this case the window procedure halts all further cursor processing. You could also use the WM_SETCURSOR intercept to install your own cursor or cursors; however, the disadvantage of this approach is that WM_SETCURSOR does not provide information about the cursor's screen location.

An alternate method is to perform cursor manipulations at one of the mouse message intercepts, or any other message handler for that matter. For example, code can implement cursor changes at WM_MOUSEMOVE. In this case the lParam contains the cursor's horizontal and vertical position. Child windows can use this intercept to display their own cursors. In this case the hCursor field of the WNDCLASSEX structure is usually set to NULL, and the application takes on full responsibility for handling the cursor.

Applications that manipulate the cursor often start by setting a new program cursor during WM_CREATE processing. In cursor processing there are several ways of achieving the same purpose. The methods described here are those that we have found to be more reliable. To create and display one of the built-in cursors you need a variable to store the handle to the cursor. The LoadCursor() and SetCursor() functions can then be used to load and display the cursor. To load and display the IDC_APPSTARTING cursor (see Figure 5-1) code can be as follows:

```
HCURSOR    aCursor;
.
.
.
aCursor = LoadCursor(NULL, IDC_APPSTARTING);
SetCursor (aCursor);
```

The first parameter of the LoadCursor() function is the handle to the program instance. This parameter is set to NULL to load one of the built-in cursors. Any of the symbolic names in Figure 5-1 can be used. The cursor is not displayed until the SetCursor() function is called, using the cursor handle as a parameter.

Graphics applications sometimes need one or more special cursors to suit their own needs. In the Visual C++ development environment, the image editor makes creating a custom cursor easy. The process described for creating a program icon in Chapter 3, in the section, "Creating a Program Resource," is almost identical to the one for creating a custom cursor. The following steps review this process briefly:

1. In the Insert menu, select the Resource command and then the Cursor resource type.
2. Use the editor to create a cursor. Note that all cursors are defined in terms of a 32 by 32 bit monochrome bitmap.
3. A button on the top bar of the editor allows the positioning of the cursor's hot spot. The default position for the hot spot is the upper-left corner.
4. In the process of creating a cursor, Developer Studio also creates a new script file, or adds the information to an existing one. You must manually insert the script file into the project by selecting the Add to Project command from the Project menu and then selecting the Files option. In the "Insert Files into Project" dialog box, select the script file and then click the OK button. The script file now appears on the Source Files list in the Files View window of the Project Workspace.
5. In addition to the script file, Developer Studio also creates a header file for resources. The default name of this file is *resource.h*. In order for resources to be available to the code you must enter an `#include` statement for the resource.h file in your source.

In order to use the custom cursor in your code you must know the symbolic name assigned to this resource, or its numeric value. This information can be obtained by selecting the Resource Symbols command from the View menu, or clicking the corresponding button on the toolbar.

The `LoadCursor()` function parameters are different for a custom cursor than for a built-in one. In the case of a custom cursor, you must enter the handle to the instance as the first parameter, and use the `MAKEINTRESOURCE` macro to convert the numeric or symbolic value into a compatible resource type. For example, if the symbolic name of the custom cursor is `IDC_CURSOR1`, and the handle to the instance is stored in the variable `pInstance` (as is the case in the template files furnished in this book), you can proceed as follows:

```
HCURSOR       aCursor;      // handle to a cursor
 .
 .
 .
aCursor = LoadCursor(pInstance,
                     MAKEINTRESOURCE(IDC_CURSOR1));
SetCursor(aCursor);
```

Mouse and Cursor Demonstration Program

The program named MOU_DEMO, located in the *Mouse Demo* project folder of the book's CD ROM, is a demonstration of some of the mouse-handling operations previously described. At this point in the book we have not yet covered the graphics services, or the implementation of user-interface functions. For these reasons, it is difficult to find a meaningful demonstration for mouse operations.

MOU_DEMO monitors the left and the right mouse buttons. Clicking the left button displays one of the built-in cursors. The cursors displayed are the same as those in Figure 5-1. Clicking the right mouse button displays a customized cursor in the form of the letter "A." The hot spot of the custom cursor is the vertex of the "A." When the mouse is moved in the client area, its position is displayed on the screen. Figure 5-2 is a screen dump of the MOU_DEMO program.

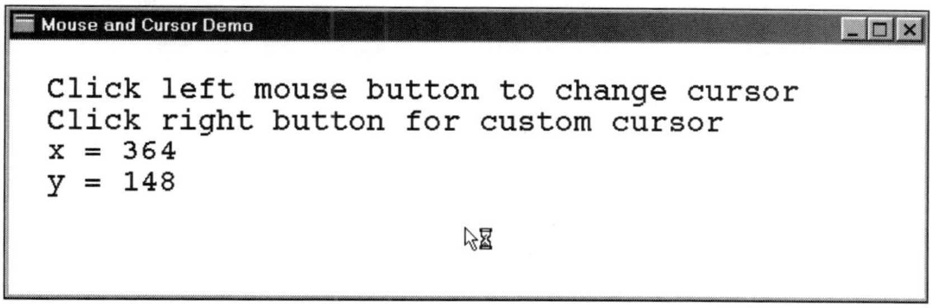

Figure 5-2: Screen dump of the MOU_DEMO program

The program's first interesting feature is that no class cursor is defined in the `WNDCLASSEX` structure. Instead, the `hCursor` variable is initialized as follows:

```
wndclass.hCursor     = NULL;
```

Since the program has no class cursor, one is defined during `WM_CREATE` processing with the following statements:

```
// Select and display a cursor
aCursor = LoadCursor(NULL, IDC_UPARROW);
SetCursor(aCursor);
```

In this code, the variable `aCursor`, of type `HCURSOR`, is declared in the windows procedure. Toggling the built-in cursors is performed in the `WM_LBUTTONDOWN` message intercept. The coding is as follows:

```
case WM_LBUTTONDOWN:
curNum++;       // bump to next cursor

switch (curNum) {
case 1:
   aCursor = LoadCursor(NULL, IDC_WAIT);
   SetCursor(aCursor);
   break;
```

```
case 2:
   aCursor = LoadCursor(NULL, IDC_APPSTARTING);
   SetCursor(aCursor);
   break;
case 3:
   aCursor = LoadCursor(NULL, IDC_CROSS);
   SetCursor(aCursor);
   break;
.
.
.
case 12:
   aCursor = LoadCursor(NULL, IDC_UPARROW);
   SetCursor(aCursor);
   curNum = 0;
   break;
}
```

Note that the static variable `curNum`, defined in the window procedure, is used to keep track of the cursor being displayed and to index through all 13 cursor images. The custom cursor is created using the cursor editor that is part of Visual Studio. The display of the custom cursor is implemented during `WM_RBUTTONDOWN` processing:

```
case WM_RBUTTONDOWN:
   aCursor = LoadCursor(pInstance,
             MAKEINTRESOURCE(IDC_CURSOR1));
   SetCursor(aCursor);
   return 0;
```

In the MOU_DEMO program, the movement of the mouse in the client area is detected by intercepting the `WM_MOUSEMOVE` message. The processing consists of obtaining the cursor coordinates from the low-order and high-order words of `lParam`, and converting the numeric values into ASCII strings for display. The code uses `_itoa()` for this purpose. The uu values are placed on the corresponding string arrays. The processing is as follows:

```
case WM_MOUSEMOVE:
   cursorX = LOWORD(lParam);
   cursorY = HIWORD(lParam);
   // Convert integer to ASCII string
   _itoa(cursorX, CurXStr + 4, 10);
   _itoa(cursorY, CurYStr + 4, 10);
   // Display x coordinate of mouse cursor
   // First initialize rectangle structure
```

```
    SetRect (&textRect,        // address of structure
       2 * cxChar,       // x for start
       3 * cyChar,        // y for start
       cxClient -(2 * cxChar),  // x for end
       cyClient);          // y for end
    // Erase the old string
    DrawText( hdc, CurXBlk, -1, &textRect,
        DT_LEFT | DT_WORDBREAK);
    // Display new string
    DrawText( hdc, CurXStr, -1, &textRect,
        DT_LEFT | DT_WORDBREAK);
  // Display y coordinate of mouse cursor
  .
  .
  .
  return 0;
```

In order to avoid having Windows change the cursor as it moves into the client area, the code intercepts the `WM_SETCURSOR` message, as follows:

```
case WM_SETCURSOR:
   return 1;
```

When running the MOU_DEMO program, notice that if the cursor is moved at a rather fast rate out of the client area, toward the left side or the top of the screen, the last value displayed for the diminishing coordinate may not be zero. This is due to the fact, mentioned earlier in this section, that `WM_MOUSEMOVE` messages are not sent to the window for every pixel of screen travel. Mouse programming must also take this into account and use greater-than and smaller-than comparisons to determine screen areas of cursor travel.

Window Styles and Controls

One of the members of the `WNDCLASSEX` structure is the windows style. In Chapter 3 we briefly discussed windows styles, and Table 3-2 is a summary of the constants that can be used to define this member. Since the 11 style constants can be ORed with each other, many more windows styles can result. Furthermore, when you create a window using the `CreateWindow()` function, there are 27 window style identifiers (see Table 3-5). In addition, the `CreateWindowEx()` function provides 21 style extensions (see Table 3-4). Although the number of possible combinations of all these elements is very large, in practice, about 20 Windows window styles, with unique properties, are clearly identified; all of which are occasionally used. Some authors have attempted to further simplify this matter: Rector and Newcommer (see bibliography) describe three general classes (overlapped, pop-up, and child windows) and three variations (owned, unowned, and child), which gives rise to five major styles:

- overlapped windows (owned and unowned)
- pop-up windows (owned and unowned)
- child windows

In the sections that follow we discuss four specific windows styles:

- **Unclassed child windows.** These are windows that are related to a parent window, but that do not belong to one of the predefined classes.
- **Basic controls.** These are child windows that belong to one of the standard control classes: BUTTON, Combo box, EDIT, LISTBOX, MDICLIENT, SCROLLBAR, and STATIC.
- **Dialog boxes.** A special type of pop-up window, that usually includes several child-window controls, typically used to obtain and process user input.
- **Common controls.** A type of controls introduced in Windows 3.1, which include status bars, toolbars, progress bars, animation controls, list and tree view controls, tabs, property sheets, wizards, rich edit controls, and a new set of dialog boxes.

Several important topics related to child windows and window types are not discussed at this time, among them are OLE control extensions, ActiveX controls, and multiple document interface (MDI). OCX controls relate to OLE automation and ActiveX controls are used mostly in the context of Web pages. The MDI controls are a Microsoft specification that defines a relationship between frame windows and client windows. MDI allows the user to work with several screen objects simultaneously. The reason for not including MDI in the contents is that its most common use is in text-handling applications, although the structure of the MDI does not preclude its use in a graphics context.

Child Windows

Conceptually, the simplest of all child windows is one that has a parent but does not belong to any of the predefined classes. Sometimes these are called "unclassed" child windows. However, if we refer to the "classed" child windows as controls, then the "unclassed" windows can be simply called "child windows." These are the designations used in the rest of the book: we refer to unclassed child windows simply as child windows and the classed variety as controls.

A child window must have a parent, but it cannot be an owned or an unowned window. The child window can have the appearance of a main window; that is, it can have a sizing border, a title bar, a caption, one or more control buttons, an icon, a system menu, a status bar, and scroll bars. The one element it cannot have is a menu because an application can have a single menu and it must be on the main window. On the other hand, a child window can be defined just as an area of the parent window. Moreover, a child window can be transparent; therefore, invisible on the screen. The conclusion is that it is often impossible to identify a child window by its appearance.

A child window with a caption bar can be moved inside its parent client area; however, it will be automatically clipped if moved outside the parent. The child window overlays a portion of its parent client area. When the cursor is over the child, Windows sends messages to the child, not to the parent. By the same token, mouse action on the child window's controls, or its system menu, is sent to the child. A child window can have its own window procedure and perform input processing operations independently of the parent. When the child window is created or destroyed, or when a mouse-button-down action on the child occurs, a `WM_PARENTNOTIFY` message is sent to the parent window. One exception to parent notification is if the child is created with the `WS_EX_NOPARENTNOTIFY` style.

A child window is created in a similar manner as the parent window, although some important variations exist. Creating a child window involves the same steps as creating the main window. You must first initialize the members of the `WNDCLASSEX` structure. Then the window class must be registered. Finally, the window is actually created and displayed when a call is made to `CreateWindow()` or `CreateWindowEx()` function.

There are not many rules regarding when and where an application creates a child window. The child window can be defined and registered in `WinMain()` and displayed at the same time as the main window. Or the child window can be created as the result of user input or program action. We have already mentioned the great number of windows styles and style combinations that can be used to define a child window. Some of these styles are incompatible, and others are ineffective when combined. The styles used in creating the child window determine how it must be handled by the code. For example, if a child window is created with the `WS_VISIBLE` style, then it is displayed as it is created. If the `WS_VISIBLE` style is not used, then to display the child window you have to call `ShowWindow()` with the handle to the child window as the first parameter, and `SW_SHOW`, `SW_SHOWNORMAL`, or one of the other predefined constants, as the second parameter.

In operation, the child window provides many features that facilitate program design. For instance, a child window has its own window procedure, which can do its own message processing. This procedure receives the same parameters as the main window procedure and is notified of all the windows messages that refer to the child. The child window can have its own attributes, such as icons, cursors, and background brush. If the main window is defined with an arrow cursor and the child window with a cross cursor, the cursor changes automatically to a cross as it travels over the child, and back to an arrow as it leaves the child's client area. The fact that each windows does its own message processing considerably simplifies the coding. Screen environments with multiple areas, such as the ones in Visual Studio, Windows Explorer, and many other applications, are implemented by means of child windows.

Parent and child windows can share the same display context or have different ones. In fact, each window can have any of the display contexts described in Chapter 4. If the child window is declared with the class style `CS_PARENTDC`, then it uses the parent's display context; output performed by the child takes place in the parent's client area, and the child has no addressable client area of its own. On the other hand, parent and child can have separate device contexts. If both windows are declared with the class style `CS_OWNDC`, discussed in Chapter 4, then each has its own display context with a unique set of attributes. If more than one child window exists, they can be declared with the class style `CS_CLASSDC`, and the children share a single device context, which can be different from the one of the parent window.

Each child window is given its own integer identifier at the time it is created. Because child windows can have no menus, the `HMENU` parameter passed to `CreateWindows()` or `CreateWindowsEx()` serves this purpose. The child window uses this identifier in messages sent to its parent, which enables the parent to know to which child window the message belongs, if more than one is enabled. If multiple child windows are given the same numeric identification, it may be impossible for the parent to tell them apart.

Child Windows Demonstration Program

The program named CHI_DEMO, located in the *Child Window Demo* project folder on the book's CD-ROM, is a demonstration of a program with a child window. The program displays an overlapped child window inside the parent window. When the left mouse button is clicked inside the child window, a text message is displayed in its client area. The same thing happens when the left mouse button is clicked in the parent's client area. At the same time, the old messages in the parent or the child windows are erased. Figure 5-3 is a screen dump of the CHI_DEMO program.

Figure 5-3: Screen dump of the CHI_DEMO program

The program uses a child window, which is defined using the WS_OVERLAPPEDWINDOW style. This style, which is the same one used in the parent window, gives both the parent and the child a title bar with caption, a system menu, a border, and a set of control buttons to close, minimize and restore. The child window is created during WM_CREATE message processing of the parent window, as follows:

```
LRESULT CALLBACK WndProc(HWND hwnd, UINT iMsg, WPARAM wParam,
                         LPARAM lParam) {
  PAINTSTRUCT ps ;
  WNDCLASSEX  chiclass ;
  switch (iMsg) {
    case WM_CREATE:
      hdc = GetDC (hwnd) ;
      // The system monospaced font is selected
      SelectObject (hdc, GetStockObject (SYSTEM_FIXED_FONT)) ;
      // Create a child window
      chiclass.cbSize        = sizeof (chiclass) ;
      chiclass.style         = CS_HREDRAW | CS_VREDRAW
                               | CS_OWNDC;
      chiclass.lpfnWndProc   = ChildWndProc ;
      chiclass.cbClsExtra    = 0 ;
      chiclass.cbWndExtra    = 0 ;
      chiclass.hInstance     = pInstance ;
      chiclass.hIcon         = NULL;
      chiclass.hCursor       = LoadCursor (NULL, IDC_CROSS) ;
      chiclass.hbrBackground = (HBRUSH) GetStockObject
                               (WHITE_BRUSH);
      chiclass.lpszMenuName  = NULL;
      chiclass.lpszClassName = "ChildWindow" ;
      chiclass.hIconSm       = NULL;
      RegisterClassEx (&chiclass) ;
        hChild = CreateWindow ("ChildWindow",
                "A Child Window",  // caption
                 WS_CHILD | WS_VISIBLE |
                 WS_OVERLAPPEDWINDOW ,
                 40, 40,        // x and y of window location
                 400, 100,      // x and y of window size
                 hwnd,          // handle to the parent window
                 (HMENU) 1001, // child window designation
                 pInstance,     // program instance
                 NULL) ;
      // Make sure child window is valid
```

```
    assert(hChild != NULL);
    return 0 ;
    .
    .
    .
```

Note that the child is defined with the styles WS_CHILD, WS_VISIBLE, and WS_OVERLAPPEDWINDOW. The WS_VISIBLE class style ensures that the child becomes visible as soon as CreateWindows() is executed. The child window is assigned the arbitrary value 1001 in the HMENU parameter to CreateWindow(). The child has a private DC, the same as the parent, but the DCs are different. The assert statement ensures, during program development, that the child window is a valid one.

During the parent's WM_PAINT message processing a call is made to UpdateWindow() with the handle of the child window as a parameter. The result of this call is that the child's window procedure receives a WM_PAINT message.

The window procedure for the child, named ChildWndProc() in the demo program, is prototyped in the conventional manner and its name defined in the lpfnWndProc member of the child's WNDCLASSEX structure. The child's window procedure is coded as follows:

```
LRESULT CALLBACK ChildWndProc (HWND hChild, UINT iMsg, WPARAM
wParam,
                               LPARAM lParam) {
 switch (iMsg) {
  case WM_CREATE:
      childDc = GetDC(hChild);
      SelectObject (childDc, GetStockObject
                   (SYSTEM_FIXED_FONT)) ;
      return 0;

  case   WM_LBUTTONDOWN:
     // Display message in child and erase text in parent
     TextOut(childDc, 10, 10, "Mouse action in child ", 22);
     TextOut(hdc, 10, 10, "                      ", 22);
return 0;

  case WM_DESTROY:
       return 0;
  }
 return DefWindowProc (hChild, iMsg, wParam, lParam) ;
}
```

During the WM_CREATE processing of the child's windows procedure, the code obtains a handle to the child's DC. Also, the system fixed font is selected into the DC at this time.

In the CHI_DEMO program we have declared several public variables: the handles to the windows of the parent and the child, and the handles to their display context. This stretches one of the fundamental rules of Windows programming: to keep public data at a minimum. In this case, however, we achieve a substantial simplification in the coding because now the parent can have access to the child's device context, and vice versa. Therefore, when the user clicks the left mouse button in the child's client area, a text message is displayed in the child window and the one in the parent window is simultaneously erased. Similar processing takes place when the left mouse button is clicked in the parent's client area.

Basic Controls

These are the traditional controls that have been around since the Win16 APIs. They are predefined child windows that belong to one of the standard window classes. Table 5-3 lists the predefined classes used for controls.

TABLE 5-3 PREDEFINED CONTROL CLASSES

Class Name	Meaning
`BUTTON`	A small rectangular child window representing a button. The user clicks a button to turn it on or off. Button controls can be used alone or in groups, and they can be labeled or not. Button controls typically change appearance when clicked.
`COMBOBOX`	Consists of a list box and a selection field similar to an edit control (see description). Depending on its style, you can or cannot edit the contents of the selection field. If the list box is visible, typing characters into the selection field highlights the first list box entry that matches the characters typed. By the same token, selecting an item in the list box displays the selected text in the selection field.
`EDIT`	A rectangular child window into which you type text. You select the edit box and give it the keyboard focus by clicking it or moving to it by pressing the Tab key. You can enter text into an Edit control if it displays a flashing caret. You use the mouse to move the cursor inside the box, to select characters to be replaced, or to position the cursor for inserting new characters. The Backspace key deletes characters. Edit controls use a variable-pitch system font and display characters from the ANSI character set. The `WM_SETFONT` message can be used to change the default font. During input, tab characters are expanded into as many spaces as are required to move the caret to the next tab stop. Tab stops are preset eight spaces apart.

Continued

TABLE 5-3 PREDEFINED CONTROL CLASSES *(Continued)*

Class Name	Meaning
`LISTBOX`	A list of character strings. It presents a list of names, such as filenames, from which you can select. Selection is made by clicking an item in the list box. The selected string is highlighted, and a notification message is sent to the parent window. When the item list is too long for the window, you can use a vertical or horizontal scroll bar. If the scroll bar is not needed, it is automatically hidden.
`SCROLLBAR`	A rectangular control with a scroll box and direction arrows at both ends. The scroll bar sends a notification message to its parent window whenever the user clicks it. The parent window is responsible for updating the position of the scroll box when necessary. Scroll-bar controls have the same appearance and function as scroll bars used in ordinary windows. Unlike scroll bars, however, scroll-bar controls can be positioned anywhere in a window and for any purpose. The scroll-bar class also includes size-box controls, which are small rectangles that you can expand to change the size of the window.
`STATIC`	A simple text field, box, or rectangle, used to label, group, or separate other controls. Static controls take no input and provide no output.

The MDICLIENT control is not listed in Table 5-3 for reasons discussed earlier in this section. Figure 5-4 shows buttons of several types, a list box, a combo box, and a scroll-bar control.

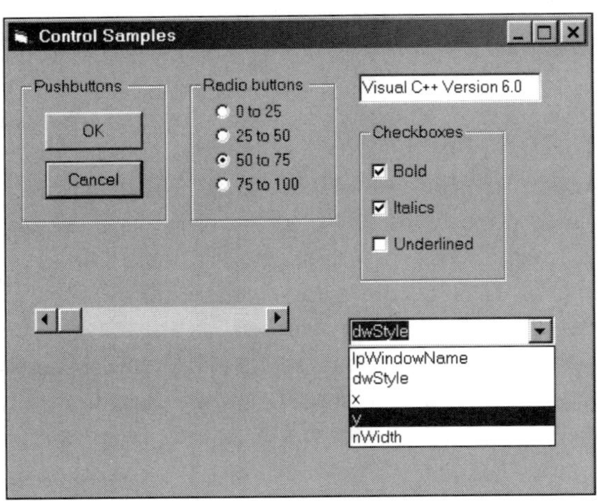

Figure 5-4: Buttons, list box, combo box, and scroll-bar controls

In conventional Windows programming, basic controls are not frequently used in the client area of the main window. Most often you see them in message boxes or input boxes, described later in this chapter. For this reason, Developer Studio does not provide a resource editor for inserting controls in the client area, although it does contain a powerful editor for dialog boxes. In spite of this, the use of basic controls in child windows adds considerable power to a programmer's toolkit. The result is a completely customizable message, dialog box, toolbar, or other child window, in which you are free of all the restrictions of the built-in versions of these components. The price for this power and control is that you must implement all the functionality in your own code.

The `CreateWindow()` or `CreateWindowEx()` functions are used to build any one of the controls in Table 5-3. If the control is created using the `WS_VISIBLE` window style, then it is displayed immediately on the window whose handle is passed as a parameter to the call. If not, then the `ShowWindow()` function has to be called to display it. The call returns a handle to the created control, or NULL if the operation fails. The following is a code fragment for creating a button control.

```
static HWND    hwndRadio1;     // Handle to control
  .
  .
  .
hwndRadio1 = CreateWindow (
      "BUTTON",         // Control class name
      "Radio 1",                 // Button name text
       WS_CHILD | WS_VISIBLE | BS_RADIOBUTTON
       | WS_SIZEBOX,
       20,                  // x coordinate of location
       60,                  // y coordinate
       100, 30,             // button size
       hChild,              // Handle to parent window
       (HMENU) 201,         // control id number
       pInstance,           // Instance handle
       NULL) ;              // Pointer to additional data
```

Because controls belong to predefined classes, they need not be registered as a window class. Therefore, the `WNDCLASSEX` structure and the call to `RegisterClass()` or `RegisterClassEx()` are not required in this case. In the case of a main window, the eighth parameter of `CreateWindow()` is the handle to its menu. Because controls cannot have a menu, this parameter is for the control's numeric designation, the same as with a child window. Thereafter, this numeric value, which can also be a predefined constant, identifies the control. If the control is to be addressable, this identification number should be unique.

In addition to the general window style, each of the predefined control classes has its own set of attributes. The prefixes are shown in Table 5-4.

TABLE 5-4 PREFIX FOR PREDEFINED WINDOW CLASSES

Prefix	Control Type
BS	button
CBS	combo box
ES	edit box
LBS	list box
SBS	scroll bar
SS	static

In addition, dialog-box attributes use the DS prefix.

The class-specific styles are ORed with the window style constants passed in the third parameter to CreateWindow(). Note that in the previous code fragment the BS_RADIOBUTTON constant is included in the field. Several variations of the button class exist. The buttons in the first group of Figure 5-4, labeled *Pushbuttons*, are plain push buttons. They appear raised when not pushed and sunken after being pushed by the user. Push buttons operate independently. These buttons are usually created with the BS_PUSHBUTTON and BS_DEFPUSHBUTTON styles.

Radio buttons are reminiscent of the buttons in the radios of old-style automobiles: pushing one button automatically pops out all the others. The styles BS_RADIOBUTTON and BS_AUTORADIOBUTTONS are used for creating this type of button. Radio buttons contain a circular area with a central dot that indicates the button's state (see Figure 5-4).

Another variation is the checkbox. A checkbox can have two or three states. A two-state checkbox can be checked or unchecked, while the three-state style can also be grayed. Checkboxes, like regular buttons, operate independently of each other. Two-state checkboxes are created with the BS_CHECKBOX style. The three-state version requires ORing the BS_3STATE constant with BS_CHECKBOX.

A unique style of button is the groupbox, which is enabled with the button style BS_GROUPBOX. A groupbox encloses several buttons or controls in a labeled frame. It is unique in the sense that it is defined as a button, but a groupbox does not respond to user input, nor does it send messages to the parent window. Figure 5-4 shows three groupboxes, one for each type of button.

Three types of controls are designed for manipulating text: the edit box, the combo box, and the list box. You select an edit-box control for input by clicking it or tabbing until it has the input focus. When a caret is displayed, you can enter text until the rectangle is filled. If the edit-box control is created with the ES_AUTOSCROLL style, then you can enter more characters than will fit in the box since the text automatically scrolls to the left, although this practice is not recommended since part of the input disappears from the screen. If the edit box is defined with the ES_MULTILINE style, you can enter more than one text line. However, this style can create conflicts if the active window contains a default push button that also responds to the Enter key. The built-in solution to this problem is that the default style of edit box requires the Ctrl+Enter key combination to end an input line. However, if the edit box is created with the style ES_WANTRETURN, then the Enter key alone serves as a line terminator.

The list-box control displays a list of text items from which the user can select one or more. Code can add or remove strings from the list box. Scroll bars can be requested for a list box. If the list box is created with the LBS_NOTIFY style, then the parent window receives a message whenever the user clicks or double-clicks an item. The LBS_SORT style makes the list box sort items alphabetically.

The combo box is a combination of a textbox and a list box. The user can enter text on the top portion of the combo box, or drop-down the list box and select an item from it. Alternatively, the edit function of the combo box can be disabled. Figure 5-4 shows a combo box.

Scroll-bar controls can be vertical or horizontal and can be aligned at the bottom, top, left, or right of a rectangle defined at call time. At this point, we must distinguish between window and control scroll bars. Any window can have scroll bars if it is defined with the WS_VSCROLL or WS_HSCROLL styles. Scroll-bar controls are individual scroll bars which can be positioned anywhere on the parent's client area. Both windows and control scroll bars send messages to the parent window whenever a user action takes place. Scroll-bar controls are of little use by themselves, but provide a powerful and convenient way of obtaining user input. For example, a scroll-bar control that allows the user to move up or down a numeric range without typing values. In this case the scroll bar is usually combined with another control that displays the selected value. The CON_DEMO program, in this chapter, has an example of this use of a scroll-bar control.

Static controls do not interact with the user since they cannot receive mouse or keyboard input. The principal use of static controls is to display rectangular frames of several colors and borders, and to provide feedback from another control. The CON_DEMO program, described later in this chapter, which is found in the *Controls Demo* project folder on the book's CD-ROM, has a child window with a static control that displays the position of a scroll bar.

Communicating with Controls

Controls are child windows and child windows can communicate with their parents. As is the case in all Windows functions, controls communicate with their parent window by means of a message-passing mechanism. The messages passed to the parent window depend on the type of control. This communication works both ways: a control sends a message to its parent window informing it that a certain user action has taken place, or the parent window sends a message to a control requesting that it take a certain action or report some item of information stored internally. For example, when the user clicks on a push-button control, a WM_COMMAND message is sent to the parent window. When a parent window needs to know if a radio button is checked or unchecked it sends a BM_GETCHECK message to the radio button control.

WM_COMMAND informs the parent window of action on a menu, on a control, or of an accelerator keystroke. The high-order word of the wParam is zero if the message originates in a menu, and one if it originates in an accelerator keystroke. If the message originated in a control, then the high-word of the wParam is a control-specific notification code. Table 5-5 lists the notification codes for the button controls.

TABLE 5-5 NOTIFICATION CODES FOR BUTTON CONTROLS

Notification Code	Action
BN_CLICKED	Button was clicked
BN_DBLCLK	Button was double-clicked
BN_SETFOCUS	Button has gained keyboard focus
BN_KILLFOCUS	Button has lost keyboard focus

In the case of a control, the low-order word of the wParam contains the control identifier. This identifier is the number assigned to the control in the hMenu parameter of CreateWindows() or CreateWindowsEx(). Usually, an application defines a symbolic constant for each control because this is a mnemonic aid and helps to make sure that no two controls are assigned the same value. One or more #define statements can be used as follows:

```
#define    WARMBUTTON      101
#define    HOTBUTTON       102
#define    COLDBUTTON      103
```

A switch statement on the low word of wParam can later be used to tell which button been pressed by the user, for example:

```
int buttonID, buttonNotify;
.
.
```

```
.
case WM_COMMAND:
    buttonID =      LOWORD(wParam);
    buttonNotify =  HIWORD(wParam);
    //eliminate non-control actions
    if(buttonNotify <= 1)
      return 0;
    switch (buttonID):
      case WARMBUTTON:
        if(buttonNotify == BN_CLICKED)
     // ASSERT:
     //    Tested button was clicked
    .
    .
    .
```

Some controls store information about their state or other data. For example, a three-state checkbox can be in a checked, unchecked, or indeterminate state. Table 5-6 lists the checkbox constants that define the three settings. These are used with three-state checkboxes and radio buttons.

TABLE 5-6 NOTIFICATION CODES FOR THREE-STATE CONTROLS

Notification Code	Action
BST_CHECKED	Control is checked
BST_INDETERMINATE	Control is checked and grayed
BST_UNCHECKED	Control is unchecked

If you send a BM_GETCHECK message to a three-state checkbox or radio button, it responds with one of the above values. Suppose there is a three-state checkbox, with identification code CHKBOX1, and handle hwndChkBox1, which you want to change from the checked to indeterminate state; it can be coded as follows:

```
LRESULT butMsg;
int     buttonID, buttonNotify;
.
.
.
case WM_COMMAND:
```

```
buttonID =      LOWORD(wParam);
buttonNotify =  HIWORD(wParam);

//eliminate non-control actions
if(buttonNotify <= 1)
  return 0;
switch (buttonID):
  case CHKBOX1:
    butMsg = SendMessage(hwndChkBox1,  // handle
                         BM_GETCHECK,  // message
                         0, 0L);       // must be zero
    if(butMsg == BST_CHECKED)
    // ASSERT:
    //     checkbox is in checked state
    SendMessage(hwndChkBox1,
            BM_SETCHECK,        // order to set new state
            BST_INDETERMINATE,  // change to this state
            0, 01);
  .
  .
  .
```

Note, in the previous code fragment, that we used the SendMessage() function to communicate with the control. SendMessage() sends a message to a window or windows bypassing the message queue. In contrast, the PostMessage() function places the message in the thread's message queue. In communicating with a control, the first parameter to SendMessage() is the control's handle and the second one is the message to be sent. The third parameter is zero when we wish to obtain information from a control, and it contains a value or state when we wish to change the data stored. The BM_GETCHECK message returns a value, of type LRESULT, which is one of the notification codes in Table 5-6. The BM_SETCHECK message changes the button's state.

Scroll-bar controls have a unique way of communicating with the parent window. Like main windows scroll bars, scroll-bar controls send the WM_VSCROLL and WM_HSCROLL messages, the first one in the case of a vertical scroll bar action and the second one in the case of a horizontal scroll bar. The lParam is set to zero in windows scroll bars and to the scroll- bar handle in the case of a scroll-bar control. The high-order word of the wParam contains the position of the scroll box and the low-order word the scroll box value, which is one of the SB prefix constants listed in Table 5-7.

TABLE 5-7 CONSTANTS INDICATING USER SCROLL REQUEST

Value	Meaning
SB_BOTTOM	Scroll to the lower right
SB_ENDSCROLL	End scrolling
SB_LINELEFT	Scroll left by one unit
SB_LINERIGHT	Scroll right by one unit
SB_PAGELEFT	Scroll left by the width of the window
SB_PAGERIGHT	Scroll right by the width of the window
SB_THUMBPOSITION	Scrolls to the absolute position. The current position is specified by the nPos parameter
SB_THUMBTRACK	Drags scroll box to the specified position. The current position is specified by the nPos parameter
SB_TOP	Scroll to the upper left

In processing scroll-bar controls, the first step is to make sure that the message originates in the control being monitored. When the scroll action does not originate in windows scroll bars, or on those of another control, the processing usually consists in determining the new position for the scroll box. Two functions in the Windows API, SetScrollInfo() and GetScrollInfo(), provide all the necessary functionality for scroll-bar operation. SetScrollInfo() sets the minimum and maximum positions for the scroll box, to define the page size, and to set the scroll box to a specific location. GetScrollInfo() retrieves the information regarding these parameters. Four other functions, SetScrollPos(), SetScrollRange(), GetScrollPos(), and GetScrollRange() are furnished. In theory, these last four functions are furnished for backward compatibility, although they are often easier to implement in code than the new versions.

A program that implements a horizontal scroll bar usually starts by creating a scroll-bar control. You can use the SBS_HORZ scroll-bar style and determine its vertical and horizontal size in the sixth and seventh parameters to CreateWindows(), as follows:

```
#define  SCROLLBAR   401         // scroll bar id code
static   HWND        hwndSB;     // handle for the scroll bar
   .
```

```
   .
   .
// create a scroll bar class child window
   hwndSB = CreateWindow ("SCROLLBAR",  // Control class name
            "",                        // Button name text
            WS_CHILD | WS_VISIBLE | SBS_HORZ ,
            20,                 // x coordinate of location
            140,                // y coordinate
            150, 25,            // dimensions
            hChild,             // handle to parent window
            (HMENU) SCROLLBAR,  // child window id.
            pInstance,          // instance handle
            NULL) ;
```

Once the scroll bar is created, you must determine its range, set the initial position of the scroll box, and define its page size, if page operations are implemented. This last value determines how much the scroll box moves when the bar itself is clicked. All of these operations can be done with a single call to `SetScrollInfo()`, in which case the parameters are stored in a `SCROLLINFO`-type structure, as follows:

```
// Store parameters in SCROLLINFO structure members
   scinfo.cbSize = sizeof(SCROLLINFO);   // structure size
   scinfo.fMask  = SIF_POS | SIF_RANGE | SIF_PAGE; mask
   scinfo.nMin   = 0;                  // minimum value
   scinfo.nMax   = 99;                 // maximum value
   scinfo.nPage  = 0;                  // page size
   scinfo.nPos   = 50;                 // initial position
// Store scroll bar information
   SetScrollInfo(hwndSB, SB_CTL, &scinfo, TRUE);
   //              |       |       |         |___ redraw
   //              |       |       |____ address of SCROLLINFO
   //              |       |______ refers to a scroll bar
   //                              control
   //              |______________ handle to the scroll bar control
```

Manipulating the scroll bar requires intercepting the corresponding scroll-bar messages. The current position of the scroll box is usually stored in a local variable; in this case, the variable is named `sbPos`. Because this is a horizontal scroll bar, you can intercept the `WM_HSCROLL` message and then make sure that it refers to the scroll bar you are monitoring.

```
static  int       sbPos;       // position of scroll box
   .
   .
   .
```

```
case WM_HSCROLL:
     // Make sure action refers to local scroll bar
     // not the Windows scroll bars
     if(hwndSB == (HWND) lParam) {
           switch (LOWORD (wParam))  // Scroll code
           {
        case SB_LINELEFT:      // Scroll left one unit
           if(sbPos > 0)
           sbPos--;
           break;
        case SB_LINERIGHT:     // Scroll right one unit
           if(sbPos < 99)
           sbPos++;
           break;
        // Processing for user dragging the scroll box
         case SB_THUMBTRACK:
         case SB_THUMBPOSITION:
            sbPos = HIWORD (wParam);
            break;
         }
        // Display scroll box at new position
           SetScrollPos(hwndSB,
                        SB_CTL,
                        sbPos,
                        TRUE);
        }
        return 0;
```

Finally, consider the static class of controls often used for text fields, for labeling boxes, and for drawing frames and rectangles. Although static controls are frequently limited to labeling and simple drawing operations, they can be made to receive mouse input by means of the `SS_NOTIFY` style. Furthermore, the text in a static control can be changed at run time. The CON_DEMO program, described in the following section, located in the *Controls Demo* project folder on the book's CD-ROM, has two static controls. One displays the position of the scroll bar, and the other one is a black frame that surrounds the scroll-bar buttons.

The Controls Demonstration Program

The program named CON_DEMO is a demonstration of some basic controls described in previous sections and of the programming required to operate them. The controls are contained in a child window, much like the one created in the CHI_DEMO program already described. Figure 5-5 is a labeled screen dump of the CON_DEMO program.

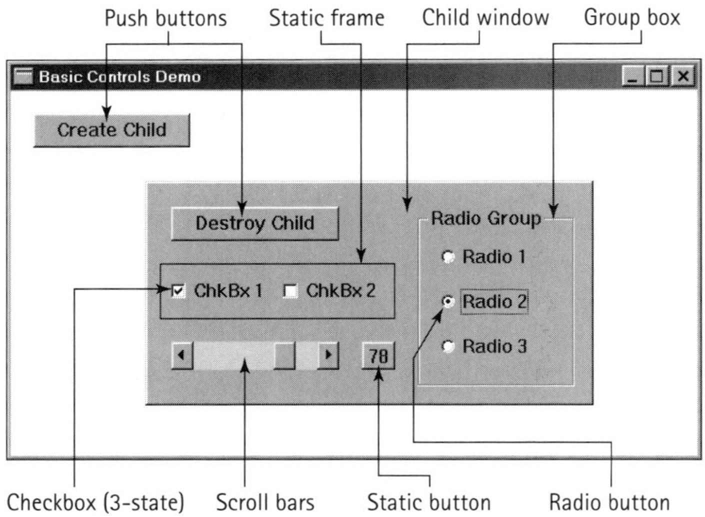

Figure 5-5: Labeled screen dump of the CON_DEMO program

The program's main screen contains a push button that displays the child window. In the remainder of this section we have selected some excerpts from the program code to demonstrate the processing.

At the start of the code, the child windows and controls are defined as symbolic names. This is a useful simplification in applications that manipulate several resources or program elements identified by numeric values. The advantage is that the information is centralized for easy access and that it ensures that no values are repeated.

```
// Constants for child windows and controls
#define  CHILD1      1001
#define  CREATEWIN   102
#define  DESTROYWIN  103
#define  RADGROUP    104
#define  RADIO1      201
#define  RADIO2      202
#define  RADIO3      203
#define  CHKBOX1     301
#define  CHKBOX2     302
#define  SCROLLBAR   401
#define  SCRBARWIN   501
#define  FRAME       502
```

The numeric values assigned to individual controls are arbitrary; it is a good idea, however, to follow a pattern for numbering resources and controls because this avoids chaos in large programs. For example, child windows can be assigned a four-digit number, controls a three-digit number, and so forth. We recommend that you use a dense set of integers for representing related controls because some Windows functions operate on this assumption. Following this rule, the radio buttons in the CON_DEMO program are numbered 201, 202, and 203, and the checkboxes have numbers 301 and 302.

The creation of the child window in the CON_DEMO program is almost identical to the one in CHI_DEMO, previously described. The individual controls are created in the child window using the `CreateWindow()` function with the parameter set required in each case. The handles for the individual controls are defined as static variables in the child windows procedure, as follows:

```
LRESULT CALLBACK ChildWndProc (HWND hChild, UINT iMsg, WPARAM
                              wParam, LPARAM lParam) {
  static HWND  hwndChildBut1;     // Handle to child's button
  static HWND  hwndRadio1, hwndRadio2, hwndRadio3;
  static HWND  hwndChkBx1, hwndChkBx2;
  static HWND  hwndSB, hwndVal;
  static HWND  hwndGrpBox1;
  static HWND  hwndFrame;
  .
  .
  .
```

The code in the child window intercepts the `WM_CREATE` message. During message processing it installs the system's fixed font in the display context and then proceeds to create the individual controls. A bool-type variable, named `childStatus`, serves to store the state of the child window. This variable is TRUE if the child window is displayed. This avoids creating more than one copy of the child. The first control created in the child window is the push button that destroys it and returns execution to the parent. Before that, the system's fixed font is selected into the display context. Coding is as follows:

```
switch (iMsg) {
   case WM_CREATE:
    // Test that child window is not already displayed
    if(childStatus)
      return 0;
    // ASSERT:
    //      child window is not displayed
    childStatus = TRUE;    // child window is displayed
    childDc = GetDC(hChild);   // handle to private DC
        SelectObject (childDc,
```

```
                    GetStockObject (SYSTEM_FIXED_FONT));
  // Place destroy button on child window
  hwndChildBut1 = CreateWindow (
    "BUTTON",                // Control class name
    "Destroy Child",          // Button name text
    WS_CHILD | WS_VISIBLE | BS_PUSHBUTTON,
    20, 20,                  // x and y location
    150,                     // Window width
    30,                      // Window height
    hChild,                  // Handle to parent window
    (HMENU) DESTROYWIN,      // Child window id.
    pInstance,               // Instance handle
    NULL) ;
    .
    .
    .
```

The user interaction with the controls is monitored and processed in the WM_COMMAND message intercept of the child window. First, the notification code and the button identifier are stored in local variables. A switch statement on the button identification code allows directing the processing to the routines for each of the buttons. The code examines the notification code to make sure that the intercept is due to action on a button control, and not on an accelerator key or a menu item.

```
case WM_COMMAND:
  buttonID = LOWORD (wParam);
  buttonNotCode = HIWORD (wParam);
  switch (buttonID) {
    if(buttonNotCode <= 1)
      return 0;

   case DESTROYWIN:
     if(buttonNotCode == BN_CLICKED) {
       childStatus = FALSE;
       DestroyWindow(hChild);
       UpdateWindow(hwnd);
       }
       break;
   // Radio button # 1 action
   case RADIO1:
      // Set radio button ON
         SendMessage(hwndRadio1, BM_SETCHECK, 1, 0L);
         SendMessage(hwndRadio2, BM_SETCHECK, 0, 0L);
```

```
SendMessage(hwndRadio3, BM_SETCHECK, 0, 0L);
break;
    .
    .
    .
```

Menus

The menu is one of the most important elements of the Windows user interface. It occupies the line below the title bar. Often, only the program's main window has a top-level menu. There has been considerable uncertainty regarding the names of the various elements in a menu. The following designations are based on Microsoft's *The Windows Interface Guidelines for Software Design* (see bibliography).

- The **menu bar** is a screen line directly below the title bar, which contains entries called the *menu titles,* or just the *menus.*
- Each **menu title** (menu) activates a drop-down box, which contains one or more *menu items.* Menu items are usually arranged in a single column, although Windows supports multiple column menus.
- **Menu items** can be of three types: *menu commands, child menus,* and *separators.* A menu command is a menu item that executes a program function directly. A child menu, also called a *cascading* or *hierarchical menu,* is a submenu, which can in turn contain menu commands, child menus, and separators. Items that activate a child menu are usually marked by a triangular arrow to the right of its name. A separator is a screen line that groups related menu items.
- **Pop-up menus** are activated by clicking the second mouse button. They are usually unrelated to the program's menu bar.
- **Access keys** are keystrokes that can be used instead of mouse button action to access menu items. Access keys are underscored in the menu title and in menu items. To activate a menu title by means of the access key you must hold down the Alt key. Once a drop-down menu is displayed, access to the contained items is obtained by pressing the corresponding access key. The Alt key is not required in this case.
- **Shortcut keys** are keystroke combinations that allow accessing a menu item directly. Shortcut keys are usually a Ctrl + key combination or a function key. Windows documentation sometimes calls these shortcut keys *accelerators,* but *The Windows Interface Guidelines for Software Design* prefers the former name.

Style should be considered regarding the design and implementation of menus. Although the design of the user interface is a topic outside the scope of this book, several general principles are worth mentioning.

- A menu title should be a single word that represents the items that it contains. Each menu title should have an access key, which activates the menu when used in conjunction with the Alt key. Access keys are underlined in the menu bar. No two menu titles should have the same access key.
- Cascading menus should be used sparingly since they add complexity to the interface. Their purpose is to reduce the number of entries in the main menu and to logically organize hierarchical entries. The user should never have to navigate through more than two levels of cascading menus to reach a command.
- Menu items that are not active or are currently unavailable should be disabled and displayed in gray characters. Alternatively, a permanently inactive item can be removed from a menu.
- If a menu command requires additional data to execute, it should be followed by an ellipsis (...). The ellipsis serves as a visual key that information for executing a command is incomplete. Typically, commands with ellipses display a dialog box where the additional data is supplied. However, commands that obviously generate other informational actions should not be followed by ellipses; for example, a Properties command is expected to display information, therefore it should not have an ellipsis.
- Checkboxes are used in menus to indicate the status of a menu item. A checked item signals that it is functional. Code should check and uncheck items during processing to update their status.
- All menu items should have access keys, but items on the same drop-down menu cannot have the same access key. The first choice for an access key is the first character in the menu title or entry. If the first character in the item name is already used as an access key, then select the next one that is not used as an access key.
- Shortcut keys that activate menu commands are best implemented with the Crtl key followed by a mnemonic letter associated with the entry. Function keys can also be used. For example, Ctrl + S can be used for a Save command and Ctrl + P for a Print command. The most-used commands should be assigned a shortcut.

Figure 5-6 shows some of the most common elements in a menu.

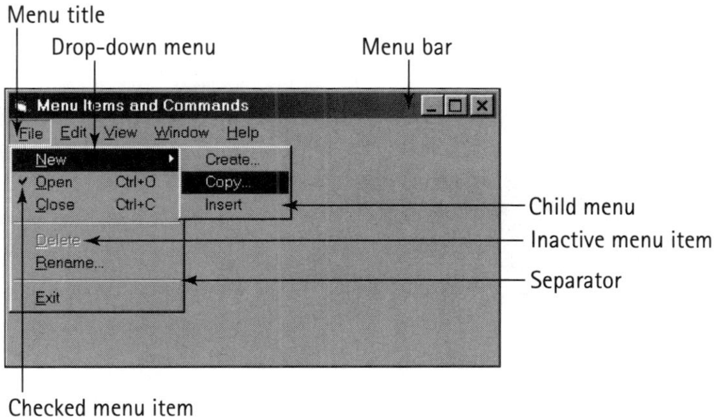

Figure 5-6: Common menu elements

Creating a Menu

There are several ways to create a menu. Before the Visual Studio and other development environments came into existence, menus were created using API functions. `CreateMenu()` creates an empty menu and returns its handle. `InsertMenuItem()` can be used to populate the menu with components. `AppendMenu()` adds a component to an existing menu. Other functions, such as `DeleteMenu()`, `DestroyMenu()`, `DrawMenuBar()`, `ModifyMenu()` and `RemoveMenu()` are also available. Finally, the LoadMenuIndirect() function can be used to load a menu from a memory resident menu template.

The visual development environments include tools that facilitate the development of program menus with little compromise on their functionality. In Visual C++ Developer Studio, the menu editor function creates a menu-type resource that can be easily implemented in code. In fact, with these facilities, the menu becomes one of the easiest elements to create in the user interface. The following steps can be used to create a menu:

1. From the Developer Studio Insert menu, select the Resource command. Select the Menu resource typethe dialog box, and click New.
2. Create the main menu entries in your program (the menu titles) as well as the menu items in each of the drop-down menus. At this time you can assign an identification code to each menu item, define child menus (called pop-up in the input form), determine if the item is initially grayed, checked, or inactive, assign shortcut keys, and other menu attributes. Details on how to use the menu editor are available in Developer Studio online Help. Figure 5-7 shows the Developer Studio menu editor screen.

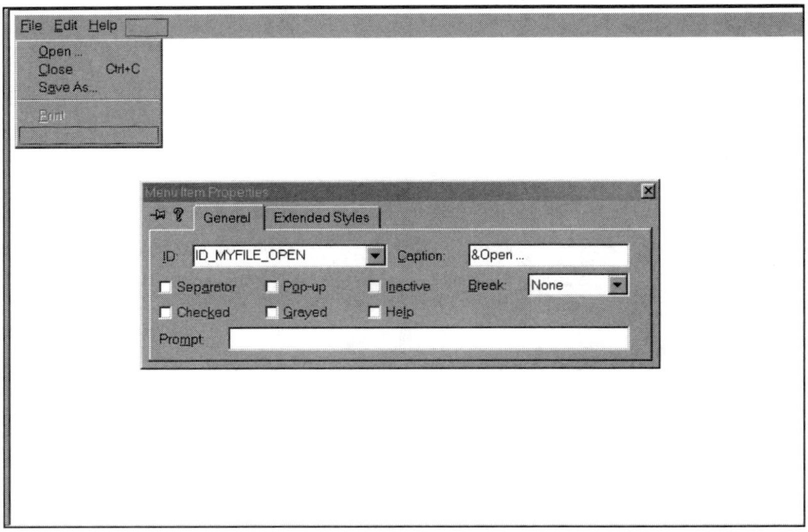

Figure 5-7: Developer Studio menu editor screen

3. Once you have finished creating the menu, click on the close button of the menu editor window. If the application already has a script file, the new menu is added to it. If not, Developer Studio prompts you to save the new script file.

4. Skip this step if a script file has already been inserted into the project. If not, open the Project menu and select Add to Project, and then Files. In the Insert Files into Project dialog box, select the script file and then click OK. The script file now appears in the project workspace window.

5. Select the Resource View button in the project workspace pane and click + on Script Resources. Click + on Menu. Note the identifier name for the menu resource, which is IDR_MENU1 if this is the first menu created.

6. Enter the menu identifier in the wndclass structure defined in WinMain(), as follows:

   ```
   wndclass.lpszMenuName   = MAKEINTRESOURCE(IDR_MENU1);
   ```

7. Developer Studio creates a header file named resource.h which assigns numeric values to the program resources. The file is saved under the name "resource.h" and stored in the project's main directory. The main source file must reference this header file in an include statement, such as:

   ```
   #include "resource.h"
   ```

8. To recompile the program with the new menu, select Rebuild All from the Build menu.

9. To edit the menu, double-click the corresponding IDR_MENU1 icon.

If you receive a redefinition of symbol error at build time, two possible solutions exist: one is to comment-out the redefined symbol in the file named afxres.h located in Msdev\Mfc\Include directory. The other one is to edit the resource, in this case the menu, and change the name in the ID: field. Changing the afxres.h file is a permanent way of avoiding this error, but the development system cannot be used for MFC applications if afxres.h has been altered.

Menu Item Processing

There are several intercept messages related to application menu processing. `WM_MENUSELECT` is sent when the mouse cursor moves among the menu items, and WM_INITITEM when the user selects an item from a menu. However, most applications do all of their menu processing in the `WM_COMMAND` message intercept. In the case of a menu, the `lParam` is 0 and the `wParam` contains the menu ID code, which is the identification number and its corresponding string constant found in the resource.h file. System menus notify the application through the `WM_SYSCOMMAND` message. The following code fragment shows the intercept routine for the item named Open in the File menu:

```
case WM_COMMAND:
   switch (LOWORD (wParam)) {
   case ID_MYFILE_OPEN:
       // ASSERT:
       //   Menu item resource named ID_MYFILE_OPEN
       //   was activated by user
   .
   .
   .
```

An important fringe benefit of using the menu editor in Developer Studio is that access keys are automatically detected and vectored to the corresponding handler. Suppose that in the preceding code fragment the Open command was defined so that the letter O was preceded by the & symbol in the editor screen. In this case, when the user presses the "O" key while the File menu is open, a `WM_COMMAND` message with the key code `ID_MYFILE_OPEN` is sent to the handler.

Shortcut Keys

Shortcut keys require a special treatment so that the keystrokes are vectored to the desired handler. It is recommended that shortcut keys be listed in the same line as the menu item. To do so, you must insert the text for the control keystroke, preceded by \t in the caption window of the Menu Item Properties editor screen. In this case \t indicates a Tab code which displays the following text on the next Tab field. Figure 5-8 shows the insertion of a shortcut key designation in Developer Studio menu editor.

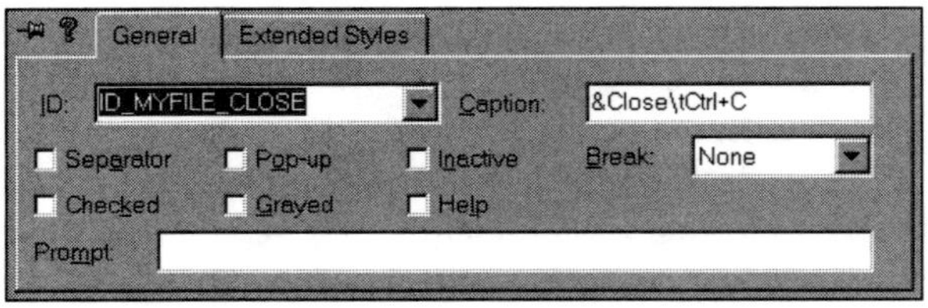

Figure 5-8: Developer Studio menu editor screen showing the insertion of a shortcut key code

But the shortcut key label is only a caption and has no effect on the processing. To associate a shortcut key with a menu item, you must create an accelerator table. The following steps can be followed:

1. Select Resource from the Developer Studio Insert menu. Select the Accelerator resource type in the dialog box and click New.
2. Create an accelerator table. The table includes an identification field that contains the resource ID, a key field for the keystroke that activates the shortcut, and a type field that specifies the properties of the key. Figure 5-9 shows the Accel Properties dialog box in the accelerator editor.

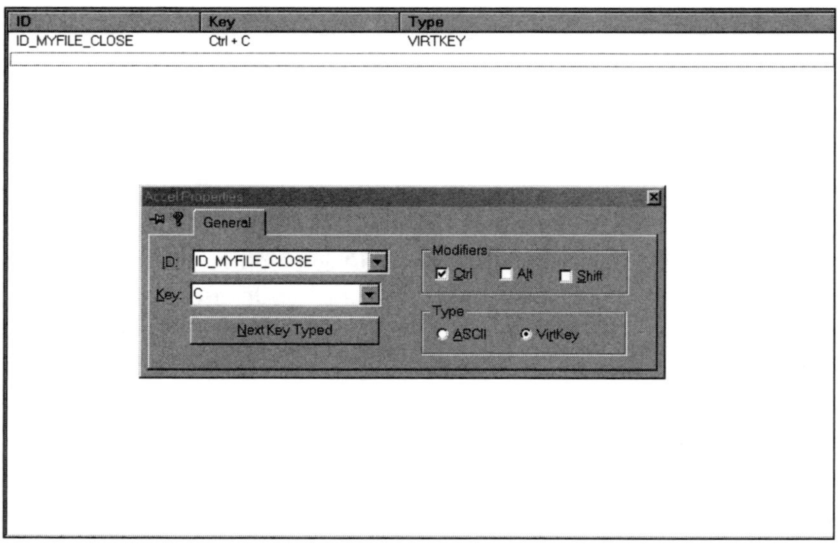

Figure 5-9: Developer Studio accelerator editor

3. Once created, the accelerator table becomes a program resource whose name can be found in the Resource tab of Developer Studio project workspace pane, or by clicking the Resource Symbols command in the View menu or its corresponding toolbar button. Developer Studio assigns the name `IDR_ACCELERATOR1` to the first accelerator table – normally only one per application.

4. The accelerator table must now be loaded into the application and processed so that the corresponding messages are sent to the windows procedure. This requires using the `LoadAccelerator()` function. Its parameters are the handle to the program's instance and an identifier of the accelerator table. `LoadAccelerator()` returns a handle to the accelerator, of type `HACCEL`. Processing of accelerator keys is by means of the `TranslateAccelerator()` function, which takes as parameters the handle to the window whose messages are to be translated, the handle to the accelerator table returned by `LoadAccelerator()`, and a pointer to a message structure. Both functions are usually included in `WinMain()`, as in the following code fragment:

```
LRESULT CALLBACK WinMain (HINSTANCE hInstance, HINSTANCE
                         hPrevInstance, PSTR szCmdLine,
                         int iCmdShow) {
     static char szAppName[] = "Demo" ;
     HWND        hwnd ;
     MSG         msg ;
     HACCEL      hAccel;         // Handle to accelerator
    .
    .
    .
     ShowWindow (hwnd, iCmdShow) ;
     UpdateWindow (hwnd) ;
    // Load accelerators
       hAccel = LoadAccelerators (hInstance,
                   MAKEINTRESOURCE (IDR_ACCELERATOR1));
     // Message loop
     while (GetMessage (&msg, NULL, 0, 0)) {
          if (!TranslateAccelerator (hwnd, hAccel, &msg)) {
             TranslateMessage (&msg) ;
             DispatchMessage (&msg) ;
          }
     }
     return msg.wParam ;
}
```

Pop-up Menus

A pop-up menu is a context-sensitive submenu activated by clicking the right mouse button. The pop-up menu is unrelated to the application's main menu and implemented differently. The items in a pop-up menu should be related to the context in which the right mouse button is pressed. Therefore, in a full-featured application, the processing usually requires calculating the screen coordinates where the mouse action takes place, or the object currently selected, to determine which, among several pop-up menus, is to be activated.

As with the program's main menu, several methods can create a pop-up menu. You can use the menu editor to create a pop-up menu, but a little trickery is required since pop-up menus have no title and the menu editor does not allow creating menu items without first entering the title. The following steps can be used to create and install a simple pop-up menu:

1. Use the menu editor to create the pop-up menu. To create a drop-down menu you have to enter a temporary menu title. Because this title is used by Developer Studio name mangler to create the item id, it may be a good idea to used the menu title "popup1."
2. Under the temporary menu title (popup1 is the suggested one), enter the menu items as you would for a program menu. You can use all of the attributes available and there can be child menus in the pop-up. Once you have finished creating the menu, double-click the temporary menu title (popup1) and erase all the characters in the caption field. This creates a drop-down menu with no menu title. To see the drop-down menu you have to click on the left corner of the menu editor's title bar. This can be a little deceptive because at times it may seem like the drop-down menu has disappeared.
3. When you close the menu editor, a new menu resource appears in the Resource tab of the Program window. If this is your second menu it is named IDR_MENU2. The new menu is now included in your script resource file.
4. You need to load the pop-up menu and obtain its handle. This can be done in the `WM_CREATE` message intercept of the window that contains it. It requires the use of the `LoadMenu()` function, which returns a handle to the menu resource. The `GetSubMenu()` function converts this handle into a submenu handle, which can then be used by the code. Processing usually occurs as follows:

```
static  HMENU   pMenu;     // Handle to pop-up menu
        .
```

```
     .
     .
case WM_CREATE:
    hdc = GetDC(hwnd);
    // Get handle to pop-up menu
    pMenu = LoadMenu(pInstance,
                   (MAKEINTRESOURCE(IDR_MENU2)));
    pMenu = GetSubMenu(pMenu, 0);
    return 0;
```

5. Once you have its handle, the pop-up menu can be displayed. The TrackPopupMenu() function defines the screen location where the pop-up menu is shown, its position relative to the mouse cursor, and which mouse button actions, if any, are tracked when an item is selected. If the pop-up menu is activated by the right mouse button, as is usually the case, then the menu display code can be placed at the corresponding message intercept, as in the following code fragment:

```
case WM_RBUTTONDOWN:
    // Get mouse coordinates
    aPoint.x = LOWORD(lParam);
    aPoint.y = HIWORD(lParam);
    ClientToScreen(hwnd, &aPoint);
    TrackPopupMenu(pMenu,
                   TPM_LEFTALIGN | TPM_TOPALIGN |\
                   TPM_LEFTBUTTON,
                   aPoint.x, aPoint.y,
                   0,
                   hwnd,
                   NULL);
    return 0;
```

In the preceding code sample we start by obtaining the mouse coordinates from the lParam. One problem is that TrackPopupMenu() requires the horizontal and vertical coordinates in screen units, and the WM_RBUTTONDOWN message intercept reports the mouse position in client area units. For this reason, the ClientToScreen() function is necessary to convert client area into screen coordinates.

The TrackPopupMenu() function displays the pop-up menu. Its first parameter is the handle to the menu obtained during WM_CREATE processing. The second parameter is one or more bitwise constants. In this case we have established that the display position is relative to the upper-left corner of the menu box, and that the left mouse button is the one tracked for menu selections. The display points are entered as the third and fourth parameters to the call. The fifth one is reserved (must be zero), the sixth one is the handle to the window that owns the pop-up menu, and the last one defines a RECT-type structure in which the user can click without erasing the pop-up menu. If this value is NULL then the shortcut menu disappears if the user clicks outside its area.

6. Intercepting action on the pop-up menu is at WM_COMMAND message processing. For example, if the id of the first item in the pop-up menu is ID_POPUP1_UNDO, then the case statement at the intercept point has this label, as follows:

```
case WM_COMMAND:
    switch (LOWORD (wParam)) {
    .
    .
    .
    case ID_POPUP1_UNDO:
    // Assert:
    //   User clicked "undo" item on pop-up menu
```

The Menu Demonstration Program

The program named MEN_DEMO, contained in the *Menu Demo* project folder on the book's CD-ROM, is a trivial demonstration of an application with a main menu, a shortcut key (accelerator) to access one of the menu items, and a pop-up menu displayed when the user right-clicks on the client area. Processing consists of a message box that lists the menu item selected by the user.

Dialog Boxes

Dialog boxes are a programming aid; they provide no new functionality. Everything that can be done in a dialog box can also be done in a child window, as described earlier in this chapter.

Dialog boxes prepackage a series of frequently needed functions for the programmer. Also, dialog boxes perform much of the processing and housekeeping operations for you. They handle the keyboard focus, passing keyboard input from one control to another one, they monitor mouse movements, and they provide a special procedure for tracking action on the controls contained in the dialog box. When used in conjunction with the dialog box editor in Developer Studio, dialog boxes are easy to create and implement in code.

Windows 3.1 introduced an extension to the concept of dialog boxes, usually called the *common dialog boxes*. The common dialog boxes are a set of prepackaged services for operations that are required often in different applications. These include opening and saving files, selecting a font, selecting or changing color attributes, searching and replacing text strings, and controlling the printer. The common dialog boxes are discussed later in this section.

Modal and Modeless

There are two general types of dialog boxes: those that suspend the application until the user interacts with the dialog box, and those that do not. The first type, which are the most common, are called *modal dialog boxes*. The second type, which are often seen in floating toolbars, are called *modeless dialog boxes*. Modal dialog boxes do not prevent the user from switching to another application. Although, upon return to the original thread, it is the modal dialog box that retains the foreground. *The Windows Interface Guidelines for Software Design* (see bibliography) recommends that modal dialog boxes should have an OK button, to accept and process input, and a Cancel button to abort execution and discard the user's action with the dialog box.

The Message Box

The simplest of all dialog boxes displays a message on the screen, which the user acknowledges having read by pressing a button. A special function in the Windows API enables the creation of message boxes directly, without having to use the dialog box editor or manipulate a program resource. The message box contains a title, a message, any one of several predefined icons, and one or more push buttons. The general form of the function call is as follows:

```
int MessageBox(hwnd, lpText, lpCaption, uType);
int MessageBox(
          HWND hWnd,          // 1
          LPCTSTR lpText,     // 2
          LPCTSTR lpCaption,  // 3
          UINT uType          // 4
                         );
```

in which `hwnd` is the handle to the window that owns the message box, `lpText` is a pointer to the text message to be displayed (or the message string itself), `lpCaption` is a pointer to the caption (or the caption string itself), and `uType` is one of several bit flags that control the behavior of the message box. Table 5-8 lists the most useful bit flags used in the `MessageBox()` function.

Table 5-8 MOST-USED MESSAGE BOX BIT FLAGS

Symbolic Constant	Meaning
MB_ABORTRETRYIGNORE	Contains three push buttons: Abort, Retry, and Ignore.
MB_OK	Contains one push button: OK. This is the default.
MB_OKCANCEL	Contains two push buttons: OK and Cancel.
MB_RETRYCANCEL	The message box contains two push buttons: Retry and Cancel.
MB_YESNO	Contains two push buttons: Yes and No.
MB_YESNOCANCEL	Contains three push buttons: Yes, No, and Cancel.
Icon Flags	
MB_ICONEXCLAMATION	Exclamation-point icon.
MB_ICONWARNING	Exclamation-point icon.
MB_ICONINFORMATION	Question mark icon.
MB_ICONASTERISK	Lowercase letter i icon in a circle.
MB_ICONQUESTION	Question-mark icon.
MB_ICONSTOP	Stop-sign icon.
MB_ICONERRO	Hand icon.
MB_ICONHAND	Hand icon.
Default Button Flags:	
MB_DEFBUTTON1	The first button is the default button.
MB_DEFBUTTON2	The second button is the default button.
MB_DEFBUTTON3	The third button is the default button.
MB_DEFBUTTON4	The fourth button is the default button.
Modality Flags	
MB_APPLMODAL	User must respond to the message box before continuing work in the window. However, the user can move to the windows of other applications and work in those windows.
MB_SYSTEMMODAL	Same as MB_APPLMODAL except that the message box has the WS_EX_TOPMOST style. Use system-modal message boxes to notify the user of serious errors that require immediate attention.

Symbolic Constant	Meaning
Modality Flags *(Continued)*	
MB_TASKMODAL	Same as MB_APPLMODAL except that all the top-level windows belonging to the current task are disabled if the hwnd parameter is NULL.
Other Flags:	
MB_HELP	Adds a Help button to the message box. Choosing the Help button or pressing F1 generates a Help event.
MB_RIGHT	The text is right-justified.
MB_SETFOREGROUND	The message box becomes the foreground window. Internally, Windows calls the SetForegroundWindow function for the message box.
MB_TOPMOST	Message box is created with the WS_EX_TOPMOST window style.

For example, the following statement creates a message box labeled "Menu Action," with the text string "File Close Requested," which contains an exclamation sign icon, and a button labeled OK:

```
MessageBox (hwnd,
           "File Close Requested",
           "Menu Action",
            MB_ICONEXCLAMATION | MB_OK);
```

Figure 5-10 shows the resulting message box.

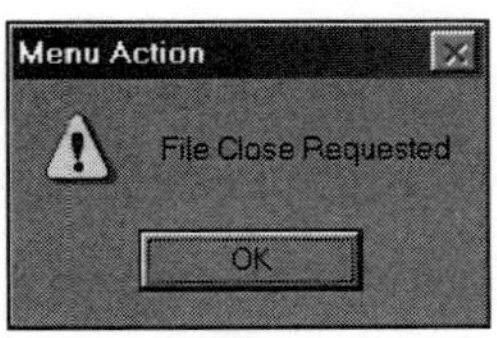

Figure 5-10: Simple message box

Creating a Modal Dialog Box

Developer Studio provides a dialog box editor, which is a tool for creating dialog boxes. When the dialog box has been created, it becomes another program resource that can be referenced in the code. The dialog box editor can be used to create simple message boxes; however, in this case it is easier to use the `MessageBox()` function described in the previous section. Dialog boxes are useful when they are used to obtain user input.

A unique feature of dialog boxes is that they contain their own processing. In a sense, the dialog box procedure is like your window procedure, although the dialog box processing takes place inside Windows.

You create a modal dialog box by means of the `DialogBox()` function, with the following standard form:

```
int DialogBox (hInstance, lpTemplate, hwndParent, lpDiaProc);
```

in which `hInstance` is the handle to the program instance that contains the dialog box, `lpTemplate` identifies the dialog box template or resource, `hwndParent` is the handle to the owner window, and `lpDiaProc` is the name of the dialog box procedure. It is this procedure that receives control when the dialog box is created. The following code fragment shows the creation of a dialog box at the time that a menu command with the id `ID_DIALOG_ABOUT` is intercepted:

```
ID_DIALOG_ABOUT:
  DialogBox (pInstance,
             MAKEINTRESOURCE (IDD_DIALOG1),
             hwnd,
             (DLGPROC) AboutDlgProc);
```

In this case the dialog box resource is named `IDD_DIALOG1`, and the dialog box procedure that receives control is `AboutDlgProc()`. The dialog box procedure's general form is as follow:

```
BOOL DialogProc (hwndDlg, uMsg, wParam, lParam);
BOOL CALLBACK DialogProc(
             HWND hwndDlg,  // 1
             UINT uMsg,     // 2
             WPARAM wParam, // 3
             LPARAM lParam  // 4
             );
```

in which `DialogProc` is the name of the procedure defined in the `lpDiaProc` field of the `DialogBox()` function. The first parameter passed to the dialog procedure (`hwndDlg`) is the handle to the dialog box. The second one is the Windows message.

The wParam and lParam values contain message-specific information, as is the case in the window procedure.

As soon as the dialog box is created, and before it is displayed, Windows sends the WM_INITDIALOG message to the dialog box procedure. Typically, the dialog box procedure intercepts the message to initialize controls and perform other housekeeping functions. In j the wParam contains the handle to the control that has focus, which is the first visible and not disabled control in the box. The application returns TRUE to accept this default focus. Alternatively, the application can set the focus to another control, in which case it returns FALSE.

The dialog box procedure receives messages for the controls in the dialog box. These messages can be intercepted in the same manner as those sent to the window procedure. The following code fragment is a dialog box procedure for a dialog box that contains a single button:

```
BOOL CALLBACK AboutDlgProc (HWND hDlg, UINT iMsg, WPARAM wParam,
                            LPARAM lParam) {
 switch (iMsg) {
    case WM_INITDIALOG :
      return TRUE ;
    // Dialog box controls message intercepts
    case WM_COMMAND :
      switch (LOWORD (wParam)) { // Get control id
         case IDOK :
           EndDialog (hDlg, 0) ;
           return TRUE ;
         }
    break ;
    }
  return FALSE ;
  }
```

Notice that, unlike a window function, AboutDlgProc() does not return control via the default window procedure. In general, a dialog box procedure returns FALSE to indicate that default processing is to be provided by Windows and TRUE when no further processing is required. The exception is the WM_INITDIALOG message in which the return value refers to the acceptance or rejection of the default focus, as discussed previously.

NOTE: Dialog procedures, like all window procedures, have to be of type CALLBACK. Failing to declare a window procedure, or a callback procedure, with this type, can be the source of unpredictable errors, such as the General Protection Fault.

You can create a dialog box by means of the following steps:

1. Select Resource from theDeveloper Studio Insert menu. Select the Dialog resource type in the dialog box and click New.
2. The dialog box editor executes by displaying a blank form and a floating toolbox containing controls that can be inserted in the dialog box. If the toolbar is not visible, you can show it on the editor screen by opening the Tools menu, then selecting Customize, and checking the Controls box in the Toolbars tab. The controls include all those already mentioned and some others. To add a control to the dialog box, you drag it onto the form and then use the handles to size it. Double-clicking on the form, or on one of the controls, displays a Dialog Properties window which allows defining the attributes of that particular element. Figure 5-11 shows the dialog box editor with the Dialog Properties windows for the form and the Controls toolbox.

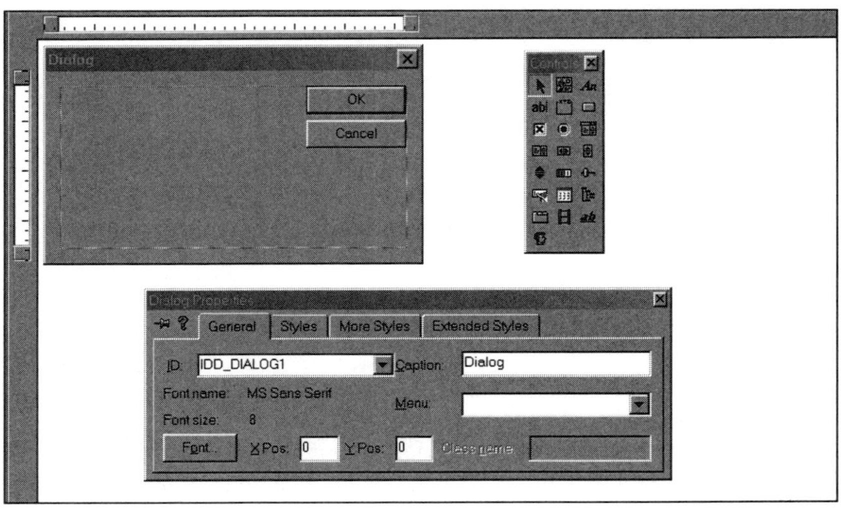

Figure 5-11: Developer Studio dialog editor

3. Once you have finished creating the dialog box, click the Close button of the menu editor window. If the application already has a script file, the dialog box is added to it. If not, Developer Studio prompts you to save the new script file.
4. Skip this step if a script file has already been inserted into the project. If not, open the Project menu, select Add to Project, and then select Files.

In the Insert Files into Project dialog box, select the script file and then click OK. The script file now appears in the Developer Studio project workspace pane.

4. Select Resource View button in project workspace pane and click + on Script Resources. Click + on Dialog. Note the identifier name for the dialog box resource, (usually IDD_DIALOG1) if this is the first dialog box created.

5. Your code must now create the dialog box, usually by intercepting the corresponding menu command and calling DialogBox(). Also, the dialog box procedure has to intercept the WM_INITDIALOG message and provide handlers for the controls contained in the box, as previously described.

Creating a Modeless Dialog Box

A modeless dialog box creates a window independent from its owner and acts much like its peer. A modeless dialog box does not disable the owner window; therefore the user can alternatively interact with either the parent or the modeless child window. This characteristic makes modeless dialog boxes particularly useful for creating toolboxes and other program elements that remain displayed while the main application is on the screen. For example, the find-and-replace function found in most word-processing programs is usually implemented by means of a modeless dialog box.

Modeless dialog boxes often include a caption bar, caption bar buttons, and a system menu box. The style constants most frequently used with modeless dialog boxes are WP_POPUP, WS_CAPTION, WS_SYSMENU, and WS_VISIBLE. If the WS_VISIBLE style constant is not included, then code must call ShowWindow() to display the modeless box. The caption bar allows moving the dialog box on the screen. If you are using Developer Studio for creating the dialog box, as explained in the preceding section, then you use the Dialog Properties box to select the box style.

Several functions and macros can be used to create a modeless dialog box, including CreateDialog(), CreateDialogIndirect(), CreateDialogParam(), and CreateDialogIndirectParam(). The first one, CreateDialog(), which is actually a macro for CreateDialogParam(), is by far the most common one. It allows creating a dialog box from a program resource. Its general form is as follows:

```
HWND CreateDialog(
                    HINSTANCE hInstance,        // 1
                    LPCTSTR lpTemplate,         // 2
                    HWND hWndParent,            // 3
                    DLGPROC lpDialogFunc        // 4
                    );
```

The first parameter identifies an instance of the module whose executable file contains the dialog box template. The second parameter refers to the dialog box template. This parameter is either the pointer to a null-terminated character string that specifies the name of the dialog box template or an integer value that specifies the corresponding resource identifier. You can use the MAKEINTRESOURCE macro to create this value from the resource. The third parameter identifies the window that owns the dialog box. The fourth parameter is a pointer to the dialog box procedure.

If the function succeeds, the return value is the handle to the dialog box. The function returns NULL if it fails.

CreateDialog() uses the CreateWindowEx() to create the dialog box. CreateDialog() then sends a WM_INITDIALOG message to the corresponding dialog box procedure. If the template specifies the WS_VISIBLE style, then the dialog box is displayed. If this style is not used, then the application displays the dialog box by calling ShowWindow().

Modeless dialog box processing takes place in the dialog box procedure, which is the same one previously described for modal dialog boxes. One difference between modal and modeless dialog boxes is that messages for modeless boxes are received through the application's message loop. This requires modifying the message loop so that it checks for messages intended for the modeless dialog box. The IsDialogMessage() function performs this function. Its general form reads as follows:

```
BOOL IsDialogMessage(
                    HWND hDlg,          // 1
                    LPMSG,lpMsg         // 2
                    );
```

The first parameter identifies the dialog box. The second one points to a structure variable of type MSG that contains the message to be checked.

Applications that use modeless dialog boxes usually maintain a global variable to indicate whether the modeless box is active. This prevents IsDialogMessage() being called with an invalid handle. The same variable can be used elsewhere in the program to determine if the modeless dialog box is currently displayed. When the box is destroyed in the dialog box procedure, the variable can be set to zero. The following code fragment shows the processing for a modeless dialog box in the *Dialog Box Demo* project program on the book's CD-ROM.

```
// Global variables
HWND          hDlgModeless;          // Handle to modeless DB
int           modeless = 0;          // Modeless state
   .
   .
```

```
  .
// The message loop is modified to handle the modeless
// dialog box messages
     while (GetMessage (&msg, NULL, 0, 0))
          {
        if (hDlgModeless == 0 ||
                   !IsDialogMessage (hDlgModeless, &msg))
            {
                TranslateMessage (&msg) ;
                DispatchMessage (&msg) ;
              }
          }
   .
   .
   .
   /*******************************
      Dialog menu processing
    *******************************/
    // Modeless dialog box command
        case ID_DIALOG_MODELESS:
             if (modeless == 0) {
                 modeless = 1;
                 hDlgModeless = CreateDialog (pInstance,
                        MAKEINTRESOURCE (IDD_DIALOG4), hwnd,
                        (DLGPROC) TestDlgProc);
              }
        return 0 ;
   .
   .
   .
/*******************************************
     Modeless box dialog box procedure
*******************************************/
BOOL CALLBACK TestDlgProc (HWND hDlg,
                           UINT iMsg,
                           WPARAM wParam,
                           LPARAM lParam)
{
   switch (iMsg)
     {
       case WM_INITDIALOG :
         BringWindowToTop(hDlg);
```

```
        SetFocus(hDlg);
        SendMessage(hDlg, DM_REPOSITION, 0, 0);
        return TRUE ;

      case WM_COMMAND :
        switch (LOWORD (wParam)) {
           case ID_BOX_CLOSE:
           case WM_CLOSE:
              MessageBeep(0);
              modeless = 0;       // Modeless box closed
              DestroyWindow (hDlg) ;

            return TRUE ;
        }
      break ;
   }
  return FALSE ;
}
```

Common Dialog Boxes

Windows 3.1 introduced the common dialog boxes as a set of prepackaged services for performing routine operations required in many applications. The idea behind them is to standardize frequent input functions so that they appear the same in different program functions and even in different applications. For example, the common dialog box used to select a filename and to browse through the disk storage system is the same if you are opening or saving a file. Furthermore, two applications that manipulate files can use the same common dialog box, giving the user a familiar interface. The following operations can be performed by means of common dialog boxes: opening and saving files, selecting fonts, selecting or changing color attributes, searching and replacing text strings, and controlling the printer. Common dialog boxes have a modal behavior, that is, the program is suspended until the user closes the dialog box.

Common dialog boxes are processed internally by Windows; therefore, they do not have a dialog box procedure.

The identification for the menu item or other resource that activates the common dialog box usually serves as the message intercept. The processing is done directly in the intercept routine. Each common dialog box is associated with a structure that serves to pass information to it and to receive the results of the user's action. Programs that use common dialog boxes should include the commdlg.h header file.

For example, the menu item `ID_DIALOG_COLORSELECTOR` can intercept user action in `WM_COMMAND` message processing and then proceed to fill a variable of the structure type `CHOOSECOLOR` (see Appendix A) as in the following code fragment:

```
LRESULT CALLBACK WndProc (HWND hwnd, UINT iMsg, WPARAM wParam,
                          LPARAM lParam) {
  HDC          hdc ;
  TEXTMETRIC   tm ;
  HBRUSH       hBrush;      // Handle to brush

  // Variables for color and font common dialog
  static CHOOSECOLOR cc ;   // Structure
  static COLORREF    custColors[16] ; // Array for custom
                                      // colors
  int    i;            // counter for custom color display
  switch (iMsg) {
     .
     .
     .
    case WM_COMMAND:
       switch (LOWORD (wParam)) {
        // Color Selector common dialog
         case ID_DIALOG_COLORSELECTOR:
         cc.lStructSize    = sizeof (CHOOSECOLOR) ;
         cc.hwndOwner      = hwnd ;
         cc.hInstance      = NULL ;
         cc.rgbResult      = RGB (0x80, 0x80, 0x80) ;
         cc.lpCustColors   = custColors ;
         cc.Flags          = CC_RGBINIT | CC_FULLOPEN ;
         cc.lCustData      = 0L ;
         cc.lpfnHook       = NULL ;
         cc.lpTemplateName = NULL ;
         .
         .
         .
```

Once the structure variable is filled with the necessary data, the application can call the `ChooseColor()` function to display the common dialog box. `ChooseColor()` requires a single parameter: the address of the previously mentioned structure. Most of the structure members are obvious. The `lpCustColors` member is an array of 16 `COLORREF`-type values that holds the RGB values for the custom colors in the dialog box. The Flags members are bit flags that determine the operation of the dialog box. In the previous example we set `CC_RGBINIT` bit so that the `rgbREsult` member holds the initial color selection. The values 0 by 80 for each of the red, green, and blue components produce a middle gray color. The last three members of the structure are used for customizing the dialog box. The constant `CC_FULLOPEN` causes the dialog box to open in the full display mode, that is, with the controls necessary for the user to create custom colors.

`ChooseColor()` returns TRUE if the user clicks the OK button on the dialog box. Therefore, the coding continues as follows:

```
if (ChooseColor (&cc) == TRUE) {
// ASSERT:
//   structure members have color data selected by user
// Clear the client window
hdc = GetDC(hwnd);
InvalidateRect (hwnd, NULL, TRUE) ;
UpdateWindow (hwnd) ;
```

The colors selected by the user are stored in two members of the `CHOOSECOLOR` structure: `rbgResult` holds the solid color box, and the array variable `custColor` holds the 16 custom colors. The code now creates a solid brush, using the color stored in the `rgbResult` member, and displays a rectangle filled with this color. Then a loop displays the first eight of the 16 custom colors:

```
  hBrush = CreateSolidBrush(cc.rgbResult);
  // Select the brush in the DC
  SelectObject (hdc, hBrush) ;
  // Draw a rectangle using the brush
  Rectangle (hdc, 20, 20, 100, 100) ;
  // Display first eight custom colors using the
  // color triplets stored in the custColors array
      for (i = 0; i < 8; i++) {
          hBrush = CreateSolidBrush(custColors[i]);
                   SelectObject (hdc, hBrush) ;
                   Rectangle (hdc, 20+(20 * i), 120,
                   40+(20 * i), 140) ;
           }
       // Clear and exit
       DeleteObject (SelectObject (hdc, hBrush)) ;
       ReleaseDC (hwnd, hdc);
  }
return 0 ;
    .
    .
    .
```

Figure 5-12 shows the color dialog box as displayed by this code.

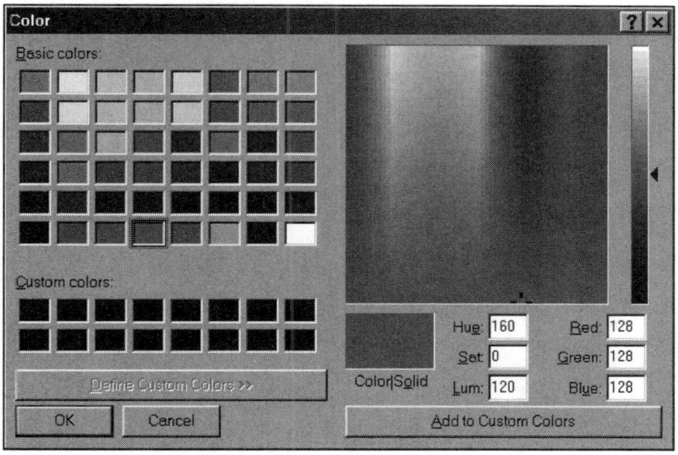

Figure 5-12: Color common dialog box

The Dialog Box Demonstration Program

The program named DIA_DEMO, contained in the *Dialog Box Demo* project folder on the book's CD-ROM, is a trivial demonstration of several dialog boxes. The Dialog menu contains commands for creating a modeless dialog box, three different modal dialog boxes (one of them with a bitmap), and for the color and font common dialog boxes. The code demonstrates how information obtained by modal and common dialog boxes is passed to the application.

Common Controls

Windows 95 introduced a new set of controls that supplement the ones that existed previously. They are also available in Windows NT version 3.51 and later. These controls, sometimes referred to as the *new common controls*, allow the implementation of status bars, toolbars, trackbars, progress bars, animation controls, image lists, list-view controls, tree-view controls, property sheets, tabs, wizards, and rich-edit controls. It is evident from this list that one could devote an entire volume to their discussion. Table 5-9 is a list of the Windows common controls first implemented in Windows 95.

Table 5-9 COMMON CONTROLS INTRODUCED IN WINDOWS 95

Control	Description
Frame Window Controls	
toolbar	Displays a window with command-generating buttons
ToolTip	Small pop-up window that describes purpose of a toolbar button or other tool
status bar	Displays status information at the bottom screen line
Explorer-type Controls	
list view	Displays a list of text with icons
tree view	Displays a hierarchical list of items
Miscellaneous Controls	
animation	Displays successive frames of an AVI video clip
header	Appears above a column of text. Controls width of text displayed
hotkey	Enables user to perform an action quickly
image list	A collection of images used to manage large sets of icons or bitmaps. It isn't really a control, but supports lists used by other controls
progress bar	Indicates progress of a long operation
rich edit	Allows the user to edit with character and paragraph formatting
slider	Displays a slider control with optional tick marks
spin button	Displays a pair of arrow buttons user can click to increment or decrement a value
tab	Displays divider-like elements used in tabbed dialog boxes or property sheets

Before we can implement the new common controls, some preliminary steps are required. The reason is that the common controls library is not automatically referenced at link time, nor is it initialized for operation. The following sequence of operations is necessary:

1. The common controls library, named Comctl32.lib, must be included in the list of libraries referenced by the linker program. This is accomplished

by opening the Project menu and selecting the Settings command. In the Project Settings dialog box, open the Link tab. The "Object/library modules" edit box contains a list of all the referenced libraries, separated from one another by a space. Position the caret between two library entries and type "Comctl32.lib." Click the OK button.

2. The program code must include the common controls header file. This is accomplished with the statement:

```
#include <commctrl.h>
```

3. The InitCommonControls() function must be called before the common controls are used. This function takes no parameters and returns nothing. The initialization can be placed in `WinMain()`, as follows:

```
InitCommonControls();
```

4. Rich edit controls reside in their own library, named Riched32.dll and have their own header file, named richedit.h. To use library controls your program must include the statement:

```
LoadLibrary ("RICHED32.DLL");
```

At this point the application can implement common controls. In this section we sample some of the common controls more frequently found in graphics applications, namely toolbars and ToolTip controls. These, together with the status bar controls, are sometimes called the *frame window controls*. Some common controls are available in the toolbar of Developer Studio dialog box editor. The resource editor contains a specific toolbar editor for creating this type of common control. Most common controls can also be created by means of the `CreateWindow()` or `CreateWindowEx()` functions. Others have a dedicated function, such as `CreateToolbarEx()`.

Common Controls Message Processing

Most common controls send `WM_NOTIFY` messages. One notable exception is the toolbar controls, which send `WM_COMMAND`. In processing common controls messages we follow methods similar to those in processing menu selections.

The `WM_NOTIFY` message contains the ID of the control in `wParam` and a pointer to a structure in `lParam`. The structure is either an `NMHDR` structure, or more frequently, a larger structure that has an `NMHDR` structure as its first member. The common notifications (whose names start with `NM_`) and the ToolTip control's `TTN_SHOW` and `TTN_POP` notifications, are the only cases in which the `NMHDR` structure is actually used by itself. The format of the `NMHDR` structure is as follows:

```
typedef struct tagNMHDR {
    HWND hwndFrom;
    UINT idFrom;
```

```
    UINT code;
} NMHDR;
```

in which hwndFrom is the handle to the controls sending the message, idFrom is the control identifier, and code is one of values in Table 5-10.

TABLE 5-10 NOTIFICATION CODE FROM COMMON CONTROLS

Code	Action in Control or Results
NM_CLICK	User clicked left mouse button
NM_DBLCLK	User double-clicked left mouse button
NM_RCLICK	User clicked right mouse button
NM_RDBLCLK	User double-clicked right mouse button
NM_RETURN	User pressed the Enter key
NM_SETFOCUS	Control has been given input focus
NM_KILLFOCUS	Control has lost input focus
NM_OUTOFMEMORY	Control could not complete an operation because there was not enough memory available

Most often notifications pass a pointer to a larger structure that contains an NMHDR structure as its first member. For example, the list view control uses the LVN_KEYDOWN notification message, which is sent when a key is pressed. In this case the pointer is to an LV_KEYDOWN structure, defined as follows:

```
typedef struct tagLV_KEYDOWN {
    NMHDR hdr;
    WORD wVKey;
    UINT flags;
} LV_KEYDOWN;
```

Since the NMHDR member is the first one in this structure, the pointer in the notification message can be cast to either a pointer to an NMHDR or a pointer to an LV_KEYDOWN.

Toolbars and ToolTips

A toolbar is a window containing graphics buttons or other controls. It is usually located between the client area and the menu bar. Although Windows applications have been using toolbars for a long time, there was no system support for toolbars until the release of the WIN-32 API. The most common use of toolbars is to provide fast access to menu commands. Toolbars often include separators, which are spaces in the toolbar that allow grouping associated buttons. A ToolTip is a small pop-up window displayed when the mouse is left on a toolbar button for more than one-half second. ToolTips usually consist of a short text message that explains the function of the toolbar button or control. Figure 5-13 shows a program containing a toolbar with nine buttons.

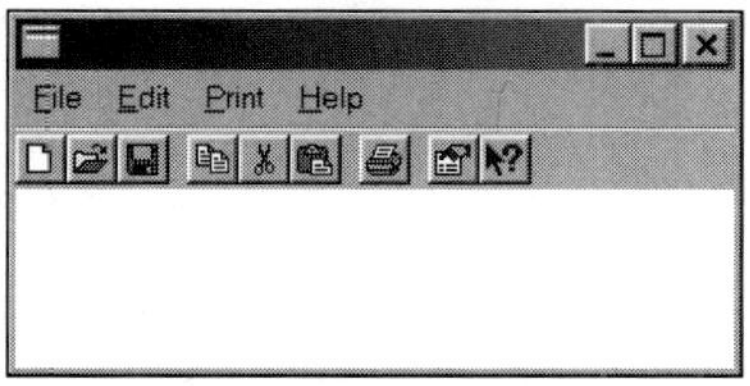

Figure 5-13: Screen dump of a program containing a toolbar

Note that in Figure 5-13 separators are used to group the toolbar buttons. In this case, the first group of buttons correspond with functions in the File menu, the second group with functions in the Edit menu, and so forth. Normally, not all menu commands have a toolbar button, but only the ones most often used.

Creating a Toolbar

There are several ways to create a toolbar. You can define the toolbar in code, using standard buttons furnished in Visual C++. You can use a premade bitmap of toolbar buttons, which can be converted into a toolbar resource and then edited. You can create custom buttons using the toolbar editor. Or you can use a combination of these methods. In this section we follow the simplest method, but even then, you must be careful to perform the steps in the same order in which we list them. The toolbar creation tools in Developer Studio are designed to be used in MFC programming; therefore, the system makes assumptions regarding the order in which the steps are performed. If you are careless in this respect, you may end up having to do some manual editing of the resource files.

We must accept that complications in creating a toolbar outside the MFC exist. However, much suffering can be avoided if the toolbar is not created until the program menu has been defined. The idea is to use the same identification codes for the toolbar as for the corresponding menu items, such that message processing takes place at the same intercept routine. For example, if the first toolbar button in Figure 5-13 corresponds to the New command in the File menu, then both the button and the menu item could be named `ID_FILE_NEW`. The same applies to the other buttons in the toolbar. In the following description about the creation of a toolbar we assume that the identification strings have been defined for the corresponding menu entries:

```
File menu:
         ID_FILE_NEW
         ID_FILE_OPEN'
         ID_FILE_SAVE
Edit menu:
         ID_EDIT_CUT
         ID_EDIT_COPY
         ID_EDIT_PASTE
Print menu:
         ID_PRT_PRINT
Help menu:
         ID_HLP_ABOUT
         ID_HLP_HELP
```

All of the toolbar buttons in Figure 5-13 correspond to standard buttons contained in Developer Studio. These buttons can be loaded into the toolbar by referencing their system names, or by loading a bitmap that contains them. In the current example we use the bitmap approach.

Toolbars require that each of the buttons be defined in a structure of type TBBUTTON (see Appendix A). Your program, usually in the window procedure, creates an array of structures, with one entry for each button in the toolbar. The button separators must be included. In the case of the screen in Figure 5-13, the array of TBBUTTON structure looks as follows:

```
// Array for attributes for toolbar buttons
 TBBUTTON tbb[] = {
0, ID_FILE_NEW,    TBSTATE_ENABLED, TBSTYLE_BUTTON, 0, 0, 0, 0,
1, ID_FILE_OPEN,   TBSTATE_ENABLED, TBSTYLE_BUTTON, 0, 0, 0, 0,
2, ID_FILE_SAVE,   TBSTATE_ENABLED, TBSTYLE_BUTTON, 0, 0, 0, 0,
0, 0,              TBSTATE_ENABLED, TBSTYLE_SEP,    0, 0, 0, 0,
3, ID_EDIT_CUT,    TBSTATE_ENABLED, TBSTYLE_BUTTON, 0, 0, 0, 0,
4, ID_EDIT_COPY,   TBSTATE_ENABLED, TBSTYLE_BUTTON, 0, 0, 0, 0,
5, ID_EDIT_PASTE,  TBSTATE_ENABLED, TBSTYLE_BUTTON, 0, 0, 0, 0,
0, 0,              TBSTATE_ENABLED, TBSTYLE_SEP,    0, 0, 0, 0,
6, ID_PRT_PRINT,   TBSTATE_ENABLED, TBSTYLE_BUTTON, 0, 0, 0, 0,
0, 0,              TBSTATE_ENABLED, TBSTYLE_SEP,    0, 0, 0, 0,
7, ID_HLP_ABOUT,   TBSTATE_ENABLED, TBSTYLE_BUTTON, 0, 0, 0, 0,
8, ID_HLP_HELP,    TBSTATE_ENABLED, TBSTYLE_BUTTON, 0, 0, 0, 0, }; /*
 | |------| |-------| |------| | see note |
 |     |             |               |         below
 |     |             |               |-- One or more
 |     |             |                     button styles
 |     |             |------- One or more state flags
```

```
 |       |—————————— Command ID mapped to
 |                                button
 |————————- Zero-based index to button image in
 |                       bitmap (excluding separators)
Note:
      0, 0, 0, 0
      |  |  |  |————— index of button string
      |  |-|—————- application defined value
      |——————- Reserved
*/
```

Table 5-11 lists the style flags used with toolbars.

TABLE 5-11 TOOLBAR AND TOOLBAR BUTTONS STYLE FLAGS

Toolbar Styles	Description
BSTYLE_ALTDRAG	Allows the user to change the position of a toolbar button by dragging it while holding down the Alt key. If this style is not specified, the user must hold down the Shift key while dragging a button. Note that the CCS_ADJUSTABLE style must be specified to enable toolbar buttons to be dragged.
TBSTYLE_TOOLTIPS	Creates a ToolTip control that an application can Use to display descriptive text for the buttons in the toolbar.
TBSTYLE_WRAPABLE	Creates a toolbar that can have multiple lines of buttons. Toolbar buttons can "wrap" to the next line when the toolbar becomes too narrow to include all buttons on the same line. Wrapping occurs on separation and non-group boundaries.
TBSTYLE_BUTTON	Creates a standard push button.
TBSTYLE_CHECK	Button toggles between the pressed and not-pressed states each time the user clicks it. The button has a different background color when it is in the pressed state.
TBSTYLE_CHECKGROUP	Creates a check button that stays pressed until another button in the group is pressed.
TBSTYLE_GROUP	Creates a button that stays pressed until another button in the group is pressed.
TBSTYLE_SEP	Creates a separator. A button that has this style does not receive user input and is not assigned a button number.

Table 5-12 lists the toolbar states.

TABLE 5-12 TOOLBAR STATES

Toolbar State	Description
TBSTATE_CHECKED	The button has the TBSTYLE_CHECKED style and is being pressed.
TBSTATE_ENABLED	The button accepts user input. A button not having this state does not accept user input and is grayed.
TBSTATE_HIDDEN	The button is not visible and cannot receive user input.
TBSTATE_INDETERMINATE	The button is grayed.
TBSTATE_PRESSED	The button is being pressed.
TBSTATE_WRAP	A line break follows the button. The button must also have the TBSTATE_ENABLED state.

The bitmap for the toolbar in Figure 5-13 is furnished with Developer Studio. We have made a copy of this bitmap and you can find it in the Resource directory on the book's CD-ROM. The name of the bitmap is *toolbar.bmp*. The process of creating a toolbar from a toolbar bitmap requires that you follow a certain sequence. The price to pay for changing the order of operations is that you may end up with incorrect resource files that must be manually edited. The following operations result in the toolbar resource:

1. Select Resource from the Insert menu. Select the Bitmap resource type and click the Import button.
2. In the Import Resource dialog editor, edit the filename field for that of a bitmap file. This is accomplished by entering "*.bmp". Now you can search though the file system until you find the toolbar bitmap. In this case the desired bitmap has the name "toolbar.bmp." Select the bitmap and click on the button labeled Import.
3. The toolbar bitmap is now loaded into the bitmap editor. The toolbar bitmap is shown in Figure 5-14. The buttons are labeled according to the identifications assigned in the TBBUTTON structure members listed previously.

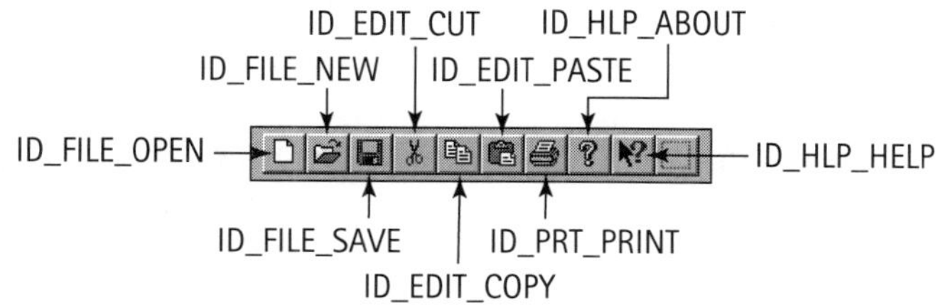

Figure 5-14: The toolbar bitmap "Toolbar.bmp" with button identification codes

4. Now you must convert the bitmap into a toolbar resource. This is accomplished by opening the Image menu and clicking on the Toolbar editor command. The New Toolbar Resource dialog box with the pixel size of normal toolbar buttons is displayed, which is 16 pixels wide and 15 pixels high. Click OK and the toolbar editor appears with the bitmap converted into a toolbar.

5. You can now proceed to edit the toolbar and assign identification codes to each of the buttons. Note the blank button at the end of the toolbar, which is for creating custom buttons. You can click on the blank button and use the editor to create a new button image. To delete a button, click on it and drag it off the toolbar. To reposition a button, click on it and drag it to it new location. To create a space in the toolbar, drag the button so that it overlaps half the width of its neighbor button. To assign an identification code to a toolbar button, double-click the button and enter the new identification in the ID: edit box of the Toolbar Button Properties dialog box. At this time you may enter the corresponding identification codes for all the buttons in the toolbar. Figure 5-15 shows the toolbar editor once the separators have been inserted.

   Figure 5-15 also shows the Toolbar Button Properties dialog box open and the new identification code in the ID: edit box.

6. Once the identification codes have been assigned to all the buttons, click the button labeled X to close the editor. Also close the next screen and save the resource file under the default name, or assign it a new one. Some programmers like to give the resource file the same base name as the application's main module. The extension for the resource file must be .RC.

7. The next step is one that you have already done for other resources: open the Project menu, click the Add To Project command, select Files, and add the resource file to the project. The toolbar is now in the project. You can use the Resource Symbols command in the View menu, or the corresponding toolbar button, to make sure that the identification codes are correct and coincide with those in the `BBUTTON` structure, and the menu items.

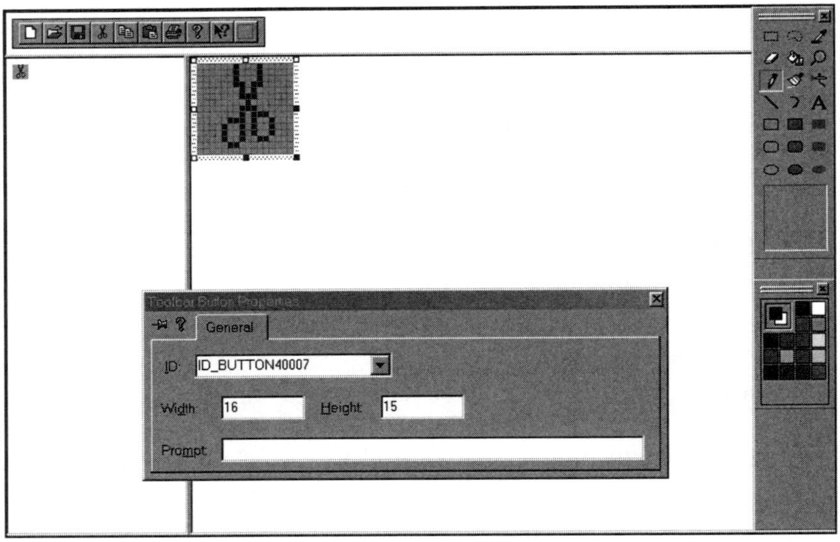

Figure 5-15: Developer Studio toolbar editor

8. Displaying the toolbar requires a call to the `CreateToolbarEx()` function. The call returns a handle to the toolbar, which is of type `HWND` since the toolbar is a window. In this example, the call is as follows:

```
#define      ID_TOOLBAR    400   // Toolbar id number
    .
    .
    .
HWND         tbHandle;      // Handle to the toolbar
    .
    .
    .
case WM_CREATE:
  // Create toolbar
  tbHandle = CreateToolbarEx (hwnd,  // Handle to window
             WS_CHILD | WS_VISIBLE |
             WS_CLIPSIBLINGS |
             CCS_TOP | TBSTYLE_ToolTipS, // Window styles
             ID_TOOLBAR,             // Toolbar identifier
             9,                      // Number of button
images
                                     // in toolbar bitmap
             hInst,                  // Module instance
             IDB_BITMAP1,            // Bitmap ID
             tbb,                    // TBBUTON structure
```

```
                12,                     // Number of buttons
                                        // plus separators
                0, 0, 0, 0,
                sizeof (TBBUTTON));
```

The second parameter in the call refers to controls bits that define the style, position, and type of toolbar. The window style `WS_CHILD` is always required and most toolbars use `WS_VISIBLE` and `WS_CHILDREN`. The bits with the `CCS_` prefix are common control styles. Table 5-13 lists the common control styles that refer to toolbars.

TABLE 5-13 TOOLBAR COMMON CONTROL STYLES

Style	Description
`CCS_ADJUSTABLE`	Allows toolbars to be customized by the user. If this style is used, the toolbar's owner window must handle the customization notification messages sent by the toolbar.
`CCS_BOTTOM`	Causes the toolbar to position itself at the bottom of the parent window's client area and sets the width to be the same as the parent window's width.
`CCS_NODIVIDER`	Prevents a two-pixel highlight from being drawn at the top of the control.
`CCS_NOHILITE`	Prevents a one-pixel highlight from being drawn at the top of the control.
`CCS_NOMOVEY`	Causes the toolbar to resize and move itself horizontally, but not vertically, in response to a `WM_SIZE` message. If the `CCS_NORESIZE` style is used, this style does not apply.
`CCS_NOPARENTALIGN`	Prevents the toolbar from automatically moving to the top or bottom of the parent window. Instead, it keeps its position within the parent window despite changes to the size of the parent window.
`CCS_NORESIZE`	Prevents the toolbar from using the default width and height when setting its initial size or a new size. Instead, the control uses the width and height specified in the request for creation or sizing.
`CCS_TOP`	Causes the control to position itself at the top of the parent window's client. The width is set to the size of the parent window. This is the default style.

In the current call to `CreateToolbarEx()` we used CCS_TOP and the `TBSTYLE_TOOLTIPS` to create a toolbar displayed above the application's client area, and to provide ToolTip support.

Standard Toolbar Buttons

The common controls library contains bitmaps for standard toolbar buttons that can be referenced by name and used by application code. In this case no toolbar bitmap is required; therefore, the button images cannot be edited in Developer Studio. There are a total of fifteen button images in two sizes, 24 by 24 pixels and 16 by 16 pixels. When using the standard toolbar buttons, the `TBBUTTON` structure must be filled differently than when using a toolbar bitmap resource. The parameters of `CreateToolbarEx()` are also different. The following code fragment shows the `TBBUTTON` structure for loading all fifteen standard toolbar buttons:

```
TBBUTTON tbb[] = {
 // File group
 STD_FILENEW,   ID_FILE_NEW,    TBSTATE_ENABLED, TBSTYLE_BUTTON,
                                0, 0, 0, 0,
 STD_FILEOPEN,  ID_FILE_OPEN,   TBSTATE_ENABLED, TBSTYLE_BUTTON,
                                0, 0, 0, 0,
 STD_FILESAVE,  ID_FILE_SAVE,   TBSTATE_ENABLED, TBSTYLE_BUTTON,
                                0, 0, 0, 0,
 0,             0,              TBSTATE_ENABLED, TBSTYLE_SEP,
                                0, 0, 0, 0,
 // Edit group
 STD_COPY,      ID_EDIT_COPY,   TBSTATE_ENABLED, TBSTYLE_BUTTON,
                                0, 0, 0, 0,
 STD_CUT,       ID_EDIT_CUT,    TBSTATE_ENABLED, TBSTYLE_BUTTON,
                                0, 0, 0, 0,
 STD_PASTE,     ID_EDIT_PASTE,  TBSTATE_ENABLED, TBSTYLE_BUTTON,
                                0, 0, 0, 0,
 STD_FIND,      ID_EDIT_FIND,   TBSTATE_ENABLED, TBSTYLE_BUTTON,
                                0, 0, 0, 0,
 STD_REPLACE,   ID_EDIT_REPLACE,  TBSTATE_ENABLED,
                                TBSTYLE_BUTTON,
                                0, 0, 0, 0,
 STD_UNDO,      ID_EDIT_UNDO,   TBSTATE_ENABLED, TBSTYLE_BUTTON,
                                0, 0, 0, 0,
 STD_REDOW,     ID_EDIT_REDO,   TBSTATE_ENABLED, TBSTYLE_BUTTON,
                                0, 0, 0, 0,
 STD_DELETE,    ID_EDIT_DELETE, TBSTATE_ENABLED,
                                TBSTYLE_BUTTON,
                                0, 0, 0, 0,
 0,             0,              TBSTATE_ENABLED, TBSTYLE_SEP,
```

```
                                0, 0, 0, 0,
// Print group
STD_PRINTPRE, ID_PRINT_PREVIEW, TBSTATE_ENABLED,
                                TBSTYLE_BUTTON,
                                0, 0, 0, 0,
STD_PRINT,     ID_PRINT_PRINT, TBSTATE_ENABLED,
                                TBSTYLE_BUTTON,
                                0, 0, 0, 0,
0,             0,               TBSTATE_ENABLED, TBSTYLE_SEP,
                                0, 0, 0, 0,
// Help and properties group
STD_PROPERTIES,ID_PROPS,        TBSTATE_ENABLED, TBSTYLE_BUTTON,
                                0, 0, 0, 0,
STD_HELP,       ID_HELP,        TBSTATE_ENABLED, TBSTYLE_BUTTON,
                                0, 0, 0, 0, } ;
```

The call to CreateToolbarEx() is also different. The fourth parameter, which indicates the number of button images in the toolbar bitmap is set to zero in the case of standard buttons. The fifth parameter, which in the case of a toolbar bitmap is set to the application instance, is now the constant HINST_COMMCTRL defined in the common controls library. The sixth parameter is the constant IDB_STD_SMALL_COLOR. The resulting call to CreateToolbarEx() is as follows:

```
tbHandle = CreateToolbarEx (hwnd,
           WS_CHILD | WS_VISIBLE | CCS_TOP |
           TBSTYLE_WRAPABLE,
           ID_TOOLBAR,          // Toolbar ID number
           0,                   // Number of bitmaps (none)
           (HINSTANCE)HINST_COMMCTRL, // Special resource
                                      // instance for
                                      // standard buttons
           IDB_STD_SMALL_COLOR, // Bitmap resource ID
           tbb,                 // TBBUTTON variable
           18,                  // Count of buttons plus
                              // separators
           0, 0, 0, 0,          // Not required for standard
                                // buttons
           sizeof (TBBUTTON));
```

The program named TB1_DEMO, located in the *Toolbar Demo No 1* project folder in the book's CD-ROM, is a demonstration of using the standard toolbar buttons. When you click on any of the toolbar buttons, a message box is displayed which contains the button's name. Figure 5-16 is a screen dump of the TB1_DEMO program.

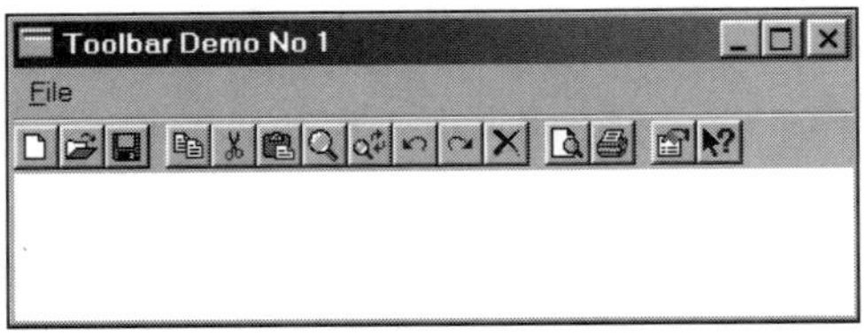

Figure 5-16: Screen dump of the TB1_DEMO program

Combo Box in a Toolbar

Windows programs, including Developer Studio, often contain a combo box as part of the toolbar. This application of the combo box is a powerful one. For example, the combo box on the Developer Studio standard menu bar serves to remember search strings that have been entered by the user. At any time, you can inspect the combo box and select one of the stored strings for a new search operation. Not only does it save you the effort of retyping the string, but it is also a record of past searches.

The position of the combo box in the toolbar is an important consideration. If the combo box is to the right of the last button in the toolbar, then it is a matter of calculating the length of the toolbar to position the combo box. However, if, as is often the case, the combo box is located between buttons in the toolbar, or at its start, then code must make space in the toolbar. The method suggested by Nancy Cluts in her book *Programming the Windows 95 User Interface* (see bibliography) is based on adding separators to make space for the combo box. Because each separator is eight pixels wide, we can calculate that for a 130-pixels wide combo box we would need at least 17 separators. In many cases a little experimentation may be necessary to find the correct number of separators.

The creation of the combo box requires calling `CreateWindow()` with "COMBOBOX" as the fist parameter. If the combo box is to have a series of string items, as is usually the case, then it is created with the style `CBS_HASSTRINGS`. If the combo box is to have an edit box feature, then the `CBS_DROPDOWN` style is used. If it is to have a list of selectable items but no editing possibilities, the `CBS_DROPDOWNLIST` style is used. The following code fragment shows the creation of a combo box in a toolbar:

```
static HWND  cbHandle;      // Handle to combo box
static HWND  tbHandle;      // Handle to toolbar
  .
  .
  .
cbHandle = CreateWindow ("COMBOBOX",
           NULL,                      // No class name
           WS_CHILD | WS_VISIBLE | WS_BORDER |
           CBS_HASSTRINGS |CBS_DROPDOWNLIST,
```

```
        0,                   // x origin
        0,                   // y origin
        130,                 // width
        144,                 // height
        tbHandle,            // Parent window handle
        (HMENU) IDR_MENU1,   // Menu resource ID
        pInstance,           // Application instance
        NULL);
```

Once the combo box is created, we need to add the text strings with which the combo box is originally furnished. This is accomplished by a series of calls to `SendMessage()` with the message code `CB_INSERTSTRING`. Typical coding reads as follows:

```
char *szStrings[] = { "Visual C++",
                      "Borland C",
                      "Pascal",
                      "Fortran 80",
                      "Visual Basic" };
  .
  .
  .
//Add strings to combo box
  for (i=0; i < 5; i++)
      SendMessage(cbHandle,
                  CB_INSERTSTRING,
                  (WPARAM)-1,
                  (LPARAM)szStrings[i]);
```

The program TB2_DEMO, located in the *Toolbar Demo No 2* project folder on the book's CD-ROM, demonstrates the creation of a toolbar that includes a combo box.

ToolTip Support

A ToolTip is a small window that contains a brief descriptive message. Although ToolTips can be activated in relation to any screen object, we are presently concerned with ToolTips associated with a toolbar. For a toolbar to support ToolTips, it must have been created with the `TBSTYLE_TOOLTIPS`, listed in Table 5-11.

Providing ToolTip support for toolbar buttons is straightforward and simple. However, when you need to furnish ToolTips for other elements in the toolbar, such as the combo box previously mentioned, then ToolTip processing may get more complicated. The first step in creating ToolTips to retrieve a handle for the ToolTip window. This is usually performed in the `WM_CREATE` message intercept. It consists of calling `SendMessage()` with the first parameter set to the toolbar handle and the second parameter set to the `TB_GETTOOLTIPS` message identifier. The following code fragment shows the creation of a three-button toolbar and its corresponding ToolTip window:

```
LRESULT CALLBACK WndProc (HWND hwnd, UINT iMsg, WPARAM wParam,
                          LPARAM lParam) {
  static HWND    tbHandle;    // Handle to toolbar
  static HWND    hWndTT;      // Handle to ToolTip
     .
     .
     .
   switch (iMsg)
         {
   case WM_CREATE:
      // Create a toolbar
      tbHandle = CreateToolbarEx (hwnd,  // Handle to window
                 WS_CHILD | WS_VISIBLE |
                 WS_CLIPSIBLINGS |
                 CCS_TOP | TBSTYLE_TOOLTIPSS, // Window styles
                 0,                  // Toolbar identifier
                 3,                  // Number of button images
                                     // in toolbar bitmap
                 pInstance,          // Module instance
                 IDB_BITMAP1,        // Bitmap ID
                 tbb,                // TBBUTON structure
                 3,                  // Number of buttons
                                     // plus separators
                 0, 0, 0, 0,         // Not required
                 sizeof (TBBUTTON));
      // Get the handle to the ToolTip window.
          hWndTT = (HWND)SendMessage(tbHandle,
                            TB_GETToolTipS, 0, 0);
              .
              .
              .
```

Once you create the ToolTip window and obtain its handle, the next step is to create and initialize a structure of type `TOOLINFO` (see Appendix A). The coding proceeds as follows:

```
if (hWndTT) {
  // Fill in the TOOLINFO structure.
  lpToolInfo.cbSize = sizeof(lpToolInfo);
  lpToolInfo.uFlags = TTF_IDISHWND | TTF_CENTERTIP;
  lpToolInfo.hwnd = hwnd;
  lpToolInfo.uId = (UINT)tbHandle;
```

```
  lpToolInfo.hinst = pInstance;
  lpToolInfo.lpszText = LPSTR_TEXTCALLBACK;
}
```

The first flag, TTF_IDISHWND, indicates that the fourth structure member (uId) is a handle to a window, in this case, the toolbar. The flag TTF_CENTERTIP determines that the ToolTip is displayed following the window specified in the uId member, here again, the toolbar. Finally, the lpszText member is set to the constant LPSTR_TEXTCALLBACK, which makes the control send the TTN_NEEDTEXT notification message to the owner window. The values entered in the other structure members are self-explanatory.

Processing of ToolTip messages, as is the case with most controls, takes place at the WM_NOTIFY message intercept. At the time the message handler receives control, the lParam is a pointer to a structure of type HMHDR (see Appendix A), or to a larger structure that has NMHDR as its first member. The third member of the HMHDR structure contains the control-specific notification code. This parameter is TTN_NEEDTEXT when text is required for a ToolTip. Therefore, code can switch on this structure member and provide processing in a case statement, as shown in the following code fragment:

```
LPNMHDR        pnmh;        // Pointer to HMHDR structure
TOOLTIPINFO    lpToolTipInfo;
LPTOOLTIPTEXT lpToolTipText;
static char    szBuf[128]; // Buffer for ToolTip text
.
.
.
 case WM_NOTIFY:
    pnmh = (LPNMHDR) lParam;
    switch  (pnmh->code) {
        case TTN_NEEDTEXT:
        // Display ToolTip text.
           lpToolTipText = (LPTOOLTIPTEXT)lParam;
           LoadString (pInstance,
                      lpToolTipText->hdr.idFrom,
                      szBuf,
                      sizeof(szBuf));
                      lpToolTipText->lpszText = szBuf;
           break;
         default:
            return TRUE;
            break;
     }
   return 0;
 break;
```

Note that the `TTN_NEEDTEXT` message intercept contains a pointer to a structure of type `TOOLTIPTEXT` in the `lParam` (see Appendix A). The first member of `TOOL1TIPTEXT` (`hdr`) is a structure of type `NMHDR`, and the `idFrom` member of `HMHDR` is the identifier of the control sending the message. Code uses this information and the `LoadString()` function to move the text into the buffer named `szBuf`. The text moved into `szBuf` comes from the `lpszText` member of a structure variable of type `TOOLTIPTEXT`. This second member is a pointer to a text string defined as a string resource in the application's executable.

The string resource that contains the messages displayed with each ToolTip is the last missing element of ToolTip implementation. You create the string resource by opening the Insert menu and selecting the Resource command. In the Insert Resource dialog box select String Table and then click on the New button. An example of a resource table is shown in Figure 5-17.

ID	Value	Caption
ID_FILE_NEW	40001	Create a new file
ID_FILE_OPEN	40002	Open current file
ID_FILE_SAVE	40003	Save current file

Figure 5-17: Developer Studio Resource Table editor

The resource table consists of three entries: the id, the value, and the caption fields. You fill the id field so that it contains the same identification code as the button for which you are providing a ToolTip. In the caption field, you enter the text to be displayed at the ToolTip. Developer Studio automatically fills the value field for the one assigned to the corresponding toolbar button. Double-clicking on the entry displays a dialog box where these values can be input.

The program named TT_DEMO, located in the *ToolTip Demo* project folder on the book's CD-ROM, is a demonstration of the processing required for the implementation of ToolTip controls.

Summary

In this chapter you learned how to program many of the components used in Windows applications, including graphics ones. It is difficult to image a graphics program that does not require a mouse, and that does not contain child windows, menus, toolbars, and dialog boxes of one kind or another.

However, in the course of one chapter we have been unable to cover all the topics related to the Windows graphical user interface programming. It is easy to fill a full-sized volume with this material, and several such books have been published. Perhaps the most comprehensive one on the new controls and interface elements is *Programming the Windows 95 User Interface* (see bibliography).

This is the last chapter of Part I. We have now concluded with the preparatory material and you should feel comfortable with the fundamentals of Windows API programming. From this point on, the book focuses entirely on Windows graphics. In Part II, you will learn to use the graphics functions that are part of the Windows API: programming the Graphics Device Interface, vector drawings, and bitmap graphics.

Part II

API Graphics

Chapter 6

Drawing Pixels, Lines, and Curves

IN THIS CHAPTER

- The basic architecture of a graphics application
- Graphics Device Interface attributes
- The Device Context
- Graphic Objects: pens, brushes, mix modes, pen position, and arc direction
- Drawing pixels, lines, and curves using GDI functions

THIS IS THE FIRST chapter on graphics programming that uses the services in the Windows Graphics Device Interface. The simpler of these services is discussed, which are used for reading and setting individual pixels and for drawing lines and curves in a two-dimensional space. Although the described graphics functions are simple, they are among the most-used in conventional Windows graphics.

To use these drawing primitives, first you have to learn about the architecture of a Windows graphics application, about the GDI itself, as well as expand your familiarity with the Device Context. It is in the Device Context that system-level graphics information is stored. Applications must often read these attributes. How to obtain Device Context information is discussed in this chapter.

You must also learn about Windows graphics objects and their attributes. The Windows graphics objects are pens, brushes, bitmaps, palettes, fonts, paths, and regions. In this chapter we discuss pens and brushes. It is also to learn about some of the attributes of the Device Context: color, mix mode, background mode, pen position, and arc direction. These attributes determine how graphics output takes place.

After these preliminaries have been covered, we get into the graphics-programming functions and cover the pixel-level operations and 10 GDI primitives used for drawing lines and curves.

Drawing in a Window

In Chapter 2 we discussed the event-driven architecture of a Windows program. At that time we mentioned that Windows applications share resources with all other running programs and with the operating system. This means that a graphics program cannot make exclusive use of the display, or of other system resources, because these are all part of a pool that is accessible to all code in a multitasking environment. The following implications result from this architecture:

- A typical Windows application must obtain information about the system and the display device before performing output operations. The application must know the structure and dimensions of the output surface, as well as its capabilities, to manage the display function.
- In Windows, output to devices is performed by means of a logical link between the application, the device driver, and the hardware components. This link is called a *device context*. A *display context* is a special device context for the display device. Applications that draw to a window using conventional Windows functions must first obtain the display context. The handle to this display context is passed as a parameter to all API drawing functions.
- Unlike a DOS program, a Windows application cannot draw to the screen and assume that the resulting image remains undisturbed for unlimited time. On the contrary, a Windows program must take into account that the video display is a shared resource. Windows notifies the application that its client area needs to be painted or repainted by posting a `WM_PAINT` message to the program's message queue. A well-designed Windows program must be able to redraw its client area upon receiving this message.

The first two of these topics – obtaining the device-context handle and the display-device attributes – are discussed in a separate section later in this chapter. Here we are concerned with the mechanisms used by Windows applications for accessing the display device in a way that is consistent with the multitasking nature of the environment.

The Redraw Responsibility

Windows applications are burdened with the responsibility of redrawing their client area at any given time. This is an obligation to be taken seriously because it implies that code must have ways for reconstructing the display on demand. The data structures and other controls necessary to redraw the screen, and how code handles this responsibility, depend on the application itself. In some programs the screen redraw burden is met simply by keeping tabs of which of several possible displays is active. In other applications the screen redraw obligation can entail such elaborate processing that it becomes a major consideration in program design.

The operating system, or your own code, sends the WM_PAINT message whenever the client area, or a portion thereof, needs to be redrawn. Application code responds to its screen-redraw responsibility during the WM_PAINT message intercept. The following events cause the operating system to send WM_PAINT:

- The user has brought into view a previously hidden area of the application window. This happens when the window has been moved or uncovered.
- The user has resized the window.
- The user has scrolled the window contents.

The WM_PAINT message is not produced when a window is merely moved to another position on the desktop because the client area has not been changed by the translation. Therefore, the operating system is able to maintain the screen contents because no new graphics elements were introduced or removed, and the screen size remained the same. However, the operating system cannot anticipate how an application will handle a screen-resizing operation. You have several processing possibilities: Are the screen contents scaled to the new dimension of the client area, or is their original size maintained? Are the positions of the graphics elements changed as a consequence of the resize operation, or do they remain in the same place? Not knowing how these situations are to be handled, the operating system responds by sending WM_PAINT to the application and letting it take whatever redraw action considers appropriate. The same logic applies when the client area is scrolled or when portions of the window are uncovered.

Sometimes Windows attempts to restore the application's screen, but may occasionally post the WM_PAINT message if it fails in this effort. This occurs when a message or dialog box is displayed, when a menu is pulled down, or when a tooltip is enabled. Finally, cases exist in which Windows always saves and restores the screen automatically. For example, when the mouse cursor or a program icon is dragged or moved across the client area.

The Invalid Rectangle

In an effort to minimize the processing, Windows keeps tabs on which portion of the application's client area needs to be redrawn. Windows does this because it is wasteful for application code to repaint the entire screen when only a small portion of the program's client area needs to be redrawn. In practice, for simpler programs, it is often easier to assume that the entire client area needs redrawing rather than to get into the complications of repainting parts of the screen. However, in more complex applications – particularly those that use multiple child windows – it may save considerable time and effort if code can determine which of these elements need redrawing and which can be left unchanged.

The screen area that needs to be redrawn is called the *update region*. The smallest rectangle that binds the update region is called the *invalid rectangle*. When the WM_PAINT message is placed in the message queue, Windows attaches to it a structure of type RECT that contains the dimensions and location of the invalid rectangle. If another screen area becomes invalid before WM_PAINT is posted, Windows then makes the necessary correction in the invalid rectangle. This scheme prevents the posting of more than one WM_PAINT message on the queue. Applications can call GetUpdateRect() to obtain the coordinates of the top-left and bottom-right corners of the update region.

An application can force Windows to send a WM_PAINT message to its own window procedure. This is accomplished by means of the InvalidateRect() or InvalidateRgn() functions. InvalidateRect() has the effect of adding a rectangle to a window's update region. The function has the following general form:

```
BOOL InvalidateRect(
          HWND hWnd,            // 1
          CONST RECT* lpRect,  // 2
          BOOL bErase           // 3
          );
```

The first parameter identifies the window whose update region has changed. The second parameter is a pointer to a structure variable of type RECT that contains the coordinates of the rectangle to be added to the update region. If this parameter is NULL, then the entire client area is added to the update region. The third parameter is a flag that indicates whether Windows should erase or not erase the background. If this parameter is TRUE, then the background is erased when the BeginPaint() function is called by the application. If it is FALSE, the background remains unchanged.

Designing for On-demand Screen Update

The standard reply of an application that has received a WM_PAINT message is the redrawing of its own client area. This implies that the application has been designed so that a screen update takes place every time a WM_PAINT message is received. In this case the application design has to take into account the message-driven characteristic of a Windows program.

Consider a program that contains three menu commands: one to display a circle, another to display a rectangle, and a third to display a triangle. When the user clicks on any one of the three menu items, a WM_COMMAND message is posted to the application's message queue. The low word of the WPARAM encodes which one of the menu items was selected. Application code usually switches on this value to field all possible commands. However, the screen should not be updated during WM_COMMAND processing. At this point, code can set a switch that indicates the selected command. In this example a static variable of type int, named drawMode, could be set to 1 to indicate a circle-drawing request, to 2 to indicate a rectangle, and to 3 to indicate a triangle. After this switch is set according to the menu command entered by the user, code calls InvalidateRect() so that Windows posts WM_PAINT to the application's own message queue. The application then processes WM_PAINT inspecting the value of the drawMode variable. If the value is 1 it draws a circle, if its is 2 it draws a rectangle, and if it is 3 it draws a triangle.

To a non-Windows programmer this may appear to be a roundabout way of doing things. Why not draw the geometrical figures at the time that the menu commands are received? The problem with drawing the figures as the commands are received is that if the window is resized or covered, no mechanism is in place to restore its screen image. The result would be either a partially or a totally blank client area. However, if the screen updates take place during WM_PAINT message processing, when Windows sends WM_PAINT to the application because of a screen contents change, the application redraws itself and the client area is correctly restored.

On the other hand, not all screen-drawing operations can take place during WM_PAINT message processing. Applications sometimes have to perform display functions that are directly linked to a user action; an example being a rubber-band image that is drawn in direct and immediate response to a mouse movement. In this case, code cannot postpone the drawing until WM_PAINT is received.

WM_PAINT Message Intercept

In Chapter 3 we discussed the basic structure of the WM_PAINT message. The message is generated only for windows that were created with the styles CS_HREDRAW or CS_VREDRAW. Receiving WM_PAINT indicates to application code that all or part of the client area must be repainted. The message can originate in Windows, typically because the user has minimized, overlapped, or resized the client area. Or possibly because the application itself has produced the message by calling InvalidateRect() or InvalidateRgn(),as previously discussed.

Typically, WM_PAINT processing begins with the BeginPaint() function. BeginPaint() prepares the window for a paint operation. First it fills a variable of type PAINTSTRUCT, which is defined as follows:

```
typedef struct tagPAINTSTRUCT {
    HDC     hdc;              // Identifies display device
    BOOL    fErase;           // TRUE if background must be
                              // erased
    RECT    rcPaint;          // Rectangle structure specifying
                              // the update region
    BOOL    fRestore;         // RESERVED
    BOOL    fIncUpdate;       // RESERVED
    BYTE    rgbReserved[32];  // RESERVED
} PAINTSTRUCT;
```

If the screen erasing flag is set, BeginPaint() uses the window's background brush to erase the background. When execution returns from BeginPaint(),code can assume that the update region has been erased. At this point the application can call GetClientRect() to obtain the coordinates of the update region, or proceed on the assumption that the entire client area must be redrawn.

Processing ends with EndPaint(). EndPaint() notifies Windows that the paint operation has concluded. The parameters passed to EndPaint() are the same ones passed to BeginPaint(): the handle to the window and the address of the structure variable of type PAINTSTRUCT. One important consequence of the EndPaint() function is that the invalid region is validated. By themselves, drawing operations have no validating effect. Placing the drawing operations between BeginPaint() and EndPaint() functions automatically validates the invalid region so that other WM_PAINT messages are not produced. In fact, placing the BeginPaint() EndPaint() functions in the WM_PAINT intercept, with no other processing operation, has the effect of validating the update region. The DefWindowProc() function operates in this manner.

The project *Pixel and Line Demo* in the book's CD-ROM demonstrates image display and update in response to WM_PAINT messages. The processing uses a static variable to store the state of the display. A switch construct in the WM_PAINT routine performs the screen updates, as shown in the following code fragment:

```
// Drawing command selector
static int   drawMode = 0;
//                   0 = no menu command active
//                       Active menu command:
//                   1 = Set Pixel
//                   2 = LineTo
//                   3 = Polyline
//                   4 = PolylineTo
//                   5 = PolyPolyline
//                   6 = Arc
//                   7 = AngleArc
//                   8 = PolyBezier
//                   9 = PolyDraw
   .
   .
   .
    //******************************
//     menu command processing
    //******************************
case WM_COMMAND:
switch (LOWORD (wParam)) {
    //******************************
//    SetPixel command
```

```
          //***************************
case ID_DRAWOP_PIXELDRAW:
drawMode = 1;   // Command to draw line
InvalidateRect(hwnd, NULL, TRUE);
break;
          //***************************
//    LineTo command
          //***************************
case ID_DRAWOP_LINE_LINETO:
drawMode = 2;   // Command to draw line
InvalidateRect(hwnd, NULL, TRUE);
break;
    .
    .
    .
     //******************************
//     WM_PAINT processing
     //******************************
case WM_PAINT :
BeginPaint (hwnd, &ps) ;
switch(drawMode)
          {
// 1 = SetPixel command
case 1:
pixColor = RGB(0xff, 0x0, 0x0); // Red
for (i = 0; i < 1000; i++) {
x = i * cxClient / 1000;
y = (int) (cyClient / 2 *
(1- sin (pix2 * i / 1000)));
SetPixelV (hdc, x, y, pixColor);
                }
break;
// 2 = LineTo command
case 2:
// Create a solid blue pen, 4 pixels wide
SelectObject(hdc, bluePen4);
MoveToEx (hdc, 140, 140, NULL);
LineTo (hdc, 300, 140);
LineTo (hdc, 300, 300);
LineTo (hdc, 140, 300);
LineTo (hdc, 140, 140);
break;
    .
    .
```

Graphics Device Interface

The *Graphics Device Interface* (GDI) consists of a series of functions and related data structures that applications can use to generate graphics output. The GDI can output to any compatible device, but most frequently the device is either the video display, a graphics hard copy device (such as a printer or plotter), or a metafile in memory GDI functions enable you to draw lines, curves, closed figures, paths, bitmapped images, and text. The objects are drawn according to the style selected for drawing objects, such as pens, brushes, and fonts. The pen object determines how lines and curves are drawn; the brush object determines how the interiors of closed figures are filled. Fonts determine the attributes of text.

Output can be directed to physical devices, such as the video display or a printer, or to a logical device, such as a metafile. A metafile is a memory object that stores output instructions so they can later be used to produce graphics on a physical device. It works much like a tape recording that can be played back at any time, any number of times.

The GDI is one of the layers between the application and the graphics hardware. It ensures device-independence and frees the programmer from having to deal with hardware details of individual devices. The device context, mentioned in Chapter 4, is one of the fundamental mechanisms used by the GDI to implement device-independent graphics. The GDI is a two-dimensional interface, which contains no 3D graphics primitives or transformations. It is also a static system, with very little support for animation. Therefore, the GDI is not capable of doing everything that a graphics programmer may desire, but within these limitations, it provides a convenient and easy-to-use toolkit of fundamental functions.

GDI functions can be classified into the following three very general categories:

- Functions that relate to the device context. These are used to create and release the DC, to get information about it, and to get and set its attributes.
- Drawing primitives. These are used to draw lines and curves, fill areas, and display bitmaps and text.
- Functions that operate on GDI objects. These perform manipulation of graphics objects such as pens, brushes, and bitmaps, which are not part of the device context.

Device Context Attributes

The GDI can output to any compatible device, including hard-copy graphics devices and memory. For this reason, when referring to the GDI functions, we always use the term *device context*, instead of the more restrictive *display context*. In Chapter 4 we discussed the fundamentals of the device context and developed a template file TEMPL02.CPP, found in the Templates directory on the book's CD-ROM. TEMPL02.CPP creates a program that uses a private device context. A private device context has the advantages that it need be retrieved only once and that attributes assigned to it are retained until they are explicitly changed. In the following examples and demonstration programs, we continue to use a private device context to take advantage of these simplifications.

In Chapter 4, we also introduced the mapping modes as one of the most important attributes of the device context. Two scalable mapping modes, named `MM_ANISOTROPIC` and `MM_ISOTROPIC`, are used in shrinking and expanding graphics by manipulating the coordinate system. They provide a powerful image-manipulation mechanism and are discussed in Chapter 7. For now, we continue to use the default-mapping mode, `MM_TEXT`, in these demonstrations and examples.

Device context operations may be classified as one of two types: those that obtain information and those that set attributes. For example, the GDI function `GetTextColor()` retrieves the current text color from the device context, while the function `SetTextColor()` is used to change the text-color attribute. Although these functions are sometimes referred to as get- and set-types, the function names do not always begin with these words. For example, the `SelectObject()` function is used to both get and set the attributes of pens, brushes, fonts, and bitmaps.

Graphics applications often need to obtain information regarding the device context. For example, a program may need to know the screen resolution or the number of display colors. One of the most useful functions for obtaining information regarding the capabilities of a device context is `GetDeviceCaps()`. The call to `GetDeviceCaps()` requires two parameters: the first one is the handle to the device context, and the second one is an index value that identifies the capability being queried. Table 6-1 lists some of the most useful information returned by this function.

TABLE 6-1 MOST USEFUL INFORMATION RETURNED BY GETDEVICECAPS()

Index	Meaning	
DRIVERVERSION	Version number of device driver.	
TECHNOLOGY	Any one of the following:	
	Value	**Meaning**
	DT_PLOTTER	Vector plotter
	DT_RASDISPLAY	Raster display
	DT_RASPRINTER	Raster printer
	DT_RASCAMERA	Raster camera

Continued

TABLE 6-1 MOST USEFUL INFORMATION RETURNED BY GETDEVICECAPS() *(Continued)*

Index	Meaning	
	Value	**Meaning**
	DT_CHARSTREAM	Character stream
	DT_METAFILE	Metafile
	DT_DISPFILE	Display file
HORZSIZE	Width of the physical screen (millimeters).	
VERTSIZE	Height of the physical screen (millimeters).	
HORZRES	Width of the screen (pixels).	
VERTRES	Height of the screen (raster lines).	
LOGPIXELSX	Number of pixels per logical inch along the screen width.	
LOGPIXELSY	Number of pixels per logical inch along the screen height.	
BITSPIXEL	Number of color bits per pixel.	
PLANES	Number of color planes.	
NUMBRUSHES	Number of device-specific brushes.	
NUMPENS	Number of device-specific pens.	
NUMFONTS	Number of device-specific fonts.	
NUMCOLORS	Number of entries in the color table, if the device has a color depth of no more than 8 bits per pixel. Otherwise, -1 is returned.	
ASPECTX	Relative width of a device pixel used for line drawing.	
ASPECTY	Relative height of a device pixel used for line drawing.	
ASPECTXY	Diagonal width of the device pixel used for line drawing.	
CLIPCAPS	Flag indicating clipping capabilities of the device. Value is 1 if the device can clip to a rectangle. Otherwise, it is 0.	
SIZEPALETTE	Number of entries in the system palette.	
NUMRESERVED	Number of reserved entries in the system palette.	
COLORRES	Actual color resolution of the device, in bits per pixel.	

Index	Meaning	
PHYSICALWIDTH	For printing devices: the width of the physical page, in device units.	
PHYSICALHEIGHT	For printing devices: the height of the physical page, in device units.	
PHYSICALOFFSETX	For printing devices: the distance from the left edge of the physical page to the left edge of the printable area, in device units.	
PHYSICALOFFSETY	For printing devices: the distance from the top edge of the physical page to the top edge of the printable area, in device units.	
RASTERCAPS	Value that indicates the raster capabilities of the device, as follows:	
	Capability	**Meaning**
	RC_BANDING	Requires banding support.
	RC_BITBLT	Capable of transferring bitmaps.
	RC_BITMAP64	Supports bitmaps larger than 64K.
	RC_DI_BITMAP	Supports SetDIBits() and GetDIBits functions.
	RC_DIBTODEV	Capable of supporting the SetDIBitsToDevice function.
	RC_FLOODFILL	Capable of performing flood fills.
	RC_PALETTE	Palette-based device.
	RC_SCALING	Capable of scaling.
	RC_STRETCHBLT	Capable of performing the StretchBlt function.
	RC_STRETCHDIB	Capable of performing the StretchDIBits function.
CURVECAPS	Indicates the curve capabilities of the device, as follows:	
	Value	**Meaning**
	CC_NONE	Does not support curves.

Continued

Table 6-1 MOST USEFUL INFORMATION RETURNED BY GETDEVICECAPS() (*Continued*)

Index	Meaning	
	Capability	**Meaning**
	CC_CIRCLES	Device can draw circles.
	CC_PIE	Device can draw pie wedges.
	CC_CHORD	Device can draw chord arcs.
	CC_ELLIPSES	Device can draw ellipses.
	CC_WIDE	Device can draw wide borders.
	CC_STYLED	Device can draw styled borders.
	CC_WIDESTYLED	Device can draw wide and styled borders.
	CC_INTERIORS	Device can draw interiors.
	CC_ROUNDRECT	Device can draw rounded rectangles.
LINECAPS	Indicates the line capabilities of the device, as follows:	
	Value	**Meaning**
	LC_NONE	Does not support lines.
	LC_POLYLINE	Device can draw a polyline.
	LC_MARKER	Device can draw a marker.
	LC_POLYMARKER	Device can draw multiple markers.
	LC_WIDE	Device can draw wide lines.
	LC_STYLED	Device can draw styled lines.
	LC_WIDESTYLED	Device can draw lines that are wide and styled.
	LC_INTERIORS	Device can draw interiors.
POLYGONALCAPS	Indicates the polygon capabilities of the device, as follows:	
	Value	**Meaning**
	PC_NONE	Does not support polygons.
	PC_POLYGON	Device can draw alternate-fill polygons.

Index	Meaning	
	Value	**Meaning**
	PC_RECTANGLE	Device can draw rectangles.
	PC_WINDPOLYGON	Device can draw winding-fill polygons.
	PC_SCANLINE	Device can draw a single scanline.
	PC_WIDE	Device can draw wide borders.
	PC_STYLED	Device can draw styled borders.
	PC_WIDESTYLED	Device can draw borders that are wide and styled.
	PC_INTERIORS	Device can draw interiors.
TEXTCAPS	Indicates the text capabilities of the device, as follows:	
	Value	**Meaning**
	TC_OP_CHARACTER	Device is capable of character output precision.
	TC_OP_STROKE	Device is capable of stroke output precision.
	TC_CP_STROKE	Device is capable of stroke clip precision.
	TC_CR_90	Device is capable of 90-degree character rotation.
	TC_CR_ANY	Device is capable of any character rotation.
	TC_SF_X_YINDEP	Device can scale independently in the x- and y-directions.
	TC_SA_DOUBLE	Device is capable of doubled character for scaling.
	TC_SA_INTEGER	Device uses integer multiples only for character scaling.
	TC_SA_CONTIN	Device uses any multiples for exact character scaling.

Continued

TABLE 6-1 MOST USEFUL INFORMATION RETURNED BY GETDEVICECAPS() *(Continued)*

Index	Meaning	
	Value	**Meaning**
	`TC_EA_DOUBLE`	Device can draw double-weight characters.
	`TC_IA_ABLE`	Device can italicize.
	`TC_UA_ABLE`	Device can underline.
	`TC_SO_ABLE`	Device can draw strikeouts.
	`TC_RA_ABLE`	Device can draw raster fonts.
	`TC_VA_ABLE`	Device can draw vector fonts.
	`TC_SCROLLBLT`	Device cannot scroll using a bit-block transfer.

DC Info Demonstration Program

The program named DCI_DEMO, located in the *DC Info Demo* project folder on the book's CD-ROM, shows how to obtain device context information. The menu labeled "DC Info" contains commands for displaying the most-used general device-context capabilities, the device driver version, as well as the specific line and curve drawing capabilities. Figure 6-1 shows the various menu commands in the DCI_DEMO program.

The Capabilities command in the DC Info menu displays the device-context values for some of the most-used elements returned by the `GetDeviceCaps()` function. To simplify the programming, the data required during processing is stored in a header file named DC_Caps.h, which can be found in the project directory. The header file is formatted as follows:

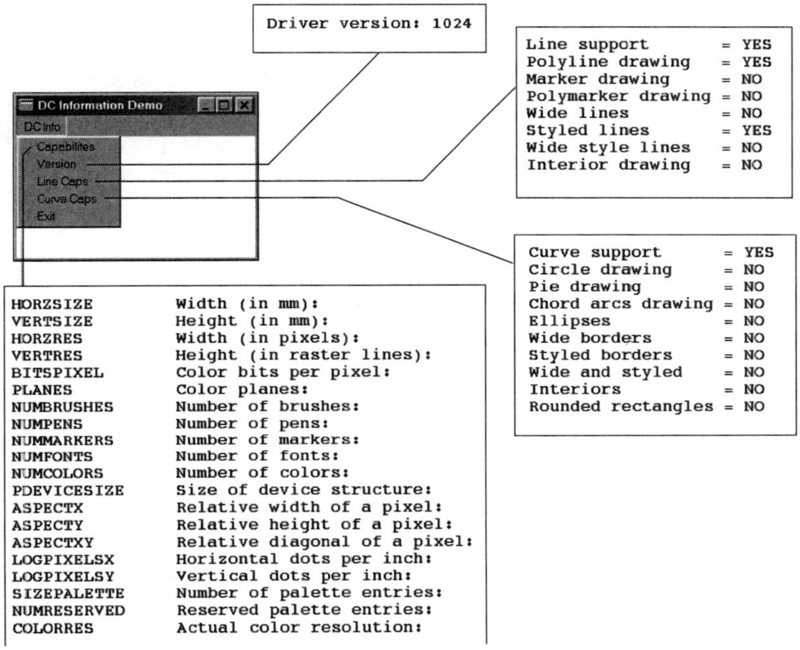

Figure 6-1: Screen dumps of the DC Info demonstration program

```
// Header file for DC Info Demo project
// Contains array of structures

#define LINES ((int) (sizeof DCcaps / sizeof DCcaps [0]))
struct
     {
int  iIndex ;
char *szLabel ;
char *szDesc ;
     }
DCcaps [] =
          {
          HORZSIZE,      "HORZSIZE",      "Width (in mm):",
          VERTSIZE,      "VERTSIZE",      "Height (in mm):",
          HORZRES,       "HORZRES",       "Width (in pixels):",
          .
          .
          .
          NUMRESERVED,   "NUMRESERVED",   "Reserved palette
entries:",
          COLORRES,      "COLORRES",      "Actual color resolution:"
          } ;
```

Each entry in the array of structures contains three elements. The first one (int iIndex) is the index name required in the GetDeviceCaps() call. The two other elements are strings used at display time. Processing takes place in a loop in which the number of iterations is determined by the constant LINES, which is calculated by dividing the number of entries in the structure by the number of elements in each entry. This coding enables us to change the number of entries in the array without having to change the loop.

```
// Obtain and display DC capabilities
for (i = 0 ; i < LINES ; i++) {
TextOut (hdc, cxChar, cyChar * (1 + i),
DCcaps[i].szLabel,
strlen (DCcaps[i].szLabel)) ;
TextOut (hdc, cxChar + 16 * cxCaps, cyChar * (1 + i),
DCcaps[i].szDesc,
strlen (DCcaps[i].szDesc)) ;
SetTextAlign (hdc, TA_RIGHT | TA_TOP) ;
TextOut (hdc, cxChar + 16 * cxCaps + 40 * cxChar,
cyChar * (1 + i), szBuffer,
wsprintf (szBuffer, "%5d",
GetDeviceCaps (hdc, DCcaps[i].iIndex))) ;
SetTextAlign (hdc, TA_LEFT | TA_TOP) ;
       }
break;
```

In the previous code fragment, the first TextOut() call displays the szLabel variable in the DCcaps structure. The second call to TextOut() displays the szDesc string. The value in the device context is obtained with the GetDeviceCaps() function that is part of the third call to TextOut(). In this case the iIndex element in the array is used as the second parameter to the call. The wsprintf() function takes care of converting and formatting the integer value returned by GetDeviceCaps() into a displayable string.

Obtaining and displaying the driver version is much simpler. The coding reads as follows:

```
// Get driver version
_itoa(GetDeviceCaps(hdc, DRIVERVERSION),
szVersion + 16, 10);
// Initialize rectangle structure
    SetRect (&textRect,                    // address of structure
             2 * cxChar,                   // x for start
             cyChar,                       // y for start
             cxClient,                     // x for end
             cyClient);                    // y for end
```

```
DrawText( hdc, szVersion, -1, &textRect,
DT_LEFT | DT_WORDBREAK);
break;
```

In this case we use the `_itoa()` function to convert the value returned by `GetDeviceCaps()` into a string. `SetRect()` and `DrawText()` are then used to format and display the string.

Obtaining and displaying the curve- and line-drawing capabilities of the device context requires different processing. These values (see Table 6-1) are returned as bit flags associated with an index variable. For example, we make the call to `GetDeviceCaps()` using the index constant `CURVECAPS` as the second parameter. The integer returned by the call contains all the bit flags that start with the prefix `CC` (`CurveCaps`) in Figure 6-1. Code can then use a bitwise AND to test for one or more curve-drawing capabilities. The following code fragment shows one possible approach for obtaining curve-drawing capabilities:

```
// Get curve drawing capabilities
curvecaps = GetDeviceCaps (hdc, CURVECAPS);
// Test individual bit flags and change default
// string if necessary
if (curvecaps & CC_NONE)
strncpy(szCurvCaps + 21, strNo, 3);
if (curvecaps & CC_CIRCLES)
strncpy(szCurvCaps + (26 + 21), strYes, 3);

    .
    .
    .

if (curvecaps & CC_ROUNDRECT)
strncpy(szCurvCaps + (9 * 26 + 21), strYes, 3);
// Initialize rectangle structure
        SetRect (&textRect,                 // address of
                                            // structure
                2 * cxChar,                 // x for start
                cyChar,                     // y for start
                cxClient,                   // x for end
                cyClient);                  // y for end

DrawText( hdc, szCurvCaps, -1, &textRect,
DT_LEFT | DT_WORDBREAK);
break;
```

Each of the if statements in the processing routine tests one of the bit flags returned by `GetDeviceCaps()`. If the bit is set, then a text string containing the words YES or NO is moved into the display string. When all the bits have been examined, the message string named `szCurvCaps` is displayed in the conventional manner.

Color in the Device Context

Monochrome displays are a thing of the past. Virtually all Windows machines have a color display and most of them can have up to 16.7 million displayable colors. In graphics programming you will often have to investigate the color capabilities of a device as well as select and manipulate colors.

In Chapter 1 we discussed the primary and the complementary color components of white light. In Windows programming, colors are defined by the relative intensity of the red, green, and blue primary components. Each color value is encoded in 8 bits; therefore, all three primary components require 24 bits. Since no C++ data type is exactly 24 bits however, the color value in Windows is stored in a type called `COLORREF`, which contains 32 bits. The resulting encoding is said to be in RGB format, in which the letters stand for the red, green, and blue components, respectively. Figure 6-2 shows the bit structure of the `COLORREF` type.

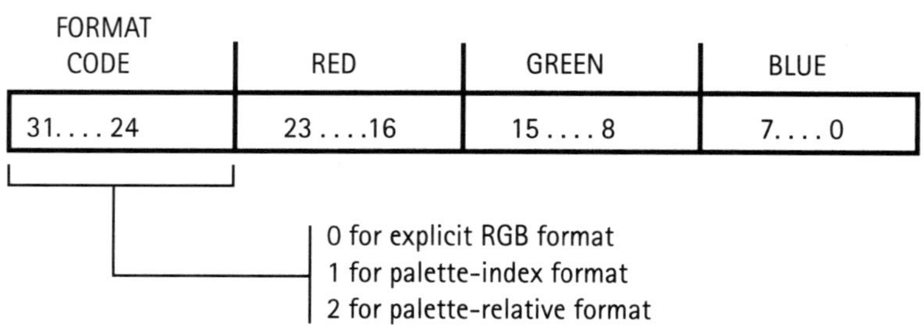

Figure 6-2: Bitmap of the COLORREF data type

Windows provides a macro named RGB defined in the *windows.h* header file; it simplifies entering the color values into a data variable of type `COLORREF`. The macro takes care of inserting the zeros in bits 24 to 31, and in positioning each color in its corresponding field. As the name RGB indicates, the first value corresponds to the red primary, the second one to the green, and the third one to the blue. For example, to enter a middle-gray value, in which each of the primary colors is set to 128, proceed as follows:

```
COLORREF     midGray;  // Variable of type COLORREF
midGray = RGB(128, 128, 128);
```

The COLORREF data type is also used to encode palette colors. Windows uses the high-order 8 bits to determine if a color value is in explicit RGB, palette-index, or palette-relative format. If the high-order byte is zero, then the color is an explicit RGB value; if it is 1 then it is a palette-index value; if it is 2 then the color is a palette-relative value. Using the RGB macro when creating explicit-RGB values ensures that the high-order byte is set correctly.

Obtaining color information from the device context requires careful consideration. Note in Table 6-1 that the index constant NUMCOLORS is valid only if the color depth is no more than 8 bits per pixel. The device queried in Figure 6-1 has 16 bits per pixel; therefore, the NUMCOLORS value is set to -1. By the same token, the COLORRES index constant is valid only if the device sets the RC_PALETTE bit. In Figure 6-1 the value of this field is 0. The two most useful constants for obtaining general color depth information are PLANES and BITPIXEL. PLANES returns the number of color planes and BITPIXEL returns the number of bits used in encoding each plane.

Graphic Objects and GDI Attributes

We should first mention that Windows graphics objects are not objects in the object-oriented sense. Windows graphics objects are pens, brushes, bitmaps, palettes, fonts, paths, and regions. Of these, pens and brushes are the objects most directly related to pixel and line-drawing operations.

Pens

The pen graphics object determines a line's color, width, and style. Windows uses the pen currently selected in the device context with any of the pen-based drawing functions. Three stock pens are defined: BLACK_PEN, WHITE_PEN, and NULL_PEN. The default pen is BLACK_PEN, which draws solid black lines. Applications refer to a pen by means of its handle, which is stored in a variable of type HPEN. The GetStockObject() function is used to obtain a handle to one of the stock pens. The pen must be selected into the device context before it is used, as follows:

```
HPEN     aPen;        // handle to pen
   .
   .
   .
aPen = GetStockObject (WHITE_PEN);
SelectObject (hdc, aPen);
```

The two functions can be combined in a single statement, as follows:

```
SelectObject (hdc, GetStockObject (WHITE_PEN));
```

In this case, no pen-handle variable is required. SelectObject() returns the handle to the pen previously installed in the device context. This can be used to save the original pen so that it can be restored later.

Drawing applications sometimes require one or more custom pens, which have a particular style, width, and color. Custom pens can be created with the functions CreatePen(), CreatePenIndirect(), and ExtCreatePen(). In the CreatePen() function, the pen's style, width, and color are passed as parameters. CreatePenIndirect() uses a structure of type LOGPEN to hold the pen's style, width, and color. ExtCreatePen(), introduced in Windows 95, is the most powerful of the three. The iStyle parameter is a combination of pen type, styles, end-cap style, and line-join attributes. The constants used in defining this parameter are listed in Table 6-2.

TABLE 6-2 VALUES DEFINED FOR THE EXTCREATEPEN() ISTYLE PARAMETER

Pen Type	Description
PS_GEOMETRIC	Pen is geometric.
PS_COSMETIC	Pen is cosmetic. Same as those created with CreatePen() and CreatePenIndirect(). Width must be 1 pixel.
Pen Style	
PS_ALTERNATE	Windows NT: Pen sets every other pixel. (Cosmetic pens only.) Windows 95: Not supported.
PS_SOLID	Pen is solid.
PS_DASH	Pen is dashed.
PS_DOT	Pen is dotted.
PS_DASHDOT	Pen has alternating dashes and dots.
PS_DASHDOTDOT	Pen has alternating dashes and double dots.
PS_NULL	Pen is invisible.
PS_USERSTYLE	Windows NT: Pen uses a styling array supplied by the user. Windows 95: Not supported.
PS_INSIDEFRAME	Pen is solid. The dimensions of the figure are shrunk in any drawing function that takes a bounding rectangle, so that the figure fits entirely in the bounding rectangle. Geometric pens only.

Pen Type	Description
End Cap Style (only in stroked paths)	
PS_ENDCAP_ROUND	End caps are round.
PS_ENDCAP_SQUARE	End caps are square.
PS_ENDCAP_FLAT	End caps are flat.
Join Style (only in stroked paths)	
PS_JOIN_BEVEL	Joins are beveled.
PS_JOIN_MITER	Joins are mitered when they are within the current limit set by the SetMiterLimit() function. If it exceeds this limit, the join is beveled. SetMiterLimit() is discussed in Chapter 7.
PS_JOIN_ROUND	Joins are round.

The standard form of the ExtCreatePen() function reads as follows:

```
HPEN ExtCreatePen (iStyle,     // pen style
                   iWidth,     // pen width
                   &aBrush,    // pointer to a LOGBRUSH
                               // structure (next section)
dwStyleCount,// length of next parameter
lpStyle);    // dot-dash pattern array
```

The second parameter to ExtCreatePen() defines the pen's width. If the pen is a geometric pen, then its width is specified in logical units. If it is a cosmetic pen then the width must be set to 1.

A geometric pen created with ExtCreatePen() has brush-like attributes. The third parameter is a pointer to LOGBRUSH. The LOGBRUSH structure, described in the following section, is defined as follows:

```
struct tagLOGBRUSH {
UINT      lbStyle;
COLORREF  lbColor;
LONG      lbHatch;
} LOGBRUSH
```

If the pen is a cosmetic pen, then the `lbStyle` member must be `BS_SOLID` and the `lbColor` member defines the pen's color. In this case the `lbHatch` member, which sets a brush's hatch pattern, is ignored. If the pen is geometric, then all three structure members are meaningful and must be used to specify the corresponding attributes.

The fourth parameter, `dwStyleCount`, determines the length of the fifth parameter. The fifth parameter, `lpStyle`, is a pointer to an array of doubleword values. The first value in the array is the length of the first dash of a user-defined pen style, the second one is the length of the first space, and so on. If the pen style does not contain the `PS_USERSTYLE` constant, then the fourth parameter must be zero, and the fifth parameter must be NULL. Note that `PS_USERSTYLE` is supported in Windows NT but not in Windows 95 or 98.

The end cap styles determine the appearance of the line ends. Three constants are defined for round, square, and flat line ends. The end join style determines the appearance of the connecting point of two lines. Both styles are available only for geometric pens. Figure 6-3 shows the pen styles and the effects of the different end caps and joins.

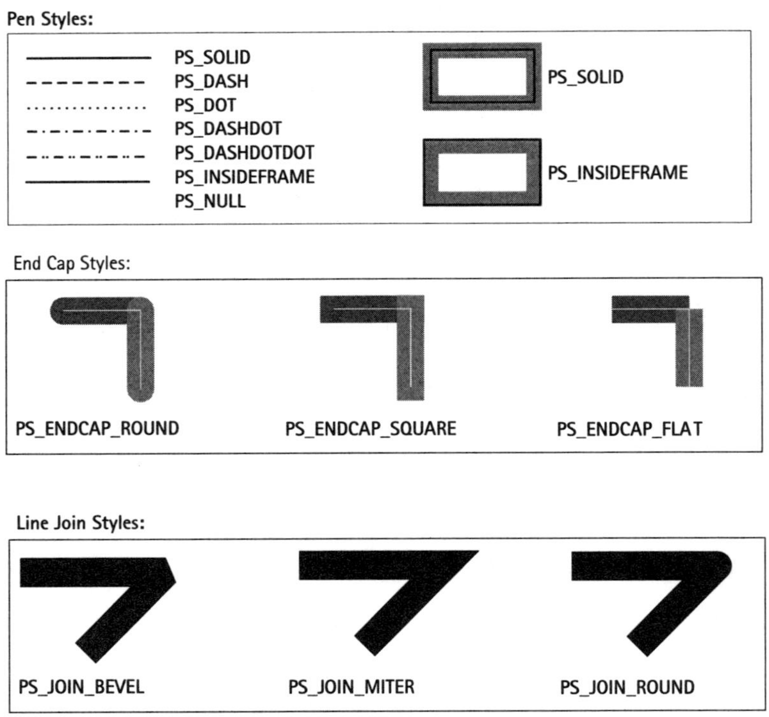

Figure 6-3: Pen styles, end caps, and joins

Note in Figure 6-3 that the difference between square and flat caps is that the square style extends the line by one-half its width. The white lines in the end cap style insert are drawn with the white stock pen to better show the style's effect. The NULL_PEN style creates a pen that draws with transparent ink, so it leaves no mark as it moves on the drawing surface. This style is occassionaly used in creating figures that are filled with a particular brush style but have no border.

Brushes

The brush object determines the attributes used in filling a solid figure. The outlines of these figures are determined by the brush selected in the device context. A brush has a style, color, and hatch pattern. The different kinds of stock brushes are: WHITE_BRUSH, LTGRAY_BRUSH, GRAY_BRUSH, DKGRAY_BRUSH, BLACK_BRUSH, and NULL_BRUSH. All stock brushes are solid; that is, they fill the entire enclosed area of the figure. The NULL_BRUSH is used to draw figures without filling the interior. If a solid figure is drawn with the NULL_PEN, then it is filled but has no outline.

Applications refer to a brush by its handle, which is stored in a variable of type HBRUSH. The GetStockObject() function is used to obtain a handle to one of the stock brushes. The brush must be selected into the device context before use, shown as follows:

```
HBRUSH     aBrush;       // handle to brush
   .
   .
   .
aBrush = GetStockObject (WHITE_BRUSH);
SelectObject (hdc, aBrush);
```

As in the case of a pen, the two functions can be combined in a single statement, shown as follows:

```
SelectObject (hdc, GetStockObject (WHITE_BRUSH));
```

In this case, no brush-handle variable is required. SelectObject() returns the handle to the brush previously installed in the device context. This can be used to save the original brush so that it can later be restored.

A custom brush is created by means of the CreateBrushIndirect() function. The call returns a handle to the brush, of type HBRUSH. The only parameter is a pointer to a structure of type LOGBRUSH which holds the brush style, color, and hatch pattern. The LOGBRUSH structure is also used by the ExtCreatePen() previously described. Table 6-3 lists the predefined constants used for members of the LOGBRUSH structure.

Table 6-3 CONSTANTS USED IN THE LOGBRUSH STRUCTURE MEMBERS

Brush Style	**Description**
BS_DIBPATTERN	A pattern brush defined by a device-independent bitmap (DIB). If lbStyle is BS_DIBPATTERN, the lbHatch member contains a handle to a packed DIB. DIBs are discussed in Chapter 8.
BS_DIBPATTERNPT	Same as BS_DIBPATTERN but the lbHatch member contains a pointer to a packed DIB.
BS_HATCHED	Hatched brush.
BS_HOLLOW	Hollow brush.
BS_NULL	Same as BS_HOLLOW.
BS_PATTERN	Pattern brush defined by a memory bitmap.
BS_SOLID	Solid brush.
Brush Color	**Description**
DIB_PAL_COLORS	The color table consists of an array of 16-bit indices into the currently realized logical palette.
DIB_RGB_COLORS	The color table contains literal RGB values.
Hatch Style	
HS_BDIAGONAL	A 45-degree upward, left-to-right hatch.
HS_CROSS	Horizontal and vertical cross-hatch.
HS_DIAGCROSS	45-degree crosshatch.
HS_FDIAGONAL	A 45-degree downward, left-to-right hatch.
HS_HORIZONTAL	Horizontal hatch.
HS_VERTICAL	Vertical hatch.

Figure 6-4 shows the brush-hatch patterns.

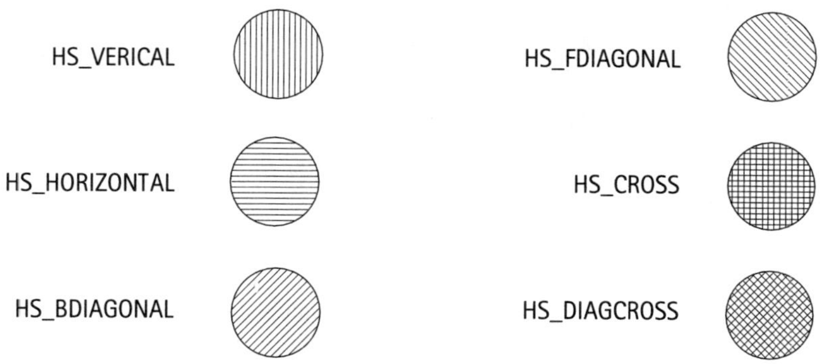

Figure 6-4: Brush-hatch patterns

Foreground Mix Mode

The foreground mix-mode attribute of the device context, also called the drawing mode, determines how Windows combines the pen or brush color with the display surface when performing drawing operations. The mixing is a raster operation based on a Boolean function of two variables: the pen and the background. For this reason it is described as a binary raster operation, or ROP2. All four Boolean primitives are used in setting the mix mode: AND, OR, NOT, and XOR. The function for setting the foreground mix mode is `SetROP2()`. `GetROP2()` returns the current mix mode in the device context. The general form of the `SetROP2()` function reads as follows:

```
int SetROP2(
            HDC hdc,          // 1
            int fnDrawMode    // 2
            );
```

The first parameter is the handle to the device context and the second parameter is one of 16 mix modes defined by Windows. The function returns the previous mix mode, which can be used to restore the original condition. Table 6-4 lists the ROP2 mix modes. The center column shows how the pen (P) and the screen (S) pixels are logically combined at draw time. The Boolean operators correspond to the symbols used in C.

Table 6-4 MIX MODES USED IN SETROP2() FUNCTION

Constant	Boolean Operator*	Description
R2_BLACK	0	Pixel is always 0.
R2_COPYPEN	P	Pixel is the pen color. This is the default mix mode.
R2_MASKNOTPEN	~P & S	Pixel is a combination of the colors common to both the screen and the inverse of the pen.
R2_MASKPEN	P & S	Pixel is a combination of the colors common to both the pen and the screen.
R2_MASKPENNOT	P & ~S	Pixel is a combination of the colors common to both the pen and the inverse of the screen.
R2_MERGENOTPEN	~P | S	Pixel is a combination of the screen color and the inverse of the pen color.
R2_MERGEPEN	P | S	Pixel is a combination of the pen color and the screen color.
R2_MERGEPENNOT	P | ~S	Pixel is a combination of the pen color and the inverse of the screen color.
R2_NOP	S	Pixel remains unchanged.
R2_NOT	~S	Pixel is the inverse of the screen color.
R2_NOTCOPYPEN	~P	Pixel is the inverse of the pen color.
R2_NOTMASKPEN	~(P & S)	Pixel is the inverse of the R2_MASKPEN color.
R2_NOTMERGEPEN	~(P | S)	Pixel is the inverse of the R2_MERGEPEN color.
R2_NOTXORPEN	~(P ^ S)	Pixel is the inverse of the R2_XORPEN color.
R2_WHITE	1	Pixel is always 1.
R2_XORPEN	P ^ S	Pixel is a combination of the colors in the pen and in the screen, but not in both.

** The symbols in this column may be understood as follows: ~ = boolean NOT; | = boolean OR; & = boolean AND; ^ = boolean XOR.*

Background Modes

Windows recognizes two background modes that determine how the gaps between dots and dashes are filled when drawing discontinuous lines, as well as with text and hatched brushes. The background modes, named `OPAQUE` and `TRANSPARENT`, are set in the device context by means of the `SetBkMode()` function. The function's general form reads as follows:

```
int SetBkMode(
            HDC hdc,       // 1
            int iBkMode    // 2
            );
```

The first parameter is the handle to the device context, and the second one the constants `OPAQUE` or `TRANSPARENT`. If the opaque mode is selected, the background is filled with the current screen background color. If the mode is `TRANSPARENT`, then the background is left unchanged.

The background mode affects lines that result from a pen created with `CreatePen()` or `CreatePenIndirect()`, but not by those created with `ExtCreatePen()`.

Current Pen Position

Many GDI drawing functions start at a screen location known as the *current pen position*, or the current position. The current pen position is an attribute of the device context. The initial position of the pen is at logical coordinates (0, 0). Two functions relate directly to the current pen position: `MoveToEx()` and `GetCurrentPosition()`. Some drawing functions change the pen position as they execute. The `MoveToEx()` function is used to set the current pen position. Its general form reads as follows:

```
BOOL MoveToEx(
            HDC hdc,            // 1
            int X,              // 2
            int Y,              // 3
            LPPOINT lpPoint     // 4
            );
```

The first parameter is the handle to the device context. The second and third parameters are the x- and y-coordinates of the new pen position, in logical units. The fourth parameter is a pointer to a structure of type `POINT` that holds the x- and y-coordinates of the previous current pen position. If this parameter is set to NULL the old pen position is not returned. The function returns a Boolean that is TRUE if the function succeeds and FALSE if it fails.

The GetCurrentPositionEx() function can be used to obtain the current pen position. Its general form reads as follows:

```
BOOL MoveToEx(
            HDC hdc,            // 1
            int X,              // 2
            int Y,              // 3
            LPPOINT lpPoint     // 4
            );
```

The second parameter is a pointer to a structure variable of type POINT that receives the coordinates of the current pen position. The function returns TRUE if it succeeds and FALSE if it fails.

Drawing functions whose names contain the word "To"use and change the current pen position, these are: LineTo(), PolylineTo(), and PolyBezierTo(). Windows is not always consistent in this use of the word "To," since the functions AngleArc() and PolyDraw() also use and update the current pen position.

Arc Direction

One start-point and one end-point on the circumference of a circle define two different arcs: one drawn clockwise and one drawn counterclockwise. The exception is when the start- and end-points coincide. Figure 6-5 shows this possible ambiguity.

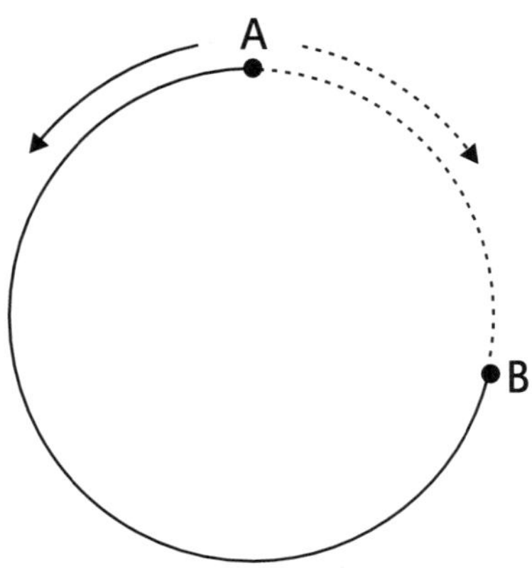

Figure 6-5: The arc drawing direction

In Figure 6-5 the solid-line arc is drawn counterclockwise from point A to point B, while the dotted-line arc is drawn clockwise between these same points. The SetArcDirection() function is used to resolve this problem. The function's general form reads as follows:

```
int SetArcDirection(
                    HDC hdc,           // 1
                    int ArcDirection   // 2
                    );
```

The second parameter is either the constant AD_CLOCKWISE, or the constant AD_COUNTERCLOCKWISE. The function returns the previous arc-drawing direction.

Drawing Pixels, Lines, and Curves

The lowest-level graphics primitives are used to set a screen pixel to a particular attribute and to read the attributes of a screen pixel. In theory, with functions to set and read a pixel, all the other graphics operations can be developed in software. For example, a line can be drawn by setting a series of adjacent pixels, a closed figure can be filled by setting all the pixels within its boundaries, and so on. However, in actual programming practice these simple primitives are not sufficient. In the first place, high-level language code requires considerable overhead in performing the pixel set and read operations. To draw lines and figures by successively calling these functions would be prohibitively time-consuming. On the other hand, sometimes the programmer must resort to pixel by pixel drawing since other higher-level functions are not available.

Eleven functions in the Windows API can be used to draw lines. For one of them, StrokePath(), we postpone the discussion until Chapter 7, since we must first discuss paths in greater detail. Table 6-5 lists the remaining 10 line-drawing functions.

Table 6-5 LINE-DRAWING FUNCTIONS

Function	Drawing Operation
LineTo()	A straight line from current position up to a point. Pen position is updated to line's end point.
PolylineTo()	One or more straight lines between the current position and points in an array. Pen position is used for the first line and updated to end point of last line.
Polyline()	A series of straight line segments between points defined in an array.
PolyPolyLine()	Multiple polylines.
ArcTo()	An elliptical arc updating current pen position.

Continued

TABLE 6-5 LINE-DRAWING FUNCTIONS *(Continued)*

Function	Drawing Operation
`Arc()`	An elliptical arc without updating current pen position.
`AngleArc()`	A segment of arc starting at current pen position.
`PolyBezier()`	One or more Bézier curves without updating the current pen position.
`PolyBezierTo()`	One or more Bézier curves updating the current pen position.
`PolyDraw()`	A set of lines and Bézier curves.
`StrokePath()`	See Chapter 7.

Pixel Operations

Two Windows functions operate on single pixels: `SetPixel()` and `GetPixel()` .`SetPixel()` is used to set a pixel at any screen location to a particular color attribute. `GetPixel()` reads the color attribute of a pixel at a given screen location. The general form of `SetPixel()` reads as follows:

```
COLORREF SetPixel(
                    HDC hdc,            // 1
                    int X,              // 2
                    int Y,              // 3
                    COLORREF crColor    // 4
                    );
```

The first parameter is the handle to the device context. The second and third parameters are the *x*- and *y*-coordinates of the pixel to set, in logical units. The fourth parameter contains the pixel color in a `COLORREF` type structure. The function returns the RGB color to which the pixel was set, which may not coincide with the one requested in the call because of limitations of the video hardware. A faster version of this function is `SetPixelV()`. It takes the same parameters but returns a Boolean value that is TRUE if the operation succeeded and FALSE if it failed. In most cases `SetPixelV()` is preferred over `SetPixel()` because of its better performance. The following code fragment shows how to draw a box of 100 by 100 pixels using the `SetPixelV()` function:

```
int x, y, i, j;         // control variables
COLORREF   pixColor;
.
```

```
.
.
x = 120;         // start x
y = 120;         // start y
pixColor = RGB(0xff, 0x0, 0x0); // Red

// Draw a 100-by-100 pixel box
for (i = 0; i < 100; i++) {
     for (j = 0; j < 100; j++) {
          SetPixelV (hdc, x, y, pixColor);
          x++;
     }
     x = 120;
     y++;
}
```

Drawing with LineTo()

The simplest of all line-drawing functions is `LineTo()`. This function requires three parameters: the handle to the device context, and the coordinates of the end points of the line. The line is drawn with the currently selected pen. The start point is the current pen position, which means that `LineTo()` is often preceded by `MoveToEx()` or another drawing function that sets the current pen position. `LineTo()` returns TRUE if the function succeeds and FALSE if it fails, but most often the return value is not used by code. If the `LineTo()` function succeeds, the current pen position is reset to the line's end point; therefore, the function can be used to draw a series of connected line segments.

The following code fragment draws a rectangle using four lines:

```
HPEN           bluePen4;      // handle for a pen
  int            x, y, i, j;    // local variables
  .
  .
  .
// Create and select pen
bluePen4 = CreatePen (PS_SOLID, 4, RGB (0x00, 0x00, 0xff);
SelectObject (hdc, bluePen4);

// Set current pen position for start point
MoveToEx (hdc, 140, 140, NULL);
  LineTo (hdc, 300, 140);      // draw first segment
  LineTo (hdc, 300, 200);      // second segment
  LineTo (hdc, 140, 300);      // third segment
  LineTo (hdc, 140, 140);      // last segment
```

Drawing with PolylineTo()

The PolylineTo() function draws one or more straight lines between points contained in an array of type POINT. The current pen position is used as a start point and is reset to the location of the last point in the array. PolylineTo() provides an easier way of drawing several connected line segments, or an unfilled closed figure. The function uses the current pen. Its general form reads as follows:

```
BOOL PolylineTo(
                HDC hdc,            // 1
                CONST POINT *lppt,  // 2
                DWORD cCount        // 3
                );
```

The second parameter is the address of an array of points that contains the *x*- and *y*-coordinate pairs. The third parameter is the count of the number of points in the array. The function returns TRUE if it succeeds and FALSE if it does not. The following code fragment shows the drawing of a rectangle using the PolylineTo() function:

```
HPEN       redPen2;
  POINT      pointsArray[4];  // array of four points
   .
   .
   .
// Create a solid red pen, 2 pixels wide
redPen2 = CreatePen (PS_SOLID, 2, RGB(0xff, 0x00, 0x00));
SelectObject (hdc, redPen2);
// Fill array of points
pointsArray[0].x = 300; pointsArray[0].y = 160;
pointsArray[1].x = 300; pointsArray[1].y = 300;
pointsArray[2].x = 160; pointsArray[2].y = 300;
pointsArray[3].x = 160; pointsArray[3].y = 160;
// Set start point for first segment
MoveToEx (hdc, 160, 160, NULL);
// Draw polyline
PolylineTo (hdc, pointsArray, 4);
```

Drawing with Polyline()

The Polyline() function is similar to PolylineTo() except that it does not use or change the current pen position. Therefore, you need one more entry in the array of points to draw a figure with Polyline() since the initial position of the drawing pen cannot be used as the starting point for the first line segment. The following code fragment shows the code for drawing a rectangle using the Polyline() function:

```
HPEN        blackPen;
  POINT       pointsArray[4];  // array of four points
  .
  .
  .
// Create a solid red pen, 2 pixels wide
blackPen = CreatePen (PS_DASH, 1, 0);
SelectObject (hdc, blackPen);
// Fill array of points
pointsArray[0].x = 160; pointsArray[0].y = 160;
pointsArray[1].x = 300; pointsArray[1].y = 160;
pointsArray[2].x = 300; pointsArray[2].y = 300;
pointsArray[3].x = 160; pointsArray[3].y = 300;
pointsArray[4].x = 160; pointsArray[4].y = 160;
// Draw polyline
Polyline (hdc, pointsArray, 5);
```

Drawing with PolyPolyline()

As the function name implies, `PolyPolyline()` is used to draw several groups of lines or "polylines." Since the points array contains sets of points for more than one polyline, the function requires an array of values that holds the number of points for each polyline. `PolyPolyline()`, like `Polyline()`, does not use or change the current pen position. The function's general form reads as follows:

```
BOOL PolyPolyline(
                  HDC hdc,                      // 1
                  CONST POINT *lppt,            // 2
                  CONST DWORD *lpdwPolyPoints,  // 3
                  DWORD cCount                  // 4
                  );
```

The second parameter is an array containing vertices of the various polylines. The third parameter is an array that contains the number of vertices in each of the polylines. The fourth parameter is the count of the number of elements in the third parameter, which is the number of polylines to be drawn. The function returns TRUE if it succeeds and FALSE otherwise. The following code fragment shows the code for the drawing of two polylines, each with five vertices, using the `PolyPolyline()` function:

```
POINT       pointsArray[10];     // array of points
 DWORD       vertexArray[2];      // vertices per polyline

// Fill array of points for first polyline
pointsArray[0].x = 160; pointsArray[0].y = 160;
```

```
pointsArray[1].x = 300; pointsArray[1].y = 160;
pointsArray[2].x = 300; pointsArray[2].y = 300;
pointsArray[3].x = 160; pointsArray[3].y = 300;
pointsArray[4].x = 160; pointsArray[4].y = 160;

// Fill array of points for second polyline
pointsArray[5].x = 160; pointsArray[5].y = 230;
pointsArray[6].x = 230; pointsArray[6].y = 160;
pointsArray[7].x = 300; pointsArray[7].y = 230;
pointsArray[8].x = 230; pointsArray[8].y = 300;
pointsArray[9].x = 160; pointsArray[9].y = 230;

// Fill number of vertices in array
vertexArray[0] = 5;
vertexArray[1] = 5;
// Draw two polylines
PolyPolyline (hdc, pointsArray, vertexArray, 2);
```

Figure 6-6 shows the figures that result from executing the previous code sample. The second polyline is shown in dashed lines to visually distinguish it from the first one. However, in an actual drawing there is no way of changing pens inside a call to `PolyPolyline()`.

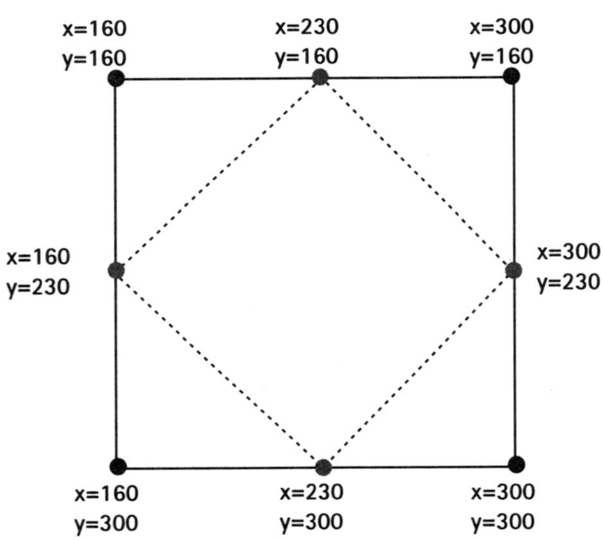

Figure 6-6: Coordinates of two polylines in the sample code

Drawing with Arc()

The Arc() function draws an elliptical arc. It is also used to draw circles, since the circle is a special case of the ellipse. The function's general form reads as follows:

```
BOOL Arc(
        HDC hdc,          // 1
        int nLeftRect,    // 2
        int nTopRect,     // 3
        int nRightRect,   // 4
        int nBottomRect,  // 5
        int nXStartArc,   // 6
        int nYStartArc,   // 7
        int nXEndArc,     // 8
        int nYEndArc      // 9
        );
```

The second and third parameters are the *x*- and *y*-coordinates of the upper-left corner of a rectangle that contains the ellipse, while the fourth and fifth parameters are the coordinates of its lower-right corner. By using a bounding rectangle to define the ellipse, the Windows API avoids dealing with elliptical semi-axes. However, whenever necessary, the bounding rectangle can be calculated from the semi-axes. The sixth and seventh parameters define the coordinates of a point that sets the start point of the elliptical arc. The last two parameters set the end points of the elliptical arc. The elliptical arc is always drawn in the counterclockwise direction. The SetArcDirectior() function has no effect in this case.

The coordinates of the start and end points of the elliptical arc need not coincide with the arc itself. Windows draws an imaginary line from the center of the ellipse to the start and end points. The point at which this line (or its prolongation) intersects the elliptical arc is used as the start or end point. If the start and end points are the same, then a complete ellipse is drawn. The following code fragment draws an elliptical arc:

```
Arc (hdc,
      150, 150,           // upper-left of rectangle
      350, 250,           // lower-right
      250, 260,           // start point
      200, 140;           // end point
```

Figure 6-7 shows the location of each of the points in the preceding call to the Arc() function and the resulting ellipse.

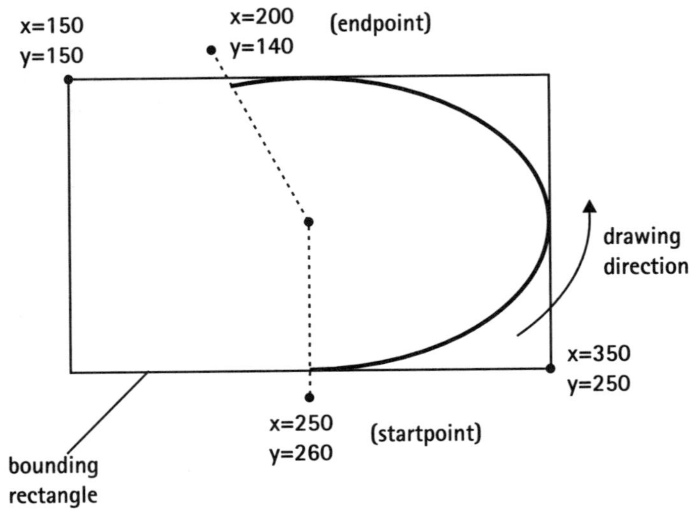

Figure 6-7: Coordinates of an elliptical arc in sample code

Drawing with ArcTo()

`ArcTo()` is a version of the `Arc()` function that updates the current pen position to the end point of the elliptical arc. This function requires Windows NT Version 3.1 or later. It is not available in Windows 95 or 98. The function parameters are identical to those of the `Arc()` function.

Drawing with AngleArc()

The `AngleArc()` function draws a straight line segment and an arc of a circle. The straight-line segment is from the current pen position to the arc's starting point. The arc is defined by the circle's radius and two angles: the starting position, in degrees, relative to the *x*-axis, and the angle sweep, also in degrees, relative to the starting position. The arc is drawn in a counterclockwise direction. The function's general form reads as follows:

```
BOOL AngleArc(
            HDC hdc,            // 1
            int X,              // 2
            int Y,              // 3
            DWORD dwRadius,     // 4
            FLOAT eStartAngle,  // 5
            FLOAT eSweepAngle   // 6
            );
```

The second and third parameters are the coordinates of the center of the circle that defines the arc, in logical units. The fourth parameter is the radius of the circle, also in logical units. The fifth parameter is the start angle in degrees, relative to the *x*-axis. The last parameter is the sweep angle, also in degrees, relative to the angle's starting position. Figure 6-8 shows the various elements in the `AngleArc()` function.

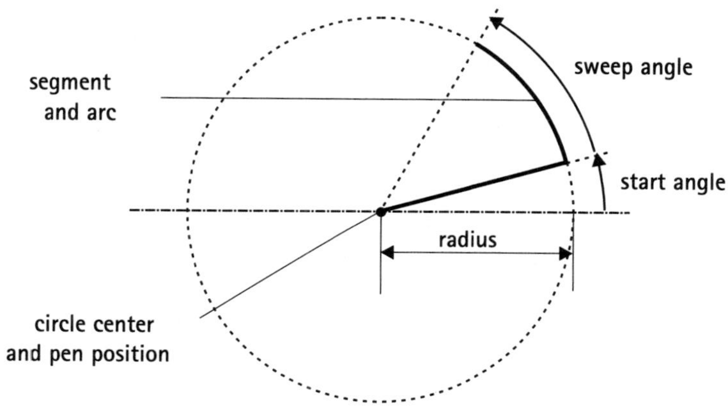

Figure 6-8: AngleArc() function elements

The `AngleArc()` function is not available in Windows 95 or 98; however, it can be emulated in code. Microsoft Developers Network contains the following listing which allows implementing the `AngleArc()` function in software:

```
BOOL AngleArc2(HDC hdc, int X, int Y, DWORD dwRadius,
               float fStartDegrees, float fSweepDegrees) {

  int iXStart, iYStart;  // End point of starting radial line
  int iXEnd, iYEnd;      // End point of ending radial line
  float fStartRadians;   // Start angle in radians
  float fEndRadians;     // End angle in radians
  BOOL bResult;          // Function result
  float fTwoPi = 2.0f * 3.141592f;

  /* Get the starting and ending angle in radians */
  if (fSweepDegrees > 0.0f) {
    fStartRadians = ((fStartDegrees / 360.0f) * fTwoPi);
    fEndRadians = (((fStartDegrees + fSweepDegrees) / 360.0f) *
          fTwoPi);
  } else {
    fStartRadians = (((fStartDegrees + fSweepDegrees)  / 360.0f) *
          fTwoPi);
```

```
    fEndRadians =  ((fStartDegrees / 360.0f) * fTwoPi);
  }

  /* Calculate a point on the starting radial line via */
  /* polar -> cartesian conversion */
  iXStart = X + (int)((float)dwRadius * (float)cos(fStartRadians));
  iYStart = Y - (int)((float)dwRadius * (float)sin(fStartRadians));

  /* Calculate a point on the ending radial line via */
  /* polar -> cartesian conversion */
  iXEnd = X + (int)((float)dwRadius * (float)cos(fEndRadians));
  iYEnd = Y - (int)((float)dwRadius * (float)sin(fEndRadians));

  /* Draw a line to the starting point */
  LineTo(hdc, iXStart, iYStart);

  /* Draw the arc */
  bResult = Arc(hdc, X - dwRadius, Y - dwRadius,
                     X + dwRadius, Y + dwRadius,
                     iXStart, iYStart,
                     iXEnd, iYEnd);

  // Move to the ending point - Arc() wont do this and ArcTo()
  // won't work on Win32s or Win16 MoveToEx(hdc, iXEnd, iYEnd,
NULL);

  return bResult;
}
```

The one documented difference between the preceding listing of `AngleArc2()`, and the GDI `AngleArc()` function, is that if the value entered in the sixth parameter exceeds 360 degrees, the software version will not sweep the angle multiple times. In most cases, this is not a problem.

The program named PXL_DEMO, in the *Pixel and Line Demo* project folder on the book's CD-ROM program, uses the `AngleArc2()` function to display a curve similar to the one in Figure 6-8.

Drawing with PolyBezier()

In mechanical drafting, a spline is a flexible edge that is used to connect several points on an irregular curve. Two French engineers, Pierre Bézier and Paul de Casteljau, almost simultaneously discovered a mathematical expression for a spline curve that can be easily adapted to computer representations. This curve is known as the Bézier spline or curve, since it was Bézier who first published his findings. The Bézier curve is defined by its end points, called the nodes, and by one or more control points. The control points serve as magnets or attractors that "pull" the curve in their direction, but never enough for the curve to intersect the control point. Figure 6-9 shows the elements of a simple Bézier curve.

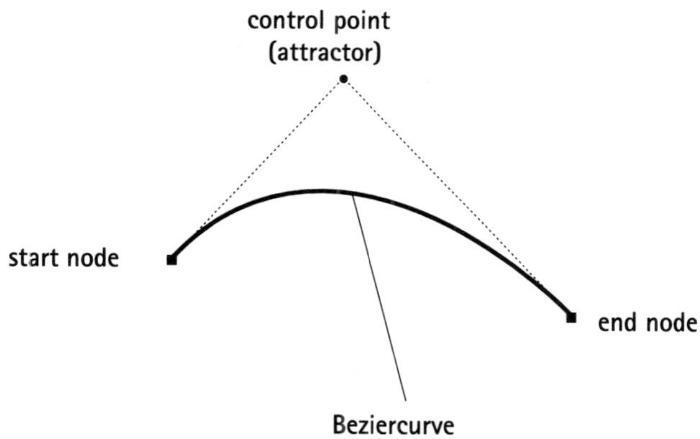

Figure 6-9: Bézier spline elements

The Bézier curve in Figure 6-9 can be generated by a geometrical method that consists of creating a series of progressively smaller line segments. The process, sometimes called the *divide and conquer method*, starts by joining the half-way points between the nodes and the attractor, thus creating a new set of nodes and a new attractor. The process continues until a sufficiently accurate approximation of the spline is reached. Figure 6-10 shows the progressive steps in creating a Bézier spline by this method.

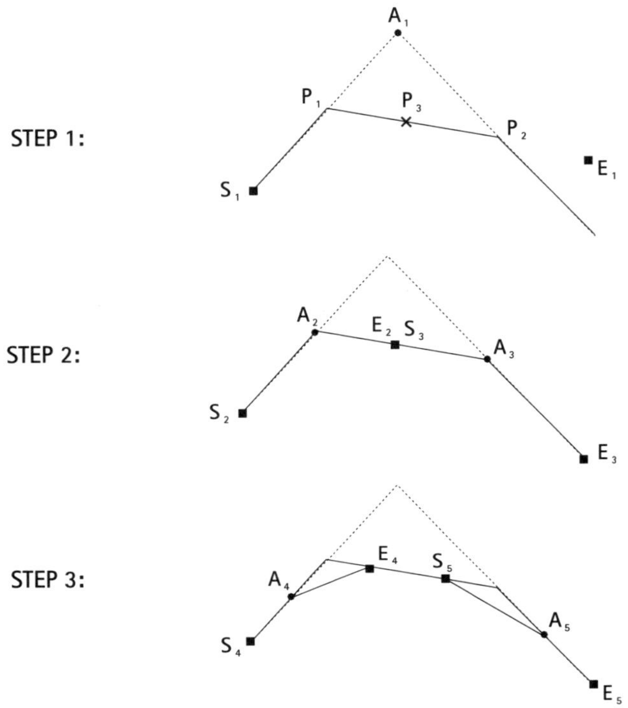

Figure 6-10: Divide-and-conquer method of creating a Bézier curve

In Step 1 of Figure 6-10, we see the start node S_1, the end node E_1, and the attractor A_1. We first find a point midway between S_1 and A_1 and label it P_1. Another point midway between A_1 and E_1 is labeled P_2. Points P_1 and P_2 are joined by a line segment whose midpoint is labeled P_3. In Step 2 we can see two new figures. The first one has nodes at S_2 and E_2, and the attractor at A_2. The second figure has nodes at S_3 and E_3, and the attractor at A_3. In Step 3 we have joined the midpoints between the nodes and the attractors with a line segment, thus continuing the process. The two new figures have their new respective nodes and attractors, so the process can be repeated. In Step 3 we can see how the resulting line segments begin to approximate the Bézier curve in Figure 6-9.

The divide and conquer process makes evident the fundamental assumption of the Bézier spline: the curve is in the same direction and tangent to straight lines from the nodes to the attractors. A second assumption is that the curve never intersects the attractors. The Bézier formulas are based on these assumptions.

The Bézier curve generated by the divide-and-conquer method is known as a quadratic Bézier. In computer graphics the most useful Bézier is the cubic form. In the cubic form the Bézier curve is defined by two nodes and two attractors. The development of the cubic Bézier is almost identical to that of the quadratic. Figure 6-11 shows the elements of a cubic Bézier curve.

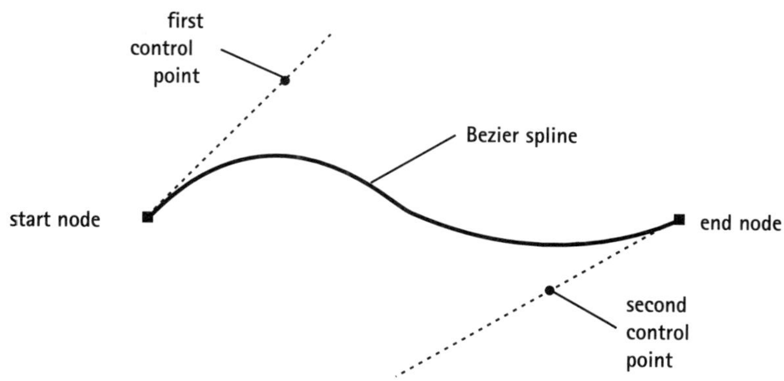

Figure 6-11: Elements of the cubic Bézier

The `PolyBezier()` function, introduced in Windows 95, draws one or more cubic Bézier curves, each one defined by its nodes and two attractors. The function can be called to draw multiple Bézier curves. In this case the first curve requires four parameters, and all the other curves require three parameters. This is because the end node of the preceding Bézier curve serves as the start node for the next one. `PolyBezier()` does not change the current pen position. The Bézier curve is drawn using the pen selected in the device context. The function's general form reads as follows:

```
BOOL PolyBezier(
                HDC hdc,             // 1
                CONST POINT *lppt,   // 2
                DWORD cPoints        // 3
                );
```

The first parameter is the handle to the device context. The second parameter is the address of an array of points that contains the *x*- and *y*-coordinate pairs for the nodes and control points. The third parameter is the count of the number of points in the array. This value must be one more than three times the number of curves to be drawn. For example, if the `PolyBezier()` function is called to draw four curves, there must be 13 coordinate pairs in the array (1 + (3 * 4)). The function returns `TRUE` if it succeeds and `FALSE` otherwise.

The Bézier data is stored in the array of points in a specific order. In the first Bézier curve, the first and fourth entries are the nodes and the second and third are attractors. Note that in the array the first and fourth entries are at offset 0 and 3 respectively, and the second and third entries are at offset 1 and 2. If other Bézier curves are in the array, the first node is not explicit in the data, since it coincides with the end node of the preceding curve. Therefore, after the first curve, the following two entries are attractors, and the third entry is the end node. Table 6-6 shows the sequence of nodes and control points for an array with multiple Bézier curves.

TABLE 6-6 ARRAY STORAGE OF BÉZIER NODES AND CONTROL POINTS FOR THE POLYBEZIER() FUNCTION

Number	Offset	Type
1	0	Start node of curve 1
2	1	First attractor of curve 1
3	2	Second attractor of curve 1
4	3	End node of curve 1
5	4	First attractor of curve 2
6	5	Second attractor of curve 2
7	6	End node of curve 2
8	7	First attractor of curve 3
9	8	Second attractor of curve 3
10	9	End node of curve 3

The following code fragment shows the drawing of a Bézier curve using the `PolyBezier()` function:

```
POINTS      pointsArray[4];  // Array of x/y coordinates
   .
   .
   .
// Fill array of points for Bezier spline
// Entries 0 and 3 are nodes
// Entries 1 and 2 are attractors
pointsArray[0].x = 150; pointsArray[0].y = 150;
pointsArray[1].x = 200; pointsArray[1].y = 75;
pointsArray[2].x = 280; pointsArray[2].y = 190;
pointsArray[3].x = 350; pointsArray[3].y = 150;

// Draw a Bezier spline
PolyBezier (hdc, pointsArray, 4);
```

The resulting Bézier curve is similar to the one in Figure 6-9.

Drawing with PolyBezierTo()

The `PolyBezierTo()` function is very similar to `PolyBezier()` except that the start node for the first curve is the current pen position, and the current pen position is updated to the end node of the last curve. The return value and parameters are the same for both functions. In the case of `PolyBezierTo()` each curve is defined by three points: two control points and the end node. Table 6-7 shows the sequence of points stored in the points array for the `PolyBezierTo()` function.

TABLE 6-7 ARRAY STORAGE OF BÉZIER NODES AND CONTROL POINTS FOR THE POLYBEZIERTO() FUNCTION

Number	Offset	Type
1	0	First attractor of curve 1
2	1	Second attractor of curve 1
3	2	End node of curve 1
4	3	First attractor of curve 2
5	4	Second attractor of curve 2
6	5	End node of curve 2
7	6	First attractor of curve 3
8	7	Second attractor of curve 3
9	7	End node of curve 3

Drawing with PolyDraw()

`PolyDraw()` is the most complex of the Windows line-drawing functions. It creates the possibility of drawing a series of line segments and Bézier curves, which can be joint or disjoint. `PolyDraw()` can be used in place of several calls to `MoveTo()`, `LineTo()`, and `PolyBezierTo()` functions. All the figures are drawn with the pen currently selected in the device context. The function's general form reads as follows:

```
BOOL PolyDraw(
            HDC hdc,                // 1
            CONST POINT *lppt,      // 2
            CONST BYTE *lpbTypes,   // 3
            int cCount              // 4
            );
```

The second parameter is the address of an array of points that contains *x*- and *y*-coordinate pairs. The third parameter is an array of type BYTE that contains identifiers that define the purpose of each of the points in the array. The fourth parameter is the count of the number of points in the array of points. The function returns TRUE if it succeeds and FALSE otherwise. Table 6-8 lists the constants used to represent the identifiers entered in the function's third parameter.

TABLE 6-8 CONSTANTS FOR POLYDRAW() POINT SPECIFIERS

Type	Meaning
PT_MOVETO	This point starts a disjoint figure. The point becomes the new current pen position.
PT_LINETO	A line is to be drawn from the current position to this point, which then becomes the new current pen position.
PT_BEZIERTO	This is a control point or end node for a Bézier curve. This constant always occurs in sets of three. The current position defines the start node for the Bézier curve. The other two coordinates are control points. The third entry is the end node.
PT_CLOSEFIGURE	The figure is automatically closed after the PT_LINETO or PT_BEZIERTO type for this point is executed. A line is drawn from the end point to the most recent PT_MOVETO or MoveTo() point. The PT_CLOSEFIGURE constant is combined by means of a bitwise OR operator with a PT_LINETO or PT_BEZIERTO constant. This indicates that the corresponding point is the last one in a figure and that the figure is to be closed.

The PolyDraw() function is not available in Windows 95 or 98. Microsoft has published the following code for implementing the function in software:

```
//****************************
// Win95 version of PolyDraw()
// as published by Microsoft
//****************************
BOOL PolyDraw95(HDC  hdc,                     // handle of a device
                                              // context
                CONST LPPOINT lppt,           // array of points
                CONST LPBYTE lpbTypes,        // line and curve
                                              // identifiers
                int  cCount)                  // count of points
```

```
{
int i;
for (i=0; i<cCount; i++)
switch (lpbTypes[i]) {
case PT_MOVETO :
MoveToEx(hdc, lppt[i].x, lppt[i].y, NULL);
break;

case PT_LINETO | PT_CLOSEFIGURE:
case PT_LINETO :
LineTo(hdc, lppt[i].x, lppt[i].y);
break;

case PT_BEZIERTO | PT_CLOSEFIGURE:
case PT_BEZIERTO :
PolyBezierTo(hdc, &lppt[i], 3);
i+=2;
break;
    }

return TRUE;
}
```

Notice that in the function `PolyDraw95()` the processing for closed and open figures takes place in the same intercepts. Therefore, there is no closing action implemented. When using this software implementation, the inclusion of the `PT_CLOSEFIGURE` constant has no effect on the drawing. We have coded the following modification, named `PolyDraw95A()`, which closes open figures:

```
//****************************
// Win95 version of PolyDraw()
//        improved!
//****************************
BOOL PolyDraw95A (HDC  hdc,              // handle to device context
                  CONST LPPOINT lppt,    // array of points
                  CONST LPBYTE lpbTypes, // array of identifiers
                  int  cCount)           // count of points
{
int i;
  static long lastPenx, lastPeny;   // Storage for last pen position
  POINT       currentPoints[1];

// Store initial position of drawing pen
GetCurrentPositionEx (hdc, currentPoints);
```

```
lastPenx = currentPoints[0].x;
lastPeny = currentPoints[0].y;

for (i=0; i<cCount; i++)
switch (lpbTypes[i]) {
case PT_MOVETO :
MoveToEx(hdc, lppt[i].x, lppt[i].y, NULL);
// Store position for closed figures
lastPenx = lppt[i].x;
lastPeny = lppt[i].y;
break;

case PT_LINETO | PT_CLOSEFIGURE:
LineTo(hdc, lppt[i].x, lppt[i].y);
LineTo(hdc, lastPenx, lastPeny);
break;

case PT_LINETO :
LineTo(hdc, lppt[i].x, lppt[i].y);
break;

case PT_BEZIERTO | PT_CLOSEFIGURE:
// Store start points of Bezier for closing
GetCurrentPositionEx (hdc, currentPoints);
lastPenx = currentPoints[0].x;
lastPeny = currentPoints[0].y;
// Draw curve
PolyBezierTo(hdc, &lppt[i], 3);
i+=2;
// Close with line
LineTo(hdc, lastPenx, lastPeny);
break;

case PT_BEZIERTO :
// Draw Bezier
PolyBezierTo(hdc, &lppt[i], 3);
i+=2;
break;
    }

return TRUE;
}
```

The following code fragment displays several open and close figures using the PolyDraw() function or its software version Polydraw95A():

```
POINT      pointsArray[16];     // array of points
 BYTE       controlArray[16];
  .
  .
  .
// In this example, pen is moved to start position externally
MoveToEx (hdc, 150, 50, NULL);

// Filling array of points for three lines
  // offset:        purpose:
  //   0            end point of line 1
  //   1            start of line 2
  //   2            end of line 2
  //   3            start of line 3
  //   4            end of line 3
pointsArray[0].x = 250; pointsArray[0].y = 50;
pointsArray[1].x = 150; pointsArray[1].y = 70;
pointsArray[2].x = 250; pointsArray[2].y = 70;
pointsArray[3].x = 150; pointsArray[3].y = 90;
pointsArray[4].x = 250; pointsArray[4].y = 90;

// Move to start node of Bezier curve
pointsArray[5].x = 150; pointsArray[5].y = 150;

// Filling array of points for first Bezier spline
pointsArray[6].x = 200; pointsArray[6].y = 75;
pointsArray[7].x = 280; pointsArray[7].y = 190;
pointsArray[8].x = 350; pointsArray[8].y = 150;

// Filling array for closed figure
pointsArray[9].x = 200; pointsArray[9].y = 200;
pointsArray[10].x = 300; pointsArray[10].y = 200;
pointsArray[11].x = 300; pointsArray[11].y = 300;
pointsArray[12].x = 200; pointsArray[12].y = 300;

// Filling array for second Bezier spline
pointsArray[13].x = 300; pointsArray[13].y = 90;
pointsArray[14].x = 350; pointsArray[14].y = 40;
pointsArray[15].x = 350; pointsArray[15].y = 40;
pointsArray[16].x = 400; pointsArray[16].y = 90;
```

```
// Filling control array
controlArray[0] = PT_LINETO;
controlArray[1] = PT_MOVETO;
controlArray[2] = PT_LINETO;
controlArray[3] = PT_MOVETO;
controlArray[4] = PT_LINETO;
controlArray[5] = PT_MOVETO;
controlArray[6] = PT_BEZIERTO;
controlArray[7] = PT_BEZIERTO;
controlArray[8] = PT_BEZIERTO;
controlArray[9] = PT_MOVETO;
controlArray[10] = PT_LINETO;
controlArray[11] = PT_LINETO;
controlArray[12] = PT_LINETO | PT_CLOSEFIGURE;
controlArray[13] = PT_MOVETO;
controlArray[14] = PT_BEZIERTO | PT_CLOSEFIGURE;
controlArray[15] = PT_BEZIERTO;
controlArray[16] = PT_BEZIERTO;

// Drawing lines and B♪zier curves
PolyDraw95A (hdc, pointsArray, controlArray, 17);
```

Figure 6-12 is an approximation of the figures that result from the previous code sample.

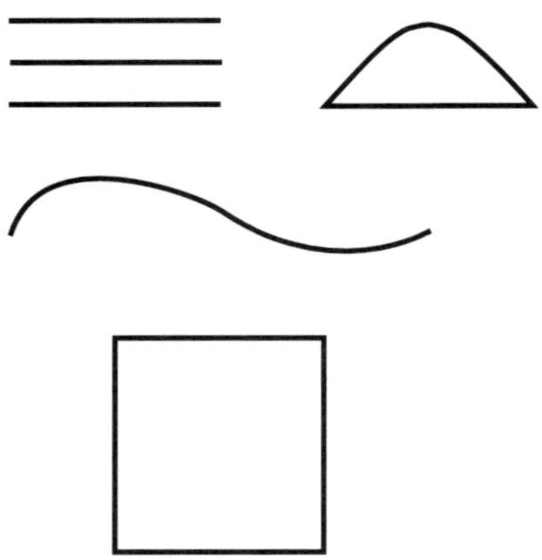

Figure 6-12: Approximate result of the PolyDraw() code sample

Pixel and Line Demonstration Program

The program named PXL_DEMO, located in the *Pixel and Line Demo* project folder of the book's CD-ROM, is a demonstration of the drawing functions discussed in this chapter. Pixel-level functions are used to display the point plot of a sine curve. Also, the program contains a function named `DrawDot()`, which uses the `SetPixelV()` function to draw a black screen dot by setting five adjacent pixels. The demo program displays a pop-up menu, named Line Functions, which has menu commands for exercising `LineTo()`, `PolyLineTo()`, `PolyLine()`, `PolyPolyLine()`, `Arc()`, `AngleArc()`, `PolyBezier()`, and `PolyDraw()`. Code for implementing `PolyDraw()` and `AngleArc()` in software is also included in the demo program.

Summary

In this chapter you have learned about the Windows GDI, the attributes of the Device Context, and about two important graphics objects: pens and brushes. You have also learned about Device Context attributes, and how to use the Windows functions for reading and setting pixels and for drawing lines and curves in two-dimensional space. We have discussed in detail 12 API services: two that take place at the pixel level and ten line- and curve-drawing primitives.

In Chapter 7 we continue GDI graphics with a discussion of regions, paths, and clipping operations. We also expand into the details of programming with the scalable mapping modes. This knowledge is then applied to the drawing of closed figures, such as rectangles, polygons, ellipses, chords, and other filled areas.

Chapter 7

Closed Regions, Figures, and Paths

IN THIS CHAPTER

- Setting the drawing attributes
- Drawing closed figures such as rectangles, ellipses, chords, pie sections, and polygons
- Drawing operations on rectangles
- Creating, combining, filling, and painting regions
- Clipping and clipping regions
- Creating, deleting, and converting paths
- Path information and rendering operations
- Filled figures Demo Program

WE CONTINUE EXPLORING the graphics functions in the Windows GDI, concentrating on solid figures. These are geometrical figures that contain an interior region and a perimeter or outline. They are more properly called *closed figures*. The interior area enables them to be filled with a given color, hatch pattern, or bitmap image. At the same time, the perimeter of a closed figure can be rendered differently than the filled area. For example, the circumference of a circle can be outlined with a 2-pixel wide black pen, and the circle's interior filled with 1-pixel wide red lines, slanted at 45 degrees, and separated from each other by 10 pixels.

In addition to being outlined and filled, closed figures enable other graphics manipulations. For instance, a solid figure can be used to define the output area to which Windows can perform drawing operations. This area, called the *clipping region*, enables you to produce unique and interesting graphics effects, such as geometrical figures filled with text or pictures.

Some solid figures are geometrically simple: a rectangle, an ellipse, or a symmetrical polygon. More complex figures are created by combining simpler ones. A *region* is an area composed of one or more rectangles, polygons, or ellipses. Regions are used to define irregular areas that can be filled – to clip output – or to establish an area for mouse input.

Paths are relatively new graphics objects – they were introduced with Windows NT, and are also supported in Windows 95/98. A *path* is the route the drawing instrument follows in creating a figure, or set of figures. It is used to define the outline of a graphics object. After a path is created, you can draw its outline (called *stroking the path*), fill its interior, or both. A path can also be used in clipping, or converted into a region. Paths and regions add a powerful dimension to Windows graphics.

Closed Figures and Areas

A closed figure has both a perimeter and an interior. The perimeter of a closed figure is drawn using the current pen and the GDI line-related attributes discussed in Chapter 6. The interior is filled using the current brush, also discussed in Chapter 6. Several closed figures can be drawn with the Windows GDI; among them are ellipses, polygons, chords, pies, and rectangles. Later in this chapter we learn that the Windows names for some of these figures are not geometrically correct. Areas bound by complex lines, such as irregular polygons, Bézier curves, and text characters, can also be filled.

Like lines and curves, closed figures have attributes that determine their characteristics. Most of the attributes that relate to closed figures are described in Chapter 6. These include the mix mode, the background mode, the arc direction, the brush pattern, the pen styles, as well as the brush, pen, and background colors. Two attributes that are specific to closed figures are the brush origin and the polygon-filling mode.

Brush Origin

Figure 6-4 shows the various hatch patterns that can be used with a brush. Windows locates the hatch pattern in reference to coordinates (0,0). It is important to know that this origin is in device units, not in logical units. The hatch pattern is a bitmap. In Windows 95/98, the bitmap is 8 by 8 pixels. In Windows NT, it can have any size. The painting process consists of repeating the bitmap horizontally and vertically until the area is filled.

In some cases, the default origin of the bitmap produces undesirable results. This usually happens when the alignment of a filled figure does not coincide with that of the brush-hatch pattern. Figure 7-1 shows two rectangles, one filled with an unaligned hatch pattern and the other one filled with an aligned hatch pattern.

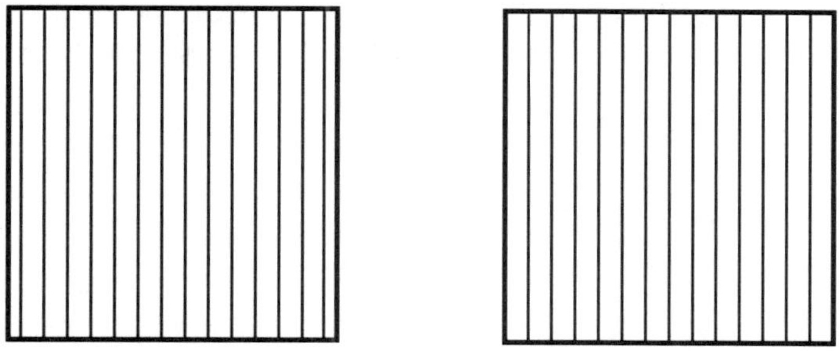

Figure 7-1: Unaligned and aligned hatch patterns

The `SetBrushOrgEx()` function can be used to reposition the hatch bitmap in relation to the origin of the client area. The function's general form reads as follows:

```
BOOL SetBrushOrgEx(
                    HDC hdc,          // 1
                    int nXOrg,        // 2
                    int nYOrg,        // 3
                    LPPOINT lppt      // 4
                   );
```

The second parameter specifies the *x*-coordinate of the new brush origin. In Windows 95/98, the range is 0 to 7. In Windows NT, the range cannot be greater than the width of the bitmap. In either case, if the entered value exceeds the width of the bitmap, it is adjusted by performing the modulus operation:

```
xOrg = xOrg % bitmap width
```

The third parameter is the *y*-coordinate of the new brush origin. Its range and adjustments are the same as for the second parameter. The fourth parameter is a pointer to a POINT structure that stores the origin of the brush previously selected in the device context. If this information is not required, NULL can be entered in this parameter. The function returns TRUE if the operation succeeds and FALSE otherwise.

A call to `SetBrushOrgEx()` sets the origin of the *next* brush that an application selects into the device context. Note that the first parameter of the `SetBrushOrgEx()` function is the handle to the device context, and that the brush variable is nowhere to be found in the parameter list. Therefore, the brush origin is associated with the device context, not with a particular brush. The origin in the device context is assigned to the next brush created.

The following code fragment shows the display of two rectangles. The brush origin is changed for the second one. The `Rectangle()` function is described later in this chapter.

```
static HBRUSH      vertBrush1, vertBrush2;
LOGBRUSH           brush1;
.
.
.
// Create a brush
brush1.lbStyle = BS_HATCHED;
brush1.lbColor = RGB(0x0, 0xff, 0x0);
brush1.lbHatch = HS_VERTICAL;
vertBrush1 = CreateBrushIndirect (&brush1);
SelectObject (hdc, (HGDIOBJ)(HBRUSH) vertBrush1);
// Draw a rectangle with this brush
Rectangle (hdc, 150, 150, 302, 300);

// Create a new hatched brush with offset origin
brush1.lbStyle = BS_HATCHED;
brush1.lbColor = RGB(0x0, 0x0, 0x0);
brush1.lbHatch = HS_VERTICAL;
// Offset the new brush 6 pixels
SetBrushOrgEx (hdc, 5, 0, NULL);
vertBrush2 = CreateBrushIndirect (&brush1);
SelectObject (hdc, (HGDIOBJ)(HBRUSH) vertBrush2);
// Draw a rectangle with the new brush
Rectangle (hdc, 350, 150, 502, 300);
```

The results of executing this code are similar to the rectangles in Figure 7-1. The `GetBrushOrg()` function can be used to retrieve the origin of the current brush.

> **NOTE:** Windows documentation recommends that to avoid brush misalignment an application should call `SetStretchBltMode()` with the stretching mode set to `HALFTONE` before calling `SetBrushOrgEx()`.

Object Selection Macros

The Windows header file `windowsx.h` contains four macros that can be used in selecting a pen, brush, font, or bitmap. The advantage of using these macros is that the objects are automatically typecast correctly. The macros are named

SelectPen(), SelectBrush(), SelectFont() and SelectBitmap(). They are all defined similarly. The SelectBrush() macro reads as follows:

```
#define SelectBrush (hdc, hbr) \
       ((HBRUSH) SelectObject ((hdc, (HGDIOBJ)(HBRUSH)(hbr)))
```

You can use these macros to easily produce correct code that is more portable. Programs that use the object selection macros must contain the statement:

```
#include <windowsx.h>
```

Polygon-fill Mode

The polygon-fill mode attribute determines how overlapping areas of complex polygons and regions are filled. The polygon-fill mode is set with the SetPolyFillMode() function. The function's general form reads as follows:

```
int SetPolyFillMode(
                    HDC hdc,            // 1
                    int iPolyFillMode   // 2
                   );
```

The second parameter is one of two constants: ALTERNATE and WINDING. ALTERNATE defines a mode that fills between odd-numbered and even-numbered polygon sides, or in other words, those areas that can be reached from the outside of the polygon by crossing an odd number of lines, excluding the vertices. This fill algorithm is based on what is called the *parity rule.*

The WINDING mode is based on the nonzero winding rule. In the WINDING mode, the direction in which the figure is drawn determines whether an area is to be filled. A polygon line segment is drawn either in a clockwise or a counterclockwise direction. The term *winding* relates to the clockwise and counterclockwise drawing of the polygon segments. An imaginary line, called a *ray,* is extended from an enclosed area in the figure, to a point distant from and outside of the figure. The ray must be on a positive x-direction. Every time the ray crosses a clockwise winding, a counter is incremented. The same counter is decremented whenever the line crosses a counterclockwise winding. The winding counter is examined when the ray reaches the outside of the figure. If the winding counter is nonzero, the area is filled.

In figures that have a single interior region the fill mode is not important. This is not the case with figures that have enclosed areas. A typical case is a polygon in the shape of a five-pointed star with an enclosed pentagon. In this case, the ALTERNATE mode does not fill the interior pentagon, while the WINDING fill mode does. In more complex figures the same rules apply, although they may not be immediately evident. Figure 7-2 shows the results of the polygon-fill modes in two different figures. Recall that in the WINDING fill mode, the direction in which the line segments are drawn is significant.

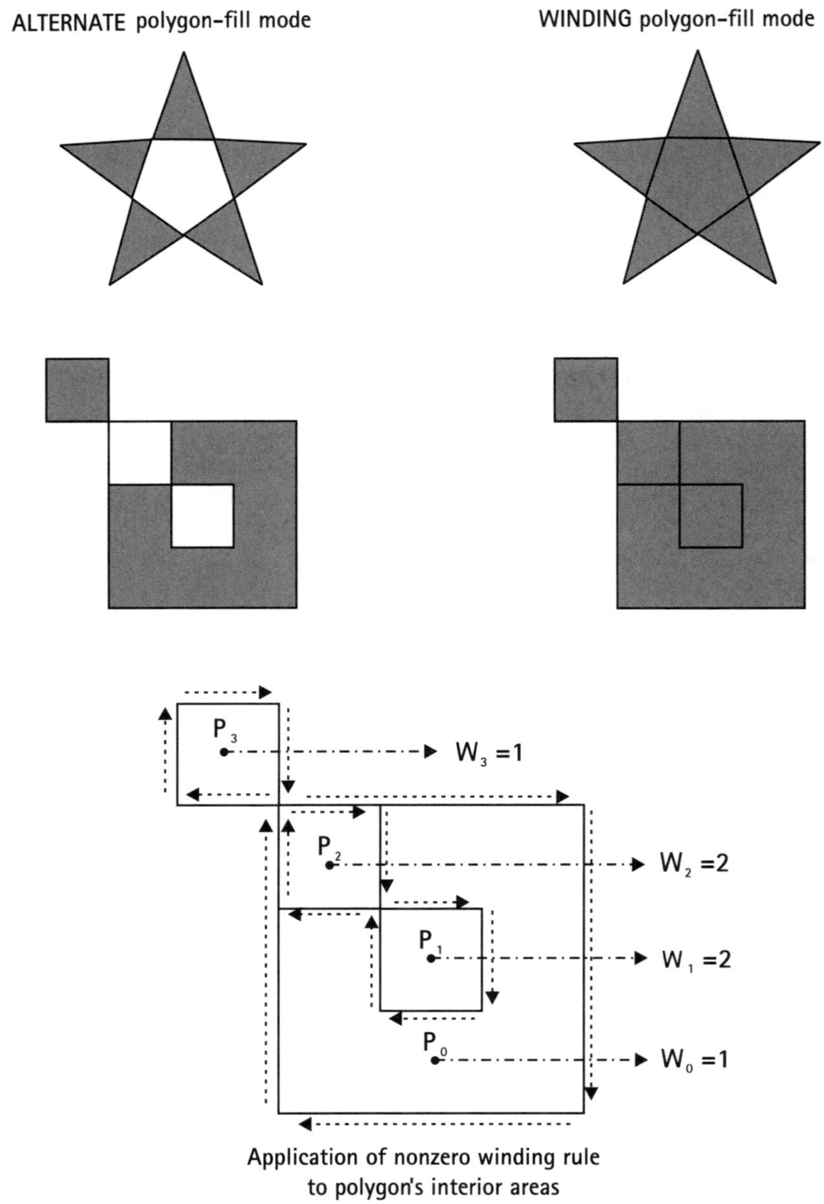

Figure 7-2: Effects of the polygon-fill modes

In Figure 7-2 you can see the application of the nonzero winding rule to the interior areas of a complex polygon. For example, the ray from point P_1 to the exterior of the figure crosses two clockwise segments (windings). Therefore, it has a winding value of 2. Because the winding is nonzero, the area is filled. The same rule can be applied to other points in the figure's interior, as shown in Figure 7-2.

> **NOTE:** Some Windows documentation states that in the WINDING mode, all interior areas of a figure are filled. This oversimplification is not correct. If the interior segments of the polygon in Figure 7-2 were drawn in the opposite direction, some areas would have zero winding and would not be filled. The program named FIL_DEMO, located in the *Filled Figure Demo* project folder of the book's CD-ROM, contains the menu command Polygon (2), on the Draw Figures pop-up menu, which displays a complex polygon that has an unfilled interior in the WINDING mode.

You can retrieve the current polygon fill mode with the GetPolyFillMode() function. The only parameter to the call is the handle to the device context. The value returned is either ALTERNATE or WINDING.

Creating Custom Brushes

In Chapter 6 we mentioned that a logical brush can be created with the CreateBrushIndirect() function. CreateBrushIndirect() has the following general form:

```
HBRUSH CreateBrushIndirect (
CONST LOGBRUSH* lplb // 1
);
```

The only parameter of the function is the address of a structure of type LOGBRUSH. The structure members are divided into three groups: brush style, brush color, and hatch style. The function returns the handle to the created brush. Table 7-1 lists the members of the LOGBRUSH structure.

TABLE 7-1 LOGBRUSH STRUCTURE MEMBERS

Brush Style	Description
BS_DIBPATTERN	A pattern brush defined by a device-independent bitmap. If lbStyle is BS_DIBPATTERN, the lbHatch member contains a handle to a packed DIB.
BS_DIBPATTERNPT	Same a BS_DIBPATTERN but the lbHatch member contains a pointer to a packed DIB.
BS_HATCHED	Hatched brush.

Continued

TABLE 7-1 LOGBRUSH STRUCTURE MEMBERS *(Continued)*

Brush Style	Description
BS_HOLLOW	Hollow brush.
BS_NULL	Same as BS_HOLLOW.
BS_PATTERN	Pattern brush defined by a memory bitmap.
BS_SOLID	Solid brush.
Brush Color	**Description**
DIB_PAL_COLORS	The color table consists of an array of 16-bit indices into the currently realized logical palette.
DIB_RGB_COLORS	The color table contains literal RGB values.
Hatch Style	**Description**
HS_BDIAGONAL	A 45-degree upward, left-to-right hatch.
HS_CROSS	Horizontal and vertical cross-hatch.
HS_DIAGCROSS	A 45-degree crosshatch.
HS_FDIAGONAL	A 45-degree downward, left-to-right hatch.
HS_HORIZONTAL	Horizontal hatch.
HS_VERTICAL	Vertical hatch.

Once the brush is created, it can be selected into the device context by either calling the `SelectObject()` function or the `SelectBrush()` macro discussed previously in this chapter. In addition, you can create specific types of brushes more easily by using the functions `CreateSolidBrush()`, `CreateHatchBrush()`, or `CreatePatternBrush()`. `CreateSolidBrush()` is used to create a brush of a specific color and no hatch pattern. The function's general form reads as follows:

```
HBRUSH CreateSolidBrush (COLORREF colorref);
```

The only parameter is a color value in the form of a `COLORREF` type structure. The color value can be entered directly using the RGB macro. For example, the following code fragment creates a solid blue brush:

```
static HBRUSH       solidBlueBrush;
.
```

```
.
.
solidBlueBrush = CreateSolidBrush ( RGB (0x0, 0x0, 0xff));
```

`CreatehatchBrush()` creates a logical brush with a hatch pattern and color. The function's general form reads as follows:

```
HBRUSH CreateHatchBrush(
                          int fnStyle,      // 1
                          COLORREF clrref   // 2
                         );
```

The first parameter is one of the hatch style identifiers listed in Figure 7-2. The second parameter is a color value of `COLORREF` type. The function returns the handle to the logical brush.

If an application requires a brush with a hatch pattern different from the ones predefined in Windows, it can create a custom brush with its own bitmap. In Windows 95/98, the size of the bitmap cannot exceed 8 by 8 pixels, but there is no size restriction in Windows NT. The function's general form reads as follows:

```
HBRUSH CreatePatternBrush (
                            HBITMAP hbmp    // 1
                           );
```

The function's only parameter is a handle to the bitmap that defines the brush. The bitmap can be created with `CreateBitmap()`, `CreateBitmapIndirect()` or `CreateCompatibleBitmap()` functions. These functions are described in Chapter 8.

Drawing Closed Figures

Seven Windows functions draw closed figures; Table 7-2 lists them.

Table 7-2 WINDOWS FUNCTIONS FOR DRAWING CLOSED FIGURES

Function	Figure
`Rectangle()`	Rectangle with sharp corners
`RoundRect()`	Rectangle with rounded corners
`Ellipse()`	Ellipse or circle

Continued

TABLE 7-2 WINDOWS FUNCTIONS FOR DRAWING CLOSED FIGURES *(Continued)*

Function	Figure
`Chord()`	Solid figure created by an arc on the circumference of an ellipse connected by a chord
`Pie()`	Pie-shaped wedge created by joining the end points of an arc on the perimeter of an ellipse with the center of the arc
`Polygon()`	Closed polygon
`PolyPolygon()`	Series of closed polygons, possibly overlapping

All functions that draw closed figures use the pen currently selected in the device context for the figure outline, and the current brush for filling the interior. All of the line attributes discussed in Chapter 6 apply to the perimeter of solid figures. The programmer has control of the width of the perimeter, its line style, and its color. By selecting NULL_PEN you can draw a figure with no perimeter. The current brush determines the fill. Windows approximates the color of the brush according to the device capabilities. This often requires manipulating dot sizes by a process called *dithering*.

> NOTE: Dithering is a technique that creates the illusion of colors or shades of gray by treating the targeted areas as a dot pattern. The process takes advantage of the fact that the human eye tends to blur small spots of different color by averaging them into a single color or shade. For example, mixing red and white dots can produce a pink color effect.

The brush can be any one of the stock brushes: WHITE_BRUSH, LTGRAY_BRUSH, GRAY_BRUSH, DKGRAY_BRUSH, BLACK_BRUSH, and NULL_BRUSH. All stock brushes are solid. NULL_BRUSH is used to draw figures without filling the interior. The GetStockObject() function is used to obtain a handle to one of the stock brushes. Because stock brushes need not be stored locally, the stock brush is commonly retrieved and installed in the device context at the time it is needed. SelectBrush() and GetStockObject() can be combined as follows:

```
SelectBrush (hdc, GetStockObject (WHITE_BRUSH));
```

The creation and installation of custom brushes was discussed previously in this chapter.

Drawing with Rectangle()

The simplest solid-figure drawing function is Rectangle(). This function draws a rectangle using the current pen for the outline and fills it with the current brush. The function's general form reads as follows:

```
BOOL Rectangle(
               HDC hdc,          // 1
               int nLeftRect,    // 2
               int nTopRect,     // 3
               int nRightRect,   // 4
               int nBottomRect   // 5
              );
```

The second and third parameters are the coordinates of the upper-left corner of the rectangle. The fourth and fifth parameters are the coordinates of the lower-right corner. The function returns TRUE if it succeeds and FALSE if it fails. Figure 7-3 shows a rectangle drawn using this function.

Figure 7-3: Figure definition in the Rectangle() function

Drawing with RoundRect()

The RoundRect() function draws a rectangle with rounded corners. Like all of the solid figure-drawing functions, it uses the current pen for the outline and fills the figure with the current brush. The function's general form reads as follows:

```
BOOL RoundRect(
               HDC hdc,          // 1
               int nLeftRect,    // 2
               int nTopRect,     // 3
```

```
    int nRightRect,  // 4
    int nBottomRect, // 5
    int nWidth,      // 6
    int nHeight      // 7
   );
```

The second and third parameters are the coordinates of the upper-left corner of the bounding rectangle. The fourth and fifth parameters are the coordinates of the lower-right corner. The sixth parameter is the width of the ellipse that is used for drawing the rounded corner arc. The seventh parameter is the height of this ellipse. The function returns TRUE if it succeeds and FALSE if it fails. Figure 7-4 shows the values that define a rounded-corner rectangle drawn using this function.

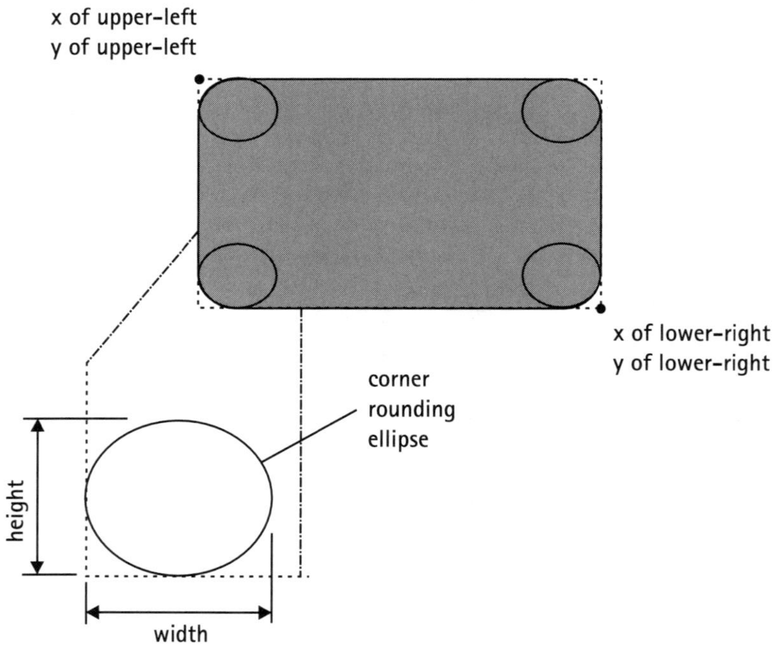

Figure 7-4: Figure definition in the RoundRect() function

Drawing with Ellipse()

The Ellipse() function draws a solid ellipse. Ellipse() uses the current pen for the outline and fills the figure with the current brush. The function's general form reads as follows:

```
BOOL Ellipse(
            HDC hdc,         // 1
```

```
    int nLeftRect,  // 2
    int nTopRect,   // 3
    int nRightRect, // 4
    int nBottomRect // 5
   );
```

The second and third parameters are the coordinates of the upper-left corner of a rectangle that binds the ellipse. The fourth and fifth parameters are the coordinates of the lower-right corner of this rectangle. The function returns TRUE if it succeeds and FALSE if it fails. Figure 7-5 shows an ellipse drawn using this function.

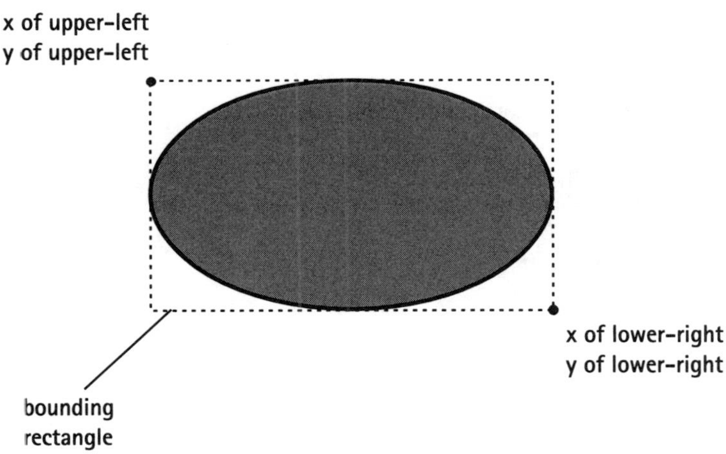

Figure 7-5: Figure definition in the Ellipse() function

Drawing with Chord()

Chord() draws a solid figure composed of an arc of an ellipse whose ends are connected to each other by a straight line, called a *secant*. The Chord() function is related to the Arc() function described in Chapter 6. The parameters that define the elliptical arc are the same for the Arc() as for the Chord() function. The function's general form reads as follows:

```
BOOL Chord(
          HDC hdc,          // 1
          int nLeftRect,    // 2
          int nTopRect,     // 3
          int nRightRect,   // 4
          int nBottomRect,  // 5
          int nXRadial1,    // 6
          int nYRadial1,    // 7
```

```
    int nXRadial2,    // 8
    int nYRadial2     // 9
   );
```

The second and third parameters are the *x*- and *y*-coordinates of the upper-left corner of a rectangle that contains the ellipse, while the fourth and fifth parameters are the coordinates of its lower-right corner. The sixth and seventh parameters define the coordinates of a point that sets the start point of the secant. The last two parameters set the end points of the secant. The elliptical arc is always drawn in the counterclockwise direction. The `SetArcDirection()` function has no effect in this case.

The coordinates of the start and end points of the secant need not coincide with the elliptical arc, because Windows prolongs the secant until it intersects the elliptical arc. Figure 7-6 shows the elements that define the figure.

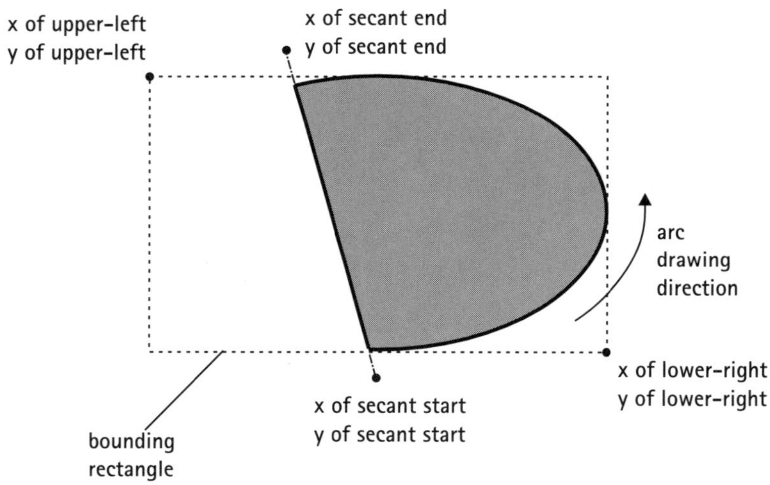

Figure 7-6: Figure definition in the Chord() function

> **NOTE:** The name of the `Chord()` function does not coincide with its mathematical connotation. Geometrically, a chord is the portion of a secant line that joins two points on a curve, not a solid figure.

Drawing with Pie()

`Pie()` draws a solid figure composed of the arc of an ellipse whose ends are connected to the center by straight lines. In Windows terminology the two straight lines are called *radials*. The `Pie()` function is related to the `Arc()` function described in Chapter 6. The parameters that define the elliptical arc are the same for the Arc() as for the Pie() function. It is also similar to the Chord() function previously described. The difference between Chord() and Pie() is that in Chord() the line points are connected to each other, and in Pie() they are connected to the center of the ellipse. The function's general form reads as follows:

```
BOOL Pie(
        HDC hdc,           // 1
        int nLeftRect,     // 2
        int nTopRect,      // 3
        int nRightRect,    // 4
        int nBottomRect,   // 5
        int nXRadial1,     // 6
        int nYRadial1,     // 7
        int nXRadial2,     // 8
        int nYRadial2      // 9
        );
```

The second and third parameters are the *x*- and *y*-coordinates of the upper-left corner of a rectangle that contains the ellipse, while the fourth and fifth parameters are the coordinates of its lower-right corner. The sixth and seventh parameters define the coordinates of the end point of the start radial line. The last two parameters set the coordinates of the end points of the end radial line. The elliptical arc is always drawn in the counterclockwise direction. The SetArcDirection() function has no effect in this case.

The coordinates of the start and end points of the radials need not coincide with the elliptical arc, because Windows prolongs these lines until they intersect the elliptical arc. Figure 7-7 shows the elements that define the figure.

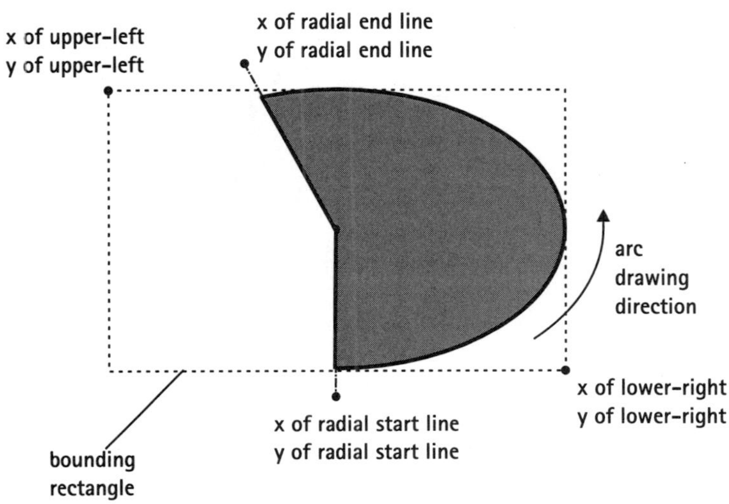

Figure 7-7: Figure definition in the Pie()function

Drawing with Polygon()

The Polygon() function is similar to the Polyline() function described in Chapter 6. The main difference between a polygon and a polyline is that the polygon is closed automatically by drawing a straight line from the last vertex to the first one. The polygon is drawn with the current pen and filled with the current brush. The inside of the polygon is filled according to the current polygon fill mode, which can be ALTERNATE or WINDING. Polygon fill modes are discussed in detail earlier in this chapter. The function's general form reads as follows:

```
BOOL Polygon(
            HDC hdc,                // 1
            CONST POINT *lpPoints,  // 2
            int nCount              // 3
           );
```

The second parameter is the address of an array of points that contains the *x*- and *y*-coordinate pairs of the polygon vertices. The third parameter is the count of the number of vertices in the array. The function returns TRUE if it succeeds and FALSE if it fails.

When drawing the lines that define a polygon you can repeat the same segment. It is not necessary to avoid going over an existing line. When the WINDING fill mode is selected, however, the direction of each edge determines the fill action. The following code fragment shows the drawing of a complex polygon that is defined in an array of structures of type POINT.

```
// Arrays of POINT structures for polygon vertices
POINT  polyPoints1[] = {
      { 100, 100 }, // 1
      { 150, 100 }, // 2
      { 150, 150 }, // 3
      { 300, 150 }, // 4
      { 300, 300 }, // 5
      { 150, 300 }, // 6
      { 150, 150 }, // 7
      { 200, 150 }, // 8
      { 200, 200 }, // 9
      { 250, 200 }, // 10
      { 250, 250 }, // 11
      { 200, 250 }, // 12
      { 200, 200 }, // 13
      { 150, 200 }, // 14
      { 150, 150 }, // 15
      { 100, 150 }  // 16
 } ;
```

```
.
.
.
// Draw the polygon using array data
SetPolyFillMode (hdc, ALTERNATE);
Polygon (hdc, polyPoints1, 17);
```

Figure 7-8 shows the figure that results from this code when the ALTERNATE fill mode is active. The polygon vertices are numbered and labeled.

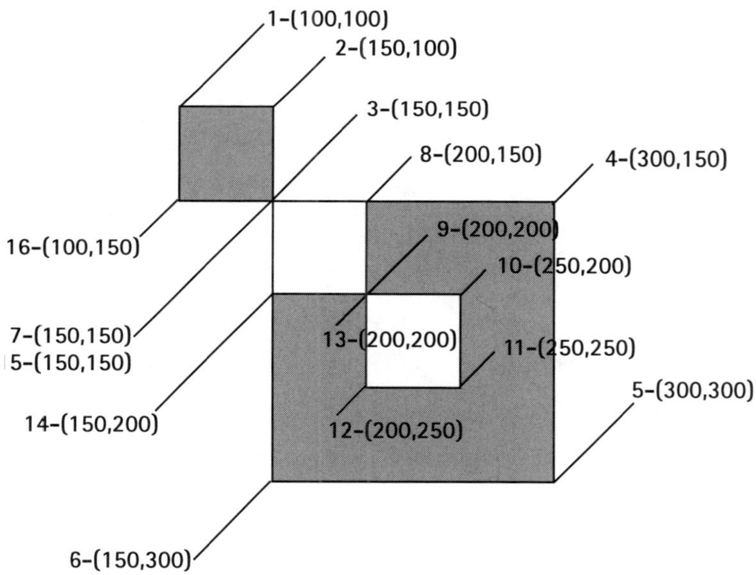

Figure 7-8: Figure generated by the Polygon() sample code

Drawing with PolyPolygon()

As the function name implies, PolyPolygon() is used to draw several closed polygons. The outlines of all the polygons are drawn with the current pen and the interiors are filled with the current brush and according to the selected fill mode. The polygons can overlap. Unlike the Polygon() function, the figures drawn with PolyPolygon() are not automatically closed. The PolyPolygon() function is similar to the PolyPolyline() function described in Chapter 6. Like the PolyPolyline() function, PolyPolygon() requires an array of values that holds the number of points for each polygon. The function's general form reads as follows:

```
BOOL PolyPolygon(
                    HDC hdc,                    // 1
```

```
        CONST POINT *lpPoints,    // 2
        CONST INT *lpPolyCounts,  // 3
        int nCount                // 4
       );
```

The second parameter is an array containing the vertices of the various polygons. The third parameter is an array that contains the number of vertices in each of the polygons. The fourth parameter is the count of the number of elements in the third parameter, which is also the number of polygons to be drawn. The function returns `TRUE` if it succeeds and `FALSE` if it fails. The following code fragment shows the drawing of four polygons, each one with four vertices, using the `PolyPolygon()` function.

```
// Arrays of POINT structures for holding the vertices
// of all four polygons
POINT  polyPoly1[] = {
   { 150, 150 }, // 1  |
   { 300, 150 }, // 2  |
   { 300, 300 }, // 3  |- first polygon
   { 150, 300 }, // 4  |
   { 150, 150 }, // 5  |

   { 200, 200 }, // 6  |
   { 250, 200 }, // 7  |
   { 250, 250 }, // 8  |- second polygon
   { 200, 250 }, // 9  |
   { 200, 200 }, // 10 |

   { 150, 150 }, // 11 |
   { 200, 150 }, // 12 |
   { 200, 200 }, // 13 |- third polygon
   { 150, 200 }, // 14 |
   { 150, 150 }, // 15 |

   { 100, 100 }, // 11 |
   { 150, 100 }, // 12 |
   { 150, 150 }, // 13 |- fourth polygon
   { 100, 150 }, // 14 |
   { 100, 100 }, // 15 |
  } ;

// Array holding the number of segments in each
// polygon
int  vertexArray[] = {
   { 5 },
```

```
    { 5 },
    { 5 },
    { 5 }
  };
  .
  .
  .
  // Draw the polygon using array data
  SetPolyFillMode (hdc, ALTERNATE);
  PolyPolygon (hdc, polyPoly1, vertexArray, 4);
```

The resulting polygon is identical to the one in Figure 7-8.

Operations on Rectangles

Rectangular areas are often used in Windows programming. Child windows are usually in the form of a rectangle, as are message and input boxes as well as many other graphics components. For this reason, the Windows API includes several functions that operate on rectangles. These are listed in Table 7-3.

TABLE 7-3 WINDOWS FUNCTIONS FOR RECTANGULAR AREAS

Function	Figure
`FillRect()`	Fills the interior of a rectangle using a brush defined by its handle
`FrameRect()`	Draws a frame around a rectangle
`InvertRect()`	Inverts the pixels in a rectangular area
`DrawFocusRect()`	Draws rectangle with special dotted pen to indicate that the object has focus

A common characteristic of all the rectangular functions is that the rectangle coordinates are stored in a structure of type `RECT`. The use of a `RECT` structure is a more convenient way of defining a rectangular area than by passing coordinates as function parameters. It allows the application to easily change the location of a rectangle, and to define a rectangular area without hard-coding the values, thus making the code more flexible. The RECT structure reads as follows:

```
typedef struct _RECT {
  LONG   left;     // x coordinate of upper-left corner
```

```
  LONG   top;      // y of upper-left corner
  LONG   right;    // x coordinate of bottom-right corner
  LONG   bottom;   // y of bottom-right
} RECT;
```

Drawing with FillRect()

The `FillRect()` function fills the interior of a rectangular area, whose coordinates are defined in a `RECT` structure. The function uses a brush specified by its handle. The filled area includes the upper-left corner of the rectangle but excludes the bottom-right corner. The function's general form reads as follows:

```
int FillRect(
            HDC hDC,            // 1
            CONST RECT *lprc,   // 2
            HBRUSH hbr          // 3
           );
```

The second parameter is a pointer to a structure of type `RECT` that contains the rectangle's coordinates. The third parameter is the handle to a brush or a system color. If it is a handle to a brush, it must have been obtained with the `CreateSolidBrush()`, `CreatePatternBrush()`, or `CreateHatchBrush()` functions described previously. Additionally, you may use a stock brush and obtain its handle by means of `GetStockObject()`. The function returns `TRUE` if it succeeds and `FALSE` if it fails. Table 7-4 lists the constants that are used to identify the system colors in Windows.

TABLE 7-4 SYSTEM COLORS

Value	Meaning
COLOR_3DDKSHADOW	Dark shadow display elements
COLOR_3DFACE,	
COLOR_BTNFACE	
COLOR_3DHILIGHT,	
COLOR_3DHIGHLIGHT,	
COLOR_BTNHILIGHT,	Face color for display elements
COLOR_BTNHIGHLIGHT	Highlight color for edges facing the light source

Value	Meaning
COLOR_3DLIGHT	Light color for edges facing the light source
COLOR_3DSHADOW,	
COLOR_BTNSHADOW	Shadow color for edges facing away from the light source
COLOR_ACTIVEBORDER	Active window border
COLOR_ACTIVECAPTION	Active window caption
COLOR_APPWORKSPACE	
COLOR_BACKGROUND,	Background color of multiple document interface (MDI) applications
COLOR_DESKTOP	Desktop color
COLOR_BTNTEXT	Text on push buttons
COLOR_CAPTIONTEXT	Text in caption, size box, and scroll-bar arrow box
COLOR_GRAYTEXT	Grayed (disabled) text Set to 0 if the current display driver does not support a solid gray color
COLOR_HIGHLIGHT	Item(s) selected in a control
COLOR_HIGHLIGHTTEXT	Text of item(s) selected in a control
COLOR_INACTIVEBORDER	Inactive window border
COLOR_INACTIVECAPTION	Inactive window caption
COLOR_INACTIVECAPTIONTEXT	Color of text in an inactive caption
COLOR_INFOBK	Background color for ToolTip controls
COLOR_INFOTEXT	Text color for ToolTip controls
COLOR_MENU	Menu background
COLOR_MENUTEXT	Text in menus
COLOR_SCROLLBAR	Scroll bar gray area
COLOR_WINDOW	Window background
COLOR_WINDOWFRAME	Window frame
COLOR_WINDOWTEXT	Text in windows

A value of 1 must be added to the chosen color, as in the following statement:

```
FillRect (hdc, &aRect, (HBRUSH) (COLOR_MENU+ 1));
```

Drawing with FrameRect()

The `FrameRect()` function draws border around a rectangular area, whose coordinates are defined in a `RECT` structure. The width and height of this border are one logical unit. The border is drawn with a brush, not with a pen. The brush is specified by its handle. The function's general form is as follows:

```
int FrameRect(
            HDC hDC,            // 1
            CONST RECT *lprc,   // 2
            HBRUSH hbr          // 3
           );
```

The second parameter is a pointer to a structure of type `RECT` that contains the coordinates. The third parameter is the handle to a brush, which must have been obtained with `CreateSolidBrush()`, `CreatePatternBrush()`, or `CreateHatch Brush()` functions described previously. Additionally, you may use a stock brush and obtain its handle by means of `GetStockObject()`. The function returns `TRUE` if it succeeds and `FALSE` if it fails.

Because the borders of the rectangle are drawn with a brush, rather than with a pen, the function is used to produce figures that can not be obtained by other means. For example, if you select a brush with the vertical hatch pattern `HS_VERTICAL`, the resulting rectangle has dotted lines for the upper and lower segments because this is the brush pattern. The vertical segments of the rectangle are displayed as solid lines only when the rectangle's side coincides with the brush's bitmap pattern. Another characteristic of the `FrameRect()` function is that dithered colors can be used to draw the rectangle's border.

Drawing with DrawFocusRect()

The `DrawFocusRect()` function draws a rectangle of dotted lines. The rectangle's interior is not filled. The function's name relates to its intention, not to its operation, because the drawn rectangle is not given the keyboard focus automatically. The `DrawFocusRect()` function uses neither a pen nor a brush to draw the perimeter. The dotted lines used for the rectangle are one pixel wide, one pixel high, and are separated by one pixel. The function's general form reads as follows:

```
BOOL DrawFocusRect(
                HDC hDC,            // 1
                CONST RECT *lprc    // 2
               );
```

The second parameter is a pointer to a structure of type RECT that contains the coordinates. The function returns TRUE if it succeeds and FALSE if it fails. Figure 7-9 shows a rectangle drawn with the DrawFocusRect() function.

Figure 7-9: Rectangle drawn with DrawFocusRect() function

The DrawFocusRect() function has several unique features. The most important feature is that the rectangle is displayed by means of an XOR operation on the background pixels. This ensures that it is visible on most backgrounds. Also, that the rectangle can be erased by calling the function a second time with the same parameters. This is a powerful feature of this function because an application can call DrawFocusRect() to draw a rectangle around an object or background, and then erase the rectangle and restore the display without having to preserve the overdrawn area.

The area that contains a rectangle drawn with DrawFocusRect() cannot be scrolled. To scroll this area you can call DrawFocusRect() a second time to erase the rectangle, scroll the display, then call the function again to redraw the focus rectangle.

Auxiliary Operations on Rectangles

Windows provides several auxiliary functions designed to facilitate manipulating structures of type RECT. Although these functions have no unique functionality, they do simplify the coding. Table 7-5 lists these auxiliary functions.

TABLE 7-5 AUXILIARY RECTANGLE FUNCTIONS

Function	Figure
SetRect()	Fills a RECT structure variable with coordinates
CopyRect()	Copies the data in a RECT structure variable to another one

Continued

TABLE 7-5 AUXILIARY RECTANGLE FUNCTIONS *(Continued)*

Function	Figure
`SetEmptyRect()`	Fills a `RECT` structure variable with zeros thus creating an empty rectangle
`OffsetRect()`	Translates a rectangle along the *x*- and *y*-axis
`InflateRect()`	Increases or decreases the width and height of a rectangle
`IntersectRect()`	Creates a rectangle that is the intersection of two other rectangles
`UnionRect()`	Creates a rectangle that is the union of two other rectangles
`SubratctRect()`	Creates a rectangle that is the difference between two other rectangles
`IsRectEmpty()`	Determines if a rectangle is empty
`PtInRect()`	Determines if a point is located within the perimeter of a rectangle
`EqualRect()`	Determines if two rectangles are equal

The function `SetRect()` is used to set the coordinates in a `RECT` structure. It is equivalent to entering these values into the structure member variables. The function's general form reads as follows:

```
BOOL SetRect(
            LPRECT lprc, // 1
            int xLeft,   // 2
            int yTop,    // 3
            int xRight,  // 4
            int yBottom  // 5
           );
```

The first parameter is a pointer to the structure variable that references the rectangle that is to be set. The second and third parameters are the *x* and *y*-coordinates of the upper-left corner. The fourth and fifth parameters are the coordinates of the lower-right corner.

The `CopyRect()` function is used to copy the parameters from one rectangle structure variable to another one. The function's parameters are the addresses of the destination and source structures. Its general form reads as follows:

```
BOOL CopyRect(
            LPRECT lprcDst,      // 1
```

```
    CONST RECT *lprcSrc   // 2
   );
```

The first parameter is a pointer to a structure of type RECT that receives the copied coordinates. The second parameter is a pointer to the structure that holds the source coordinates.

The function SetRectEmpty() takes as a parameter the address of a structure variable of type RECT and sets all its values to zero. The result is an empty rectangle that does not show on the screen. Its general form reads as follows:

```
BOOL SetEmptyRect (LPRECT rect);
```

The function's only parameter is the address of the RECT structure that is to be cleared.

> **NOTE** There is a difference between an empty rectangle and a NULL rectangle. An empty rectangle is one with no area, that is, one in which the coordinate of the right side is less than or equal to that of the left side, or the coordinate of the bottom side is less than or equal to that of the top side. A NULL rectangle is one in which all the coordinates are zero. The Foundation Class Library contains different member functions for detecting an empty and a NULL rectangle. The Windows API, however, has no function for detecting a NULL rectangle.

OffsetRect() translates a rectangle along both axes. The function's general form reads as follows:

```
BOOL OffsetRect(
            LPRECT lprc,  // 1
            int dx,       // 2
            int dy        // 3
           );
```

The first parameter is a pointer to a structure variable of type RECT that contains the parameters of the rectangle to be moved. The second parameter is the amount to move the rectangle along the *x*-axis. The third parameter is the amount to move the rectangle along the *y*-axis. Positive values indicate movement to the right or down. Negative values indicate movement to the left or up.

In reality, the OffsetRect() function does not move the rectangle, but simply changes the values in the RECT structure variable referenced in the call. Another call to a rectangle display function is necessary to show the translated rectangle on the screen. Figure 7-10 shows the effect of OffsetRect().

Figure 7-10: Effect of the OffsetRect() function

In Figure 7-10, the light-gray rectangle shows the original figure. The `OffsetRect()` function was applied to the data in the figure's `RECT` structure variable, adding 50 pixels along the *x*-axis and subtracting 50 pixels along the *y*-axis. The resulting rectangle is shown with a dark-gray fill.

`InflateRect()` serves to increase or decrease the size of a rectangle. The function's general form reads as follows:

```
BOOL InflateRect(
                    LPRECT lprc,  // 1
                    int dx,       // 2
                    int dy        // 3
                   );
```

The first parameter is a pointer to a structure variable of type `RECT` that contains the rectangle to be resized. The second parameter is the amount to add or subtract from the rectangle's width. The third parameter is the amount to add or subtract from the rectangle's height. In both cases, positive values indicate an increase of the dimension and negative values a decrease. The `InflateRect()` function does not change the displayed rectangle, but modifies the values in the `RECT` structure variable referenced in the call. Another call to a rectangle display function is necessary to show the modified rectangle on the screen. Figure 7-11 shows the effect of the `InflateRect()` function.

In Figure 7-11, the light-gray rectangle shows the original 150 by 150–pixels figure. The `InflateRect()` function was applied to increase the width by 100 pixels and decrease the height by 75 pixels. The results are shown in the dark-gray rectangle.

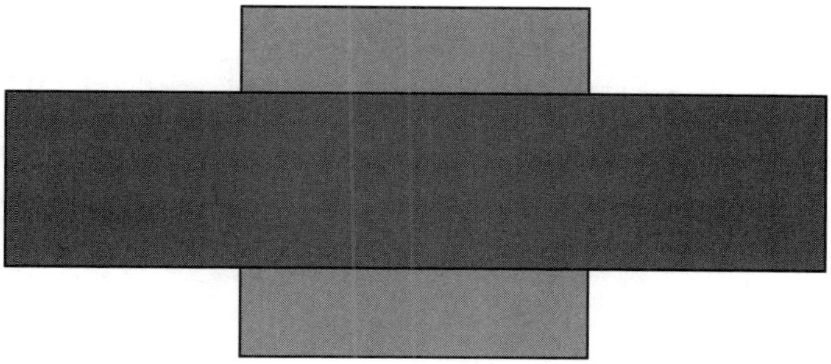

Figure 7-11: Effect of the InflateRect() function

The `IntersectRect()` function applies a logical AND operation on two rectangles to create a new rectangle that represents the intersection of the two figures. If no common points in the source rectangles exist, then an empty rectangle is produced. The function's general from reads as follows:

```
BOOL IntersectRect(
LPRECT lprcDst,                    // 1
CONST RECT *lprcSrc1,// 2
CONST RECT *lprcSrc2        // 3
);
```

The first parameter is the address of a `RECT` structure variable where the intersection coordinates are placed. The second parameter is a pointer to a RECT structure variable that holds the coordinates of the first rectangle. The third parameter is a pointer to a `RECT` structure variable with the coordinates of the second rectangle. Figure 7-12 shows the effect of the `IntersectRect()` function.

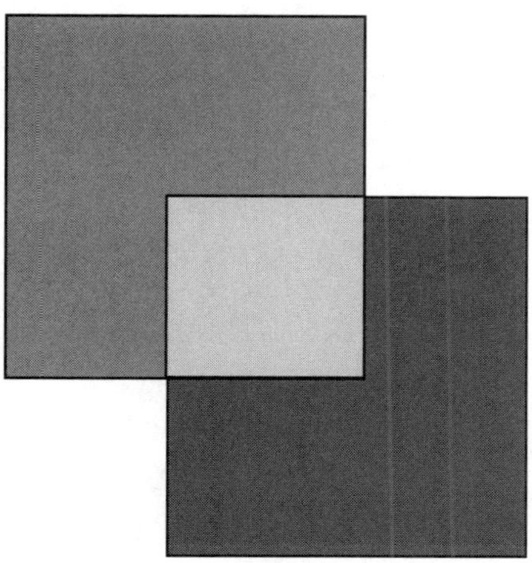

Figure 7-12: Effect of the IntersectRect() function

The UnionRect() function applies a logical OR operation on two rectangles to create a new rectangle that represents the union of the two figures. If no common points in the source rectangles exist, then an empty rectangle is produced. The resulting image is the smallest rectangle that contains both sources. The function's general form reads as follows:

```
BOOL UnionRect(
               LPRECT lprcDst,          // 1
               CONST RECT *lprcSrc1,    // 2
               CONST RECT *lprcSrc2     // 3
              );
```

The first parameter is the address of a RECT structure variable where the union rectangle coordinates are placed. The second parameter is a pointer to a RECT structure variable that holds the coordinates of the first rectangle, and the third parameter is a pointer to a RECT structure variable with the coordinates of the second rectangle. Figure 7-13 shows the effect of the UnionRect() function.

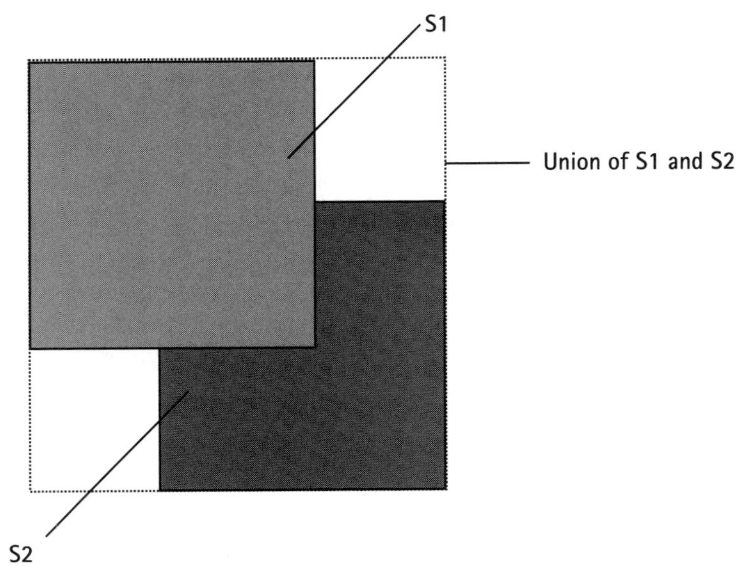

Figure 7-13: Effect of the UnionRect() function

The SubtractRect() function creates a new rectangle by subtracting the coordinates of two source rectangles. The function's general form reads as follows:

```
BOOL SubtractRect(
                  LPRECT lprcDst,          // 1
                  CONST RECT *lprcSrc1,    // 2
```

```
    CONST RECT *lprcSrc2    // 3
   );
```

The first parameter is the address of a RECT structure variable where the resulting coordinates are placed. The second parameter is a pointer to a RECT structure variable that holds the coordinates of the first source rectangle. It is from this rectangle that the coordinates of the second source rectangle are subtracted. The third parameter is a pointer to a RECT structure variable with the coordinates of the second source rectangle. The coordinates of this rectangle are subtracted from the ones of the first source rectangle.

The result of the operation must be a rectangle, not a polygon or any other nonrectangular surface. This imposes the restriction that the rectangles must completely overlap in either the vertical or the horizontal direction. If not, the coordinates of the resulting rectangle are the same as those of the first source rectangle. Figure 7-14 shows three possible cases of rectangle subtraction.

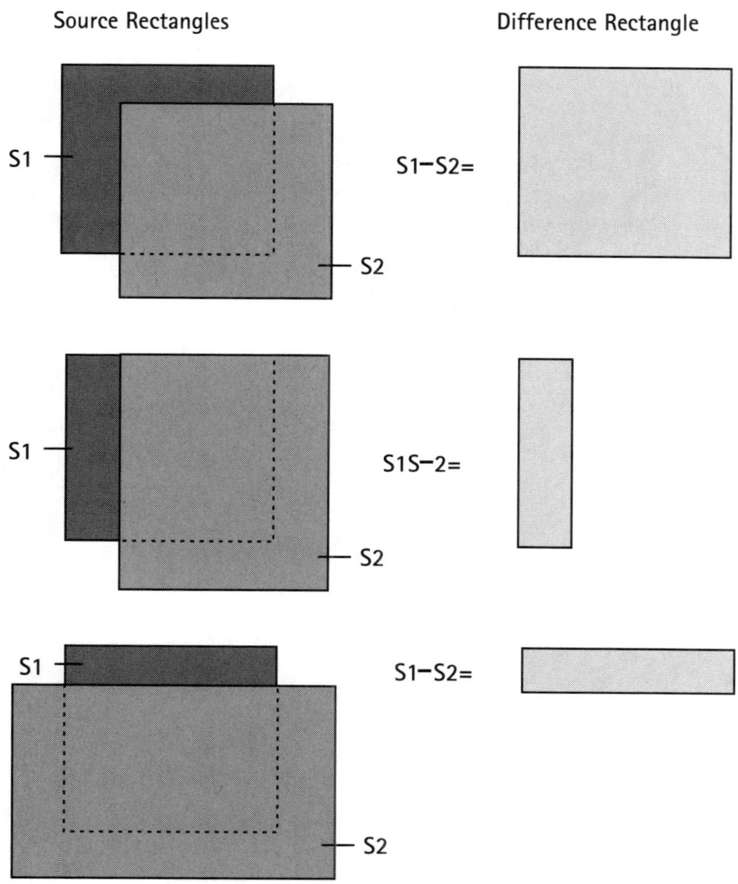

Figure 7-14: Three possible cases in the SubtractRect() function

The `IsRectEmpty()` function determines whether a rectangle is empty. An empty rectangle is one with no area, that is, one in which the width and/or the height are zero or negative. The function's general form reads as follows:

```
BOOL IsRectEmpty(
                 CONST RECT *lprc   // 1
                );
```

The only parameter is the address of the `RECT` structure variable that contains the rectangle's parameters. The function returns `TRUE` if the rectangle is empty and `FALSE` otherwise.

The `PtInRect()` function determines whether a point lies within a rectangle. A point that lies on the rectangle's top or left side is considered to be within the rectangle, but a point within the right or bottom side is not. The function's general form reaads[Please check spelling Au] as follows:

```
BOOL PtInRect(
              CONST RECT *lprc,  // 1
              POINT pt           // 2
             );
```

The first parameter is the address of a `RECT` structure variable that contains the rectangle's dimensions. The second parameter is a structure of type `POINT` that holds the coordinates of the point being tested. The function returns `TRUE` if the point is within the rectangle and `FALSE` otherwise.

The `EqualRect()` function determines whether two rectangles are equal. For two rectangles to be equal, all their coordinates must be identical. The function's general form reads as follows:

```
BOOL EqualRect(
               CONST RECT *lprc1,  // 1
               CONST RECT *lprc2   // 2
              );
```

The first parameter points to a `RECT` structure variable that contains the parameters of one rectangle. The second parameter points to a `RECT` structure variable with the parameters of the second rectangle. The function returns `TRUE` if both rectangles are equal and `FALSE` otherwise.

Updating the Rectangle() Function

All of the rectangle operations described in the preceding section receive the coordinates in a structure of type RECT. The basic rectangle-drawing function, Rectangle(), receives the figure coordinates as parameters to the call. This difference in data formats, which is due to the evolution of Windows, makes it difficult to transfer the results of a rectangle operation into the Rectangle() function. To solve this problem we have coded a rectangle-drawing function, called DrawRect(), which takes the figure coordinates from a RECT structure. The function reads as follows:

```
BOOL DrawRect (HDC hdc, LPRECT aRect) {
  return (Rectangle (hdc, aRect->left,
                     aRect->top,
                     aRect->right,
                     aRect->bottom));
}
```

Because DrawRect() uses Rectangle() to draw the figure, the return values are the same for both functions.

Regions

A region is an area composed of one or more polygons or ellipses. Because a rectangle is a polygon, a region can also be (or contain) a rectangle, or even a rounded rectangle. In Windows programming, regions are used for three main purposes:

- To fill or frame an irregular area
- To clip output to an irregular area
- To test for mouse input in an irregular area

From these uses we can conclude that the main role of a region is to serve as a boundary. Regions can be combined logically, copied, subtracted, and translated to another location. In Windows 95/98 and NT, a new region can be produced by performing a rotation, scaling, reflection, or shearing transformation on another region. Transformations are discussed in Chapter 9. Here, we deal with the simpler operations on regions. There is a rich set of functions that relate to regions and region operations. These are listed in Table 7-6.

Table 7-6 REGION-RELATED FUNCTIONS

Function	Action
Creating Regions	
`CreateRectRgn()`	Creates a rectangular-shaped region, given the four coordinates of the rectangle
`CreateRectRgnIndirect()`	Creates a rectangular-shaped region, given a `RECT` structure with the coordinates of the rectangle
`CreateRoundRectRgn()`	Creates a region shaped like a rounded-corner rectangle, given the coordinates of the rectangle and the dimensions of the corner ellipse
`CreateEllipticRgn()`	Creates an elliptically-shaped region from a bounding rectangle
`CreateEllipticRegion Indirect()`	Creates an elliptically-shaped region from the parameters of a bounding rectangle in a `RECT` structure
`CreatePolygonRgn()`	Creates a polygon-shaped region from an array of points that define the polygon
`CreatePolyPolygonRgn()`	Creates one or more polygon-shaped regions from an array of points that define the polygons
`PathToRegion()`	Converts the current path into a region
`ExtCreateRgn()`	Creates a region based on a transformation performed on another regions (Windows 95/98 and NT only)
Combining Regions	
`CombineRgn()`	Combines two regions into one by performing a logical, subtraction, or copy operation
Filling and Painting Regions	
`FillRgn()`	Fills a region using a brush
`GetPolyFillMode()`	Gets fill mode used by `FillRgn()`
`SetPolyFillMode()`	Sets the fill mode for `FillRgn()`
`FrameRgn()`	Frames a region using a brush
`PaintRgn()`	Paints the interior of a region with the brush currently selected in the device context

Function	Action
Filling and Painting Regions	
InvertRgn()	Inverts the colors in a region
Region Status and Control	
SetWindowRgn()	Sets the window regions. The window region is the area where the operating system enables drawing operations to take place
GetWindowRgn()	Retrieves the window region established by SetWindowRgn()
OffsetRgn()	Moves a region along the *x*- or *y*-axis
SelectClipRgn()	Makes a region the current clipping region
ExtSelectClipRgn()	Combines a region with the current clipping region
GetClipRgn()	Gets handle of the current clipping region
ValidateRgn()	Validates the client area removing the area in the region from the current update region
InvalidateRgn()	Forces a WM_PAINT message by invalidating a screen area defined by a region
Obtain Region Data	
PtInRegion()	Tests if a point is located within a region
RectInRegion()	Tests if a given rectangle overlaps any part of a region
EqualRgn()	Tests if two regions are equal
GetRgnBox()	Retrieves a region's bounding box
GetRegionData()	Retrieves internal structure information about a region

In the sections that follow we discuss some of the region-related functions. Other region operations are discussed, in context, later in the book.

Creating Regions

A region is a GDI object, hence, it must be explicitly created. The functions that create a region return a handle of type HRGN (handle to a region). With this handle you can perform many region-based operations, such as filling the region, drawing its outline, and combining it with another region. You often create two or more simple regions by calling their primitive functions, and then combine them into a more complex region, usually by means of the `CombineRgn()` function.

`CreateRectRgn()` is used to create a rectangular region. The function's general form reads as follows:

```
HRGN CreateRectRgn(
                    int nLeftRect,   // 1
                    int nTopRect,    // 2
                    int nRightRect,  // 3
                    int nBottomRect  // 4
                   );
```

The first and second parameters are the coordinates of the upper-left corner of the rectangle. The third and fourth parameters are the coordinates of the lower-right corner.

`CreateRectRgnIndirect()` creates a rectangular-shaped region, identical to the one produced by `CreateRectRgn()`; the only difference being that `CreateRectRgnIndirect()` receives the coordinates in a `RECT` structure variable. The function's general form reads as follows:

```
HRGN CreateRectRgnIndirect(
                            CONST RECT *lprc   // 1
                           );
```

`CreateRoundRectRgn()` creates a region shaped like a rounded-rectangle. Its general form reads as follows:

```
HRGN CreateRoundRectRgn(
                         int nLeftRect,      // 1
                         int nTopRect,       // 2
                         int nRightRect,     // 3
                         int nBottomRect,    // 4
                         int nWidthEllipse,  // 5
                         int nHeightEllipse  // 6
                        );
```

The first and second parameters are the coordinates of the upper-left corner of the bounding rectangle. The third and fourth parameters are the coordinates of the lower-right corner. The fifth parameter is the width of the ellipse that is used for drawing the rounded corner arc. The sixth parameter is the height of this ellipse. The shape of the resulting region is the same as that of the rectangle in Figure 7-4.

CreateEllipticRgn() creates an elliptically-shaped region. The function's general form reads as follows:

```
HRGN CreateEllipticRgn(
                        int nLeftRect,    // 1
                        int nTopRect,     // 2
                        int nRightRect,   // 3
                        int nBottomRect   // 4
);
```

The first and second parameters are the coordinates of the upper-left corner of a rectangle that bounds the ellipse. The third and fourth parameters are the coordinates of the lower-right corner of this bounding rectangle. The shape of the resulting region is similar to the one in Figure 7-5.

CreateEllipticRegionIndirect() creates an elliptically-shaped region identical to the one produced by CreateEllipticRgn() except that in this case the parameters are read from a RECT structure variable. The function's general form reads as follows:

```
HRGN CreateEllipticRgnIndirect(
                                CONST RECT *lprc    // 1
                              );
```

CreatePolygonRgn() creates a polygon-shaped region. The call assumes that the polygon is closed; no automatic closing is provided. The function's general form reads as follows:

```
HRGN CreatePolygonRgn(
                      CONST POINT *lppt,  // 1
                      int cPoints,        // 2
                      int fnPolyFillMode  // 3
                    );
```

The first parameter is the address of an array of points that contains the *x*- and *y*-coordinate pairs of the polygon vertices. The second parameter is the count of the number of vertices in the array. The third parameter specifies the polygon-fill mode, which can be ALTERNATE or WINDING. ALTERNATE defines a mode that fills between odd-numbered and even-numbered polygon sides, that is, those areas that can be reached from the outside of the polygon by crossing an odd number of lines. WINDING mode fills all internal regions of the polygon. These are the same constants that are used in the SetPolyFillMode() function described earlier in this chapter. In the CreatePolygonRgn() function call the fill mode determines which points are included in the region.

CreatePolyPolygonRgn() creates one or more polygon-shaped regions. The call assumes that the polygons are closed figures. No automatic closing is provided. CreatePolyPolygonRgn() is similar to PolyPolygon(). The function's general form reads as follows:

```
HRGN CreatePolyPolygonRgn(
                          CONST POINT *lppt,           // 1
                          CONST INT *lpPolyCounts,     // 2
                          int nCount,                  // 3
                          int fnPolyFillMode           // 4
                         );
```

The first parameter is a pointer to an array containing vertices of the various polygons. The second parameter is a pointer to an array that contains the number of vertices in each of the polygons. The third parameter is the count of the number of elements in the second parameter, which is the same as the number of polygons to be drawn. The fourth parameter specifies the polygon fill mode, which can be ALTERNATE or WINDING. These two constants have the same effect as that described in the CreatePolygonRgn() function.

All the region-creation functions discussed so far return the handle to the region if the call succeeds, and NULL if it fails.

A region can be created from a path by means of the PathToRegion() function. Paths are discussed later in this chapter. The ExtCreateRgn() function enables the creation of a new region by performing a transformation on another region. Transformations are discussed in Chapter 9.

Combining Regions

Sometimes a region consists of a simple, primitive area such as a rectangle, an ellipse, or a polygon. On other occasions a region is a complex figure, composed of two or more simple figures of the same or different types, which can overlap, be adjacent, or disjoint. The CombineRgn() function is used to create a complex region from two simpler ones. The function's general form reads as follows:

```
int CombineRgn(
               HRGN hrgnDest,        // 1
               HRGN hrgnSrc1,        // 2
               HRGN hrgnSrc2,        // 3
               int fnCombineMode     // 4
              );
```

The first parameter is the handle to the resulting combined region. The second parameter is the handle to the first source region to be combined. The third parameter is the handle to the second source region to be combined. The fourth parameter is one of five possible combination modes, listed in Table 7-7.

TABLE 7-7 REGION COMBINATION MODES

Mode	Effect
RGN_AND	The intersection of the two combined regions
RGN_COPY	A copy of the first source region
RGN_DIFF	Combines the parts of the first source region that are not in the second source region
RGN_OR	The union of two combined regions
RGN_XOR	The union of two combined regions except for any overlapping area

CombineRgn() returns one of four integer values, as shown in Table 7-8.

TABLE 7-8 REGION-TYPE RETURN VALUES

Value	Meaning
NULLREGION	The region is empty
SIMPLEREGION	The region is a single rectangle
COMPLEXREGION	The region is more complex than a single rectangle
ERROR	No region was created

One property of CombineRgn() is that the destination region, expressed in the first parameter, must exist as a region prior to the call. Creating a memory variable to hold the handle to this region is not sufficient. The region must have been first created by means of one of the region-creation functions, otherwise CombineRgn()

returns ERROR. The following code fragment shows the required processing for creating two simple regions and then combining them into a complex region using the RGN_AND combination mode:

```
HRGN      rectRgn, ellipRgn, resultRgn;
.
.
.
// Create a rectangular region
rectRgn = CreateRectRgn (100, 100, 300, 200);
// Create an elliptical region
ellipRgn = CreateEllipticRgn (200, 100, 400, 200);
// Create a dummy region for results. Skipping this
// step results in an ERROR from the CombineRgn() call
resultRgn = CreateRectRgn (0, 0, 0, 0);
// Combine regions and fill
CombineRgn (resultRgn, rectRgn, ellipRgn, RGN_AND);
FillRgn (hdc, resultRgn, redSolBrush);
```

Figure 7-15 shows the results of applying the various region combination modes on two simple, overlapping regions.

In addition to the CombineRgn() function, the *windowsx.h* header files defines several macros that facilitate region combinations. These macros implement the five combination modes that are entered as the last parameter of the CombineRgn() call. They read as follows:

```
CopyRgn      (hrgnDest, hrgnScr1);
IntersectRgn (hrgnDest, hrgnSrc1, hrgnSrc2);
SubtractRgn  (hrgnDest, hrgnScr1, hrgnScr2);
UnionRgn     (hrgnDest, hrgnSrc1, hrgnSrc2);
XorRgn       (hrgnDest, hrgnSrc1, hrgnScr2);
```

In all of the macros, hrgnDest is the handle to the destination region, while hrgnScr1 and hrgnSrc2 are the handles to the source regions.

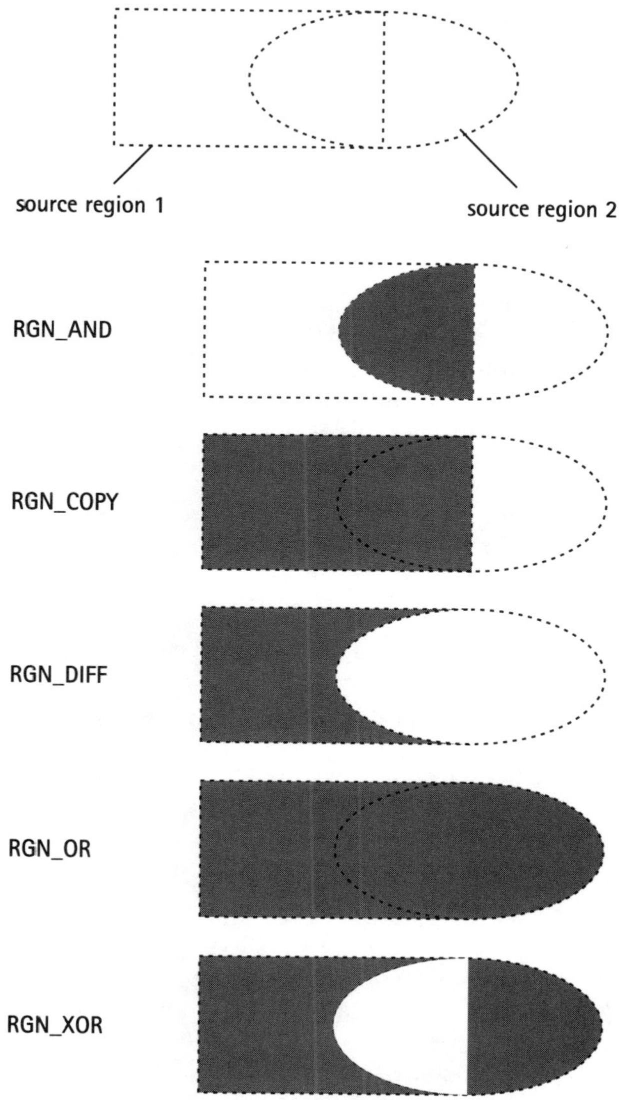

Figure 7-15: Regions resulting from the five CombineRgn() modes

Filling and Painting Regions

Several functions relate to filling, painting, and framing regions. The difference between filling and painting is that fill operations require a handle to a brush, while paint operations use the brush currently selected in the device context.

The FillRgn() function fills a region using a brush defined by its handle. The function's general form reads as follows:

```
BOOL FillRgn(
            HDC hdc,     // 1
            HRGN hrgn,   // 2
            HBRUSH hbr   // 3
           );
```

The first parameter is the handle to the device context. The second one is the handle to the region to be filled. The third parameter is the handle to the brush used in filling the region. The function returns TRUE if it succeeds and FALSE if it fails.

PaintRgn() paints the interior of a region with the brush currently selected in the device context. The function's general form reads as follows:

```
BOOL PaintRgn(
            HDC hdc,     // 1
            HRGN hrgn    // 2
           );
```

The second parameter is the handle to the region to be filled. The function returns TRUE if it succeeds and FALSE if it fails.

FrameRgn() draws the perimeter of a region using a brush defined by its handle. The function's general form reads as follows:

```
BOOL FrameRgn(
            HDC hdc,       // 1
            HRGN hrgn,     // 2
            HBRUSH hbr,    // 3
            int nWidth,    // 4
            int nHeight    // 5
           );
```

The second parameter is the handle to the region to be filled. The third one is the handle to the brush used in filling the region. The fourth parameter specifies the width of the brush, in logical units. The fifth parameter specifies the height of the brush, also in logical units. The function returns TRUE if it succeeds and FALSE if it fails. If the width and height of the brush are different, then oblique portions of the image are assigned an intermediate thickness. The result is similar to using a calligraphy pen. Figure 7-16 shows a region drawn with the FrameRgn() function.

Figure 7-16: Region border drawn with the FrameRgn() function

The `InvertRgn()` function inverts the colors in a region. In a monochrome screen, inversion consists of turning white pixels to black and black pixels to white. In a color screen, inversion depends on the display technology. In general, inverting a color produces its complement. Therefore, inverting blue produces yellow, inverting red produces cyan, and inverting green produces magenta. The function's general form reads as follows:

```
BOOL InvertRgn(
                HDC hdc,     // 1
                HRGN hrgn    // 2
              );
```

The second parameter is the handle to the region to be inverted. The function returns `TRUE` if it succeeds and `FALSE` if it fails.

Region Manipulations

Several functions allow the manipulation of regions. These manipulations include moving a region, using a region to define the program's output area, setting the clipping region, obtaining the clipping-region handle, and validating or invalidating a screen area defined by a region. The region manipulations related to clipping are discussed in the following section.

A powerful, but rarely used function in the Windows API is `SetWindowRgn()`. It enables you to redefine the window area of a window, thus redefining the area where drawing operations take place. In a sense, `SetWindowRgn()` is a form of clipping that includes not only the client area, but the entire window. The `SetWindowRgn()` function enables you to create a window that includes only part of the title bar, or to eliminate one or more of the window borders, as well as many other effects. The function's general form reads as follows:

```
int SetWindowRgn(
                  HWND hWnd,     // 1
                  HRGN hRgn,     // 2
                  BOOL bRedraw   // 3
                );
```

The first parameter is the handle to the window whose region is to be changed. The second parameter is the handle to the region that is to be used in redefining the window area. If this parameter is NULL then the window has no window area; thereby, becoming invisible. The third parameter is a redraw flag. If set to `TRUE`, the operating system automatically redraws the window to the new output area. If the window is visible the redraw flag is usually `TRUE`. The function returns nonzero if it succeeds and zero if it fails.

The function `GetWindowRgn()` is used to obtain the window area of a window, which has usually been set by `SetWindowRgn()`. The function's general form reads as follows:

```
int GetWindowRgn(
                    HWND hWnd, // 1
                    HRGN hRgn  // 2
                  );
```

The first parameter is the handle to the window whose region is to be obtained. The second parameter is the handle to a region that receives a copy of the window region. The return value is one of the constants listed in Table 7-8.

The `OffsetRgn()` function is used to move a region to another location. The function's general form reads as follows:

```
int OffsetRgn(
                 HRGN hrgn,      // 1
                 int nXOffset,   // 2
                 int nYOffset    // 3
               );
```

The first parameter is the handle to the region that is to be moved. The second parameter is the number of logical units that the region is to be moved along the *x*-axis. The third parameter is the number of logical units along the *y*-axis. The function returns one of the constants listed in Table 7-8.

Sometimes the `OffsetRgn()` function does not perform as expected. It seems that when a region is moved by means of this function, some of the region attributes are not preserved. For example, assume a region that has been filled red is moved to a new location that does not overlap the old position. If we now call `InvertRgn()` on the translated window, the result is not a cyan-colored window, but one that is the reverse of the background color. In this case the red fill attribute of the original window was lost as it was translated into a new position, and the translated window has no fill. If the translated window partially overlaps the original one, however, then the overlap area's original color is negated when the `InvertRgn()` function is called on the translated region. Figure 7-17 shows the result of inverting a region translated by means of `OffsetRgn()`.

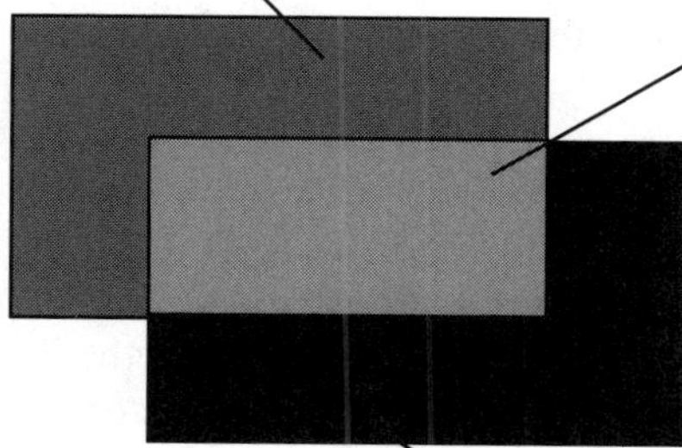

Figure 7-17: Effect of OffsetRgn() on region fill

Two functions, `SelectClipRgn()` and `ExtSelectClipRgn()`, refer to the use of regions in clipping. These functions, along with clipping operations, are discussed later in this chapter.

The `InvalidateRgn()` function adds the specified region to the current update region of the window. The invalidated region is marked for update when the next `WM_PAINT` message occurs. The function's general form reads as follows:

```
BOOL InvalidateRgn(
                    HWND hWnd,    // 1
                    HRGN hRgn,    // 2
                    BOOL bErase   // 3
                   );
```

The first parameter is the handle to the window that is to be updated. The second parameter is the handle to the region to be added to the update area. If this parameter is `NULL` then the entire client area is added to the update area. The third parameter is an update flag for the background area. If this parameter is `TRUE`, then the background is erased. The function always returns a nonzero value.

The `ValidateRgn()` function removes the region from the update area. It has the reverse effect as `InvalidateRgn()`. The function's general form is as follows:

```
BOOL ValidateRgn(
                  HWND hWnd,  // 1
                  HRGN hRgn   // 2
);
```

The first parameter is the handle to the window. The second parameter is the handle to the region to be removed from the update area. If this parameter is NULL then the entire client area is removed from the update area. The function returns TRUE if it succeeds and FALSE if it fails.

Obtaining Region Data

A few region-related functions are designed to provide region data to application code. The GetRegionData() function is used mainly in relation to the ExtCreateRegion() function. Both of these functions relate to geometric transformations and are discussed in Chapter 9.

PtInRegion() tests if a point defined by its coordinates is located within a region. The function's general form reads as follows:

```
BOOL PtInRegion(
               HRGN hrgn,  // 1
               int X,      // 2
               int Y       // 3
              );
```

The first parameter is the handle to the region to be examined. The second and third parameters are the *x*- and *y*-coordinates of the point. If the point is located within the region, the function returns TRUE. If not, the function returns FALSE.

The RectInRegion() function determines if any portion of a given rectangle is within a specified region. The function's general form reads as follows:

```
BOOL RectInRegion(
 HRGN hrgn,          // 1
CONST RECT *lprc     // 2
);
```

The first parameter is the handle to the region to be examined. The second parameter is a pointer to a RECT structure that holds the coordinates of the rectangle. If any part of the specified rectangle lies within the region, the function returns TRUE. If not, the function returns FALSE.

EqualRgn() tests if two regions are identical in size and shape. The function's general form reads as follows:

```
BOOL EqualRgn(
             HRGN hSrcRgn1,  // 1
             HRGN hSrcRgn2   // 2
            );
```

The first parameter identifies one of the regions and the second parameter the other region. If the two regions are identical, the function returns TRUE. If not, the function returns FALSE.

The GetRgnBox() function retrieves the bounding rectangle that encloses the specified region. The function's general form is as follows:

```
int GetRgnBox(
            HRGN hrgn,    // 1
            LPRECT lprc   // 2
           );
```

The first parameter is the handle to the region. The second parameter is a pointer to a RECT structure variable that receives the coordinates of the bounding rectangle. The function returns one of the first three constants listed in Table 7-8. If the first parameter does not identify a region then the function returns zero.

Clipping Operations

One of the fundamental graphics manipulations is *clipping.* In Windows programming, clipping is associated with regions because the clip action is defined by a region. In practice, a clipping region is often of rectangular shape, which explains why some clipping operations refer specifically to rectangles. Figure 7-18 shows the results of a clipping operation.

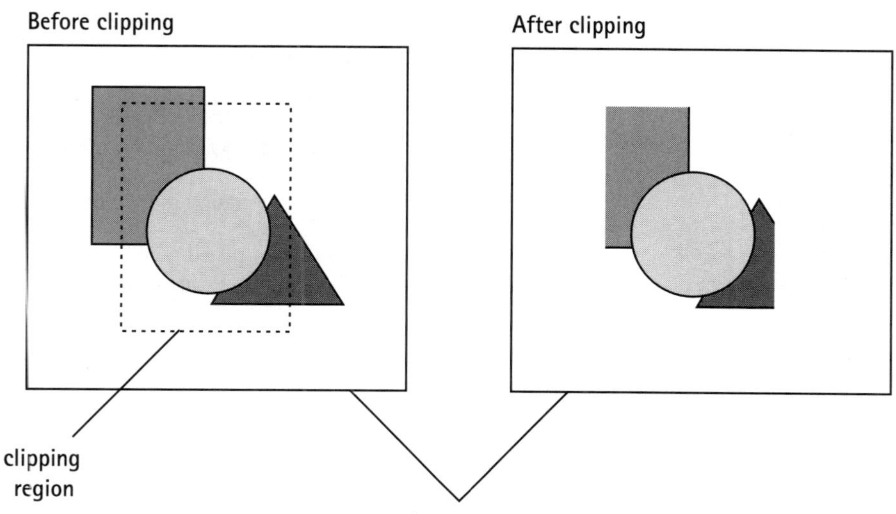

Figure 7-18: Results of a clipping operation

A clipping region is an object of the device context. The default clipping region is the client area. Not all device contexts support a predefined clipping region. If the device context is supplied by a call to BeginPaint(), then Windows creates a default clipping region and assigns to it the area of the window that needs to be repainted. If the device context was created with a call to `CreateDC()` or `GetDC()`, as is the case with a private device context, then no default clipping region exists. In this case an application can explicitly create a clipping region. Table 7-9 lists the functions that relate to clipping.

TABLE 7-9 CLIPPING FUNCTIONS

Function	Action
CREATING OR MODIFYING A CLIPPING REGION	
`SelectClipRgn()`	Makes a region the clipping region for a specified device context
`ExtSelectClipRgn()`	Combines a specified region with the clipping region according to a predefined mode
`IntersectClipRect()`	Creates a new clipping region from the interception of a rectangle and the current clipping region in a device context
`ExcludeClipRect()`	Subtracts a rectangle from the clipping region
`OffsetClipRgn()`	Moves the clipping region horizontally or vertically
`SelectClipPath()`	Appends the current path to the clipping region of a device context, according to a predefined mode
OBTAIN CLIPPING REGION INFORMATION	
`GetClipBox()`	Retrieves the bounding rectangle for the clipping region
`GetClipRgn()`	Retrieves the handle of the clipping region for a specified device context
`PtVisible()`	Determines if a specified point is within the clipping region of a device context
`RectVisible()`	Determines whether any part of a rectangle lies within the clipping region
METAREGION OPERATIONS	
`GetMetaRgn()`	Retrieves the metaregion for the specified device context
`SetMetaRgn()`	Creates a metaregion, which is the intersection of the current metaregion and the clipping region

> **NOTE:** Metaregions were introduced in Windows NT and are supported in Windows 95/98. However, very little has been printed about their meaning or possible uses. Microsoft documentation for Visual C++ — up to the May prerelease of version 6.0 — has nothing on metaregions beyond a brief mentioning of the two related functions listed in Table 7-9. For this reason, it is impossible to determine at this time if a metaregion is a trivial alias for a conventional region, or some other concept not yet documented. Metaregions are not discussed in the text.

Creating or Modifying a Clipping Region

In order for a region to be used to clip output, it must be selected as such in a device context. The `SelectClipRgn()` function is the primary method of achieving clipping. The region must first be defined and a handle for it obtained. Then the handle to the device context and the handle to the region are used to enforce the clipping. The function's general form reads as follows:

```
int SelectClipRgn(
                   HDC hdc,     // 1
                   HRGN hrgn    // 2
                  );
```

The first parameter is the handle to the device context that is to be clipped. The second parameter is the handle to the region used in clipping. This handle is obtained by any of the region-creating calls listed in Table 7-6. The function returns one of the values in Table 7-8.

Once the call is made, all future output is clipped; however, the existing screen display is not automatically changed to reflect the clipping area. Some unexpected or undesirable effects are possible during clipping. Once a clipping region is defined for a device context, then all output is limited to the clipping region. This requires that clipping be handled carefully, usually by installing and restoring clipping regions as necessary.

When a call is made to `SelectClipRgn()`, Windows preserves a copy of the previous clipping region. The newly installed clipping region can be removed from the device context by means of a call to `SelectClipRgn()` specifying a `NULL` region handle.

The `ExtSelectClipRgn()` function enables the combiningof the current clipping region with a new one, according to one of five predefined modes. The function's general form is as follows:

```
int ExtSelectClipRgn(
                    HDC hdc,          // 1
                    HRGN hrgn,        // 2
                    int fnMode        // 3
                   );
```

The first parameter is the handle to the device context that is to be clipped. The second parameter is the handle to the region used in clipping. The third parameter is one of the constants listed in Table 7-10.

TABLE 7-10 CLIPPING MODES

Value	Action:
RGN_AND	The resulting clipping region combines the overlapping areas of the current clipping region and the one identified in the call, by performing a logical AND between the two regions.
RGN_COPY	The resulting clipping region is a copy of the region identified in the call. The result is identical to calling `SelectClipRgn()`. If the region identified in the call is NULL, the new clipping region is the default clipping region.
RGN_DIFF	The resulting clipping region is the difference between the current clipping region and the one identified in the call.
RGN_OR	The resulting clipping region is the result of performing a logical OR operation on the current clipping region and the region identified in the call.
RGN_XOR	The resulting clipping region is the result of performing a logical XOR operation on the current clipping region and the region identified in the call.

The clipping regions that result from these selection modes are the same as those used in the `CombineRgn()` function, as shown in Figure 7-15. The `ExtSelectClipRgn()` function returns one of the values in Table 7-8.

The `IntersectClipRect()` function creates a new clipping region by performing a logical AND between the current clipping region and a rectangular area defined in the call. The function's general form reads as follows:

```
int IntersectClipRect(
                      HDC hdc,            // 1
                      int nLeftRect,      // 2
                      int nTopRect,       // 3
                      int nRightRect,     // 4
                      int nBottomRect     // 5
                     );
```

The second and third parameters are the coordinates of the upper-left corner of the rectangle. The fourth and fifth parameters are the coordinates of the lower-right corner. The function returns one of the values in Table 7-8.

The function `ExcludeClipRect()` subtracts a rectangle specified in the call from the clipping region. The function's general form reads as follows:

```
int ExcludeClipRect(
                    HDC hdc,          // 1
                    int nLeftRect,    // 2
                    int nTopRect,     // 3
                    int nRightRect,   // 4
                    int nBottomRect   // 5
                   );
```

The second and third parameters are the coordinates of the upper-left corner of the rectangle. The fourth and fifth parameters are the coordinates of the lower-right corner. The function returns one of the values in Table 7-8.

The function `OffsetClipRgn()` translates the clipping region along the horizontal or vertical axes. The function's general form reads as follows:

```
int OffsetClipRgn(
                  HDC hdc,        // 1
                  int nXOffset,   // 2
                  int nYOffset    // 3
                 );
```

The second parameter is the amount to move the clipping region along the *x*-axis. The third parameter is the amount to move along the *y*-axis. Positive values indicate movement to the right or down. Negative values indicate movement to the left or up. The function returns one of the values in Table 7-8.

The SelectClipPath() function appends the current path to the clipping region of a device context, according to a predefined mode. The function's general form reads as follows:

```
BOOL SelectClipPath(
                    HDC hdc,     // 1
                    int iMode    // 2
                   );
```

The second parameter is one of the constants listed in Table 7-10. The function returns TRUE if it succeeds and FALSE if it fails. Paths are discussed later in this chapter.

Obtaining Clipping Region Information

Code that uses clipping often needs to obtain information about the clipping region. Several functions are available for this purpose. The GetClipBox() function retrieves the bounding rectangle for the clipping region. This rectangle is the smallest one that can be drawn around the visible area of the device context. The function's general form reads as follows:

```
int GetClipBox(
               HDC hdc,       // 1
               LPRECT lprc    // 2
              );
```

The second parameter is a pointer to a RECT structure that receives the coordinates of the bounding rectangle. The function returns one of the values in Table 7-8.

The GetClipRgn() function retrieves the handle of the clipping region for a specified device context. The function's general form reads as follows:

```
int GetClipRgn(
               HDC hdc,            // 1
               HRGN hrgn           // 2
              );
```

The first parameter is the handle to the device context whose clipping region is desired. The second parameter is the handle to an existing clipping region that holds the results of the call. The function returns zero if there is no clipping region in the device context. The return value 1 indicates that there is a clipping region and that the function's second parameter holds its handle. A return value of -1 indicates an error. The function refers to clipping regions that result from SelectClipRgn() or ExtSelectClipRgn() functions. Clipping regions assigned by the system on calls to the BeginPaint() function are not returned by GetClipRgn().

The `PtVisible()` function is used to determine if a specified point is within the clipping region of a device context. The function's general form reads as follows:

```
BOOL PtVisible(
              HDC hdc,  // 1
              int X,    // 2
              int Y     // 3
             );
```

The first parameter is the handle to the device context under consideration. The second and third parameters are the *x*- and *y*-coordinates of the point in question. The function returns `TRUE` if the point is within the clipping region, and `FALSE` otherwise.

The function `RectVisible()` is used to determine whether any part of a rectangle lies within the clipping region of a device context. The function's general form reads as follows:

```
BOOL RectVisible(
                HDC hdc,            // 1
                CONST RECT *lprc    // 2
               );
```

The first parameter is the handle to the device context under consideration. The second parameter is a pointer to a structure variable of type `RECT` that holds the coordinates of the rectangle in question. The function returns `TRUE` if any portion of the rectangle is within the clipping region, and `FALSE` otherwise.

Paths

In Chapter 3, we first encountered the notion of paths, which were lightly discussed at that time. The project folder *Text Demo No 3* on the book's CD-ROM contains a program that uses paths to achieve graphics effects in text display. We now revisit paths in a more rigorous manner, and apply paths to other graphics operations.

Paths were introduced with Windows NT and are also supported by Windows 95/98. As its name implies, a path is the route the drawing instrument follows in creating a particular figure or set of figures. A path, which is stored internally by the GDI, can serve to define the outline of a graphics object. For example, if we start at coordinates 100, 100, and move to the point at 150, 100, then to 150, 200, from there to 100, 200, and finally to the start point, we have defined the path for a rectangular figure. We can now *stroke* the path to draw the rectangle's outline, *fill* the path to produce a solid figure, or both stroke and fill the path to produce a figure with both outline and fill. In general, there are path-related functions to perform the following operations:

- To draw the outline of the path using the current pen.
- To paint the interior of the path using the current brush.
- To draw the outline and paint the interior of a path.
- To modify a path converting curves to line segments.
- To convert the path into a clip path.
- To convert the path into a region.
- To flatten the path by converting each curve in the path into a series of line segments.
- To retrieve the coordinates of the lines and curves that compose a path.

The path is an object of the device context, such as a region, a pen, a brush, or a bitmap. One characteristic of a path is that there is no default path in the device context. Another one is that there is only one path in each device context; this determines that there is no need for a path handle. Every path is initiated by means of the `BeginPath()` function. This clears any old path from the device context and prepares to record the drawing primitives that create the new path, sometimes called the *path bracket*. Any of the functions listed in Table 7-11 can be used for defining a path in Windows NT. The subset of functions that can be used in paths in Windows 95/98 is listed in Table 7-12.

TABLE 7-11 PATH-DEFINING FUNCTIONS IN WINDOWS NT

AngleArc()	LineTo()	Polyline()
Arc()	MoveToEx()	PolylineTo()
ArcTo()	Pie()	PolyPolygon()
Chord()	PolyBezier()	PolyPolyline()
CloseFigure()	PolyBezierTo()	Rectangle()
Ellipse()	PolyDraw()	RoundRect()
ExtTextOut()	Polygon()	TextOut()

TABLE 7-12 PATH-DEFINING FUNCTIONS IN WINDOWS 95/98

ExtTextOut()	PolyBezierTo()	PolyPolygon()
LineTo()	Polygon()	PolyPolyline()
MoveToEx()	Polyline()	TextOut()
PolyBezier()	PolylineTo()	

Because paths are mostly utilized in clipping operations, the `CloseFigure()` function is generally used to close an open figure in a path. After all the figures that form the path have been drawn into the path bracket, the application calls `EndPath()` to select the path into the specified device context. The path can then be made into a clipping region by means of a call to `SelectClipPath()`.

> **NOTE:** The term *clip path*, or *clipping path*, sometimes found in the Windows documentation, can be somewhat confusing. It is better to say that the `SelectClipPath()` function converts a path to a clipping region, thus eliminating the notion of a clip path as a separate entity.

Table 7-13 lists the paths-related functions.

TABLE 7-13 PATH-RELATED FUNCTIONS

Function	Action
PATH CREATION, DELETION, AND CONVERSION	
BeginPath()	Opens a path bracket
EndPath()	Closes the path bracket and selects the path into the device context
AbortPath()	Closes and discards any open path bracket on the device context
SelectClipPath()	Makes the current path into a clipping region for a specified device context. Combines the new clipping region with any existing one according to a predefined mode
PathToRegion()	Closes an open path and converts it to a region

Continued

Table 7-13 PATH-RELATED FUNCTIONS *(Continued)*

Function	Action
PATH-RENDERING OPERATIONS	
`StrokePath()`	Renders the outline of the current path using the current pen
`FillPath()`	Closes and opens figure in the current path and fills the path interior with the current brush, using the current polygon-fill mode
`StrokeAndFillPath()`	Renders the outline of the current path using the current pen and fills the interior with the current brush
`CloseFigure()`	Draws a line from the current pen position to the figure's start point. The closing line is connected to the figure's first line using the current line-join style
`PolyDraw()`	Draws lines and curves that result from `GetPath()` (Windows NT only)
PATH MANIPULATIONS	
`FlattenPath()`	Converts curves in the current path into line segments
`WidenPath()`	Redefines the current path in a given device context as the area that would be painted if the path were stroked with the current pen
`SetMiterLimit()`	Sets the length of the miter joins for the specified device context
OBTAIN PATH INFORMATION	
`GetPath()`	Retrieves the coordinates of the endpoints of lines and control points of curves in a path
`GetMiterLimit()`	Returns the limit for the length of the miter joins in the specified device context
`GetPolyFillMode()`	Returns the current polygon-fill mode

Creating, Deleting, and Converting Paths

A path is initiated by calling the `BeginPath()` function. The call discards any existing path in the device context and opens a path bracket. The function's general form reads as follows:

```
BOOL BeginPath (HDC hdc);
```

The only parameter is the handle to the device context. The function returns TRUE if it succeeds and FALSE if it fails. After the call to BeginPath() is made, an application can call any of the functions in Table 7-11 or 7-12, according to the operating system platform.

The EndPath() function closes a path bracket and selects the path into the specified device context. The function's general form reads as follows:

```
BOOL EndPath (HDC hdc);
```

The only parameter is the handle to the device context. The function returns TRUE if it succeeds and FALSE if it fails.

The AbortPath() functions closes and discards any open path bracket on the specified device context. The function's general form reads as follows:

```
BOOL AbortPath (HDC hdc);
```

The only parameter is the handle to the device context.

A path bracket is created by calling BeginPath(), followed by one or more of the drawing functions listed in Table 7-11 and 7-12, and closed by a call to EndPath(). At this point applications usually proceed to stroke, fill, or stroke-and-fill the path or to install it as a clipping region. Two possible methods can be followed for converting a path into a clipping region. One method is to use PathToRegion() to create a region and then call ExtSelectClipRgn() to make the region a clipping region. Alternatively, code can call SelectClipPath() and perform both functions in a single call.

SelectClipPath() makes the current path into a clipping region for a specified device context, according to a predefined combination mode. The function's general form reads as follows:

```
BOOL SelectClipPath(
                  HDC hdc,     // 1
                  int iMode    // 2
                 );
```

The second parameter is one of the values listed in Table 7-7. The function returns TRUE if it succeeds and FALSE if it fails.

The PathToRegion() function closes an open path and converts is to a region. The function's general form reads as follows:

```
HRGN PathToRegion (HDC hdc);
```

The function's only parameter is the handle to the device context. The call assumes that the path in the device context is closed. PathToRegion() returns the handle to the created region. Because no path handles exist, this function provides a way of identifying a particular path, although it must first be converted into a region. Unfortunately, there is no method for converting a region into a path.

Path-rendering Operations

After a path is created it is possible to render it as an image by stroking it, filling it, or both. In Windows NT it is also possible to directly draw line segments and Bézier curves that form a path, whose end and control points are stored in an array of type `POINT`.

The `StrokePath()` function renders the outline of the current path using the current pen. The function's general form reads as follows:

```
BOOL StrokePath (HDC hdc);
```

The only parameter is the handle to the device context that contains a closed path. Because a device context can only have a single path, there is no need for further specification. The path is automatically discarded from the device context after it is stroked. The function returns `TRUE` if it succeeds and `FALSE` if it fails.

> **NOTE:** Microsoft Visual C++ documentation does not mention that `StrokePath()` discards the path automatically. What is worse, the remarks on the `StrokeAndFillPath()` function suggest that it is possible to first stroke and then fill the same path by making separate calls to the `StrokePath()` and `FillPath()` function. In reality, the `StrokePath()` function destroys the path before exiting execution. A subsequent call to `FillPath()` has no effect, because there is no longer a path in the device context. This is the reason why the `StrokeAndFillPath()` function exists. Without this function it would be impossible to both stroke and fill a path.

The `FillPath()` function closes an open figure in the current path and fills the path interior with the current brush, using the current polygon-fill mode. The function's general form reads as follows:

```
BOOL FillPath (HDC hdc);
```

The only parameter is the handle to the device context that contains a valid path. Because a device context can only have a single path, there is no need for further specification. The path is automatically discarded from the device context after it is filled. The function returns `TRUE` if it succeeds and `FALSE` if it fails.

The `StrokeAndFillPath()` function closes an open figure in the current path, strokes the path outline using the current pen, and fills the path's interior with the current brush, using the current polygon-fill mode. The function's general form reads as follows:

```
BOOL StrokeAndFillPath (HDC hdc);
```

The only parameter is the handle to the device context that contains a valid path. The path is automatically discarded from the device context after it is stroked and filled. `StrokeAndFillPath()` provides the only way for both stroking and filling a path in Windows, because `StrokePath()` and `FillPath()` destroy the path after they execute. The function returns `TRUE` if it succeeds and `FALSE` if it fails.

The `CloseFigure()` function draws a line from the current pen position to the figure's start point. The closing line is connected to the figure's first line using the current line-join style. The function's general form reads as follows:

```
BOOL CloseFigure (HDC hdc);
```

The only parameter is the handle to the device context that contains a valid path. A figure in a path is open unless the `CloseFigure()` call has been made, even if the figure's starting point and the current point coincide. Usually, the starting point of the figure is the one in the most recent call to `MoveToEx()`.

The effect of closing a figure using the `CloseFigure()` function is not the same as using a call to a drawing primitive. For example, when the figure is closed with a call to the `LineTo()` function, end caps are used at the last corner, instead of a join. If the figure is drawn with a thick, geometric pen, the results can be quite different. Figure 7-19 shows the difference between closing a figure by calling `LineTo()` or by calling `CloseFigure()`.

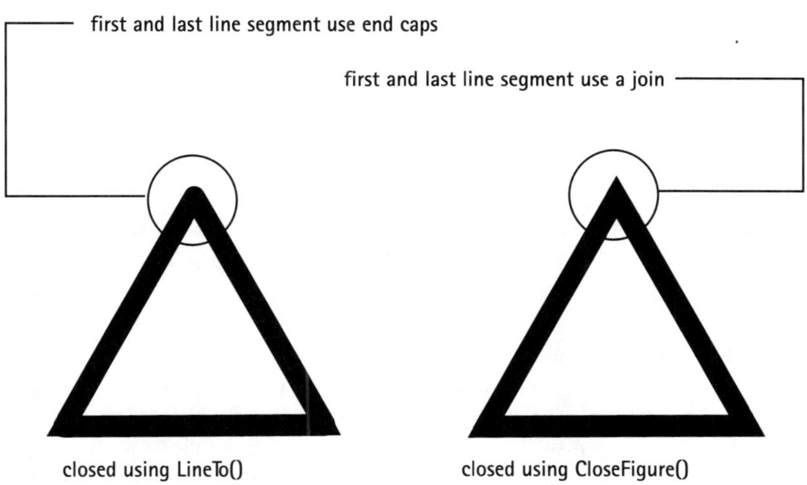

Figure 7-19: Differences in figure closing

The triangles in Figure 7-19 are both drawn with a pen style that has a miter join and a round-end cap. One of the figures is closed using the `LineTo()` drawing function and the other one with `CloseFigure()`. The apex of the triangle closed using the `LineTo()` function is rounded while the one closed using the `CloseFigure()` function is mitered. This is due to the fact that two segments drawn with LineTo() do not have a join at a common end point. In this case, the appearance of the apex is determined by the figure's round-end cap. On the other hand, when the figure is closed with the CloseFigure() function, the selected join is used in all three vertices.

The PolyDraw() function, available only in Windows NT, draws lines segments and Bezier curves. Because of its limited portability we do not discuss it here.

Path Manipulations

Several functions allow the modification of existing paths or the determination of the path characteristics. FlattenPath() converts curves in the current path into line segments. The function's general form reads as follows:

```
BOOL FlattenPath (HDC hdc);
```

The only parameter is the handle to the device context that contains a valid path. The function returns TRUE if it succeeds and FALSE if it fails. Few documented uses for the FlattenPath() function exist. The screen appearance of a flattened path is virtually undetectable. The documented application of this function is to fit text on a curve. Once a curved path has been flattened, a call to GetPath() retrieves the series of line segments that replaced the curves of the original path. Code can now use this information to fit the individual characters along the line segments.

The WidenPath() function redefines the current path in a given device context as the area that would be painted if the path were stroked with the current pen. The function's general form reads as follows:

```
BOOL WidenPath (HDC hdc);
```

The only parameter is the handle to the device context that contains a valid path. Any Bezier curves in the path are converted to straight lines. The function makes a difference when the current pen is a geometric pen or when it has a width or more than one device unit. WidenPath() returns TRUE if it succeeds and FALSE if it fails. This is another function with few documented uses. The fact that curves are converted into line segments suggests that it can be used in text-fitting operations, such as the one described for the FlattenPath() function.

The SetMiterLimit() function sets the length of the miter joins for the specified device context. The function's general form reads as follows:

```
BOOL SetMiterLimit(
                    HDC hdc,            // 1
                    FLOAT eNewLimit,    // 2
                    PFLOAT peOldLimit   // 3
                  );
```

The first parameter is the handle to the device context. The second parameter specifies the new miter limit. The third parameter is a pointer to a floating-point variable that holds the previous miter limit. If this parameter is NULL the value of the previous miter limit is not returned. The function returns `TRUE` if it succeeds and `FALSE` if it fails.

The miter length is the distance from the intersection of the line walls on the inside of the join to the intersection of the line walls on the outside of the join. The miter limit is the ratio between the miter length, to the line width. Figure 7-20 shows the miter length, the line width, and the miter limit.

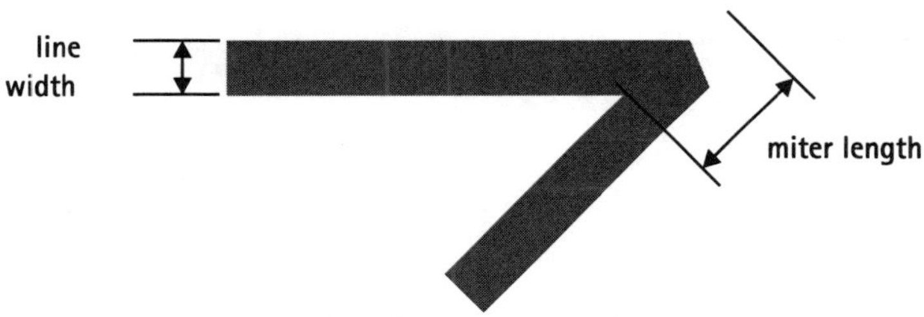

$$\text{miter limit} = \frac{\text{miter length}}{\text{line width}}$$

Figure 7-20: Miter length, line width, and miter limit

The miter limit determines if the vertex of a join that was defined with the `PS_JOIN_MITER` style (see Figure 6-3) is drawn using a miter or a bevel join. If the miter limit is not exceeded, then the join is mitered. Otherwise, it is beveled. Mitered and beveled joins apply only to pens created with the `ExtCreatePen()` function and to stroked paths. The following code fragment shows the creation of two joins:

```
static HPEN    fatPen;    // Handle for pen
static FLOAT   oldMiter;  // Storage for miter limit
.
.
.
// Create a special pen
fatPen = ExtCreatePen (PS_GEOMETRIC | PS_SOLID |
         PS_ENDCAP_ROUND | PS_JOIN_MITER,
         15,
         &fatBrush, 0, NULL);
SelectBrush (hdc, GetStockObject (LTGRAY_BRUSH));
SelectPen (hdc, fatPen);
```

```
// Draw first angle
BeginPath (hdc);
MoveToEx (hdc, 100, 100, NULL);
LineTo (hdc, 250, 100);
LineTo (hdc, 150, 180);
EndPath (hdc);
StrokePath (hdc);
// Draw second angle
GetMiterLimit (hdc, &oldMiter);
SetMiterLimit (hdc, 2, &oldMiter);
BeginPath (hdc);
MoveToEx (hdc, 300, 100, NULL);
LineTo (hdc, 450, 100);
LineTo (hdc, 350, 180);
EndPath (hdc);
StrokePath (hdc);
SetMiterLimit (hdc, oldMiter, NULL);
```

Figure 7-21 is a screen snapshot of the execution of the preceding code fragment.

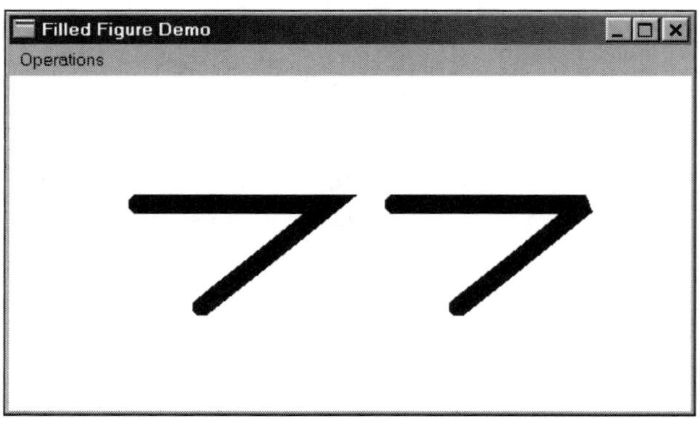

Figure 7-21: Effect of the SetMiterLimit() function

Notice in Figure 7-21 that the figure on the left – in which the default miter limit of 10 is used – is drawn with a miter join. In the right-hand figure the miter limit was changed to 1, therefore, the figure is drawn with a bevel join.

Obtaining Path Information

Several functions provide information about the path, or about GDI parameters that affect the path. The `GetPath()` function retrieves the coordinates of the endpoints of lines and control points of curves in a path. The function's structure is quite similar to the PolyDraw() function discussed in Chapter 6. GetPath() is related to the PolyDraw() function mentioned earlier. The function's general form reads as follows:

```
int GetPath(
            HDC hdc,            // 1
            LPPOINT lpPoints,   // 2
            LPBYTE lpTypes,     // 3
            int nSize           // 4
           );
```

The first parameter identifies the device context. The second parameter is a pointer to an array of POINT structures that contains the endpoints of the lines and the control points of the curves that form the path. The third parameter is an array of type BYTE that contains identifiers that define the purpose of each of the points in the array. The fourth parameter is the count of the number of points in the array of points. The function returns TRUE if it succeeds and FALSE otherwise. Table 7-14 lists the constants used to represent the identifiers entered in the function's third parameter.

TABLE 7-14 CONSTANTS FOR THE GETPATH() VERTEX TYPES

Type	Meaning
PT_MOVETO	This point starts a disjoint figure. The point becomes the new current pen position.
PT_LINETO	A line is to be drawn from the current position to this point, which then becomes the new current pen position.
PT_BEZIERTO	This is a control point or end node for a Bézier curve. This constant always occurs in sets of three. The current position defines the start node for the Bézier curve. The other two coordinates are controlpoints. The third entry (if coded) is the end node.
PT_CLOSEFIGURE	The figure is automatically closed after the PT_LINETO or PT_BEZIERTO type for this point is executed. A line is drawn from the end point to the most recent PT_MOVETO or MoveTo( ) point. The PT_CLOSEFIGURE constant is combined by means of a bitwise OR operator with a PT_LINETO or PT_BEZIERTO constant. This indicates that the corresponding point is the last one in a figure and that the figure is to be closed.

The GetMiterLimit() function, which was mentioned in regards to SetMiterLimit(), returns the limit for the length of the miter join in the specified device context. The function's general form reads as follows:

```
BOOL GetMiterLimit(
                    HDC hdc,          // 1
                    PFLOAT peLimit    // 2
                   );
```

The first parameter is the handle to the device context. The second parameter stores the current miter limit. The function returns TRUE if it succeeds and FALSE if it fails.

The GetPolyFillMode() returns the current polygon-fill mode. The only parameter is the handle to the device context. The value returned is either ALTERNATE or WINDING. The fill mode affects the operation of the FillPath() and StrokeAndFillPath() functions.

Filled Figures Demo Program

The program named FIL_DEMO, located in the *Filled Figures Demo* project folder of the book's CD-ROM, is a demonstration of the graphics functions and operations discussed in this chapter. The first entry in the *Operations* menu shows offseting the hatch origin to visually improve a filled rectangle. The main menu contains several pop-up menus that demonstrate most of the graphics primitives discussed in the text. These include drawing solid figures, operations on rectangles, regions, clipping, and paths. Another menu entry demonstrates the use of the SetMiterLimit() function. Many of the illustrations used in this chapter were taken from the images displayed by the demonstration program.

Summary

In this chapter we explored a rather extensive set of GDI graphics functions. The topics discussed are related, somewhat loosely, to solid figures. We started with brushes and polygon-fill modes, then proceeded to the drawing primitives, with one section devoted entirely to rectangle operations because these are so often encountered in Windows programming. We also discussed regions and clipping operations. The chapter concludes with a discussion of paths and how these are used in graphics programming.

The next chapter is about bitmaps and bitmapped graphics.

Chapter 8

Bitmapped Graphics

IN THIS CHAPTER

- Raster and vector graphics on the PC
- Windows bitmap formats and structures
- Bitmap programming and the bitblt operation
- Manipulating and transforming bitmaps

THIS CHAPTER IS DEVOTED entirely to bitmaps. A bitmap is a digitized image in which each dot is represented by a numeric value. Bitmap images are used in graphics programming at least as frequently as vector representation. The high resolution and extensive color range of current video display systems enables the encoding of bitmapped images with photo-realistic accuracy. The powerful storage and processing capabilities of the modern-day PC make it possible for software to rapidly and effectively manipulate and transform bitmaps. Computer simulations, virtual reality, artificial life, and electronic games are all fields of application that rely heavily on bitmap operations.

Raster and Vector Graphics

The two possible ways of representing images on a computer screen, or a digital graphics device, are based on vector and raster graphics technologies. All of the graphics primitives discussed in Chapters 6 and 7 are based on vector techniques. Commercially speaking, vector graphics are associated with drawing programs, while raster graphics are associated with painting programs. The vector representation of a line consists of its start and end points and its attributes, which usually include width, color, and type. The raster representation of the same line is a mapping of adjacent screen dots. Most current computer systems are raster based, that is, the screen is a two-dimensional pixel grid and all graphics objects are composed of individual screen dots, as described in Chapter 1. Vector graphics are a way of logically defining images, but the images must be rasterized at display time.

Vector and raster representations have their advantages and drawbacks. Vector images can be transformed mathematically (as you will see in Chapter 9); they can also be scaled without loss of quality. Furthermore, vector images are usually more compact. Many images can be conveniently represented in vector form, such as an engineering drawing composed of geometrical elements that can be mathematically defined. The same applies to illustrations, and even to artwork created by combining geometrical elements.

Bitmaps

An image of Leonardo da Vinci's "Mona Lisa," or a photograph of the Crab nebulae, can hardly be vectorized. When geometrical elements are not present, or when the image is rich in minute details, vector representations cease to be practical. In such cases it is better to encode the image as a data structure containing all the individual picture elements. This pixel-by-bit encoding is called a *bitmap.*

A bitmap is a form of raster image. A raster image can be defined as pixel-by-pixel enumeration, usually in scan-line order. A bitmap is a formatted raster image encoded according to some predefined standard or convention. A raster image, on the other hand, can be in raw format. For example, a scanning instrument onboard a satellite or spacecraft acquires and transmits image data in raster form. Once received, the raster data can be processed and stored as bitmaps that can be easily displayed on a computer screen. Television images are in raster form.

A bitmap is a memory object, not a screen image. It is the memory encoding of an image at the pixel level. Although bitmaps are often represented in image form, it is important to remember that a bitmap is a data construct. Bitmaps cannot be easily transformed mathematically – as is the case with vector images – nor can they be scaled without some loss of information. However, bitmaps offer a more faithful reproduction of small details than is practical in vector representations.

In bitmapping, one or more memory bits are used to represent the attribute of a screen pixel. The simplest and most compact scheme is that in which a memory bit represents a single screen pixel: if the bit is set, so is the pixel. This one-bit-to-one-pixel representation leaves no choice about pixel attributes, that is, a pixel is either set or not. In a monochrome video system a set bit can correspond to a bright pixel and a reset bit to a black one. Figure 8-1 shows a bit-to-pixel image and bitmap.

Most current video systems support multiple attributes per screen pixel. PC color video systems are usually capable of representing 16, 256, 65,535, and 16.7 million colors. Shades of gray can also be encoded in a bitmap. The number of bits devoted to each pixel determines the attribute range. Sixteen colors or shades of gray can be represented in four bits. Eight bits can represent 256 colors. Sixteen bits encode 65,535 colors. So-called true color systems, which can display approximately 16.7 million colors, require 24 data bits per screen dot. Some color data formats use 32 bits per pixel, but this representation is actually 24 bits of pixel data plus 8 bits of padding. Figure 8-2 shows an image and bitmap in which each pixel is represented by two memory bits.

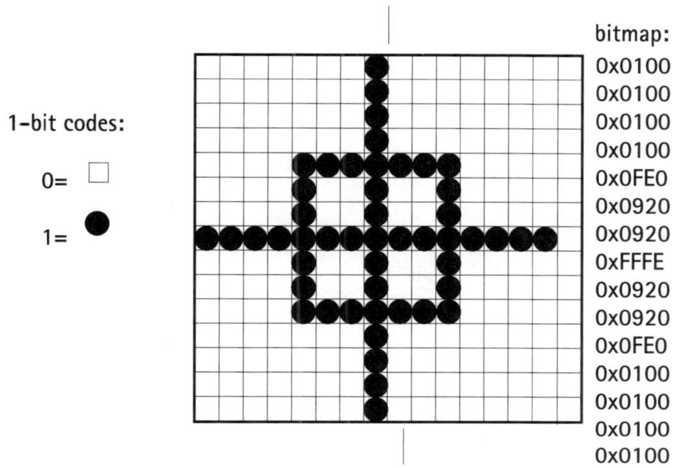

Figure 8-1: One bit-per-pixel image and bitmap

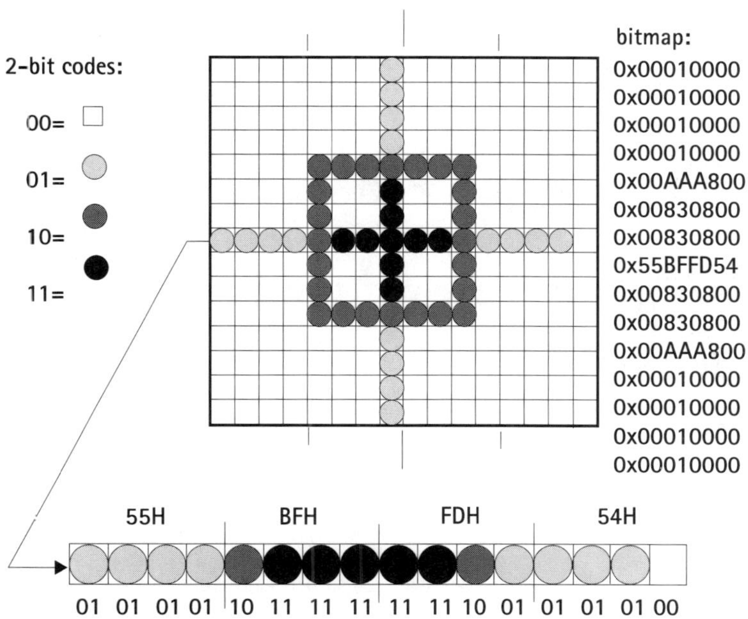

Figure 8-2: Two bits-per-pixel image and bitmap

In Figure 8-2, each screen pixel can be in one of four attributes: background, light gray, dark gray, or black. To represent these four states it is necessary to assign a 2-bit field for each screen pixel. The 4-bit combinations that correspond with the attribute options are shown on the left side of Figure 8-2. At the bottom of the illustration is a map of one of the pixel rows, with the corresponding binary codes for each pixel, as well as the hexadecimal digits of the bitmap.

Image Processing

The fact that raster images can't be transformed mathematically does not mean that they can't be manipulated and processed. Image Processing is a major field of computer graphics. It deals exclusively with the manipulation and analysis of two-dimensional pictorial data in digital form. In practice, this means processing raster data. Although digital-image processing originated in the science programs of the National Aeronautics and Space Administration (NASA), it has since been applied to many other technological fields, including biological research, document processing, factory automation, forensics, medical diagnostics, photography, prepress-publishing operations, space exploration, and special effects on film and video.

Bitblt Operations

The fundamental bitmap operation is the bit block transfer, or *bitblt* (pronounced bit-blit). In the bitblt a rectangular block of memory bits, representing pixel attributes, is transferred as a block. If the destination of the transfer is screen memory, then the bitmapped image is displayed. At the time of the transfer, the source and destination bit blocks can be combined logically or arithmetically, or a unary operation can be performed on the source or the destination bit blocks. Figure 8-3 shows several binary and unary operations on bit blocks.

Windows Bitmap Constructs

Several Windows data structures and concepts relate to bitmaps:

- Bitmap formats
- Structures for bitmap operations
- Creating bitmap resources

You must understand these concepts to be able to manipulate and display bitmaps.

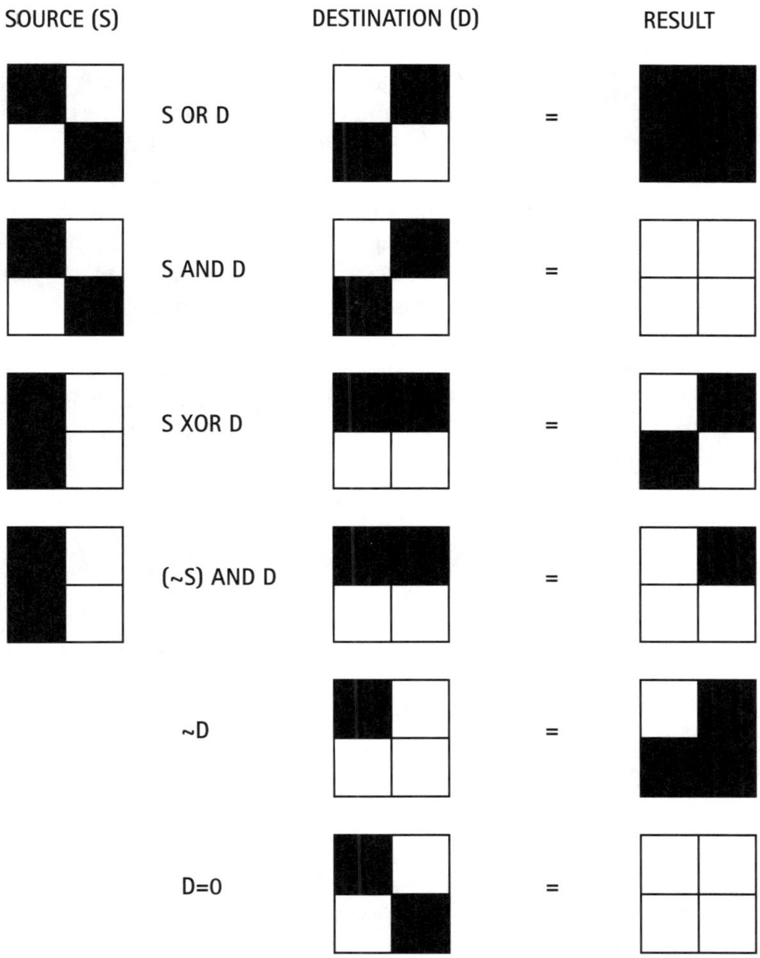

Figure 8-3: Binary and unary operations on bit blocks

Bitmap Formats

The computer establishment has created hundreds of bitmap-image formats over the past two or three decades. Among the best known are GIF, PCX, Targa, TIFF, and Jpeg. Windows does not provide support for manipulating image files in any commercial format. The only bitmap formats that can be handled are those specifically created for Windows. These are the original device-specific bitmaps (extension BMP) and the newer device-independent bitmaps (extension DIB).

The device-specific bitmap format was created in Windows 3.0. It can store images with up to 24-bit color. Files in BMP format are uncompressed, which makes it quick to read and display them. The disadvantage of uncompressed files is that they take up considerable memory and storage space. Another objection to using the device-specific bitmap is that the BMP header cannot directly encode the original colors in the bitmap. For this reason, the format works well for copying parts of the screen to memory and pasting them back to other locations. But problems often occur when the device-specific bitmap must be saved in a disk file and then output to a different device, because the destination device may not support the same colors as the original one. For this reason it is usually preferable to use the device-independent format, although its data structures are slightly larger.

Note that many Windows bitmap functions operate both on device-specific and device-independent bitmaps. The *Bitmap Demo* project on the book's CD-ROM displays bitmaps in BMP and DIB format using the same Windows functions. In the remainder of this chapter we deal exclusively with device-independent bitmaps encoded in DIB format, although device-independent bitmaps can also be stored in .BMP files.

Bitmap Structures

Eleven structures directly or indirectly related to Windows bitmaps are listed in Table 8-1.

TABLE 8-1 BITMAP-RELATED STRUCTURES

Structure	Contents
`BITMAP`	Defines the width, height, type, format, and bit values of a bitmap.
`BITMAPCOREHEADER`	Contains information about the dimensions and color format of a DIB.
`BITMAPCOREINFO`	Contains a `BITMAPCOREHEADER` structure and a `RGBTRIPLE` structure array with the bitmap's color intensities.
`BITMAPFILEHEADER`	Contains information about a file that holds a DIB.
`BITMAPINFO`	Defines the dimensions and color data of a DIB. Includes a `BITMAPINFOHEADER` structure and a `RGBQUAD` structure.
`BITMAPINFOHEADER`	Contains information about the dimensions and color format of a DIB.
`COLORADJUSTMENT`	Defines the color adjustment values used by the `StrtchBlt()` and `StretchDIBits()` functions.

Structure	Contents
DIBSECTION	Contains information about a bitmap created by means of the CreateDIBSection() function.
RGBQUAD	Describes the relative intensities of the red, green, and blue color components. The fourth byte of the structure is reserved.
RGBTRIPLE	Describes the relative intensities of the red, green, and blue color components. The BITMAPCOREINFO structure contains an array of RGBTRIPLE structures.
SIZE	Defines the width and height of a rectangle, which can be used to represent the dimensions of a bitmap.

Some of the structures in Table 8-1 are listed and described in this chapter. All of them appear in Appendix A.

The Bitmap as a Resource

In Visual C++ a bitmap can be a program resource. Developer Studio includes a bitmap editor that can be used for creating and editing bitmaps that do not exceed a certain size and color range. Bitmaps in BMP or DIB format created with other applications can also be imported into a program. In this case you can select the Resource command in the Insert menu, and then select the bitmap resource type and click the Import button. The dialog box that appears enables you to browse through the file system to locate the bitmap file. It is usually better to copy the bitmap file into the project's folder, thus ensuring that it is not deleted or modified inadvertently.

Once a bitmap has been imported in the project, it is listed in the Resource tab of the Project Workspace pane. At this point it is possible to use the MAKEINTRESOURCE macro to convert it into a resource type that can be managed by the application. Because the final objective is to obtain the handle to a bitmap, code usually proceeds as follows:

```
HBITMAP       aBitmap;
.
.
.
aBitmap = LoadBitmap (pInstance,
                      MAKEINTRESOURCE (IDB_BITMAP1));
```

In this case, IDB_BITMAP1 is the resource name assigned by Developer Studio when the bitmap was imported. It is listed in the Bitmap section of the Resource tab in the Project Workspace pane and also by the Resource Symbols command in the View menu.

Bitmap Programming Overview

The bitmap is an object of the device context, such as a brush, a pen, a font, or a region. Bitmap manipulations and display functions in Windows are powerful, but not without some limitations and complications. This overview presents a preliminary discussion of simple bitmap programming. Later in this chapter we get into more complicated operations.

Creating the Memory DC

One unique characteristic of a bitmap is that it can be selected only into a memory device context. The memory DC is defined as a device context with a display surface. It exists only in memory and is related to a particular device context. To use a memory device context you must first create it. The CreateCompatibleDC() function is used for this purpose. Its general form reads as follows:

```
HDC CreateCompatibleDC (HDC hdc);
```

Its only parameter is the handle to the device context with which the memory device context is to be compatible. This parameter can be NULL if the memory device context is to be compatible with the video screen. If the function succeeds, it returns the handle to the memory device context. The call returns NULL if it fails. CreateCompatibleDC() assumes that the device context supports raster operations, which is true in all PC video systems, but not necessarily so for other graphics devices, such as a plotter. The GetDeviceCaps() function with the RASTERCAPS constant can be used to determine if a particular device supports raster operations (see Table 6-4).

Like the device context, a memory device context has a mapping-mode attribute. Applications often use the same mapping mode for the memory device context and for the device context. In this case the SetMapMode() and GetMapMode() functions can be combined as follows:

```
HDC        hdc;       // Handle to device context
HDC        memDC;     // Handle to memory device context
.
.
.
SetMapMode (memDC, GetMapMode (hdc));
```

Selecting the Bitmap

When the memory device context is created, it is assigned a display surface of a single monochrome pixel. The single pixel acts as a placeholder until a real one is selected into the memory DC. The `SelectObject()` function – discussed in Chapter 6 – can be used to select a bitmap into a memory device context, but the `SelectBitmap()` macro, discussed in Chapter 7, serves the same purpose. Both `SelectObject()` and `SelectBitmap()` have the same interface. For `SelectBitmap()` the code reads as follows:

```
HBITMAP SelectBitmap (HDC, HBITMAP);
                       |    ----
                       |     |
                       1     2
```

The first parameter must be the handle of a memory device context. The second parameter is the handle to the bitmap being installed. If the call succeeds, the macro returns the handle to the device context object being replaced. If the call fails, it returns NULL. Using the `SelectBitmap()` macro instead of the `SelectObject()` function produces code that is correct and the coding is made easier. Recall that programs that use the object selection macros must include the *windowsx.h* file.

The handle to the bitmap used in the `SelectBitmap()` macro is usually obtained with the `LoadBitmap()` function previously discussed.

Obtaining Bitmap Dimensions

Bitmap functions often require information about the dimensions and other characteristics of the bitmap. For example, the function most often used to display a bitmap is `BitBlt()`; it requires the width and height of the bitmap. If the bitmap is loaded as a resource from a file, the application must obtain the bitmap dimensions before blitting it to the screen. The `GetObject()` function is used to obtain information about a bitmap. The function's general form reads as follows:

```
int GetObject(
          HGDIOBJ hgdiobj,   // 1
          int cbBuffer,      // 2
          LPVOID lpvObject   // 3
         );
```

The first parameter is the handle to a graphics object – in this case – the handle to a bitmap. The second parameter is the size of the buffer that holds the information returned by the call. In the case of a bitmap, this parameter can be coded as `sizeof (BITMAP)`. The third parameter is a pointer to the buffer that holds the information returned by the call. In the case of a bitmap, the buffer is a structure variable of type BITMAP. The BITMAP structure is defined as follows:

```
typedef struct tagBITMAP {
   LONG   bmType;        // Must be zero
   LONG   bmWidth;       // bitmap width (in pixels)
   LONG   bmHeight;      // bitmap height  (in pixels)
   LONG   bmWidthBytes;  // bytes per scan line
   WORD   bmPlanes;      // number of color planes
   WORD   bmBitsPixel;   // bits per pixel color
   LPVOID bmBits;        // points to bitmap values array
} BITMAP;
```

The structure member bmType specifies the bitmap type. It must be zero. The member bmWidth specifies the width, in pixels, of the bitmap. Its value must be greater than zero. The member bmHeight specifies the height, in pixels, of the bitmap. The height must be greater than zero. The bmWidthBytes member specifies the number of bytes in each scan line. Because Windows assumes that the bitmap is word-aligned, its value must be divisible by two. The member bmPlanes specifies the number of color planes. The member bmBitsPixel specifies the number of bits required to indicate the color of a pixel. The member bmBits points to the location of the bit values for the bitmap. It is a long pointer to an array of character-size values.

When the target of the GetObject() call is a bitmap, the information returned is the structure members related to the bitmap width, height, and color format. The GetObject() function cannot be used to read the value of the pointer to the bitmap data in the bmBits structure member. GetDIBits() retrieves the bit data of a bitmap.

The mapping mode can also be a factor in regard to bitmap data. The GetObject() function returns the bitmap width and height in the BITMAP structure. The values returned are in pixels, which are device units. This works well if the mapping mode of the memory device context is MM_TEXT, but is not acceptable in any of the mapping modes that use logical units. The DPtoLP() function facilitates the conversion of device coordinates (pixels) into logical coordinates for a particular device context. The function's general form reads as follows:

```
BOOL DPtoLP(
            HDC hdc,           // 1
            LPPOINT lpPoints,  // 2
            int nCount         // 3
           );
```

The first parameter identifies the device context. In the case of a bitmap, it is a memory device context. The second parameter points to an array of POINT structures that holds the transformed values for the *x*- and *y*-coordinates. The third parameter holds the number of points in the array specified in the second parameter. The function returns TRUE if it succeeds and FALSE if it fails.

A bitmap size is defined by two values: the *x*-coordinate is the width and the *y*-coordinate the height. When a call to DPtoLP() is made to obtain the bitmap size, the third parameter is set to 1. This indicates that the coordinates to be transformed refer to a single point. By the same token, the second parameter is a pointer to a single POINT structure that holds the bitmap width in the *x* member and the bitmap height in the *y* member.

Blitting the Bitmap

Once a bitmap has been selected onto a memory device context, and the code has obtained the necessary information about its width and height, it is possible to display it at any screen position by blitting the memory-stored bitmap onto the screen. The BitBlt() function is the simplest and most direct method of performing the bitmap display operation. The function's general form reads as follows:

```
BOOL BitBlt(
            HDC hdcDest, // 1
            int nXDest,  // 2
            int nYDest,  // 3
            int nWidth,  // 4
            int nHeight, // 5
            HDC hdcSrc,  // 6
            int nXSrc,   // 7
            int nYSrc,   // 8
            DWORD dwRop  // 9
           );
```

The first parameter identifies the destination device context. If the call to BitBlt() is made to display a bitmap, this will be the display context. The second and third parameters are the *x*- and *y*-coordinates of the upper-left corner of the destination rectangle, which is also the screen location where the upper-left corner of the bitmap is displayed. The fourth and fifth parameters are the width and height of the bitmap, in logical units. The sixth parameter is the source device context. In the case of a bitmap-display operation, this parameter holds the memory device context where the bitmap is stored. The seventh and eighth parameters are the *x*- and *y*-coordinates of the source bitmap. Because the blitted rectangles must be of the same dimensions, as defined by the fourth and fifth parameters, the seventh and eighth parameters are usually set to zero.

The ninth parameter defines the raster operation code. These codes are called ternary raster operations. They differ from the binary raster operation codes (ROP2) discussed in Chapter 6 in that the ternary codes take into account the source, the destination, and a pattern determined by the brush currently selected in the device context. Two hundred fifty-six possible raster operations exist, fifteen of which have symbolic names defined in the *windows.h* header file. The raster operation code determines how the color data of the source and destination rectangles, together with the current brush, are to be combined. Table 8-2 lists the 15 raster operations with symbolic names.

TABLE 8-2 SYMBOLIC NAMES FOR RASTER OPERATION CODES

Name	Description
BLACKNESS	Fills the destination rectangle using the color associated with index 0 in the physical palette. The default value is black.
DSTINVERT	Inverts the destination rectangle.
MERGECOPY	Merges the colors of the source rectangle with the specified pattern using an AND operation.
MERGEPAINT	Merges the colors of the inverted source rectangle with the colors of the destination rectangle using an OR operation.
NOTSRCCOPY	Inverts the bits in the source rectangle and copies it to the destination.
NOTSRCERASE	Combines the colors of the source and destination rectangles using an OR operation, and then inverts the result.
PATCOPY	Copies the specified pattern to the destination bitmap.
PATINVERT	Combines the colors of the specified pattern with the colors of the destination rectangle using an XOR operation.
PATPAINT	Combines the colors of the pattern with the colors of the inverted source rectangle using an OR operation. The result of this operation is combined with the colors of the destination rectangle using an OR operation.
SRCAND	Combines the colors of the source and destination rectangles using an AND operation.
SRCCOPY	Copies the source rectangle directly to the destination rectangle. This is, by far, the most-used mode in bitblt operations.
SRCERASE	Combines the inverted colors of the destination rectangle with the colors of the source rectangle using an AND operation.
SRCINVERT	Combines the colors of the source and destination rectangles using an XOR operation.

Name	Description
SRCPAINT	Combines the colors of the source and destination rectangles using an OR operation.
WHITENESS	Fills the destination rectangle using the color associated with index 1 in the physical palette. The default value is white.

Appendix B lists all 256 raster operations codes and the Boolean operations performed by each one. Applications can reference the ternary ROP codes by means of their symbolic names or by using the 32-bit ROP codes listed in Appendix B.

Developing a Bitmap Display Function

Displaying a bitmap is a multistage process that includes the following operations:

1. Creating a memory device context
2. Selecting the bitmap into the memory device context
3. Obtaining the bitmap dimensions and converting device units to logical units
4. Blitting the bitmap onto the screen according to a ternary raster operation code

Many graphics applications can make use of a function that performs all of the previous operations. The function named `ShowBitmap()` is used in the Bitmap Demo project on the book's CD-ROM. The function's prototype reads as follows:

```
void ShowBitmap (HDC, HBITMAP, int, int, DWORD);
                  |  ----     |    |   ---
                  |     |      |    |     |
                  1     2      3    4     5
```

The first parameter is the handle to the device context. The `ShowBitmap()` function creates its own memory device context. The second parameter is the handle to the bitmap that is to be displayed. The third and fourth parameters are the screen coordinates for displaying the upper-left corner of the bitmap. The fifth parameter is the ternary `ROP` code used in blitting the bitmap. If this parameter is NULL then the bitmap is displayed using the `SRCCOPY` raster operation. The following is a listing of the `ShowBitmap()` function:

```
void ShowBitmap (HDC hdc, HBITMAP hBitmap, int xStart, int yStart,\
                 DWORD rop3) {

BITMAP      bm;               // BITMAP structure
HDC         memoryDc;         // Handle to memory DC
POINT       ptSize;           // POINT for DC
POINT       ptOrigin;         // POINT for memory DC
int         mapMode;          // Mapping mode

    // Test for NULL ROP3 code
    if (rop3 == NULL)
        rop3 = SRCCOPY;

    memoryDc = CreateCompatibleDC (hdc); // Memory device
                                         // handle
    mapMode = GetMapMode (hdc);          // Obtain mapping
                                         // mode
    SetMapMode (memoryDc, mapMode);      // Set memory DC
                                         // mapping mode

    // Select bitmap into memory DC
    // Note: assert statement facilitates detecting invalid
    //       bitmaps during program development
    assert (SelectBitmap (memoryDc, hBitmap));

    // Obtain bitmap dimensions
    GetObject (hBitmap, sizeof(BITMAP), (LPVOID) &bm);

    // Convert device units to logical units
    ptSize.x = bm.bmWidth;
    ptSize.y = bm.bmHeight;
    DPtoLP (hdc, &ptSize, 1);

    ptOrigin.x = 0;
    ptOrigin.y = 0;
    DPtoLP (memoryDc, &ptOrigin, 1);

    // Bitblt bitmap onto display memory
    BitBlt( hdc, xStart, yStart, ptSize.x, ptSize.y, memoryDc,
            ptOrigin.x, ptOrigin.y, rop3);

    // Delete memory DC with bitmap
    DeleteDC (memoryDc);
}
```

Bitmap Manipulations

In addition to displaying a bitmap stored in a disk file, graphics applications often need to perform other bitmap-related operations. The following are among the most common operations:

- Creating and displaying a hard-coded bitmap
- Creating a bitmap in heap memory
- Creating a blank bitmap and filling it by means of GDI functions
- Creating a system-memory bitmap that applications can access directly
- Using a bitmap to create a pattern brush

Hard-coding a Monochrome Bitmap

With the facilities available in Developer Studio for creating bitmaps, the programmer is seldom forced to hard-code a bitmap. Our rationale for discussing this option is that hard-coding bitmaps is a basic skill for a graphics programmer, and it also helps you to understand bitmaps in general.

A monochrome bitmap has one color plane and is encoded in a one-bit-per-pixel format. In Windows, a monochrome bitmap is displayed by showing the 0-bits in the foreground color and the 1-bits in the background color. If the screen has a white foreground and a black background, 0-bits in the bitmap are displayed as white pixels, and vice versa. If the bitmap is to be blitted on the screen using the `BitBlt()` function, the action of the bits can be reversed by changing the raster operation code. This gives the programmer the flexibility of using either zero or one bits for background or foreground attributes. Figure 8-4 shows a hard-coded monochrome bitmap.

In Figure 8-4 the dark pixels in the image are represented by 0-bits in the bitmap. The resulting data structure has five bytes per scan line and a total of 10 scan lines. The illustration shows how eight pixels in the bottom row of the image are represented by eight bits (one byte) of the bitmap. The dark pixels are encoded as 0-bits and the light pixels as 1-bits. To display this bitmap so that the letters are black on a white screen background, the black and white pixels have to be reversed by changing the raster operation mode from the default value, `SCRCOPY`, to `NOTSCRCOPY`, as previously explained.

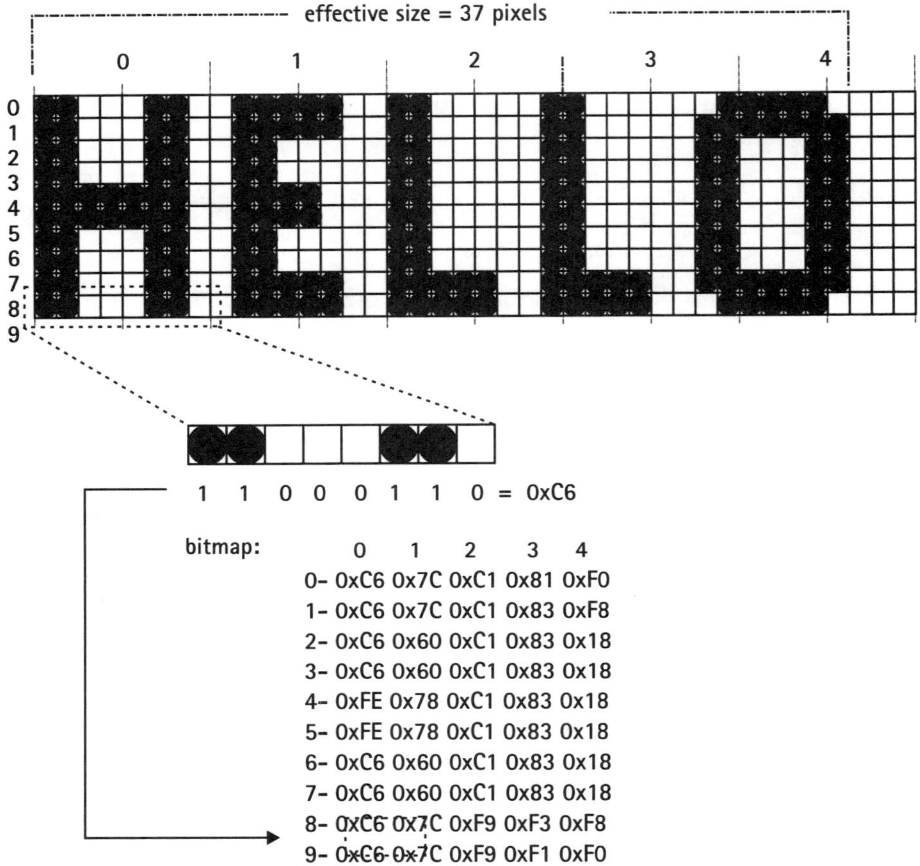

Figure 8-4: A hard-coded, monochrome bitmap

Once the bit image of a monochrome bitmap has been calculated, we can proceed to store this bit-to-pixel information in an array of type `BYTE`. Windows requires that bitmaps be word-aligned; therefore, each scan line in the array must have a number of bytes divisible by two. In regards to the bitmap in Figure 8-4, you would have to add a padding byte to each scan line to satisfy this requirement. The resulting array could be coded as follows:

```
//                              0     1     2     3     4     5
static BYTE hexBits[] = {0xc6, 0x7c, 0xc1, 0x81, 0xf0, 0x0,
                          0xc6, 0x7c, 0xc1, 0x83, 0xf8, 0x0,
                          0xc6, 0x60, 0xc1, 0x83, 0x18, 0x0,
                          0xc6, 0x60, 0xc1, 0x83, 0x18, 0x0,
                          0xfe, 0x78, 0xc1, 0x83, 0x18, 0x0,
                          0xfe, 0x78, 0xc1, 0x83, 0x18, 0x0,
```

```
                              0xc6, 0x60, 0xc1, 0x83, 0x18, 0x0,
                              0xc6, 0x60, 0xc1, 0x83, 0x18, 0x0,
                              0xc6, 0x7c, 0xf9, 0xf3, 0xf8, 0x0,
                              0xc6, 0x7c, 0xf9, 0xf1, 0xf0, 0x0};
//                                                           |
//                                  padding byte ---------- -|
```

The CreateBitmap() function can be used to create a bitmap given the bit-to-pixel data array. The function's general form is as follows:

```
HBITMAP CreateBitmap(
                  int nWidth,         // 1
                  int nHeight,        // 2
                  UINT cPlanes,       // 3
                  UINT cBitsPerPel,   // 4
                  CONST VOID *lpvBits // 5
                 );
```

The first parameter is the actual width of the bitmap, in pixels. In relation to the bitmap in Figure 8-4, this value is 37 pixels, as shown in the illustration. The second parameter is the number of scan lines in the bitmap. The third parameter is the number of color planes. In the case of a monochrome bitmap this value is 1. The fourth parameter is the number of bits per pixel. In a monochrome bitmap this value is also 1. The fifth parameter is a pointer to the location where the bitmap data is stored. If the function succeeds, the return value is the handle to a bitmap. If the function fails, the return value is NULL. The following code fragment initializes a monochrome bitmap using the bitmap data in the hexBits[] array previously listed:

```
static HBITMAP      bmImage1;
.
.
.
// Initialize monochrome bitmap
bmImage1 = CreateBitmap (37, 10, 1, 1, hexBits);
```

Alternatively, a bitmap can be defined using a structure of type BITMAP, listed previously in this chapter and in Appendix A. Before the bitmap is created the structure members must be initialized – as is done in the following code fragment:

```
static BITMAP       monoBM;
.
.
.
```

```
// Initialize data structure for a monochrome bitmap
monoBM.bmType = 0;          // must be zero
monoBM.bmWidth = 37;        // actual pixels used
monoBM.bmHeight = 10;       // scan lines
monoBM.bmWidthBytes = 6;    // width (must be word aligned)
monoBM.bmPlanes = 1;        // 1 for monochrome bitmaps
monoBM.bmBitsPixel = 1;     // 1 for monochrome bitmaps
monoBM.bmBits = (LPVOID) &hexBits; // address of bit field
```

When the bitmap data is stored in a structure of type `BITMAP`, the bitmap can be created by means of the `CreateBitmapIndirect()` function. The function's general form reads as follows:

```
HBITMAP CreateBitmapIndirect(
                              CONST BITMAP *lpbm    // 1
                             );
```

The function's only parameter is a pointer to a structure of type `BITMAP`. If the function succeeds, the returned value is the handle to a bitmap. If the function fails, the return value is NULL. The following code fragment uses `CreateBitmapIndirect()` to initialize a monochrome bitmap using the bitmap data in the `hexBits[]` array previously listed:

```
static HBITMAP      bmImage1;
.
.
.
// Initialize monochrome bitmap
bmImage1 = CreateBitmapIndirect (&monoBM);
```

Whether the bitmap was created using `CreateBitmap()` or `CreateBitmapIndirect()`, it can now be displayed by means of the `ShowBitmap()` function developed and listed previously in this chapter.

Bitmaps in Heap Memory

A bitmap can take up a considerable amount of memory or storage resources. For example, a 1200 by 1200 pixel bitmap encoded in 32-bit color takes up approximately 5.7 MB. Applications that store large bitmaps in their own memory space can run into memory management problems. One possible solution is to store large bitmaps in dynamically allocated memory, which can be freed as soon as the bitmap is no longer needed. Note that freeing memory where the bitmap is stored does not affect the screen image.

Several programming techniques can be used to allocate and release heap memory for a bitmap. The one most suitable depends on the particular needs of each particular programming problem. In one case you may allocate heap memory for a bitmap during `WM_CREATE` message processing, and then use this allocated space to create or copy different bitmaps during program execution. The allocated memory can then be freed during `WM_DESTROY` processing. Another option is to allocate memory at the time it is required, create or copy the bitmap to this allocated space, and deallocate the memory when the bitmap is no longer needed.

Many fables and fantastic theories have originated in the complications and misunderstandings of Windows memory management. Although most of these problems were corrected in Windows 3.1, an entire programming subculture still thrives on discussions related to these topics. A programmer encountering memory management in Windows finds that three separate sets of memory allocation and deallocation operators exist that serve apparently identical purposes: the C++ operators *new* and *delete*, the traditional C operators *malloc* and *free*, and the Windows kernel functions `LocalAlloc()`, `GlobalAlloc()`, `LocalFree()`, and `GlobalFree()`.

In Win32 programming, the first simplification is a result of the fact that there is no difference between the global and the local heaps. Therefore, `GlobalAlloc()` and `LocalAlloc()`, as well as `GlobalFree()` and `LocalFree()`, actually perform virtually identical functions. Because of their greater flexibility we will use `GlobalAlloc()` and `GlobalFree()` instead of `new` and `delete` or `malloc` and `free` operators from the C++ and C libraries. Another reason for this preference is that most Windows compilers implement `malloc` and `new` in terms of `GlobalAlloc()`; therefore, the traditional operators offer no advantage.

Traditionally, three types of memory are documented as being available to applications: *fixed* memory, *moveable* memory, and *discardable* memory. The justification for preferring moveable memory disappeared with Windows 95, in which a memory block can be moved in virtual memory while retaining the same address. For the same reason, the use of fixed memory no longer needs to be avoided. Discardable memory is only indicated when the data can be easily recreated, which is not usually the case with image data structures. In conclusion, fixed memory is usually quite suitable for dynamically storing bitmaps and other image data.

> **NOTE:** Both *moveable* and *movable* are accepted spellings, although movable is preferred. However, the Windows API contains the constants `GMEM_MOVEABLE` and `LMEM_MOVEABLE`. For this reason we have used the former.

In this section we discuss the bare essentials of memory allocation and deallocation in Windows. The topic of Windows memory management can easily fill a good-size volume. Graphics applications are often memory-intensive and may require sophisticated memory management techniques. A graphics programmer should have a thorough knowledge of Win32 memory architecture, virtual memory, and heap management. The book *Advanced Windows*, by Richter (see bibliography) has chapters devoted to each of these topics.

The `GlobalAlloc()` function is used to allocate memory from the default heap. The default heap is initially 1MB, but under Windows, this heap grows as it becomes necessary. The function's general form reads as follows:

```
HGLOBAL GlobalAlloc(
                    UINT uFlags,     // 1
                    DWORD dwBytes    // 2
                   );
```

The first parameter is a flag that determines how memory is allocated to the caller. Table 8-3 lists the most commonly used allocation flags. The second parameter is the number of bytes of memory to be allocated. If it succeeds, the function returns the handle to the allocated memory object. If the allocation flag is `GMEM_FIXED`, the handle can be directly cast into a pointer and the memory used. If the allocated memory is not fixed, then it must be locked using `GlobalLock()` before it can be used by code. The function returns NULL if the allocation request fails.

TABLE 8-3 COMMONLY USED MEMORY ALLOCATION FLAGS IN WIN32

Flag	Meaning
`GMEM_FIXED`	Allocates fixed memory. This flag cannot be combined with the `GMEM_MOVEABLE` or `GMEM_DISCARDABLE` flag. The return value is a pointer to the memory block.
`GMEM_MOVEABLE`	Allocates moveable memory. This flag cannot be combined with the `GMEM_FIXED` flag. The return value is the handle of the memory object, which is a 32-bit quantity private to the calling process.
`GMEM_DISCARDABLE`	Allocates discardable memory. This flag cannot be combined with the GMEM_FIXED flag. Win32-based operating systems ignore this flag. This is provided only for compatibility with old 16-bit source code. It is ignored on all Win32 operating systems.
`GMEM_ZEROINIT`	Initializes memory to 0.
`GPTR`	Combines the `GMEM_FIXED` and `GMEM_ZEROINIT` flags.
`GHND`	Combines the `GMEM_MOVEABLE` and `GMEM_ZEROINIT` flags.

The process of creating a bitmap in heap memory and displaying it on the video screen can be accomplished by the following steps:

1. Dynamically allocate the memory required for the bitmap and the corresponding data structures.
2. Store the bitmap data and the bitmap dimensions and color information, thus creating a DIB.
3. Convert the device independent bitmap (DIB) into a device dependent bitmap using `CreateDIBitmap()`.
4. Display the bitmap using `SetDIBitsToDevice()`.

Suppose you wanted to create a 200-pixel wide bitmap, with 255 scan lines, in 32-bit color. Because each pixel requires four bytes, each scan line consists of 800 bytes, and the entire bitmap occupies 204,000 bytes. A `BITMAPINFO` structure variable is used to hold the bitmap information. Notice that because this is a true-color bitmap, the `RGBQUAD` structure is not necessary. In this case the memory allocation operations can be coded as follows:

```
static PBITMAPINFO  pDibInfo;    // pointer to BITMAPINFO structure
static BYTE         *pDib;       // pointer to bitmap data
.
.
.
pDibInfo = (PBITMAPINFO) LocalAlloc(LMEM_FIXED, \
                         sizeof(BITMAPINFOHEADER));
pDib = (BYTE*) LocalAlloc(LMEM_FIXED, 204000);
```

At this point the code has allocated memory for both the bitmap and the `BITMAPINFOHEADER` structure variable that is to hold the bitmap format information. The pointers to each of these memory areas can be used to fill them in. First the bitmap information:

```
pDibInfo->bmiHeader.biSize = (LONG) sizeof(BITMAPINFOHEADER);
pDibInfo->bmiHeader.biWidth = (LONG) 200;      // pixel width
pDibInfo->bmiHeader.biHeight = (LONG) 255;     // pixel height
pDibInfo->bmiHeader.biPlanes = 1;              // number of planes
pDibInfo->bmiHeader.biBitCount = 32;           // bits per pixel
```

Assume that the bitmap is to represent a blue rectangle with 255 decreasing intensities of blue, along the scan lines. The code to fill this bitmap can be coded as follows:

```
int    i, j, k;        // counters
```

```
BYTE  shade;          // shade of blue
.
.
.
// Fill the bitmap using 32-bit color data
// <——- 200 pixels (4 bytes each) ——>
// |
// | ... 255 scan lines
shade = 0;
  for (k = 0; k < 255; k++){        // Counts 255 scan lines
     for (i = 0; i < 200; i++){     // Counts 200 pixels
        for(j = 0; j < 4; j++) {    // Counts 4 bytes
            pDib[((k*800)+(i*4)+0] = shade; // blue
            pDib[((k*800)+(i*4)+1] = 0;     // green
            pDib[((k*800)+(i*4)+2] = 0;     // red
            pDib[((k*800)+(i*4)+3] = 0;     // must be zero
            };
        };
     shade++;
  };
```

Now that the bitmap data structures have been initialized and the bitmap data entered into the allocated heap memory, it is time to create the device-dependent bitmap that can be displayed on the display context. The function used for this purpose is named `CreateDIBitmap()`. This name is somewhat confusing because it actually creates a dependent device from a device-independent bitmap. The function's general form reads as follows:

```
HBITMAP CreateDIBitmap(
                       HDC hdc,                          // 1
                       CONST BITMAPINFOHEADER *lpbmih,   // 2
                       DWORD fdwInit,                    // 3
                       CONST VOID *lpbInit,              // 4
                       CONST BITMAPINFO *lpbmi,          // 5
                       UINT fuUsage                      // 6
                      );
```

The first parameter is the handle to the device context for which the device-dependent bitmap is to be configured. The second parameter is a pointer to a `BITMAPINFOHEADER` structure variable that contains the bitmap data. The third parameter is a flag that determines how the operating system initializes the bitmap bits. If this parameter is zero, the bitmap data is not initialized and parameters 4 and 5 are not used. If it is set to `CBM_INIT`, then parameters 4 and 5 are used as pointers to the data used in initializing the bitmap bits. The fourth parameter is a pointer to the array of type BYTE that contains the bitmap data. The fifth parameter is a pointer to a BITMAPINFO structure that contains the bitmap size and color data. The sixth parameter is a flag that determines whether the bmiColors member of the BITMAPINFO structure contains explicit color values in RGB format or palette indices. In the first case the constant DIB_RGB_COLORS is used for this parameter, and in the second case the constant is DIB_PAL_COLORS. The function returns the handle to the bitmap if it succeeds, or NULL if it fails.

In the example that we have been following, the device dependent bitmap is created as follows:

```
static HBITMAP      hBitmap;     // handle to a bitmap
.
.
.

hBitmap = CreateDIBitmap ( hdc,
            (LPBITMAPINFOHEADER) &pDibInfo->bmiHeader,
            CBM_INIT,
            (LPSTR) pDib,
            (LPBITMAPINFO) pDibInfo,
            DIB_RGB_COLORS );
```

Having obtained its handle, the bitmap can be displayed using the ShowBitmap() function developed earlier in this chapter. Alternatively, you can use SetDIBitsToDevice() to set the screen pixels. The function's general form reads as follows:

```
int SetDIBitsToDevice(
                    HDC hdc,                    //  1
                    int XDest,                  //  2
                    int YDest,                  //  3
                    DWORD dwWidth,              //  4
                    DWORD dwHeight,             //  5
                    int XSrc,                   //  6
                    int YSrc,                   //  7
                    UINT uStartScan,            //  8
                    UINT cScanLines,            //  9
                    CONST VOID *lpvBits,        // 10
                    CONST BITMAPINFO *lpbmi,    // 11
                    UINT fuColorUse             // 12
                   );
```

The first parameter is the handle to the display context to which the bitmap is to be output. The second and third parameters are the *x*- and *y*-coordinates of the destination rectangle, in logical units. This is the screen location where the bitmap is displayed. The fourth and fifth parameters are the width and height of the DIB. These values are often read from the corresponding members of the BITMAPINFOHEADER structure variable that defines the bitmap. The sixth and seventh parameters are the *x*- and *y*-coordinates of the lower-left corner of the DIB. The eighth parameter is the starting scan line of the DIB. The ninth parameter is the number of scan lines. The tenth parameter is a pointer to the bitmap data, and the eleventh parameter is a pointer to the BITMAPINFO structure variable that describes the bitmap. The twelfth parameter is a flag that determines whether the bmiColors member of the BITMAPINFO structure contains explicit color values in RGB format or palette indices. In the first case the constant DIB_RGB_COLORS is used, and in the second case the constant DIB_PAL_COLORS. If the function succeeds the return value is the number of scan lines displayed. The function returns NULL if it fails.

In the current example, the bitmap can be displayed with the following call to SetDIBitsToDevice():

```
SetDIBitsToDevice (hdc, 50, 50,
        pDibInfo->bmiHeader.biWidth,
        pDibInfo->bmiHeader.biHeight,
        0, 0, 0,
        pDibInfo->bmiHeader.biHeight,
        pDib,
        (BITMAPINFO FAR*) pDibInfo,
        DIB_RGB_COLORS);
```

Operations on a Blank Bitmap

Sometimes an application needs to fill a blank bitmap using GDI functions. The functions can include all the drawing and text-display primitives discussed in previous chapters. You can take several different programming approaches to creating a bitmap on which GDI operations can be performed. The simplest approach is to select a bitmap into a memory device context and then perform the draw operation on the memory device context. Note that all the drawing functions discussed previously require a handle to the device context. When the drawing takes place on a memory DC, the results are not seen on the video display until the memory DC is blitted to the screen. In this approach, the following steps are required:

1. The bitmap is selected into a memory device context using the SelectObject() function.
2. The bitmap is cleared or otherwise painted using the PatBlt() function.
3. Drawing operations are performed on the memory device context that contains the bitmap.
4. Display the bitmap by blitting it on the screen, typically with BitBlt().

The `CreateCompatibleBitmap()` function has the following general form:

```
HBITMAP CreateCompatibleBitmap(
                              HDC hdc,         // 1
                              int nWidth,      // 2
                              int nHeight      // 3
                             );
```

The first parameter is the handle to the device context with which the created bitmap is to be compatible. If the bitmap is to be displayed this parameter is set to the display context. The second and third parameters are the width and height of the bitmap, in pixels. If the function succeeds it returns the handle to the bitmap. The function returns `NULL` if it fails.

In the following code sample we create a blank, 300 by 300 pixel bitmap, draw a rectangle and an ellipse on it, and then blit it to the screen. First we start by creating the blank bitmapwith the following code:

```
static HDC        aMemDC;          // memory device context
static HBITMAP    bmBlank;         // handle to a bitmap
static HGDIOBJ    oldObject;       // storage for current object
.
.
.
// Preliminary operations
aMemDC = CreateCompatibleDC (NULL);  // Memory device handle
mapMode = GetMapMode (hdc);          // Obtain mapping mode
SetMapMode (aMemDC, mapMode);        // Set memory DC mapping mode
// Create the bitmap
bmBlank = CreateCompatibleBitmap (hdc, 300, 300);
oldObject = SelectObject (aMemDC, bmBlank);
```

Note that we use a generic handle (`HGDIOBJ`) to store the current handle in the device context.

There is no guarantee that the bitmap thus created and selected into the device is initialized. The `PatBlt()` function can be used to set all the bitmap bits to a particular attribute or to a predefined pattern. The function's general form reads as follows:

```
BOOL PatBlt(
            HDC hdc,       // 1
            int nXLeft,    // 2
            int nYLeft,    // 3
            int nWidth,    // 4
            int nHeight,   // 5
            DWORD dwRop    // 6
           );
```

The first parameter is the handle to the device context, which can be a memory device context. The second and third parameters are the *x*- and *y*-coordinates of the upper-left corner of the rectangle to be filled. The fourth and fifth parameters are the width and height of the bitmap, in logical units. The sixth parameter is one of the following constants: `PATCOPY`, `PATINVERT`, `DSTINVERT`, `BLACKNESS`, or `WHITENESS`. The constants are defined in Table 8-2. The call returns `TRUE` if it succeeds and `FALSE` if it fails.

The following call clears the bitmap and sets all bits to the white attribute:

```
PatBlt (aMemDC, 0, 0, 300, 300, WHITENESS);
```

At this point in the code we can start performing drawing operations on the bitmap. The only requirement is that the drawing primitives reference the handle to the memory device context where the blank bitmap was selected, as in the following example:

```
Ellipse (aMemDC, 10, 10, 210, 110);
Polyline (aMemDC, rectangle, 5);
```

Once you have finished drawing on the blank bitmap, it can be displayed by means of a bitblt, as in the following example:

```
BitBlt(hdc, 50, 50, 300, 300, aMemDC, 0, 0, SRCCOPY);
```

In this case, the call references both the display context (`hdc`) and the memory device context containing the bitmap (`aMemDC`).

Clean-up operations consist of reselecting the original object to the memory device context, then deleting the device context and the bitmap.

Creating a DIB Section

The methods described in the preceding section are satisfactory when the bitmap area requires drawing operations that can be implemented by GDI functions, but code has no direct access to the bitmap itself. This is due to the fact that `CreateCompatibleBitmap()` does not return a pointer to the bitmap data area. The `CreateDIBSection()` function, first introduced in Win32 and formalized in Windows 95, enables the creation of a device-independent bitmap that applications can access directly.

NOTE: The original Windows documentation for Win32 contained incorrect information about the `CreateDIBSection()` function and the associated `DIBSECTION` structure. Some of the errors and omissions were later corrected so that current documentation is more accurate, although not very clear.

Before CreateDIBSection(), an application would access bitmap data by calling the GetDIBits() function, which copies the bitmap into a buffer supplied by the caller. At the same time, the bitmap size and color data are copied into a BITMAPINFO structure from which the application can read these values. After the bitmap is changed, the SetDIBits() function is used to redisplay the bitmap. Both functions, GetDIBits() and SetDIBits(), enable the selection of the first scan line and the number of scan lines. When operating on large bitmaps, this feature makes it possible to save memory by reading and writing portions of it at a time.

The modification of bitmaps at run time using GetDIBits() and SetDIBits() has several shortcomings. The most obvious one is that the system bitmap must be copied into the application's memory space, then back into system memory. The process is wasteful and inefficient. If the entire bitmap is read during the GetDIBits() call, two copies of the same data exist, thus wasting memory. If it is broken down into regions to reduce the waste, then processing speed suffers considerably. The solution offered by CreateDIBSection() is to create a bitmap that can be accessed by both the system and the application. Figure 8-5 shows both cases.

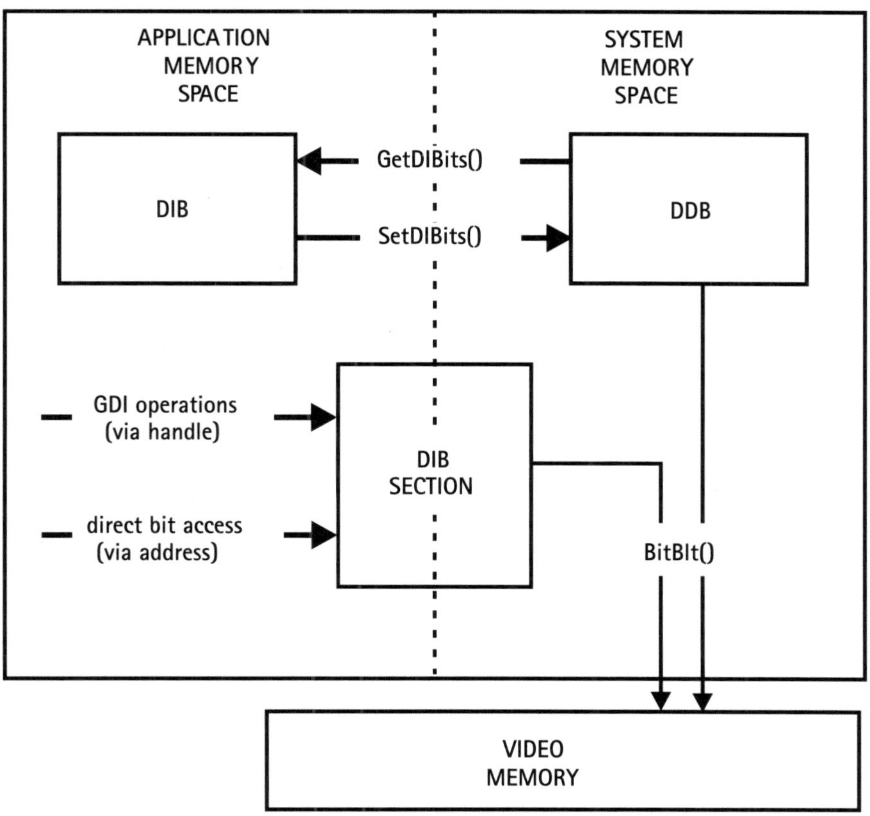

Figure 8-5: Memory image of conventional and DIB section bitmaps

NOTE: Although CreateDIBSection() provides a better alternative than GetDIBits() and SetDIBits(), it is by no means the ultimate in high-performance graphics. DirectDraw methods, discussed starting in Chapter 9, provide ways of accessing video memory directly and of taking advantage of raster graphics hardware accelerators.

In the following example, we create a DIB section, using the pointer returned by the CreateDIBSection() call to fill the bitmap, and the bitmap handle to perform GDI drawing functions on its memory space. The bitmap is 50 pixels wide and 255 scan lines long. It is encoded in 32-bit true color format. The code starts by defining the necessary data structures, initializing the variables, and allocating memory.

```
HDC                 aMemDC;         // Memory DC
static HBITMAP      aBitmap;
static BYTE*        lpBits;


BITMAPINFOHEADER    bi;
BITMAPINFOHEADER*   lpbi;
HANDLE              hDIB;
int                 shade;
static int BMScanLines;      // Bitmap y-dimension
static int BMWidth;          // Bitmap x-dimension
.
.
.
// Initialize size variables
BMScanLines = 255;
BMWidth = 50;
// Initialize BITMAPINFOHEADER structure
bi.biSize = sizeof(BITMAPINFOHEADER);
bi.biWidth = BMWidth;
bi.biHeight = BMScanLines;
bi.biPlanes = 1;
bi.biBitCount = 32;
bi.biCompression = BI_RGB;
bi.biSizeImage = 0;
bi.biXPelsPerMeter = 0;
bi.biYPelsPerMeter = 0;
bi.biClrUsed = 0;
bi.biClrImportant = 0;
```

```
// Allocate memory for DIB
hDIB = GlobalAlloc (GMEM_FIXED, sizeof(BITMAPINFOHEADER));
// Initialize bitmap pointers
lpbi = (BITMAPINFOHEADER*) hDIB;
*lpbi = bi;
```

At this point everything is ready to call CreateDIBSection(). The function's general form is as follows:

```
HBITMAP CreateDIBSection(
                            HDC hdc,                  // 1
                            CONST BITMAPINFO *pbmi,   // 2
                            UINT iUsage,              // 3
                            VOID *ppvBits,            // 4
                            HANDLE hSection,          // 5
                            DWORD dwOffset            // 6
                           );
```

The first parameter is the handle to a device context associated with the DIB section. The second parameter is a pointer to a structure variable of type BITMAPINFO-HEADER, which holds the bitmap attributes. The first five members of the BITMAPINFOHEADER structure are required; the other ones can often be omitted, although it is usually a good idea to fill in the entire structure. The third parameter is either the constant DIB_PAL_COLORS or DIB_RGB_COLORS. In the first case the bmiColors array member of the RGBQUAD structure in BITMAPINFO is a set of 16-bit palette color indices. In the second case the bmiColors member is not used and the colors are encoded directly in the bitmap. The fourth parameter is a pointer to a pointer to type VOID that contains the location of the bitmap values. This parameter is incorrectly documented in the Windows help files as a pointer to type VOID. If the parameter is not correctly typecast to (VOID**) the CreateDIBSection() call fails.

The fifth parameter is a handle to a file-mapping object. In file mapping, a physical file on disk is associated with a portion of the virtual address space of a process. The *file-mapping object* is the mechanism that maintains this association. Its main purpose is to share data between applications and to facilitate access to files. Although file mapping is a powerful mechanism, it is outside the scope of this book and is not discussed any further. If no file mapping is used, the fifth parameter is set to NULL, and the sixth one, which sets the offset of the file-mapping object, is set to zero.

The call to CreateDIBSection() is coded as follows:

```
aBitmap = CreateDIBSection (hdc,
          (LPBITMAPINFO)lpbi,  // Pointer to
                               // BITMAPINFOHEADER
```

```
          DIB_RGB_COLORS,       // True color in RGB format
          (VOID**) &lpBits,     // Pointer to bitmap data
          NULL,                 // File mapping object
          (DWORD) 0);           // File mapping object offset
assert (aBitmap);
assert (lpBits);
```

The two assertions that follow the call ensure that a valid bitmap and pointer are returned. If the call succeeds we now have a handle to a bitmap and its address in system memory. Using the address, we can fill the bitmap. The following code fragment uses the soft-coded bitmap parameters to fill the entire bitmap, scan line by scan line, with increasing intensities of blue. The access to the bitmap is by means of the pointer (`lpBits`) returned by the previous call.

```
// Fill the bitmap using 32-bit color data
// <——- BMWidth * 4 ——>
// |
// | ... BMScanLines

shade = 0;
for (k = 0; k < BMScanLines; k++){     // Counts 255 lines
   for (i = 0; i < BMWidth; i++){      // Counts 50 pixels
      for(j = 0; j < 4; j++) {  //Counts 4 bytes per pixel
        lpBits[(k*(BMWidth*4))+(i*4)+0] = shade; // blue
        lpBits[(k*(BMWidth*4))+(i*4)+1] = 0x0;   // green
        lpBits[(k*(BMWidth*4))+(i*4)+2] = 0x0;   // red
        lpBits[(k*(BMWidth*4))+(i*4)+3] = 0;     // zero
        };
      };
    shade++;
};
```

Because we have also acquired the handle to the bitmap, we can use GDI functions to perform drawing operations on its surface. As described earlier in this chapter, the GDI functions require that the bitmap be first selected into a memory device context. The following code fragment shows one possible processing method:

```
aMemDC = CreateCompatibleDC (NULL); // Memory device handle
mapMode = GetMapMode (hdc);         // Obtain mapping mode
SetMapMode (aMemDC, mapMode);       // Set memory DC
                                    // mapping mode
// Select the bitmap into the memory DC
oldObject = SelectObject (aMemDC, aBitmap);
```

Drawing operations can now take place, as follows:

```
// Draw on the bitmap
blackPenSol = CreatePen (PS_SOLID, 2, 0);
redPenSol = CreatePen (PS_SOLID, 2, (RGB (0xff, 0x0, 0x0)));
SelectPen (aMemDC, blackPenSol);
Polyline (aMemDC, rectsmall, 5);     // Draw a rectangle
SelectPen (aMemDC, redPenSol);
Ellipse (aMemDC, 4, 4, 47, 47);      // Draw a circle
```

You may be tempted to display the bitmap at this time; the display operation, however, cannot take place until the memory device context has been deleted. In the following instructions we re-select the original object in the memory device context and then delete it. We also delete the pens used in the drawing operations.

```
// Erase bitmap and free heap memory
SelectObject (aMemDC, oldObject);
DeleteDC (aMemDC);
DeleteObject (redPenSol);
DeleteObject (blackPenSol);
```

Displaying the bitmap can be performed by any of the methods already discussed. In this code fragment we use the `ShowBitmap()` function developed earlier in the chapter. A necessary precaution relates to the fact that some versions of Windows NT place GDI calls that return a Boolean value in a batch for later execution. In this case, it is possible to attempt to display a DIB section bitmap before all the calls in the GDI batch have been executed. To prevent this problem, it is a good idea to flush the GDI batch buffer before displaying a DIB section bitmap, as shown in the following code:

```
GdiFlush();        // Clear the batch buffer
ShowBitmap (hdc, Abitmap, 50, 50, SRCCOPY);
```

Now that you have finished displaying the bitmap, a tricky problem arises: how to free the system memory space allocated by `CreateDIBSection()`. The solution is easy. Because the bitmap resides in system memory, all we have to do in application code is delete the bitmap; Windows takes care of freeing the memory. On the other hand, if the `BITMAPINFOHEADER` structure was defined in heap memory, your code must take care of freeing this memory space in the conventional manner. Processing reads as follows:

```
// Erase bitmap and free heap memory
// Note: deleting a DIB section bitmap also frees
//       the allocated memory resources
```

```
DeleteObject (aBitmap);    // Delete the bitmap
GlobalFree (hDIB);
```

Figure 8-6 is a screen dump of a program that executes the listed code. The listing can be found in the *Bitmap Demo* project folder on the book's CD-ROM.

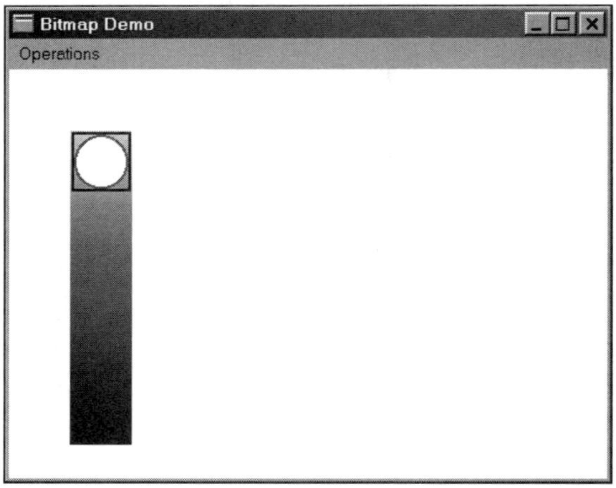

Figure 8-6: Screen dump of a DIB-section bitmap manipulation

Creating a Pattern Brush

In Chapter 7 we mentioned that applications can create a brush with a hatch pattern different than the ones predefined in Windows. This is done by using a bitmap to define the brush pattern. In Windows 95/98 the size of the bitmap cannot exceed 8-by-8 pixels, but there is no size restriction in Windows NT. The function's general form reads as follows:

```
HBRUSH CreatePatternBrush (HBITMAP hbitmap);
```

The function's only parameter is a handle to the bitmap that defines the brush. The bitmap can be created with `CreateBitmap()`, `CreateBitmapIndirect()`, or `CreateCompatibleBitmap()` functions. It can also be a bitmap drawn using Developer Studio bitmap editor, or any other similar utility, and loaded with the `LoadBitmap()` function. The one type of bitmap that is not allowed is one created with the CreateDIBSection() function. `CreatePatternBrush()` returns the handle to the brush if it succeeds, and `NULL` if it fails.

Once the handle to the brush has been obtained, the pattern brush is selected into the device context. Thereafter, all GDI drawing functions that use a brush use the selected pattern brush. The following code fragment shows the creation of a pattern brush from a bitmap resource named IDC_BITMAP5. The pattern brush is then used to draw a rectangle.

```
static HBITMAP     brushBM1;  // Handle to a bitmap
static HBRUSH      patBrush;  // Handle to a brush
.
.
.
brushBM1 = LoadBitmap (pInstance,
                       MAKEINTRESOURCE (IDB_BITMAP5);
patBrush = CreatePatternBrush (brushBM1);
SelectBrush (hdc, patBrush);
Rectangle (hdc, 10, 10, 110, 160);
DeleteObject (patBrush);
```

In displaying solid figures that use a pattern brush, Windows sets the origin of the brush bitmap to the origin of the client area. The `SetBrushOrgEx()` function is used to reposition the brush bitmap in relation to the origin of the client area. This matter was discussed in Chapter 7 in relation to brush-hatch patterns.

Bitmap Transformations

In addition to manipulating bitmaps, Windows provides functions that transform the bitmaps themselves. You have already seen that the `BitBlt()` function enables you to define a ternary raster operation code that determines how the source bitmap and a pattern are combined to form the destination bitmap. In this section we discuss the following transformations that are useful in bitmap programming:

- Painting a bitmap using a raster operation based on the brush selected in the device context
- Stretching or compressing a bitmap according to the dimensions of a destination rectangle, a predefined stretch mode, and the selected ternary raster operation code

Windows NT provides two powerful bitmap transforming functions named `MaskBlt()` and `PlgBlt()`. Because the scope of this book includes functions that are available only in Windows 95/98, these functions are not discussed.

Pattern Brush Transfer

A pattern brush transfer consists of transferring the pattern in the current brush into a bitmap. The `PatBlt()` function is used in this case. If the `PATCOPY` raster operation code is selected, as is usually the case, the brush pattern is copied to the destination bitmap. If the `PATINVERT` raster operation code is used, then the brush and the destination bitmap are combined by performing a Boolean XOR operation. The remaining raster operation codes that are documented for the `PatBlt()` function with symbolic names (DSTINVERT, BLACKNESS, and WHITENESS) ignore the brush and are useless in a pattern block transfer. The raster operation performed by PatBlt() is a binary one because it combines a pattern and a destination. In theory, any of the raster operations codes listed in Appendix B that do not have a source operand can be used in PatBlt(), although it may be difficult to find a useful application for most of them.

Note that there is a not-so-subtle difference between a rectangle filled with a pattern brush, and a bitmap created by means of a pattern transfer. Although the results can be made graphically identical by drawing the rectangle with a NULL pen, the possibilities of further manipulating and transforming a bitmap are not possible with a figure created by means of a GDI drawing function.

The following code fragment creates a blank bitmap in a memory device context and fills it with a pattern brush. Because the processing is based on functions already discussed, the following code listing needs little comment.

```
static HBITMAP     brushBM1;  // Handle to a bitmap
static HBRUSH      patBrush;  // Handle to a brush
.
.
.
// Create the brush pattern bitmap from a resource
brushBM1 = LoadBitmap (pInstance,
                       MAKEINTRESOURCE (IDB_BITMAP5);
// Create a pattern brush
patBrush = CreatePatternBrush (patBM1);
// Create a memory device context
aMemDC = CreateCompatibleDC (NULL);   // Memory DC
mapMode = GetMapMode (hdc);           // Obtain mapping mode
SetMapMode (aMemDC, mapMode);         // Set memory DC
                                      // mapping mode
// Create the bitmap
bmBlank = CreateCompatibleBitmap (hdc, 300, 300);
oldObject = SelectObject (aMemDC, bmBlank);
// Select the pattern brush into the memory DC
SelectBrush (aMemDC, patBrush);
// Blit the pattern onto the memory DC
PatBlt (aMemDC, 0, 0, 300, 300, PATCOPY);
// Display the bitmap
BitBlt(hdc, 50, 50, 300, 300, aMemDC, 0, 0, SRCCOPY);
// Clean-up
SelectObject (aMemDC, oldObject);
DeleteDC (aMemDC);
DeleteObject (bmBlank);
```

The demonstration program named *Bitmap Demo* – on the book's CD-ROM – displays a pattern bitmap using code very similar to the one listed.

Bitmap Stretching and Compressing

Occasionally, an application must fit a bitmap into a destination rectangle that is of different dimensions, and even of different proportions. To do this, the source bitmap must be either stretched or compressed. One possible use of bitmap stretching or compressing is adapting imagery to a display device that has a different aspect ration than the one for which it was created. The method can also be used to accommodate a bitmap to a resizable window, as well as for producing intentional distortions, such as simulating the effect of a concave or convex mirror, or other special visual effects.

The `StretchBlt()` function, one of the more elaborate ones in the API, allows stretching or compressing a bitmap if this is necessary to fit it into a destination rectangle. `StretchBlt()` is a variation of `BitBlt()`; therefore, it is used to stretch or compress, and later display the resulting bitmap. `StretchBlt()` is also used to reverse (vertically) or invert (horizontally) a bitmap image. The stretching or compressing is done according to the stretching-mode attribute selected in the device context. The stretch mode is selected by means of the `SetStretchBltMode()` function, which has the following general form:

```
int SetStretchBltMode(
                        HDC hdc,            // 1
                        int iStretchMode    // 2
                       );
```

The first parameter is the handle to the device context to which the stretch mode attribute is applied. The second parameter is a predefined constant that corresponds to one of four possible stretching modes. All stretching modes have an old and a new name. Table 8-4 lists and describes the stretching modes. The new, preferred names are listed first.

TABLE 8-4 STRETCHING MODES

Name	Description
STRETCH_ANDSCANS BLACKONWHITE	Performs a logical AND operation using the color values for the dropped pixels and the retained ones. If the bitmap is a monochrome bitmap, this mode preserves black pixels at the expense of white ones.

Continued

TABLE 8-4 STRETCHING MODES *(Continued)*

Name	Description
STRETCH_DELETESCANS COLORONCOLOR	Deletes the pixels. This mode deletes all dropped pixel lines without trying to preserve their information. This mode is typically used to preserve color in a color bitmap.
STRETCH_HALFTONEHALFTONE	Maps pixels from the source rectangle into blocks of pixels in the destination rectangle. The average color over the destination block of pixels approximates the color of the source pixels. Windows documentation recommends that after setting the HALFTONE stretching mode, an application must call the SetBrushOrgEx() function to avoid brush misalignment.
STRETCH_ANDSCANS WHITEONBLACK	Performs a logical OR operation using the color values for the dropped and preserved pixels. If the bitmap is a monochrome bitmap, this mode preserves white pixels at the expense of black ones.

On many systems the entire discussion on stretch modes is purely academic because Microsoft has reported a Windows 95 bug in which the StretchBlt() function always uses the STRETCH_DELETESCANS mode, no matter which one has been selected by means of SetStretchBltMode(). The Microsoft Knowledge Base article describing this problem is number Q138105. At the time of this writing we have found no other Microsoft Knowledge Base update regarding this matter.

The actual stretching or compression of the bitmap is performed by means of the StretchBlt() function. The function's general form reads as follows:

```
BOOL StretchBlt(
                HDC hdcDest,       // 1
                int nXOriginDest,  // 2
                int nYOriginDest,  // 3
                int nWidthDest,    // 4
                int nHeightDest,   // 5
                HDC hdcSrc,        // 6
                int nXOriginSrc,   // 7
```

```
    int nYOriginSrc,  // 8
    int nWidthSrc,    // 9
    int nHeightSrc,   // 10
    DWORD dwRop       // 11
   );
```

The first parameter is the destination device context and the sixth parameter is the source device context. The second and third parameters are the *x*- and *y*-coordinates of the upper-left corner of the destination rectangle. The fourth and fifth parameters are the width and height of the destination rectangle. The seventh and eighth parameters are the *x*- and *y*-coordinates of the upper-left corner of the source rectangle. The ninth and tenth parameters are the width and height of the source rectangle. The eleventh parameter is one of the ternary raster operation codes listed in Table 8-2 and in Appendix B.

Although the function's parameter list is rather large, it can be easily simplified. Parameters 1 through 5 are the handle to the device context and the location and size of the destination rectangle. Parameters 6 through 10 contain the same information in regards to the source rectangle. The last parameter defines the raster operation code, which is usually set to `SRCCOPY`.

If the source and destination width parameters have opposite signs, the bitmap is flipped about its vertical axis. In this case the left side of the original bitmap is displayed starting at the right edge. If the source and destination height parameters have opposite signs, the image is flipped about its horizontal axis. If both, the width and the height parameters have opposite signs, the original bitmap is flipped about both axes during the transfer. Figure 8-7 shows the image changes in each case.

The following example takes an existing bitmap and stretches or compresses it to fit the size of the client area. Code assumes an existing bitmap resource named `IDB_BITMAP2`. The code starts by creating a bitmap from the resource and storing its dimensions in a structure variable of type `BITMAP`. The dimensions of the client area, which serves as a destination bitmap, are also retrieved and stored in a structure variable of type `RECT`.

```
BITMAP              bm;       // Storage for bitmap data
RECT                rect;     // Client area dimensions
static  HBITMAP     hstScope; // Handle for a bitmap
.
.
.
// Create bitmap from resource
hstScope = LoadBitmap (pInstance, MAKEINTRESOURCE (IDB_BITMAP2);
// Get bitmap dimensions into BITMAP structure variable
GetObject (hstScope, sizeof(BITMAP), &bm);
// Get client area dimensions
GetClientRect (hwnd, &rect);
```

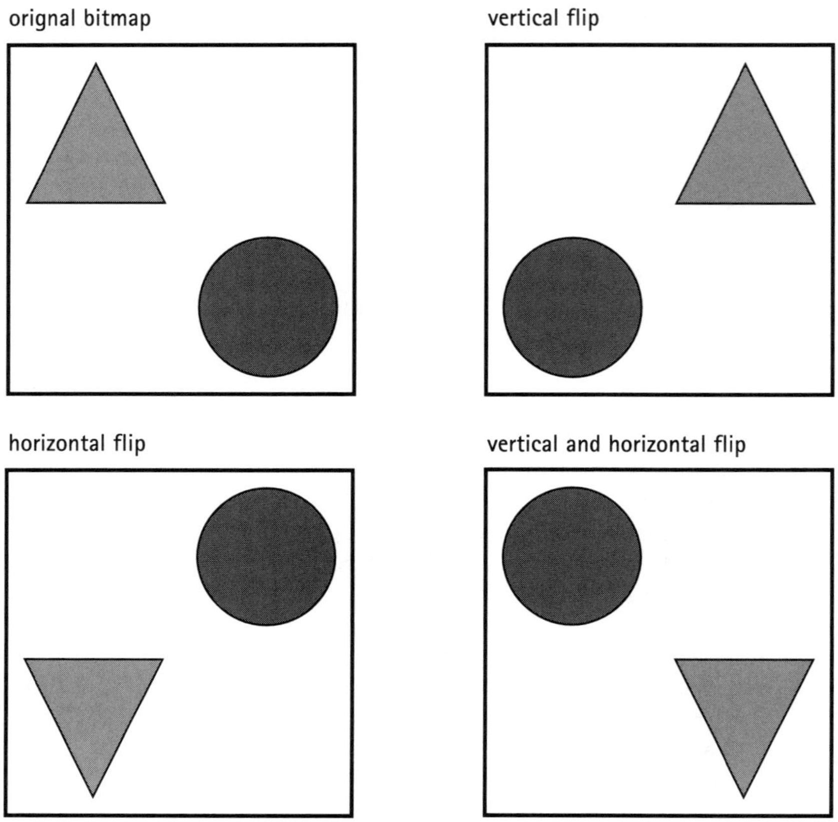

Figure 8-7: Horizontal and vertical bitmap inversion with StretchBlt()

The `StretchBlt()` function requires two device contexts: one for the source bitmap and another one for the destination. In this case we create a memory device context and select the bitmap into it. This device context is the source rectangle. The code also sets the stretch mode.

```
aMemDC = CreateCompatibleDC (hdc);
SelectObject (aMemDC, hstScope);
SetStretchBltMode (hdc, STRETCH_DELETESCANS);
```

All that is left is to display the bitmap using `StretchBlt()`. Once the bitmap is blitted, the destination device context can be deleted. If the bitmap is not necessary, it can also be erased at this time.

```
StretchBlt(hdc,                    // Destination DC
           0, 0, rect.right, rect.bottom,  // dest. dimensions
           aMemDC,                 // Source DC
```

```
        0, 0, bm.bmWidth, bm.bmHeight,  // Source dimensions
        SRCCOPY);
DeleteDC (aMemDC);
```

Bitmap Demonstration Program

The program named BMP_DEMO, located in the *Bitmap Demo* project folder of the book's CD-ROM, is a demonstration of the bitmap operations and functions discussed in this chapter. The Operations menu contains commands that correspond to all the bitmap programming primitives, manipulations, and transformations discussed in the text.

Summary

With this chapter we conclude our discussion of GDI graphics. You have now learned to read and write individual pixels, to draw lines, curves, and solid figures with pens and brushes, to program using regions and paths, to use clipping operations, and to create, display, manipulate, and transform bitmaps. These are the core operations of a graphics programmer's toolkit. If performance and execution speed were not a consideration, the material covered would suffice to develop most graphics applications. But graphics programs usually have requirements that exceed those of conventional code. DirectDraw, the topic of the next part of this book, enables the programmer to take advantage of the hardware features of the video card, to manage multiple resolutions and color depths, and to access system and video memory, thus improving control, performance, and functionality of graphics applications.

Part III

DirectDraw Programming

Chapter 9

Direct Draw Concepts

IN THIS CHAPTER

- Computer games and Windows programming
- Obtaining and using the DirectX 6 SDK
- Overview of DirectDraw features
- DirectDraw architecture
- DirectDraw concepts
- Configuring and initializing a DirectDraw application
- Developing the first demonstration program that uses DirectDraw

IN THIS CHAPTER we begin our discussion of DirectDraw programming. DirectDraw is one of the components of Microsoft's DirectX Software Development Kit, version 6, usually called the DirectX 6 SDK. DirectDraw provides graphics programmers with direct access to video memory and to special hardware features that may be available in the video card, which results in applications with much better performance and a higher level of control. On the other hand, the direct access to the video memory and hardware complicates programming and reintroduces a certain degree of device dependency.

Games and Windows Programming

Game programmers have always pushed the performance limits of computer hardware. The reason is that most games require interactive graphics and animation effects, and these functions are usually hungry for CPU cycles and video resources. In pressing the boundaries of machine performance, game programmers have not always behaved according to the desires of hardware manufacturers and operating system vendors. In the original Technical Reference Manual for the PC, IBM strongly stated that programmers should not access video memory directly, because these addresses were likely to change in the future. But programmers did not heed the warning, and before long, many applications were improving performance by doing what IBM had condemned. The result was that IBM and other hardware manufacturers were forced to maintain the video buffer addresses, even to this date. In fact, in subsequent editions of the Technical Reference, IBM contradicted its own original statement by saying that programmers should feel free to use the video area addresses because they would be maintained in the future.

Hardware and operating system companies had no way of preventing DOS programmers from accessing system resources. In the DOS environment, an application cannot be prevented from executing any instruction or using any legal operand available in the instruction set. In DOS, the running application is the "god" of the machine. However, this can be dangerous. A DOS program can accidentally or intentionally destroy files and resources that it does not own, including the operating system itself. For this reason, the newer generations of Intel microprocessors, starting with the 286, come equipped with hardware features that allow the operating system to detect and prevent access to restricted memory areas and to disallow instructions that are considered dangerous to the environment's stability. It is this operating system control that prevents PC game programmers from doing in Windows what they were accustomed to doing in DOS; namely, accessing video memory directly and controlling the video system hardware.

The result of the access and control restrictions imposed by Windows was that game developers continued to design and code their products for the DOS environment. In spite of the fact that Windows users constituted a large customer base for their products, game programmers felt that Windows graphics performance at the GDI level was so poor that it was impossible to produce game software of even marginal quality in this medium. This status also determined that DOS gained a new lease on life, probably beyond what Microsoft had originally planned. An unexpected revival of computer games added to this revived interest in DOS.

Microsoft took notice of this situation and decided that the only possible solution was to provide game programmers with a way of accessing video memory, and possibly other video hardware features, with as little compromise as possible of the device-independence principles on which Windows is based. The first effort made in this direction was the introduction of a new set of APIs which Microsoft named WinG in reference to *Windows for Games*. WinG was first made available in 1994 and it required Win32 in Windows 3.1. WinG allowed the game programmer to rapidly transfer bitmaps from system memory into video memory. This feature alone made possible the creation of Windows games that executed with much better performance. Due to the success of WinG, Microsoft developed a more elaborate product called the Game Software Development Kit, or Game SDK.

DirectX 6 SDK

After the first release of the Game SDK it became evident that the usefulness of direct access to video memory and hardware was not limited to games. Many multimedia applications, and other graphics programs that required high performance, could benefit from these enhanced facilities. In response, Microsoft renamed the new version of the Game SDK, calling it DirectX 2. Other versions later released were named DirectX 3, DirectX 5, and the current version, DirectX 6. Note that no DirectX 4 version exists. DirectX version 6 SDK, released in August 1998, is the only one discussed in this book.

The functionality of the DirectX SDKs is available to applications running in Windows 95/98 and Windows NT 3.1 and later. In fact, the full functionality of DirectX 6 SDK is incorporated into Windows 98 and will also be found in Windows 2000 (previously known as NT 5.0), when it is released. This means that applications running under Windows 95/98 or NT 4.0 and later will be able to execute programs that use DirectX without the loading of additional drivers or other support software. In addition, Microsoft provides a setup utility with the DirectX SDK that enables the upgrading of a compatible machine to a new version of DirectX. The DirectSetup component of DirectX is discussed in detail in Chapter 13.

Obtaining and Installing the SDK

Several versions of the DirectX SDK are available for download, at no cost, on the Microsoft Web sites. DirectX has grown in size during its evolution. The current version takes up approximately 409 MB, which requires several hours online, even with the fastest commercial modems. For this reason, we have included the DirectX 6 SDK on the book's CD-ROM. DirectX SDK CD-ROMs can also be ordered from Microsoft.

DirectX 6 contains an installation utility that loads and sets up the software on the target system. Microsoft recommends that any previous versions of the SDK be uninstalled before the setup program is executed; however, only the most recent versions of the SDK are equipped with uninstall utilities. The SDK installs to a default folder c:\mssdk. Certain uncommon features of the SDK directory structure are designed for compatibility with Microsoft Developers Network (MSDN) Platform SDK, which duplicates most of DirectX 6.

Compiler Support

DirectX 6 is compatible with Microsoft Visual C++ version 4.2 and later as well as with Watcom 11.0 and Borland C Builder 3. Visual C++ project files (.mdp) are included in the demonstration programs contained in the package. Microsoft states in the SDK documentation that some of the sample programs are not compatible with Borland or Watcom systems.

Testing Installation

The folder mssdk\bin\DXUtils of the installed DirectX 6 SDK contains several programs that can be used for testing DirectX in the host system. The most useful utility, named *dxdiag*, enables the testing of the DirectDraw, Direct3D, and DirectSound components of the SDK. The tests also provide a brief demonstration of the capabilities of each of these components. Figure 9-1 shows the "Display" test tab of the DirectX diagnostics program.

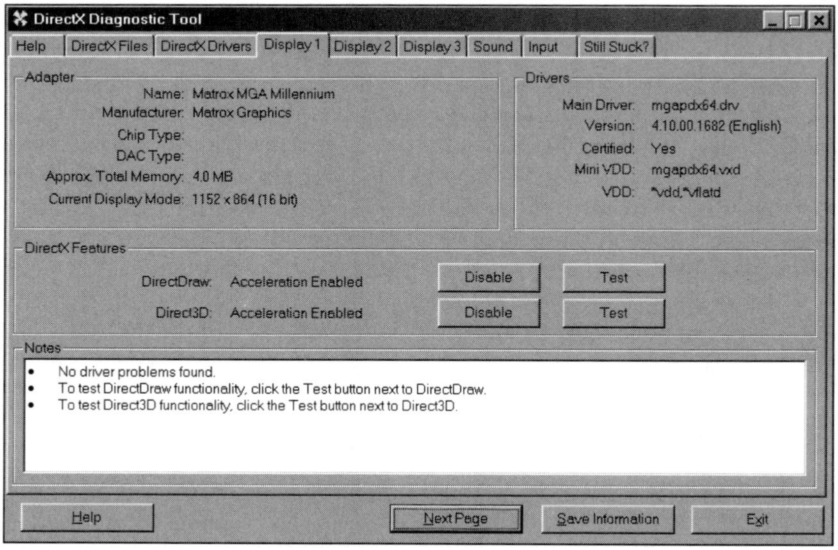

Figure 9-1: Display test function of the DirectX 6 diagnostics program

When the Test button associated with the DirectDraw function is clicked, the program executes several tests to determine compatibility. A series of tests related to the Direct3D function activate when the corresponding test button is selected. In the "Still Stuck?" tab, the program provides several troubleshooting options. Figure 9-2 shows the initial display of the troubleshooting screen.

DirectX Components

The DirectX SDK includes the following components:

- **DirectDraw** provides hardware acceleration and direct access to video memory. It enables you to perform fast bit block transfers (bitblts) and buffer flipping. These features are particularly useful in animation techniques because they considerably improve the graphics performance.
- **DirectSound** provides hardware and software sound-mixing and playback.
- **DirectMusic** works with message-based musical data. It supports the Musical Instrument Digital Interface (MIDI) and provides authoring tools for creating interactive music.
- **DirectPlay** makes it possible to connect to applications over a modem link or a network.

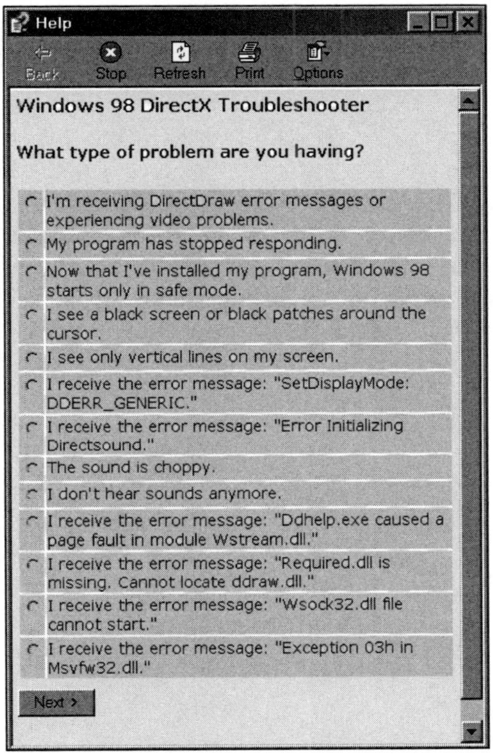

Figure 9-2: Troubleshooting screen of the DirectX 6 diagnostics program

- **Direct3D** is a 3D graphics package that provides a high-level Retained Mode interface that enables you to implement a complete 3-D graphical system. It also contains a low-level Immediate Mode interface that lets applications take complete control over the rendering pipeline.
- **DirectInput** provides support for input devices including joystick, mouse, keyboard, and game controllers. It also provides support for feedback game devices.
- **DirectSetup** provides a simple installation procedure for DirectX. It simplifies the process of updating display and audio drivers and makes sure that no software or hardware conflicts exist.
- **AutoPlay** enables you to create a CD-ROM that installs automatically once inserted in the drive. AutoPlay is not unique to DirectX because it is part of the Microsoft Win32 API.

The SDK also includes several sample programs with the corresponding source code.

Throughout Part III of this book, "Direct Draw Graphics," we mainly discuss the DirectDraw component. DirectSetup and DirectInput are discussed in Chapters 13 and 14.

DirectX and COM

Microsoft's Component Object Model (COM) is a foundation for an object-oriented system that attempts to improve on the C++ model. COM is also an object model at the operating system level, which supports and promotes the reuse of interfaces. DirectDraw is presented to the programmer using the Component Object Model. The COM object is a data structure that contains a pointer to the associated functions. Because it is not specific to C++, a program written in C, or even in a non-C development system, can use APIs based on the COM protocol.

The graphics programmer using the DirectX API has several options regarding access to the COM interface. From C++, the COM object appears like an abstract class. In this case, access is by means of the pointer to the DirectDraw COM object. On the other hand, when using straight C, the function must pass the pointer to the COM object as an additional parameter. In addition, the call must include a pointer to a property of the COM object called the *vtable*. Because there is no reason for these additional complications, in this book we use the simpler C++ interface to the COM.

DirectDraw Overview

DirectDraw is perhaps the most important component of DirectX. It is designed to allow an application to access display memory as well as some of the hardware functions in the video card. The intention is to allow a Windows program to obtain a high level of graphics performance without sacrificing device independence, and while maintaining compatibility with the GDI. DirectDraw is implemented as a software interface to the card's video memory and graphics functions. Although its original intention was merely to facilitate game development under Windows, many graphics applications can benefit from the higher degree of control and the performance gains that it provides.

DirectDraw can be viewed as a display memory manager that also furnishes access to some hardware acceleration features and other graphics facilities that may be available on the video card. Most current video cards used in the PC support DirectDraw to some degree, but this support is not standard by any means. There is no uniform set of acceleration features and graphics functions that all devices must provide. For these reasons, the decision to use DirectDraw also entails the burden of accommodating varying degrees of DirectDraw functionality. DirectDraw provides services that allow you to query the capabilities of a particular video card as well as the level of hardware support. Most features not supported by the hardware are emulated in software by DirectX, but at a substantial performance penalty.

DirectDraw is implemented in hardware and in software emulation, each one with its own capabilities. Applications can query DirectDraw to retrieve the hardware and software capabilities of the specific implementation in the particular video card. DirectDraw is furnished as a 32-bit dynamic link library named DDRAW.DLL.

DirectDraw Features

The following are the most important features of DirectDraw, listed in approximate order of importance:

- Direct access to video memory
- Manipulation of multiple display surfaces
- Page flipping
- Back buffering
- Palette management
- Clipping operations
- Querying the video system support level

Advantages and Drawbacks

The following are possible advantages of using DirectDraw

1. DirectDraw enables you to have direct access to video memory, thus increasing performance and allowing the graphics programmer a higher level of control. This feature also makes it easier to port some DOS graphics programs and routines into the Windows environment.
2. DirectDraw improves application performance by making use of video hardware capabilities whenever possible. For example, if the video card supports hardware blits, DirectDraw uses this feature. DirectDraw also provides a *hardware emulation layer* (HEL) to simulate features that are not supported by the hardware.
3. DirectDraw uses 32-bit flat memory addressing of video memory. This model is much easier to handle by code than one based on the Intel segmented architecture.
4. In full-screen, exclusive-mode applications, DirectDraw supports page flipping with multiple back buffers. This enables you to implement animation effects, often with satisfactory performance. In windowed programs, DirectDraw supports clipping, hardware-assisted overlays, image stretching, and other graphics manipulations.

The major disadvantages of using DirectDraw include:

1. Programming in DirectDraw is more complicated and difficult than using the Windows GDI. Programs that do not need the additional performance or control provided by DirectDraw do not benefit enough from its use to justify the added complexity.
2. Graphics features emulated by DirectDraw are often slower than those in the GDI.
3. Applications that rely on DirectDraw are less portable than those that do not.

DirectDraw Architecture

The architecture of DirectDraw is defined by its interface, its object composition, the hardware abstraction layer (HAL), and the hardware emulation layer (HEL).

DirectDraw Interface

DirectDraw provides services through COM-based interfaces. The various versions of this interface are named `IDirectDraw`, `IDirectDraw2`, and `IDirectDraw4`. Note that IDirectDraw3 does not exist, although it is mentioned in some Microsoft documents. These interfaces to DirectDraw correspond to different releases of the Game SDK and of DirectX.

Programs can gain access to DirectDraw by means of the `DirectDrawCreate()` function or by the `CoCreateInstance()` COM function. In this book, we use `DirectDrawCreate()`, which is the more common function. Later in this chapter, we discuss how a program can ask at run time which of the three DirectDraw interfaces is available.

Object Composition

DirectX APIs are sometimes implemented as instances of COM objects. Communication with these objects is by means of methods; for example, if IDirectDraw4 is the interface, the method `SetDisplayMode` is accessed through the interface as follows:

```
IDirectDraw4::SetDisplayMode
```

COM interfaces are derived from a base class called `IUnknown`. The following DirectDraw object types are currently defined: `DirectDraw`, `DirectDrawSurface`, `DirectDrawPalette`, `DirectDrawClipper`, and `DirectDrawVideoPort`. Figure 9-3 shows the object composition of the DirectDraw interface.

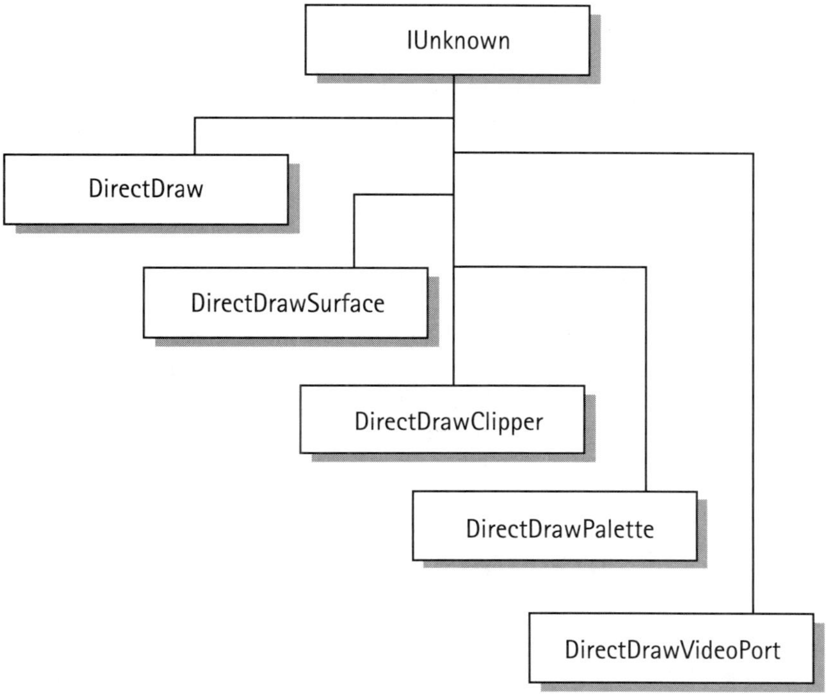

Figure 9-3: DirectDraw object types

The various DirectDraw objects can be described as follows:

- **DirectDraw** is the basic object of all Direct X applications. It can be viewed as representing the display adapter card. The corresponding COM object is named IDirectDraw. This is the first object created by a program and it relates to all other DirectDraw objects. The `DirectDrawCreate()` function is used to obtain the DirectDraw object. If the call is successful it returns a pointer to either IDirectDraw, IDirectDraw2, or IDirectDraw4 interfaces.
- **DirectDrawSurface** object, sometimes called a "surface," represents an area in memory. The COM object name is IDirectDrawSurface. This object holds the image data to be displayed, or images to be moved to other surfaces. Applications usually create a surface by calling the `IDirectDraw::CreateSurface` method of the DirectDraw object.
- **DirectDrawPalette** object, sometimes referred to as a "palette," represents a 16- or 256-color indexed palette. The palette object simplifies palette manipulations. It contains a series of indexed RGB triplets that describe colors associated with values within a surface. Palettes are limited to surfaces that use a pixel format of 8 bits or less. Palette objects are usually

associated with a corresponding surface object, whose color attributes the palette object defines.

- **DirectDrawClipper** object, sometimes referred to as a "clipper," serves to prevent applications from drawing outside a predefined area. Clipper objects are often used when a DirectDraw application is displayed in a window. In such a case, the clipper object prevents the application from drawing outside of its client area.
- **DirectDrawVideoPort** object was introduced in DirectX5, making it the most recent DirectDraw object. The object represents the video-port hardware present in some systems. It enables you to have direct access to the frame buffer without intervention of the CPU or the PCI bus. Video ports are a low-level interface to the video system, and are not intended for mainstream graphics programming. Video-port objects are not discussed in this book.

The Hardware Abstraction Layer (HAL)

DirectDraw ensures device independence by implementing a *Hardware Abstraction Layer*, or HAL. The HAL is provided by the video card manufacturer, board manufacturer, or OEM, according to Microsoft's DirectDraw specifications. However, applications have no direct access to the HAL, they have access only to the interfaces exposed by DirectDraw. It is this indirect access mechanism that ensures HAL consistency and reliability.

In Windows 95/98, device manufacturers implement the HAL in both 16-bit and 32-bit code. Under Windows NT the HAL is always in 32-bit code. It can be furnished as part of card's display driver or a separate DLL. The HAL contains device-dependent code. It performs no emulation and provides no programmer-accessible services. The only point of contact between an application and the HAL is when the application needs to query DirectDraw to find out what capabilities are supported by the HAL.

The Hardware Emulation Layer (HEL)

DirectDraw attempts to emulate in software those basic features that are not supported through the HAL. The hardware emulation layer is the part of DirectDraw that provides this functionality. As with the HAL, applications do not access the HEL directly. The emulated functions are presented as DirectDraw functions. Whether a given functionality is provided through hardware features, or through emulation, it is transparent to an application using DirectDraw. Code must specifically query DirectDraw to determine the origin of a given functionality. The `GetCaps()` function, discussed later in this chapter, furnishes this information.

Unfortunately, some combinations of hardware-supported and emulated functions may lead to slower performance than pure emulation. DirectDraw documentation cites an example in which a display device driver supports DirectDraw but not stretch blitting. When the stretch blit function is emulated in video memory, a noticeable performance loss occurs. The reason is that video memory is often slower than system memory; therefore, the CPU is forced to wait when accessing video memory surfaces. Cases like this highlight one of the greatest drawbacks of DirectDraw, which is that applications must provide alternate processing for hardware dependencies.

Component Relations

Several Windows graphics components lay between the application code and the video-card hardware. Figure 9-4 shows the relations between the various Windows graphics components.

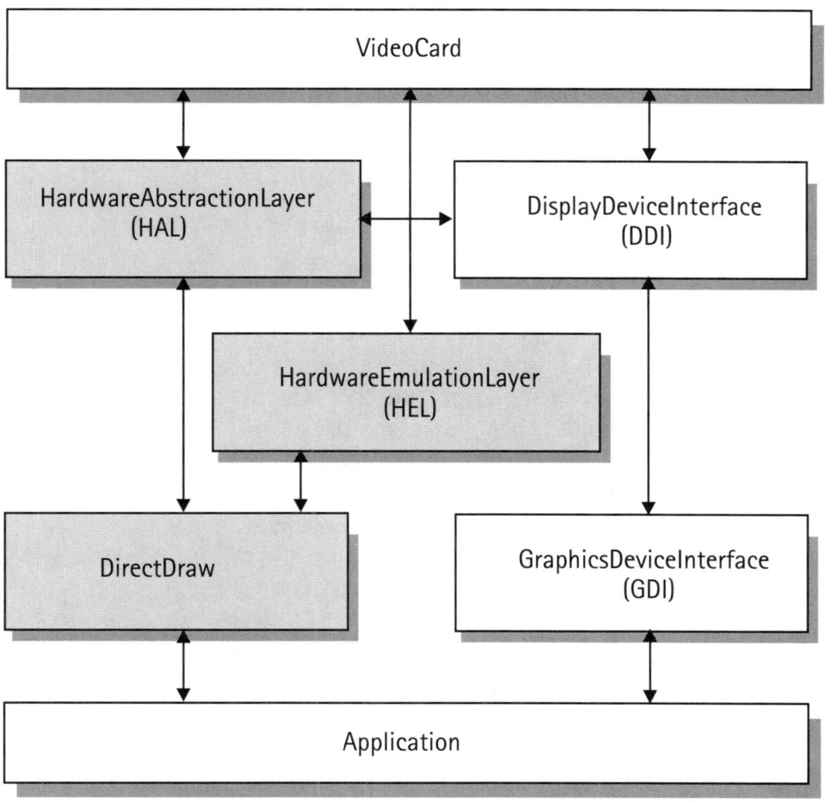

Figure 9-4: Relations between Windows graphics components

As shown on the right-hand side of Figure 9-4, an application can access the Windows video functions through the GDI and the Display Device Interface.

Alternatively, an application can access the video functions through DirectDraw, which makes use of the Hardware Abstraction Layer and the Hardware Emulation Layer to provide the necessary functionality. Applications that use DirectDraw can also use the GDI functions provided by Windows, because both channels of video-card access are open simultaneously.

DirectDraw Basic Concepts

In addition to the notion of a DirectDraw object, several topics relate specifically to DirectDraw. Understanding these concepts is a prerequisite to successful DirectDraw programming. The following concepts are the essential ones:

- Cooperative levels
- Display modes
- Surfaces
- Palettes
- Clippers

Cooperative Levels

The notion of cooperative levels refers to the relation between DirectDraw and other Windows applications. A DirectDraw program can execute full-screen, with exclusive access to the display, or it can execute in a window and share the video resources with other applications. In this case, the DirectDraw application and the other Windows programs executing concurrently must cooperate in their use of the video resources. When a DirectDraw application requests and obtains total control of the video functions, it is said to execute in exclusive mode.

The `SetCooperativeLevel()` function, described later in this chapter, is used by an application to set cooperative level. The predefined constants `DDSCL_FULLSCREEN` and `DDSCL_EXCLUSIVE` allow the application to execute full-screen and to ensure control of the display mode and the palette. In this case, the DirectDraw program has almost exclusive control of the video resources.

DirectDraw cooperative levels also have the following effects:

- A DirectDraw application can be enabled to use a non-standard VGA resolution known as Mode X. Mode X, which executes in 320 by 240 pixels in 256 colors, was a very popular mode with DOS game programmers.
- In the exclusive mode a DirectDraw application can be prevented from responding to CTRL + ALT + DEL keystrokes.

- A DirectDraw application can be enabled to minimize or maximize itself.

Microsoft considers the normal cooperative level the one in which the DirectDraw application cooperates as a windowed program. But at this cooperative level the application is not able to change the display mode or perform page flipping. Display-mode control and page flipping are essential to many high-performance graphics programs, especially those that use animation. For this reason, most high-performance DirectDraw programs execute in exclusive mode.

Display Modes

Display modes were introduced with the first video system used in the PC. The Video Graphics Array (VGA) video system, first made public in 1987, supports 18 display modes. A display mode is a hardware configuration of the video system's internal registers that enables a particular resolution and color depth. Display modes are described by their pixel-width, height, and bit-depth. For example, VGA mode 18H has a resolution of 640 by 480 by 4. This means that it displays 640 pixel columns and 480 pixel rows in 16 colors. The last digit of the mode specification is the number of bits used in the pixel color encoding. In this case, the range of 16 colors is the maximum number of combinations of 4 binary digits.

Display modes can be palettized and nonpalettized. In palettized display modes each color value is an index into an associated palette. In this case, the bit depth of the display mode determines the number of colors in the palette. For instance, in a 4-bit palettized display mode, such as VGA mode 18H, each pixel attribute is a value from 0 to 15, which makes possible a palette with 16 entries. The actual colors displayed depend on the palette settings. Nonpalettized display modes, on the other hand, encode pixel colors directly. In this case, the bit depth represents the total number of color attributes that can be assigned to each pixel.

The higher the resolution and the color depth of a display mode, the more video memory required in the adapter. Because not all video adapters contain the same amount of memory, not all of them support the same video modes. The DirectDraw `EnumDisplayModes()` function can be used to list all the display modes supported by a device, or to confirm if a particular display mode is available in the video card.

Applications using DirectDraw can set the display mode by means of the `SetDisplayMode()` function. The parameters passed to the call describe the dimensions, bit depth, and refresh rate of the mode to be set. A fifth parameter indicates special options for the given mode. Currently, this parameter is used only to differentiate between Mode 13H, with 320 by 200 resolution and 16 colors, and Mode X, also with 320 by 200 resolution but in 256 colors. Although an application can request a specific display-mode resolution and bit depth, it cannot specify how the pixel depth is achieved by the hardware. After a mode is set, the application can call the `GetDisplayMode()` function to determine if the mode is palettized and to examine the pixel format.

DirectDraw programs that do not execute in exclusive mode allow other applications to change the video mode. However, an application can change the bit depth of the display mode only if it has exclusive access to the DirectDraw object. DirectDraw applications that execute in exclusive mode allow other applications to allocate `DirectDrawSurface` objects and to use DirectDraw and GDI services. However, only applications that execute at the exclusive cooperative level can change the display mode or manipulate the palette.

A DirectDraw application can explicitly restore the display hardware to its original mode by calling the `RestoreDisplayMode()` function. Starting with the DirectDraw2 interface, an application that sets the display mode by calling `SetDisplayMode()`, and that uses the exclusive cooperative level, can automatically restore the original display mode by calling `RestoreDisplayMode()`. Code that uses earlier interfaces must explicitly indicate the mode being restored.

DirectDraw supports all screen resolutions and pixel depths that are available in the card's device driver. Thus, a DirectDraw application can change to any mode supported by the display driver, including all 24- and 32-bit true-color modes.

Surfaces

A DirectDraw surface is a linear memory area used to hold image data. A `DirectDrawSurface` object is a COM object derived from `IUnknown`, as shown in Figure 9-3. Surfaces can reside in display memory, which is located in the video card, or in system memory. Applications create a DirectDraw surface by calling the `CreateSurface()` function. The call can create a single-surface object, a complex surface-flipping chain, or a three-dimensional surface. The `IDirectDrawSurface` interface enables an application to indirectly access memory through blit methods, such as `Blt()` and `BltFast()`. In addition, a surface provides a device context to the display, which can be used with GDI functions.

Some `IDirectDrawSurface` surface functions directly access display memory. Applications use the `Lock()` function to retrieve the address of an area of display memory and to ensure exclusive access to this area, or in other words, to "lock it." The address of a display memory area can be a pointer to the memory area mapped to the video display, usually called the primary surface. It can also be a pointer to a nondisplayed area, called an off-screen or overlay surface. Nonvisible buffers usually reside in display memory, but they can be created in system memory if DirectDraw is performing a hardware emulation, or if it is otherwise necessary due to hardware limitations. Surface objects that use a pixel depth of 8 bits or less are assigned a palette that defines the color attributes in the encoding. Figure 9-5 shows the surface-based layout of video memory.

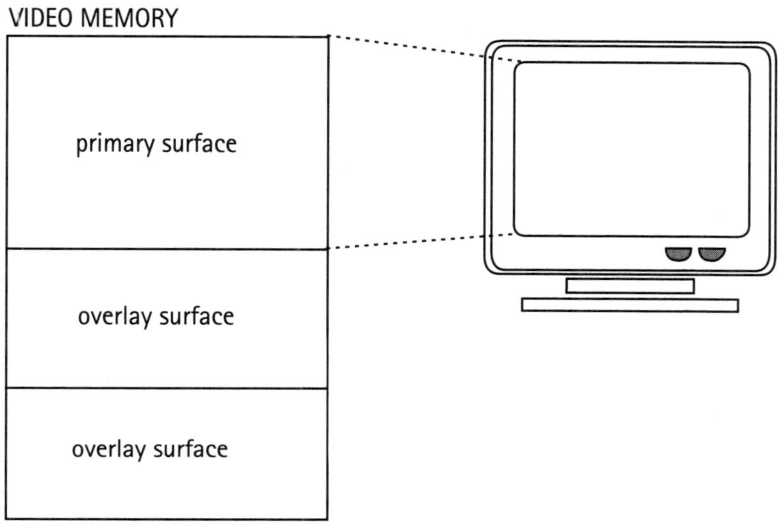

Figure 9-5: Primary and overlay surfaces in video memory

Once a DirectDraw application receives a pointer to video memory, it can use this pointer to draw on the screen, with considerable gain in control and performance. However, a program that accesses video memory directly must concern itself with many details of the video system layout that are transparent at a higher level of programming. The first complicating factor is that the video-buffer mapping is different in two modes with the same resolution but different color depths. The reason is that the video buffer stores pixel attributes; therefore, if an attribute is encoded in 8 bits, then the buffer requires one byte per pixel. On the other hand, if the pixel attribute is stored in 24 bits, then the buffer requires 3 bytes per pixel. Figure 9-6 shows two video modes with different pixel depths. In the 8-bits-per-pixel mode the fourth memory byte is mapped to the fourth screen pixel. However, in the 24-bits per pixel mode it is the thirteenth through the fifteenth video memory bytes that are mapped to the fourth pixel. The calculations required to obtain the offset in video memory for a particular screen pixel will be different in each case.

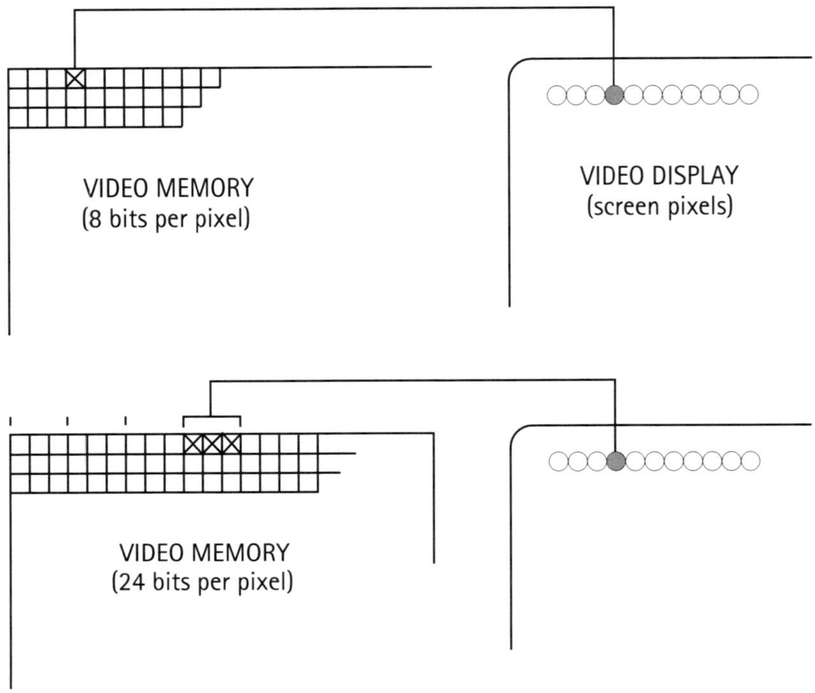

Figure 9-6: Changes in memory-to-video mapping according to pixel depth

A second complication results from the fact that in some display modes, the number of bytes in each row is not exactly the product of the number of pixels by the mode's byte depth. In other words, for design and performance reasons, some display modes have data areas in each row that are not mapped to screen pixels. For example, a display mode with a resolution of 640 pixels per row and a color depth of 24 bits per pixel requires 1920 bytes to store the data corresponding to a single row of screen pixels. However, the video-card designers may have assigned 2560 bytes of video buffer space for each screen row, so that the same buffer size could be used in a 32-bits-per-pixel mapping. The result is that in the 24-bit mode there is an area of 640 unmapped bytes at the end of each row. The term *pitch* is used to describe the actual byte length of each row in the video buffer, while the term *width* refers to the number of pixels in each screen row.

Palettes

A palette is a color look-up table. It provides an indirect mapping of pixel attributes and extends the number of displayable colors in modes with limited color depths. For example, a display mode with a 4-bits-per-pixel color depth enables the representation of 16 different color attributes. When a palette is attached to the display surface, each video buffer value serves as an index into the palette, which in turn defines the pixel color. By changing the palette, the application can now map many 16-color sets to the display attributes. Thus, the number of simultaneously displayable colors remains the same, but the actual colors mapped to the video buffer values can be changed by the application. Figure 9-7 shows how a palette provides an indirect mapping for the color attributes stored in the video buffer.

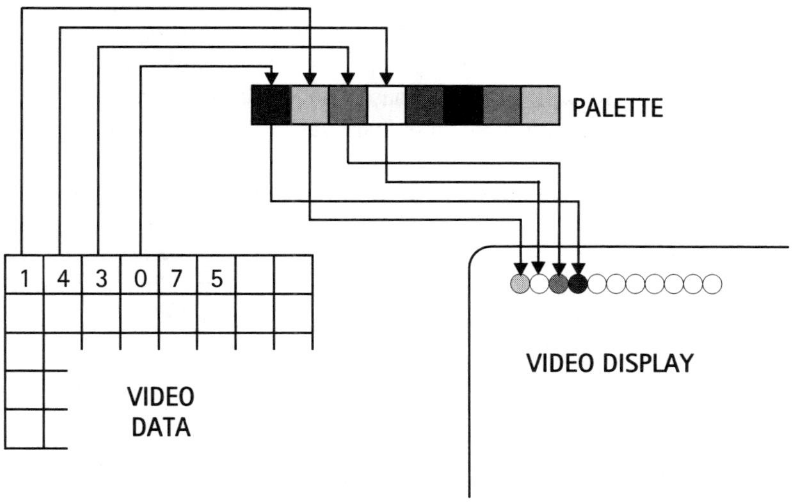

Figure 9-7: A palette provides indirect pixel-attribute mapping.

In DirectDraw, palettes are linked to surfaces. Surfaces that use a 16-bit or greater pixel format do not use palettes. Therefore, the so-called real-color modes (16 bits per pixel) and true color modes (24 and 32 bits per pixel) are nonpalettized. A DirectDraw palette can have 2, 4, 16, or 256 entries. A palette can only be attached to a surface with the same color depth. In addition, it is possible to create palettes that do not contain a color table. In these so-called index palettes, the palette values serve as an index into another palette's color table.

Each palette entry is in the form of an RGB triplet that describes the color to be used when displaying pixel values at the corresponding entry. The RGB values in the color table can be in 16- or 24-bit format. In 16-bit RGB format, each palette entry is encoded in 5-6-5 form. The first 5 pixels are mapped to the red attribute, the second 6 pixels to the green attribute, and the last 5 pixels to the blue attribute. This mapping corresponds to the real-color modes. In the 24-bit RGB palette format each of the primary colors (red, green, and blue) is mapped to 8 pixels, as is the case in the true-color modes.

An application creates a palette by calling the DirectDraw `CreatePalette()` function. At call time, the application defines whether the palette contains 2, 4, 16, or 256 entries and provides a pointer to a color table used in initializing the palette. If the call is successful, DirectDraw returns the address of the newly created

`DirectDrawPalette` object. This palette object can then be used to attach the palette to a DirectDraw surface. The same palette can be attached to multiple surfaces. Once a palette is attached to a surface, an application can call the `GetPalette()` and `SetPalette()` functions to query or change the palette entries.

One form of animation is based on changing the appearance of a surface object by modifying the palette attached to the surface that contains it. By repeatedly changing the palette, the surface object can be made to appear differently without actually modifying the contents of video memory. Two different types of palette manipulations can be used for this. The first method is based on modifying the values in a single palette. The second method is based on switching between several palettes. Because palette modifications are not hardware intensive, either method often produces satisfactory results.

The development and use of palettes was a direct consequence of the memory limitations of the original video systems used in the PC. In VGA, the video space was about a few hundred kilobytes, while the low-end PCs of today are furnished with video cards that have 2 and 4MB of onboard video memory. This amount of video memory makes palette modes almost obsolete. We therefore devote little space to palette programming in this book.

Clipping

In the context of DirectDraw programming, *clipping* is the process by which video output is limited to one or more rectangularly shaped regions. DirectDraw supports clipping in applications that execute in either exclusive mode or windowed mode. The term "clippers" is often used to refer to `DirectDrawClipper` objects. A single bounding rectangle is sometimes used to limit the display to the application's client area. Several associated bounding rectangles are called a *clip list.*

Perhaps the most common use for a clipper is to define the boundaries of the screen or of a rectangular window. A DirectDraw clipper can be used to define the screen area of an application to ensure that a bitmap is progressively displayed as it moves into this area. If a clipping area is not defined, then the blit fails because the destination drawing surface is outside the display limits. However, when the boundaries of the video display area are defined as a clipper, DirectDraw knows not to display outside of this area and the blit succeeds. Blitting a bitmap to unclipped and clipped display areas is shown in Figure 9-8.

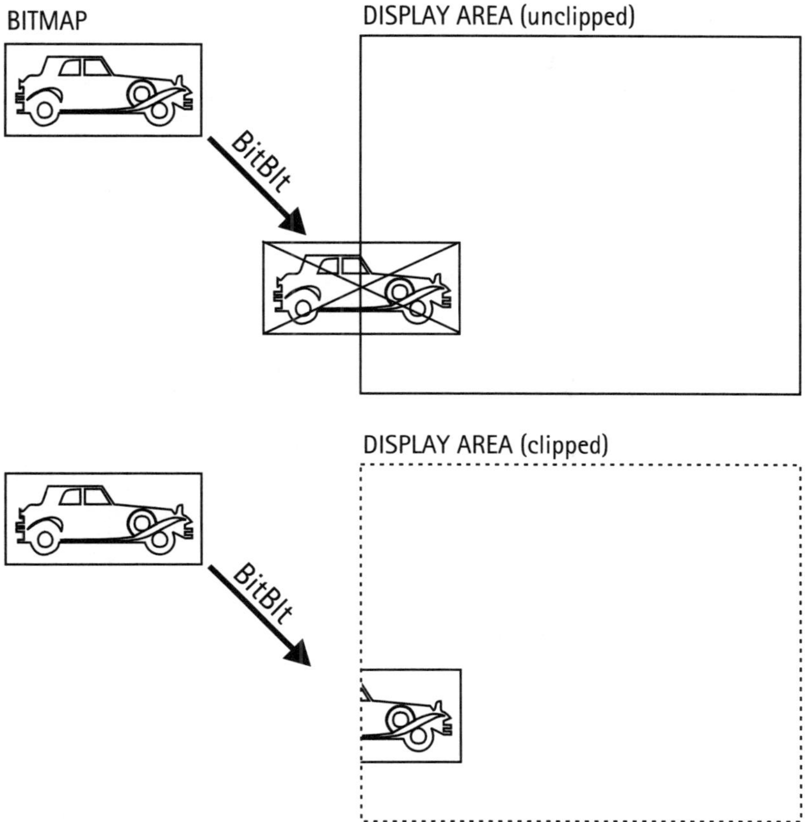

Figure 9-8: Blitting a bitmap to unclipped and clipped display areas

Figure 9-8 shows that clipping makes it possible to display the bitmap of the automobile as it progressively enters the screen area, instead of making it pop onto the screen. In DirectDraw, all that is required is to create a clipper with the screen rectangle is its clip list. Trimming of the bitmap is automatic in this case. Clipper objects are also used to designate areas within a destination surface. The designated areas are tagged as writable, while DirectDraw automatically crops images that fall outside this area. Figure 9-9 shows a display area with a clipper defined by two rectangles. When the text bitmap is blitted onto the screen, only those parts that fall inside the clipper are displayed. The pixel data is preserved in the screen areas not included in the clipper. In this case, the clip list consists of the two rectangles for which output is validated.

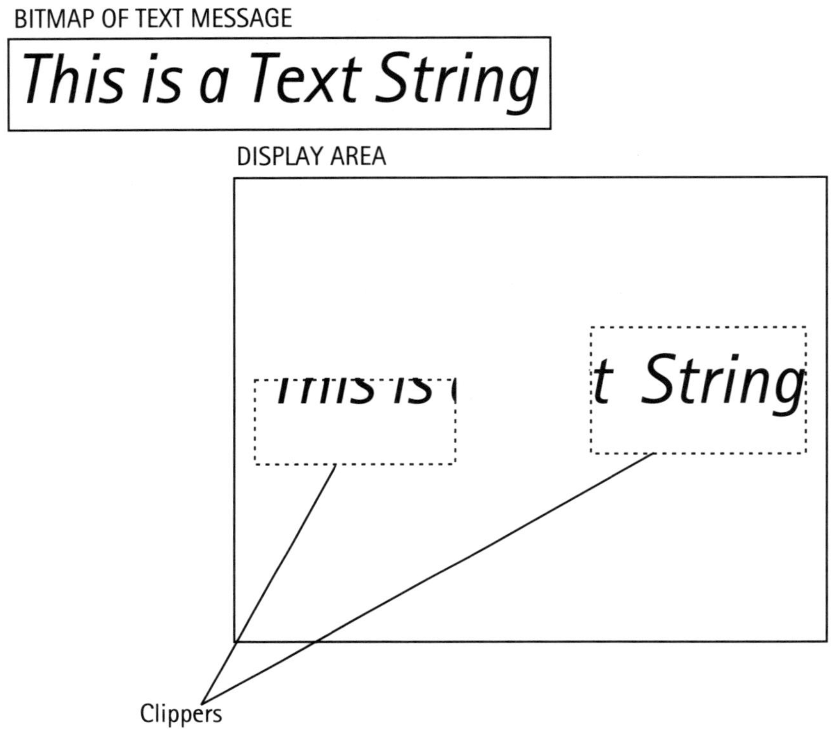

Figure 9-9: Action of a clipper consisting of two rectangular areas

Configuring DirectDraw

Before an application can use the DirectDraw services, it must initialize the software and perform a series of configuration tests to determine how the program cooperates with concurrent Windows programs. The following are the most important steps during program initialization:

- Set up Developer Studio to access DirectDraw
- Create the DirectDraw object
- Determine the interface version
- Set the level of interaction with concurrent applications
- Obtain the critical hardware capabilities
- Set the DirectDraw display mode

Setting Up Developer Studio

Before you can develop a DirectDraw program, you must first set up your development system so that it accesses the corresponding header and library files. The first step for an application that uses DirectDraw is to include the DirectDraw header file named ddraw.h. The file is furnished with the DirectX package and also with the newer versions of the Windows operating system.

As a system is updated with newer versions of the DirectX SDK, and perhaps with operating system patches and new releases, it is not uncommon to find several versions of the ddraw.h file on the same machine. The developer needs to make sure that the software is using the most recent release of the header file. One way to do this is to use the file-finding feature of Windows Explorer, or of a similar program, and then rename or delete the older versions of ddraw.h. In most cases the directory path, the date stamp, and the file size can be used to determine the most recent version. It is unwise to assume that the installation program for the operating system, the SDK, or the development environment, performs the necessary setup operations.

If, after this operation, the development software fails to find the ddraw.h header, then the file can be moved to the corresponding include directory, or the path can be changed to make it accessible. In Visual C++, the directories searched by the development system can be seen by selecting the Options command from the Tools menu. In this case, the "Show directories for:" scroll box should be set for include files. You may now enter the path to the DirectDraw include and library files in the edit box at the bottom of the Directories: window. Once entered, the boxes can be dragged to the top of the list so that these directories are searched first. If DirectX is installed in the default drive and path, then the results are as shown in Figure 9-10.

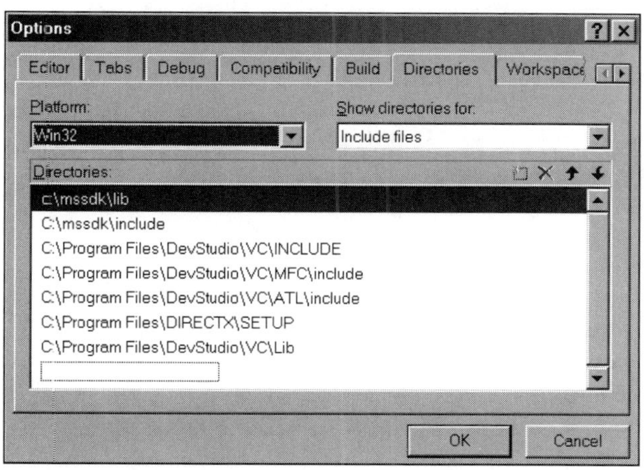

Figure 9-10: The Directories tab in Developer Studio Options dialog box

The second software element necessary for creating DirectDraw programs is the ddraw.lib library file. What was said in relation to possible duplicate versions of ddraw.h also applies to ddraw.lib. Here again, a search function can be used to find the duplicate files. Once the most recent library file is identified, the older ones can be deleted or renamed. If, after this step, the development system is unable to locate the library files, you must copy ddraw.lib to the corresponding include directory or modify the path.

In addition to finding the newest version of the library, and installing it in the development system's library path, Visual C++ users must also make sure that the development system is set up to look for the DirectDraw libraries. To ensure this, you can inspect the dialog box that is displayed when the Settings command is selected in Developer Studio Project menu. The ddraw.lib and dxguid.lib files must be listed in both the Object/Library Modules and the Project Options windows of the Link tab in the Project Settings dialog box, as shown in Figure 9-11. If not, you can manually insert the library names in the Object/Library Modules edit box. The library names are automatically copied to the Project Options box.

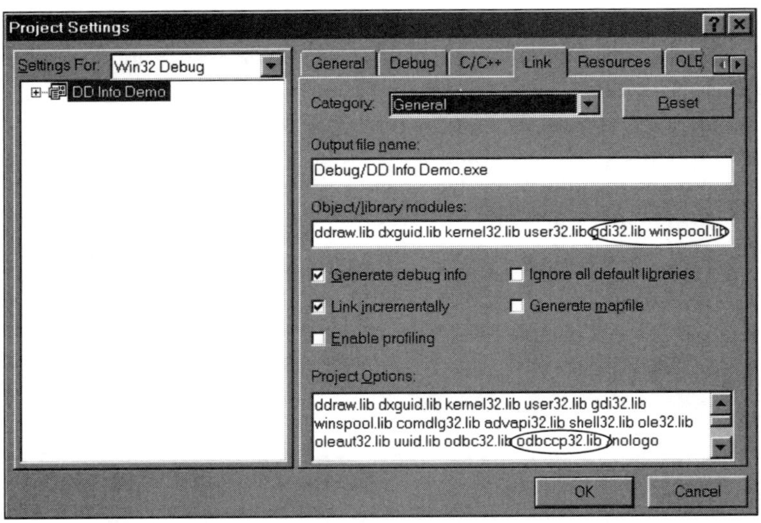

Figure 9-11: The Link tab in Developer Studio Project Settings dialog box

The ddraw.lib library contains the DirectDraw functions, and dxguid.lib has the GUID identifiers required for accessing the various interface versions, as described later in this chapter. Once access to the DirectDraw header file and the libraries is in place, the development system is ready for coding of DirectDraw applications.

Creating the DirectDraw Object

In order to use DirectDraw, an application must first create a DirectDraw object. This object is actually a pointer to the DirectDraw interface as implemented in the video card. The pointer is required for accessing all other DirectDraw functions; therefore, a DirectDraw application can do little else without this object. The DirectDrawCreate() function creates an instance of the DirectDraw object. The function's general form reads as follows:

```
HRESULT WINAPI DirectDrawCreate(
                         GUID FAR *lpGUID,          // 1
                         LPDIRECTDRAW FAR *lplpDD,  // 2
                         IUnknown FAR *pUnkOuter    // 3
                        );
```

The first parameter is the address of a globally unique identifier (GUID) that represents the driver to be created. If this parameter is NULL then the call refers to the active display driver. The newer versions of DirectDraw enable the passing of one of the two following flags in this parameter to control the behavior of the active display:

- DDCREATE_EMULATIONONLY: DirectDraw uses only emulation. Hardware-support features are not used.
- DDCREATE_HARDWAREONLY: DirectDraw object does not use emulated features. If a hardware-supported feature is not available, the call returns DDERR_UNSUPPORTED.

The second parameter is a pointer that the call initializes if it succeeds. This is the object returned by DirectDrawCreate(). The third parameter is provided for future compatibility with the COM interface. At present, it should be set to NULL. The call returns DD_OK if it succeeds. If it fails, one of the following predefined constants is returned:

DDERR_DIRECTDRAWALREADYCREATED

DDERR_GENERIC

DDERR_INVALIDDIRECTDRAWGUID

DDERR_INVALIDPARAMS

DDERR_NODIRECTDRAWHW

DDERR_OUTOFMEMORY

On systems with multiple monitors, specifying NULL for the call's first parameter causes the DirectDraw object to run in emulation mode. In these systems, the call must specify the device's GUID to use hardware acceleration. The use of multiple monitors is discussed in Chapter 15.

Retrieving the Interface Version

The Component Object Model (COM) requires that objects update their functionality by means of new interfaces that provide the new features, rather than by changing methods within existing interfaces. The objective is to keep existing interfaces static so that older applications continue to be compatible with the newer interfaces. DirectX, and therefore DirectDraw, follow the Component Object Model.

Although the availability of various interfaces facilitates component updating, it also brings about some coding complications. For example, the DirectDraw surface object currently supports three different interfaces, named IDirectDrawSurface, IDirectDrawSurface2, and IDirectDrawSurface4. Each version supports all the methods of its predecessor and adds new ones for the new features. For an application to use these new features, it must query DirectDraw to determine which interface or interfaces are available in the host, then provide alternative processing routes for each case. The processing is further complicated by the fact that at least in some instances, a new interface may not support methods provided in a previous one. The result is a return to device-dependent programming, which is what Windows proposed to avoid.

Once the DirectDraw application has obtained a pointer to the DirectDraw object by means of the DirectDrawCreate() function, COM has a mechanism to find out whether the object supports other interfaces. The QueryInterface() method of IUnknown enables you to determine whether or not an object supports a particular interface; if so, it returns a pointer to this interface. It is through this pointer that code gains access to the methods of the new interface. If the QueryInterface method returns a null pointer or an error, then the calling code must decide a) if it can use the previous interface, b) if it provides some sort of work-around for the missing functionality, or c) if it must abort execution for lack of processing capabilities. The processing usually consists of one or more tests and the contingency code required in each case.

The QueryInterface() function determines whether or not the object supports a particular COM interface. The function has the following general form:

```
HRESULT QueryInterface(
                         REFIID riid,         // 1
                         LPVOID* obp          // 2
                        );
```

The first parameter is a reference identifier for the object being queried. The calling code must know this unique identifier before the call is made. The second parameter is the address of a variable that will contain a pointer to the new interface if the call is successful. The return value is S_OK if the call succeeds or one of the following error messages if it fails:

DDERR_INVALIDOBJECT

DDERR_INVALIDPARAMS

DDERR_OUTOFMEMORY

The DDERRR_OUTOFMEMORY error message is returned by IDirectDrawSurface2 and IDirectDrawSurface4 objects only. If after making the call the application determines that it does not need to use the interface, it must call the Release() function to free it.

At this time, three IDirectDraw interfaces are implemented. The corresponding reference identifiers are IID_DirectDraw, IID_DirectDraw2, and IID_DirectDraw4. Mixing methods from two or more interfaces is not recommended because the results are sometimes unpredictable. Furthermore, it is virtually impossible to code a DirectDraw application of any substance that executes in more than one implementation. In the first place, the pointers returned by the various versions are often of formally different types. For example, IID_DirectDraw returns a pointer of type LPDIRECTDRAW, IID_DirectDraw2 returns a type LPDIRECTDRAW2, and IID_DirectDraw4 returns a pointer of type LPDIRECTDRAW4. The same is true of other objects and data structures, as well as the parameters to some calls. For instance, the SetDisplayMode() function takes three parameters in IID_DIRECTDRAW and five parameters in IID_DIRECTDRAW2 and IID_DIRECTDRAW4.

Microsoft attempts to ensure the portability of applications that commit to a specific DirectX implementation by furnishing an installation utility that upgrades the host system to the newest components. Diagnostics and installation programs, as well as the drivers and library files that serve to update a system to the corresponding version of the SDK are in the DirectSetup element of DirectX. DirectSetup also includes a ready-to-use installation utility that copies all the system components to the corresponding directories of the client's hard drive and performs the necessary modifications in the Windows registry. In the DirectX SDK, Microsoft also provides all of the required project files for a sample installation application named *dinstall*. The DirectX programmer can use the source code of the dinstall program as a base on which to create a customized installation utility for DirectX. DirectSetup is discussed in detail in Chapter 13.

The following code fragment shows the processing necessary to obtain the version of DirectX installed in the host system:

```
// Global variables for DirectDraw operations
HRESULT          DDConnect;
```

```
// Interfaces pointers
LPDIRECTDRAW         lpDD;
LPDIRECTDRAW2        lpDD2;
LPDIRECTDRAW4        lpDD4;
int                  dDLevel = 0;     // Implementation level
.
.
.
//************************
//   DirectDraw Init
//************************
// Create a DirectDraw object
  DDConnect = DirectDrawCreate ( NULL,
              &lpDD,         // Pointer to object
              NULL);
// Querying the interface to determine most recent
// version
   if(DDConnect == DD_OK) {
      dDLevel = 1;               // Store level
   // Query the next interface level
     DDConnect = lpDD->QueryInterface(
                 IID_IDirectDraw2,
                 (LPVOID *) &lpDD2);
   }
   if(DDConnect == S_OK){
      dDLevel = 2;           // Update level
      lpDD->Release();       // Release old pointer
   // Query the next interface level
      DDConnect = lpDD2->QueryInterface(
                  IID_IDirectDraw4,
                  (LPVOID *) &lpDD4);
    }
    if(DDConnect == S_OK){
       dDLevel = 4;            // Update level
       lpDD2->Release();       // Release old pointer
       lpDD4->Release();       // and current one
    }
// ASSERT:
//  dDlevel holds the current interface levels (values are
//  1, 2 or 4). If dDLevel == 0, then no DirectDraw interface
//  was found.
//  All pointers to interfaces have been released
```

Some of the examples in the DirectDraw literature use the return value from the `DirectDrawCreate()` or `QueryInterface()` calls to determine if a DirectDraw object is available. In the previous code fragment, we use the `dDlevel` variable for this same purpose. If this variable is zero, then no DirectDraw object has been created and DirectDraw functions are unavailable. Notice in the code that as each new valid object is found, the preceding one is released by means of the `Release()` function. The reason for this call is that the COM interface maintains a count of the number of objects created. `IUnknown` contains a function named `AddRef()` that increments the object's reference count by 1 when an interface or an application binds itself to an object. The `Release()` function then decrements the object's reference count by 1 when it is no longer needed. When the count reaches 0, the object is deallocated.

Normally, every function that returns a pointer to an interface calls `AddRef()` to increment the object reference count. By the same token, the application calls `Release()` to decrement the object reference count. When an object's reference count reaches 0, it is destroyed and all interfaces to it become invalid. In the previous sample code we don't need to call the `AddRef()` method because `QueryInterface()` implicitly calls `AddRef()` when a valid object is found. However, the code must still call `Release()` to decrement the reference object count and destroy the pointer to the interface.

Setting the Cooperative Level

A DirectDraw application can obtain almost exclusive control over the hardware resources that normal Windows applications must share. Control over the video system is necessary for implementing some types of interactive, animated games and other high-performance graphics programs. These are applications that must squeeze the last drop of the system's processing power as well as ensure that they retain control of the video system. On the other hand, other DirectDraw programs may not need this special functionality and may behave more like a normal Windows program. The `SetCooperativeLevel()` function is used to request a specific level of resource control, and thus, to establish its level of cooperation with other Windows programs.

The function `SetCooperativeLevel()` has slightly different implementations in the DirectDraw, DirectDraw2, and DirectDraw4 interfaces, which can cause some portability problems. The fundamental decision that is made at the time of calling `SetCooperativeLevel()` is whether the application is to run full-screen, with exclusive access to the display resources, or as a normal windowed program. In addition, DirectDraw cooperative levels also allow you to enable the use of Mode X resolutions, prevent DirectDraw from releasing exclusive control of the display, allow rebooting if the user presses CTRL + ALT + DEL, and enable DirectDraw to minimize or maximize the application in response to user events. Table 9-1 lists the predefined constants that are recognized by the `SetCooperativeLevel()` function.

TABLE 9-1 SYMBOLIC CONSTANTS USED IN SETTING THE COOPERATIVE LEVEL DEFINED IN THE IDIRECTDRAW4 INTERFACE.

Flag	Description
DDSCL_ALLOWMODEX	Enables the use of Mode X display modes. This flag can only be used with the DDSCL_EXCLUSIVE and DDSCL_FULLSCREEN modes.
DDSCL_ALLOWREBOOT	Enables the CTRL+ALT+DEL keystroke to function while in exclusive mode.
DDSCL_CREATEDEVICEWINDOW	DirectDraw creates and manages a default device window for this DirectDraw object. Supported by Windows 98 and NT 5.0 only.
DDSCL_EXCLUSIVE	Requests the exclusive level. Must be used with DDSCL_FULLSCREEN.
DDSCL_FPUSETUP	Indicates that the DirectDraw application maintains the math unit set up for single precision and exceptions disabled, which is the best setting for optimal Direct3D performance.
DDSCL_FULLSCREEN	The exclusive-mode owner is responsible for the entire primary surface. GDI is ignored. Must be used with DDSCL_EXCLUSIVE.
DDSCL_MULTITHREADED	Requests multithread-safe DirectDraw behavior. This causes Direct3D to take the global critical section more frequently.
DDSCL_NORMAL	Indicates a regular Windows application. Cannot be used with the DDSCL_ALLOWMODEX, DDSCL_EXCLUSIVE, or DDSCL_FULLSCREEN flags. Applications executing in this mode cannot perform page flipping or change the primary palette.
DDSCL_NOWINDOWCHANGES	Prevents DirectDraw from minimizing or restoring the application window.
DDSCL_SETDEVICEWINDOW	The hWnd parameter is the window handle of the device window for this DirectDraw object. This flag cannot be used with the DDSCL_SETFOCUSWINDOW flag. Supported by Windows 98 and NT 5.0 only.

Flag	Description
CDSCL_SETFOCUSWINDOW	The hWnd parameter is the window handle of the focus window for the DirectDraw object. Cannot be used with the DDSCL_SETDEVICEWINDOW flag. Supported by Windows 98 and NT 5.0 only.

The SetCooperativevel() function's general form is as follows:

```
HRESULT SetCooperativeLevel(
                          HWND hWnd,        // 1
                          DWORD dwFlags     // 2
                         );
```

The first parameter is the handle to the application window; however, if an application requests DDSCL_NORMAL in the second parameter, it can use NULL for the window handle. The second parameter is one or more of the flags defined by the symbolic constants listed in Table 9-1. The function returns DD_OK if the call succeeds, or one of the following error messages if it doesn't:

DDERR_EXCLUSIVEMODEALREADYSET

DDERR_HWNDALREADYSET

DDERR_HWNDSUBCLASSED

DDERR_INVALIDOBJECT

DDERR_INVALIDPARAMS

DDERR_OUTOFMEMORY

The DDERR_EXCLUSIVEMODEALREADYSET message refers to the fact that only one application can request the exclusive mode. If this message is received, then there is another application that has been granted the exclusive mode, and code should provide alternative processing or an exit.

Full-screen applications receive the DDERR_NOEXCLUSIVEMODE return value if they lose exclusive device access, as is the case when the user presses ALT+TAB to switch to another program. In this event one possible coding alternative is to call TestCooperativeLevel() function in a loop, exiting only when it returns DD_OK, which indicates that exclusive mode is now available.

Applications that use the normal cooperative level (DDSCL_NORMAL flag) receive DDERR_EXCLUSIVEMODEALREADYSET if another application has taken exclusive device access. In this case, a windowed application can be coded to loop until TestCooperativeLevel() returns DD_OK.

The two most common flag combinations used in the SetCooperativeLevel() call are for programs that execute in exclusive mode and those that are normal Windows applications. The following code fragment shows the call to SetCooperativeLevel() for a DirectDraw application that requests exclusive mode:

```
LPDIRECTDRAW      lpDD4;     // DirectDraw object
HWND              hwnd;      // Handle to the window
...
lpDD4->SetCooperativeLevel(hwnd, DDSCL_EXCLUSIVE |
DDSCL_FULLSCREEN);
```

To set the cooperative level to the normal mode the code reads as follows:

```
LPDIRECTDRAW      lpDD4;     // DirectDraw object
...
lpDD4->SetCooperativeLevel(NULL, DDSCL_NORMAL);
```

Note that exclusive-mode applications pass the handle to the window (hwnd) parameter so that Windows has a way of recovering from conditions that freeze the otherwise disabled video system. This is not required for normal Windows programs that use conventional recovery procedures.

Obtaining Hardware Capabilities

Often in conventional Windows programming, application code ignores the system's video hardware. This is not the case, however, in programs that use DirectDraw. Video cards that support DirectDraw do so at varying degrees of hardware compatibility and of DirectDraw functionality. In most cases, an application needs to know what level of DirectDraw hardware support is available in a particular machine, as well as the amount of video memory, before deciding if the code is compatible with the host, or deciding how to proceed if a given functionality is not present.

DirectDraw works with a wide variety of display hardware. Applications can enumerate the capabilities of the hardware to determine the supported hardware-accelerated features. Most features that are not implemented in hardware are emulated by DirectX; however, there are a few features where this is not the case. This emulation makes possible some degree of device independence. The DirectDraw GetCaps() function returns run-time information about video resources and hardware capabilities. By examining these capabilities during the initialization stage, an application can decide whether the available functionality is insufficient and abort execution, or make other adjustments, to provide the best possible performance over varying levels of support. This kind of processing, which can be called "best-option" programming, is discussed in Chapter 12.

It has been documented that, sometimes, a particular combination of hardware-supported features and emulation can result in worse performance than emulation alone. For example, if the device driver does not support stretch blitting from video memory, noticeable performance losses occur. The reason is that video memory is usually slower than system memory, which forces the CPU to wait when accessing video memory surfaces. For this reason, applications that use features not supported by the hardware are usually better off creating surfaces in system memory, rather than in video memory.

The `GetCaps()` function returns the capabilities of the device driver for the hardware (HAL) and for the hardware emulation layer (HEL). The general form of the `GetCaps()` function reads as follows:

```
HRESULT GetCaps(
                LPDDCAPS lpDDDriverCaps,     // 1
                LPDDCAPS lpDDHELCaps         // 2
               );
```

The first parameter is the address of a structure of type `DDCAPS` that is filled with the capabilities of the hardware abstraction layer (HAL), as reported by the device driver. Code can set this parameter to `NULL` if the hardware capabilities are not to be retrieved. The second parameter is the address of a structure, also of type `DDCAPS`, which is filled with the capabilities of the hardware emulation layer (HEL). This parameter can also be set to `NULL` if these capabilities are not to be retrieved. Code can only set one of the two parameters to `NULL`. If the method succeeds, the return value is `DD_OK`. If the method fails, the return value is one of the following error constants:

```
DDERR_INVALIDOBJECT
DDERR_INVALIDPARAMS
```

The `DDCAPS` structure is a large one indeed: it contains 58 members in the DirectDraw4 version. The structure is defined as follows:

```
typedef struct _DDCAPS {
  DWORD    dwSize;            // size of structure DDCAPS
  DWORD    dwCaps;            // driver-specific caps
  DWORD    dwCaps2;           // more driver-specific caps
  DWORD    dwCKeyCaps;        // color key caps
  DWORD    dwFXCaps;          // stretching and effects caps
  DWORD    dwFXAlphaCaps;     // alpha caps
```

```
DWORD     dwPalCaps;          // palette caps
DWORD     dwSVCaps;           // stereo vision caps
DWORD     dwAlphaBltConstBitDepths;
                                     // alpha bit-depth members
DWORD     dwAlphaBltPixelBitDepths;        //  .
DWORD     dwAlphaBltSurfaceBitDepths;      //  .
DWORD     dwAlphaOverlayConstBitDepths;    //  .
DWORD     dwAlphaOverlayPixelBitDepths;    //  .
DWORD     dwAlphaOverlaySurfaceBitDepths;  //  .
DWORD     dwZBufferBitDepths;      // Z-buffer bit depth
DWORD     dwVidMemTotal;           // total video memory
DWORD     dwVidMemFree;            // total free video memory
DWORD     dwMaxVisibleOverlays;    // maximum visible
                                   // overlays
DWORD     dwCurrVisibleOverlays;   // overlays currently
                                   // visible
DWORD     dwNumFourCCCodes;        // number of supported
                                   // FOURCC codes
DWORD     dwAlignBoundarySrc;      // overlay alignment
                                   // restrictions
DWORD     dwAlignSizeSrc;          //  .
DWORD     dwAlignBoundaryDest;     //  .
DWORD     dwAlignSizeDest;         //  .
DWORD     dwAlignStrideAlign;      // stride alignment
DWORD     dwRops[DD_ROP_SPACE];    // supported raster ops
DWORD     dwReservedCaps;          // reserved
DWORD     dwMinOverlayStretch;     // overlay stretch factors
DWORD     dwMaxOverlayStretch;     //  .
DWORD     dwMinLiveVideoStretch;   // obsolete
DWORD     dwMaxLiveVideoStretch;   //  .
DWORD     dwMinHwCodecStretch;     //  .
DWORD     dwMaxHwCodecStretch;     //  .
DWORD     dwReserved1;             // reserved
DWORD     dwReserved2;             //  .
DWORD     dwReserved3;             //  .
DWORD     dwSVBCaps;               // system-to-video blit
                                   // related caps
DWORD     dwSVBCKeyCaps;           //  .
DWORD     dwSVBFXCaps;             //  .
DWORD     dwSVBRops[DD_ROP_SPACE]; //  .
DWORD     dwVSBCaps;               // video-to-system blit
                                   // related caps
                                   // caps
DWORD     dwVSBCKeyCaps;           //  .
```

```
  DWORD     dwVSBFXCaps;              //  .
  DWORD     dwVSBRops[DD_ROP_SPACE]; //  .
  DWORD     dwSSBCaps;                // system-to-system blit
                                      // related caps
  DWORD     dwSSBCKeyCaps;            //  .
  DWORD     dwSSBCFXCaps;             //  .
  DWORD     dwSSBRops[DD_ROP_SPACE]; //  .
  DWORD     dwMaxVideoPorts;          // maximum number of live
                                      // video ports
  DWORD     dwCurrVideoPorts;         // current number of live
                                      // video ports
  DWORD     dwSVBCaps2;               // additional
                                      // system-to-video blit
                                      // caps
  DWORD     dwNLVBCaps;               // nonlocal-to-local video
                                      // memory
                                      //  blit caps
  DWORD     dwNLVBCaps2;              //  .
  DWORD     dwNLVBCKeyCaps;           //  .
  DWORD     dwNLVBFXCaps;             //  .
  DWORD     dwNLVBRops[DD_ROP_SPACE];//  .
  DDSCAPS2 ddsCaps;                   // general surface caps
DDCAPS,FAR* LPDDCAPS;
```

Most applications are only concerned with a few of the capabilities of a DirectDraw device. Table 9-2 lists some of the most-often needed capabilities.

TABLE 9-2 MOST-OFTEN USED DEVICE CAPABILITIES REPORTED BY THE GETCAPS() FUNCTION

Item	Description
dwCaps Member Constants	
DDCAPS_3D	Display hardware has 3-D acceleration.
DDCAPS_ALPHA	Display hardware supports alpha-only surfaces.
DDCAPS_BANKSWITCHED	Display hardware is bank-switched. Therefore it is very slow at random access operations to display memory.
DDCAPS_BLT	Display hardware is capable of blit operations.

Continued

Table 9-2 MOST-OFTEN USED DEVICE CAPABILITIES REPORTED BY THE GETCAPS() FUNCTION *(Continued)*

Item	Description
dwCaps Member Constants	
DDCAPS_BLTCOLORFILL	Display hardware is capable of color filling with a blitter.
DDCAPS_BLTSTRETCH	Display hardware is capable of stretching during blit operations.
DDCAPS_CANBLTSYSMEM	Display hardware is capable of blitting to or from system memory.
DDCAPS_CANCLIP	Display hardware is capable of clipping with blitting.
DDCAPS_CANCLIPSTRETCHED	Display hardware is capable of clipping while stretch blitting.
DDCAPS_COLORKEY	System supports some form of color key in either overlay or blit operations.
DDCAPS_GDI	Display hardware is shared with GDI.
DDCAPS_NOHARDWARE	No hardware support.
DDCAPS_OVERLAY	Display hardware supports overlays.
DDCAPS_OVERLAYCANTCLIP	Display hardware supports overlays but cannot clip.
DDCAPS_PALETTE	DirectDraw is capable of creating and supporting `DirectDrawPalette` objects for more surfaces than the primary one.
DDCAPS_READSCANLINE	Display hardware is capable of returning the current scan line.
DDCAPS_ZBLTS	Supports the use of z-buffers with blit operations.
dwCaps2 member constants	
DDCAPS2_VIDEOPORT	Display hardware supports live video.
DDCAPS2_WIDESURFACES	Display surfaces supports surfaces wider than the primary surface.

Item	Description
dwPalCaps Member Constants	
DDPCAPS_1BIT	Supports 2-color palettes.
DDPCAPS_2BIT	Supports 4-color palettes.
DDPCAPS_4BIT	Supports 16-color palettes.
DDPCAPS_8BIT	Supports 256-color palettes.
DDPCAPS_8BITENTRIES	Specifies an index to an 8-bit color index. This field is valid only when used with the DDPCAPS_1BIT, DDPCAPS_2BIT, or DDPCAPS_4BIT capability.
DDPCAPS_ALPHA	Supports palettes that include an alpha component.
DDPCAPS_ALLOW256	Supports palettes that can have all 256 entries defined.
DDPCAPS_PRIMARYSURFACE	The palette is attached to the primary surface. Changing the palette has an immediate effect on the display unless the DDPCAPS_VSYNC capability is specified and supported.
Other Structure Members	
dwVidMemTotal	Total amount of display memory.
dwVidMemFree	Amount of free display memory.
dwMaxVisibleOverlays	Maximum number of visible overlays or overlay sprites.
dwCurrVisibleOverlays	Current number of visible overlays or overlay sprites.
dwReservedCaps	Reserved. Prior to DirectX 6.0, this member contained general surface capabilities.
dwMinOverlayStretch dwMaxOverlayStretch	Minimum and maximum overlay stretch factors multiplied by 1000. For example, 1.3 = 1300.
dwSVBCaps	Driver-specific capabilities for system-memory-to-display-memory blits.

Continued

Table 9-2 MOST-OFTEN USED DEVICE CAPABILITIES REPORTED BY THE GETCAPS() FUNCTION *(Continued)*

Item	Description
Other Structure Members	
dwVSBRops	Raster operations supported for display-memory-to-system-memory blits.
dwSSBCaps	Driver-specific capabilities for system-memory-to-system-memory blits.

The following code fragment shows the processing required to read the hardware capabilities using the DirectDraw `GetCaps()` function. The code reads various capabilities and displays the corresponding screen messages. After each message is displayed, the screen position is indexed by one or more lines. The project named *DD Info Demo*, on the book's CD-ROM, uses similar processing.

```
DDCAPS          DrawCaps;      // DDCAPS structure
LPDIRECTDRAW4   lpDD4;          // DirectDraw object
.
.
.
//*********************************
// DirectDraw hardware capabilities
//*********************************
DrawCaps.dwSize = sizeof ( DrawCaps );
// Call to capabilities function
   lpDD4->GetCaps (&DrawCaps, NULL );

// Video memory
    strcpy ( message, " Total Video Memory: ");
    sprintf ( message+strlen(" Total Video Memory: "),
              "%i",DrawCaps.dwVidMemTotal );
    TextOut ( hdc, text_x, text_y, message,
              strlen (message) );
    text_y += tm.tmHeight+tm.tmExternalLeading;
// Free video memory
   strcpy ( message, " Free Video Memory: ");
   sprintf ( message+strlen(" Free Video Memory: "),
               "%i",DrawCaps.dwVidMemFree );
```

```
 TextOut ( hdc, text_x, text_y, message,
           strlen (message) );
 text_y += tm.tmHeight+tm.tmExternalLeading;
 text_y += tm.tmHeight+tm.tmExternalLeading;

// Video card hardware
 strcpy ( message,
         " Video card hardware support as follows:");
 TextOut ( hdc, text_x, text_y, message,
           strlen (message) );
 text_y += tm.tmHeight+tm.tmExternalLeading;
 text_x = 16;
 if (DrawCaps.dwCaps & DDCAPS_NOHARDWARE)
 {
 strcpy ( message, "  No DirectDraw hardware support
          available" );
     TextOut ( hdc, text_x, text_y, message,
               strlen (message) );
     text_y += tm.tmHeight+tm.tmExternalLeading;
     return;
 }
 if (DrawCaps.dwCaps & DDCAPS_3D)
 {
     strcpy ( message, "  3D support" );
     TextOut ( hdc, text_x, text_y, message,
               strlen (message) );
     text_y += tm.tmHeight+tm.tmExternalLeading;
 }
else
 {
     strcpy ( message, "  No 3D support" );
     TextOut ( hdc, text_x, text_y, message,
               strlen (message) );
     text_y += tm.tmHeight+tm.tmExternalLeading;
 }
 if (DrawCaps.dwCaps & DDCAPS_BLT)
 {
     strcpy ( message, "  Hardware Bitblt support" );
     TextOut ( hdc, text_x, text_y, message,
               strlen (message) );
     text_y += tm.tmHeight+tm.tmExternalLeading;
 }
else
 {
```

```
        strcpy ( message, "  No hardware Bitblt support" );
        TextOut ( hdc, text_x, text_y, message,
                  strlen (message) );
        text_y += tm.tmHeight+tm.tmExternalLeading;
    }
    if (DrawCaps.dwCaps & DDCAPS_OVERLAY)
    {
        strcpy ( message, "  Hardware overlays supported");
        TextOut ( hdc, text_x, text_y, message,
                  strlen (message) );
        text_y += tm.tmHeight+tm.tmExternalLeading;
    }
   else
    {
        strcpy ( message, "  No hardware overlays ");
        TextOut ( hdc, text_x, text_y, message,
                  strlen (message) );
        text_y += tm.tmHeight+tm.tmExternalLeading;
    }

   if (DrawCaps.dwCaps & DDCAPS_CANCLIP)
    {
        strcpy ( message, "  Clipping supported in hardware");
        TextOut ( hdc, text_x, text_y, message,
                  strlen (message) );
        text_y += tm.tmHeight+tm.tmExternalLeading;
    }
   else
    {
        strcpy ( message, "  No hardware clipping support ");
        TextOut ( hdc, text_x, text_y, message,
                  strlen (message) );
        text_y += tm.tmHeight+tm.tmExternalLeading;
    }
    if (DrawCaps.dwCaps & DDCAPS_BANKSWITCHED)
    {
        strcpy ( message, "  Memory is bank switched");
        TextOut ( hdc, text_x, text_y, message,
                  strlen (message) );
        text_y += tm.tmHeight+tm.tmExternalLeading;
    }
   else
    {
        strcpy ( message, "  Memory not bank switched");
        TextOut ( hdc, text_x, text_y, message,
```

```
                strlen (message) );
        text_y += tm.tmHeight+tm.tmExternalLeading;
    }
        if (DrawCaps.dwCaps & DDCAPS_BLTCOLORFILL)
    {
        strcpy ( message, "  Color fill Blt support");
        TextOut ( hdc, text_x, text_y, message,
                  strlen (message) );
        text_y += tm.tmHeight+tm.tmExternalLeading;
    }
   else
    {
        strcpy ( message, "  No Blt color fill support");
        TextOut ( hdc, text_x, text_y, message,
                  strlen (message) );
        text_y += tm.tmHeight+tm.tmExternalLeading;
    }
    if (DrawCaps.dwCaps & DDCAPS_COLORKEY)
    {
        strcpy ( message, "  Color key hardware support ");
        TextOut ( hdc, text_x, text_y, message,
                  strlen (message) );
        text_y += tm.tmHeight+tm.tmExternalLeading;
    }
   else
    {
        strcpy ( message, "  No color key support");
        TextOut ( hdc, text_x, text_y, message,
                  strlen (message) );
        text_y += tm.tmHeight+tm.tmExternalLeading;
    }
    if (DrawCaps.dwCaps & DDCAPS_ALPHA)
    {
        strcpy ( message, "  Alpha channels supported");
        TextOut ( hdc, text_x, text_y, message,
                  strlen (message) );
        text_y += tm.tmHeight+tm.tmExternalLeading;
    }
   else
    {
        strcpy ( message, "  No Alpha channels support");
        TextOut ( hdc, text_x, text_y, message,
                  strlen (message) );
        text_y += tm.tmHeight+tm.tmExternalLeading;
    }
```

Obtaining the Display Modes

Earlier in this chapter we discussed display modes in DirectDraw programming. In this context, a display mode is defined by its resolution and color depth. Therefore, a display mode of 640 by 480 by 8 executes with a resolution of 640 pixel rows, 480 pixel columns, and encodes the pixel attribute in 8 bits, corresponding to a range of 256 colors. DirectDraw applications can obtain the available display modes. An application that executes in exclusive mode can also set a display mode and restore the previous one when it concludes.

Not all devices support all display modes. To determine the display modes supported on a given system, an application can call the `EnumDisplayModes()` function. `EnumDisplayModes()` can be used to list all supported display modes or to confirm that a single display mode is available in the hardware. The function's general form reads as follows:

```
HRESULT EnumDisplayModes(
                    DWORD dwFlags,                                   // 1
                    LPDDSURFACEDESC lpDDSurfaceDesc,                 // 2
                    LPVOID lpContext,                                // 3
                    LPDDENUMMODESCALLBACK lpEnumModesCallback        // 4
                  );
```

The first parameter determines the function's options by means of two flags. `DDEDM_REFRESHRATES` enumerates separately the modes that have different refresh rates, even if they have the same resolution and color depth. The second flag, `DDEDM_STANDARDVGAMODES`, enumerates Mode X and VGA Mode 13H as different modes. This parameter can be set to 0 to ignore both of these options. The second parameter is the address of a `DDSURFACEDESC2` structure, listed in Appendix A. The structure is used to store the parameters of a particular display mode, which is confirmed or not by the call. Applications that request a listing of all available modes set this parameter to NULL. The third parameter is a pointer to an application-defined structure that is passed to the callback function associated with `EnumDisplayModes()`. This provides a mechanism whereby the application code can make local data visible to the callback function. If not used, as is most often the case, then the third parameter is set to `NULL`. The fourth parameter is the address of a special callback function, of prototype `EnumModesCallback2()`. This function is called every time a supported mode is found. Applications use this callback function to provide the necessary processing for each display mode found by the call.

The callback function, whose address your code supplies when it calls `EnumDisplayModes()`, must match the prototype for `EnumModesCallback2()`. Each time that a supported mode is found, the callback function receives control. The function's general form is:

```
HRESULT WINAPI EnumModesCallback(
                              LPDDSURFACEDESC lpDDSurfaceDesc,  // 1
                              LPVOID lpContext                  // 2
                            );
```

The first parameter is the address of a DDSURFACEDESC2 structure that describes the display mode (see Appendix A). The second parameter is the address of the application-defined data structure, which may have been passed in the third parameter of the EnumDisplayModes() function call. Code can examine the values in the DDSURFACEDESC2 structure to determine the characteristics of each available display mode. The most important members of the DDSURFACEDESC2 structure are dwWidth, dwHeight, and ddpfPixelFormat. The dwWidth and dwHeight hold the display mode's dimensions. The ddpfPixelFormat member is a DDPIXELFORMAT structure that contains information about the mode's bit depth and describes whether the display mode is palettized or not. If the dwFlags member contains the DDPF_PALETTEINDEXED1, DDPF_PALETTEINDEXED2, DDPF_PALETTEINDEXED4, or DDPF_PALETTEINDEXED8 flag, then the display mode's bit depth is 1, 2, 4, or 8 bits. In this case the pixel value is an index into the corresponding palette. If dwFlags contains DDPF_RGB, then the display mode's bit depth in the dwRGBBitCount member of the DDPIXELFORMAT structure is valid.

Applications that call EnumDisplayModes() usually do most of the processing in the EnumModesCallback() function. For example, a program can list all of the DirectDraw display modes on the screen by storing the display modes data in one or more arrays each time the callback function receives control. When execution returns to the caller, then all modes have been stored or a predetermined maximum was reached. The calling code can now read the mode data from the arrays and display the values on the screen. In this case, the callback function could be coded as follows:

```
// Global variables for DirectDraw operations
HRESULT          DDConnect;
DDCAPS           DrawCaps;
.
.
.
// DirectDraw object
LPDIRECTDRAW2  lpDD4;
int            DDLevel = 0;  // DirectDraw implementation
// DirectDraw modes data
int modesCount = 0;          // Counter for DirectDraw modes
static int MAX_MODES = 30;  // Maximum number of modes
DWORD modesArray[90];        // Array for mode parameters
.
```

```
.
.
//**************************************************************
// Callback function for EnumDisplayModes()
//**************************************************************
static WINAPI ModesProc(LPDDSURFACEDESC aSurface,
                        LPVOID Context)
{
    static int i;         // Index into array
    i = modesCount * 3;   // Set array pointer
   // Store mode parameters in public array
   // Note: code assumes that the dwRGBBitFormat member of
   //       the DDPIXELFORMAT structure contains valid data
   modesArray[i]     = aSurface->dwWidth;
   modesArray[i + 1] = aSurface->dwHeight;
   modesArray[i + 2] = aSurface->ddpfPixelFormat.dwRGBBitCount;
   modesCount++;          // Bump display modes counter
   // Check for maximum number of display modes
   if( modesCount >= MAX_MODES )
     return DDENUMRET_CANCEL;  // Stop mode listing

   else
     return DDENUMRET_OK;  // Continue
}
```

Note that the callback function, named `ModesProc()`, uses an array of type `DWORD` to store the height, width, and color depth for each mode reported by DirectDraw. A public variable named `modesCount` keeps track of the total number of modes. In this case the calling code can be implemented in a function called `DDModes`, as follows:

```
//**************************************************************
//      DDModes - Obtain and list DD display modes
//**************************************************************
void DDModes ( HDC hdc )
{
    TEXTMETRIC  tm;
    char        message[255];
    int j;                      // Display buffer offset
    static int textLines;       // Display lines counter
    int         text_x = 0;
    int         text_y = 0;
    int         cxChar;
    GetTextMetrics ( hdc, &tm );
```

```
   cxChar = tm.tmAveCharWidth ;
// Test for no DirectDraw interface
   if (DDLevel == 0) {
   strcpy ( message, "No DirectDraw interface" );
       TextOut ( hdc, text_x, text_y, message,
                strlen (message) );
   return;
   }
 //******************************
 //  There is DirectDraw. Obtain
 //    and list display modes
 //******************************
 strcpy ( message, "        DirectDraw Display Modes" );
   TextOut ( hdc, text_x, text_y, message,
             strlen (message) );
   text_y += tm.tmHeight+tm.tmExternalLeading;
 // Call EnumDisplayModes()
 DDConnect = lpDD4->EnumDisplayModes(0, NULL,
                   NULL, ModesProc);
 if (DDConnect == DD_OK) {
 strcpy ( message, "        Number of display modes: ");
 sprintf ( message+strlen
          ("        Number of display modes: "),
          "%i", modesCount);
   TextOut ( hdc, text_x, text_y, message,
             strlen (message) );
   text_y += tm.tmHeight+tm.tmExternalLeading;
   // Format and display mode data
   // First column
   textLines = modesCount;
   if(modesCount > 15){
     textLines = modesCount - 15;
     for(int x = 0; x < 15; x++){
       j = sprintf ( message, "  %d",
                     modesArray[x*3] );
       j += sprintf (message + j, " x %d",
                     modesArray[x*3+1] );
       j += sprintf (message + j, " x %d",
                     modesArray[x*3+2] );
       TextOut ( hdc, text_x, text_y, message,
                strlen (message) );
       text_y += tm.tmHeight+tm.tmExternalLeading;
     }
   }
```

```
    if(modesCount < 16)
      return;
    // Display second column if more than 15 modes
    text_x = cxChar * 20;
    text_y = 2 * tm.tmHeight+tm.tmExternalLeading;
      for(int y = 15; y < modesCount; y++){
        j = sprintf ( message, "  %d", modesArray[y*3] );
        j += sprintf (message + j, " x %d", modesArray[y*3+1] );
        j += sprintf (message + j, " x %d", modesArray[y*3+2] );
        TextOut ( hdc, text_x, text_y, message,
                  strlen (message) );
          text_y += tm.tmHeight+tm.tmExternalLeading;
        text_x = cxChar * 20;
      }
    return;
    }
}
```

The processing calls `EnumDisplayModes()` in the statement:

```
DDConnect = lpDD4->EnumDisplayModes(0, NULL, NULL,
                                    ModesProc);
```

The first parameter is set to 0 to indicate that no special control flags are required. Therefore, the refresh rate is not taken into consideration and mode X is not reported separately. The second parameter is `NULL` to indicate that no structure data for checking against available modes is used. The `NULL` value for the third parameter relates to the fact that no user-defined data structure is being passed to the callback function. The last parameter is the address of the callback function, in this case the `ModesProc()` function previously listed. When the callback function returns, the code tests for a return value of `DD_OK`, which indicates that the call was successful, and then proceeds to display the header messages and to convert the code data stored in `ModesArray[]` into ASCII strings for display.

DirectDraw Info Demo Project

The program named DD_info.cpp, located in the *DD Info Demo* project folder of the book's CD-ROM, is a demonstration of the initialization and preparatory operations for a DirectDraw application. The program starts by initializing DirectDraw. The program's menu contains commands to read and display system hardware information and to list the available display modes. Figure 9-12 is a screen dump of both menu commands in a machine equipped with a Matrox Millennium video card and 2MB of video memory.

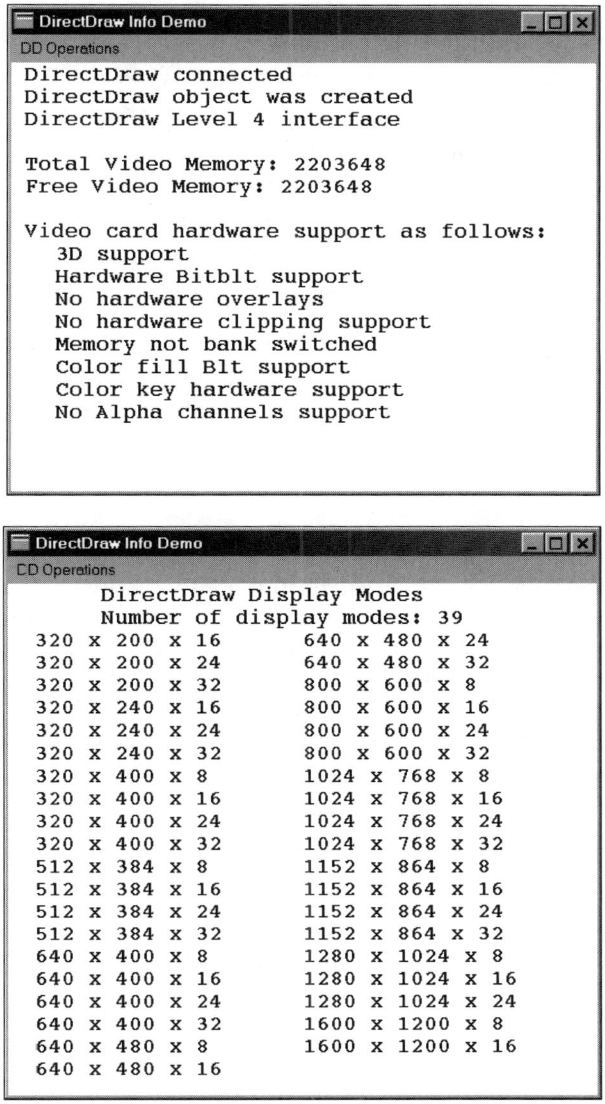

Figure 9-12: Screen dump of the DD Information and Display Modes commands in the DD Info Demo project.

> **Note:** One of the first operations performed by the DD_info.cpp program, which is the source in the *DD Info Demo* project, is to determine which version of the DirectDraw interface is installed in the target system. Then the code continues to obtain and display hardware support and lists the available display modes whatever DirectDraw interface is present. To accomplish this, the program typecasts the interface pointer, which can be of type `LPDIRECTDRAW`, `LPDIRECTDRAW2`, or `LPDIRECTDRAW4`, to a type `LPDIRECTDRAW`. This manipulation is not conventional and only works in very simple processing conditions. Application code should not typecast DirectDraw pointer into those of other interfaces.

Summary

In this chapter you have learned the essential elements of DirectDraw, as well as the fundamental steps in creating and initializing an application that uses DirectDraw functions. The discussion included topics related to computer games, Windows programming using the DirectX 6 SDK, as well as an overview of DirectDraw features, architecture, and basic concepts. The programming operations discussed have referred mainly to configuration and initialization. We have not yet discussed the use of DirectDraw to perform graphics display operations. In the next chapter, we begin graphics programming with DirectDraw.

Chapter 10

Accessing Video Memory

IN THIS CHAPTER

- Developing a program template for DirectDraw exclusive-mode programs using IDirectDraw4
- Programming for direct access
- Low-level coding using in-line assembly
- Developing direct-access primitives that perform the fundamental drawing operations
- Using raster operations in direct access

In Chapter 9 we discussed how an application is set up and initialized to use DirectDraw, we talked about the basics of DirectDraw programming, and demonstrated some fundamental DirectDraw functions in the context of a conventional, windowed program. But the basic purpose of DirectDraw is to facilitate the development of high-performance graphics. This often implies using DirectDraw to access video memory directly and to take advantage of the hardware facilities furnished in the video card. In developing an application that accesses video memory several issues must be considered, and some of the issues mentioned in Chapter 9 must be revisited in a new setting.

In developing a DirectDraw exclusive-mode application two preliminary topics must be considered. The first one is creating a `WinMain()` function suited for DirectDraw applications that execute in this mode. The second one is providing access to the up-to-date version of the interface, currently DirectX 6. This relates to the fact that DirectX 6 furnishes its DirectDraw functionality in the IDirctDraw4 interface. In Chapter 9 we mentioned that the DirectX DirectSetup component provides a version update mechanism, as well as the necessary files and drivers. The details of implementing the DirectDraw installation and version update are the topic of Chapter 13. It is the upgrade facilities provided by DirectSetup that allow an application to commit to the newest version of DirectX without loosing compatibility with existing systems. By furnishing installation software support, and by supplying the drivers at no cost, Microsoft has made it possible for applications to use the newest version of the interface with little concern for incompatibility with older systems. In this book, we generally assume that the host machine is equipped with DirectX version 6. The one exception is the diagnostic program named *DD Info Demo*, developed in Chapter 9.

DirectDraw WinMain() Function

The `WinMain()` function for a DirectDraw program that operates in exclusive mode has little use for some of the elements normally present in a conventional Windows application. On the other hand, it needs to perform several DirectDraw-specific initializations that are not found in standard Windows programming. The result is that we must develop a new template for DirectDraw exclusive-mode programming, so that it includes a customized implementation of the `WinMain()` function that suits its particular purposes.

If the program's main window is created by means of the DirectDraw interface, then a reasonable approach is to perform most of the initialization and setup operations in `WinMain()`. In addition to the usual windows initialization operations, the following DirectDraw-specific steps are typically required:

- Obtain the DirectDraw4 interface and store the pointer object for future use.
- Check that the desired mode is available in the host machine.
- Set the cooperative level.
- Set the display mode.
- Create the drawing surfaces. Most DirectDraw programs require at least a primary surface.
- Obtain the DirectDraw device context if the program is to execute GDI functions.

The WinMain() Backbone

The first task is coding the backbone for a `WinMain()` function that creates an application window compatible with a DirectDraw exclusive mode program. In addition to this backbone, the `WinMain()` function can perform DirectDraw-specific initialization and output operations. This code is usually placed before the message loop. The fundamental parts of this backbone, as follows, are the same as those of any Windows program:

- Creating and filling the members of a data structure of type `WNDCLASS`.
- Registering the window class.
- Creating the DirectDraw-compatible window.

- Setting the window's show state.
- Providing a program message loop.

In the following discussion, we stress the elements of WinMain() that are specific to a DirectDraw program. A general discussion of the WinMain() function is found in Chapter 3.

The WINDCLASSEX structure contains window class information. In WinMain() it is used with the RegisterClassEx() functions. There are few differences between the WNDCLASSEX structure that we have been using in conventional Windows programming and the one required for an exclusive mode DirectDraw application. One such difference relates to the fact that a DirectDraw window class does not use a private device context; therefore, the CS_OWNDC constant is not present in the style member of the WNDCLASSEX structure. The only other structure member that requires comment is hbrBackground. In this case, the application can select a standard brush to color the initial program background. In the template file, the structure is filled as follows:

```
WNDCLASSEX  wndclass ;
 wndclass.cbSize        = sizeof (wndclass) ;
 wndclass.style         = CS_HREDRAW | CS_VREDRAW;
 wndclass.lpfnWndProc   = WndProc ;
 wndclass.cbClsExtra    = 0 ;
 wndclass.cbWndExtra    = 0 ;
 wndclass.hInstance     = hInstance ;
 wndclass.hIcon         = LoadIcon (NULL, IDI_APPLICATION) ;
 wndclass.hCursor       = LoadCursor (NULL, IDC_ARROW) ;
 wndclass.hbrBackground = (HBRUSH) GetStockObject
                          (GRAY_BRUSH) ;
 wndclass.lpszMenuName  = szAppName;
 wndclass.lpszClassName = szAppName;
 wndclass.hIconSm       = LoadIcon (NULL, IDI_APPLICATION) ;
```

The window class is a template that defines the characteristics of a particular window. It also defines the address of the window procedure, as in the preceding code fragment. Having filled the structure members, code can now register the class with the following call:

```
RegisterClass(&wndclass);
```

It is now time to create the window using the CreateWindowEx() function. Many combinations of parameters can be used in the call, according to the characteristics desired for the particular application window that is to be created. However, in the case of a DirectDraw exclusive-mode application, many of the predefined values are meaningless.

The extended style WS_EX_TOPMOST defines a window that is placed above all non-topmost windows. For a DirectDraw exclusive mode program, WS_EX_TOPMOST is usually the appropriate style. The window style parameter is usually WS_POPUP. If the DirectDraw application is to execute full screen, which is always the case in exclusive mode, then the horizontal and vertical origins are set to zero and the xsize and ysize parameters are filled using GetSystemMetrics(). The GetSystemMetrics() call returns the full pixel size of the screen area. In the template file, the structure is filled as follows:

```
hWnd = CreateWindowEx(
       WS_EX_TOPMOST,         // Extended style
       szAppName,             // Application name
       "DirectDraw Demo No. 2",
       WS_POPUP,              // Window style
       0,                     // Horizontal origin
       0,                     // Vertical origin
       GetSystemMetrics(SM_CXSCREEN), // x size
       GetSystemMetrics(SM_CYSCREEN), // y size
       NULL,              // Handle of parent
       NULL,              // Handle to menu
       hInstance,         // Application instance
       NULL);             // Additional data
if (!hWnd)
   return FALSE;
```

By calling the ShowWindow() function, the code specifies how the window is to be shown. CreateWindowEx() creates the window internally but does not display it. To display the window, a conventional Windows program usually calls ShowWindow() to set the show state, and then UpdateWindow() to update the client area by sending a WM_PAINT message to the window procedure. It is different in the case of a DirectDraw exclusive-mode application. Because the DirectDraw interface has not been yet established, no WM_PAINT message can be sent at this point in the code. Therefore, the template file makes the call to the ShowWindow() function, but not the one to UpdateWindow(). The code reads as follows:

```
ShowWindow (hwnd, iCmdShow) ;
```

The first parameter is the handle to the window returned by the CreateWindowEx() function. The second parameter is the window's display mode parameter. In this first call to ShowWindow(), applications must use the value received by WinMain().

The coding is now at a point in which WinMain() can initialize DirectDraw and perhaps perform some preliminary display operations. The processing details in the case of the sample program are discussed in the following section. The last step in WinMain() is the ever-present message loop. In a standard DirectDraw exclusive-mode application, the message loop is no different than the one in a conventional windows program. In Chapter 12 we discuss a different type of message loop, used in DirectDraw programs that implement animation. The present code reads as follows:

```
    while (GetMessage(&msg, NULL, 0, 0))
    {
        TranslateMessage(&msg);
        DispatchMessage(&msg);
    }
    return msg.wParam;
}
```

DirectDraw Initialization

A DirectDraw exclusive-mode application is often initialized inside `WinMain()`. The reason behind this approach is that the exclusive-mode application cannot perform display operations until it has obtained the interface and set the cooperative level and the display mode. If display operations are to be performed by means of GDI functions, then the application must also obtain the DirectDraw device context. Note that some DirectDraw applications draw on the screen using both GDI and direct-memory access methods.

The DirectDraw initialization for exclusive-mode operation typically includes the following steps:

- Obtain the current interface. In DirectX 6 this is `IDirectDraw4`.
- Check that the desired display mode is available in the host machine.
- Set the cooperative level.
- Set the display mode.
- Create the drawing surfaces. This usually means at least a primary surface, but often other surfaces are also necessary.
- Display some initial screen text or graphics. This can be accomplished by means of conventional GDI functions, by direct access to video memory, by DirectDraw specific functions, or by a combination of these methods. Programs of greater complexity usually perform other initialization, setup, and initial display functions at this time. The example used in this chapter has minimal DirectDraw functionality. In the chapters that follow, we develop DirectDraw programs with a greater level of complexity.

An important thing to do in preliminary DirectDraw operations is to provide a mechanism whereby the application can recover if a terminal condition is encountered during the initialization process. In the DirectDraw template program we have included a function named `DDInitFailed()` that creates a message box with the corresponding diagnostic prompt and waits for the user to press the OK button. When the user acknowledges, the terminal error handler destroys the application window and returns control to the operating system. The function is coded as follows:

```
//***************************************
// Name: DDInitFailed()
// Desc: This function is called if an
//       initialization operation fails
//***************************************
HRESULT DDInitFailed(HWND hWnd, HRESULT hRet, LPCTSTR szError)
{
    char   szBuff[128];
    sprintf(szBuff, szError);
    ReleaseObjects();
    MessageBox(hWnd, szBuff, "DirectDraw Access Demo", MB_OK);
    DestroyWindow(hWnd);
    return hRet;
}
```

The parameters for the `DDInitFailed()` function are the handle to the window, the result code from the call that caused the failure, and a string pointer with the diagnostic text to be displayed in the message box. All DirectDraw initialization calls performed in the template code test for a valid result code; if no valid code is found, they exit execution through the `DDInitFailed()` function. The same is true of the DirectDraw examples used in the rest of the book.

The first processing step is to obtain the DirectDraw object that corresponds to the current version of the interface. It is usually a good idea to store the pointer in a global variable, which can be accessed by other program elements. The function named `DD4Interface()` attempts to find this object. It is coded as follows:

```
// Global data
LPDIRECTDRAW4     lpDD4;    // Pointer to current interface
.
.
.
//****************************************
// Name: DD4Interface()
// Desc: Finds DirectDraw4 object
// PRE CONDITIONS:
//   lpDD4 is a global variable of type
//   LPDIRECTDRAW4
//
// POST CONDITIONS:
//   returns 0 if no DirectDraw4 interface
//   returns 1 if DirectDraw4 found
```

```
//***************************************
int DD4Interface()
{

  HRESULT         DDConnect;
  LPDIRECTDRAW    lpDD;        // Pointer to DirectDraw
 DDConnect = DirectDrawCreate ( NULL, &lpDD, NULL);
 if(DDConnect != DD_OK)
  return 0;
    // Attempt to locate DirectDraw4 interface
    DDConnect = lpDD->QueryInterface( IID_IDirectDraw4,
                                      (LPVOID *) &lpDD4);
    if(DDConnect != S_OK)
    return 0;
    lpDD->Release();       // Release old pointer
      return 1;
  }
```

Note that the code releases the local pointer to DirectDraw if the DirectDraw4 pointer is found. In this manner the application code need only be concerned with releasing the object actually in use. Also that the pointer to the DirectDraw4 interface is defined globally so that it can be seen throughout the application. In `WinMain()`, the call to the `DD4Interface()` function reads as follows:

```
// Attempt to fetch the DirectDraw4 interface
   hRet = DD4Interface();
     if (hRet == 0)
     return DDInitFailed(hWnd, hRet,
                        "QueryInterface() call failed");
```

If the DirectDraw4 interface is not found, then the program exits through the `DDInitFailed()` function previously described. In the template file the diagnostic messages simply express the name of the failed function. In your own programs, you may want to substitute these text messages for more appropriate ones. For example, the failure of the `QueryInterface()` call can be interpreted to mean that the user needs to upgrade the host system to DirectX 6. A more detailed diagnostics may be advisable in this case. If the call succeeds, then we have obtained a pointer to the DirectDraw4 interface. This pointer can be used in all other DirectDraw function calls.

The fact that we have a pointer to the newest version of the DirectDraw interface does not mean that the application is guaranteed to execute correctly. DirectDraw programming sometimes introduces hardware dependencies that are not a factor in conventional Windows programming. This fact is evident in operations related to the display mode. For this reason, before we attempt to set a display mode, it is usually a good idea to find out if the desired mode is available in the host system. This gives our code the opportunity to select an alternative mode if the ideal one is not available, or to exit with a diagnostic message if no satisfactory display mode is found.

In Chapter 9 we explored the use of the `EnumDisplayModes()` function; at that time it was used to list the display modes available in a system. The same function can be used to determine if a particular mode is available. The code used in the template file reads as follows:

```
//*****************************************************
// Name: ModesProc
// Desc: Callback function for EnumDisplayModes()
//*****************************************************
HRESULT WINAPI ModesProc(LPDDSURFACEDESC2 aSurface,
          LPVOID Context)
{
   static int i;         // Index into array of mode data
   i = modesCount * 3;   // Set array pointer
   if( modesCount >= MAX_MODES )
    return DDENUMRET_CANCEL;  // Stop mode listing
   // Store mode parameters in public array
   // Note: code assumes that the dwRGBBitFormat member if
   //       the DDPIXELFORMAT structure contains valid data
   modesArray[i]     = aSurface->dwWidth;
   modesArray[i + 1] = aSurface->dwHeight;
   modesArray[i + 2] =
                   aSurface->ddpfPixelFormat.dwRGBBitCount;
   modesCount++;         // Bump display modes counter
   return DDENUMRET_OK;  // Continue
}
//*******************************************************
// Name: hasDDMode
// Desc: Tests for mode availability
//*******************************************************
// PRE CONDITIONS:
// 1. Public variable modesArray[] to store mode data
// 2. Public int variable modesCount to store number of
//    display modes
// 3. ModesProc() is an associated function that stores
//    mode data in array and count modes
//
// POST CONDITIONS:
//  1. Returns 1 if mode is available
//******************************************************
int HasDDMode(DWORD pixWidth, DWORD pixHeight, DWORD pixBits)
{
```

```
 static HRESULT DDConnect;
    // Call EnumDisplayModes()
 if(MODES_ON == 0){
  MODES_ON = 1;          // set switch
  DDConnect = lpDD4->EnumDisplayModes(0, NULL, NULL,
                                      ModesProc);
 }
// Modes are now stored in modeArray[] as triplets encoding
// width, height, and pixel bit size
// Variable modesCount holds the total number of display modes
 for(int x = 0; x < (modesCount * 3); x += 3){
  if(modesArray[x]==pixWidth && modesArray[x+1]==pixHeight\
                     && modesArray[x+2]==pixBits)
   return 1;
 }
 return 0;
}
```

NOTE: DirectDraw documentation states that the `EnumDisplayModes()` function can be passed the address of a `DDSURFACEDESC2` structure that is checked for a specific mode. In our tests we have found that this variation of the DirectX API is not always reliable. For this reason, our `HasDDMode()` function loads all the available modes into a global array variable and then searches the array for the desired mode.

In the `WinMain()` template, the call to the `HasDDMode()` function is coded as follows:

```
// Check for available mode (640 by 480 in 24-bit color)
 if (HasDDMode(640, 480, 24) == 0)
       return DDInitFailed(hWnd, hRet,
                           "Display mode not available");
```

We have provided for no alternative processing for the case in which the desired true-color mode is not available in the system. In your own programs you may want to provide alternative modes if the ideal one is not found. This type of alternative processing, which can be called "best-option" logic, is discussed in Chapter 12. Again, you should note that this programming style creates device-dependent code that may bring about other major complications.

If the desired mode is available, then the code must determine the cooperative level and proceed to set the mode. Exclusive mode DirectDraw programs require the constants DDSLC_EXCLUSIVE and DDSCL_FULLSCREEN, which were discussed in Chapter 9. The processing reads as follows:

```
// Set cooperative level to exclusive and full screen
   hRet = lpDD4->SetCooperativeLevel(hWnd, DDSCL_EXCLUSIVE
                                     | DDSCL_FULLSCREEN);
   if (hRet != DD_OK)
       return DDInitFailed(hWnd, hRet,
                      "SetCooperativeLevel() call failed");
   // Set the video mode to 640 x 480 x 24
   hRet = lpDD4->SetDisplayMode(640, 480, 24, 0, 0);
   if (hRet != DD_OK)
       return DDInitFailed(hWnd, hRet,
                      "SetDisplayMode() call failed");
```

In Chapter 9 we first encountered the concept of DirectDraw surfaces. At that time we defined a drawing surface as an area of video memory, typically used to hold image data, and DirectDrawSurface as a COM object in itself. Most DirectDraw4 applications require at least two types of COM objects: one of type LPDIRECTDRAW4 is a pointer to the DirectDraw object. The second one of type LPDIRECTDRAWSURFACE4 is a pointer to a surface. All surface-related functions use this second pointer type, while the core DirectDraw calls require the first one. Applications that manipulate several surfaces often cast a pointer for each surface. A third type of object – a DirectDraw palette object – is necessary for programs that perform palette manipulations, while DirectDraw clipper objects are used in clipping operations.

Before accessing a DirectDraw surface, you must create it by means of a call to the CreateSurface() function. The call can produce a single surface object, a complex surface-flipping chain, or a 3-D surface. The call to CreateSurface() specifies the dimensions of the surface, whether it is a single surface or a complex surface, and the pixel format. These characteristics are previously stored in a DDSURFACEDESC2 structure, whose address is included in the call's parameters. The function's general form reads as follows:

```
HRESULT CreateSurface(
                      LPDDSURFACEDESC lpDDSurfaceDesc,          // 1
                      LPDIRECTDRAWSURFACE FAR *lplpDDSurface,  // 2
                      IUnknown FAR *pUnkOuter                   // 3
                     );
```

The first parameter is the address of a structure variable of type LPDDSURFACEDESC2. This structure is listed in Appendix A. The CreateSurface() API requires that all unused members of the structure be set to zero. In the code sample that follows you will see how this can easily be accomplished. The second parameter is the address of a variable of type LPDIRECTDRAWSURFACE4, which is set to the interface address if the call succeeds. This is the pointer used in the calls that relate to this surface. Applications often store this pointer in a global variable so that it is visible throughout the code. The third parameter is provided for future expansion of the COM. Presently, applications must set this parameter to NULL or an error results.

If the call succeeds, the return value is DD_OK. If it fails, the following self-explanatory error values can be returned:

DDERR_INCOMPATIBLEPRIMARY

DDERR_INVALIDCAPS

DDERR_INVALIDOBJECT

DDERR_INVALIDPARAMS

DDERR_INVALIDPIXELFORMAT

DDERR_NOALPHAHW

DDERR_NOCOOPERATIVELEVELSET

DDERR_NODIRECTDRAWHW

DDERR_NOEMULATION

DDERR_NOEXCLUSIVEMODE

DDERR_NOFLIPHW

DDERR_NOMIPMAPHW

DDERR_NOOVERLAYHW

DDERR_NOZBUFFERHW

DDERR_OUTOFMEMORY

DDERR_OUTOFVIDEOMEMORY

DDERR_PRIMARYSURFACEALREADYEXISTS

DDERR_UNSUPPORTEDMODE

DirectDraw always attempts to create a surface in local video memory. If there is not enough local video memory available, then DirectDraw tries to use non-local video memory. Finally, if no video memory is available at all, then the surface is created in system memory. The call to CreateSurface() can explicitly request that a surface be created in a certain type of memory. This is done by means of the appropriate flags in the associated DDSCAPS2 structure. DDSCAPS2 structure is part of DDSURFACEDESC2 (see Appendix A).

The primary surface is the one currently displayed on the monitor. It is identified by the DDSCAPS_PRIMARYSURFACE flag. There is only one primary surface for each

DirectDraw object. The dimensions and pixel format of the primary surface must match the current display mode. It is not necessary to explicitly enter these values when calling `CreateSurface()`. In fact, specifying these parameters generates an error even if they match the ones in the current display mode. In this template program we create the simplest possible surface object, which is the one that corresponds to a primary surface. The code reads as follows:

```
// Global data
LPDIRECTDRAWSURFACE4      lpDDSPrimary = NULL; // DirectDraw primary
DDSURFACEDESC2            ddsd;
     .
     .
     .
 // Create a primary surface
 // ddsd is a structure of type DDSRUFACEDESC2
 // First, zero all structure variables using the ZeroMemory()
 // function
    ZeroMemory(&ddsd, sizeof(ddsd));
 // Now fill in the required members
    ddsd.dwSize = sizeof(ddsd);      // Structure size
    ddsd.dwFlags = DDSD_CAPS ;
    ddsd.ddsCaps.dwCaps = DDSCAPS_PRIMARYSURFACE;

    hRet = lpDD4->CreateSurface(&ddsd, &lpDDSPrimary, NULL);
    if (hRet != DD_OK)
        return DDInitFailed(hWnd, hRet,
                     "CreateSurface() call failed");
```

If the call succeeds, we obtain a pointer by which to access the functions that relate to DirectDraw surfaces. The pointer, named `lpDDSPrimary`, is stored in a global variable of type `LPDIRECTDRAWSURFACE4`. The surface pointer can be used to obtain a DirectDraw device context, which enables the use of GDI graphics in the application, or to lock the surface for direct access and retrieve its base address and pitch.

For example, if the application now needs to display some screen text, such as a "Hello World" message, it has to obtain a handle to the device context. The DirectDrawSurface4 interface contains a function called `GetDC()` that can be used for this purpose. This function is not the same one as `GetDC()` in the general Windows API. Its general form reads as follows:

```
HRESULT GetDC( HDC );
```

The function's only parameter is the address of the handle to the device context that is associated with the surface. If the call succeeds, it returns `DD_OK`. If it fails, it returns one of the following error codes:

DDERR_DCALREADYCREATED

DDERR_GENERIC

DDERR_INVALIDOBJECT

DDERR_INVALIDPARAMS

DDERR_INVALIDSURFACETYPE

DDERR_SURFACELOST

DDERR_UNSUPPORTED

DDERR_WASSTILLDRAWING

Note that the GetDC() function uses an internal version of the IDirectDrawSurface4::Lock function to lock the surface. The surface remains locked until the IDirectDrawSurface4::ReleaseDC function is called. In the template program the code proceeds as follows:

```
static char szDDMessage1[] =
 "Hello World - Press <Esc> to end program";
  .
  .
  .
// Display some text on the primary surface
if(lpDDSPrimary->GetDC(&hdc) != DD_OK)
 return DDInitFailed(hWnd, hRet, "GetDC() call failed");
// Display screen message
   SetBkColor(hdc, RGB(0, 0, 255));        // Blue background
   SetTextColor(hdc, RGB(255, 255, 0));    // Yellow letters
   TextOut(hdc, 120, 200, szDDMessage1,
          lstrlen(szDDMessage1));
   lpDDSPrimary->ReleaseDC(hdc);
```

The DD Template Project

The project file named *DD Template* project on the book's CD-ROM contains the program DD_templ.cpp, which can be used as a template for developing simple DirectDraw applications. The template contains all of the support functions previously mentioned, that is, functions to find a DirectDraw4 interface object, to test for availability of a particular display mode, to release objects, and to handle terminal errors during DirectDraw initialization. The processing consists of displaying a screen message using the text output GDI service. The code also includes a skeletal window procedure to handle keyboard input, disable the cursor, and terminate execution.

Direct-access Programming

The described program, found in the *DD Template Project* directory, initializes DirectDraw, defines the cooperative level, sets a display mode, and draws text on the screen using a GDI function. These operations are necessary in many DirectDraw applications, but have few advantages over conventional Windows programming. There is not much gained in performance and control by a DirectDraw application that is limited to the GDI functions. The purpose of DirectDraw is to obtain a higher level of control and to improve graphics performance. Neither of these is achieved by merely setting a display mode and displaying text or graphics to the screen using the GDI services. Before an application can enjoy the advantages derived from the DirectDraw interface, it must gain access to video memory. The second level of DirectDraw advantages, those that result from using the hardware features in the video card, are discussed in the chapters that follow.

Memory-mapped Video

Graphics programming in DOS is based on the fact that PC video functions are mapped to a specific area of system memory. The DOS graphics programmer determines the base address to which the video system is mapped and the pixel format used in the current display mode. The code then proceeds to store pixel data in this memory area and the video hardware takes care of automatically updating the display by reflecting the contents of the memory region to which it is mapped. The process is simple, although in some display modes the manipulations can become relatively complicated.

One of the fundamental difficulties of graphics programming in DOS relates to the segmented architecture of the Intel CPUs. Each DOS segment is limited to 64k. A display mode of 640 by 480 pixels, in which each pixel is stored in one byte of data, requires 307,200 bytes, which far exceeds the span of a single segment. In fact, 307,200 data bytes require five segments for storing the pixel information. This forces the programming into the so-called *banking mechanisms*. By switching a hardware element called the bank, this scheme enables several areas of system memory to be mapped to the same segment of video memory. The programming appears difficult, but once the access routines are developed for a particular display mode, the code can set any screen pixel to any desired color attribute by just passing the pixel's screen column and row address and the desired color code.

Until the advent of DirectDraw, Windows graphics programmers had no way of accessing video memory directly. Even if a Windows programmer had been able to find the address to which the video display was mapped in a particular system, any attempt to access this area of memory would generate a general protection fault at the operating system level. DirectDraw solves both problems: it temporarily relaxes the operating system's access restriction, and it provides information about the location and mapping of the video system. Furthermore, in Win32 versions of DirectDraw, the video display area is defined in a flat, unsegmented memory space. Once the application obtains the base address of video memory, and its bit-to-pixel mapping, it proceeds to perform display operations without any banking complications nor the attribute-mapping schemes that plague DOS graphics systems.

Mapping in Hi-color Modes

The development of SuperVGA video cards, with more video memory than the standard VGA, made possible display modes with a much richer color range than had been previously available on the PC. Those modes that devote 16 or more bits for the color encoding of each screen pixel have been called the hi-color modes. Although no formal designation for these modes has ever been established, the 16-bit per pixel modes are usually referred to as *real-color* modes, and those with 24- and 32-bits per pixel are called the *true-color* modes. An adapter with 4MB of video memory, which is less than average in today's hardware, enables several real-color and true-color modes. The screen dump in Figure 9-12, which corresponds to a video card with 4MB of memory, shows real-color modes with a resolution of up to1600 by 1200 pixels and true-color modes up to 1280 by 1024 pixels. The conclusion is that the graphics programmer working with current video system technology can safely assume that most PCs support real-color and true-color modes with standard resolutions.

> NOTE: The names hi-color, true-color, and real-color in relation to display modes have been used rather imprecisely in graphics programming literature. Some articles and books refer to 16-bit display modes as "hi-color" and others use real-color and true-color, hyphenated or not, with different meanings from the ones we have described. The designations we have adopted seem the most reasonable and generally accepted. Also note that true-color video modes were not supported in the original Game SDK; therefore, they are not mentioned often in some articles and books of the period.

In Windows, all display modes with a resolution of 16-bits per pixel or higher are nonpalettized. Palettes were developed mostly to increase the colors available in modes with limited pixel depth. For general graphics programming, the use of palette-independent display modes considerably simplifies the design and coding effort. In today's video cards, with several megabytes of display memory, there is little justification for using palettized modes. All real-color and true-color modes are, by definition, nonpalettized. Figure 10-1 shows the mapping of video memory bits to pixel attributes in a real-color and a true-color mode.

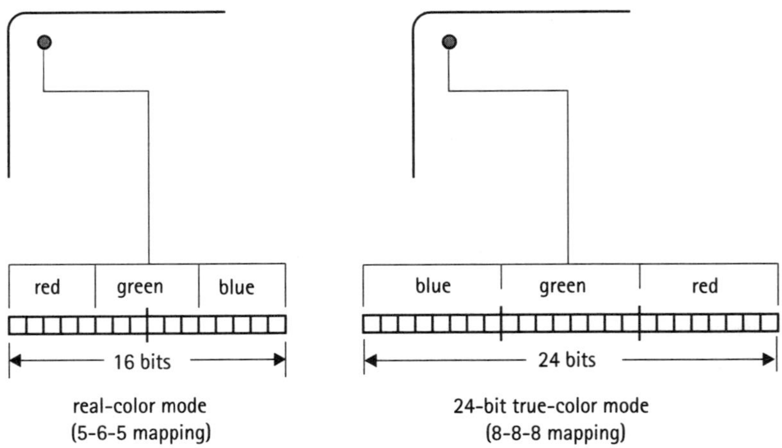

Figure 10-1: Bit-to-pixel mapping in real-color and 24-bit true-color display modes

Real-color modes are often mapped differently in the various SuperVGA cards. The basic problem is that 16 bits is not an exact multiple of the three primary colors. One possible solution is to leave one bit unused and map each primary color to a 5-bit field. A more reasonable alternative is to map green to a 6-bit field, because the human eye is more sensitive to this color than to red and blue. This scheme, usually called a 5-6-5 mapping, is the one shown in Figure 10-1.

Programming in the real-color modes directly is not without complications. In these modes the primary colors do not coincide with a byte boundary. Therefore, the code must perform bitwise operations to set the corresponding fields to the required values. On the other hand, in the true-color modes eight bits are mapped to each of the primary colors. This makes the access operations much easier to implement in code.

True-color Modes

The true-color modes are those in which each primary color (red, green, and blue) is mapped to an 8-bit field. The name true-color relates to the fact that these modes reproduce a color range on the video display that is approximately equivalent to the sensitivity of the human eye. It is often said that these modes produce a color rendition that is of photographic quality. Two different mappings are used in the true-color modes. The 24-bit mapping, shown in Figure 10-1, uses three consecutive bytes to represent each of the primary colors. In the 32-bit mappings there is an extra byte, which is unused, at the end of each pixel field. The 32-bit true-color mapping is shown in Figure 10-2.

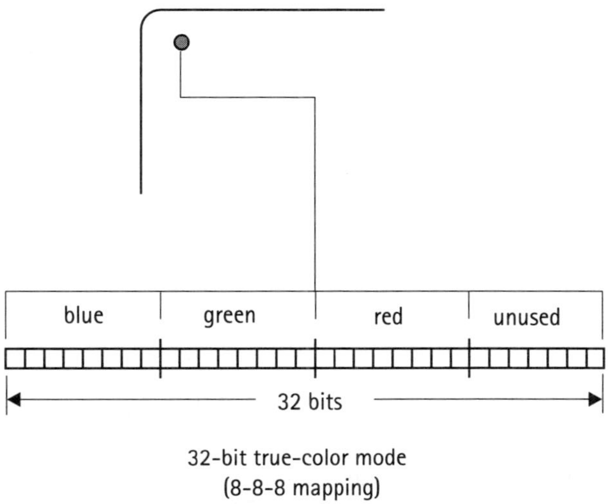

Figure 10-2: Bit-to-pixel mapping in 32-bit true-color display mode

The reason for the unused byte in the 32-bit true-color modes relates to the 32-bit architecture of the Intel CPUs, which also happens to be the bus width of most video cards. Devoting 32 bits to encoding the color attribute makes it possible to fill a pixel with a single memory transfer. In the case of the Intel CPUs, a low-level program can store the pixel attribute in an extended machine register, such as EAX, and then transfer it into video memory with a single move instruction. A C or C++ program can place the value into a variable of type `LONG` and use a pointer to `LONG` to move the data – also in a single operation. In the 32-bit mapping scheme, memory storage space is sacrificed for the sake of faster access.

Locking the Surface

Applications directly access the video buffer, or any surface memory area, by first calling the `Lock()` function. The `Lock()` function returns a pointer to the top-left corner of the rectangle that defines the surface, as well as the surface pitch and other relevant information necessary for accessing the surface. When calling the `Lock()` function, the application can define a rectangular area within the surface, or the entire surface. If the surface is a primary surface, and the entire area is requested, then `Lock()` returns the base address of the video buffer and the number of bytes in each buffer row. This last parameter is called the surface pitch. At this point, the DirectDraw application gains total control as well as direct access to the video display.

The Lock() function is related to the surface; therefore, it is accessed by means of the surface object returned by the call to CreateSurface(), not by a DirectDraw object. The function's general form reads as follows:

```
HRESULT Lock(
            LPRECT lpDestRect,                  // 1
            LPDDSURFACEDESC lpDDSurfaceDesc,    // 2
            DWORD dwFlags,                      // 3
            HANDLE hEvent                       // 4
           );
```

The first parameter is a pointer to a RECT structure that describes a rectangular area on the surface that is to be accessed directly. This parameter is set to NULL to lock the entire surface. If more than one rectangle is to be locked, they cannot overlap. The second parameter is the address of a structure variable of type DDSURFACEDESC2, which is filled with all the information necessary to access the surface memory directly. The information returned in this structure includes the base address of the surface, its pitch, and its pixel format. The third parameter contains one or more flags that define the function's mode of operation. Table 10-1 lists the constants currently implemented in the IDirectDrawSurface4 interface.

> **NOTE:** Applications should never make assumptions about the surface pitch, because this value changes according to the location of surface memory and even the version of the DirectDraw driver.

TABLE 10-1 FLAGS USED IN THE IDIRECTDRAWSURFACE4::LOCK FUNCTION

Flag	Meaning
DDLOCK_NOSYSLOCK	Do not take the Win16Mutex. This flag is ignored when locking the primary surface.
DDLOCK_READONLY	The surface being locked will only be read.
DDLOCK_SURFACEMEMORYPTR	A valid memory pointer to the top-left corner of the specified rectangle should be returned. If no rectangle is specified, a pointer to the top of the surface is returned. This is the default and need not be entered explicitly.
DDLOCK_WAIT	If blit operation is in progress, lock is retried.
DDLOCK_WRITEONLY	The surface being locked will be write-enabled.

The fourth parameter to the `Lock()` call was originally documented to be a handle to a system event that is triggered when the surface is ready to be locked. The newest version of the DirectDraw documentation states that it is not used and should always be set to `NULL`.

The `DDLOCK_NOSYSLOCK` flag relates to the fact that while a surface is locked, DirectDraw usually holds the Win16Mutex (also known as the Win16Lock) so that gaining access to surface memory can occur safely. The Win16Mutex in effect shuts down Windows GDI used by other applications for the time lapse between the `Lock()` and the `Unlock()` calls. If the `DDLOCK_NOSYSLOCK` flag is present, then the Win16Mutex does not take place if the locked surface is not the primary surface. If a blit is in progress when the `Lock()` call takes place, the function returns an error. This can be prevented by including the `DDLOCK_WAIT` flag, which causes the call to wait until a lock can be successfully obtained.

`Lock()` returns `DD_OK` if it succeeds, or returns one of the following error codes if it fails:

```
DDERR_INVALIDOBJECT

DDERR_INVALIDPARAMS

DDERR_OUTOFMEMORY

DDERR_SURFACEBUSY

DDERR_SURFACELOST

DDERR_WASSTILLDRAWING
```

When `Lock()` succeeds, the application can retrieve a surface memory pointer and other necessary data and start accessing surface memory directly. Code can continue to access surface memory until a call to the `Unlock()` function is made. As soon as the surface is unlocked, the surface memory pointer becomes invalid. While the lock is in progress, applications cannot blit to or from surface memory. GDI functions fail when used on a locked surface.

Reading Locked Surface Data

When the `Lock()` call returns `DD_OK`, the application can access the corresponding members of the `DDSURFACEDESC2` structure variable passed in the call to obtain the data necessary for direct access. Assuming that application code knows the display mode and its corresponding pixel format, then the two data elements necessary for accessing the locked surface are its base address and its pitch. The surface address is returned in a structure member of type `LPVOID`, and the surface pitch is returned in a structure member of type `LONG`. Applications that plan to de-reference the surface pointer typically cast it into one that matches the surface's color format. For example, a program that has set a 24-bit true-color mode is likely to access surface memory in byte-size units. In this case the pointer can be cast into a variable of type

LPBYTE. On the other hand, an application executing in a 16-bit real-color mode typecasts the pointer into an LPWORD type, and one that has set a 32-bit true-color mode may typecast into an LPLONG data type.

The following code fragment shows the use of the Lock() function in a routine that fills a 50 by 50 pixel box in a 24-bit true-color video mode. The box is arbitrarily located at screen row number 80 and pixel column number 300. The pixels are filled with the red attribute by setting each third surface byte to 0xff and the other three color-bytes to 0x0.

```
LONG       localPitch;    // Local variable for surface pitch
LPBYTE     localStart;    // and for buffer start
LPBYTE     lastRow;       // Storage for row start
.
.
.
// Attempt to lock the surface for direct access
if (lpDDSPrimary->Lock(NULL, &ddsd, DDLOCK_WAIT, NULL)\
                       != DD_OK)
   return DDInitFailed(hWnd, hRet, "Lock() call failed");
// Store video system data
   vidPitch = ddsd.lPitch;        // Pitch
   vidStart = ddsd.lpSurface;     // Buffer address
// Surface is locked. Global video data is as follows:
// vidPitch holds surface pitch
// vidStart holds video buffer start
// Copy to local variables typecasting void pointer
   localPitch = vidPitch;
   localStart = (LPBYTE) vidStart;

// Index to row 80
   localStart = localStart + (80 * localPitch);
// Move right 300 pixels
   localStart += (400 * 3);
// Display 50 rows, 50 times
   for(int i = 0; i < 50; i++){
     lastRow = localStart;         // Save start of row
   for(int j = 0; j < 50; j++) {
     *localStart = 0x0;            // blue attribute
     localStart++;
     *localStart = 0x0;            // green attribute
     localStart++;
     *localStart = 0xff;           // red attribute
     localStart++;
   }
```

```
 localStart = lastRow + localPitch;
}

lpDDSPrimary->Unlock(NULL);
```

Low-level Coding for Direct Access

The maximum advantages of direct access to video memory are realized when the code is highly optimized: this means programming in 80 by 86 assembly language. Although an entire Windows application can be coded in assembly language, this approach usually entails more difficulties and complications than can be justified by the relatively few advantages. On the other hand, most C and C++ compilers provide in-line assemblers that allow embedding assembly language code in a C or C++ program. The result is an easy-to-produce multi-language program with the advantages of both environments.

An additional benefit of in-line assembly is that the assembly code can reference, by name, any C++ language variable or function that is in scope. This makes it easier to access data and processing routines than when the assembly language source is in a module that must be assembled and linked separately. In-line assembly avoids many of the complication and portability problems usually associated with parameter passing conventions in multi-language programming. The resulting development environment has all the advantages of high-level programming, as well as the power and flexibility of low-level code. A graphics programmer cannot ignore the potential of this language combination. Visual C++ and Borland C Builder both support in-line assembly.

The most frequent objection to assembly language programming is that it is difficult to learn and use. Pentium assembly language contains an instruction set of over one hundred opcodes, with operand forms and addressing modes that can appear arcane and enigmatic to a programmer unfamiliar with assembly-language constructs. Low-level languages are also incapable of performing many of the simple processing operations that we take for granted in high-level code; even decimal arithmetic becomes a chore. Although these complexities are undeniable, it is also true that they do not apply to using in-line assembly for developing simple graphics primitives. In this case the in-line approach makes the interface between C++ and assembly virtually transparent to the code. Furthermore, for simple graphics routines we need but a small subset of the available opcodes and we use mostly the simplest addressing modes. Finally, the advantages in control and performance are so great that they cannot be ignored.

Assembly language coding in Windows applications becomes an attractive option because of DirectDraw; it is the direct access to video memory made possible by DirectX that opens the possibility of using assembly language to maximize performance and control. In conventional GDI programming there is little justification for using low-level code.

The _asm Keyword

In Visual C++ the _asm keyword is used to produce assembly language instructions, one at a time or in blocks. Upon encountering the _asm symbol, the in-line assembler is invoked by the compiler and the resulting opcodes are inserted into the object file. In this process, the development system limits its action to that of an assembler program; no modification of the coding takes place and no interpretation or optimization effort is made. Thus, the programmer is certain that the resulting code is identical to the source. The fact that no separate assembly or linking is necessary considerably simplifies the development process.

Although the _asm keyword can precede a single instruction, it is more common to use it to generate a block of several assembly language lines. In this case braces delimit the source, as in the following simple example:

```
_asm
{
  ; Assembly language code follows:
    PUSH    EBX           ; EBX to stack
    MOV     EAX,vidPitch  ; vidPitch is a C variable
    MOV     EBX,80        ; Constant to register
    MUL     EBX           ; Integer multiply
    POP     EBX           ; Restore EBX
}
```

The second instruction of the preceding code fragment loads a variable defined in C++ code into a machine register. Accessing high-level language variables is one of the most convenient features of in-line assembly. By the same token, assembly language code can perform other manipulations and store results in high-level variables.

Coding Restrictions

There are a few rules and conventions that assembly language in-line code must follow. The most important one relates to preserving registers that are used by C++. The major source of problems is when the C++ program is compiled with the _fastcall switch or the /Gr compiler option. In these cases, arguments to functions are passed in the ECX and EDX machine registers; therefore, they must be preserved by the assembly-language program section. The easiest way to avoid this concern is to make sure that programs that use in-line assembly are not compiled with either of these options. In Visual C++, the compiler options can be examined by selecting the Settings command in the Project Menu and then clicking on the C/C++ tab. The Project Options window in this dialog box shows the compiler switches and options that are active. Make sure that you inspect the settings for both the Release and the Debug options, as shown in the "Settings For:" scroll box. Figure 10-3 is a screen dump of the Project Settings dialog box.

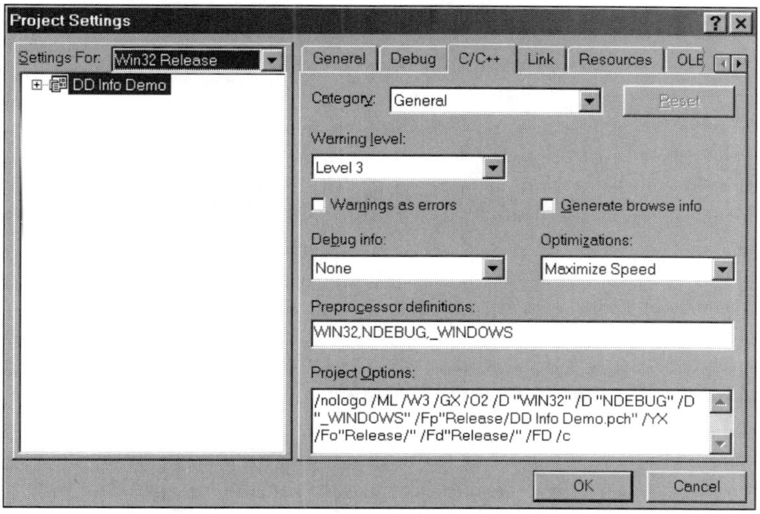

Figure 10-3: Inspecting compiler switches and options in the Project Settings dialog box

It has been consistently documented that programs that do not use the `_fastcall` switch or the /Gr compiler options can assume that the four general-purpose registers need not be preserved. Therefore, EAX, EBX, ECX, and EDX are free and available to the assembly-language code. In regards to the pointer registers and the direction flag, the Microsoft documentation is inconsistent. Some versions of the *Visual C++ Programmers Guide* state that ESI and EDI must be preserved, while other versions state the contrary. Regarding the direction flag, the original Microsoft C++ compilers required that the flag be cleared before returning, while the most recent manuals say that the state of the direction flag must be preserved. These newer documents also state that all other registers must be preserved.

In view of these discrepancies, and in fear of future variations, the safest approach is to use the general purpose registers freely (EAX, EBX, ECX, and EDX), but to preserve all other machine registers and the direction flag. This means that on entry to the routine, the in-line assembly code must push on the stack the registers that must be preserved, as well as the flags, and restore them before exiting the `_asm` block. This is the approach that we use in the book's sample code. The processing in a routine that uses the ESI and EDI registers could read as follows:

```
_asm
{
    PUSH     ESI          ; Save context
    PUSH     EDI
    PUSHF
    ; Processing operations go here
```

```
    ; .
    ; .
    ; .
    ; Exit code
    POPF                ; Restore context
    POP        EDI
    POP        ESI
}
```

Assembly-language Functions

Often the low-level processing routines can be conveniently located in functions that can be called by the C++ code. When the assembly code is not created by means of the online feature of the compiler, that is, when it is written for a separate assembler, then the assembly-language routine and the C++ must interface following the calling conventions adopted by the compiler. The usual procedure is that C++ places the parameters in the stack at the time the call is made, and the assembly-language routine removes them from the stack, making sure that the stack integrity is preserved. In this case, the assembly and the C++ code usually reside in separate files that are referenced at link time.

For applications that use in-line assembly, the inter-language protocol can be considerably simplified by creating a C++ function shell to hold the assembly code. In this case the use of the stack for parameter passing becomes unnecessary, because the assembly code can reference the C++ variables directly. One possible drawback is that the in-line assembler does not allow the use of the data definition directives `DB`, `DW`, `DD`, `DQ`, and `DT` or the `DUP` operator. Therefore, the data elements used by the assembly-language code must be defined as C++ variables. The following trivial example is an assembly-language routine to add three integers and return the sum to the calling code. The processing is contained in a C++ function shell, and reads as follows:

```
int SumOf3(int x, int y, int z)
  {
   int total;          // C++ variable to hold sum
    _asm
    {
    MOV     EAX,x          ; move first parameter to accumulator
    ADD     EAX,y          ; add second parameter
    ADD     EAX,z          ; and third parameter
    MOV     total,EAX      ; store sum
    }
   return total;
}
```

The calling code could read as follows:

```
int     aSum;           // local variable for sum
.
.
.
aSum = SumOf3(10, 20, 30);
```

This example shows that the assembly-language code can access the parameters passed to the C++ function, as well as store data in a local variable that is also accessible to C++. This easy mechanism for sharing data is one of the major advantages of the in-line assembler.

Developing Direct-access Primitives

An application that uses direct access to the video buffer can usually benefit from a few primitive functions that perform the core processing operations. Depending on performance requirements, these primitives can be coded in C++, or with in-line assembly. The primitive routines are mode-specific, and the code assumes that a particular display mode is available and has been selected. It is impossible to predict the specific functions and the number of primitives that are necessary for a particular graphics program. Among other factors, this depends on what portion of the processing is performed using direct access to video memory, and also on the size and scope of the application. The resulting complexity can range from a few simple routines to a full-size, stand-alone graphics package. In this section we consider the following several direct-access primitives that can be generally useful:

- Function to lock a DirectDraw primary surface and store the video buffer's base address and pitch
- Function to release a DirectDraw primary surface
- Function to set an individual screen pixel at given coordinates and color attributes and to read the attributes of a screen pixel located at given coordinates
- Function to lock a DirectDraw primary surface, fill a pixel rectangle, at given coordinates, dimensions, and color attributes, then release the surface
- Function to lock a DirectDraw primary surface, draw a single-line box at given coordinates, dimensions, and color attributes, then release the surface

Many of the routines that access video memory directly must perform calculations to determine the offset of a particular pixel in the display surface. For example, a call to fill a screen rectangle passes the address of its top-left corner as parameters. The processing must convert this address, often in column/row format, into a video memory offset. It is possible to develop a primitive function that calculates this pixel offset, but this approach introduces a call-return overhead that adversely affects performance. More often, the address calculations are part of the processing routine. Therefore, before attempting to develop the direct-access primitives, we take a closer look at the operations necessary for calculating pixel addresses.

Pixel-address Calculations

A display mode's resolution, color depth, and pitch determine the location of each pixel on the surface. Therefore, pixel address calculations are specific to a display mode. In the case of the hi-color modes, the variables that enter into the calculation of a pixel offset are the number of bytes per pixel and the surface pitch. In addition, the horizontal and vertical resolution of the display mode can be used to check for invalid input values, because it is the responsibility of direct-access routines not to read or write outside of the locked surface area. Figure 10-4 shows the parameters that define the location of a screen pixel and the formula used for calculating its offset.

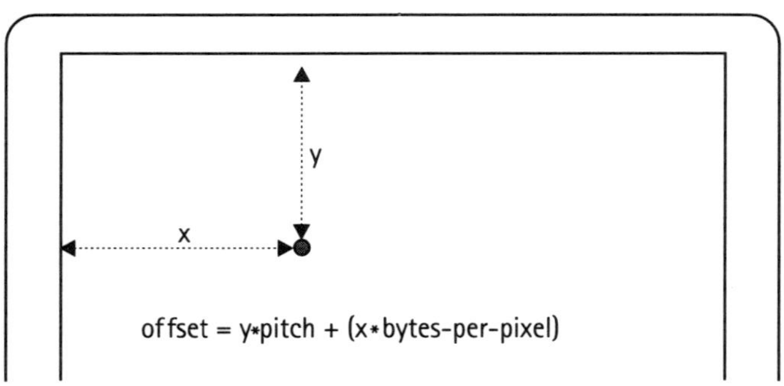

Figure 10-4: Pixel-offset calculation

Direct-access Lock Function

The DirectDraw `Lock()` function is used to lock the surface so that it can be accessed directly. The call also returns a pointer to the top-left corner of the rectangle that defines the surface, as well as its pitch. In the case of a primary surface, when the entire area is requested, `Lock()` returns the base address of the video buffer. The pitch in this case is the number of bytes in each screen buffer row.

Another essential effect of the `Lock()` call is that Windows relaxes its normal protection over video display memory. If a successful `Lock()` call has not been previously made, any instruction that attempts to access video memory immediately generates a protection violation exception and the application is summarily terminated. This is important to keep in mind while designing direct-access functions because it is this feature that makes the `Lock()` call necessary if a previous `Lock()` has been released. This is true even when the video buffer address and pitch have been previously obtained and stored. On the other hand, the surface lock can be retained during more than one access to video memory. This means that a routine that sequentially sets several screen pixels need only call the `Lock()` function once. Once the pixel sequence is set, then the lock can be released. Also recall that the `Lock()` call requires a pointer to an `IDirectDrawSurface4` object, which is usually obtained by a call to the `CreateSurface()` function. The following is a simple locking function for the entire primary surface:

```
// Global variables for surface pitch and base address
LONG        vidPitch;
LPVOID    vidStart;
   .
   .
   .
//*******************************************************
// Name: LockSurface
// Desc: Function to lock the entire DirectDraw primary
//       surface and store the direct access parameters
//
// PRE CONDITIONS:
// 1. First parameter is a pointer to DirectDraw surface
// 2. Video display globals have been declared as follows:
//    LONG    vidPitch; // Pitch
//    LPVOID  vidStart; // Buffer address
//
// POST CONDITIONS:
// Returns 1 if call succeeds and 0 if it fails
//*******************************************************
int LockSurface(LPDIRECTDRAWSURFACE4  lpSurface)
{
    // Attempt to lock the surface for direct access
       if (lpSurface->Lock(NULL, &ddsd, DDLOCK_WAIT, NULL)\
                            != DD_OK)
       return 0;                      // Lock failed
    // Store video system data
       vidPitch = ddsd.lPitch;        // Pitch
       vidStart = ddsd.lpSurface;     // Buffer address
       return 1;                      // Surface locked
}
```

Direct-access Release Function

A function to release the locked surface is also necessary. In this case the processing is quite simple. In addition to the call to the `Unlock()` function, the code resets the access variables to zero. This makes it easier to determine if a lock is being held, because a zero value is invalid for either variable. The routine itself tests one of these variables before attempting to release the lock:

```
//***************************************************************
// Name: ReleaseSurface
// Desc: Function to release locked surface
// PRE CONDITIONS:
// 1. Parameter is pointer to locked DirectDraw surface
// 2. Video display globals as follows:
//    LONG   vidPitch;   // Pitch
//    LPVOID  vidStart;  // Buffer address
//***************************************************************
void ReleaseSurface(LPDIRECTDRAWSURFACE4  lpSurface)
{
   if(vidStart != 0) {
        lpSurface->Unlock(NULL);
        // Clear global variables
        vidPitch = 0;
        vidStart = 0;
   }
   return;
}
```

This version of the `ReleaseSurface()` function assumes that the object of the lock was the entire surface.

Direct-access Pixel-level Functions

Pixel-level operations are the lowest-level graphics routines available, to the point that they are sometimes considered device-driver components rather than primitives. Using pixel read and pixel write routines, it is possible to construct any graphics routine desired. In Chapter 6 we described GDI functions to set and read a single pixel. The objection to the GDI pixel-level functions is that they are extremely slow. A drawing operation that repeatedly calls GDI `SetPixel()` or `ReadPixel()` functions is likely to execute at an unacceptably slow speed. However, direct-access pixel-level routines execute several hundred times faster than the GDI counterparts. This determines that in some cases, a routine based on direct-access pixel-level primitives may show satisfactory performance. The code for the pixel-level read and write primitives reads as follows:

```
// Global variables for surface pitch and base address
LONG        vidPitch;
LPVOID    vidStart;
   .
   .
   .
//****************************************************************
// Name: DASetPixel
// Desc: Assembly language code to set a single screen pixel
//       using direct access to the video buffer
//
// PRE CONDITIONS:
// 1. Successful Lock() of surface
//    Video display globals are stored as follows:
//    LONG    vidPitch;    // Pitch
//    LPVOID    vidStart;    // Buffer address
// 2. First and second parameters are the pixel coordinates
// 3. Last three parameters are pixel RGB attributes
// 4. Assumes true color mode 640 by 480 by 28
//
// POST CONDITIONS:
// None
//****************************************************************
void DASetPixel( int xCoord, int yCoord,
              BYTE redAtt, BYTE greenAtt, BYTE blueAtt)
{
    _asm
     {
    PUSH   ESI                  ; Save context
    PUSHF
    MOV    EAX,yCoord           ; Row number to EAX
    MUL    vidPitch;
    MOV    EBX,EAX              ; Store in EBX
    MOV    EAX,xCoord           ; x coordinate
    MOV    CX,3
    MUL    CX                   ; 3 bytes per pixel
    ADD    EAX,EBX              ; move right to x coordinate
    MOV    ESI,vidStart
    ADD    ESI,EAX
  ; Load color attributes into registers
    MOV    AL,blueAtt
    MOV    DH,greenAtt
    MOV    DL,redAtt
  ; Set the pixel
```

```
    MOV    [ESI],AL        ; Set blue attribute
    INC    ESI
    MOV    [ESI],DH        ; Set green
    INC    ESI
    MOV    [ESI],DL        ; Set red
    POPF                   ; Restore context
    POP    ESI
    }
  return;
}
//*************************************************************
// Name: DAReadPixel
// Desc: Assembly language code to read a single screen pixel
//       using direct access to the video buffer
//
// PRE CONDITIONS:
// 1. Successful Lock() of surface
//    Video display globals are stored as follows:
//    LONG    vidPitch;    // Pitch
//    LPVOID    vidStart;    // Buffer address
// 2. First and second parameters are the pixel coordinates
//    values are returned in public variables named
//    pixelRed, pixelGreen, and pixelBlue
// 3. Assumes true color mode 640 by 480 by 28
//
// POST CONDITIONS:
//    None
//*************************************************************
void DAReadPixel( int xCoord, int yCoord)
{
    _asm
    {
    PUSH    ESI            ; Save context
    PUSHF
    MOV    EAX,yCoord     ; Row number to EAX
    MUL    vidPitch
    MOV    EBX,EAX        ; Store in EBX
    MOV    EAX,xCoord     ; x coordinate
    MOV    CX,3
    MUL    CX             ; 3 bytes per pixel
    ADD    EAX,EBX        ; move right to x coordinate
    MOV    ESI,vidStart
    ADD    ESI,EAX
   ; Read and store pixel attributes
```

```
    MOV     AL,[ESI]          ; Get blue attribute
    INC     ESI
    MOV     DH,[ESI]          ; green
    INC     ESI
    MOV     DL,[ESI]          ; and red
    MOV     pixelBlue,AL      ; Store blue
    MOV     pixelGreen,DH     ; green
    MOV     pixelRed,DL       ; and red
    POPF                      ; Restore context
    POP     ESI
    }
  return;
}
```

Rectangle-fill Function

Filling rectangular areas with a particular color attribute is such a useful manipulation that most applications that access memory directly can profit from such a primitive. To define a screen rectangle you can use the coordinates of its diagonally opposite corners, or the coordinates of one corner and the rectangle's dimensions. The following listed function adopts the second approach. The routine also needs to know the values for the RGB color attributes to use in the fill. The code reads as follows:

```
//*************************************************************
// Name: DARectangle
// Desc: Assembly language code to draw a rectangle on the
// screen using direct access to the video buffer
//
// PRE CONDITIONS:
// 1. First parameter is pointer to surface
// 2. Second and third parameters are rectangle's x and y
//    coordinates
// 3. Fourth parameter is rectangle width, in pixels
// 4. Fifth parameter is rectangle height, in pixels
// 5. Last three parameters are RGB attributes
// 6. Assumes true color mode is 640 by 480 by 24
// POST CONDITIONS:
// Returns 1 if lock succeeded and 0 if it failed
//*************************************************************
int DARectangle(LPDIRECTDRAWSURFACE4 lpPrimary,
     int yCoord, int xCoord,
     int width, int height,
     BYTE redAtt, BYTE greenAtt, BYTE blueAtt)
{
```

```
// Attempt to lock the surface for direct access
if (!LockSurface(lpPrimary))
      return 0;                    // Lock failed

_asm
{
      PUSH     ESI              ; Save context
      PUSHF
      MOV      EAX,yCoord       ; Row number to EAX
      MUL      vidPitch;
      MOV      EBX,EAX          ; Store in EBX
      MOV      EAX,xCoord       ; x coordinate
      MOV      CX,3
      MUL      CX               ; 3 bytes per pixel
      ADD      EAX,EBX          ; move right to x coordinate
      MOV      ESI,vidStart
      ADD      ESI,EAX
      ; Load color attributes into registers
      MOV      AL,blueAtt
      MOV      DH,greenAtt
      MOV      DL,redAtt
      MOV      EBX,height      ; number of lines in rectangle
NEXT_LINE:
      PUSH     ESI             ; Save start of line
      MOV      ECX,width       ; x dimension of rectangle
SET_PIX:
      MOV      [ESI],AL        ; Set blue attribute
      INC      ESI             ; Next pixel
      MOV      [ESI],DH        ; Set green
      INC      ESI             ; Next pixel
      MOV      [ESI],DL        ; Set red
      INC      ESI             ; Next pixel
      LOOP     SET_PIX
    ; Pixel line is set
      POP      ESI
      ADD      ESI,vidPitch
      DEC      EBX
      JNZ      NEXT_LINE
      POPF                    ; Restore context
      POP      ESI
  }
ReleaseSurface(lpPrimary);
return 1;      // Exit
}
```

Observe that the DARectangle() calls the LockSurface() and ReleaseSurface() functions previously developed. Alternatively, the function could be easily modified to call Lock() and Unlock() directly.

Box-drawing Function

Drawing a box is a little more difficult than filling a rectangle. The actual processing can be based on two simple routines: one to draw a horizontal line and another one to draw a vertical line. The core routine sets up the machine registers with the necessary data and then calls the horizontal and vertical line routines to do the actual drawing. You would probably find other uses for the vertical and horizontal line-drawing functions. The parameters to the box drawing routine are the same as those for the rectangle fill. They include the pointer to the surface, the box coordinates, its dimensions, and the color attributes. The code reads as follows:

```
//***********************************************************
// Name: DABox
// Desc: Assembly language code to draw a screen box with
//       single-pixel wide lines, using direct access to the
//       video buffer
//
// PRE CONDITIONS:
// 1. First parameter is pointer to surface
// 2. Second and third parameters are the coordinates of the
//    top-left corner of the box
// 3. Fourth parameter is box width, in pixels
// 4. Fifth parameter is box height, in pixels
// 5. Last three parameters are RGB attributes
// 6. True color mode is 640 by 480 by 24
//
// POST CONDITIONS:
// Returns 1 if lock succeeds and 0 if it fails
//***********************************************************
int DABox(LPDIRECTDRAWSURFACE4 lpPrimary,
      int xCoord, int yCoord,
      int width, int height,
      BYTE redAtt, BYTE greenAtt, BYTE blueAtt)
{
  // Attempt to lock the surface for direct access
  if (!LockSurface(lpPrimary))
        return 0;                   // Lock failed

  _asm
  {
```

```
PUSH    ESI             ; Save context
PUSHF
MOV     EAX,yCoord      ; Row number to EAX
MUL     vidPitch;
MOV     EBX,EAX         ; Store in EBX
MOV     EAX,xCoord      ; x coordinate
MOV     CX,3
MUL     CX              ; 3 bytes per pixel
ADD     EAX,EBX         ; move right to x coordinate
MOV     ESI,vidStart
ADD     ESI,EAX
; Load color attributes into registers
MOV     AL,blueAtt
MOV     DH,greenAtt
MOV     DL,redAtt
; Draw top horizontal line
MOV     ECX,width        ; x dimension of rectangle
CALL    DAHorLine
; Draw bottom horizontal line
PUSH    ESI              ; Save top left corner address
PUSH    EAX              ; Save color
PUSH    EDX
MOV     EAX,height       ; Number of lines to EAX
MUL     vidPitch;        ; Times the length of each line
ADD     ESI,EAX          ; Add to start
MOV     ECX,width        ; x dimension of rectangle
POP     EDX              ; Restore color
POP     EAX
CALL    DAHorLine        ; Draw line
POP     ESI              ; Restore start of rectangle
; Draw left vertical line
MOV     EBX,vidPitch     ; Pitch to EBX
MOV     ECX,height       ; Pixel height of vertical line
CALL    DAVerLine
; Draw right vertical line
; ESI holds address of top-left corner
PUSH    EAX              ; Save color
PUSH    EDX
MOV     EAX,width        ; Number of lines to EAX
MOV     CX,3             ; Pixels per line
MUL     CX
ADD     ESI,EAX          ; Add to start
MOV     ECX,height       ; Line y dimensions
INC     ECX              ; One more pixel
POP     EDX              ; Restore color
```

```
    POP     EAX
    CALL    DAVerLine       ; Draw line
    POPF                    ; Restore context
    POP     ESI
    }
    ReleaseSurface(lpPrimary);
  return 1;                // Exit
}

//***************************************************************
// Name: DAHorLine
// Desc: Assembly language support function for DABox()
//             draws a horizontal pixel line
// PRE CONDITIONS:
//    ESI holds buffer address of start of line
//    ECX hold pixel length of line
//    AL = blue attribute
//    DH = green attribute
//    DL = red attribute
// POST CONDITIONS:
//    ECX is destroyed
//    All others are preserved
//***************************************************************
void DAHorLine()
{
    _asm
    {
    PUSH     ESI             ; Save start of line
DRAW_HLINE:
    MOV     [ESI],AL         ; Set blue attribute
    INC     ESI
    MOV     [ESI],DH         ; Set green
    INC     ESI
    MOV     [ESI],DL         ; Set red
    INC     ESI
    LOOP    DRAW_HLINE
    POP     ESI
    }
    return;
}

//***************************************************************
// Name: DAVerLine
// Desc: Assembly language support function for DABox()
//      draws a vertical pixel line
```

```
// PRE CONDITIONS:
//    ESI holds buffer address of start of line
//    ECX hold pixel height of line
//    EBX holds surface pitch
//    AL = blue attribute
//    DH = green attribute
//    DL = red attribute
// POST CONDITIONS:
//    ECX is destroyed
//    All others are preserved
//***************************************************************
void DAVerLine()
{
    _asm
    {
    PUSH     ESI              ; Save start of line
DRAW_VLINE:
    PUSH     ESI              ; Save start address
    MOV      [ESI],AL         ; Set blue attribute
    INC      ESI
    MOV      [ESI],DH         ; Set green
    INC      ESI
    MOV      [ESI],DL         ; Set red
    POP      ESI              ; Restore start
    ADD      ESI,EBX          ; Index to next line
    LOOP     DRAW_VLINE
    POP      ESI
    }
  return;
}
```

Raster Operations in Direct Access

Direct access to video memory, combined with low-level coding, provides the programmer with a powerful graphics toolkit. One of the many possibilities consists of using logical operations to combine object and screen data. These are sometimes called *raster operations*, raster ops, or mixes. A raster operation determines how two or more source images are combined to produce a destination image. Arithmetic and logical operators are used to produce the desired effect. The simplest operation is to replace the destination with the source. This is what takes place when we write a pixel value to the video screen, as in the preceding examples. When we use a MOV instruction to write a color value to the screen, we are actually replacing the destination with the source. The simplest way to replace the destination with the source pixel is as follows:

```
MOV    [ESI],AL
```

In many cases, a raster operation requires a read-modify-write sequence. For example, we could increase the brightness of a pixel value by adding a constant to its value:

```
MOV    AL,[ESI]        ; Read pixel
ADD    AL,20           ; Modify
MOV    [ESI],AL        ; Write
```

The problem with this type of processing is that the read-modify-write cycle takes considerable processing time. For this reason, some graphics processors perform raster operations in hardware.

Nevertheless, the Pentium CPU has several logical operators that enable you to combine foreground and background data by means of a single instruction. For example, a logical `AND` operation can be used to combine foreground bits (object data) and background data. The result is that the background bits are preserved whenever the foreground bit is zero, and vice versa. The object data is sometimes referred to as a mask. For example, a graphics application can overlay a white grid over an existing image by ANDing a mask consisting of 1-bits in the solid portion of the grid and of 0-bits in the transparent portion. The Pentium contains opcodes for `AND`, `OR`, `XOR`, and `NOT` operations. For example, the following operation ANDs the value in the AL register with the screen data contained in the address pointed at by ESI:

```
AND    [ESI],AL
```

In C++ programming, the bitwise operators perform a similar action. In the following sections, we examine the `XOR` mix, which is one of the most popular raster operations in graphics programming.

XOR Animation

Animating a screen object often requires that its image be erased from the current screen position before being redrawn at its new location. Graphics programmers sometimes call this sequence the *save-draw-redraw* cycle. If the object is not erased before it is redrawn, its apparent movement leaves an undesirable image track on the display surface. We can make an object appear to move laterally, left to right, by progressively redrawing and erasing its screen image at consecutively larger *x* coordinates. To do this in a conventional manner we have to perform a rather complex sequence of operations:

1. Preserve the screen image data in the area where the object is to be displayed.
2. Draw the object.
3. Erase the object by restoring the original screen image.

Step 1 requires that you read all data in the screen area that is to be occupied by the animated object, while Step 3 requires you to redisplay the saved image. Both operations are time consuming, and in computer animation, time is always in short supply.

Several hardware and software techniques have been devised for performing the save-draw-redraw cycle. In later chapters, we explore DirectDraw animation techniques that are powerful and versatile. These methods are based on flipping surfaces containing images and on taking advantage of the hardware blitters that are available in most video cards. Right now we are concerned with the simplest possible approach to figure animation. This technique, which is made feasible by the high performance obtained with direct-access-to-video memory, is based on the properties of the logical exclusive, or `XOR`, operation. Although it is theoretically possible to perform `XOR` animation using high-level code, the most efficient and powerful technique requires assembly language.

The action of the logical `XOR` can be described by saying that a bit in the result is set if both operands contain opposite values. It follows that XORing the same value twice restores the original contents, as in the following case:

```
             10000001 <= original value  —|
XOR value => 10110011                      |
             ———-                         |
             00110010  <= first result     |
XOR value => 10110011                      |
             ———-                         |
             10000001  <= final result  ——|
```

`XOR`, like all bitwise operations, takes place on a bit-by-bit basis. In this example, the final result (10000001) is the same as the original value.

Animation techniques can be based on this property of the bitwise `XOR` because it provides a convenient and fast way for consecutively drawing and erasing a screen object. The object is drawn on the screen by XORing it with the background data. XORing a second time erases the object and restores the original background. Therefore, the save-draw-redraw cycle now becomes an XOR-XOR cycle, which is considerably faster and simpler to implement. The `XOR` method is particularly useful when more than one animated object can coincide on the same screen position, because it ensures that the original screen image is automatically preserved.

There are disadvantages to using XOR in computer animation. Most importantly, the resulting image changes according to the background. This is due to the fact that each individual pixel in the object is determined both by the XORed value and by the destination pixel. For example, the following XOR operation produces a red object (in RGB format) on a bright, white screen background:

```
               R G B
background =>  1 1 1  ( white)
 XOR value =>  0 1 1
               ----
    result =>  1 0 0  ( red )
```

However, if the same XOR operation is applied over a black background the results are as follows:

```
               R G B
background =>  0 0 0  ( black )
 XOR value =>  0 1 1
               ----
    result =>  0 1 1  ( cyan )
```

This property of the XOR operation, which makes the object's color change as it moves over different backgrounds, can be both an advantage or a disadvantage. For example, an object displayed by conventional methods can disappear as it moves over a background of its same color, while if this object is XORed onto the screen, it remains visible over most backgrounds. On the other hand, it may happen that the color of a graphics object is an important characteristic. In this case the changes brought about by XOR display operations may not be acceptable. Figure 10-5 shows how the XOR operation changes the attributes of an object (circle) as it is displayed over different backgrounds.

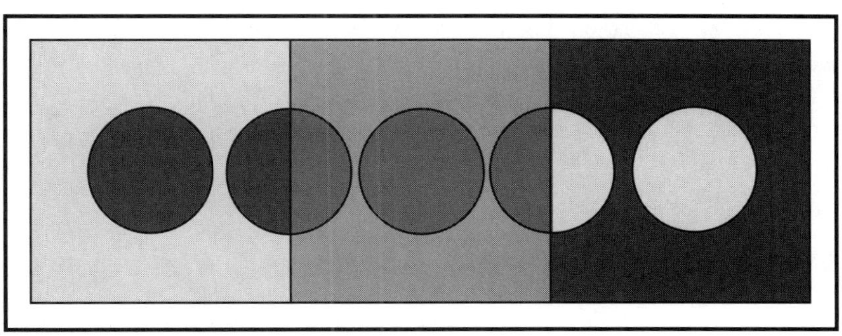

Figure 10-5: Effect of XOR operation on figure color

XORing a Bitmap

One of the many possible uses of the XOR raster operation is to project a bitmap over an existing background. The graphics programmer can take advantage of the automatic draw-erase action of the XOR function to animate cursors and small sprites with minimal processing. The main drawback has already been mentioned: that the object's color is partially determined by the background color. The following function XORs a variable-size bitmap onto the video display, at any desired screen location. The function assumes a true-color display mode in 640 by 480 by 24 format.

```
// Cross-shaped bitmap for demonstrating the DAXorBitmap()
// function
// 2 by 8 Bitmap      0    1    2    3    4    5    6    7
BYTE mapData[] = { 0x00,0x00,0x00,0x7f,0x7f,0x00,0x00,0x00,
                   0x00,0x00,0x00,0x7f,0x7f,0x00,0x00,0x00,
                   0x00,0x00,0x00,0x7f,0x7f,0x00,0x00,0x00,
                   0x7f,0x7f,0x7f,0x7f,0x7f,0x7f,0x7f,0x7f,
                   0x7f,0x7f,0x7f,0x7f,0x7f,0x7f,0x7f,0x7f,
                   0x00,0x00,0x00,0x7f,0x7f,0x00,0x00,0x00,
                   0x00,0x00,0x00,0x7f,0x7f,0x00,0x00,0x00,
                   0x00,0x00,0x00,0x7f,0x7f,0x00,0x00,0x00};
         .
         .
         .
//**************************************************************
// Name: DAXorBitmap
// Desc: Assembly language code to XOR a bitmap onto the
/        screen using direct access to the video buffer
//
// PRE CONDITIONS:
// 1. First parameter is pointer to surface
// 2. Second and third parameters are x and y screen
//    coordinates
// 3. Fourth parameter is bitmap width, in pixels
// 4. Fifth parameter is bitmap height, in pixels
// 5. Sixth parameter is pointer to bitmap
// 6. Assumes true-color mode 640 by 480 by 28
//
// POST CONDITIONS:
// Returns 1 if call succeeds and 0 if it fails
//**************************************************************
int DAXorBitmap(LPDIRECTDRAWSURFACE4 lpPrimary,
                int xCoord, int yCoord,
                int bmWidth, int bmHeight,
```

```
              LPBYTE bitMapPtr)
{
    // Attempt to lock the surface for direct access
    if (!LockSurface(lpPrimary))
        return 0;                       // Lock failed

    _asm
    {
    PUSH    ESI                 ; Save context
    PUSH    EDI
    PUSHF
    MOV     EAX,yCoord          ; Row number to EAX
    MUL     vidPitch;
    MOV     EBX,EAX             ; Store in EBX
    MOV     EAX,xCoord          ; x coordinate
    MOV     CX,3
    MUL     CX                  ; 3 bytes per pixel
    ADD     EAX,EBX             ; move right to x-coordinate
    MOV     EDI,vidStart
    ADD     EDI,EAX
    MOV     ESI,bitMapPtr       ; Pointer to bitmap
    MOV     EBX,bmHeight        ; number of lines in bitmap
NEXT_BM_LINE:
    PUSH    EDI                 ; Save start of line
    MOV     ECX,bmWidth         ; x-dimension of bitmap
XOR_PIX_LINE:
    MOV     AL,[ESI]            ; Bitmap data to AL
    XOR     [EDI],AL            ; Set blue attribute
    INC     EDI
    XOR     [EDI],AL            ; Set green
    INC     EDI
    XOR     [EDI],AL            ; Set red
    INC     EDI
    INC     ESI                 ; Bitmap pointer to next byte
    LOOP    XOR_PIX_LINE
; End of line
    POP     EDI                 ; Pointer to start of line
    ADD     EDI,vidPitch        ; Index to next line
    DEC     EBX                 ; EBX is Lines counter
    JNZ     NEXT_BM_LINE
    ; Done!
    POPF                        ; Restore context
    POP     EDI
    POP     ESI
   }
```

```
    ReleaseSurface(lpPrimary);
    return 1;                          // Exit
}
```

In this function, a single bitmap attribute is XORed with all three background colors. This keeps the bitmap small but limits the range of possible results. It would be quite easy to modify the routine so that the bitmap contains a byte value for each color attribute.

DirectDraw Access Demo Project

The program named DD_Access.cpp, located in the *DD Access Demo* project folder of the book's CD-ROM, is a demonstration of the direct-access techniques discussed in this chapter. The program contains all the functions listed in this chapter, plus some other ones not mentioned in the text. It executes in exclusive, full-screen display mode. The text messages are displayed using GDI graphics and the geometrical figures using the direct-access functions developed in this chapter. Figure 10-6 is a screen snapshot of the demo program. The labels list the program functions that perform the corresponding operations.

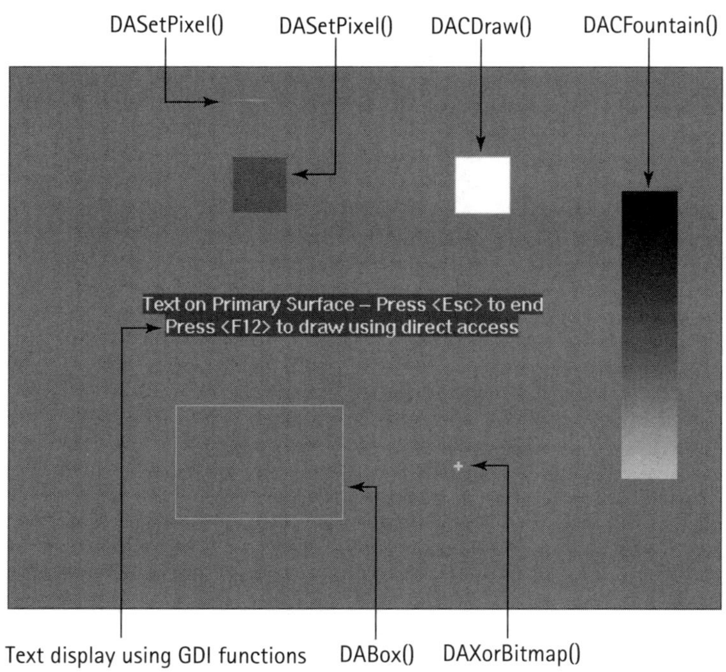

Figure 10-6: Screen dump of the DD Access Demo project program

Summary

In this chapter, you have learned how to gain direct access to the video buffer using the facilities provided by DirectX 6. Direct access methods give the Windows programmer a level of control and the advantages of high-performance coding that have been characteristic of DOS graphics. At the same time, direct access techniques in Windows have greater coding facilities and operating system support. In the case of Windows programming, the main disadvantages are that direct access is more difficult and that it introduces device-dependency concerns. Whether to use direct access, and if so, how much to use, are questions that must be answered in the context of each particular application. Fortunately, conventional Windows graphics and direct access techniques can be combined in DirectDraw applications that execute in exclusive mode.

In the following chapter we look at off-screen surfaces and bitblt operations in DirectDraw. These are the fundamental mechanisms that support the fast manipulation of graphics images, one of the most important advantages of DirectDraw.

Chapter 11

Rendering Operations

IN THIS CHAPTER

- Surfaces are revisited in greater detail
- Image transparency and color key operations
- The DirectDraw blits: `BltFast()` and `Blt()`
- Blit-time transformations: color fills, scaling, mirroring, and raster operations
- Rendering bitmaps
- Coding DirectDraw windowed applications, including DirectDraw windowed mode rendering by clipping and by blit-time scaling

TO RENDER IS TO REPRESENT, transform, or express graphically. This concept encompasses most of the manipulations and display operations of graphics programming. In this chapter, we discuss the DirectDraw proprietary operations used in the static transformation and display of bitmapped images. We exclude the manipulations related to animation, which is the topic of Chapter 12.

The fundamental rendering operation is the *blit*, which we first encountered in Chapter 8 as a GDI function. DirectDraw provides its own versions of the blit, in the form of two functions named `Blt()` and `BltFast()`. A third variation, called `BltBatch()`, has been announced for future versions of the DirectX SDK. Another rendering operation is the *overlay*. As the name implies, overlays are like a drawing on transparent media, which can be placed over an image and then removed, restoring the original. The overlay technique simplifies many graphics-rendering operations. Unfortunately, overlays are currently supported by few video cards, and those that implement it do so inconsistently. For this reason, we do not discuss overlays in this book.

Surfaces Revisited

Before beginning the discussion of DirectDraw blits, we must expand some of the notions related to DirectDraw surfaces, first presented in Chapter 9. The following are the fundamental concepts introduced in this section:

- Surface operations
- Primary and off-screen surfaces
- Enumerating surfaces
- Loosing and restoring surfaces
- Experimenting with surfaces

Surface Operations

In Chapter 9, we defined a DirectDraw surface as a linear area of video memory most frequently used to hold image data. We also saw that a `DirectDrawSurface` is a COM object in itself—with its own interface—and that this interface is referenced in all surface-related operations. Applications create a DirectDraw surface by calling the `CreateSurface()` function. If the call is successful, it returns a pointer to the surface. In DirectX 6, this pointer is of type `LPDIRECTDRAWSURFACE4`. It is this pointer that is used in calling the functions of the `IDirectDrawSurface4` interface. Table 11-1 lists these functions.

Table 11-1 SURFACE-RELATED FUNCTIONS IN DIRECTDRAW

Type or Topic	Function Name
Allocating memory	`Initialize()`
	`IsLost()`
	`Restore()`
Attaching surfaces	`AddAttachedSurface()`
	`DeleteAttachedSurface()`
	`EnumAttachedSurfaces()`
	`GetAttachedSurface()`

Type or Topic	Function Name
Blitting	`Blt()`
	`BltBatch()` (not implemented in DirectX 6)
	`BltFast()`
	`GetBltStatus()`
Color keys	`GetColorKey()`
	`SetColorKey()`
Device contexts	`GetDC()`
	`ReleaseDC()`
Flipping	`Flip()`
	`GetFlipStatus()`
Locking surfaces	`Lock()`
	`PageLock()`
	`PageUnlock()`
	`Unlock()`
Overlays	`AddOverlayDirtyRect()`
	`EnumOverlayZOrders()`
	`GetOverlayPosition()`
	`SetOverlayPosition()`
	`UpdateOverlay()`
	`UpdateOverlayDisplay()`
	`UpdateOverlayZOrder()`
Private data	`FreePrivateData()`
	`GetPrivateData()`
	`SetPrivateData()`
Capabilities	`GetCaps()`
Clipper	`GetClipper()`
	`SetClipper()`

Continued

TABLE 11-1 SURFACE-RELATED FUNCTIONS IN DIRECTDRAW *(Continued)*

Type or Topic	Function Name
Characteristics	`ChangeUniquenessValue()`
	`GetPixelFormat()`
	`GetSurfaceDesc()`
	`GetUniquenessValue()`
	`SetSurfaceDesc()`
Miscellaneous	`GetDDInterface()`

Primary and Off-screen Surfaces

DirectDraw first attempts to create a surface in local video memory. If there is not enough video memory available to hold the surface, then DirectDraw tries to use non-local video memory, and finally it creates the surface in system memory if no better option is available. Code can also explicitly request that a surface be created in a certain type of memory by including the appropriate flags in the `CreateSurface()` call.

The primary surface is the one visible on the monitor. It is identified by the `DDSCAPS_PRIMARYSURFACE` flag. There can be only one primary surface for each DirectDraw object. The size and pixel format of the primary surface matches the current display mode. Therefore, the surface dimensions, mode, or pixel depth are not specified in the `CreateSurface()` call for a primary surface. In fact, the call fails if these dimensions are entered, even if they match those of the display mode.

Off-screen surfaces are often used to store bitmaps, cursors, sprites, and other digital imagery. Off-screen surfaces can reside in video memory or in system memory. In order for off-screen surfaces to exist in video memory, the total memory on the card must exceed the memory mapped to the video display. For example, a video card with 2MB of video memory (2,097,152 bytes), which is executing in 640 by 480 by 24 mode, requires 921,600 bytes for storing the displayed image (assuming that there are no unused areas in the pixel mapping). In this case, there are 1,175,552 bytes of memory left on the video card that can be used as off-screen memory.

A common type of off-screen surface, called a *back buffer*, can be created if the amount of free video memory is sufficient to store a second displayable image. As in the previous case, it is possible to create one back buffer since the display area requires 921,600 bytes, and there are 1,175,552 bytes of additional video memory available on the card. Back buffers are frequently used in animation, the subject of Chapter 12.

Off-screen surfaces are created with the `CreateSurface()` function. In this case, the call needs to specify the surface dimensions, which means that it must include the `DDSD_WIDTH` and `DDSD_HEIGHT` flags. The corresponding values must have been previously entered in the dwWidth and dwHeight members of the DDSURFACEDESC2 structure. In addition, the call must include the DDSCAPS_OFFSCREENPLAIN flag in the DDSCAPS2 structure. If possible, DirectDraw creates a surface in display memory. If there is not enough video memory available, it creates the surface in system memory. Code can explicitly choose display or system memory by including the DDSCAPS_SYSTEMMEMORY or DDSCAPS_VIDEOMEMORY flags in the dwCaps member of the DDSCAPS2 structure. The call fails, returning an error, if DirectDraw cannot create the surface in the specified location. Figure 11-1 shows different types of DirectDraw surfaces.

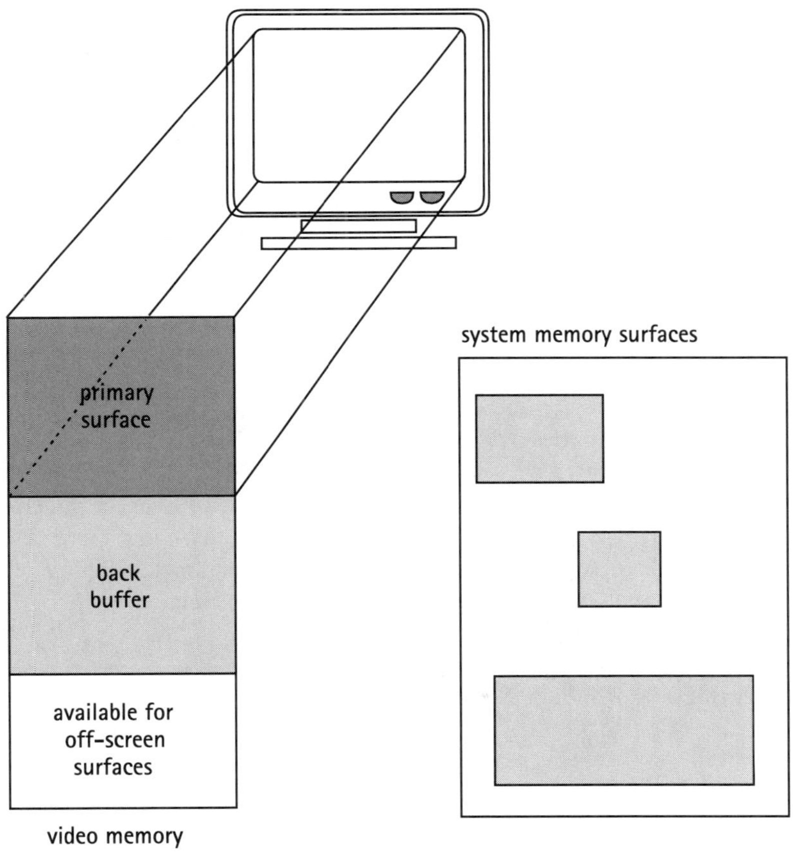

Figure 11-1: Types of DirectDraw surfaces

A surface is lost when the display mode is changed or when another application receives exclusive mode. The Restore() function can be used to recreate lost surfaces and reconnect them to their DirectDrawSurface object. Applications using the IDirectDraw4 interface can restore all lost surfaces by calling the RestoreAllSurfaces() function. Note that restoring a surface does not reload bitmaps that may have existed before the surface was lost. It is up to the application to reconstitute the graphics on the surfaces.

When a surface is no longer needed, it should be released by calling the `Release()` function. Each surface must be explicitly released, since there is no call to release all surfaces.

Enumerating Surfaces

A typical DirectDraw application operates on several surfaces during its execution. In these manipulations, an application often needs to know if a surface can be created that matches certain characteristics. On other occasions, the application may need a list of the existing surfaces and their properties. The `IDirectDraw4 EnumSurfaces()` function is used to enumerate surfaces, similar to the way in which `EnumDisplayModes()` (discussed in Chapter 9) is used in regards to display modes. The function's general form reads as follows:

```
HRESULT EnumSurfaces(
            DWORD dwFlags,                                          // 1
            LPDDSURFACEDESC lpDDSD,                                 // 2
            LPVOID lpContext,                                       // 3
            LPDDENUMSURFACESCALLBACK lpEnumSurfacesCallback         // 4
           );
```

The first parameter is a combination of one search-type flag and one matching flag. The search-type flag determines how the method searches for surfaces. Code can search for surfaces that are created by using the description in the second parameter or it can search for existing surfaces that already match that description. The matching flag determines whether the method enumerates all surfaces, those that match, or those that do not match the description specified in the second parameter. Table 11-2 lists the search and matching flags used in the `EnumSurfaces()` function.

Table 11-2 FLAGS USED IN THE EnumSurfaces() FUNCTION

Flag	Function Name
Search-type Flags	
DDENUMSURFACES_CANBECREATED	Enumerates the first surface that can be created and that meets the specifications in the second parameter. This flag can only be used with the DDENUMSURFACES_MATCH flag.
DDENUMSURFACES_DOESEXIST	Enumerates the already existing surfaces that meet the specification in the second parameter.

Flag	Function Name
Matching-type Flags	
DDENUMSURFACES_ALL	Enumerates all of the surfaces that meet the specification in the second parameter. This flag can only be used with the DDENUMSURFACES_DOESEXIST search type flag.
DDENUMSURFACES_MATCH	Searches for any surface that matches the specification in the second parameter.
DDENUMSURFACES_NOMATCH	Searches for any surface that does not match the specification in the second parameter.

The second parameter to EnumSurfaces() is the address of a structure variable of type DDSURFACEDESC2 that defines the characteristics of the surface. If the first parameter includes the DDENUMSURFACES_ALL flag, then this second parameter must be NULL. The third parameter is the address of an application-defined structure that is passed to each enumeration member. The fourth parameter is the address of a callback function, of type lpEnumSurfacesCallback, that is called every time the enumeration procedure finds a surface matching the predefined characteristics.

If the call succeeds, the return value is DD_OK. If it fails, the return value may be one of the following errors:

DDERR_INVALIDOBJECT

DDERR_INVALIDPARAMS

Implementing the callback function for EnumSurfaces() is very similar to the processing described in Chapter 9 for the EnumDisplayModes() callback function. The *DD Info Demo* project contained on the book's CD-ROM contains sample code of the EdnumDisplayModes() callback.

An application often needs to know if a surface of certain characteristics is possible before it attempts to create it. In this case, code can combine the DDENUMSURFACES_CANBECREATED and DDENUMSURFACES_MATCH flags when it calls EnumSurfaces(). The DDSURFACEDESC2 structure variable is initialized to contain the desired surface characteristics. If the characteristics include a particular pixel format, then the DDSD_PIXELFORMAT flag must also be present in the dwFlags member of the DDSURFACEDESC2 structure. In addition, the DDPIXELFORMAT structure in the surface description must be initialized and the flags set to the desired pixel format flags. These can be DDPF_RGB, DDPF_YUV, or both. In order to specify surface dimensions, code must include the DDSD_HEIGHT and DDSD_WIDTH flags in DDSURFACEDESC2. The dimensions are then specified in the dwHeight and dwWidth structure members. If the dimension flags are not included, DirectDraw uses the dimensions of the primary surface.

The following code fragment shows a call to EnumSurfaces() to determine if a 640 by 480 by 24 bits RGB surface is available in the card's video memory space:

```
// Public variables
DDSURFACEDESC2      ddsd;
int                 surfCount = 0;
.
.
.
// Determine if a surface of 640 by 480 pixels, in 24-bits
// RGB color can be created in video memory
ZeroMemory(&ddsd, sizeof(ddsd));
  ddsd.dwSize  = sizeof(ddsd);
  ddsd.dwFlags = DDSD_CAPS |
                 DDSD_PIXELFORMAT |
                 DDSD_HEIGHT |
                 DDSD_WIDTH;
  ddsd.ddpfPixelFormat.dwFlags = DDPF_RGB;
  ddsd.ddpfPixelFormat.dwRGBBitCount = 24;
  ddsd.ddsCaps.dwCaps = DDSCAPS_VIDEOMEMORY |
                        DDSCAPS_LOCALVIDMEM;
  ddsd.dwHeight = 480;
  ddsd.dwWidth  = 640;
lpDD4->EnumSurfaces(
       DDENUMSURFACES_CANBECREATED | DDENUMSURFACES_MATCH,
       &ddsd, NULL,
       (LPDDENUMSURFACESCALLBACK2) SurfacesProc);
  if (surfCount == 0)
      DDInitFailed(hWnd, hRet,
       "Surface not available");
   .
   .
   .
//*******************************************
//    Callback function for EnumSurfaces()
//*******************************************
static BOOL WINAPI SurfacesProc(LPDIRECTDRAWSURFACE4 aSurfPtr,
                   LPDDSURFACEDESC2 aSurface, LPVOID Context)
{
     surfCount++;
     return DDENUMRET_OK;  // Continue
}
```

Because the DDENUMSURFACES_MATCH flag is present in the call, the callback function, in this case named SurfacesProc(), receives control only if a surface can be created. Therefore, we made each iteration of the callback function increment the variable surfCount, which holds the number of similar surfaces that can be created, or zero if none can be created. The calling code inspects this variable to determine the results of the EnumSurfaces() call. The previous code fragment uses the DDInitFailed() function, developed and listed in Chapter 10, to provide a terminal exit in case the surface cannot be created. In practice, an application may take another action, such as creating the surface in system memory instead of video memory. Note that the fourth parameter of EnumSurfaces() has to be typecast into a type LPDDENUMSURFACESCALLBACK2, otherwise a compiler error is generated.

> NOTE: The call to EnumSurfaces() attempts to create a temporary surface that has the desired characteristics. You should be careful not to assume that a surface is unsupported just because it is not enumerated. DirectDraw attempts to create a temporary surface with the memory constraints that exist at the time of the call. This can result in a surface not being enumerated, even when the driver actually supports it.

Losing and Restoring Surfaces

The surface memory associated with a DirectDrawSurface object may be freed, while the DirectDrawSurface objects representing these pieces of surface memory are not released. Several DirectDraw functions return DDERR_SURFACELOST in this case. Surfaces can be lost because the display mode was changed, or because another application requested and obtained exclusive mode and freed all of the currently allocated surface memory. The DirectDraw Restore() function recreates these lost surfaces and reconnects them to their DirectDrawSurface object. If the application uses more than one surface, code can call the RestoreAllSurfaces() function to restore all surfaces at once. Restoring a surface does not reload any imagery that may have previously existed in the surface. Code must reload bitmaps and other image elements to the surfaces in order to reconstruct the display.

Experimenting with Surfaces

Most DirectDraw operations relate to surfaces; therefore, it is important for the programmer to gain familiarity with surface construction and characteristics. The DirectDraw application named ddtest, furnished with DirectX 6, allows you to experiment with DirectDraw options such as surfaces, blits, display modes, and capabilities, without actually writing code.

To create and examine a surface, you must first execute ddtest and then click the Connect button to establish a DirectDraw interface. If the interface is realized, you can now click the Create button. On the Create DirectDraw Surface dialog box, select the desired capabilities, dimensions, and pixel format for the surface, then click OK. If the surface creation fails, a message is posted on the DirectDraw Test Application main screen and the Surface and Surface Info fields are blank. If the surface is created, then the surface box of the main screen contains the surface pointer and the Surface Info boxes have the pertinent surface information. Figure 11-2 shows two dialog boxes of the ddtest program.

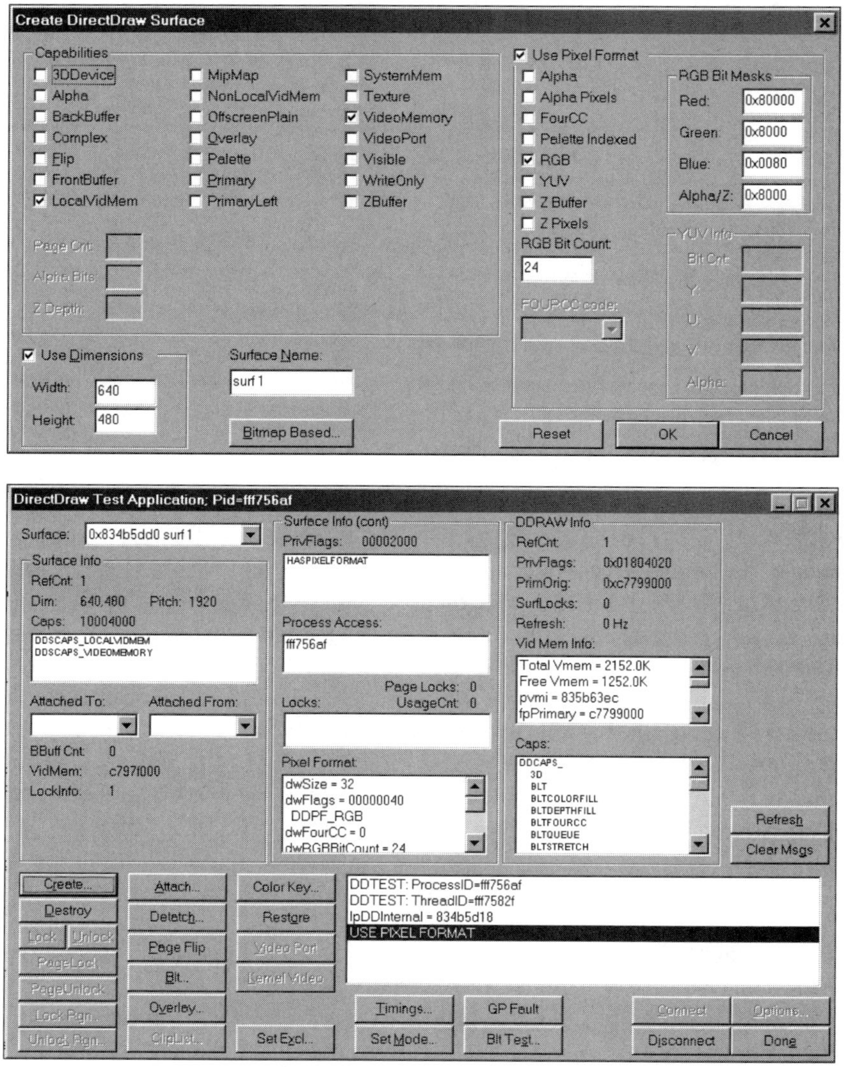

Figure 11-2: Experimenting with surfaces using Microsoft's ddtest program

Transparency and Color Keys

In graphics programming, we often need to display a new bitmap over an existing one. For example, the bitmap of an airplane is shown over a background of mountains, sky, and clouds, contained in another bitmap. Since bitmaps are rectangular areas, the airplane bitmap is actually a rectangle of some uniform color that contains the image of the airplane. If we were to display the airplane by simply projecting its rectangular bitmap over the background, the result would be quite unnatural. The solution is to select the color of the framing rectangle of the airplane bitmap so that it is different from the colors used in drawing the airplane. The software can then be programmed to ignore the framing color while displaying the airplane bitmap. The processing logic is as follows:

If bitmap pixel is equal to framing color, then leave the background pixel undisturbed. Else, replace background pixel with foreground image pixel.

The result is that the image of the airplane behaves as if it had been drawn on a sheet of transparent plastic. The selection of a framing color, called the *color key*, plays an important role in the result. If a color key can be found that is not present in the foreground image, then the transparency is perfectly achieved. If not, some pixels of the foreground image will not be shown. The greater the color range, the easier it is to find a satisfactory color key. It is difficult to imagine a 24-bit color bitmap (16.7 million colors) that will not have a single color value that is absent in the image.

An alternative option to achieve transparency is based on a color key located in the background image, also called the destination. In this case, the color key determines whether or not the foreground image pixel is used. The logic is as follows:

If background pixel is color key, then use foreground pixel over background. Else, leave background undisturbed.

The result of using a destination color key is a window on which the foreground image is displayed. Here again, the programmer must find an attribute for the color key that is not used in the background.

DirectDraw supports both source and destination color-keying for blits and overlay surfaces. Code supplies either a single color or a color range for source or destination color-keying. Source and destination color keys can be combined on different surfaces. For example, a destination color key can be attached to a surface in order to create a window on which the mountains, sky, and clouds are visible. Then a source color key can be used in another surface in order to display the airplane bitmap transparently over this background. Figure 11-4 shows transparency based on the simultaneous use of source and destination color keys.

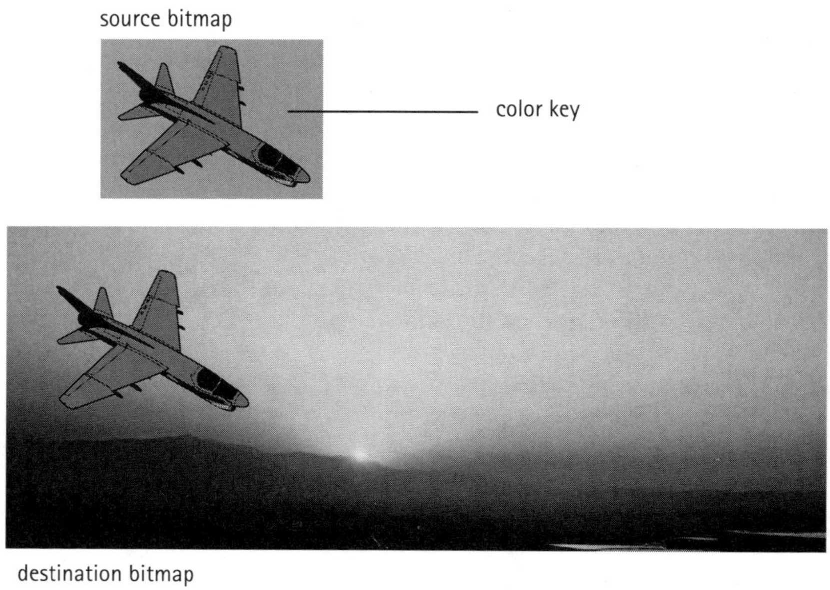

Figure 11-3: Transparency using a source color key

In Figure 11-4, we are manipulating three surfaces that implement source and destination color-key transparency. Surface 1 contains a window in which a destination color key has been defined. Surface 2 is a bitmap image. Surface 3 is a sprite representing an airplane in which the background is a source color key. This sprite is transparently blitted onto the bitmap on surface 2, and then surface 2 is transparently blitted onto surface 1. The resulting image is shown at the bottom of the illustration.

Setting the Color Key

In DirectDraw, a color key is always associated with a surface. Code can set the color keys for a surface when it is created, or afterward. To set a color key or keys when creating a surface, you must first assign the desired color values to one or both of the `ddckCKSrcBlt` and `ddckCKDestBlt` members of the `DDSURFACEDESC2` structure. When `CreateSurface()` is called, the color keys are automatically assigned. If the color key is to be used in blitting, one or both `DDSD_CKSRCBLT` and `DDSD_CKDESTBLT` must be included in the `dwFlags` member.

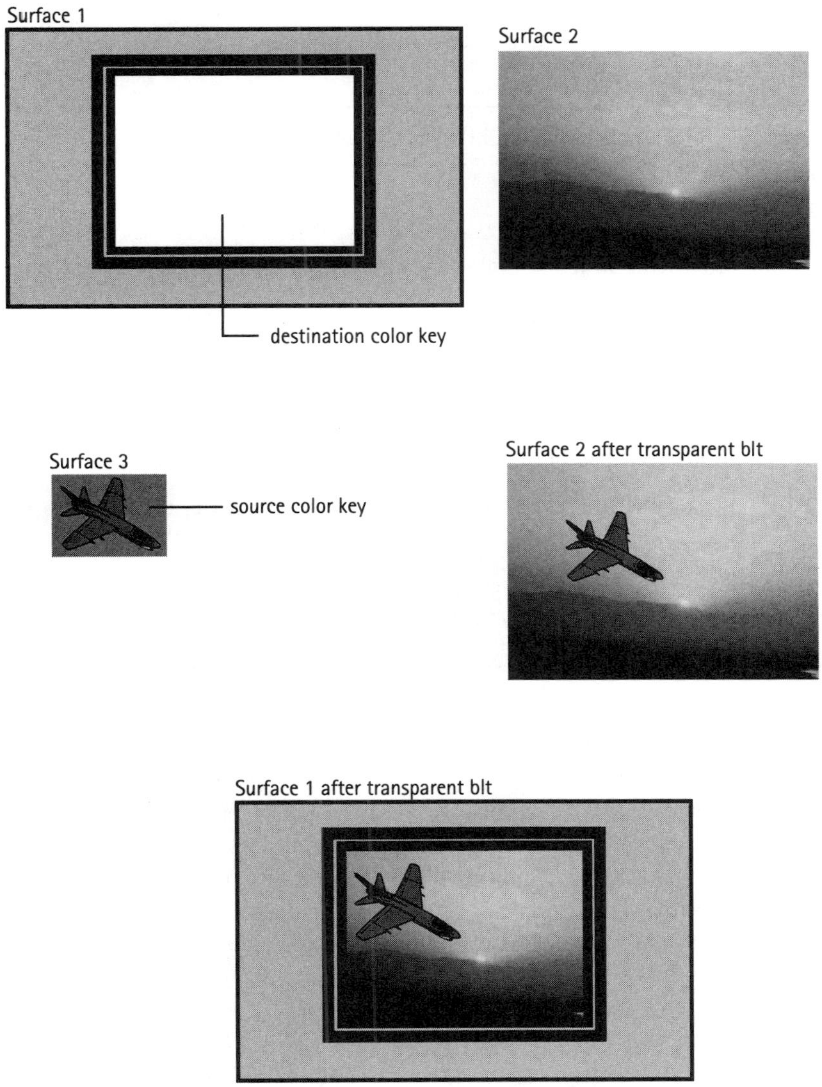

Figure 11-4: Transparency using source and destination color keys

The DirectDraw function `SetColorKey()` sets the color key for an existing `DirectDrawSurface` object. The function's general form reads as follows:

```
HRESULT SetColorKey(
                     DWORD dwFlags,                // 1
                     LPDDCOLORKEY lpDDColorKey     // 2
                    );
```

The first parameter is a flag that determines the type of color key to be used. Table 11-3 lists the predefined constants used in this parameter.

TABLE 11-3 CONSTANTS USED IN SETCOLORKEY() FUNCTION

Constant	Action
DDCKEY_COLORSPACE	The structure contains a color range. Not set if the structure contains a single color key.
DDCKEY_DESTBLT	The structure specifies a color key or color space to be used as a destination color key for blit operations.
DDCKEY_DESTOVERLAY	The structure specifies a color key or color space to be used as a destination color key for overlay operations.
DDCKEY_SRCBLT	The structure specifies a color key or color space to be used as a source color key for blit operations.
DDCKEY_SRCOVERLAY	The structure specifies a color key or colorspace to be used as a source color key for overlay operations.

Color keys are used in two different types of DirectDraw bitmap display operations: blits and overlays. Because overlays are currently supported by few video cards, they are not discussed in this book. The second parameter is the address of a structure variable of type DDCOLORKEY structure that contains the new color key values for the DirectDrawSurface object. If this value is NULL, then the existing color key is removed from the surface.

If the call to SetColorKey() succeeds, the function returns DD_OK. If it fails, one of the following error codes is returned:

DDERR_GENERIC

DDERR_INVALIDOBJECT

DDERR_INVALIDPARAMS

DDERR_INVALIDSURFACETYPE

DDERR_NOOVERLAYHW

DDERR_NOTAOVERLAYSURFACE

DDERR_SURFACELOST

DDERR_UNSUPPORTED

DDERR_WASSTILLDRAWING

The color key is described in a DDCOLORKEY structure. The structure is used for a source color key, a destination color key, or a color range. A single color key is specified when both structure members have the same value. The structure is defined in the Windows header files as follows:

```
typedef struct _DDCOLORKEY{
    DWORD dwColorSpaceLowValue;
    DWORD dwColorSpaceHighValue;
} DDCOLORKEY,FAR* LPDDCOLORKEY;
```

The member dwColorSpaceLowValue contains the low value (inclusive) of the color range that is to be used as the color key. The member wColorSpaceHighValue contains the high value (also inclusive). If both members have the same value then the color key is a single color, not a range.

Color keys are specified using the pixel format of the surface. If a surface is palettized, then the color key is an index or a range of indexes. If the surface is in a 16-bit color space mode (hi-color), then the color key is a word-size value. If the surface's pixel format is RGB or YUV, then the color key is specified in an RGBQUAD or YUVQUAD structure, as in the following code fragments:

```
// Hi color mode is the single color key.
dwColorSpaceLowValue = 0xf011;
dwColorSpaceHighValue = 0xf011;

// RGB color 255,128,128 is the single color key.
dwColorSpaceLowValue = RGBQUAD(255,128,128);
dwColorSpaceHighValue = RGBQUAD(255,128,128);

// YUV color range used as a color key
dwColorSpaceLowValue = YUVQUAD(120,50,50);
dwColorSpaceHighValue = YUVQUAD(140,50,50);
```

NOTE: The YUV format was developed to more easily compress motion video data. It is based on the physics of human vision, where the eye is more sensitive to brightness levels than to specific colors. The YUV acronym refers to a three-axis coordinate system. The *Y*-axis encodes the luminance component, while the *U* and *V* axes encode the chrominance, or color, element. Although several different implementations of the YUV format are available, no single format is directly supported by DirectDraw.

The YUV color example listed above uses a color range that extends from 120-50-50 to 150-50-50. In this case, any pixel with a *Y* value between 120 and

150, and *U* and *V* values of 50, serves as a color key. Range values for color keys are often used when working with video data or photographic images, because in this case, there are often variations in the background color values. Artwork composed with draw or paint programs often uses single-key colors.

Color Key Support

Transparency and color keys are supported by the HEL; therefore, these functions are always available; however, support for a color key range is hardware-dependent. Code should check the `dwCKeyCaps` member of the `DDCAPS` structure. The `DDCAPS_COLORKEY` constant of the `dwCaps` member identifies some form of color key support for either overlay or blit operations. The `dwCKeyCaps` member defines the options listed in Table 11-4.

TABLE 11-4 COLOR KEY CAPABILITIES IN DWCKEYCAPS MEMBER OF DDCAPS STRUCTURE

Constant	Meaning
`DDCKEYCAPS_DESTBLT`	Supports transparent blitting. Color keyidentifies the replaceable bits of the destination surface for RGB colors.
`DDCKEYCAPS_DESTBLTCLRSPACE`	Supports transparent blitting. Color space identifies the replaceable bits of the destination surface for RGB colors.
`DDCKEYCAPS_DESTBLTCLRSPACEYUV`	Supports transparent blitting. Color space identifies the replaceable bits of the destination surface for YUV colors.
`DDCKEYCAPS_DESTBLTYUV`	Supports transparent blitting. Color key identifies the replaceable bits of the destination surface for YUV colors.
`DDCKEYCAPS_DESTOVERLAY`	Supports overlaying with color keying of the replaceable bits of the destination surface being overlaid for RGB colors.
`DDCKEYCAPS_DESTOVERLAYCLRSPACE`	Supports a color space as the color key for the destination of RGB colors.
`DDCKEYCAPS_DESTOVERLAYCLRSPACEYUV`	Supports a color space as the color key for the destination of YUV colors.
`DDCKEYCAPS_DESTOVERLAYONEACTIVE`	Supports only one active destination color key value for visible overlay surfaces.

Constant	Meaning
DDCKEYCAPS_DESTOVERLAYYUV	Supports overlaying using color keying of the replaceable bits of the destination surface being overlaid for YUV colors.
DDCKEYCAPS_NOCOSTOVERLAY	No bandwidth trade-offs for using the color key with an overlay.
DDCKEYCAPS_SRCBLT	Supports transparent blitting using the color key for the source with this surface for RGB colors.
DDCKEYCAPS_SRCBLTCLRSPACE	Supports transparent blitting using a color space for the source with this surface for RGB colors.
DDCKEYCAPS_SRCBLTCLRSPACEYUV	Supports transparent blitting using a color space for the source with this surface for YUV colors.
DDCKEYCAPS_SRCBLTYUV	Supports transparent blitting using the color key for the source with this surface for YUV colors.
DDCKEYCAPS_SRCOVERLAY	Supports overlaying using the color key for the source with this overlay surface for RGB colors.
DDCKEYCAPS_SRCOVERLAYCLRSPACE	Supports overlaying using a color space as the source color key for the overlay surface for RGB colors.
DDCKEYCAPS_SRCOVERLAYCLRSPACEYUV	Supports overlaying using a color space as the source color key for the overlay surface for YUV colors.
DDCKEYCAPS_SRCOVERLAYONEACTIVE	Supports only one active source color key value for visible overlay surfaces.
DDCKEYCAPS_SRCOVERLAYYUV	Supports overlaying using the color key for the source with this overlay surface for YUV colors.

Some hardware supports color ranges only for YUV pixel data, which is usually video. The transparent background in video footage (the "blue screen" against which the subject was photographed) might not be a pure color, so a range of colors in the color key is desirable in this case.

DirectDraw Blits

In Chapter 8, we discussed the GDI bit block transfer operation, called a bitblt or blit. In the blit, a rectangular block of memory bits, called the source, is transferred as a block into a rectangular memory area called the destination. If the destination of the transfer is screen memory, then the bitmapped image is immediately displayed. The source and destination bit blocks can be combined logically or arithmetically, or a unary operation can be performed on the source or the destination bit blocks.

GDI blits can be used in DirectDraw programming, and sometimes they are. However, DirectDraw contains its own blit functions that are usually more suitable to the programming environment and execute faster than their GDI counterparts. The DirectDraw blit functions are named `Blt()` and `BltFast()`. They are both associated with DirectDraw surface objects. Microsoft has announced a third method, called `BltBatch()`, which is to be implemented in future versions of DirectDraw. In the context of DirectDraw programming, blit operations usually originate in an off-screen surface and have as a destination either the back buffer or a primary surface. In fact, much of the processing time of a typical DirectDraw application is spent blitting imagery. Also, the performance capability (also called the bandwidth) of a particular blitter often determines the quality of the application's video output. Figure 11-5 shows the most common forms of the DirectDraw blit operation.

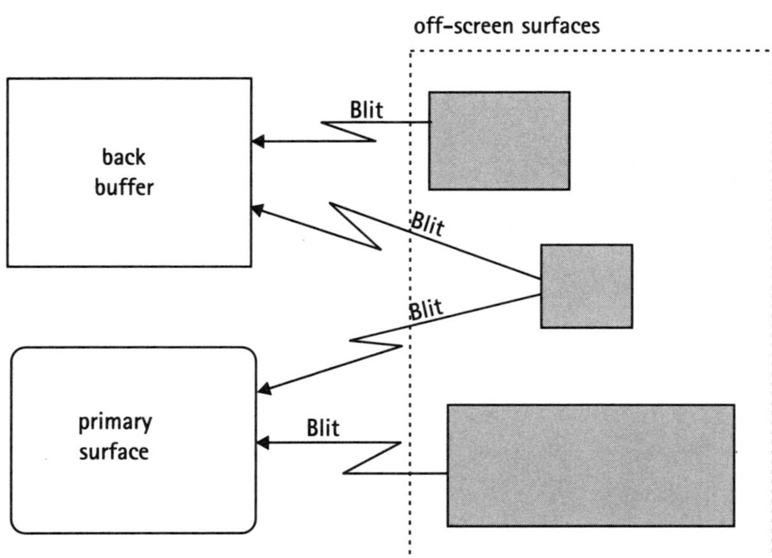

Figure 11-5: DirectDraw blit operations

Both blit functions, `Blt()` and `BltFast()`, operate on a destination surface, which is referenced in the call, and receive the source surface as a parameter. It is possible for both source and destination to be the same surface. In this case, DirectDraw preserves all source pixels before overwriting them. `Blt()` is more flexible, but `BltFast()` is faster, especially if there is no hardware blitter. Applications can determine the blitting capabilities of the hardware from the `DDCAPS` structure obtained by means of the `GetCaps()` function. If the `dwCaps` member contains `DDCAPS_BLT`, the hardware supports blitting.

BltFast()

`BltFast()` requires a valid rectangle in the source surface from which the pixels are to be copied. If the entire surface is to be copied, then the source rectangle is `NULL`. It also requires *x*- and *y*-coordinates in the destination surface. If the source rectangle is larger than the destination, the call fails and `BltFast()` returns `DDERR_INVALIDRECT`. `BltFast()` cannot be used on surfaces that have an attached clipper. Nor does it support stretching, mirroring, or other effects that can be performed with `Blt()`.

The function's general form reads as follows:

1 2 3 4

```
HRESULT BltFast(
          DWORD dwX                                 // 1
          DWORD dwY,                                // 2
          LPDIRECTDRAWSURFACE3 lpDDSrcSurface,      // 3
          LPRECT lpSrcRect,                         // 4
          DWORD dwTrans                             // 5
);
```

The first and second parameters are the *x*- and *y*-coordinates on which to blit on the destination surface. The third parameter is the address of a `IDirectDrawSurface4` interface for the `DirectDrawSurface` object that is the source of the blit. The fourth parameter is a `RECT` structure that defines the upper-left and lower-right points of the rectangle on the source surface. The fifth parameter defines the type of blit, as listed in Table 11-5.

TABLE 11-5 TYPE OF TRANSFER CONSTANTS IN BLTFAST()

Constant	Action
DDBLTFAST_DESTCOLORKEY	Transparent blit that uses the destination's color key.
DDBLTFAST_NOCOLORKEY	Normal copy blit with no transparency.
DDBLTFAST_SRCCOLORKEY	Transparent blit that uses the source's color key.
DDBLTFAST_WAIT	Does not produce a DDERR_WASSTILLDRAWING message if the blitter is busy. Returns as soon as the blit can be set up or another error occurs.

If the call succeeds, `BltFast()` returns `DD_OK`. If it fails, it returns one of the following self-explanatory values:

DDERR_EXCEPTION

DDERR_GENERIC

DDERR_INVALIDOBJECT

DDERR_INVALIDPARAMS

DDERR_INVALIDRECT

DDERR_NOBLTHW

DDERR_SURFACEBUSY

DDERR_SURFACELOST

DDERR_UNSUPPORTED

DDERR_WASSTILLDRAWING

`BltFast()` always attempts an asynchronous blit if it is supported by the hardware. The function works only on display memory surfaces and cannot clip when blitting. According to Microsoft, `BltFast()` is ten percent faster than the `Blt()` method if there is no hardware support, but there is no speed difference if the display hardware is used. Figure 11-6 is a diagram that shows the parameters and operation of the `BltFast()` function

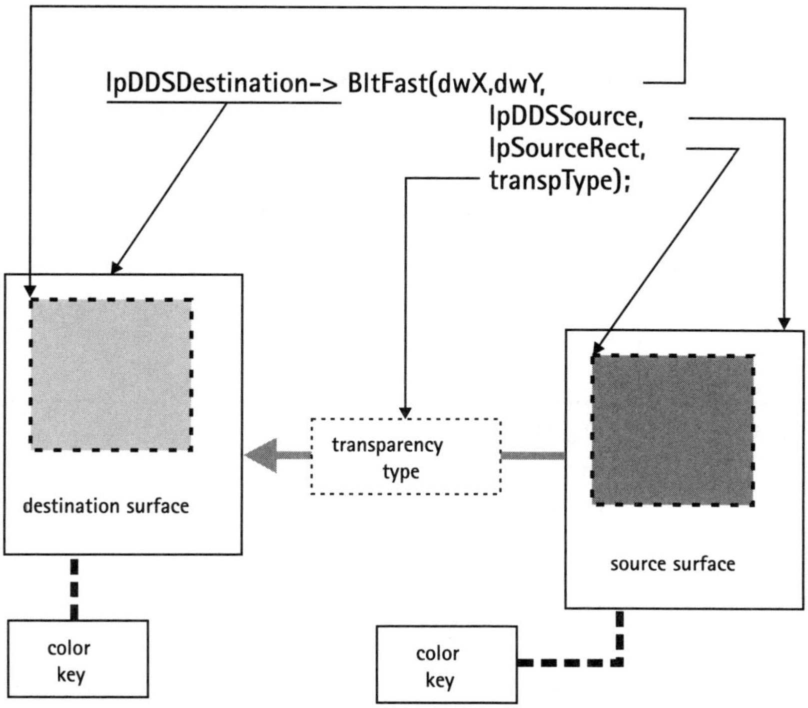

Figure 11-6: Diagram of the DirectDraw BltFast() function

Blt()

`Blt()` is the more flexible and powerful of the two DirectDraw blit functions. Like `BltFast()`, `Blt()` performs a bit block transfer from a source surface into a destination surface. `Blt()` allows a clipper to be attached to the destination surface, in which case clipping is performed if the destination rectangle falls outside of the surface. `Blt()` can also be used to automatically scale the source image to fit the destination rectangle. Scaling is disabled when both surfaces are of the same size. The function's general form reads as follows:

```
HRESULT Blt(
            LPRECT lpDestRect,                   // 1
            LPDIRECTDRAWSURFACE3 lpDDSrcSurface,  // 2
            LPRECT lpSrcRect,                     // 3
            DWORD dwFlags,                        // 4
            LPDDBLTFX lpDDBltFx                   // 5
);
```

The first parameter is the address of a RECT structure that defines the upper-left and lower-right points of the source rectangle. If this parameter is NULL, the entire destination source surface is used. The second parameter is the address of the IDirectDrawSurface4 interface for the DirectDrawSurface object that is the source of the blit. The third parameter is the address of a RECT structure that defines the upper-left and lower-right points of the source rectangle from which the blit is to take place. If this parameter is NULL, then the entire source surface is used. The fourth parameter is one or more flags that determine the valid members of the associated DDBLTFX structure, which specifies color-key information or requests a special behavior. Three types of flags are currently defined: validation flags, color-key flags, and behavior flags. Table 11-6 lists the predefined constants for this parameter.

TABLE 11-6 FLAGS FOR THE BLT() FUNCTION

Flags	Meaning
Validation Flags	
DDBLT_COLORFILL	The dwFillColor member of the DDBLTFX structure is the RGB color that fills the destination rectangle.
DDBLT_DDFX	The dwDDFX member of the DDBLTFX structure specifies the effects to use for the blit.
DDBLT_DDROPS	The dwDDROP member of the DDBLTFX structure specifies the raster operations (ROPS) that are not part of the Win32 API.
DDBLT_DEPTHFILL	The dwFillDepth member of the DDBLTFX structure is the depth value with which to fill the destination rectangle.
DDBLT_KEYDESTOVERRIDE	The ddckDestColorkey member of the DDBLTFX structure is the color key for the destination surface.
DDBLT_KEYSRCOVERRIDE	The ddckSrcColorkey member of the DDBLTFX structure is the color key for the source surface.
DDBLT_ROP	The dwROP member of the DDBLTFX structure is the ROP for this blit. The ROPs are the same as those defined in the Win32 API.
DDBLT_ROTATIONANGLE	The dwRotationAngle member of the DDBLTFX structure is the rotation angle, in 1/100th of a degree units, for the surface.

Flags	Meaning
Color Key Flags	
DDBLT_KEYDEST	The color key is associated with the destination surface.
DDBLT_KEYSRC	The color key is associated with the source surface.
Behavior Flags	
DDBLT_ASYNC	Blit asynchronously in the FIFO order received. If no room is available in the FIFO hardware, the call fails.
DDBLT_WAIT	Postpones the DDERR_WASSTILLDRAWING return value if the blitter is busy, and returns as soon as the blit can be set up or another error occurs.

The fifth parameter is the address of a structure variable of type DDBLTFX that defines special effects during the blit, including raster operation codes (ROP) and override information. Because of their complexity, special effects during blit operations are discussed in a separate section. Figure 11-7 shows the parameters and operation of the Blt() function.

If the call succeeds, the return value is DD_OK. If it fails, the return value is one of the following error codes:

DDERR_GENERIC DDERR_NOMIRRORHW

DDERR_INVALIDCLIPLIST DDERR_NORASTEROPHW

DDERR_INVALIDOBJECT DDERR_NOROTATIONHW

DDERR_INVALIDPARAMS DDERR_NOSTRETCHHW

DDERR_INVALIDRECT DDERR_NOZBUFFERHW

DDERR_NOALPHAHW DDERR_SURFACEBUSY

DDERR_NOBLTHW DDERR_SURFACELOST

DDERR_NOCLIPLIST DDERR_UNSUPPORTED

DDERR_NODDROPSHW DDERR_WASSTILLDRAWING

The Blt() function is capable of synchronous or asynchronous blits for either display memory to display memory, display memory to system memory, system memory to display memory, or system memory to system memory. The default is asynchronous. The function supports both source and destination color keys. If the source and the destination rectangles are not the same size, `Blt()` performs the necessary stretching. `Blt()` returns immediately with an error if the blitter is busy. If the code specifies the `DDBLT_WAIT` flag, then a synchronous blit takes place and the call waits until the blit can be set up or until another error occurs.

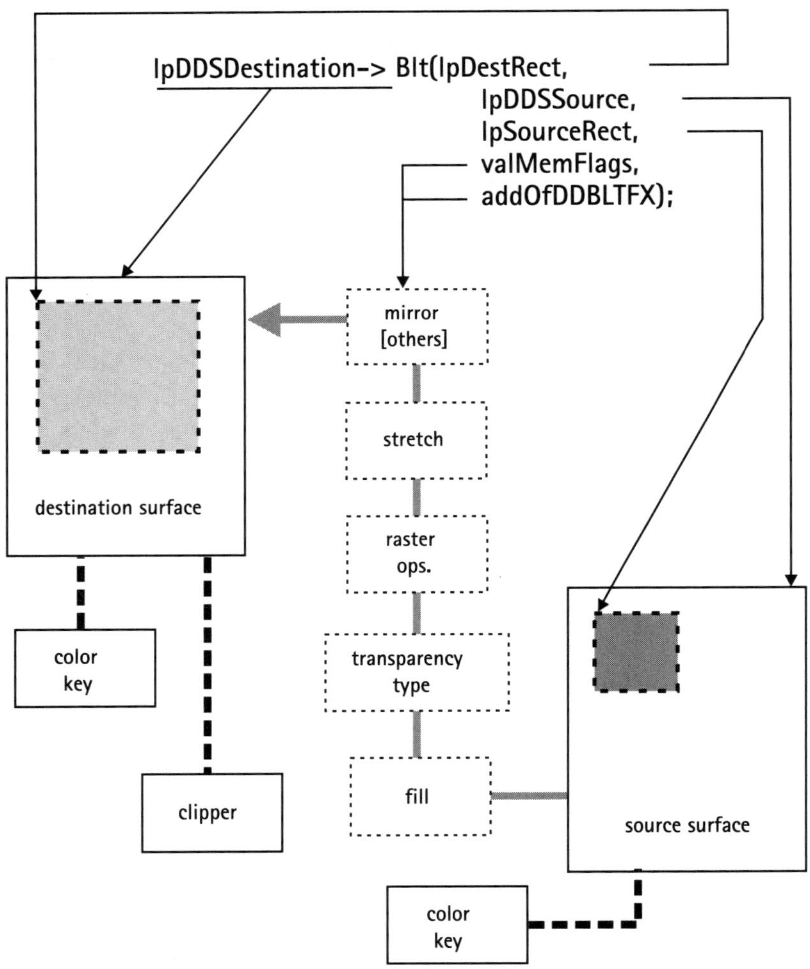

Figure 11-7: Diagram of the DirectDraw Blt() function

To use the Blt() function, code must supply a valid rectangle in the source surface (or NULL to specify the entire surface), and a rectangle in the destination surface to which the source image is copied. Here again, NULL means the destination rectangle is the entire surface. If a clipper is attached to the destination surface, then the bounds of the destination rectangle can fall outside the surface and clipping is automatically performed. If there is no clipper, the destination rectangle must fall entirely within the surface or else the method fails with DDERR_INVALIDRECT.

Blt() vs. BltFast()

The Blt() function allows maximum control of the blit operation, while BltFast() executes faster and is easier to set up. The number of flags listed in Table 11-6 gives an idea of the level of control provided by Blt(). In fact, many of the flags available in Blt() relate to transparency, Z-buffers, and other features not yet implemented in DirectDraw. In addition, Blt() supports stretching, mirroring, raster operations, and fill controls which are not possible using BltFast(). Which function to use is determined by the functionality necessary in the blit. Since BltFast() is documented to execute about 10 percent faster than Blt(), it should be used whenever possible. However, if hardware support for blit operations is available, both functions take approximately the same time.

Blit-time Transformations

DirectDraw supports several transformations that take place at blit-time. The most important ones are color fills, scaling, mirroring, and raster operations. Other effects, such as rotation, are not available in the HEL; therefore, they cannot be used if the hardware does not support them. Applications that do not require any special blit-time transformations other than scaling can pass NULL as in the fourth parameter of the Blt() function. Code can determine the hardware support for blit-time transformations by means of the GetCaps() function.

Applications that require a particular blit-time transformation must pass the corresponding value in one of the members of the DDBLTFX structure. The appropriate flags must also be included in the fourth parameter to Blt(), which determines which members of the structure are valid. Some transformations require only setting a single flag, while others require several of them.

The dwFlags member of DDBLTFX named DDBLTFX_NOTEARING can be used when blitting images directly to the front buffer. The action of this flag is to time the blit so that it coincides with the screen's vertical retrace cycle, thus minimizing the possibility of tearing. Tearing and screen-update timing are discussed in Chapter 12.

Applications that use surface color keys when calling BltFast() or Blt() must set one or both of the DDBLTFAST_SRCCOLORKEY or DDBLTFAST_DESTCOLORKEY flags in the corresponding function parameter. Alternatively, code can place the appropriate color values in the ddckDestColorkey and ddckSrcColorkey members of the DDBLTFX structure that is passed to the function in the lpDDBltFx parameter. In this case, it is also necessary to set either the DBLT_KEYSRCOVERRIDE or DBLT_KEYDESTOVERRIDE flag, or both, in the dwFlags parameter. The resulting action is that the selected color keys are taken from the DDBLTFX structure rather than from the surface properties.

Color Fills

Applications can use the blitter to fill the entire surface, or a part of it, with a single color. This operation is useful for creating backgrounds when using a destination color key, and for clearing large screen areas. When Blt() is used to perform a color fill, the call must reference the DDBLT_COLORFILL flag. The following code fragment fills an entire surface with the color blue. Code assumes that lpDDS is a valid pointer to an IDirectDrawSurface4 interface.

```
 HRESULT         ddrval;
 DDBLTFX         ddbltfx;
 .
 .
 .
 ZeroMemory(&ddbltfx, sizeof(ddbltfx));
 ddbltfx.dwSize = sizeof(ddbltfx);
 ddbltfx.dwFillColor = ddpf.dwBBitMask; // Pure blue
 ddrval = lpDDS->Blt(
                 NULL,     // Destination is entire surface
                 NULL,     // No source surface
                 NULL,     // No source rectangle
                 DDBLT_COLORFILL, &ddbltfx);
if(ddrval != DD_OK)
// Error handler goes here
```

Scaling

The Blt() function automatically scales the source image to fit the destination rectangle. Scaling is implemented in the HEL, so it is always available. Some video cards have hardware support for scaling operations. Applications can inspect the dwCXCaps member of the DDCAPS structure to determine if hardware support is available and of which type. Table 11-7 lists the predefined constants used in the scaling capabilities flag.

TABLE 11-7 SCALING FLAGS FOR THE BLT() FUNCTION

Flag	Meaning
DDFXCAPS_BLTALPHA	Supports alpha-blended blit operations.
DDFXCAPS_BLTARITHSTRETCHY	Arithmetic operations, rather than pixel-doubling techniques, are used to stretch and shrink surfaces along the *y*-axis.
DDFXCAPS_BLTARITHSTRETCHYN	Arithmetic operations, rather than pixel-doubling techniques, are used to stretch and shrink surfaces along the *y*-axis. Stretching must be integer-based.
DDFXCAPS_BLTSHRINKX	Arbitrary shrinking of a surface along the *x*-axis (horizontally).
DDFXCAPS_BLTSHRINKXN	Integer shrinking of a surface along the *x*-axis.
DDFXCAPS_BLTSHRINKY	Arbitrary shrinking of a surface along the *y*-axis.
DDFXCAPS_BLTSHRINKYN	Integer shrinking of a surface along the *y*-axis.
DDFXCAPS_BLTSTRETCHX	Arbitrary stretching of a surface along the *x*-axis.
DDFXCAPS_BLTSTRETCHXN	Integer stretching of a surface along the *x*-axis.
DDFXCAPS_BLTSTRETCHY	Arbitrary stretching of a surface along the *y*-axis (vertically).
DDFXCAPS_BLTSTRETCHYN	Supports integer stretching of a surface along the *y*-axis.

Scaling is automatically disabled when the source and destination rectangles are exactly the same size. An application can use the `BltFast()` function, instead of `Blt()`, in order to avoid accidental scaling due to different sizes of the source and destination rectangles.

Some video cards support arithmetic scaling. In this case the scaling operation is performed by interpolation rather than by multiplication or the deletion of pixels. For example, if an axis is being increased by one-third, the pixels are recolored to provide a closer approximation to the original image than would be produced by doubling every third pixel on that axis. Code has little control over the type of scaling performed by the driver. The only possibility is to set the `DDBLTFX_ARITHSTRETCHY` flag in the `dwDDFX` member of the `DDBLTFX` structure passed to `Blt()`. This flag requests that arithmetic stretching be done on the *y*-axis. Arithmetic stretching on the *x*-axis and arithmetic shrinking are not currently supported in the DirectDraw API, but a driver may perform them on its own.

Mirroring

Another blit-time transformation supported by the HEL is *mirroring*; applications can assume that mirroring is available even if it not supported in the hardware. Mirroring is defined in the *x*-axis and the *y*-axis of the blit rectangle. Figure 11-8 shows mirroring along both axes.

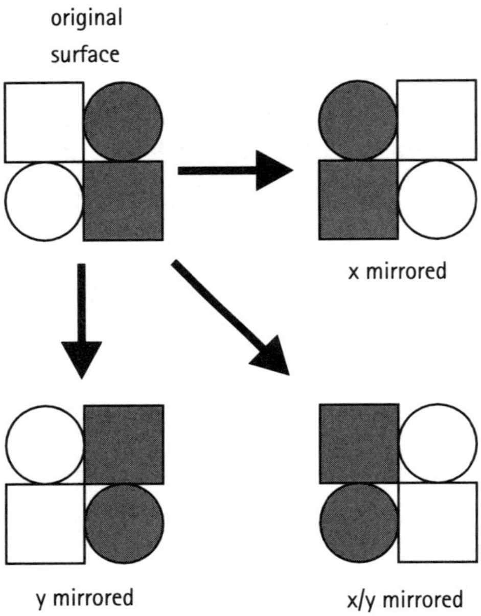

Figure 11-8: Mirroring transformations

Table 11-8 lists the predefined constants used in mirroring transformations during `Blt()`.

TABLE 11-8 MIRRORING FLAGS FOR THE BLT() FUNCTION

Flag	Meaning
`DDBLTFX_MIRRORLEFTRIGHT`	Mirrors on the *y*-axis. The surface is mirrored from left to right.
`DDBLTFX_MIRRORUPDOWN`	Mirrors on the *x*-axis. The surface is mirrored from top to bottom.

Applications sometimes need several versions of a symmetrical sprite, in which the image faces in different directions. Rather than creating a bitmap for each image, it is possible to generate them by mirroring the original. Hardware support for mirroring can be determined by the presence of the `DDFXCAPS_BLTMIRRORLEFTRIGHT` and `DDFCAPS_BLTMIRRORUPDOWN` identifiers in the `dwFXCaps` member of the `DDCAPS` structure.

Raster Operations

Blit-time transformations can include some of the standard raster operations (ROPs) used by the GDI `BitBlt()` functions. At present, HEL supports only `SRCCOPY` (the default), `BLACKNESS`, and `WHITENESS`. Hardware support for other raster operations can be determined by examining the `DDCAPS` structure. Code that uses any of the standard ROPS with the `Blt()` method must set the corresponding flag in the `dwROP` member of the `DDBLTFX` structure. The `dwDDROP` member of the `DDBLTFX` structure is for specifying ROPs specific to DirectDraw. No such ROPs have been defined at this time.

Rendering Windows Bitmaps

Bitmaps are one of the most powerful tools available to the graphics programmer. In today's technological world, with an abundance of real-color and true-color modes, bitmaps can be used to encode images with photo-realistic accuracy. The processing capabilities available in this generation of PCs make possible the effective manipulation of bitmapped images. DirectDraw implements a new dimension of functionality in bitmap processing and display operations. Many types of applications rely heavily on bitmaps; these include image processing, simulations, virtual reality, artificial life, and electronic games.

In DirectDraw programming, bitmap manipulations consist of four basic steps:

1. Loading the bitmap into application memory.
2. Obtaining bitmap data necessary for displaying it on the screen.
3. Loading a bitmap onto a DirectDraw surface.
4. Blitting the bitmap onto the video display.

Loading a Bitmap

Loading a bitmap onto the application's memory space is an operation of GDI graphics, not actually part of DirectDraw. In the demonstration program named Bitmap Demo, contained on the book's CD-ROM, we load several bitmaps during `WM_CREATE` message processing. In this case, we used Developer Studio to define the bitmaps as program resources, and then used `LoadBitmap()` to load them into the application's memory space. We revisit this topic now with a different approach:

instead of defining the bitmap as a program resource, we use the `LoadImage()` function to load the bitmap directly from the disk file in which it is stored.

In addition, we also perform certain preliminary checks to make sure that the DirectDraw surface is compatible with the bitmap to be displayed. Note that the sample code requires that the surface be nonpalettized The `GetSurfaceDesc()` DirectDraw function is used to fill a `DDSURFACEDESC2` structure, discussed in Chapter 10 and described in Appendix A. The `DDPIXELFORMAT` structure, which is part of `DDSURFACEDESC2`, contains two relevant values: the flag `DDPF_RGB` indicates that the RGB data is valid, and the `dwRGBBitCount` member contains the number of RGB bits per pixel. If the `DDPF_RGB` flag is set and `dwRGBBitCount` is greater than 15, we can assume that the surface is nonpalettized, and therefore, compatible.

> The `LoadImage()` function does not return palette information. Microsoft Knowledge Base Article Q158898 lists the function `LoadBitmapFromBMP-File()`, which uses the DIBSection's color table to create a palette. If no color table is present, then a half-tone palette is created. The source for this function can be found in the MSDN 6.0 Library that is part of Visual C++ version 6.

Once code has determined that a compatible surface is available, it can proceed to load the bitmap. The general form of the `LoadImage()` function reads as follows:

```
HANDLE LoadImage(
           HINSTANCE hinst,                // 1
           LPCTSTR lpszName,               // 2
           UINT uType,                     // 3
           int cxDesired,                  // 4
           int cyDesired,                  // 5
           UINT fuLoad                     // 6
);
```

The first parameter is a handle to an instance of the module that contains the image to be loaded. In the case of an image contained in a file, this parameter is set to zero. The second parameter is a pointer to the image to load. If it is non-null and the sixth parameter (described later) does not include `LR_LOADFROMFILE`, then it is a pointer to a null-terminated string that contains the filename of the image resource. The third parameter is the image type. It can be one of the following constants:

```
IMAGE_BITMAP

IMAGE_CURSOR

IMAGE_ICON
```

The fourth and fifth parameters specify the pixel width and height of the bitmap, cursor, or icon. If the fifth is zero and the sixth parameter is `LR_DEFAULTSIZE`, then the function uses the `SM_CXICON` or `SM_CXCURSOR` system metric value to set the width. If the fifth parameter is zero, and if `LR_DEFAULTSIZE` is present in the sixth parameter, then the function uses the actual width and height of the bitmap.

The sixth and last parameter is one or more flags represented by the predefined constants listed in Table 11-9.

TABLE 11-9 PREDEFINED CONSTANTS IN LOADIMAGE() FUNCTION

Constant	Meaning
`LR_DEFAULTCOLOR`	Default flag. Does nothing.
`LR_CREATEDIBSECTION`	When the third parameter is `IMAGE_BITMAP`, this flag causes the function to return a DIB section bitmap rather than a compatible bitmap. It is useful for loading a bitmap without mapping it to the colors of the display device.
`LR_DEFAULTSIZE`	For cursors and icons, the width or height values are those specified by the system metric values, but only if the fourth and fifth parameters are set to zero. If this flag is not specified and the fourth and fifth parameters are set to zero, the function uses the actual resource size.
`LR_LOADFROMFILE`	Loads the image from the file specified by the second parameter. If this flag is not specified, `lpszName` is the name of the resource.
`LR_LOADMAP3DCOLORS`	Searches the color table for the image and replaces the following shades of gray with the corresponding 3D color. Color — RGB value — Replaced With Dk Gray — RGB(128,128,128) — `COLOR_3DSHADOW` Gray — RGB(192,192,192) — `COLOR_3DFACE` Lt Gray — RGB(223,223,223) — `COLOR_3DLIGHT`
`LR_LOADTRANSPARENT`	Retrieves the color value of the top-left pixel in the image and replaces the corresponding entry in the color table with the default window color (`COLOR_WINDOW`). All pixels in the image that use that entry become the default window color. This value applies only to images that have corresponding color tables.

Continued

Table 11-9 PREDEFINED CONSTANTS IN LOADIMAGE() FUNCTION *(Continued)*

Constant	Meaning
LR_MONOCHROME	Converts the image to black and white pixels.
LR_SHARED	Shares the image handle if the image is loaded multiple times. If LR_SHARED is not used, a second call to LoadImage for the same resource will load the image again and return a different handle. LR_SHARED should not be used for images that have nonstandard sizes that may change after loading, or that are loaded from a file. In Windows 95 and Windows 98, LoadImage() finds the first image with the requested resource name in the cache, regardless of the size requested.
LR_VGACOLOR	Uses true VGA colors.

LoadImage() returns the handle of the newly loaded image if the call succeeds. If the function fails, the return value is NULL. Although the system automatically deletes all resources when the process that created them terminates, applications can save memory by releasing resources that are no longer needed. DeleteObject() is used to release a bitmap; DestroyIcon() is used to release an icon; and DestroyCursor() is used to release cursor resources.

The following function is used to load a bitmap into the application's memory space and obtain its handle. In this case, the code checks for a surface compatible with a nonpalettized bitmap.

```
//**************************************************************
// Name: DDLoadBitmap
// Desc: Loads a bitmap file into memory and returns its
//       handle
//
// PRE CONDITIONS:
// 1. Parameter 1 is pointer to a DirectDraw surface
//    Parameter 2 is pointer to bitmap filename string
//
// POST CONDITIONS:
// Returns handle to bitmap
//
// ERROR CONDITIONS:
// All errors exit through DDInitFailed() function
//**************************************************************
HBITMAP DDLoadBitmap( LPDIRECTDRAWSURFACE4 lpDDS,
```

```
  LPSTR szImage)
{
    HBITMAP         hbm;
    DDSURFACEDESC2  ddsd;
    ZeroMemory( &ddsd, sizeof( ddsd ) );
    ddsd.dwSize = sizeof( ddsd );
    if ( lpDDS->GetSurfaceDesc( &ddsd ) != DD_OK )
         DDInitFailed(hWnd, hRet,
         "GetSurfaceDesc() call failed in DDLoadBitmap()");
    // Test for compatible pixel format
    if ( ( ddsd.ddpfPixelFormat.dwFlags != DDPF_RGB ) ||
         ( ddsd.ddpfPixelFormat.dwRGBBitCount < 16 ) )
           DDInitFailed(hWnd, hRet,
          "Incompatible surface in DDLoadBitmap()");
    // Load the bitmap image onto memory
    hbm = ( HBITMAP )LoadImage( NULL, szImage,
            IMAGE_BITMAP, 0, 0, LR_LOADFROMFILE );
    if ( hbm == NULL )
         DDInitFailed(hWnd, hRet,
          "Bitmap load failed in DDLoadBitmap()");
    return hbm;
}
```

Note that in DDLoadBitmap(), all errors are considered terminal and are directed through the DDInitFailed() function, which was developed and listed in Chapter 10. This mode of operation can be changed if you want the code to provide alternate processing in these cases.

Obtaining Bitmap Information

In order to display and manipulate a bitmap, the processing routines usually require information about its size and organization. The GDI GetObject() function is used for this purpose. This function, which is described in Chapter 8, fills a structure of type BITMAP, defined as follows:

```
typedef struct tagBITMAP {
   LONG   bmType;         // Must be zero
   LONG   bmWidth;        // bitmap width (in pixels)
   LONG   bmHeight;       // bitmap height (in pixels)
   LONG   bmWidthBytes;  // bytes per scan line
   WORD   bmPlanes;       // number of color planes
   WORD   bmBitsPixel;   // bits per pixel color
   LPVOID bmBits;         // points to bitmap values array
} BITMAP;
```

The bmWidth member specifies the width, in pixels, of the bitmap, while bmHeight specifies the height, also in pixels. Both values must be greater than zero. The bmWidthBytes member specifies the number of bytes in each scan line. Windows assumes that the bitmap is word-aligned; therefore, this value must be divisible by 2. The member bmPlanes specifies the number of color planes. The member bmBitsPixel specifies the number of bits required to indicate the color of a pixel. The member bmBits points to the location of the bit values for the bitmap. It is a long pointer to an array of char-size (one byte) values.

The amount of information in the BITMAP structure that is used depends on the type of bitmap processing performed by the application. The direct access operations described in Chapter 10 allow code to manipulate bitmap data directly. In this case, most of the BITMAP structure members are required in order to locate and access the bitmap data. On the other hand, applications can use high-level functions to display a bitmap. Such is the case with the BitBlt() GDI function described in Chapter 8, and the DirectDraw Blt() and BltFast() functions. When high-level functions are used, usually only the bmWidth and bmHeight members are necessary.

Loading a Bitmap onto a Surface

Blit operations in DirectDraw take place between surfaces. Therefore, a useful function is one that loads a bitmap onto a surface. The function, named DDBmapToSurf(), copies a memory-resident bitmap, specified by its handle, into a DirectDraw surface.

```
//**********************************************************
// Name: DDBmapToSurf
// Desc: Moves a bitmap to a DirectDraw Surface
// PRE CONDITIONS:
// 1. Parameter 1 is pointer to a DirectDraw surface
//    Parameter 2 is handle to the bitmap
//
// POST CONDITIONS:
// Bitmap is moved to surface
// Returns 1 if successful
// /
// ERROR CONDITIONS:
// All errors exit through DDInitFailed() function
//**********************************************************
HRESULT DDBmapToSurf(LPDIRECTDRAWSURFACE4 pdds, HBITMAP hbm)
{
    HDC                     hdcImage;
    HDC                     hdc;
    DDSURFACEDESC2          ddsd;
    HRESULT                 hr = 1;
```

```
    BOOL                    retValue;
    if (hbm == NULL || pdds == NULL)
     DDInitFailed(hWnd, hRet,
           "Invalid surface or bitmap in DDBmapToSurf");
   // Create compatible DC and select bitmap into it
   hdcImage = CreateCompatibleDC(NULL);
     if (!hdcImage)
       DDInitFailed(hWnd, hRet,
           "CreateCompatibleDC() failed in DDBmapToSurf");
   SelectObject(hdcImage, hbm);

   // Get size of surface
   ddsd.dwSize = sizeof(ddsd);
   ddsd.dwFlags = DDSD_HEIGHT | DDSD_WIDTH;
   pdds->GetSurfaceDesc(&ddsd);
   if ((hr = pdds->GetDC(&hdc)) != DD_OK)
     DDInitFailed(hWnd, hRet,
           "GetDC() failed in DDBmapToSurf");
   retValue = BitBlt(hdc, 0, 0, ddsd.dwWidth, ddsd.dwHeight,
                     hdcImage, 0, 0, SRCCOPY);
   // Release surface immediately
   pdds->ReleaseDC(hdc);
   if(retValue == FALSE)
       DDInitFailed(hWnd, hRet,
           "BitBlt() failed in DDBmapToSurf");
        DeleteDC(hdcImage);
    return hr;
}
```

Displaying the Bitmap

The `BitBlt()` GDI function described in Chapter 8 provides a flexible, yet slow, mechanism for displaying bitmaps. In the case of DirectDraw applications executing in exclusive mode, the device context must be obtained with the DirectDraw-specific version of the `GetDC()` function. `IDirectDrawSurface4::GetDC` not only returns a GDI-compatible device context, but also locks the surface for access. The following function displays a bitmap using a DirectDraw device context:

```
//***********************************************************
// Name: DDShowBitmap
// Desc: Displays a bitmap using a DirectDraw device context
//
// PRE CONDITIONS:
```

```
// 1. Parameter 1 is pointer to a DirectDraw surface
//    Parameter 2 is handle to the bitmap
//    Parameters 3 and 4 are the display location
//    Parameters 5 and 6 are the bitmap dimensions
//
// POST CONDITIONS:
// Returns TRUE if successful
//
// ERROR CONDITIONS:
// All errors exit through DDInitFailed() function
//************************************************************
BOOL DDShowBitmap( LPDIRECTDRAWSURFACE4 lpDDS,
                   HBITMAP hBitmap,
                   int xLocation, int yLocation,
                   int bWidth, int bHeight)
{
    HDC              hdcImage = NULL;
    HDC              hdcSurf  = NULL;
    HDC              thisDevice = NULL;
    // Create a DC and select the image into it.
    hdcImage = CreateCompatibleDC( NULL );
    SelectObject( hdcImage, hBitmap);

    // Get a DC for the surface.
    if(lpDDS->GetDC(&hdcSurf) != DD_OK) {
        DeleteDC( hdcImage );
        DDInitFailed(hWnd, hRet,
            "GetDC() call failed in DDShowBitmap()");
        }
    // BitBlt() is used to display bitmap
    if ( BitBlt( hdcSurf, xLocation, yLocation, bWidth,
         bHeight, hdcImage, 0, 0, SRCCOPY ) == FALSE ) {
            lpDDS->ReleaseDC( hdcSurf );
            DeleteDC( hdcImage );
         // Take terminal error exit
         DDInitFailed(hWnd, hRet,
             "BitBlt() call failed in DDShowBitmap()");
         }
    // Release device contexts
       lpDDS->ReleaseDC( hdcSurf );
       DeleteDC( hdcImage );
       return TRUE;
}
```

The following code fragment shows the processing required for loading and displaying a bitmap onto the primary surface, as implemented in the project named *DD Bmap Demo* contained on the book's CD-ROM.

```
// Load bitmap named nebula.bmp
aBitmap = DDLoadBitmap(lpDDSPrimary, "nebula.bmp");

// Get bitmap data for displaying
GetObject(aBitmap, sizeof (BITMAP), &bMap1);
// Display bitmap
DDShowBitmap(lpDDSPrimary, aBitmap, 130, 50,
             (int) bMap1.bmWidth,
             (int) bMap1.bmHeight);
```

DirectDraw Windowed Applications

The maximum power and functionality of DirectDraw is available only to applications that execute in exclusive mode. This explains why we usually associate DirectDraw programming with exclusive mode. However, this does not preclude conventional Windows applications from using many DirectDraw functions, usually with a considerable gain in performance. DirectDraw functions also allow some image manipulations that are not possible in GDI code. We should also consider the fact that DirectDraw programming in windowed mode restores most of the device-independence that is lost in exclusive mode. This also means that program coding must return to the conventional multitasking, message-based paradigm that is characteristic of Windows.

Programs that run in a window can be totally or partially obscured by another program, they can lose focus, they can have surfaces that become unbound from their memory assignments, and they can be minimized or resized by the user. Most of these circumstances, which are often ignored in exclusive mode, require careful attention in windowed DirectDraw. Following are the main differences between DirectDraw programs in exclusive and non-exclusive mode:

- Exclusive mode applications usually require a window style WS_POPUP, while windowed applications use WS_THICKFRAME if they are resizable. The combination WS_SYSMENU, WS_CAPTION, and WS_MINIMIZEBOX is used if the window cannot be resized by the user. The WS_OVERLAPPEDWINDOW style includes WS_THICKFRAME.
- Exclusive mode programs use DDSCL_FULLSCREEN and DDSCL_EXCLUSIVE cooperative level, while windowed programs use DDSCL_NORMAL.

- Exclusive mode programs can use page-flipping in implementing animation (animation techniques are covered in Chapter 12), while windowed programs have very limited flipping capabilities. This is one of the reasons why games and other animation-intensive applications are usually designed for DirectDraw exclusive mode.
- Full-screen programs can set their own display mode, while windowed programs must operate in the current desktop display mode. By the same token, exclusive mode programs can assume a particular display mode, while windowed programs must be designed with sufficient flexibility to execute in several display modes.
- Exclusive-mode applications may use clipping to produce specific graphics effects. Non-exclusive mode programs often rely on clipping to facilitate interaction with other programs and with the Windows desktop.
- While exclusive mode can be switched to the background, usually they cannot be minimized or resized by the user. Non-exclusive mode programs can be moved on the desktop, resized, minimized, or obscured by other applications.
- Exclusive-mode programs have direct control over the palette and can be designed for a particular palette. Windowed programs must use the palette manager to make changes and must accommodate palette changes made by the user or by other programs.
- Exclusive-mode programs can display or hide the system cursor but cannot use system-level mouse support, as is the case with the system menu or the buttons on the program's title bar. Furthermore, exclusive-mode programs must furnish most of the cursor processing logic. On the other hand, DirectDraw windowed applications can make use of all the cursor and cursor-related support functions in the Windows API.
- Exclusive mode applications must implement their own menus. Windows applications can use the menu facilities in the API.

In summary: although windowed programs must address some specific issues when using DirectDraw services, they do have almost unrestricted access to the functionality of a conventional application. Thus, a DirectDraw program that executes in non-exclusive mode can have a title bar, resizable borders, menus, status bar, sizing grip, scroll bars, as well as most of the other GUI components discussed earlier in the book. For this reason, there is no "standard" design for a DirectDraw windowed application. However, there are issues that are usually confronted by a typical DirectDraw application when executing in non-exclusive mode. In the following sections, we discuss the most important issues.

Initialization for Non-exclusive Mode

It is virtually impossible to design a general-purpose template for a DirectDraw non-exclusive mode application. The same applies for the initialization operations required to set up such programs. At the same time, there are certain typical initialization steps that apply to many DirectDraw applications that execute in non-exclusive mode. The project named *DD Template2*, contained on the book's CD-ROM, contains a template file with minimal initializations for a DirectDraw application in non-exclusive mode.

The first step in `WinMain()` processing is defining and filling the `WNDCLASSEX` structure variable and registering the window class. In the template file, this is accomplished as follows:

```
// Defining a structure of type WNDCLASSEX
WNDCLASSEX  wndclass ;
wndclass.cbSize        = sizeof (wndclass) ;
wndclass.style         = CS_HREDRAW | CS_VREDRAW;
wndclass.lpfnWndProc   = WndProc ;
wndclass.cbClsExtra    = 0 ;
wndclass.cbWndExtra    = 0 ;
wndclass.hInstance     = hInstance ;
wndclass.hIcon         = LoadIcon (NULL, IDI_APPLICATION) ;
wndclass.hCursor       = LoadCursor (NULL, IDC_ARROW) ;
wndclass.hbrBackground = (HBRUSH) GetStockObject
                         (WHITE_BRUSH) ;
wndclass.lpszMenuName  = szAppName;
wndclass.lpszClassName = szAppName;
wndclass.hIconSm       = LoadIcon (NULL, IDI_APPLICATION) ;

// Register the class
   RegisterClassEx(&wndclass);
```

Next, the code must create the window and define its show state. In the case of a resizable window with the three conventional buttons and the system menu box in the title bar, we can use the `WS_OVERLAPPEDWINDOW` style. Since it is impossible to predict in the template the window size and initial location, we have used `CW_USEDEFAULT` for these parameters.

```
hWnd = CreateWindowEx(0,          // Extended style
           szAppName,
           "DirectDraw in Window Template",
           WS_OVERLAPPEDWINDOW,
```

```
            CW_USEDEFAULT,
            CW_USEDEFAULT,
            CW_USEDEFAULT,
            CW_USEDEFAULT,
            NULL,               // Handle of parent
            NULL,               // Handle to menu
            hInstance,          // Application instance
            NULL);              // Additional data
if (!hWnd)
    return FALSE;
ShowWindow(hWnd, nCmdShow);
```

The processing for creating a DirectDraw object and a primary surface is similar to that used in exclusive-mode programming. In the template, we use the same support procedures previously developed. `DD4Interface()` attempts to find a `DirectDraw4` object and returns 1 if found and 0 if not. If the call is successful, a global pointer variable named `lpDD4`, of type `LPDIRECTDRAW4`, is initialized. `DDInitFailed()` provides a terminal exit for failed initialization operations. The primary surface is created by means of a call to `CreateSurface()`. The surface pointer is stored in the public variable `lpDDSPrimary`. Code reads as follows:

```
//***************************************
// Create DirectDraw object and
// create primary surface
//***************************************
// Fetch DirectDraw4 interface
hRet = DD4Interface();
if (hRet == 0)
  return DDInitFailed(hWnd, hRet,
         "QueryInterface() call failed");
// Set cooperative level to exclusive and full screen
   hRet = lpDD4->SetCooperativeLevel(hWnd, DDSCL_NORMAL);
   if (hRet != DD_OK)
      return DDInitFailed(hWnd, hRet,
          "SetCooperativeLevel() call failed");
//*********************************
//    Create the primary surface
//*********************************
// ddsd is a structure of type DDSRUFACEDESC2
  ZeroMemory(&ddsd, sizeof(ddsd));  // Clear structure
// Fill in other members
  ddsd.dwSize = sizeof(ddsd);
```

```
ddsd.dwFlags = DDSD_CAPS ;
ddsd.ddsCaps.dwCaps = DDSCAPS_PRIMARYSURFACE;
hRet = lpDD4->CreateSurface(&ddsd, &lpDDSPrimary, NULL);
if (hRet != DD_OK)
    return DDInitFailed(hWnd, hRet,
           "CreateSurface() call failed");
```

Clipping the Primary Surface

In Chapter 9 we discussed clipping as the DirectDraw operation by which output is limited to a rectangular area, usually defined in a surface. DirectDraw supports clipping in both exclusive and non-exclusive modes. Since exclusive-mode applications have control over the entire client area, clipping is used mostly as a graphics output manipulation. Windowed applications, on the other hand, often share the display with the Windows desktop and with other applications. In this case, clipping is often used to ensure that the application's output is limited to its own client area. Figure 11-9 shows the execution on the Windows desktop of three copies of a DirectDraw application that uses clipping. The program itself, whose source file DD_InWin.ccp is contained in the *DD InWin Demo* project on the book's CD-ROM, is discussed later in this session.

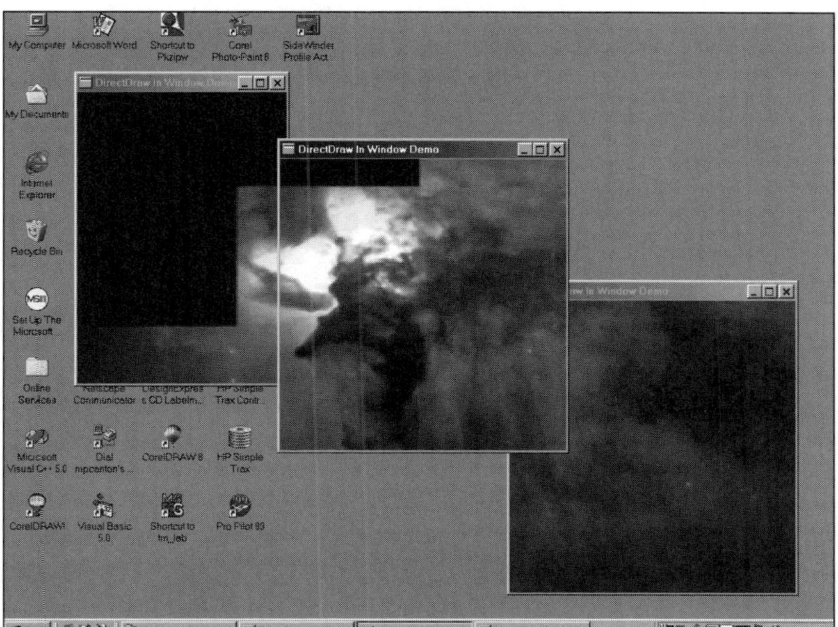

Figure 11-9: Clipping in a DirectDraw windowed application

In DirectDraw windowed applications, a clipper is used to define the program's screen boundaries. The clipper ensures that a graphics object is not displayed outside the client area. Failure to define a clipper may cause the blit operation to fail because the destination drawing surface may be outside of the display limits. When the boundaries of the primary surface are defined in a clipper, then DirectDraw knows not to display outside of this area and the blit operation succeeds, as is the case in Figure 11-9. Recall that the `Blt()` function supports clipping but that `BltFast()` does not.

In a clip list, pixel coordinates are stored in one or more structures of type `RECT`. DirectDraw uses the clipper object to manage clip lists. Clip lists can be attached to any surface by using a `DirectDrawClipper` object. The simplest clip list consists of a single rectangle that defines the area within the surface to which a `Blt()` function outputs. Figure 11-10 shows a DirectDraw surface to which a clipper consisting of a single rectangle has been attached.

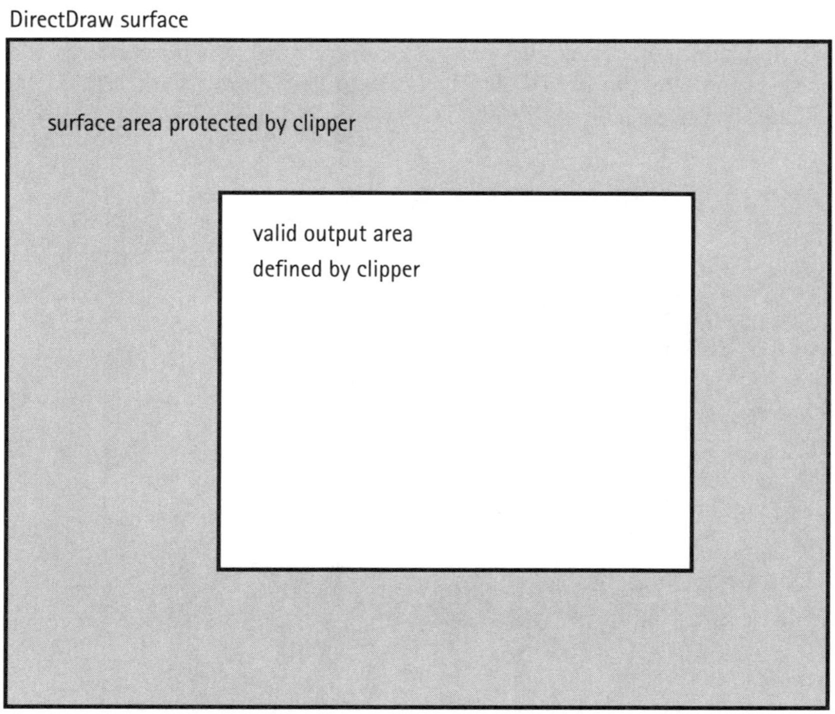

Figure 11-10: Clipper establishes a surface's valid blit area

DirectDraw's `Blt()` function copies data only to the rectangles in the clip list. Clip lists consisting of several rectangles are often necessary in order to protect a specific surface area from output. For example, if an application requires a rectangular area in the top-center of the screen to be protected from output, it would need to define several clipping rectangles. Figure 11-11 demonstrates this case.

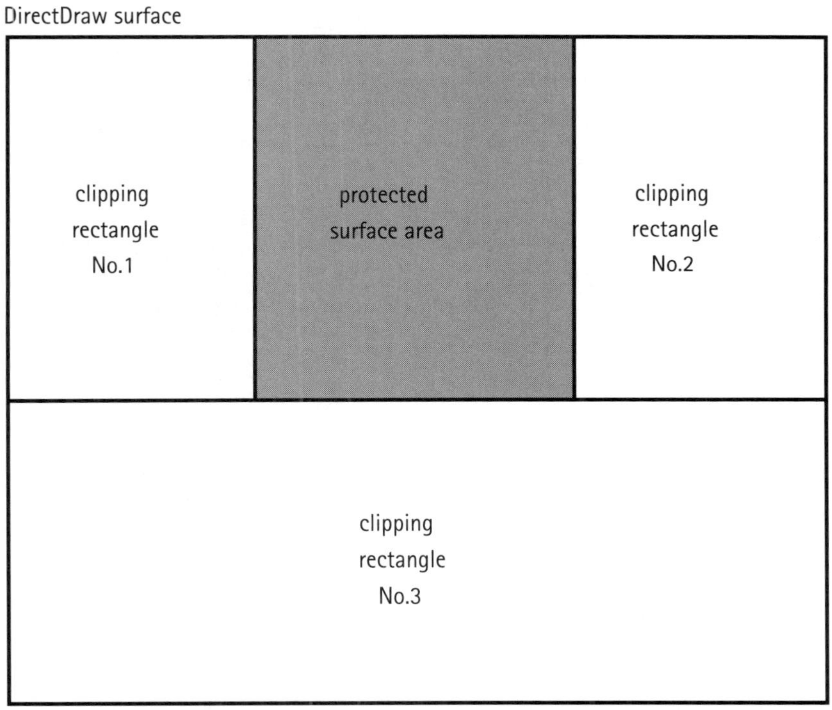

Figure 11-11: Three clipping rectangles protect an area from output

To manage a clip list the application creates a series of rectangles and stores them in a data structure of type `RGNDATA`. One of the members of `RGNDATA` is the `RGNDATAHEADER` structure, which is used to define the number of rectangles that make up the region. The function `SetClipList()` is then called with the `RGNDATA` structure variable as a parameter. To delete a clip list from a surface, the `SetClipList()` call is made using `NULL` for the `RGNDATA` parameter.

DirectDraw can automatically manage the clip list for a primary surface. Attaching a clipper to the primary surface requires the following steps:

1. Creating the clipper object.
2. Associating the clipper with the application window.
3. Associating the clipper with the primary surface.

To create the clipper object we must take into account that a clipper is a DirectDraw object in itself, which must be created using the DirectDraw4 interface object. The `CreateClipper()` function is used in this step. The function's general form reads as follows:

```
HRESULT CreateClipper(
          DWORD dwFlags,                               // 1
          LPDIRECTDRAWCLIPPER FAR *lplpDDClipper,      // 2
          IUnknown FAR *pUnkOuter                      // 3
);
```

The first and third parameters are not used in current implementations. The first parameter should be set to zero and the third one to `NULL`. The second parameter is the address of a variable of type `LPDIRECTDRAWCLIPPER`, which is set to the interface if the call succeeds; in this case, the return value is `DD_OK`. If the call fails it returns one of the following constants:

DDERR_INVALIDOBJECT

DDERR_INVALIDPARAMS

DDERR_NOCOOPERATIVELEVELSET

DDERR_OUTOFMEMORY

Once the clipper to the primary surface is created, it must be attached to the application's window. This second step requires a call to the `SetHWnd()` function. `SetHWnd()` takes two parameters: the first one must be set to zero in the current implementation and the second one is the handle to the window that uses the clipper object. This has the effect of setting the clipping region to the client area of the window and ensuring that the clip list is automatically updated as the window is resized, covered, or uncovered. Once a clipper is set to a window, additional rectangles cannot be added.

In the third step the clipper is associated with the primary surface. This is done by means of a call to the `SetClipper()` function, which takes the surface pointer as its only parameter. The code in the template program reads as follows:

```
//*********************************************
//  Create a clipper for the primary surface
//*********************************************
  hRet = lpDD4->CreateClipper(0, &lpDDClipper, NULL);
  if (hRet != DD_OK)
      return DDInitFailed(hWnd, hRet,
                    "Create clipper failed");
// Associate clipper with application window
hRet = lpDDClipper->SetHWnd(0, hWnd);
```

```
  if (hRet != DD_OK)
  return DDInitFailed(hWnd, hRet,
          "Clipper not linked to application window");
// Associate clipper with primary surface
hRet = lpDDSPrimary->SetClipper(lpDDClipper);
  if (hRet != DD_OK)
  return DDInitFailed(hWnd, hRet,
          "Clipper not linked to primary surface");
```

The remainder of the `WinMain()` function listed in the template program contains the regular message loop.

Rendering in DirectDraw Non-exclusive Mode

A simple rendering operation in DirectDraw non-exclusive mode programming consists of storing a bitmap image in an off-screen surface and then blitting it to the primary surface. It is in the blitting stage that the windowed nature of the application introduces some constraints. The DirectDraw interface allows the program to access video memory directly, while the windowed nature of the application requires that video output be limited to the application's client area. A terminal error occurs if a windowed program attempts to display outside its own space. In GDI programming, Windows takes care of clipping video output. In DirectDraw programming, these restrictions must be observed and enforced by the application itself.

The most powerful rendering function for DirectDraw windowed applications is `Blt()`. Figure 11-7 shows some of the controls and options available in this case. DirectDraw windowed applications that use `Blt()` often create a destination surface clipper, and manipulate the size and position of the source and destination rectangles in order to achieve the desired effects. The `BltFast()` function can be used in cases that do not require clippers or the other output controls that are available in `Blt()`.

In this section, we illustrate non-exclusive mode rendering with two sample programs, both contained in the *DD InWin Demo* project on the book's CD-ROM. Both programs display a bitmap of the Lagoon nebula images obtained by the Hubble Space Telescope.

Rendering by Clipping

The first variation of the *DD InWin Demo* project is contained in the source file named DD_InWin.cpp. In this case, the bitmap image is blitted to the entire primary surface and a clipper is used to restrict which portion of the image is displayed in the application's window. Figure 11-12 shows the original bitmap stretched to fill the primary surface. The clipper, which is the size of the application window, is attached to the primary surface. The lower part of the illustration shows three copies of the program on the windows desktop. Each executing copy of the program shows the underlying portion of a virtual image according to the clipper, which is automatically resized by Windows to the application's client area. This ensures that video output is limited to the application's video space.

The operation of the DD_InWin.cpp program is as follows:

The DirectDraw windowed application is initialized as described earlier in this chapter. The `wndclass.style` member of the `WNDCLASSEX` structure is set to `CS_HREDRAW` and `CS_VREDRAW` so that the entire client area is redrawn if there is vertical or horizontal resizing.

The program design calls for creating an initial application window of the same size as the bitmap. Using the size of the original bitmap is an arbitrary decision since the program window is resizable. In order to obtain the bitmap dimensions, the code must load the bitmap into memory before creating the application window. The processing reads as follows:

```
// Global handles and structures for bitmaps
HBITMAP       aBitmap;
BITMAP        bMap1;          // Structures for bitmap data
.
.
.
// Local data
RECT          progWin;        // Application window

//************************************
//      Load bitmap into memory
//************************************
// Load the bitmap image into memory
aBitmap = ( HBITMAP )LoadImage( NULL, "nebula.bmp",
            IMAGE_BITMAP, 0, 0, LR_LOADFROMFILE );
 if ( aBitmap == NULL )
     DDInitFailed(hWnd, hRet,
        "Bitmap load failed in DDLoadBitmap()");
// Get bitmap data
GetObject(aBitmap, sizeof (BITMAP), &bMap1);
// Store bitmap in RECT structure variable
progWin.left = 0;
progWin.top = 0;
progWin.right = bMap1.bmWidth;
progWin.bottom = bMap1.bmHeight;
```

Original bitmap attached to the primary surface

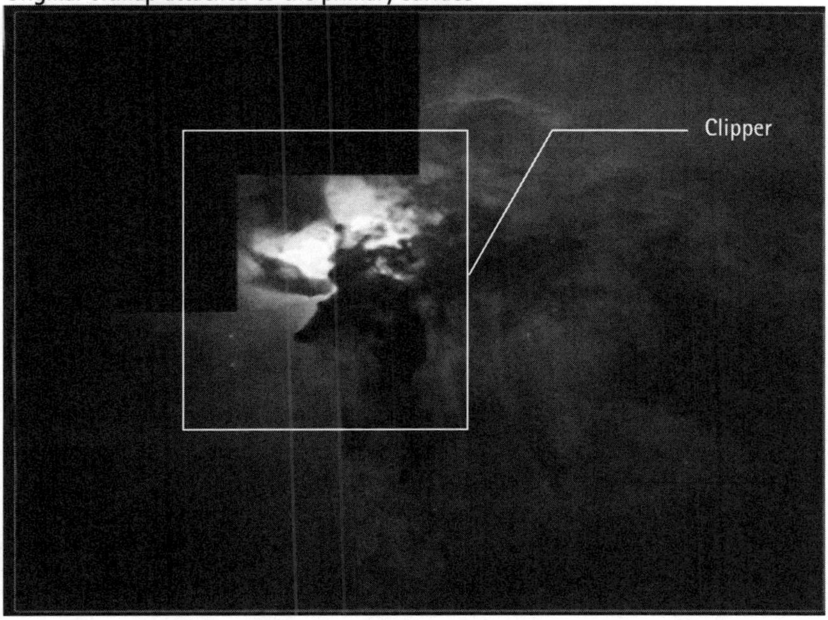

Copies of *DD InWin Demo* application on the Windows desktop

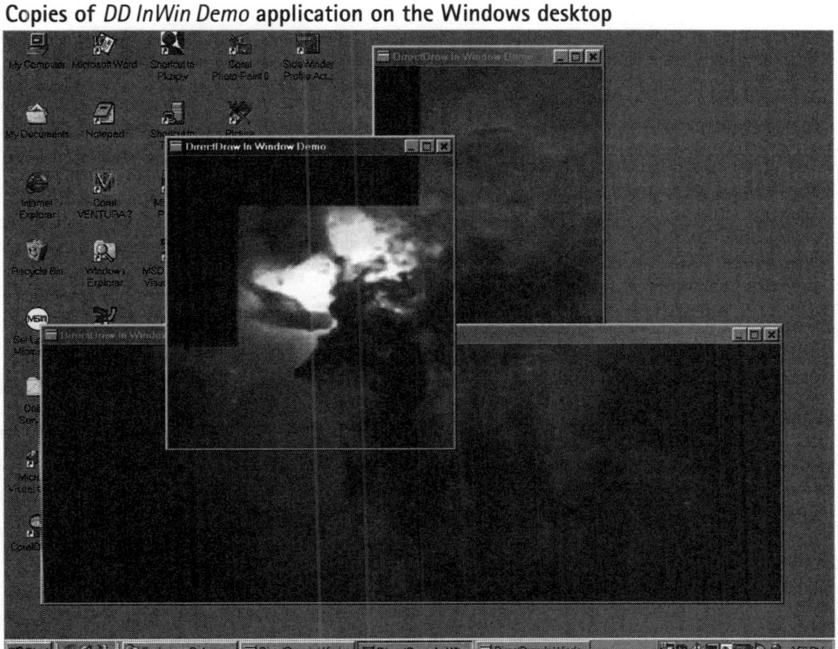

Figure 11-12: DirectDraw output control by clipping

At this point, the bitmap dimensions have been stored in a structure variable named progWin, of type RECT. However, the application window is larger than the client area, since it includes the title bar and the border. It is necessary to adjust the size by calling AdjustWindowRectEx(). This function corrects the data stored in a RECT structure variable according to the application's window style. The code reads as follows:

```
//****************************************
//   Create a window with client area
//   the same size as the bitmap
//****************************************
// First adjust the size of the client area to the size
// of the bounding rectangle (this includes the border,
// caption bar, menu, etc.)
 AdjustWindowRectEx(&progWin,
                    WS_OVERLAPPEDWINDOW,
                    FALSE,
                    0);
  hWnd = CreateWindowEx(0,        // Extended style
             szAppName,
             "DirectDraw In Window Demo",
              WS_OVERLAPPEDWINDOW,
              CW_USEDEFAULT,    // x of initial position
              CW_USEDEFAULT,    // y of initial position
              (progWin.right - progWin.left),  // x size
              (progWin.bottom - progWin.top),  // y size
               NULL,            // Handle of parent
               NULL,            // Handle to menu
               hInstance,       // Application instance
               NULL);           // Additional data
 if (!hWnd)
     return FALSE;
 ShowWindow(hWnd, nCmdShow);
```

In the call to CreateWindowEx(), we used the default initial position and arbitrarily set the Windows dimension to that of the bitmap, the size of which is stored in the progWin structure variables. The code now proceeds to create a DirectDraw object and a primary surface in the conventional manner. Note that the cooperative level in this case is DDSCL_NORMAL.

```
//*************************************
// Create DirectDraw object and
// create primary surface
```

```
//**************************************
 // Fetch DirectDraw4 interface
hRet = DD4Interface();
if (hRet == 0)
   return DDInitFailed(hWnd, hRet,
                       "QueryInterface() call failed");
 // Set cooperative level to exclusive and full screen
 hRet = lpDD4->SetCooperativeLevel(hWnd, DDSCL_NORMAL);
 if (hRet != DD_OK)
     return DDInitFailed(hWnd, hRet,
                "SetCooperativeLevel() call failed");
// Create the primary surface
// ddsd is a structure of type DDSRUFACEDESC2
   ZeroMemory(&ddsd, sizeof(ddsd));  // Clear structure
// Fill in other members
   ddsd.dwSize = sizeof(ddsd);
   ddsd.dwFlags = DDSD_CAPS ;
   ddsd.ddsCaps.dwCaps = DDSCAPS_PRIMARYSURFACE;
   hRet = lpDD4->CreateSurface(&ddsd, &lpDDSPrimary, NULL);
   if (hRet != DD_OK)
     return DDInitFailed(hWnd, hRet,
                       "CreateSurface() call failed");
```

Now the code must create a clipper associated with the application window that is attached to the primary surface, as described previously in this chapter. The surface component tells DirectDraw which surface to clip. The window element defines the clipping rectangle to the size of the application's client area. The processing reads as follows:

```
//*********************************
//    Create a clipper
//*********************************
 hRet = lpDD4->CreateClipper(0, &lpDDClipper, NULL);
 if (hRet != DD_OK)
     return DDInitFailed(hWnd, hRet,
                       "Create clipper failed");
// Associate clipper with application window
hRet = lpDDClipper->SetHWnd(0, hWnd);
 if (hRet != DD_OK)
   return DDInitFailed(hWnd, hRet,
              "Clipper not linked to application window");
 // Associate clipper with primary surface
```

```
hRet = lpDDSPrimary->SetClipper(lpDDClipper);
 if (hRet != DD_OK)
   return DDInitFailed(hWnd, hRet,
             "Clipper not linked to primary surface");
```

Although the bitmap has been loaded, it has not yet been stored in an off-screen surface. `Blt()` requires that the bitmap be located on a surface; for this reason, we have no other option in this case. Since speed is not a factor in this program, we create the surface in system memory, which allows you to run several copies of the executable simultaneously. The code reads as follows:

```
//************************************
//   Store bitmap in off screen surface
 //************************************
 // First create an off-screen surface
// in system memory
ZeroMemory(&ddsd, sizeof(ddsd));  // Clear structure
// Fill in other members
 ddsd.dwSize = sizeof(ddsd);
 ddsd.dwFlags = DDSD_CAPS | DDSD_HEIGHT | DDSD_WIDTH;
 ddsd.ddsCaps.dwCaps = DDSCAPS_OFFSCREENPLAIN |
                      DDSCAPS_SYSTEMMEMORY;
 ddsd.dwHeight = bMap1.bmHeight;
 ddsd.dwWidth = bMap1.bmWidth;
 hRet = lpDD4->CreateSurface(&ddsd, &lpDDSOffscreen, NULL);
 if (hRet != DD_OK)
     return DDInitFailed(hWnd, hRet,
            "Off Screen surface creation failed");
// Move bitmap to surface using DDBmapToSurf()function
 hRet = DDBmapToSurf(lpDDSOffscreen, aBitmap);
  if(hRet != DD_OK)
     return DDInitFailed(hWnd, hRet,
                       "DDBMapToSurf() call failed");
 // ASSERT:
 //     Bitmap is in offscreen surface -> lpDDSOffscreen
```

Finally, the bitmap stored in the off-screen surface can be blitted to the primary surface using the clipper attached to the primary surface. The `Blt()` call reads as follows:

```
//**********************************
//      Blit the bitmap
```

```
//**********************************
// Update the window with the new sprite frame. Note that the
// destination rectangle is our client rectangle, not the
// entire primary surface.
   hRet = lpDDSPrimary->Blt( NULL, lpDDSOffscreen, NULL,
                   DDBLT_WAIT, NULL );
        if(hRet != DD_OK)
           return DDInitFailed(hWnd, hRet,
                   "Blt() failed");
```

Since the window is resizable, we must also provide processing in the WM_PAINT message intercept. However, WM_PAINT is first called when the window is created; at this time, the application has not yet performed the necessary initialization operations. To avoid a possible conflict, we create a public switch variable named DDOn, which is not set until the application is completely initialized. Another consideration is that the call to BeginPaint(), often included in WM_PAINT processing, automatically sets the clipping region to the application's update region. Since we are providing our own clipping, the call to BeginPaint() is undesirable. In the sample program WM_PAINT, message processing reads as follows:

```
case WM_PAINT:
   if(DDOn)
   hRet = lpDDSPrimary->Blt( NULL, lpDDSOffscreen, NULL,
              DDBLT_WAIT, NULL );
   ValidateRect(hwnd, NULL);
   return 0;
```

Rendering by Blit-time Cropping

In the preceding section, we saw the first variation of the *DD InWin Demo* sample program (source file is named DD_InWin.cpp) in which the bitmap image is stretch-blitted to the entire primary surface. A clipper that was previously attached to the primary surface automatically restricts which portion of the image is displayed in the application's window. An alternative rendering option, which produces entirely different results, is blitted to a destination rectangle in the primary surface that corresponds to the size of the application's client area. Because the destination of the blit is restricted to the client area, there is no need for a clipper in this case, since the output is cropped by the Blt() function. Figure 11-13 graphically shows the basic operation of the two versions of the *DD InWin Demo* program.

Processing in DD_InWin.cpp sample program

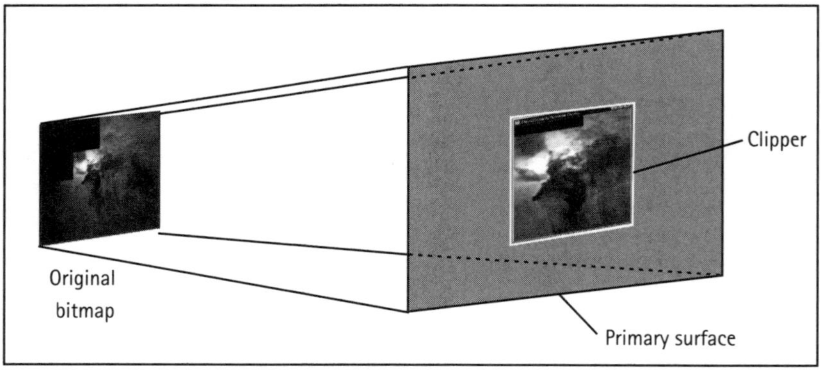

Processing in DD_InWinB.cpp sample program

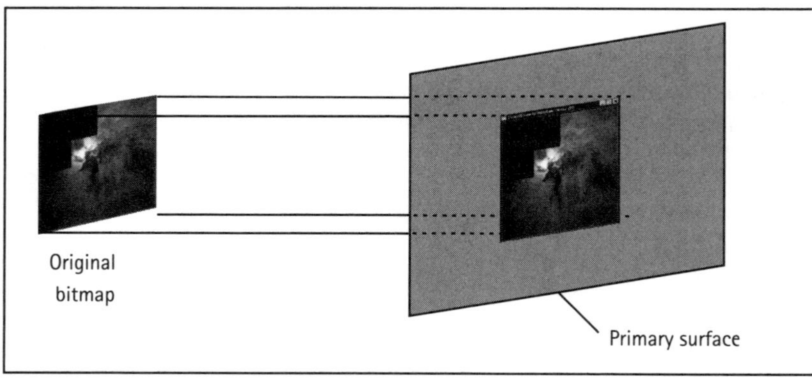

Figure 11-13: Comparing the two versions of the DD InWin Demo sample program

In the DD_InWinB.cpp version, the code proceeds as follows:

The `WNDCLASSEX` structure is defined similarly as in the first version of the sample program, except that, since the program window is not resizeable, the `CS_HREDRAW` and `CS_VREDRAW` window style constants are not necessary. The fixed size of the program window also determines that the code uses `WS_SYSMENU`, `WS_CAPTION`, and `WS_MINIMIZEBOX` as the window style constants in both the `AdjustWindowRectEx()` and `CreateWindowEx()` functions. Note that a resizable window requires the `WS_THICKFRAME` or `WS_SIZEBOX` style. Also, the `WS_OVERLAPPEDWINDOW` style, used in the first version of the sample program, includes `WS_THICKFRAME`, and therefore also produces a resizable window. In the second version, the program window is made the same size as the original bitmap, as is the case in the first version. In the first version, the size of the display area is arbitrary, since the program window is resizable anyway. In the second version, we propose to display the bitmap identically as it is stored; therefore, it is consequential that the display area correspond to the bitmap's size.

Much of the initialization and setup of the second version of the program is similar to the first version. The bitmap is loaded into memory and its size is stored in the corresponding members of a RECT structure variable. The DirectDraw4 object and the primary surface are created. In this case the clipper is not attached to the primary surface since it is not used. Then the off-screen surface is created and the bitmap is stored in it. It is now time to blit the bitmap from the off-screen surface to the primary surface. But before the blit can take place, the code must determine the screen location and the size of the application's client area.

At blit time we need to define the destination rectangle as the first parameter of the Blt() function. One way to visualize the problem is to realize that, at this point, the program window is already displayed with a blank rectangle on its client area, which is the same size as the bitmap. Also, the primary surface is the entire screen. Figure 11-14 shows the application at this stage and the dimensions necessary for locating the client area on the primary surface.

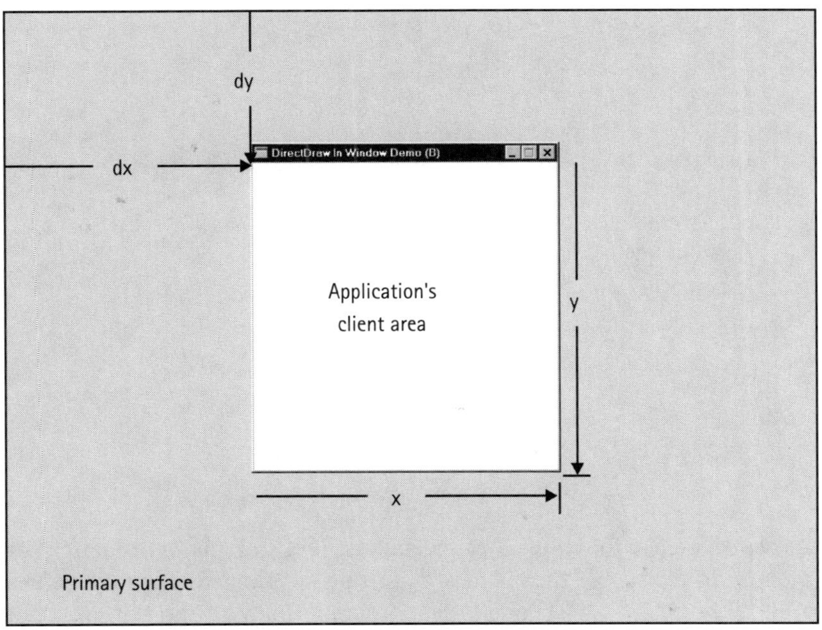

Figure 11-14: Locating the Blt() destination rectangle

The GetClientRect() API function returns the coordinates of the client area of a window. The function parameters are the handle of the target window and the address of a variable of type RECT that holds the client area dimensions. The values returned by GetClientRect() correspond to the *x* and *y* dimensions shown in Figure 11-14. Since the coordinates are relative to the application's window, the value returned by the call for the upper-left corner of the rectangle is always (0,0). This makes the value of the left and top members of the RECT structure variable passed to the call always zero. Since we need the location of application's window in the primary surface, the code must determine the values labeled *dx* and *dy* in Figure 11-14 and add them to the coordinates stored in the RECT structure.

The ClientToScreen() function performs this operation for us. Its parameters are the handle to the application's window and the address of a structure of type POINT containing two coordinate values that are to be updated to screen coordinates. ClientToScreen() actually performs an addition operation on the coordinate pair: it calculates the distances labeled *dx* and *dy* in Figure 11-14 and adds these values to those stored in the structure variable. Since the POINT structure (see Appendix A) contains two members of type LONG and the RECT structure contains four members, we can consider that the RECT structure member holds two structures of type POINT. The code in the sample program reads as follows:

```
RECT              clientArea;      // For Blt() destination
 .
 .
 .
// Obtain client rectangle and convert to screen coordinates
   GetClientRect(hWnd, &clientArea);
   ClientToScreen(hWnd, (LPPOINT) &clientArea.left);
   ClientToScreen(hWnd, (LPPOINT) &clientArea.right);
// Blit to the destination rectangle
   hRet = lpDDSPrimary->Blt( &clientArea,
                             lpDDSOffscreen, NULL,
                             DDBLT_WAIT, NULL );
    if(hRet != DD_OK)
       return DDInitFailed(hWnd, hRet,
                          "Blt() failed");
```

The ClientToScreen() function is called twice. First, for the coordinate pair that holds the top-left corner of the client area rectangle; these are the zero values returned by GetClientRect(). Then for the coordinate pair of the bottom-right corner of the client area rectangle, which correspond to the *x* and *y* dimensions in Figure 11-14. Similar processing must be performed in the WM_PAINT message intercept. Figure 11-15 shows the results of the DD_InWinB.cpp version of the demonstration program.

Figure 11-15: Screen snapshot of the DD_InWinB.cpp program version

The project folder *DD InWind Demo* on the book's CD-ROM contains both versions of the source program as well as the corresponding executable files.

Summary

In this chapter we discussed rendering operations in DirectDraw programming. We started by reviewing surfaces, because DirectDraw bitmap rendering operations always take place at the surface level. We also looked at transparency and color keys as the fundamental tool for overlaying bitmaps. The basic rendering functions, `Blt()` and `BltFast()`, were analyzed in detail, as well as the blit-time transformations consisting of color fills, scaling, mirroring, and raster operations. The chapter also includes sample programs that demonstrate rendering by clipping and by blit-time cropping.

As the chapter title indicates, we considered only static rendering. In the next chapter, we discuss dynamic rendering operations in the context of DirectDraw animation.

Chapter 12

DirectDraw Animation

IN THIS CHAPTER

- The fundamentals of computer animation in real time and the problems associated with surface tearing and rendering performance
- Obtaining a timed pulse for animation, including tick counting and system timer intercepts
- Sprite animation and generating the sprite art and image set
- Flipping techniques, including multiple buffering methods
- Flip animation programming including panning, zooming, and animated objects called sprites
- Advanced performance-tuning techniques for animated applications

ANIMATION IS THE most exacting task of graphics programming. This chapter is about computer animation using the facilities provided by DirectDraw. Before DirectDraw, animation in Windows was considered somewhat of an oxymoron. DirectDraw furnishes mechanisms and programming facilities that make possible graphics rendering at a high speed. It also provides the storage of image data in so-called back buffers, which can be rapidly flipped with the displayed surface to simulate screen movement. The result is often a smooth and natural simulation of movement that can be used in computer games, simulations, and high-performance multimedia applications.

We have excluded from discussion in this chapter some topics that we feel are not important at this time. One of these topics is palette manipulation, which has been used in the past to create primitive forms of animation. Today's video cards, even those in low-end systems, support such resolutions and color depths that palette modes are no longer needed. Overlays, on the other hand, are powerful and useful, but most video cards do not support them, and those that do support them do so inconsistently. Furthermore, overlay operations are not emulated in the HEL, so if they are not available in the hardware, they cannot be used by code. In view of these facts, we feel that overlays belong in the future of graphics programming and palette manipulations in its past. Neither topic is discussed in this chapter.

Animation Fundamentals

Computer animation is the simulation of movement or lifelike actions by the manipulation of digital objects. Animation is a complex specialty field of graphics programming on which many books have been written. Computers play different roles in animation. A computer can serve to create imagery that is later animated using other media, or it can itself produce and display the animated action. The first case is usually referred to as computer-assisted animation. An example of computer-assisted animation is the production of intermediate imagery in a morphing transformation. In this case, the computer software is given the initial and final pictures of an object, and it is then asked to generate a set of intermediate images that gradually transform one into the other. For example, a man's face is gradually transformed into that of a wolf. Morphing transformations are now a common special effect in television and motion pictures.

In another form of animation, the computer is used to simulate movement in real time. This is the way in which many computer games and simulations are implemented. In real-time animation, the imagery is displayed in the user's own time frame; there is no image storage for later playback. The animation is shown "live" as it happens. Often the user interacts with the system. For example, a flight simulator program consists of animated imagery of the aircraft's cockpit and of the pilot's view through the windshield. The actions performed by the virtual pilot flying the digital aircraft determine changes in the cockpit instruments and in the landscape seen through the windshield.

Real-time Animation

In this chapter, we are concerned with real-time animation, rather than with computer-assisted techniques. Real-time animation is found in arcade machines, simulators, trainers, electronic games, multimedia applications, and interactive programs of many kinds. In real-time animation, the computing machine is often both the image generator and the display media, although most animations rely heavily on prestored images and image sets.

Real-time animation is based on the fact that the image of an object perceived by the human eye persists in the brain for a brief period of time after the object no longer exists. This phenomenon is called *visual retention*. Smooth animation is achieved by consecutively displaying images at a faster rate than the period of visual retention. It is the sequence of rapidly displayed images that creates in our minds the illusion of a smoothly moving object.

Television and moving picture technologies have estimated the critical image update rate for smooth animation to be between 22 and 30 images per second. In animation programming, this is called the *frame rate*. Moving picture films are recorded and displayed at a rate of 24 images per second, while commercial television takes place at a slightly faster pace. The threshold rate, which is subject to individual variations, is sometimes estimated at about 17 images per second. If the consecutive images are projected at a rate slower than this threshold, the average individual perceives jerkiness in the animation and feels uncomfortable watching it.

Surface Tearing

While the animator's principal concerns are usually speed and performance, too much speed can lead to image quality deterioration. A raster scan display system scans each horizontal row of screen pixels with an electron beam. The pixel rows are refreshed starting at the top-left corner of the screen and ending at the bottom-right corner. Each pixel row is called a *scan line*. The electron beam is turned off at the end of each scan line while the gun is reaimed to the start of the next line. This period is called the *horizontal retrace*. When this process reaches the last scan line on the screen, the beam is turned off again while the gun is reaimed to the top-left screen corner. The period of time required to reaim the electron gun from the right-bottom corner of the screen to the top-left corner is known as the *vertical retrace* or *screen blanking* cycle. Figure 12-1 shows the scan and retrace cycles.

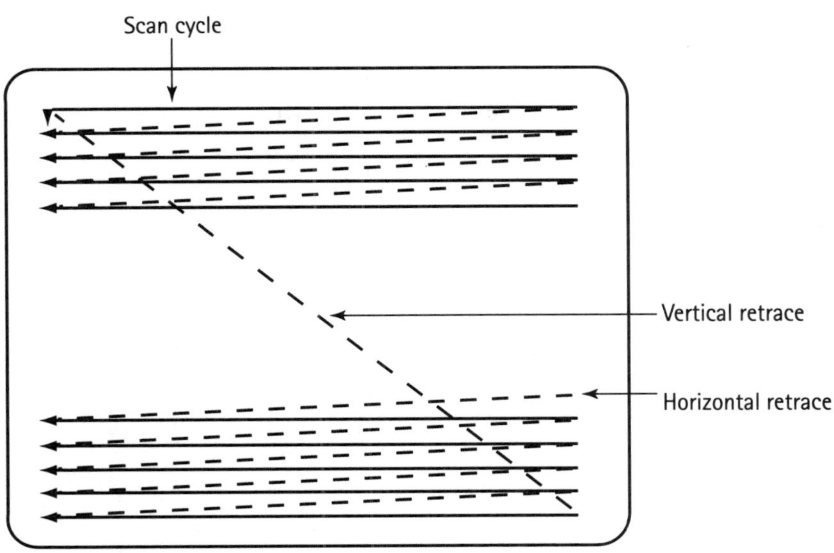

Figure 12-1: CRT scan and retrace cycles

The problem arises when video data is changed by the CPU at the same time it is being displayed by the video controller. In the PC, screen refresh rates are normally between 60Hz and 100Hz, while a modern-day CPU may be capable of executing hundreds of thousands of instructions per second. This makes it quite possible that the image in video memory is modified before the video system has finished displaying it. The result is a breaking of the image known as *tearing*. One way to avoid tearing is to limit video memory updates to the time the electron guns are turned off. In practice, this is the vertical retrace cycle, because it takes longer than the horizontal retrace.

DirectDraw programs that execute in exclusive mode can prevent or minimize tearing by using double-buffering and flipping techniques, which we discuss later in this chapter. Programs in windowed mode cannot use flipping and are limited to timing video updates with the vertical refresh cycle.

The Animator's Predicament

For all these reasons, computer animation is often a battle against time. The animation programmer must resort to every possible trick in order to squeeze out the maximum performance while executing the image update and display operations. Most of the work of the programmer-animator consists of making compromises and finding acceptable levels of undesirable effects.

The animator must often decide the following:

- How small an image satisfactorily depicts the object
- How much tearing is acceptable
- How much bumpiness can be allowed in depicting movement
- How little definition is sufficient for certain scenery
- How few colors can realistically represent an object

Obtaining a Timed Pulse

Representing movement requires a display sequence, executed frame-by-frame, that creates the illusion of motion. Figure 12-2 shows several frames in the animation of a stick figure of a walking person.

Figure 12-2: Frame-by-frame animation of a stick figure

The display of the frame-by-frame sequence in real-time animation requires a mechanism for measuring the time lapse between each frame, or in other words, an *update pulse*. In DOS programming, this can be accomplished by intercepting the system timer, which usually requires installation of a dedicated interrupt vector. The result is that a routine in the application's code receives control every time a preset timer counter expires. Because in DOS there is no multitasking, the resulting timing pulse is reasonably accurate. Windows, on the other hand, does not enable direct manipulation of the timer hardware.

A Windows application has several ways of generating a timed pulse. One is based on a program loop that reads the value in a ticker register and proceeds to update the frame whenever it matches or exceeds a predefined constant. A second approach is to enable a system timer pulse that can be intercepted in a callback function or by a window message. In the following sections we discuss both methods. We discuss other alternatives, sometimes called high-resolution timers, in the context of performance tuning later in this chapter.

Tick-counting Method

Windows maintains a counter with the number of milliseconds elapsed since the system was started. This time period, sometimes called the Windows time, is stored in a `DWORD` variable that can be read by code. Two identical functions enable you to read this counter: `GetCurrentTime()` and `GetTickCount()`. Windows documentation states that `GetCurrentTime()` is now obsolete and should not be used.

`GetTickCount()`, which takes no parameters, returns the number of milliseconds elapsed since Windows was started. Application code can determine the number of milliseconds elapsed since the last call by storing the previous value in a static or public variable, as in the following function:

```
...// Public variables for counter operation
   DWORD          thisTickCount;     // New ticker value
   DWORD          lastTickCount;     // Storage for old value
   static DWORD   TIMER_VALUE = 25;  // Constant for time lapse
   .
   .
   .
static void UpdateFrame()
{
   thisTickCount = GetTickCount();    // Read counter
   if(( thisTickCount - lastTickCount) < TIMER_VALUE)
      return;
   else
   {
      // Frame update operations go here
    lastTickCount = thisTickCount;    // Reset tick counts
```

```
    }
    return;
}
```

In order for the ticker counter reading method to produce a smooth animation, the value in the ticker counter must be polled frequently. One possible approach is to include the frame update function call as part of the application's message loop. The processing logic can be expressed in the following pseudo-code:

If the application is active, and no other messages are waiting to be processed, then call the frame update routine.

The `PeekMessage()` function is used to check the thread's message queue without pausing to wait for a message. The function's general form is as follows:

```
BOOL PeekMessage(
                  LPMSG lpMsg,          // 1
                  HWND hWnd,            // 2
                  UINT wMsgFilterMin,   // 3
                  UINT wMsgFilterMax,   // 4
                  UINT wRemoveMsg       // 5
);
```

The first parameter points to an `MSG` structure variable that contains message information. The second parameter is the handle to the window whose messages are being checked. This parameter can be set to `NULL` to check messages for the current application. The third and the fourth parameters are used to specify the lowest and highest value of the messages to be checked. If both parameters are set to 0, then all messages are retrieved. The fifth parameter is one of two predefined constants: `PM_REMOVE` is used if the message is to be removed from the queue, and `PM_NOPREMOVE` is used otherwise. The call returns `TRUE` if a message is available and `FALSE` if a message is not available.

Another API function often used in message polling routines is `WaitMessage()`. This function, which takes no parameters, suspends thread execution and does not return until a new message is placed in the queue. As a result, when the current thread has nothing to do with its CPU cycles, it yields control to other threads. `PeekMessage()` and `WaitMessage()` can be combined with `GetMessage()` in the following message polling routine:

```
MSG         msg;            // Message structure variable
int         appActive = 0;  // Application active switch
                            // initialized to inactive
.
.
.
while(1) {
```

```
  if(PeekMessage(&msg, NULL, 0, 0, PM_NOREMOVE)) {
    if(!GetMessage(&msg, NULL, 0, 0)
      return msg.wParam;
    TranslateMessage(&msg);
    DispatchMessage(&msg);
  }
  else if (appActive)
  {
  // call to read ticker counter and/or update frame
  // go here
  }
else
   WaitMessage();
}
```

In this sample code, the application must define when to set and reset the `appActive` switch. This switch determines if the frame update function is called, or if the thread just waits for another message.

The method just described – that is, reading the Windows tick count inside a program loop – is usually capable of generating a faster pulse than the system timer intercept described in the next section. On the other hand, the system timer intercept is easier to implement and more consistent with the Windows multitasking environment. Therefore, it is the preferred method if the resulting pulse rate is satisfactory.

System Timer Intercept

An alternative way of obtaining a timed pulse is by means of the Windows system timer. The `SetTimer()` function is used to define a time-out value in milliseconds. When this time-out value elapses, the application gets control either at the `WM_TIMER` message intercept or in an application-defined callback function that has the generic name `TimerProc()`. Either processing technique is satisfactory, and which one is selected is a matter of coding convenience. `SetTimer()` has the following general form:

```
UINT SetTimer(
              HWND hWnd,              // 1
              UINT nIDEvent,          // 2
              UINT uElapse,           // 3
              TIMERPROC lpTimerFunc   // 4
);
```

The first parameter is the handle to the window associated with the timer. The second parameter is the timer number. This enables more than one timer per application. The timer identifier is passed to the `WM_TIMER` intercept and to the `TimerProc()`. The third parameter is the number of milliseconds between timer intercepts. The fourth parameter is the address of the application's `TimerProc()`, if one is implemented, or `NULL` if processing is to be done in the `WM_TIMER` message intercept.

If the call succeeds, the return value is an integer identifying the new timer. This is true of 16-bit Windows, not Win32. Applications must pass this timer identifier to the `KillTimer()` function to destroy a particular timer. If the function fails to create a timer, the return value is 0. Once a system timer has been initialized, processing usually consists of calling the application's frame update function directly, because the timer tick need not be checked in this case.

> **Note:** Code cannot assume that system timer events will be generated at the requested rate, only that the events will be produced approximately at this rate and not more frequently. Windows documentation states that the minimum time between events is approximately 55 milliseconds.

Sprite Animation

In graphics programming, particularly in game programming, a sprite is defined as a rather small screen object, usually animated at display time. Sprite animation can be simple or complex. In the first case, an object represented in a single bitmap is animated by translating it to other screen positions, or the object itself performs an intrinsic action such as rotating a wheel. In complex animation, both actions are performed simultaneously; for example, a rocket moves on the screen until it reaches a point where it explodes. Sprites are typically encoded in one or more images that represent the object or its action sequence. The images can be stored in separate bitmaps, or in a single one. Figure 12-3 shows the image set of a dagger sprite that revolves around its own axis.

When the 20 images in the set of Figure 12-3 are rapidly displayed, the dagger appears to rotate 180 degrees. If the images are also translated from one screen position to another, the sprite simulates the action of throwing a dagger. This last action would be a case of complex sprite animation.

Sprites often use a source color key in order to achieve transparency. To automate sprite color keying, some applications assume that the pixel at the top-left corner of the bitmap is the color key. Later in this chapter we discuss dynamic color keys. It is possible to encode each image of the sprite image set in separate bitmaps, but this usually leads to many disk files and complicated file access operations. A better approach is to store the entire sprite image set in a single bitmap, and then use the source rectangle selection capability of either the `Blt()` or `BltFast()` functions to pick the corresponding image.

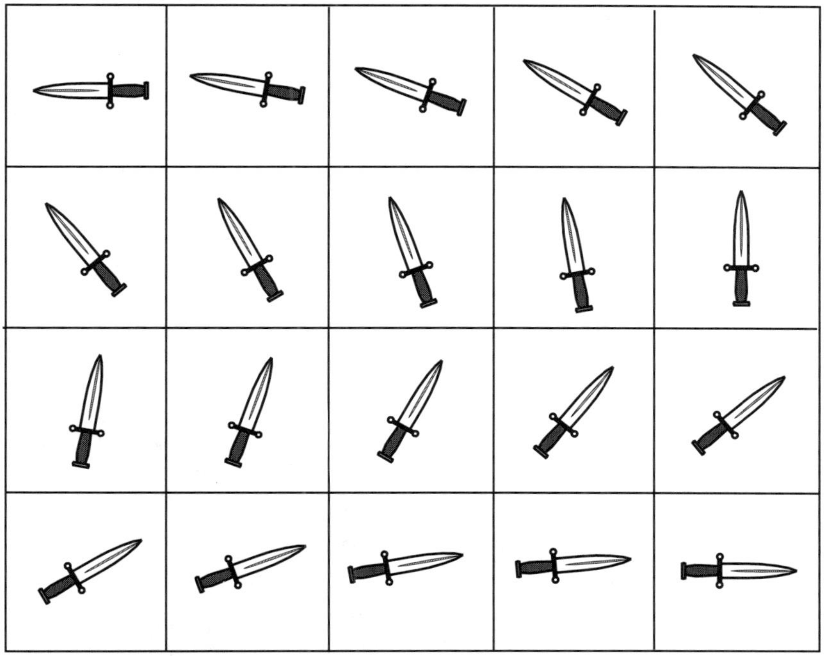

Figure 12-3: Image set for a dagger sprite

Many factors determine how a sprite is actually rendered. One of the most important factors is whether the application executes in exclusive mode or windowed mode. Exclusive mode programs can use back buffers and flipping manipulations that considerably increase performance, while windowed mode programs are much more limited in the available rendering operations. Other factors are the sprite's size, the number of images in the set, and the required rendering speed. Programmers must often juggle these and other program elements in order to come up with a satisfactory animation.

3-D Sprite Art

Animated programs spend considerable resources manipulating sprites and backgrounds. It is common sense that the better the image quality of these objects, the better the graphics that result. Because backgrounds are animated by simple panning and zooming transformations, the programmer's effort is usually limited to scanning or drawing relatively few and relatively large images. But sprites can be a more complicated matter, especially if the sprite is to have intrinsic movements or action. In this case, the individual images in the sprite set must be tied to a common point. For example, if the various daggers in Figure 12-3 do not have a common center of rotation, the resulting animation is bumpy and unpleasant. The progression between each image in the set must also be proportional. In other words, the dagger in Figure 12-3 must rotate by approximately the same angle between each image in order to generate uniform screen movement. But perhaps the most important factor in creating good sprites is the sprite itself.

A few years ago, the creation of attractive sprites was considered some sort of black art. With the popularization of 3-D graphics on the PC, it is possible to easily create solid sprites that add a new dimension to the animation. Relatively inexpensive programs are now available that generate 3-D graphics objects that can be animated. Some popular commercial drawing applications, such as CorelDraw 8, now include 3-D drawing capabilities. Figure 12-4 shows the rotation of a clipart 3-D image using CorelDraw 8. The resulting image set can be used to produce an intrinsic sprite animation.

Figure 12-4: Rotation of a 3-D image using commercial software

The Sprite Image Set

The typical computer animator spends a large portion of his or her available time designing, drawing, encoding, and testing sprites. This is true whether the sprite image is in 2-D or 3-D graphics. The process of sprite design implies several apparently contradictory decisions, for instance:

- The larger the sprite the better its image quality, but it is more difficult to animate a larger sprite.
- The more images in the sprite image set the smoother the animation, but it takes longer to display a large sprite image set.

- The higher the definition and color depth of the sprite bitmaps, the better the quality of the image, but higher quality bitmaps take up more video memory and take longer to blit.

Two hardware-dependent issues must also often be taken into consideration: the processor speed of the host system and the capabilities of the video system. The latter of these issues comprises two other issues: the amount of video memory available and the hardware support for DirectDraw operations. Once the designers have defined the minimum system capabilities and the acceptable performance levels, the next step is usually to experiment with several sprite image sets in order to determine the best possible image quality for the required levels of performance.

The details of how the sprite image sets are produced is more in the realm of graphics design than in programming. The better the drawing or painting program used and the more experienced the sprite artist, the easier it is to produce a satisfactory image set. The *DD Animation Demo* project included on the book's CD-ROM shows two rotating, meshed gears. The image set consists of 18 images. In each image, the gears are rotated by an angle of 2.5 degrees. After 18 iterations, the gears have rotated through an angle of 45 degrees. Because the gears have 8 teeth each, the images are symmetrical after a rotation of 45 degrees. For this reason, this animation requires one-eighth the number of images that would be necessary to rotate a nonsymmetrical object by the same angle. For example, to perform a complete rotation of the dagger in Figure 12-3 at 2.5 degree increments would require a total of 144 images. Figure 12-5 shows the sequence of steps that we followed in creating the image set for the *DD Animation Demo* program.

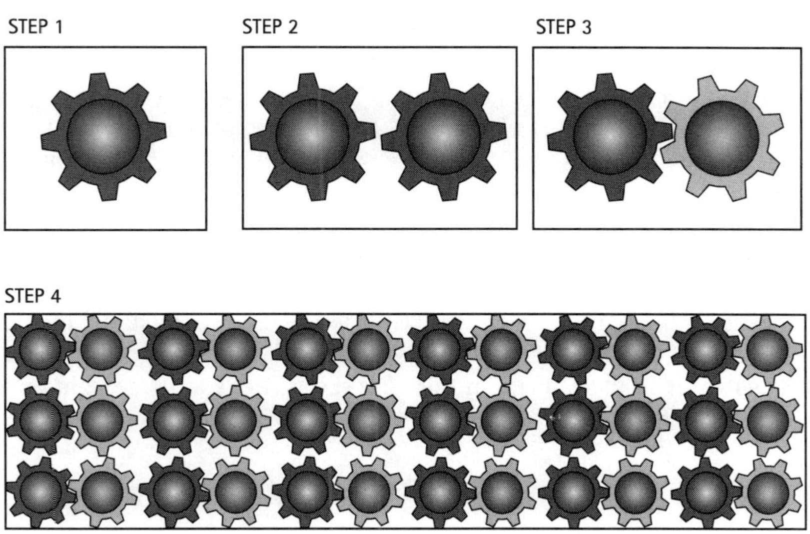

Figure 12-5: Creating the image set for DD Animation Demo program

In creating the image set of the *DD Animation Demo* program, we started with a CorelDraw 8 clipart image of a gear that was then edited and colored as shown in step 1 in Figure 12-5. In step 2 we made a copy of the original gear. The copy was colored and rotated so that the two gears would mesh, as shown in step 3. The meshed gear pair was then reproduced 18 times. In each reproduction the left-hand gear was rotated clockwise and the right-hand gear was rotated counterclockwise by 2.5 degrees. The resulting image set is shown in step 4 in Figure 12-5. This image set was then saved as a Windows bitmap for use by the code.

Sprite Rendering

The actual display of the sprite consists of obtaining a timing pulse and blitting the image onto the screen. Whether the rendering is done using `Blt()` or `BltFast()`, with or without transparency, using source or destination color keys, or applying any blit-time transformations depends on the particular case. You have seen that the sprite image sequence is usually stored in a single bitmap. It is also possible to store the various bitmaps in different disk files and then read all those files into a common surface or memory area. Either case results in a surface with multiple images. At blit time the program logic must select the corresponding image in the animation set.

The display of several images stored in a contiguous memory area or surface is made possible by the fact that both `Blt()` and `BltFast()` support the definition of a source area for the blit. In Chapter 11, you saw that a structure of type `RECT` is used to store the offset of the source rectangle in the surface. If an animation image set is stored in a rectangular bitmap, and the bitmap is then loaded onto a surface, then code can select which of the images in the set is displayed during each time-pulse iteration. This is done by assigning values to the corresponding members of the `RECT` structure variable that defines the source surface. For example, the final bitmap image set in Figure 12-5 contains a sequence of 18 individual rotations of the gears. Each of these individual bitmaps is often called an animation frame, or simply, a frame. Figure 12-6 shows the image set partitioned into six rows and three columns. The dimensions labeled *x* and *y* refer to the size of each frame in the set.

Given the number of rows and columns in the image set and the pixel size of each image, code can determine the coordinates of the `RECT` structure variable for each frame in the set. In Figure 12-6, notice the imaginary rectangle (in dotted lines) that binds each frame in the sequence. The members of a structure variable named `rect`, of type `RECT`, are calculated using the consecutive frame number and the number of columns in the bitmap. In this case the frame is number eight and the bitmap has six columns.

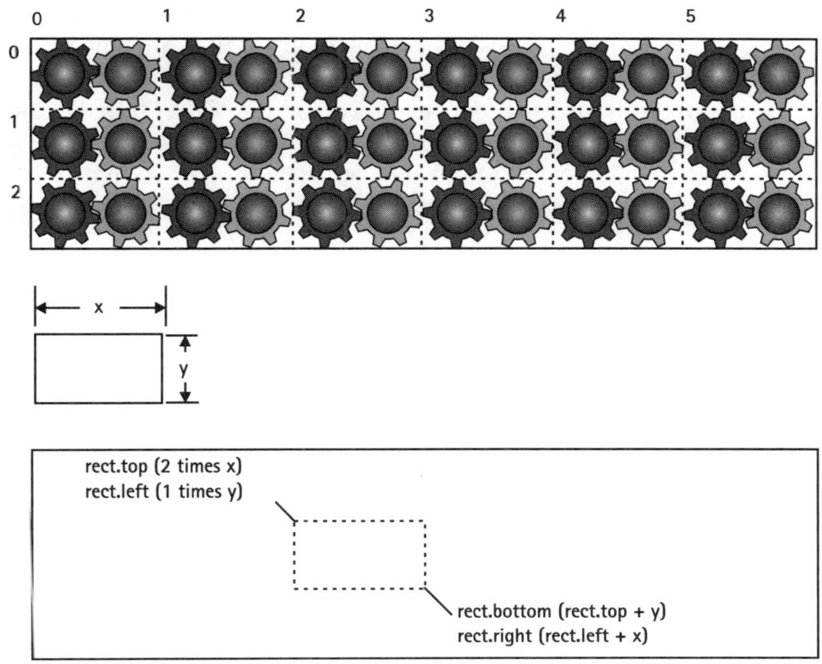

Figure 12-6: Rendering the sprite image set

In the *DD Animation Demo* program, the processing has been generalized so the code can be used to display any rectangular bitmap image set. This makes it useful for experimenting with various image sets before deciding which one is better suited for the purpose at hand. Code starts by creating global variables that define the characteristics of the image set. Code is as follows:

```
// Constants identifying the bitmap image set
static char bmapName[] = {"gearsy.bmp"};
static int          imageCols = 6;   // Number of image
// columns
static int          imageRows = 3; // Number of rows

// Variables, constants, handles, and structure for bitmaps
int          frameCount = (imageCols * imageRows) - 1;
int          bmapXSize;      // Calculated x size of bitmap
int          bmapYSize;      // Calculated y size of bitmap
HBITMAP      aBitmap;
BITMAP       bMap1;          // Structures for bitmap data
```

In this case the programmer defines the name of the bitmap and states the number of image columns and rows. Code uses these values to calculate the number of frames; this number is stored in the variable `frameCount`. The dimensions of the bitmap are obtained after it is loaded into memory. The *x* dimension is stored in the variable `bmapXSize` and the *y* dimension is stored in `bmapYSize`. The bitmap dimensions are also used in the sample program to define the size of the application window, all of which is shown in the following code fragment:

```
//************************************
//     Load bitmap into memory
//************************************
// Load the bitmap image into memory
aBitmap = ( HBITMAP )LoadImage( NULL, bmapName,
          IMAGE_BITMAP, 0, 0, LR_LOADFROMFILE );
  if ( aBitmap == NULL )
       DDInitFailed(hWnd, hRet,
        "Bitmap load failed in DDLoadBitmap()");
// Get bitmap data
GetObject(aBitmap, sizeof (BITMAP), &bMap1);

// Calculate and store bitmap and image data
bmapXSize = bMap1.bmWidth / imageCols;
bmapYSize = bMap1.bmHeight / imageRows;

// Store bitmap in RECT structure variable
progWin.left = 0;
progWin.top = 0;
progWin.right = bmapXSize;
progWin.bottom = bmapYSize;

//****************************************
//   Create window with client area
//   the same size as the bitmap
//****************************************
// First adjust the size of the client area to the size
// of the bounding rectangle (this includes the border,
// caption bar, menu, etc.)

 AdjustWindowRectEx(&progWin,
          WS_SYSMENU | WS_CAPTION,
          FALSE,
          0);

 hWnd = CreateWindowEx(0,        // Extended style
```

```
          szAppName,
          "DirectDraw Animation Demo",
          WS_SYSMENU | WS_CAPTION,
          CW_USEDEFAULT,
          CW_USEDEFAULT,
          (progWin.right - progWin.left),
          (progWin.bottom - progWin.top),
          NULL,            // Handle of parent
          NULL,            // Handle to menu
          hInstance,       // Application instance
          NULL);           // Additional data
  if (!hWnd)
      return FALSE;
```

The actual display of the bitmap is performed by a local function called `BlitSprite()`. The function begins by checking the tick counter. If the difference between the old and the new tick counts is smaller than the predefined delay, execution returns immediately. If it is equal to or larger than the delay, then the offset of the next frame in the source surface is calculated and the bitmap is blitted by means of the `Blt()` function. In this case the frame number counter is bumped; if this is the last frame in the set, the counter is restarted. Execution concludes by updating the tick counter variable. Coding is as follows:

```
//**************************************
//      update animation frame
//**************************************
static void BlitSprite()
{
  thisTickCount = GetTickCount();

  if((thisTickCount - lastTickCount) < TIMER_VALUE)
    return;
  else
 {
 // Update the sprite image with the current frame.
 bmapArea.top = ( ( frameNum / imageCols) * bmapYSize );
 bmapArea.left = ( ( frameNum % imageCols) * bmapXSize );
 bmapArea.bottom = bmapArea.top + bmapYSize;
 bmapArea.right = bmapArea.left + bmapXSize;

 hRet = lpDDSPrimary->Blt( &clientArea, lpDDSOffscreen,
        &bmapArea, DDBLT_WAIT, NULL );
        if(hRet != DD_OK)
             DDInitFailed(hWnd, hRet, "Blt() failed");
```

```
    // Update the frame counter
     frameNum++;
     if(frameNum > imageCount)
        frameNum = 0;
     lastTickCount = thisTickCount;
     return;
    }
}
```

Figure 12-7 is a screen snapshot of the *DD Animation Demo* program.

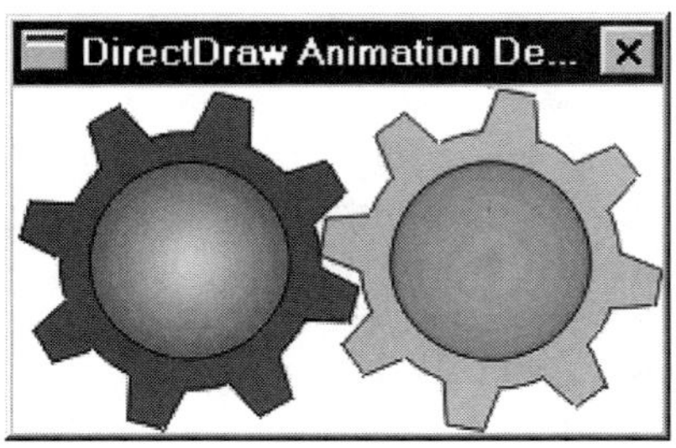

Figure 12-7: Screen snapshot of the DD Animation Demo program

Flipping

One of the most powerful animation tools provided by DirectDraw is page flipping. Page flipping is most often used in high-performance multimedia applications, in simulations, and in game software. The process is reminiscent of the schoolhouse method of drawing a series of images containing slight changes. The figures are drawn on a paper pad, and when you thumb through the stack of pages, you see the illusion of movement. In the simplest version of computerized page flipping, the programmer sets up two DirectDraw surfaces. The first one is the conventional primary surface and the second one is called a *back buffer.* Application code updates the image in the back buffer and then flips the back buffer and the primary surface. The result is usually a clean and efficient animation effect. Figure 12-8 shows the fade-out animation of a sphere.

In Figure 12-8, notice that consecutively smaller images are drawn on the back buffer, which is then flipped with the primary surface. In this illustration the arrows represent the flip operations. The back buffers are shown in dark gray rectangles. The sequence of operations is the following: draw back buffer, flip, draw back buffer, flip, and so on.

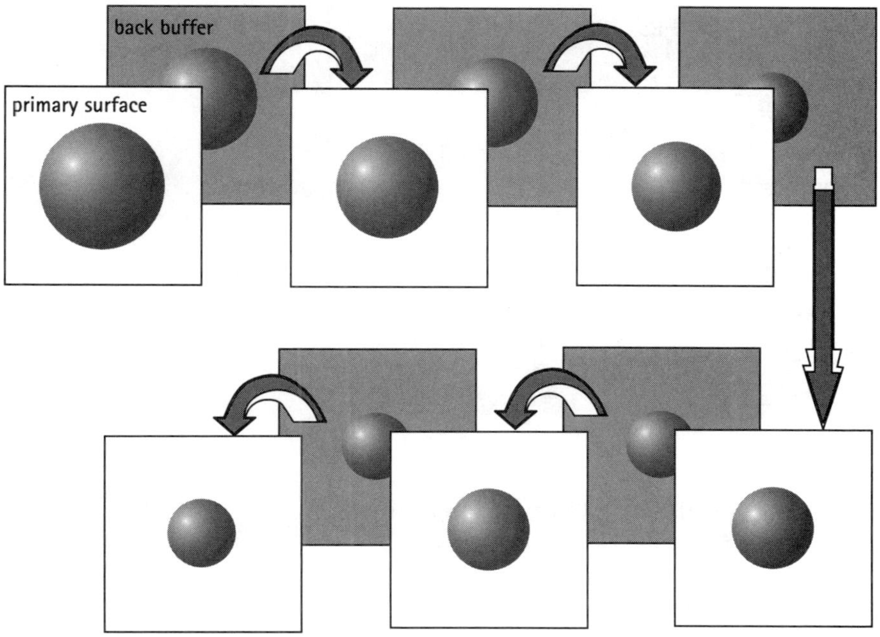

Figure 12-8: Fade-out animation by flipping

One limitation of multiple buffering and page flipping is they can only be used in DirectDraw exclusive mode. This is due to the fact that flipping requires the manipulation of video memory directly, which is unacceptable in a windowed environment. In the DirectDraw flip operation, it is the pointers to surface memory for the primary surface and the back buffers that are swapped. It is actually a switching of pointers, not a data copying operation. Exceptions are when the back buffer cannot fit into display memory, or when the hardware does not support flipping, in which cases DirectDraw performs the flip by copying the surfaces.

When programming a flip-based animation, it is important to remember that code need only access the back buffer surface in order to perform the image updates. Every time the DirectDraw `Flip()` function is called, the primary surface becomes the back buffer and vice versa. The surface pointer to the back buffer always points to the area of video memory not displayed, and the surface pointer to the primary surface or front buffer points to the video memory being displayed. If more than one back buffer is included in the flipping chain, the surfaces are rotated in circular fashion. Figure 12-9 shows a flipping chain with a primary surface and two back buffers. In this case, the flip operation rotates the surfaces as shown.

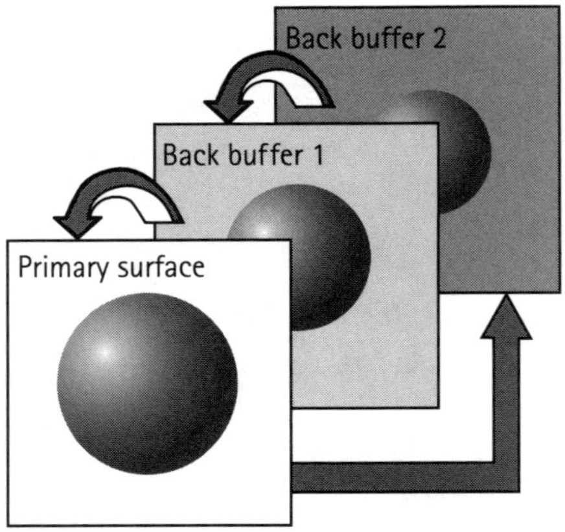

Figure 12-9: Flipping chain with two back buffers

Initializing and performing flip animation consists of several well-defined steps. In most cases the following operations are necessary:

1. Create a flipping chain.
2. Obtain a back buffer pointer.
3. Draw to the back buffer.
4. Flip the primary surface and the back buffer.

The first two steps of this sequence relate to initializing the flipping surfaces, and the second two steps refer to flip animation rendering operations. Table 12-1 lists the flipping-related functions in DirectDraw.

TABLE 12-1 FLIPPING-RELATED DIRECTDRAW FUNCTIONS

Function	Object	Action
`CreateSurface()`	`DIRECTDRAW4`	Creates surface and attached back buffers
`GetAttachedSurface()`	`DIRECTDRAWSURFACE4`	Obtains back buffer pointer
`Flip()`	`DIRECTDRAW4`	Performs flipping
`GetFlipStatus()`	`DIRECDRAWSURFACE4`	Indicates whether a surface has concluded flipping

The function FlipToGDISurface(), which is rarely used, is not discussed in this book.

Initializing the Flipping Surfaces

Any DirectDraw surface can be constructed as a flipping surface, although most flipping surfaces consist of a primary surface and at least one back buffer. The surfaces involved in the flipping are sometimes called the flipping chain. Creating the flipping chain requires two DirectDraw functions: CreateSurface() is used to create both the primary surface and the back buffer, and GetAttachedSurface() is used to obtain the back buffer pointer. The CreateSurface() function is discussed in Chapter 10 and revisited in Chapter 11. In the case of a flipping chain, the call to CreateSurface() must include the flag DDSD_BACKBUFFERCOUNT, which defines the member dwBackBufferCount, which in turn is used to set the number of back buffers in the chain. Other flags usually listed in the call are DDSCAPS_PRIMARYSURFACE, DDSCAPS_FLIP, DDSCAPS_COMPLEX, and DDSCAPS_VIDEOMEMORY. The following code shows a call to CreateSurface() for a flipping chain consisting of a primary surface and a single back buffer:

```
DDSURFACEDESC2      ddsd;
.
.
.
// Create the primary surface with a back buffer
ZeroMemory(&ddsd, sizeof(ddsd));  // Fill structure with zeros
// Fill in other members
   ddsd.dwSize = sizeof(ddsd);
   ddsd.dwFlags = DDSD_CAPS | DDSD_BACKBUFFERCOUNT;
   ddsd.ddsCaps.dwCaps = DDSCAPS_PRIMARYSURFACE |
                         DDSCAPS_FLIP |
                         DDSCAPS_COMPLEX |
                         DDSCAPS_VIDEOMEMORY;
   ddsd.dwBackBufferCount = 1;
   hRet = lpDD4->CreateSurface(&ddsd, &lpDDSPrimary, NULL);
```

If the call to CreateSurface() returns DD_OK, then the flipping chain surfaces have been created. In order to use the flipping chain, code must first obtain the pointer to the back buffer, because the call to CreateSurface() returns only the pointer to the primary surface (in its second parameter). The GetAttachedSurface() function has the following general form:

```
HRESULT GetAttachedSurface(
     LPDDSCAPS lpDDSCaps,                             // 1
     LPDIRECTDRAWSURFACE3 FAR *lplpDDAttachedSurface  // 2
);
```

The first parameter is a pointer to a DDSCAPS2 structure that contains the hardware capabilities of the surface. The second parameter is the address of a variable that is to hold the pointer, of type IDIRECTDRAWSURFACE4, retrieved by the call. The retrieved surface matches the description in the first parameter. If the function succeeds, it returns DD_OK. If it fails, it returns one of the following errors:

- DDERR_INVALIDOBJECT
- DDERR_INVALIDPARAMS
- DDERR_NOTFOUND
- DDERR_SURFACELOST

The following code fragment obtains the back buffer surface pointer for the primary surface previously described:

```
// Get back buffer pointer
   ddscaps.dwCaps = DDSCAPS_BACKBUFFER;
   hRet = lpDDSPrimary->GetAttachedSurface(&ddscaps,
                        &lpDDSBackBuf);
```

If the calls to CreateSurface() and GetAttachedSurface() are successful, DirectDraw creates two attached surfaces in display memory, and the application retrieves the pointers to each of these surfaces. The pointer to the back buffer surface is used at draw time, and the pointer to the primary surface at flip time. DirectDraw automatically switches the surface pointers transparent to application code.

Flipping Operations

Once the application has concluded drawing and the frame timer count has expired, the actual rendering is performed by calling DirectDraw Flip(). The Flip() function exchanges the surface memory of the primary surface and the back buffer. If more than one back buffer is specified when the flip chain is created, then each call to Flip() rotates the surfaces in a circular manner, as shown in Figure 12-9. When DirectDraw flipping is supported by the hardware, as is the case in most current video cards, flipping consists of changing pointers and no image data is physically moved. The function's general form is as follows:

```
HRESULT Flip(
     LPDIRECTDRAWSURFACE3 lpDDSurfaceTargetOverride,  // 1
     DWORD dwFlags                                     // 2
);
```

The first parameter, sometimes called the *target override,* is the address of the IDirectDrawSurface4 interface for any surface in the flipping chain. The default value for this parameter is NULL, in which case DirectDraw cycles through the flip chain surfaces in the order they are attached to each other. If this parameter is not NULL, then DirectDraw flips to the specified surface instead of the next surface in the flipping chain, thus overriding the default order. The call fails if the specified surface is not a member of the flipping chain.

The second parameter specifies one of the predefined constants that control flip options. The constants are listed in Table 12-2.

TABLE 12-2 DIRECTDRAW FLIP() FUNCTION FLAGS

Flag	Action
DDFLIP_EVEN	Used only when displaying video in an overlay surface. The new surface contains data from the even field of a video signal. Cannot be used with the DDFLIP_ODD flag.
DDFLIP_INTERVAL2	See action for DDFLIP_INTERVAL4.
DDFLIP_INTERVAL3	See action for DDFLIP_INTERVAL4.
DDFLIP_INTERVAL4	Indicates how many vertical retraces to wait between each flip. The default is 1. DirectDraw returns DERR_WASSTILLDRAWING until the specified number of vertical retraces has occurred. If DDFLIP_INTERVAL2 is set, DirectDraw flips on every second vertical retrace cycle. If DDFLIP_INTERVAL3 is set, DirectDraw flips on every cycle, and so on. These flags are effective only if DDCAPS2_FLIPINTERVAL is set in the DDCAPS structure for the device.
DDFLIP_NOVSYNC	DirectDraw performs the physical flip as close as possible to the next scan line. Subsequent operations involving the two flipped surfaces do not check to see if the physical flip has finished; that is, they do not return DDERR_WASSTILLDRAWING. This flag enables an application to perform flips at a higher frequency than the monitor refresh rate. The usual consequence is the introduction of visible artifacts (tearing). If DDCAPS2_FLIPNOVSYNC is not set in the DDCAPS structure for the device, DDFLIP_NOVSYNC has no effect.
DDFLIP_ODD	Used only when displaying video in an overlay surface. The new surface contains data from the odd field of a video signal. This flag cannot be used with the DDFLIP_EVEN flag.

Continued

TABLE 12-2 DIRECTDRAW FLIP() FUNCTION FLAGS *(Continued)*

Flag	Action
DDFLIP_WAIT	If the flip cannot be set up because the state of the display hardware is not appropriate, then the DDERR_WASSTILLDRAWING is immediately returned and no flip occurs. Setting this flag causes Flip() to continue trying if it receives the DDERR_ WASSTILLDRAWING. In this case, the call does not return until the flipping operation has been successfully set up, or another error, such as DDERR_SURFACEBUSY, is returned.

If the Flip() call succeeds, the return value is DD_OK. If it fails, one of the following errors is returned:

- DDERR_GENERIC
- DDERR_INVALIDOBJECT
- DDERR_INVALIDPARAMS
- DDERR_NOFLIPHW
- DDERR_NOTFLIPPABLE
- DDERR_SURFACEBUSY
- DDERR_SURFACELOST
- DDERR_UNSUPPORTED
- DDERR_WASSTILLDRAWING

The Flip() function can be called only for surfaces that have the DDSCAPS_FLIP and DDSCAPS_FRONTBUFFER capabilities. The first parameter is used in rare cases when the back buffer is not the buffer that should become the front buffer. In most cases this parameter is NULL. In its default state, the Flip() function is always synchronized with the vertical retrace cycle of the video controller. When working with visible surfaces, such as a primary surface-flipping chain, the Flip() function is asynchronous, except if the DDFLIP_WAIT flag is included.

Many applications check if Flip() returns with a DDERR_SURFACELOST error. If so, code can make an attempt to restore the surface by means of the DirectDraw Restore() function, which is discussed in Chapter 11. If the restore is successful, the application loops back to the Flip() call and tries again. If the restore is unsuccessful, the application breaks from the while loop, and returns a terminal error.

Multiple Buffering

The call to Flip() can return before the actual flip operation takes place, because the hardware waits until the next vertical retrace to actually flip the surfaces. While the Flip() operation is pending, the back buffer directly behind the currently visible surface cannot be locked or blitted to. If code attempts to call Lock(), Blt(), BltFast(), or GetDC() while a flip is pending, the call fails and the function returns DDERR_WASSTILLDRAWING. The effect of the surface update time on the frame rate is shown in Figure 12-10.

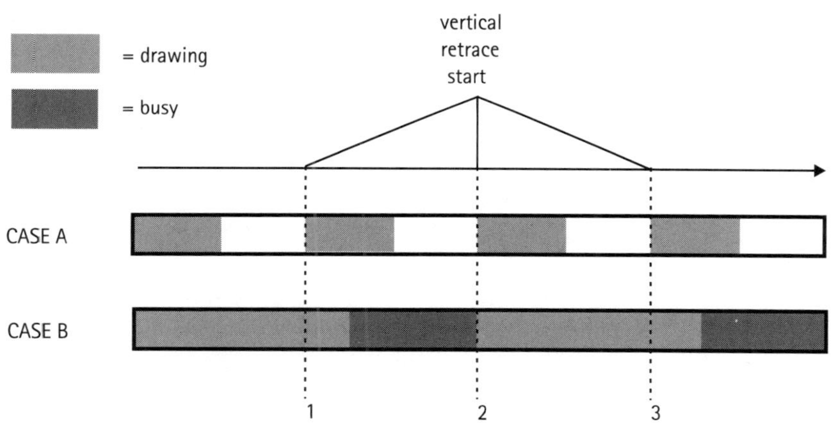

Figure 12-10: Surface update time and frame rate

Case A in Figure 12-10 shows an application with a relatively short surface update time. In this case, the rendering is finished well before the next vertical retrace cycle starts. The result is that the image is updated at the monitor's refresh rate. In Case B, the rendering time is longer than the refresh cycle. In this case, the application's frame rate is reduced to one-half the monitor's refresh rate. In such situations, any attempt to access the back buffer during the period represented by the dark gray rectangles results in the DDERR_WASSTRILLDRAWING error message.

A possible way of improving the frame rate in Case B is to use two back buffers instead of a single one. With two back buffers, the application can draw to the back buffer that is not immediately behind the primary surface, thereby reducing the wasted time as the blits to this rearmost surface are not subject to the DDERR_WASSTILLDRAWING error condition.

In coding practice, creating a flipping chain with two or more back buffers requires no different processing than with a single one. DirectDraw takes care of flipping the surfaces and the application code actually draws using the same back buffer pointer. In this case, the middle buffer or buffers can be ignored by the code, which only sees the primary surface and a back buffer. The one drawback of multiple buffering is that each back buffer requires as much display memory as the primary surface. Also, the law of diminishing returns applies to back buffers: the more back buffers, the less increase in performance for each back buffer. At some point, adding more back buffers degrades performance.

Exclusive mode applications can select a lower resolution or color depth in the display mode in order to make possible multiple back buffers. For example, in a card with 2MB of video memory executing in 640 by 480 pixel resolution in 24-bit color, we can only create one back buffer because the primary surface requires 921,600 bytes. By reducing the color depth to 16 bits, the sample application needs only 614,400 bytes for the primary surface, and we can now create two back buffers in display memory. The following code fragment shows the creation of a primary surface with two back buffers:

```
//Global variables
LPDIRECTDRAWSURFACE4         lpDDSPrimary = NULL;
LPDIRECTDRAWSURFACE4         lpDDSBackBuf = NULL;
DDSURFACEDESC2               ddsd;   // Surface description
HRESULT                      hRet;
.
.
.
// Create a primary surface with two back buffers
// ddsd is a structure of type DDSRUFACEDESC2
  ZeroMemory(&ddsd, sizeof(ddsd)); // Fill structure with
// zeros
// Fill in other members
  ddsd.dwSize = sizeof(ddsd);
  ddsd.dwFlags = DDSD_CAPS | DDSD_BACKBUFFERCOUNT;
  ddsd.ddsCaps.dwCaps = DDSCAPS_PRIMARYSURFACE |
                        DDSCAPS_FLIP |
                        DDSCAPS_COMPLEX |
                        DDSCAPS_VIDEOMEMORY;
  ddsd.dwBackBufferCount = 2;   // Two back buffers
  hRet = lpDD4->CreateSurface(&ddsd, &lpDDSPrimary, NULL);
  // At this point code can examine hRet for DD_OK and
  // provide alternate processing if the surface creation
  // call failed
  // Get backbuffer pointer
  ddscaps.dwCaps = DDSCAPS_BACKBUFFER;
  hRet = lpDDSPrimary->GetAttachedSurface(&ddscaps,
                      &lpDDSBackBuf);
  // At this point code can examine hRet for DD_OK and
  // provide alternate processing if the back buffer pointer
  // was not returned
```

Flip Animation Programming

Exclusive mode applications that use flipping animation start by initializing DirectDraw, setting a display mode, creating the flip chain, obtaining the corresponding pointers to the front and back buffers, and setting up a timer mechanism that produces the desired beat. Once these housekeeping chores are finished, the real work can begin, which consists of rendering the imagery to the back buffer, usually by means of blits from other surfaces in video memory or offscreen. The design and coding challenge of creating an animated application using DirectDraw can be broken down into two parts. The first one is to require the minimum resources that will enable the program to perform satisfactorily. The second one is to make the best use of these resources in order to produce the finest and smoothest animation possible.

Background Animation

A typical computer game or real-time simulation often contains two different types of graphics objects: backgrounds and sprites. Backgrounds consist of larger bitmaps over which the action takes place. For example, in a flight simulator program there can be several background images representing views from the cockpit. These may include landscapes, seascapes, and views of airports and runways used during take-off and landing. In a computer game that takes place in a medieval castle, the backgrounds are the various castle rooms and corridors in which the action takes place. Sprites, on the other hand, are rather small, animated objects represented in two or three dimensions. In the flight simulator program, the sprites are other aircraft visible from the cockpit and the cabin instruments and controls that are animated during the simulation. In the computer game, the sprites are medieval knights that do battle in the castle, as well as the objects animated during the battle.

Panning Animation

The design and display of background images is relatively straightforward and not complicated. The most difficult processing consists of creating backgrounds that are larger than the viewport and using clipping and blit-time rectangles to generate panning and zoom effects. Figure 12-11 shows a bitmapped mountain scene with a portion selected by a source rectangle.

The project named *DD Panning Demo* on the book's CD-ROM demonstrates panning animation of the background bitmap. The source rectangle in this program has the same vertical dimension as the background bitmap, which is 480 pixels. The image bitmap is 1280 pixels wide and the source rectangle is one-half that size (640 pixels). This creates a source window that can be moved 639 pixels to the right from its original position. The white, dotted rectangle in Figure 12-11 represents the source rectangle within the background bitmap.

Figure 12-11: Source rectangle selection in panning animation

The program DD_Pan.cpp, which is located in the *DD Panning Demo* project, uses a simple processing logic to demonstrate panning animation. The program's action is to pan to the right until the image's right border is reached, and then reverse the panning direction until the left border is reached. The primary surface and a single back buffer are created and a clipper is installed in both surfaces. The background image, which is stored in the panback.bmp bitmap, is stored in an off-screen surface. This bitmap is twice as wide as the viewport; therefore, the source rectangle can be moved horizontally within the bitmap. The panning variables and the display routine are coded as follows:

```
// Global panning animation controls
RECT         thisPan;          // Storage for source rectangle
LONG         panIteration = 0;  // panning iteration counter
LONG         panDirection = 0;  // 1 = left, 0 = right
// Constants
LONG         PAN_LIMIT_LEFT = 1;
LONG         PAN_LIMIT_RIGHT = 639;
   .
   .
   .
   //*********************************************
   // Name: PanImage
   // Desc: Update back with a source rectangle that
   //       is a portion of the background bitmap
   //       and flip to create a panning animation
   //*********************************************
   static void PanImage()
   {
```

```
thisTickCount = GetTickCount();
if((thisTickCount - lastTickCount) < TIMER_VALUE)
   return;

else
{
  lastTickCount = thisTickCount;

// Bump pan iteration according to direction
   if(panDirection == 1)
      panIteration—;
   else
      panIteration++;

// Reset panning iteration counter at limits
  if(panIteration == PAN_LIMIT_RIGHT)
     panDirection = 1;          // Pan left
  if(panIteration == PAN_LIMIT_LEFT)
     panDirection = 0;

// Set panning rectangle in source image
thisPan.left = panIteration;
thisPan.top = 0;
thisPan .right = 640 + panIteration;
thisPan.bottom = 480;

// Blit background bitmap to back buffer
   hRet = lpDDSBackBuf->Blt(NULL,
                lpDDSBackGrnd,
                &thisPan,
                DDBLT_WAIT,
                NULL);
   if(hRet != DD_OK){
      DDInitFailed(hWnd, hRet,
         "Blt() on background failed");
   return;
   }

 // Flip surfaces
    hRet = lpDDSPrimary->Flip(NULL, DDFLIP_WAIT);
    if(hRet != DD_OK){
        DDInitFailed(hWnd, hRet,
             "Flip() call failed");
    return;
```

```
            }
        return;
        }
    }
```

The function named `PanImage()` performs the panning animation. First, it bumps and checks the ticker counter. If the counter has not yet expired, execution returns immediately. Code then checks the `panDirection` variable. If the direction is 1, then panning is in the left-to-right cycle and the `panIteration` variable is decremented. If not, then panning is in the right-to-left cycle and the `panIteration` variable is incremented. When either variable reaches the limit as defined in the constants `PAN_LIMIT_LEFT` and `PAN_LIMIT_RIGHT`, the panning direction is reversed. A structure variable named `thisPan`, of type `RECT`, is used to define the source rectangle for the blit. The `panIteration` variable is used to define the offset of the source rectangle within the image bitmap. Because panning takes place on the horizontal axis only, and the display mode is defined in the code, then the image size can be hard-coded into the `thisPan` structure members. Once the image is blitted onto the back buffer, surfaces are flipped in the conventional manner.

Zoom Animation

Zooming is another background animation that can be implemented by manipulating the source or destination rectangles, or both. This is possible due to the fact that both `Blt()` and `BltFast()` perform automatic scaling when the source and destination areas are of a different size. The simplest approach to zooming animation consists of reducing the area covered by the source rectangle and letting `Blt()` or `BltFast()` perform the necessary adjustments. Figure 12-12 shows the initial and final source rectangles in zoom animation.

The program DD_Zoom.cpp, which is located in the *DD Zoom Demo* project, demonstrates zoom animation. The program action is to zoom into a bitmapped image by changing the position and progressively reducing the dimensions of the source rectangle. When the process reaches an arbitrary maximum zoom value, it reverses and the source rectangle is made progressively larger until it is restored to the original size. As in the panning animation demo program, the primary surface and a single back buffer are created, and a clipper is installed in both surfaces. The background image, which in this case is stored in the zoomback.bmp bitmap, is then moved to an offscreen surface. This bitmap is the size of the viewport. In the following code fragment we show the zoom controls and display operations that are different from the panning animation previously listed:

Figure 12-12: Source rectangle selection in zoom animation

```
// Zoom animation controls
RECT       thisZoom;    // Storage for source rectangle
LONG       zoomIteration = 0;  // panning iteration counter
LONG       zoomDirection = 0;  // 1 = left, 0 = right
// Constants
LONG       ZOOM_LIMIT_OUT = 1;
LONG       ZOOM_LIMIT_IN = 200;
.
.
.
// Bump zoom iteration according to direction
if(zoomDirection == 1)
   zoomIteration--;
else
   zoomIteration++;

// Reset zoom iteration counter at limits
if(zoomIteration == ZOOM_LIMIT_IN)
   zoomDirection = 1;          // Pan left
if(zoomIteration == ZOOM_LIMIT_OUT)
```

```
   zoomDirection = 0;

// Set zoom rectangle in source image
   thisZoom.left = zoomIteration;
   thisZoom.top = zoomIteration;
   thisZoom.right = 640 - zoomIteration;
   thisZoom.bottom = 480 - ((zoomIteration * 3)/4);
```

Notice that in dimensioning the source rectangle for zoom animation we take into account the screen's aspect ratio, which is approximately 3:4. Therefore, the *y* coordinate of the end point of the source rectangle is changed at a slower rate than the *x* coordinate. If both coordinates were reduced by the same amount, the resulting images would be stretched along this axis during the zoom.

Sprite Operations

In the context of graphics programming, a sprite is a rather small screen object, usually animated during program execution. It can be a fuel gauge on the dashboard of a race car simulation, a spaceship in a futuristic game, and so on. Designing, encoding, and manipulating sprites requires all the talents and skills of the animator.

The project named *DD Sprite Demo* on the book's CD-ROM demonstrates sprite animation by simultaneously moving three screen objects at different speeds. Figure 12-13 is a screen snapshot of the demonstration program.

The three hot-air balloons in Figure 12-13 are the sprites. During program execution the balloons rise at different speeds. The one in the center, which appears closer to the viewer, moves up one pixel during each iteration of the frame counter. The one on the left moves every second iteration and the one on the right moves every third iteration. The background is fixed in this sample.

Controlling several simultaneously displayed sprites can be a challenge in program design and data organization, but does not present any major programming problems in DirectDraw. The program named DD_Sprt.ccp, which performs the processing in the *DD Sprite Demo* project, starts by creating a primary surface and two back buffers. In this case, a second back buffer makes the program execute better in some machines. A clipper is then installed on both surfaces. The clipper makes the balloons appear to come into the display area, and disappear from it, softly and pleasantly. The background image, which is located in the bitmap named backgrnd.bmp, is stored in an offscreen surface. This bitmap is the size of the viewport. The code creates three additional surfaces, one for each of the sprites, and moves the sprite bitmaps into these surfaces. The sprite surfaces are assigned a source color key to make the bitmap backgrounds transparent at display time. To ensure a smooth animation, all the surfaces in the sample program are located in video memory.

Figure 12-13: Screen snapshot of the sprite animation demo

Sprite control in the demo program is based on a structure of type SpriteCtrl defined globally as follows:

```
// Sprite control structure
struct SpriteCtrl
{
   LONG     startY;          // Start x coordinate
   LONG     startX;          // Start y coordinate
   LONG     bmapX;           // Width of bitmap
   LONG     bmapY;           // Height of bitmap
   LONG     iterMax;         // Maximum iteration count
   LONG     skipFactor;      // Display delay
   LONG     iteration;       // Sprite iteration counter
} Sprite1, Sprite2, Sprite3;
```

Three structure variables named Sprite1, Sprite2, and Sprite3 are allocated, with one for each hot-air balloon in the animation. The sprites are numbered left to right as they are displayed, as shown in Figure 12-13. Each structure variable contains the startX and startY members that define the start coordinates for each sprite. The bmapX and bmapY members store the bitmap dimensions, which are obtained as the bitmaps are loaded from their files.

The sprite animation control is performed by the last three members of the SpriteCtrl structure. The iterMax member stores the value of the iteration counter at which the sprite is repositioned to the bottom of the screen. The skipFactor member determines how many iterations are skipped at display time. This value is used to slow down the smaller balloons. Sprite1 is assigned a skipFactor of 2. Sprite2, the largest one, has skipFactor equal to 1. Sprite3, the smallest one, has a skipFactor of 3. The iteration member keeps track of the number of frame beats corresponding to each sprite. The counters are reset when the iterMax value is reached for each sprite. The range of the iteration counters is from 0 to iterMax. The code initializes the structure members for each sprite as follows:

```
...//*****************************************************
   //   Fill SpriteCtrl structure members for each sprite
   //*****************************************************
   // Sprite1 is balloon bitmap in bMap1
   // Resolution is 640 by 480 pixels
   Sprite1.startY = 479;     // Starts at screen bottom
   Sprite1.startX = 70;      // x for start position
   Sprite1.bmapX = bMap1.bmWidth;
   Sprite1.bmapY = bMap1.bmHeight;
   Sprite1.skipFactor = 2;
   Sprite1.iterMax = (480+(bMap1.bmHeight))
* Sprite1.skipFactor;
   Sprite1.iteration = 50;    // Init iteration counter

   // Sprite2 is balloon bitmap in bMap2
   Sprite2.startY = 479;     // Starts at screen bottom
   Sprite2.startX = 240;     // x for start position
   Sprite2.bmapX = bMap2.bmWidth;
   Sprite2.bmapY = bMap2.bmHeight;
   Sprite2.skipFactor = 1;
   Sprite2.iterMax = 480+(bMap2.bmHeight);
   Sprite2.iteration = 50;    // Init iteration counter

   // Sprite3 is balloon bitmap in bMap3
   Sprite3.startY = 479;     // Starts at screen bottom
   Sprite3.startX = 500;      // x for start position
   Sprite3.bmapX = bMap3.bmWidth;
   Sprite3.bmapY = bMap3.bmHeight;
   Sprite3.skipFactor = 3;
   Sprite3.iterMax = (480+(bMap3.bmHeight))
* Sprite3.skipFactor;
   Sprite3.iteration = 20;    // Init iteration counter
```

During initialization, the dimensions of each sprite are read from the corresponding `bmWidth` and `bmHeight` members of the `BITMAP` structure for each sprite. This ensures that the code continues to work even if the size of a sprite bitmap is changed. The maximum number of iterations for each sprite is calculated by adding the number of screen pixels in the selected mode (480) to the bitmap pixel height, and then multiplying this sum by the sprite's skip factor. At display time, the surface with the background bitmap is first blitted to the back buffer. Then the code calls a local function named `SpriteAction()` for each sprite. The `FlipImages()` function is coded as follows:

```
..//**********************************************  // Name:
FlipImages
  // Desc: Update back buffer and flip
  //**********************************************

  static void FlipImages()
  {

     thisTickCount = GetTickCount();
     if((thisTickCount - lastTickCount) < TIMER_VALUE)
        return;
     else
     {
         lastTickCount = thisTickCount;

      // Blit background bitmap to back buffer
      hRet = lpDDSBackBuf->Blt(NULL,
                               lpDDSBackGrnd,
                               NULL,
                               DDBLT_WAIT,
                               NULL);
       if(hRet != DD_OK){
          DDInitFailed(hWnd, hRet,
                   "Blt() on background failed");
          return;
      }

    // Animate sprites. Farthest ones first
      SpriteAction(Sprite3, lpDDSBmap3);
      SpriteAction(Sprite2, lpDDSBmap2);
      SpriteAction(Sprite1, lpDDSBmap1);

   // Flip surfaces
       hRet = lpDDSPrimary->Flip(NULL, DDFLIP_WAIT);
```

```
        if(hRet != DD_OK){
          DDInitFailed(hWnd, hRet,
                       "Flip() call failed");
          return;
        }
      return;
    }
  }
```

The actual display of the sprites is performed by the local function named `SpriteAction()`. This function receives the `SpriteCtrl` structure variable for the sprite being animated, and the pointer to the surface that contains the sprite image. The code checks the iteration number for the sprite against the maximum count to determine if the iteration counter needs resetting. Then the position of the sprite is calculated by dividing the current iteration number by the skip factor. This information is stored in a `RECT` structure corresponding to the destination surface rectangle and the `Blt()` function is called. `SpriteAction()` code is as follows:

```
..//**********************************************
  // Name: SpriteAction
  // Desc: Animate a sprite according
  //       to its own parameters
  // PRE CONDITIONS:
  //    1. Pointer to structure containing
  //       sprite data
  //    2. Pointer to DirectDraw surface
  //       containing sprite bitmap
  //**********************************************
  void SpriteAction(SpriteCtrl &thisSprite,
            LPDIRECTDRAWSURFACE4 lpDDSBmap)
  {
      RECT        destSurf;
      LONG        vertUpdate;

     thisSprite.iteration++;

     if(thisSprite.iteration == thisSprite.iterMax)
        thisSprite.iteration = 0;

     vertUpdate = thisSprite.iteration /
  thisSprite.skipFactor;

     // Set coordinates for balloon1 display
     destSurf.left = thisSprite.startX;
```

```
    destSurf.top = thisSprite.startY - vertUpdate;
    destSurf.right = destSurf.left + thisSprite.bmapX;
    destSurf.bottom = destSurf.top + thisSprite.bmapY;

    // Use Blt() to blit bitmap from the off-screen surface
    // (->lpDDSBitamp), onto the back buffer (->lpDDSBackBuf)
    hRet = lpDDSBackBuf->Blt(&destSurf,
                             lpDDSBmap,
                             NULL,
                             DDBLT_WAIT | DDBLT_KEYSRC,
                             NULL);

      if(hRet != DD_OK){
         DDInitFailed(hWnd, hRet,
                      "Blt() on sprite failed");
     return;
    }
  return;
}
```

After the background bitmap and all three sprites have been blitted onto the back buffer, the code calls the `Flip()` function to render the results onto the primary surface.

Performance-tuning the Animation

Computer animation is a performance-critical task. The programmer's greatest concern is to produce a smooth and uniform effect with as little bumpiness, screen tearing, and interference as possible. Today's machines with 400MHz and faster CPUs; video cards with graphics coprocessors and 4 MB or 8 MB of video memory; high-speed buses; and DirectX 6 software can often produce impressive animations with straightforward code. For example, the executable in the DD Sprite Demo project on the book's CD-ROM smoothly animates three sprites, even when running on a 200MHz Pentium machine equipped with a low-end display card containing 2 MB of video memory.

The basic paradigm of animation programming implies pushing graphics performance to its limits. If the animator finds that the code can successfully manipulate three sprites, then perhaps it can manipulate four, or even five. The rule seems to be the more action, and the faster the action, the better the animation. In this section, we discuss several loosely linked topics that relate to improving program performance or to facilitating implementation.

Best-option Processing

DirectDraw has made it possible for Windows applications to achieve the graphics functionality and performance that, for a long time, was only possible in DOS. The price for greater control and speed is a higher degree of device dependency. To accommodate this device dependency, the applications developer can take several approaches. One approach is to require a minimum functionality in the host system. In this case, the code can test the hardware for these requirements and abort execution if they are not available. This kind of program seems to say: "This is what I need to run. If you don't have it, I'm out of here." Specialty and high-end programs, as well as dedicated applications, often do this. On the other hand, general-purpose programs intended for a wide audience must make the best possible use of whatever resources are available in the host machine. In this case the application seems to say: "This is what I would like to have. If it is not available, I'll make the best of what you have." The selection of the most suitable alternative among those available can be called *best-option* processing.

Programs that execute in windowed mode must accommodate the current desktop settings. If the settings are not adequate, there is little else that can be done but to notify the user and suggest changes. On the other hand, DirectDraw programs executing in exclusive mode can change display modes and hardware settings, thus controlling the execution environment to some degree. Most DirectDraw applications start by checking for a DirectDraw object and for the interface level. If DirectDraw is not installed, two actions are possible: the first one is to notify the user and to abort installation; the second one is to proceed to install the DirectX software with varying levels of user participation. The DirectX setup facilities (discussed in Chapter 13) can be used to copy the required files to the host machine and to perform the necessary initialization. Because Microsoft furnishes these files at no cost, there is little justification for any major DirectDraw application not to provide this option.

Another possibility is that the version of DirectX installed on the host machine is not the current one. On encountering this problem, you may be tempted to accommodate processing to whatever version of the SDK is already there. Although possible, the required processing presents some major complications. In the first place, the interface pointers are not generally interchangeable. That is, to use a function in the DirectDraw 4 version of the SDK you need a pointer of type `LPDIRECTDRAW4`. The same applies to clippers, surfaces, palettes, and other objects of the interface. For this reason, providing alternate processing for several interfaces amounts to furnishing separate code for each one. Here again, an easy way out is to notify the user of the problem and abort execution. A more reasonable approach is to offer installation of the updated drivers for the required SDK version. These installations are discussed in Chapter 13.

> **NOTE:** In very simple applications, such as the *DD Info Demo* project on the book's CD-ROM, it is possible to typecast a pointer to an older interface in order to access methods in a newer one. However, this approach is dangerous and should be avoided because the functions in newer interfaces often have different parameter lists, processing options, and return types. If the call does not fail at compile time, it may fail at run time.

It is difficult to provide general guidelines on how to handle DirectDraw device dependencies. Determining system capabilities is addressed in Chapter 9. The project named *DD Info Demo* contains code showing how to read these capabilities in the host machine. In DirectDraw programming, the most critical device-dependency complication results from the fact that not all hardware functionality is emulated in the HEL. For example, clipping and color fills can be implemented in hardware, but are also emulated. An application that uses these functions has better performance in a system with hardware support, but still executes in one in which these operations are furnished by the HEL. On the other hand, overlays, alpha channels, and other DirectDraw operations are not emulated in the HEL. If an application attempts to use these functions in a machine that does not provide hardware support, execution fails with unpredictable results. In this book we avoid discussing DirectDraw operations that are not emulated by the software. Applications that require these nonemulated functions should make the necessary checks and adjustments.

DirectDraw programs that execute in exclusive mode can virtually tailor the system environment to suit their own requirements. Their first and most important decision is about the display mode. The *DD Info Demo* project contains code to list all available modes. The *DD Access Demo* project contains the function `HasDDMode`, which can be used to test if a particular mode is available in the hardware. Applications can use this function in cascade fashion to determine the best available mode. Alternatively, code can attempt to set the ideal mode; if the ideal mode is not available, it can then proceed to the next preferred one, and so forth.

Mode selection is complicated by the fact that different modes use various amounts of video memory. For example, an application that requires two back buffers needs to investigate not only if a particular mode is available, but also whether there is sufficient free memory in the mode to allocate the two back buffers. You can use the `GetCaps()` function and read the `dwVidMemTotal` or `dwVidMemFree` members to determine the video memory in a system. This is how it is done in the *DD Info Demo* project program. Alternatively, code can call the `GetAvailableVidMem()` function to obtain the total amount of memory available and the amount currently free. The results are identical with either function.

The display mode and the number of surfaces necessary determine an application's video memory requirements. For example, the *DD Sprites Demo* program executes in 640 by 480 pixel resolution with a 16-bits per pixel color depth. In addition to the primary surface, it ideally requires two back buffers and space for storing four bitmaps: one for the background and three for the hot-air balloon sprites. The program's maximum memory requirements are as follows:

```
primary surface ...............   614,400 bytes
two back buffers .............. 1,228,800 bytes
background bitmap ............   614,400 bytes
Sprite 1 bitmap ...............    13,400 bytes
Sprite 2 bitmap ...............    30,600 bytes
Sprite 3 bitmap ...............     8,880 bytes
                                ==============
          Total .............. 2,510,480 bytes
```

Once the memory requirements are known, code can make sure it is available by either calling `GetCaps()` or `GetAvailableVidMem()`. The following code fragment shows processing in the *DD Sprite Demo* project program:

```
// Variables for checking available memory
DDSCAPS2         ddCapsMem;
DWORD            memTotal;
DWORD            memFree;
static DWORD     MEM_REQUIRED = 2510480;
.
.
.
// Check for necessary free video memory
   ZeroMemory(&ddCapsMem, sizeof(ddCapsMem));
   lpDD4->GetAvailableVidMem(&ddCapsMem,
                             &memTotal,
                             &memFree);
      if (memTotal < MEM_REQUIRED)
          return DDInitFailed(hWnd, hRet,
         "Insufficient video memory");
```

The code for performing display operations using one or more back buffers is identical in most cases. Applications can take advantage of this fact and start by requesting two or more back buffers. Then they can reduce the number of back buffers if the call to `CreateSurface()` fails, and try again. If you start by making sure there is sufficient memory for at least one back buffer, the processing is sure to succeed at some point. The following code shows this handling:

```
//***************************************************
// Create primary surface and one or more back buffers
//***************************************************
// ddsd is a structure of type DDSRUFACEDESC2
```

```
   ZeroMemory(&ddsd, sizeof(ddsd));  // Clear structure
// Fill in other members
   ddsd.dwSize = sizeof(ddsd);
   ddsd.dwFlags = DDSD_CAPS | DDSD_BACKBUFFERCOUNT;
   ddsd.ddsCaps.dwCaps = DDSCAPS_PRIMARYSURFACE |
                         DDSCAPS_FLIP |
                         DDSCAPS_COMPLEX |
                         DDSCAPS_VIDEOMEMORY;
// First request two back buffers
   ddsd.dwBackBufferCount = 2;
     hRet = lpDD4->CreateSurface(&ddsd,
                                &lpDDSPrimary,
                                NULL);
// If call failed, retry with one back buffer
     if (hRet == DDERR_OUTOFVIDEOMEMORY)  {
        ddsd.dwBackBufferCount = 1;
        hRet = lpDD4->CreateSurface(&ddsd,
                                   &lpDDSPrimary,
                                   NULL);
     }
   if (hRet != DD_OK)
      return DDInitFailed(hWnd, hRet,
                  "CreateSurface() call failed");
```

High-resolution Timers

At the beginning of this chapter, we examined two methods of obtaining the timed beat that is necessary for the frame updates in an animation routine. One method is based on a milliseconds counter maintained by the system, which can be read by means of the GetTickCount() function. The other method sets an interval timer that operates as an alarm clock. When the timer lapse expires, the application receives control, either in a message handler intercept or a dedicated callback function. Although both methods are often used, processing based on reading the Windows tick counter has considerably better resolution than the alarm clock approach. Windows documentation states that the resolution of the timer intercepts is approximately 55 milliseconds. This produces a beat of 18.2 times per second, which is precisely the default speed of the PC internal clock. In many cases this beat is barely sufficient to produce smooth and lifelike animations.

There are several ways of improving the frequency and reliability of the timed pulse. The multimedia extensions to Windows include a high-resolution timer with a reported resolution of 1 millisecond. Furthermore, the multimedia timer produces more accurate results because it does not rely on WM_TIMER messages posted on the queue. Each multimedia timer has its own thread, and the callback function is invoked directly regardless of any pending messages. To use the multimedia library, code must include MMSYSTEM.H and make sure that WINMM.LIB is available and referenced at link time. Several timer functions are found in the multimedia library. The most useful one in animation programming is `setTimeEvent()`. This function starts an event timer that runs in its own thread. A callback function defined in the call to `setTimeEvent()` receives control every time the counter timer expires. The function's general form is as follows:

```
MMRESULT timeSetEvent(
              UINT uDelay,                  // 1
              UINT uResolution,             // 2
              LPTIMECALLBACK lpTimeProc,    // 3
              DWORD dwUser,                 // 4
              UINT fuEvent                  // 5
);
```

The first parameter defines the event delay in milliseconds. If this value is not in the timer's valid range, the function returns an error. The second parameter is the resolution, in milliseconds, of the timer event. As the values get smaller, the resolution increases. A resolution of 0 indicates that timer events should occur with the greatest possible accuracy. Code can use the maximum appropriate value for the timer resolution in order to reduce system overhead. The third parameter is the address of the callback function that is called every time the event delay counter expires. The fourth parameter is a double word value passed by Windows to the callback procedure. The fifth parameter encodes the timer event type. This parameter consists of one or more predefined constants listed in Table 12-3.

TABLE 12-3 EVENT-TYPE CONSTANTS IN TIMESETEVENT() FUNCTION

Value	Meaning
TIME_ONESHOT	Event occurs once, after `uDelay` milliseconds.
TIME_PERIODIC	Event occurs every `uDelay` milliseconds.
TIME_CALLBACK_FUNCTION	Windows calls the function pointed to by the third parameter. This is the default.
TIME_CALLBACK_EVENT_SET	Windows calls the `SetEvent()` function to set the event pointed to by the third parameter. The fourth parameter is ignored.
TIME_CALLBACK_EVENT_PULSE	Windows calls the `PulseEvent()` function to pulse the event pointed to by the third parameter. The fourth parameter is ignored.

Notice that the multimedia timers support two different modes of operation. In one mode, TIME_ONESHOT, the timer event occurs but once. In the other mode, TIME_PERIODIC, the timer event takes place every time the timer counter expires. This mode is the one used in animation routines. If successful, the call returns an identifier for the timer event. This identifier is also passed to the callback function. Once the timer is no longer needed, applications should call the timeKillEvent() function to terminate it.

> Despite its high resolution, it has been documented that the multimedia timer can suffer considerable delays in Windows 95. One author has recorded delays of up to 100 milliseconds. Applications requiring very high timer accuracy are recommended to implement the multimedia timer in a 16-bit DLL.

The Win32 API first made available a high-resolution tick counter. These counters are sometimes called *performance monitors* because they were originally intended for precisely measuring the performance of coded routines. Using the high-performance monitors is similar to using the GetTickCount() function previously described, but with a few special accommodations. Two Windows functions are associated with performance monitor counters. QueryPerformanceFrequency() returns the resolution of the counter, which varies according to hardware. QueryPerformanceCounter() returns the number of timer ticks since the system was started. QueryPerformanceFrequency() can also be used to determine if high-performance counters are available in the hardware, although the presence of the performance monitoring function can be assumed in any Windows 95, 98, or NT machine.

The function prototypes are identical for QueryPerformanceFrequency() and QueryPerformanceCount(): the return type is of type BOOL and the only parameter is a 64-bit integer of type LARGE_INTEGER. The general forms are as follows:

```
BOOL QueryPerformanceCounter(LARGE_INTEGER*);
BOOL QueryPerformanceFrequency(LARGE_INTEGER*);
```

Although it has been stated that the performance frequency on Intel-based PCs is 0.8 microseconds, it is safer for applications to call QueryPerformanceFrequency() to obtain the correct scaling factor. The following code fragment shows this processing:

```
_int64          TIMER_DELAY = 15;  // Milliseconds
_int64          frequency;         // Timer frequency
  .
  .
```

```
.
QueryPerformanceFrequency((LARGE_INTEGER*) &frequency);
TIMER_DELAY = (TIMER_DELAY * frequency) / 1000;
```

After executing, the `TIMER_DELAY` value has been scaled to the frequency of the high-resolution timer. The `QueryPerformanceCounter()` can now be called in the same manner as `GetTickCount()`, for example:

```
_int64          lastTickCount;
_int64          thisTickCount;
.
.
.
QueryPerformanceCounter((LARGE_INTEGER*) &thisTickCount);
if((thisTickCount - lastTickCount) < TIMER_DELAY)
  return;
else {
  lastTickCount = thisTickCount;
  .
  .
  .
```

The *DD Sprite Demo* project program uses a high-performance timer to produce the animation beat.

Dirty Rectangles

Notice that in Figure 12-13 the background image is overlaid by three sprites. During every iteration of the animation pulse, code redraws the background in order to refresh those parts of the surface that have been overwritten by the sprites. The process is wasteful because most of the background remains unchanged. In fact, only the portion of the background that was covered by the sprite image actually needs to be redrawn. Figure 12-14 shows the rectangular areas that actually need refreshing in producing the next animation iteration of the image in Figure 12-13. These are called the *dirty rectangles*.

DirectDraw clipping operations can be used to identify the dirty rectangles. In this case, a clip list defines the areas that require refreshing, and these are the only ones updated during the blit. The processing is simplified by the fact that the last position of the sprite and its stored dimensions can be used to define the dirty rectangles.

Figure 12-14: Dirty rectangles in the animation of Figure 12-13

It is difficult to predict when a dirty rectangle scheme actually improves performance. The result depends on many factors: the total image area covered by the dirty rectangles, the number of rectangles, the processing overhead in calculating the rectangles and creating the clip list, and above all, the efficiency of the DirectDraw clipping operations of the particular hardware. Unfortunately, in many cases, the screen update takes longer with dirty rectangle schemes than without them. The most rational approach is to develop the animation without dirty rectangles. If the results are not satisfactory, then try the dirty rectangles technique. The comparative results can be assessed by measuring the execution time in both cases. We discuss methods for measuring performance of routines later in this section.

Dynamic Color Keys

Color keys are an integral part of sprite animation. It is difficult to imagine a sprite that can be transparently overlaid on a bitmapped background without the use of a source color key. When we create our own sprites using draw or paint programs, and these sprites are stored in 24- or 32-bit color depth bitmaps, the color key is usually known at coding time, or can be easily determined. If there is any doubt, the sprite can be loaded into a bitmap editor utility in order to inspect the RGB value of the background pixels. However, matters are not always that simple. One of the complicating factors with color keys occurs when the color depth of the application's video mode does not coincide with that of the sprite bitmap. This can be problematic in the palettized display modes, particularly when the palette changes during execution, or in applications that use best-option processing in regards to the video mode.

One possible solution is to determine the bitmap's color key dynamically, that is, at run time rather than at compile time. This method is usually based on the assumption that there is a fixed location in the bitmap that is transparent at blit time. For example, the pixel at the bitmap's upper-left corner of the sprite image rectangle is typically part of the background. Figure 12-15 shows the fixed location of the color key for one of the balloon bitmaps used in the *DD Sprite Demo* project.

Figure 12-15: Color key in a fixed bitmap location

Once the relative location of a color key pixel has been determined, code can load the bitmap onto a surface, and then read the surface data at the predefined location in order to obtain the color key. The manipulation is made possible by the direct access to memory areas that are available in DirectDraw discussed in Chapter 10. Because the application knows the color depth of the target surface, it can read the color key directly from the surface. In this case, we need not be concerned about how Windows converts a pixel value in one color depth into another one, because the code is reading the resulting color key directly. The following code is used in the *DD Sprite Demo* program for dynamically loading the color key for `Sprite1`:

```
// Video display globals
LONG      vidPitch = 0;  // Pitch
LPVOID    vidStart = 0;  // Buffer address

// Color key data
DDCOLORKEY  bColorKey;
WORD        dynamicKey;
.
.
.
//**********************************************
// move first balloon bitmap to off-screen surface
//**********************************************
// Load the bitmap into memory
ballBitmap = ( HBITMAP )LoadImage( NULL, "balloon1.bmp",
              IMAGE_BITMAP, 0, 0, LR_LOADFROMFILE );
  if ( ballBitmap == NULL )
       DDInitFailed(hWnd, hRet,
        "Balloon1 bitmap load failed");
// Get bitmap dimensions to determine surface size
   GetObject(ballBitmap, sizeof (BITMAP), &bMap1);

// Create the off-screen surface for bitmap in system memory
   ZeroMemory(&ddsd, sizeof(ddsd));  // Clear structure
// Fill in other members
   ddsd.dwSize = sizeof(ddsd);
   ddsd.dwFlags = DDSD_CAPS | DDSD_HEIGHT | DDSD_WIDTH;
   ddsd.ddsCaps.dwCaps = DDSCAPS_OFFSCREENPLAIN |
                         DDSCAPS_VIDEOMEMORY;
   ddsd.dwHeight = bMap1.bmHeight;
   ddsd.dwWidth = bMap1.bmWidth;
   hRet = lpDD4->CreateSurface(&ddsd, &lpDDSBmap1, NULL);
     if (hRet != DD_OK)
        return DDInitFailed(hWnd, hRet,
                 "Off screen surface1 creation failed ");

 // Move bitmap to surface using DDBmapToSurf()function
 hRet = DDBmapToSurf(lpDDSBmap1, ballBitmap);
   if(hRet != DD_OK)
      return DDInitFailed(hWnd, hRet,
                     "DDMapToSurf() call failed");
```

```
//****************************************
//   read color key from loaded sprite
//****************************************
// Attempt to lock the surface for direct access
if (!LockSurface(lpDDSBmap1))
      return DDInitFailed(hWnd, hRet,
                      "Surface Lock failed ");
// Surface data is stored as follows:
//   LONG      vidPitch;  // Pitch (not used here)
//   LPVOID    vidStart;  // Buffer address

_asm
{
    PUSH   ESI          ; Save context
    PUSHF
    MOV    ESI,vidStart ; Left-top pixel address
    ; Read and store pixel attributes
    MOV    AX,[ESI]        ; Get attribute
    MOV    dynamicKey,AX   ; Store value in variable
    POPF                   ; Restore context
    POP    ESI
}

ReleaseSurface(lpDDSBmap1);

// Set color key for balloon1 surface using values stored
// in variable dynamicKey
 bColorKey.dwColorSpaceLowValue = dynamicKey;
 bColorKey.dwColorSpaceHighValue = dynamicKey;
   hRet = lpDDSBmap1->SetColorKey(DDCKEY_SRCBLT,
                                   &bColorKey);
   if(hRet != DD_OK)
      return DDInitFailed(hWnd, hRet,
            "SetColorKey() for Balloon1 failed");
```

Measuring Performance

The execution time of a coded routine or function is often the factor that determines its suitability for an animation application. Several software engineering techniques enable programmers to estimate the performance and efficiency of algorithms. These methods, which are based on mathematical analysis, are usually difficult and time-consuming. Instead of performing a complicated analysis of the algorithms that underlie a particular processing routine, a programmer can often obtain the necessary performance metrics by physically measuring its execution time.

In some cases, execution time ranges from several seconds to several minutes. In these situations, execution time can sometimes be measured by observing the screen with a stopwatch in hand. More often, the time of execution is in the milliseconds order, and it may be possible to use the computer's timing mechanisms to determine the time elapsed between the start and the end of a processing routine or code segment. The `QueryPerformanceCounter()` function described previously has a resolution on the order of one-millionth of a second. In order to measure the execution time of a program segment, function, or routine, you need to read the tick counter at the start and the end of the processing routine, and then subtract these values. The difference is the approximate execution time.

Unfortunately, there are many complicating factors that can affect the accuracy of this simple scheme. In the first place, the scheduler in a multitasking environment can interrupt a thread of execution at any time, thereby delaying it. Sometimes the unit boundary at which a data item is located in memory affects the time required for a memory fetch operation. Another consideration relates to the occasional state of a memory cache, which can also change the fetch time for data. This means that the measurements should be repeated as many times as is practicable in order to obtain a more reliable value. Even with many repetitions, the resulting numbers may not be accurate. However, for many practical programming situations the data obtained in this manner is sufficient for a decision regarding which of two or more routines is more suitable for the case at hand. The following code fragment shows how to measure the execution time of two routines:

```
// Timer data
_int64          startCount;
_int64          endCount;
_int64          timeLapse1;    // First routine
_int64          timeLapse2;    // Second routine
.
.
.
// First routine starts here
QueryPerformanceCounter((LARGE_INTEGER*) &startCount);
//
// First routine code
//
QueryPerformanceCounter((LARGE_INTEGER*) &endCount);
timeLapse1 = endCount - startCount;
.
.
.
// Second routine starts here
QueryPerformanceCounter((LARGE_INTEGER*) &startCount);
//
// Second routine code
```

```
//
QueryPerformanceCounter((LARGE_INTEGER*) &endCount);
timeLapse2 = endCount - startCount;
```

The `timeLapse1` and `timeLapse2` variables now hold the number of timer ticks that elapsed during the execution of either routine. Code can display these values or a debugger can be used to inspect the variables. However, you should be aware that code executed in the context of a debugger runs significantly slower due to the additional processing.

Summary

We have now tackled some of the most difficult problems of 2-D graphics programming. Animation is one of the most exacting, as well as the most rewarding, tasks that can be undertaken in a graphics application. DirectDraw makes Windows animation possible by furnishing direct access to the video hardware as well as specialized programming facilities, such as back buffers and flip operations. With these capabilities you can create applications that simulate movement smoothly and naturally. These techniques find use in computer games, simulations, multimedia, and many high-end graphics programs.

The next and last section is about the graphics support facilities provided in the DirectX 6 SDK. The first topic is the DirectSetup component, which makes it possible to install or update DirectX in a host system. The second topic relates to obtaining input in exclusive mode by using the DirectInput element of DirectX. The third and last topic refers to multiple adapters and monitors. This powerful graphics feature is made possible by the operating system support provided by Windows 98 and NT 5, and by the specialized functions in DirectX 6.

Part IV

DirectX Graphics Support

CHAPTER 13:
DirectX Upgrade and Setup

CHAPTER 14:
Input in Exclusive Mode Applications

CHAPTER 15:
Multiple Adapters and Monitors

Chapter 13

DirectX Upgrade and Setup

IN THIS CHAPTER

- DirectSetup package components
- Installing and uninstalling DirectX drivers
- Preparing for installation
- Normal DirectX 6 installation
- Performing verbose and silent installations

TWO TOPICS ADDRESSED in the design of DirectX and the COM interface are compatibility and version upgrade. The design objective was to make possible the development of application code that uses the newest versions of the software without failing in machines that do not contain the new drivers. Past experience in PC software has shown that leaving these matters to the natural process of users acquiring and installing upgrades leads to slow adoption on the part of developers. In fact, any upgrade mechanism that is out of the developer's direct control is usually distrusted in the programming community. Microsoft's solution has been to allow software developers to redistribute the run files required for a DirectX upgrade and to provide support software that facilitates the installation process.

The version upgrade installation component of DirectX 6 is named DirectSetup. In this chapter, we discuss this setup and upgrade facility.

DirectX Upgrade Facilities

The DirectX SDK CD-ROM includes a folder named `\Redist` that contains all the DirectX run-time components. Developers can redistribute these components to end-users according to the terms of the Microsoft license agreement. The `\Redist` folder is not copied to the host system when DirectX is installed, so it must be obtained from the original SDK CD-ROM. The redistributable portion of DirectX contains all the drivers and other support software necessary to upgrade a host machine to the current DirectX implementation. The Microsoft license agreement is as follows:

The Redistributable Code is the property of Microsoft Corporation and its suppliers and is protected by copyright law and international treaty provisions. You are authorized to make and use copies of the Redistributable Code either as part of the application in which you received the Redistributable Code, or in conjunction with the application for which its use is intended. Except as expressly provided in the foregoing sentence, you are not authorized to reproduce and distribute the Redistributable Code. Microsoft reserves all rights not expressly granted. You may not reverse engineer, decompile, or disassemble the Redistributable Code, except and only to the extent that such activity is expressly permitted by applicable law notwithstanding this limitation. THE REDISTRIBUTABLE CODE IS PROVIDED TO YOU "AS IS" WITHOUT WARRANTY OF ANY KIND, EITHER EXPRESS OR IMPLIED, INCLUDING BUT NOT LIMITED TO THE IMPLIED WARRANTIES OF MERCHANTABILITY AND/OR FITNESS FOR A PARTICULAR PURPOSE. YOU ASSUME THE ENTIRE RISK AS TO THE ACCURACY AND THE USE OF THE REDISTRIBUTABLE CODE. MICROSOFT SHALL NOT BE LIABLE FOR ANY DAMAGES WHATSOEVER ARISING OUT OF THE USE OF OR INABILITY TO USE THE REDISTRIBUTABLE CODE, EVEN IF MICROSOFT HAS BEEN ADVISED OF THE POSSIBILITY OF SUCH DAMAGE.

The DirectSetup Component

In addition to the drivers, DirectX contains a component named DirectSetup, which provides functions that enable applications to easily and reliably install the DirectX run-time components. It is this mechanism that makes possible the use of the newest version of DirectX without compatibility concerns. For example, a DirectDraw program can check for the current version of DirectX in the host machine. If the SDK version found is not the one used in developing the application code, the program can offer to upgrade the user's system directly and immediately. It can even upgrade the user's system without obtaining permission or notifying the user of the change. It is up to the developer to decide how much user participation is adequate in each case, or how much feedback is furnished during the software installation process.

The installation overwrites system components from a previous version of DirectX. For example, if DirectX 6 is installed on a system that contains DirectX 5, all DirectX 5 components are replaced. In theory, this should not compromise the compatibility of programs designed and coded for a previous version of the SDK. The backward compatibility rules that are part of the Component Object Model should ensure that software written for a previous version continues to run properly. Because this is not always the case, the installation routines create a backup copy of the replaced system components and drivers, so that they can be restored if necessary. We discuss uninstalling the DirectX 6 components later in this section.

The Redistributable Package

The \Redist folder in the DirectX 6 SDK contains the following folder structure:

```
Redist
  DirectX6
    Directx
      Drivers
        Brz
        Chs
        Cht
        Cze
        Dan
        Dut
        Eng
        Fin
        Frn
        Ger
        Hun
        Itn
        Jpn
        Kor
        Nec
        Pol
        Rus
        Spa
        Swe
```

The lowest-level directories, which have three-letter designations, contain the implementations for the corresponding foreign languages. During setup, the language files are automatically selected according to the one installed on the host machine. If the proper language folder is not available, the installation fails. However, Microsoft enables the deletion of any of these language directories if they are not required in a particular case. In fact, in DirectX 6 the entire \Drivers folder can be deleted if no foreign language support is necessary. This is often desirable because the DirectX 6 language support files take up approximately 40MB of disk space. Note that the parent folder named \Directx furnishes support of American English.

Uninstalling DirectX Drivers

More than one method is available for uninstalling the DirectX 6 drivers and restoring a system to its original state. One method is to select the DirectX Drivers entry in the Windows Add/Remove Program Properties dialog box. In this case, a second dialog box is displayed that enables the user to remove either the video or the audio drivers. Alternatively, the user can double-click the DirectX icon in the Windows Control Panel. The DirectX tab of the resulting dialog box provides version information as well as a button labeled Restore Drivers. Clicking this button restores the DirectX drivers previously found in the system. Figure 13-1 is a screen snapshot of the DirectX Properties dialog box.

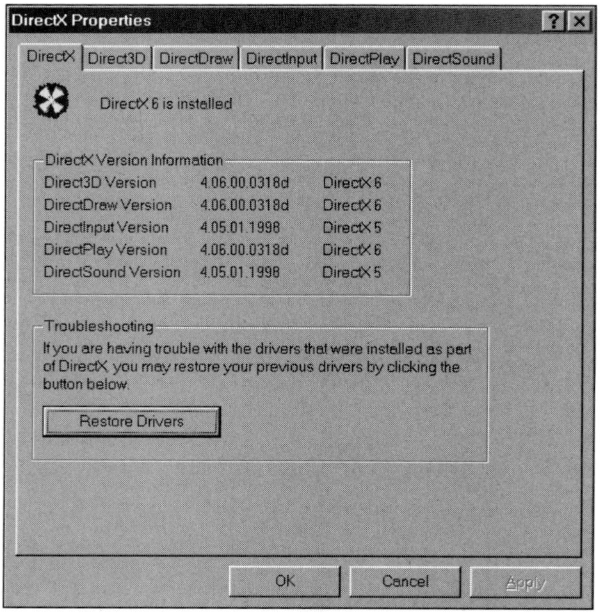

Figure 13-1: Screen snapshot of the DirectX Properties dialog box

The entire DirectX 6 package can also be uninstalled by selecting the Microsoft DirectX 6 SDK entry in the Windows Add/Remove Program Properties dialog box. You can access this dialog box by selecting the Add/Remove Programs icon in the Control Panel.

Using DirectSetup

The DirectSetup component of DirectX 6 consists of six functions that support the installation of the Microsoft redistributable. The functions are listed in Table 13-1.

Table 13-1 DIRECTSETUP FUNCTIONS

Name	Purpose
`DirectXSetup`	Installs one or more DirectX components
`DirectXSetupGetVersion`	Retrieves the version number of the current DirectX implementation
`DirectXSetupCallback`	Sets a pointer to a callback function that is optionally called by `DirectXSetup`
`DirectXRegisterApplication`	Registers a DirectPlay application
`DirectXUnregisterApplication`	Deletes the registration of a DirectPlay application

DirectPlay is the DirectX component that enables interaction over modems and networks. DirectPlay is not covered in this book. For this reason, the related functions `DirectXRegisterApplication()` and `DirectXUnregisterApplication()` are not discussed. `DirectXSetup()` can access a callback function in order to customize the installation process. In this case, the application defines a function of type `DirectXSetupCallbackFunction`. The callback function is discussed in detail later in this chapter.

Preliminary Steps

Before an application that uses DirectSetup functionality can be compiled and executed, there are several preliminary steps that must be performed. Many of the difficulties encountered with using DirectSetup originate in these preparatory operations, which are not clearly documented in the Microsoft literature.

The first step consists of copying the support software to the corresponding directories in the target system. You can find all the required files in the `\Redist` folder and its subfolders.

Applications that use DirectSetup must have access to three DLL files: dsetup.dll, desetup16.dll, and dsetup32.dll. These files are found in the `Directx6` folder of the `\Redist` folder. The three DLL files must be copied to the `Windows\system` folder, to the development system's path for executable files, or to the development folder.

The file dsetup.dll has an associated library named dsetup.lib. This library is not in the redistributable package but in the `\mssdk\lib` folder created during the installation of DirectX 6. The library must be present in order to enable programs to use DirectSetup. It is also a good idea to check the Options command in Developer Studio Tools menu to make sure the Directories tab contains a path to the location of the library file.

In addition, the dsetup.h header file must be in the development system's include file path, typically `\mssdk\include`, or in the development folder. Here again, the Options command in Developer Studio Tools menu can be used to make sure the Directories tab contains a path to the location of the header file. Programs that use DirectSetup must contain an `#include` statement for dsetup.h. If the header file is located in the system's include file path, then the `#include` statement must reference the file inside angle brackets. If the file is in the development system's path, it is typed inside double quotation marks, as follows:

```
#include <dsetup.h>    // File is in the include path
#include "dsetup.h"    // File is in the development folder
```

The final step of the preparatory phase is copying the `Directx` folder and its subfolders (if any are present) to the folder in which the executable that uses DirectSetup is located. Notice that copying the parent folder, which is named `Directx6`, is not acceptable. In its default mode, DirectSetup expects the support files to be located in a folder named `Directx` (not case sensitive), and this folder to be in the path at run time. For example, if the development environment is set up to produce an executable file in a folder named `DD_Test\Release`, then the path to the `Directx` folder must be `DD_Test\Release\Directx`.

Installation Modes

DirectSetup enables the programmer to decide how much, if any, participation the user is to have in the installation, as well as how much feedback is furnished during the process. To make changes in a host machine without the user's knowledge and consent is usually considered bad programming ethics. The recommended approach is that, once the software detects that a driver update is required or desirable, the user be given the option of installing these drivers or not.

During the installation process, the application using DirectSetup can provide no feedback, some feedback, or detailed feedback to the user. Once the installation has concluded, DirectSetup informs client code if the machine must be restarted or not. Here again it would be unconventional, to say the least, to restart the user's machine without explicit authorization.

AutoPlay is a feature of Windows 95/98 and NT that automatically starts an application when an AutoPlay-enabled CD-ROM is inserted in the drive. Using this feature, it is possible to execute the DirectX 6 driver installation or upgrade automatically in a way totally invisible to the user. Here again, the developer must decide when such an unorthodox approach may be desirable.

Preparing for DirectX Installation

The actual copying of the driver files to the target system, as well as the updating of the Windows registry, is performed by the `DirectXSetup()` function that is part of the DirectSetup component. The installation program typically consists of three steps:

- Determine if a new installation or an upgrade is required.
- Check that there is sufficient disk space for the new files.
- Obtain the user's permission and perform the installation.

The first two steps are preparatory. The third step is the actual installation of the SDK run-time components.

Obtaining the SDK Version

The DirectSetup function `DirectXSetupGetVersion()` retrieves the version of DirectX installed on the target system. This information can be used to determine if a software installation or update is required. The function's general form is as follows:

```
INT WINAPI
    DirectXSetupGetVersion(
                               DWORD *pdwVersion,    // 1
                               DWORD *pdwRevision    // 2
    );
```

The first parameter is the address of a variable that receives the SDK version number. Code can set this parameter to `NULL` if the version number is not needed. The second parameter is the address of a variable that receives the revision number. It can be `NULL` if the revision number is not wanted. If the call is successful, it returns nonzero. If it fails, the return value is 0.

The `DirectXSetupGetVersion()` function can be used before or after the call to `DirectXSetup()` function. If the `DirectXSetupGetVersion()` function is called before `DirectXSetup()`, it returns the version and revision numbers of the DirectX components currently installed. If it is called after the call to `DirectXSetup()`, but before the computer is rebooted, it returns the version and revision numbers of the DirectX components that will take effect after restarting.

The version number includes the major version number and the minor version number. The major version number is encoded in the 16 most significant bits of the `DWORD` variable. The minor version number is in the 16 least significant bits. The version numbers can be interpreted as shown in Table 13-2.

TABLE 13-2 DIRECTX VERSION NUMBERS

Version	Returned Value
DirectX 1	0x00040001
DirectX 2	0x00040002
DirectX 3	0x00040003
DirectX 5	0x00040005
DirectX 6	0x00040006

The revision number returned in the second parameter contains the release number and the build number. The release number is in the 16 most significant bits, and the build number is in the 16 least significant bits. The following code, which is used in the *DD Info Demo* project program, shows the processing for obtaining and displaying the version and revision data:

```
// DirectX version and revision data
int                 verRet;         // Storage for SDK version call
DWORD               version;
DWORD               revision;
WORD                releaseNum;
WORD                buildNum;
   .
   .
   .
//*****************************
//   SDK version/revision info
//*****************************
verRet = DirectXSetupGetVersion( &version, &revision);
// Check for call failure
      if(verRet == 0){
   strcpy ( message, " ERROR - No SDK Version information" );
   TextOut ( hdc, text_x, text_y, message, strlen (message) );
           text_y += tm.tmHeight+tm.tmExternalLeading;
           return;
       }
// DirectX version number
   strcpy ( message, " DirectX SKD Version: ");
   sprintf ( message+strlen(" DirectX SDK Version: "),
```

```
                "%x", version );
   TextOut ( hdc, text_x, text_y, message, strlen (message) );
      text_y += tm.tmHeight+tm.tmExternalLeading;
// Revision number
   buildNum = LOWORD(revision);
   releaseNum = HIWORD(revision);
// Display release number
   strcpy ( message, " DirectX SKD release: ");
   sprintf ( message+strlen(" DirectX SDK release: "),
            "%x", releaseNum );
   TextOut ( hdc, text_x, text_y, message, strlen (message) );
      text_y += tm.tmHeight+tm.tmExternalLeading;
// Display build number
   strcpy ( message, " DirectX SKD build: ");
   sprintf ( message+strlen(" DirectX SDK build: "),
            "%x", buildNum );
   TextOut ( hdc, text_x, text_y, message, strlen (message) );
```

Figure 13-2 is a screen snapshot of the DirectX Info menu command in the *DD Setup Demo* project on the book's CD-ROM.

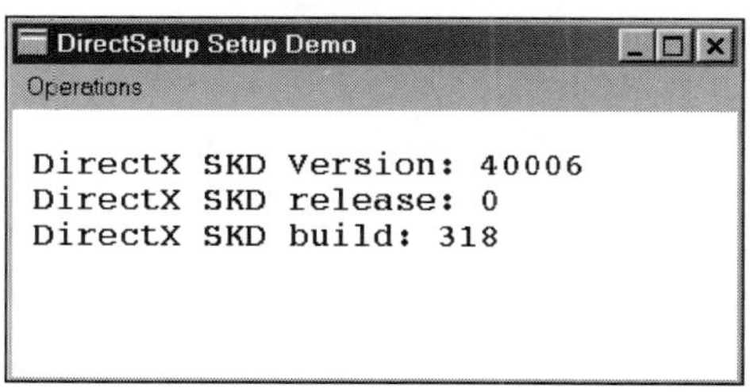

Figure 13-2: Screen snapshot of the DirectX Info menu command in the DD Setup Demo project program

The Upgrade Decision

Obtaining SDK version and revision information is straightforward, but using this information to decide if an upgrade is required is another matter. Several processing options are possible:

- Compare the version number obtained by the call to `DirectXSetup GetVersion()` with a hard-coded version number defined at compile time. Assume an upgrade is not required if the current version number is equal to or greater than the stored value.

- Use the revision number in deciding if an upgrade is necessary. This can be accomplished by appending the revision number to the version number into a 64-bit variable, or by ANDing the two values in the test condition.
- Ignore whatever value is returned by `DirectXSetupGetVersion()` and call `DirectXSetup()` anyway.

The first approach bases the update decision on the version number only, while the second approach also takes into account the revision number. Microsoft documentation seems to favor using both the version and the revision numbers in making the comparison. However, how this number is used depends on the application's purpose. An installation utility designed exclusively for upgrading DirectX can assume that the installation should proceed if the version/revision number is smaller than the one in the upgrade software. However, an application that merely wants to make sure the host system is compatible may decide that a new installation is required only if the version/revision number of the software in the host machine is smaller than the one under which the application was developed. The decision, although apparently subtle, is not without consequence; there is a risk, however small, that an application may not function correctly in a later version of the DirectX package. For this reason, the safest approach is not to install the upgrade package if the one on the host machine is compatible with the SDK version under which the program was coded.

The third option actually passes the decision on to the installation software. In this case, we call the DirectSetup software installation function named `DirectXSetup()` and let it decide how to proceed. The sample installation program furnished in the DirectX 6 SDK and our own *DX Setup Demo* project program use this approach.

Setting Up DirectX

Once the application has determined that a DirectX installation is necessary, either because there is no DirectX in the host system or because the DirectX version is not current, code can proceed to install the DirectX run-time components. At this point, a message box or other interface device should be used to inform the user that the installation is ready to proceed and to ensure that permission is granted to perform it.

DirectXSetup() Function

Applications use the `DirectXSetup()` function to copy and initialize the necessary system components into an existing Windows installation. Optionally, the function can update the display and audio drivers. The function's general form is as follows:

```
int WINAPI
        DirectXSetup(
```

```
                    HWND hwnd,            // 1
                    LPSTR lpszRootPath,   // 2
                    DWORD dwFlags         // 3
        );
```

The first parameter is the handle to the parent window that is to display the setup dialog boxes. The second parameter is a pointer to a string that contains the full path of the DirectX component files. This folder must contain the files dsetup.dll, dsetup16.dll, and dsetup32.dll, as well as a "DirectX" (not case sensitive) folder with the redistributable files. Note that the file dsetup.dll needs to be in the same directory (or in the path) of the setup program before the upgrade can take place. Optionally, the DLL files can also be located in the `\Windows\System` folder. If this value is `NULL`, the current folder is used. The third parameter contains one or more flags that define the installation mode. Table 13-3 lists the installation flags that are not considered obsolete in the Microsoft documentation.

TABLE 13-3 INSTALLATION FLAGS FOR DIRECTXSETUP() FUNCTION

Flag Name	Function
DSETUP_DDRAWDRV	Installs display drivers provided by Microsoft.
DSETUP_DIRECTX	Installs DirectX run-time components as well as DirectX-compatible display and audio drivers.
DSETUP_DSOUNDDRV	Installs audio drivers provided by Microsoft.
DSETUP_DXCORE	Installs DirectX run-time components. Does not install DirectX-compatible display and audio drivers.
DSETUP_TESTINSTALL	Performs a test installation. Does not actually install new components.

The `DSETUP_TESTINSTALL` flag is typically used during program development. Once an installation routine has been debugged and tested, it is substituted by `DSETUP_DIRECTX`, which performs a full installation of the run-time software.

If the function is successful and the software is ready for use, the call returns `DSETUPERR_SUCCESS`. If the installation is successful, but Windows must be restarted for it to take effect, it returns `DSETUPERR_SUCCESS_RESTART`. If it is not successful, it returns an error code. Table 13-4 lists the error codes returned by `DirectXSetup()`.

TABLE 13-4 ERROR CODES RETURNED BY DIRECTXSETUP() FUNCTION

Code Name	Meaning
DSETUPERR_SUCCESS	Setup was successful. No restart is required.
DSETUPERR_SUCCESS_RESTART	Setup was successful but restart is required.
DSETUPERR_BADSOURCESIZE	A file size could not be verified or was incorrect.
DSETUPERR_BADSOURCETIME	A file date or time could not be verified or was incorrect.
DSETUPERR_BADWINDOWSVERSION	DirectX does not support the Windows version on the system.
DSETUPERR_CANTFINDDIR	The setup program could not find the working folder.
DSETUPERR_CANTFINDINF	A required .inf file could not be found.
DSETUPERR_INTERNAL	An internal error occurred.
DSETUPERR_NOCOPY	A file version could not be verified or was incorrect.
DSETUPERR_NOTPREINSTALLEDONNT	The version of Windows NT on the system does not contain the current version of DirectX. An older version of DirectX may be present, or DirectX may be absent altogether.
DSETUPERR_OUTOFDISKSPACE	The setup program ran out of disk space.
DSETUPERR_SOURCEFILENOTFOUND	One of the required source files could not be found.
DSETUPERR_UNKNOWNOS	The operating system is not currently supported.
DSETUPERR_USERHITCANCEL	The Cancel button was pressed before the application was fully installed.

The call to the `DirectXSetup()` function overwrites system components from previous versions of DirectX. The function detects when DirectX components, display drivers, and audio drivers need to be upgraded. It also notices whether these components can be upgraded without adversely affecting operating system integrity. Microsoft documentation says the function performs "safe" upgrades only. It also mentions that a safe upgrade for the operating system may not be safe for the applications, and it could affect some hardware-dependent programs negatively.

DirectXSetup() does not provide an automatic uninstall feature. However, it creates a backup copy of the replaced system components and drivers so that they can be manually restored. The upgrade process is based on a Microsoft database that contains information on existing drivers and their upgrade status as provided by vendors and manufacturers of the hardware. We discussed uninstalling DirectX 6 drivers earlier in this chapter.

Normal Installation

The simplest approach is to call the DirectXSetup() function and notify the user of the results according to the returned code. In many cases, DirectXSetup() can be called without first testing the system for the current version of the SDK. In this case, which we call a normal installation, the application code calls DirectXSetup() and waits for the process to conclude. It then processes the messages returned by DirectXSetup() accordingly. During execution, DirectXSetup() provides feedback to the user directly by way of message boxes that indicate the progress of the installation. The following code fragment shows normal processing during SDK installation:

```
// By default, installation of DirectX 6 is in test mode.
// To actually perform the driver upgrade, change the
// following #define statement to 0
#define SDK_TEST_MODE 1
   .
   .
   .
//********************************
//   Install DirectX SDK drivers
//********************************
// Check for installation mode and perform real or
// simulated installation
    if(SDK_TEST_MODE)
        setupRet = DirectXSetup(hwnd,
                   NULL,  // Use current folder
                   DSETUP_TESTINSTALL);
    else
        setupRet = DirectXSetup(hwnd,
                   NULL,
                   DSETUP_DIRECTX);

    if(setupRet == DSETUPERR_SUCCESS)
    {
```

```
            MessageBox(hwnd,
                      "DirectX installed and ready",
                      "DX Setup Demo",
                      MB_OK);
            return 0;
     }
     else if(setupRet == DSETUPERR_SUCCESS_RESTART)
     {
            msgBoxRet = MessageBox(hwnd,
                        "DirectX 6 installed\n"
                        "Restart system now?",
                        "DX Setup Demo",
                         MB_YESNO);
           // Restart windows if yes
              if(msgBoxRet == IDYES)
                 ExitWindowsEx(EWX_REBOOT, 0);
           // Continue if no
              if(msgBoxRet == IDNO)
              {
                   MessageBox(hwnd,
                             "Windows must be restated\n"
                             "before using DirectX 6",
                              "DX Setup Demo",
                              MB_OK);
                   return 0;
              }
       }
       else
       {
            msgBoxRet = MessageBox(hwnd,
                        "DirectX 6 installation failed",
                        "DirectX Setup Demo",
                         MB_OK);
                return 0;
        }
```

This code fragment shows the processing in the *DX Setup Demo* project program. In this example, the constant SDK_TEST_MODE is initialized to 1 to perform a test installation. This determines that the DirectXSetup() function call is made using the DSETUP_TESTINSTALL flag. If the constant is set to 0, the call uses the SETUP_DIRECTX flag to produce a real installation.

Customized Installation

In most cases, the DirectX run-time setup is done as described in the previous section, that is, by calling `DirectXSetup()` and letting the function make installation decisions and provide user feedback. Less often, an application needs to control the installation process or customize the feedback to fit its design or to accommodate other special conditions. This is done by defining a callback function that serves as a message intercept during the installation process. The callback function is called every time a DirectX component or driver is ready to be installed or upgraded. In this mode of operation, the information that would have been used by `DirectXSetup()` to create the message, status, and dialog boxes is instead passed to the application. The application examines the messages and makes alternative decisions.

Because the callback function is an installation message intercept, it can also be used to suppress all user feedback. This creates the possibility of making a silent installation during which the user is not informed that a software update is taking place. Silent installation is discussed later in this section.

Creating the Callback Function

In order for `DirectXSetup()` to use a callback function, this function must be previously defined and coded. The function `DirectXSetupSetCallback()` receives as its single parameter a pointer to the address of the callback function in the application's space. The function is called as follows:

```
DirectXSetupSetCallback(
        (DSETUP_CALLBACK) DXSetupCallback);
```

In this case, `DXSetupCallback()` is the name of the application's callback function. You can substitute this name for that of your own setup callback function. In the current implementation, the call always returns 0. If the application does not contain a callback function, the `DirectXSetupSetCallback()` function should not be invoked. Like all functions in DirectSetup, the header file is dsetup.h and the import library is dsetup.lib.

The Callback Function

The `DirectXSetupCallbackFunction()` is a prototype to which your own callback function must conform. If present, it is called once for each step of the setup process. The prototype is defined in DirectX 6 as follows:

```
DWORD WINAPI
          DirectXSetupCallbackFunction(
              DWORD Reason,       // 1
```

```
        DWORD MsgType,      // 2
        LPSTR *szMessage,   // 3
        LPSTR *szName,      // 4
        void *pInfo         // 5
    );
```

The first parameter contains the reason for the callback intercept. Table 13-5 lists the predefined constants for this parameter.

TABLE 13-5 CONSTANTS FOR DIRECTX CALLBACK FUNCTION REASON PARAMETER

Constant	Interpretation
DSETUP_CB_MSG_BEGIN_INSTALL	DirectSetup is about to begin installing DirectX components and device drivers.
DSETUP_CB_MSG_BEGIN_INSTALL_DRIVERS	DirectSetup is about to begin installing device drivers.
DSETUP_CB_MSG_BEGIN_INSTALL_RUNTIME	DirectSetup is about to begin installing DirectX components.
DSETUP_CB_MSG_BEGIN_RESTORE_DRIVERS	DirectSetup is about to begin restoring previous drivers.
DSETUP_CB_MSG_CANTINSTALL_BETA	A component or device driver cannot be installed because the host system is a prerelease beta version of Windows 95.
DSETUP_CB_MSG_CANTINSTALL_NOTWIN32	The host's operating system is not Windows 95 or Windows NT.
DSETUP_CB_MSG_CANTINSTALL_NT	The DirectX component or device driver cannot be installed on Windows NT prior to version 4.0.
DSETUP_CB_MSG_CANTINSTALL_UNKNOWNOS	The DirectX component or driver cannot be installed because the operating system is unknown.
DSETUP_CB_MSG_CANTINSTALL_WRONGLANGUAGE	The DirectX component or driver is not compatible with language being used by Windows.

Constant	Interpretation
DSETUP_CB_MSG_CANTINSTALL_WRONGPLATFORM	The DirectX component or device driver is not compatible with the computer hardware.
DSETUP_CB_MSG_CHECK_DRIVER_UPGRADE	The current driver is being considered for upgrade. User should verify installation.
DSETUP_CB_MSG_INTERNAL_ERROR	An internal error has occurred. Setup of the DirectX component or device driver has failed.
DSETUP_CB_MSG_NOMESSAGE	No message received. The callback function should return.
DSETUP_CB_MSG_NOTPREINSTALLEDONNT	The DirectX component or device driver cannot be installed on the Windows NT version in use.
DSETUP_CB_MSG_PREINSTALL_NT	DirectX is already installed on the Windows NT version in use.
DSETUP_CB_MSG_SETUP_INIT_FAILED	Setup of the DirectX component or device driver failed.

The second parameter consists of the message box button flags that define the type of message box used by DirectXSetup(). These flags can be passed on to a MessageBox() function in the application's code space. When this parameter is 0, the code can display status information, but should not wait for input from the user.

The third parameter is a character string that contains the error or status message that was to be displayed by the DirectXSetup(). Applications can pass this message to their own message display routine or replace it with another one.

The fourth parameter is NULL unless the first parameter is DSETUP_CB_MSG_CHECK_DRIVER_UPGRADE. In this case, the fourth parameter is a string containing the name of the driver to be upgraded.

The fifth parameter is a pointer to a structure containing upgrade information. The message DSETUP_CB_MSG_CHECK_DRIVER_UPGRADE received in the first parameter indicates that the setup program is in the process of upgrading a driver and is asking the user whether to proceed with the upgrade or not. In this case, the fifth parameter points to a structure of type DSETUP_CB_UPGRADEINFO containing information about the upgrade. The structure is defined as follows:

```
typedef struct _DSETUP_CB_UPGRADEINFO
{
    DWORD UpgradeFlags;
} DSETUP_CB_UPGRADEINFO;
```

The `UpgradeFlags` member of this structure indicates the status of the upgrade. The defined values are listed in Table 13-6.

TABLE 13-6 VALUES OF THE UPGRADEFLAGS MEMBER IN DSETUP_CB_UPGRADEINFO STRUCTURE

Flag	Interpretation
DSETUP_CB_UPGRADE_CANTBACKUP	The old system components cannot be backed up. Upgrade can be performed, but it will not be possible to restore the original drivers at a later time.
DSETUP_CB_UPGRADE_DEVICE_ACTIVE	The device is currently in use.
DSETUP_CB_UPGRADE_DEVICE_DISPLAY	A display device driver is being updated.
DSETUP_CB_UPGRADE_DEVICE_MEDIA	A media device driver is being updated.
DSETUP_CB_UPGRADE_FORCE	Windows may not function correctly if the component is not upgraded. The upgrade will be performed.
DSETUP_CB_UPGRADE_HASWARNINGS	Upgrading this driver could adversely affect one or more programs on the system. The third parameter passed to the callback function contains the names of the programs that are affected. Upgrade not recommended.
DSETUP_CB_UPGRADE_KEEP	If this driver is updated, the system may fail. Upgrade not allowed.
DSETUP_CB_UPGRADE_SAFE	DirectSetup can safely upgrade this driver. Upgrade recommended.
DSETUP_CB_UPGRADE_UNKNOWN	DirectSetup does not recognize the existing driver for this device. It is strongly recommended that the upgrade not be performed.

The value returned by the callback function must conform to specific rules:

- If the second parameter (indicating the message type) is 0, the return value must be IDOK. In this case, the application has no other choice, although it is free to display a status message. This response performs the default upgrade action for the component or driver.
- If the second parameter is nonzero, the return value must be the same as would have been returned by a MessageBox() function had the user made the corresponding choice.

In the second case, code needs to determine the appropriate return value. Application code must test the second parameter for the buttons that would normally have been placed in the message box and provide the correct response for those buttons.

Coding the Message Intercept

A customized callback function is actually a message intercept handler for DirectXSetup(). Typical processing consists of testing for the callback reason passed in the first parameter to the callback function, and either producing a substitute action or allowing the default action to take place. In the following discussion, we assume the first parameter is passed in a variable named reason and the second one is passed in a variable named msgType. Processing logic is typically as follows:

1. If the first parameter is DSETUP_CB_MSG_NOMESSAGE and the second one is 0, then the callback function is required to produce the default action, which is to return IDOK. For this reason, code usually begins by testing for this case.
2. Code then tests for reason parameters that indicate terminal errors, and produces the corresponding messages to notify the user to continue or abort the installation.
3. Tests can be performed for reason parameters that indicate installation progress, such as DSETUP_CB_MSG_BEGIN_INSTALL, DSETUP_CB_MSG_BEGIN_INSTALL_RUNTIME, and DSETUP_CB_MSG_BEGIN_INSTALL_DRIVERS. The action can be to update a progress indicator or to notify the user of the action taking place.
4. The reason DSETUP_CB_MSG_CHECK_DRIVER_UPGRADE usually requires special handling. Upon detecting this reason flag, code can inspect the UpgradeFlags member of the CSETUP_CB_UPGRADEINFO structure to decide how to proceed in each case.

Intercepting and replacing the DirectXSetup() messages requires some way of displaying the replacement messages, or of notifying the user of the installation progress or the action taken. Because some of these messages do not require a response, it is common to use a modeless dialog box in this case. Alternatively, applications can produce feedback in their own client area, or by a series of modal dialog or message boxes. A modeless dialog box usually requires a dialog box procedure to initialize it and monitor the user's interaction. The creation of modeless dialog boxes and their corresponding dialog procedures is discussed in Chapter 5. In the demonstration program *named DX Setup Demo*, the callback function creates the modeless dialog box. Because the callback function can receive control more than once, a global switch named cbIteration ensures that the dialog box is displayed only one time. Code is as follows:

```
// Display modeless dialog box if first iteration of callback
if(cbIteration == 0)
  {
    hModeless1 = CreateDialog(pInstance,
                          MAKEINTRESOURCE(IDD_DIALOGBAR),
                          hWnd,
                         (DLGPROC) DlgProc);
    cbIteration = 1;    // Set iteration switch
  }
```

In the previous code fragment, the dialog box is a program resource named IDD_DIALOGBAR and the dialog box procedure is named DlgProc(). The dialog box procedure is coded as follows:

```
//*******************************************
//   Modeless box dialog box procedure
//*******************************************
BOOL CALLBACK DlgProc (HWND hDlg, UINT iMsg, WPARAM wParam,
               LPARAM lParam)
{
     switch (iMsg)
        {
        case WM_INITDIALOG :
            BringWindowToTop(hDlg);
            SetFocus(hDlg);
            SendMessage(hDlg, DM_REPOSITION, 0, 0);
            return TRUE ;
        case WM_COMMAND :
            switch (LOWORD (wParam)) {
        case IDC_BUT_CLOSE:
```

```
        case WM_CLOSE:
            hModeless1 = 0;      // Modeless box closed
            DestroyWindow (hDlg) ;
            return TRUE ;
        }
          break ;
    }
      return FALSE ;
}
```

The dialog box contains a single button labeled Close. In this case, the processing consists of initializing the dialog box and monitoring the user's action on the Close button. In the *DX Setup Demo* project program, the verbose version of the callback function is coded as follows:

```
//************************************************************
// Name: DXCallbackVerbose
// Desc: Test reason for why the callback was called and
// produce the adequate action
//************************************************************
DWORD WINAPI
DXCallbackVerbose(DWORD reason, DWORD msgType,
                  LPSTR message, LPSTR
                  name, void *pInfo)
{
    int    msgBoxRet;
    DWORD   upgrade;
// Display modeless dialog box if first iteration of
// callback
  if(cbIteration == 0)
  {
     hModeless1 = CreateDialog(pInstance,
                       MAKEINTRESOURCE(IDD_DIALOGBAR),
                       hWnd,
                       (DLGPROC) DlgProc);
    cbIteration = 1;
  }
  // Test for no message intercept
    if (reason == DSETUP_CB_MSG_NOMESSAGE && msgType == 0)
  {
  SendDlgItemMessage( hModeless1, IDC_LIST1, LB_ADDSTRING, 0,
        (LPARAM) "No Message");
    return IDOK;
  }
```

```
//*********************************
//  processing callback messages
//*********************************
switch (reason)
  {
     // Test for messages that indicate a terminal error
     case DSETUP_CB_MSG_CANTINSTALL_UNKNOWNOS:
     case DSETUP_CB_MSG_CANTINSTALL_NT:
     case DSETUP_CB_MSG_CANTINSTALL_BETA:
     case DSETUP_CB_MSG_CANTINSTALL_NOTWIN32:
     case DSETUP_CB_MSG_CANTINSTALL_WRONGLANGUAGE:
     case DSETUP_CB_MSG_CANTINSTALL_WRONGPLATFORM:
     case DSETUP_CB_MSG_PREINSTALL_NT:
     case DSETUP_CB_MSG_NOTPREINSTALLEDONNT:
     case DSETUP_CB_MSG_SETUP_INIT_FAILED:
     case DSETUP_CB_MSG_INTERNAL_ERROR:
     case DSETUP_CB_MSG_OUTOFDISKSPACE:
     case DSETUP_CB_MSG_FILECOPYERROR:
  // Copy original message to local list box
       SendDlgItemMessage( hModeless1, IDC_LIST1,
                           LB_ADDSTRING, 0,
                           (LPARAM) message);
       break;
 // Test for messages that indicate installation in progress
     case DSETUP_CB_MSG_BEGIN_INSTALL:
     case DSETUP_CB_MSG_BEGIN_INSTALL_RUNTIME:
     case DSETUP_CB_MSG_BEGIN_INSTALL_DRIVERS:
     // Copy original message to local list box
        SendDlgItemMessage( hModeless1,
                            IDC_LIST1, LB_ADDSTRING, 0,
        (LPARAM) "Installation in progress");
        break;

 // Test for driver update messages and check additional
 // data
   case DSETUP_CB_MSG_CHECK_DRIVER_UPGRADE:
       {
       upgrade = ((DSETUP_CB_UPGRADEINFO *)
                  pInfo)->UpgradeFlags
                  & DSETUP_CB_UPGRADE_TYPE_MASK;
       switch (upgrade)
       {
       case DSETUP_CB_UPGRADE_FORCE:
       case (DSETUP_CB_UPGRADE_SAFE &
```

```
                DSETUP_CB_UPGRADE_HASWARNINGS):
          case DSETUP_CB_UPGRADE_UNKNOWN:
              {
              msgBoxRet = MessageBox(hWnd,
                        "Upgrade not recognized by DirectX 6\n"
                        "Upgrade not recommended\n\n",
                        "Upgrade driver?",
                        MB_YESNO);
                 if(msgBoxRet == IDYES)
                 return IDYES;
               else
                 return IDOK;
                 break;
               }
           case DSETUP_CB_UPGRADE_KEEP:
           case DSETUP_CB_UPGRADE_SAFE:
           {
               return IDOK;
               break;
           }
          }
        return IDOK;
       }
     return IDOK;
   }
  return IDOK;
}
```

The processing performed by the DXVerboseCallback() function displays the text string "No Message" whenever the SETUP_CB_MSG_NOMESSAGE and the message type 0 are received. The purpose of this message is to show how many times this intercept takes place during execution. Normally, no display is necessary for this case. Figure 13-3 shows the modeless dialog box produced by the verbose callback mode in the *DX Setup Demo* project program. Note that the display corresponds to a simulated installation as results from using the DSETUP_TESTINSTALL flag in the call to DirectXSetup().

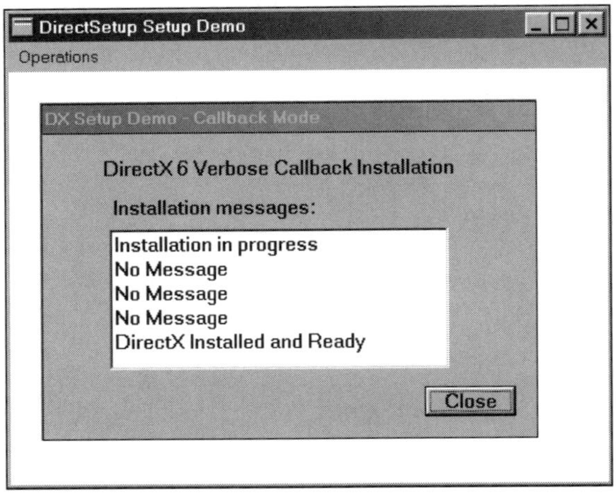

Figure 13-3: Screen snapshot of the verbose callback mode in the DX Setup Demo project program

Silent Installation

The `DirectXSetup()` function provides an alternative for those rare occasions in which a completely silent installation is indicated. The fact that defining a callback function disables the display of `DirectXSetup()` messages can be used for this purpose. All that is required for a totally silent installation is a callback function that performs no display action. In the *DX Setup Demo* project program, the silent version of the callback function is coded as follows:

```
//****************************************************************
// Name: DXCallbackSilent
// Desc: Silent DirectX installation
//****************************************************************
DWORD WINAPI
DXCallbackSilent(DWORD reason, DWORD msgType, LPSTR message,
                  LPSTR name, void *pInfo)
{
  return IDOK;
}
```

A less silent version could be based on intercepting terminal error messages only. In all cases, code would probably inspect the results of the installation as returned by `DirectXSetup()` and provide some feedback if the installation failed or if a system restart was required. In the sample program, we have also furnished a message box to indicate that the silent installation has concluded satisfactorily.

Summary

In this chapter, we discussed the software upgrade and installation facilities provided in the DirectSetup component of DirectX 6. The functions in DirectSetup enable us to provide a safe and easy upgrade mechanism for our DirectX applications. The process is made possible by Microsoft's decision to grant developers the right to redistribute the SDK run-time components, and by the backward compatibility rules that are part of the COM interface. The most important result is that programmers can develop code that uses the new features of the SDK without fear of failing in a machine that does not contain the new software.

Chapter 14

Input in Exclusive Mode Applications

IN THIS CHAPTER

- The DirectInput component of DirectX
- DirectInput preparatory operations
- Obtaining device information
- Setting device properties
- Reading input-device data
- Experimenting with DirectInput

HIGH-PERFORMANCE graphics applications, especially those coded for DirectDraw, must be capable of obtaining input effectively and of responding rapidly to user interaction. Otherwise, the display speed advantages provided by direct access to video memory and hardware resources are diminished, or even canceled, by the effects of a sluggish user interface. For example, a computer game capable of effectively animating several sprites and smoothly manipulating background images may appear to execute listlessly if the code must depend on the Windows message mechanism to receive and respond to user input. DirectX contains a component named DirectInput whose purpose is to upgrade the performance of user input and interaction functions so that they match those of the graphics-display operations. In addition, DirectInput provides support for many input devices that are not standard or supported by the Windows API.

The DirectInput component of DirectX is both powerful and complex. It is designed for maximum performance and flexibility. An entire book could easily be written on this topic. In this chapter, we discuss the essentials of DirectInput programming only.

The DirectInput Component

The DirectInput component of DirectX 6 provides support for several types of input devices, including the mouse, keyboard, and specialized game controllers usually called joysticks. In addition, DirectInput provides services for devices not supported by the Win32 API, such as force-feedback game devices. Force-feedback devices are a new generation of computer-input gadgetry that is capable of both acting and reacting during the interface process. For example, a steering wheel controller produces a force in the opposite direction in which it is being turned to simulate what the user would feel when driving a vehicle in the real world. Because of their specialized use and complexity, force-feedback devices are not considered in this book.

From an application developer's viewpoint, DirectInput's greatest advantage is that it gives faster access to input data by communicating directly with the hardware drivers. This improved performance makes it valuable in the implementation of computer games, simulations, and many other programs that execute interactively in real time.

DirectInput Architecture

Like DirectDraw and other DirectX components, DirectInput consists of an object that is compatible with the COM interface. In this case, the object is named `IDirectInput`. In addition, the `IDirectInput` object contains a device object for each input device that can provide data. In turn, each device object can have individual controls, which are implemented as switches, buttons, axes, or other gadgets.

> NOTE: In the discussion of DirectInput architecture, we deviate from the nomenclature in Microsoft documentation, which refers to an `IDirectInput` *object*, which has *objects* for every data device and *object instances* for each control on the device. Instead, we use the word object in the sense of a COM-interface entity only. We refer to the lower-level elements simply as devices, or device objects, and to the individual input components as device controls, or controls.

DirectInput accesses the device drivers directly, bypassing the conventional Windows message mechanism. The use of DirectInput also makes it possible for an application to gain access to input data while it is in the background.

Applications create the `IDirectInput` object by means of the `DirectInputCreate()` function. If the call is successful, it returns a pointer to an `IDirectInput` COM interface. Two versions of the interface are available: one for ANSI and the other one for Unicode character sets. The ANSI version is the default since it is selected if the `UNICODE` macro is not defined. Once the DirectInput object is created, code can use the methods of the interface to enumerate individual devices available to the system and to obtain a `DirectInputDevice` object for each device that is used by the program.

A `DirectInputDevice` object represents a single input device, for example, a keyboard, a mouse, or a joystick. Applications create a `DirectInputDevice` object by calling the `CreateDevice()` function. If the call is successful, it returns a pointer to the corresponding `IDirectInputDevice` interface. The functions in the interface are used to set the device properties, to obtain information about the device, and to read device data.

A device control (called an object instance in Microsoft's DirectX documentation) is one of the switches, buttons, keys, wheels, sliders, or other gadgets located on a device. For example, the two buttons and the wheel of a Microsoft Intellimouse are device controls. In the case of the keyboard, each key is considered a device control. The `EnumObjects()` function reports the number and type of controls available on a particular device.

DirectInput and Windows

Applications that use DirectInput access the device drivers directly. Since DirectInput furnishes an interface with the device hardware, it either suppresses or ignores conventional Windows messages. Like DirectDraw, DirectInput devices must establish a cooperative level that defines their interaction with other applications. The cooperative levels, discussed later in this chapter, have an exclusive and a non-exclusive mode. When DirectInput is in exclusive mode, it suppresses mouse messages. This, in turn, determines that Windows is unable to display the standard mouse cursor. DirectInput also ignores Control Panel settings, such as acceleration and swapped buttons. However, if there is a configuration that takes place in the driver itself, then it is also active in DirectInput.

Regarding keyboard processing, DirectInput ignores keyboard *typematic* rates set by the user. The typematic rate is the automatic keystroke repetition that takes place when a key is held down. When used in the buffered-data mode, DirectInput interprets each key press and release as a single event. In the immediate data mode, DirectInput is concerned only with the present physical state of the keys, not with keyboard events as interpreted by Windows.

DirectInput provides full support for devices that conform to the Human Interface Device (HID) specification under the Universal Serial Bus (USB) standard. Obtaining data from a HID device is substantially the same as from a conventional device.

DirectInput Support

Before an application can use DirectInput services, there are several preliminary steps that must be performed in order to ensure that the software support is available at compile time. First, the DirectInput library, named dinput.lib, must be located in the system library path. Use the Options command in the Developer Studio Tools menu to make sure that the Directories tab contains a path to the location of the library file.

In addition, the dinput.h header file must be in the development system's include file path, typically `\mssdk\include`, or in the development folder. Here again, the Options command in the Developer Studio Tools menu can also be used to make sure that the Directories tab contains a path to the location of the header file.

Programs that use DirectInput must contain an `#include` statement for dinput.h, as follows:

```
#include <dinput.h>    // If file is in the include path
#include "dinput.h"    // If file is in the development folder
```

Preparing for DirectInput

Before applications have access to DirectInput services, they must perform several initialization steps. The first step is usually to call `DirectInputCreate()` to originate the DirectInput object that is then used in accessing all the DirectInput devices. The call returns a pointer to an `IDirectInput` COM interface. The function's general form reads as follows:

```
HRESULT WINAPI
        DirectInputCreate(
                HINSTANCE hinst,                   // 1
                DWORD dwVersion,                   // 2
                LPDIRECTINPUT * lplpDirectInput,   // 3
                LPUNKNOWN punkOuter                // 4
        );
```

The first parameter is the handle to the application or DLL that is creating the DirectInput object. This value is used by DirectInput to determine whether the application or DLL has been certified and to establish any special behaviors that may be necessary for backward compatibility. The second parameter is the DirectInput version number of DirectInput for which the application is designed. The predefined constant `DIRECTINPUT_VERSION`, which returns the current version, is normally used here. Passing the version number of a previous version causes DirectInput to emulate that version. The third parameter is the address of a variable of type `LPDIRECTINPUT` that receives the interface pointer. The fourth parameter is a pointer to the address of the controlling object's `IUnknown` interface for COM aggregation, or `NULL` if the interface is not aggregated. Most applications pass `NULL` in this parameter.

If the call succeeds, the return value is `DI_OK` and the `LPDIRECTINPUT` variable holds the DirectInput object. If the function fails, the return value may be one of the following errors:

- `DIERR_BETADIRECTINPUTVERSION`
- `DIERR_INVALIDPARAM`
- `DIERR_OLDDIRECTINPUTVERSION`
- `DIERR_OUTOFMEMORY`

There are two specific versions of this function: one for ANSI and the other one for Unicode. The ANSI version creates an object that supports the `IDirectInputA` interface. The Unicode version creates an object that supports the `IDirectInputW` interface. Macros in the header files, which are sensitive to the two character sets, serve to map `DirectInputCreate()` to either the ANSI or the Unicode versions. By default, the ANSI version is selected if the `UNICODE` constant is not defined in the header file.

The following code fragment shows a call to the `DirectInputCreate()` function:

```
// Global variables
HINSTANCE   hinstance; // Handle to the application's
                       // instance. Usually initialized
                       // in WinMain()
HRESULT             hr;
LPDIRECTINPUT       lpDI;  // DirectInput object
    .
    .
    .
hr = DirectInputCreate(hinstance,
                       DIRECTINPUT_VERSION,
                       &lpDI,
                       NULL);
    if(hr != DI_OK)
        // Error handler goes here
```

Enumerating the Devices

Once a DirectInput object has been obtained, the next operation performed by many applications is to query the system for available input devices and determine if these devices are connected and active. Exceptions include applications that use only the keyboard and the mouse, since Windows programs usually assume that these devices are always available. Two global variables defined in the DirectInput header files, `GUID_SysMouse` and `GUID_SysKeyboard`, allow referencing the keyboard and the mouse directly.

For nonstandard input devices, such as joysticks, graphics tablets, and steering wheels, DirectInput applications must use a process called *enumeration*, which consists of listing the attached input devices. This can also be the case if the system is equipped with multiple keyboards or mice. The `EnumDevices()` function uses a callback function to list all available devices. The function's general form reads as follows:

```
HRESULT EnumDevices(
                    DWORD dwDevType,                // 1
```

```
LPDIENUMCALLBACK lpCallback,     // 2
LPVOID pvRef,                    // 3
DWORD dwFlags                    // 4
);
```

The first parameter is a flag that determines what types of devices are to be enumerated. Table 14-1 lists the most useful constants predefined for this parameter.

TABLE 14-1 DEVICE-TYPE PARAMETER CONSTANTS FOR ENUMDEVICE() FUNCTION

Constant	Refers To
DIDEVTYPE_MOUSE	A mouse or mouse-like device (such as a trackball).
DIDEVTYPE_KEYBOARD	A keyboard or keyboard-like device.
DIDEVTYPE_JOYSTICK	A joystick or similar device, such as a steering wheel.
DIDEVTYPE_DEVICE	A device that does not fall into one of the previous categories.
Mouse Subtypes	
DIDEVTYPEMOUSE_UNKNOWN	The subtype could not be determined.
DIDEVTYPEMOUSE_TRADITIONAL	A traditional mouse.
DIDEVTYPEMOUSE_FINGERSTICK	A fingerstick mouse.
DIDEVTYPEMOUSE_TOUCHPAD	A touchpad.
DIDEVTYPEMOUSE_TRACKBALL	A trackball.
Keyboard Subtypes	
DIDEVTYPEKEYBOARD_UNKNOWN	The subtype could not be determined.
DIDEVTYPEKEYBOARD_PCXT	IBM PC/XT 83-key keyboard.
DIDEVTYPEKEYBOARD_OLIVETTI	Olivetti 102-key keyboard.
DIDEVTYPEKEYBOARD_PCAT	IBM PC/AT 84-key keyboard.
DIDEVTYPEKEYBOARD_PCENH	IBM PC Enhanced 101/102-key or Microsoft Natural(r) keyboard.
DIDEVTYPEKEYBOARD_NOKIA1050	Nokia 1050 keyboard.

Constant	Refers To
Keyboard Subtypes	
DIDEVTYPEKEYBOARD_NOKIA9140	Nokia 9140 keyboard.
DIDEVTYPEKEYBOARD_NEC98	Japanese NEC PC98 keyboard.
DIDEVTYPEKEYBOARD_NEC98LAPTOP	Japanese NEC PC98 laptop keyboard.
DIDEVTYPEKEYBOARD_NEC98106	Japanese NEC PC98 106-key keyboard.
DIDEVTYPEKEYBOARD_JAPAN106	Japanese 106-key keyboard.
DIDEVTYPEKEYBOARD_JAPANAX	Japanese AX keyboard.
DIDEVTYPEKEYBOARD_J3100	Japanese J3100 keyboard.
Joystick Subtypes	
DIDEVTYPEJOYSTICK_UNKNOWN	The subtype could not be determined.
DIDEVTYPEJOYSTICK_TRADITIONAL	A traditional joystick.
DIDEVTYPEJOYSTICK_FLIGHTSTICK	A joystick optimized for flight simulation.
DIDEVTYPEJOYSTICK_GAMEPAD	A device whose primary purpose is to provide button input.
DIDEVTYPEJOYSTICK_RUDDER	A device for yaw control.
DIDEVTYPEJOYSTICK_WHEEL	A steering wheel.
DIDEVTYPEJOYSTICK_HEADTRACKER	A device that tracks the movement of the user's head.
Flags in the High Word	
DIDEVTYPE_HID	Device uses the Human Interface Device (HID) protocol.

The parameter DIDEVTYPE_HID is NULL if code wants to enumerate all devices regardless of type. Otherwise it is one of the values in Table 14-1.

The second parameter is a pointer to a programmer-defined callback function. This function is called once for each device enumerated. The placeholder name for the callback function is DIEnumDevicesProc. The third parameter to EnumDevices() is a 32-bit value that is passed to the callback function. Applications can use this parameter for their own purposes; for example, a pointer to a variable of type GUID can be passed in this parameter so that the callback can assign a keyboard instance GUID. The fourth parameter is a flag that defines the scope of the enumeration. Table 14-2 lists the predefined constants for this parameter.

TABLE 14-2 SCOPE OF ENUMERATION FLAGS IN ENUMDEVICES() FUNCTION

Flag	Meaning
DIEDFL_ALLDEVICES	Enumerate all installed devices. This is the default behavior.
DIEDFL_ATTACHEDONLY	Enumerate only attached and installed devices.
DIEDFL_FORCEFEEDBACK	Enumerate only devices that support force feedback.
DIEDFL_INCLUDEALIASES	Include devices that are aliases for other devices.
DIEDFL_INCLUDEPHANTOMS	Include placeholder (phantom) devices

The most commonly used constants for this parameter are DIEDFL_ALLDEVICES and DIEDFL_ATTACHEDONLY. The first one refers to all devices installed in the system, whether the hardware is actually attached or not at the time of the call. The DIEDFL_ATTACHEDONLY flag enumerates only devices that are plugged in and available for use.

The prototype for the EnumDevices() callback function is defined as follows:

```
BOOL CALLBACK DIEnumDevicesProc(
            LPCDIDEVICEINSTANCE lpddi,        // 1
            LPVOID pvRef                      // 2
            );
```

The first parameter passed to the callback function is a variable of the structure type DIDEVICEINSTANCE. The DIDEVICEINSTANCE structure, listed in Appendix A, contains information about the instance of a DirectInput device. This information includes the GUID instance number, the instance name, the product name, and the driver version. The least significant byte of the dwDevType member of this structure (see Appendix A) is one of the values listed in Table 14-1. The second parameter to the callback function is the 32-bit value defined by the caller. Application code can return DIENUM_CONTINUE to continue the enumeration or DIENUM_STOP to end it.

A lot of processing can be performed in the callback function. For example, it can be used to check for the presence of a device, to list all available devices, installed or not, to obtain the instance GUID for a particular device, or to check for a device with specific capabilities required in the program. In this case, the callback function can call the GetCapabilities() function for each identified device. In addition, applications that use more than one input device can take advantage of the callback to initialize devices as they are enumerated.

If the call succeeds, the return value is DI_OK. If it fails, the return value is one of the following errors:

- DIERR_INVALIDPARAM
- DIERR_NOTINITIALIZED

Creating the Device

At this point in the processing, the application has usually decided on one or more input devices. If the device is the keyboard or the mouse, it is associated with either the GUID_SysMouse or GUID_SysKeyboard identifiers. If the device was obtained by the EnumDevices() function, then the GUID is the value in the guidInstance member of the DIDEVICEINSTANCE structure variable passed to the callback function, as previously described. In either case, code now has available the instance GUID for the input device or devices that are used in the code.

The next step is called *creating the device* in the DirectInput documentation. A device is created by the CreateDevice() function, which initializes an instance of a device identified by its GUID and returns a pointer to the device interface. The functions in this interface are used by code to set up the device and to read device data. The function's general form reads as follows:

```
HRESULT CreateDevice(
          REFGUID rguid,                              // 1
          LPDIRECTINPUTDEVICE *lplpDirectInputDevice, // 2
          LPUNKNOWN pUnkOuter                         // 3
          );
```

The first parameter is an instance GUID that identifies the instance of the device for which the interface is to be created. IDirectInput has two predefined GUIDs, GUID_SysMouse and GUID_SysKeyboard, which represent the system mouse and keyboard devices. These identifiers can be passed directly to the CreateDevice() function. In this case, the application must define INITGUID before all other preprocessor directives at the beginning of the source file, or link to the Dxguid library, which is most often the case. For all other devices, the GUID is obtained by calling the EnumDevices() function.

The second parameter is the address of the variable, of type LPDIRECTINPUT DEVICE, which receives the interface pointer if the call is successful. The third parameter is the address of the controlling object's IUnknown interface for COM aggregation, or NULL if the interface is not aggregated. In most cases, code passes NULL in this parameter.

If the method succeeds, the return value is DI_OK. If the method fails, the return value is one of the following errors:

- DIERR_DEVICENOTREG
- DIERR_INVALIDPARAM
- DIERR_NOINTERFACE
- DIERR_NOTINITIALIZED
- DIERR_OUTOFMEMORY

The following code fragment shows how to create a mouse device interface:

```
// Global variables
LPDIRECTINPUTDEVICE  lpDIMouse;
HRESULT              hRes;
LPDIRECTINPUT        lpDI;     // DirectInput object
    .
    .
    .
  hRes = lpDI->CreateDevice(GUID_SysMouse, &lpDIMouse, NULL);
    if(hRes != DI_OK)
       // Error handler goes here
```

Data Formats

Data from different devices is delivered in different formats. For example, data obtained from a keyboard is different from that which originates in a mouse or a joystick. For this reason, before an application can obtain device data using DirectInput, it must define the data format. The SetDataFormat() function informs DirectInput of the device controls in use and of the data constructs. The function's general form reads as follows:

```
HRESULT SetDataFormat(
                      LPCDIDATAFORMAT lpdf
                      );
```

The function's only parameter is the address of a structure variable of type DIDATAFORMAT that describes the format for the data to be returned by DirectInput. Applications can create their own DIDATAFORMAT structure or use one of the following predefined constants shown in Table 14-3.

TABLE 14-3 GLOBAL VARIABLES USED IN THE DIDATAFORMAT STRUCTURE

Variable	Refers To	Data Type
c_dfDIKeyboard	Standard keyboard	Type char[256]
c_dfDIMouse	Standard mouse	DIMOUSESTATE
c_dfDIJoystick	Standard game controller	DIJOYSTATE.
c_dfDIJoystick2	Advanced game controller	DIJOYSTATE2.

If the function succeeds it returns DI_OK. If it fails, the return value is one of the following errors:

- DIERR_ACQUIRED
- DIERR_INVALIDPARAM
- DIERR_NOTINITIALIZED

The data format must be set before the device can be acquired by using the Acquire() function, discussed later in this section. The data format need be set only once and it cannot be changed while the device is acquired.

The following code fragment shows a call to SetDataFormat() using an initialized pointer to the mouse device object, in this case named lpDIMouse. Note that the function is accessed through a valid device object pointer, not through the IDirectDraw object.

```
// Global variables
LPDIRECTINPUTDEVICE  lpDIMouse;
HRESULT              hRes;
   .
   .
   .
   hRes = lpDIMouse->SetDataFormat(&c_dfDIMouse);
     if(hRes != DI_OK)
        // Error handler goes here
```

Cooperative Levels

In the same manner that DirectDraw applications must define how they cooperate with Windows and with other programs in the use of the video resources, a

DirectInput program must set the cooperative level regarding the use of input devices. The input cooperative level is set with the `SetCooperativeLevel()` function, which is found in the `IDirectInputDevice` interface. The function's general form reads as follows:

```
HRESULT SetCooperativeLevel(
                        HWND hwnd,         // 1
                        DWORD dwFlags      // 2
                        );
```

The first parameter is the top-level window handle to be associated with the device. This window must not be destroyed while it is still active in a DirectInput device. The second parameter contains one or more flags that define the cooperative level for the device. The valid flags are shown in Table 14-4.

TABLE 14-4 COOPERATIVE-LEVEL FLAGS IN SETCOOPERATIVELEVEL() FUNCTION

Flag	Refers To
`DISCL_FOREGROUND`	The application requests foreground access. If granted, the device is automatically unacquired when the window is moved to the background.
`DISCL_BACKGROUND`	The application requests background access. If granted, the device may be acquired at any time, even when the application's window is not active.
`DISCL_EXCLUSIVE`	The application requests exclusive access. If granted, no other instance of the device may obtain exclusive access to the same device while it is acquired. Non-exclusive access to the device is always permitted.
`DISCL_NONEXCLUSIVE`	The application requests non-exclusive access. In this case, access to the device will not interfere with the use of the device by other applications.

A foreground cooperative level establishes that the input device is available only when the application is in the foreground, which is when it has the input focus. If the application is moved to the background, the device is automatically unacquired. A background cooperative level means that the application receives input when it is either in the foreground or in the background. A device with this cooperative level can be acquired and used at any time. Most applications select foreground access only, since there is usually no reason for receiving input when another program is in the foreground.

The exclusive and non-exclusive mode selection has more subtle effects. The fact that an application uses a device at the exclusive level does not mean that other programs cannot get device data. What it does mean is that no other applications can acquire the device exclusively. One clear consequence of using the `DISCL_EXCLUSIVE` flag is in the case of two applications attempting to access the same device while both are running in the background. In this case, the `DISCL_EXCLUSIVE` flag ensures that only one application can access the device. Force-feedback requires that the application have exclusive access to the device.

DirectInput does not allow an application to have exclusive access to the keyboard, since this would disable the system-level keystrokes, such as Ctrl+Alt+Delete. On the other hand, an application can have exclusive access to the mouse. In this case, Windows does not receive mouse input, mouse messages are not generated, and the cursor disappears.

Code must specify either `DISCL_FOREGROUND` or `DISCL_BACKGROUND`, as well as `DISCL_EXCLUSIVE` or `DISCL_NONEXCLUSIVE`. This results in four possible flag combinations:

1. `DISCL_NONEXCLUSIVE | DISCL_BACKGROUND`. This is the default setting.
2. `DISCL_NONEXCLUSIVE | DISCL_FOREGROUND`. Access to data while program is in foreground only.
3. `DISCL_EXCLUSIVE | DISCL_FOREGROUND`. Exclusive access to data while in the foreground only. Not valid for keyboard.
4. `DISCL_EXCLUSIVE | DISC_BACKGROUND`. Exclusive access to data in foreground or background. Not valid for keyboard or mouse.

NOTE Applications that acquire the mouse or the keyboard in exclusive mode should always unacquire the devices when they receive the Windows messages `WM_ENTERSIZEMOVE` or `WM_ENTERMENULOOP`. If not, the user has no way of manipulating the menu or moving and resizing the window.

In spite of the fact that DirectInput uses the first flag combination listed previously as a default setting, applications should always explicitly set the cooperative level, since it is the only way to provide DirectInput with the handle to the application's window. Windows needs this handle in situations that involve messages to the application, such as when recalibrating a device.

If the function succeeds, the return value is DI_OK. If it fails, it returns one of the following errors:

- DIERR_INVALIDPARAM
- DIERR_NOTINITIALIZED

The following code fragment shows how to set the cooperative level for the mouse device:

```
// Global variables
LPDIRECTINPUTDEVICE  lpDIMouse;
HRESULT              hRes;
HWND                 hWnd;      // Handle to the window
   .
   .
   .
hRes = lpDIMouse->SetCooperativeLevel(hWnd,
                  DISCL_NONEXCLUSIVE | DISCL_FOREGROUND);
    if(hRes != DI_OK)
       // Error handler goes here
```

Acquiring the Device

The steps performed thus far are preparatory in nature; device data is not yet available to the application. In order to receive data, the application must first *acquire* the device. In this sense, acquiring a device means requesting Windows' and DirectInput's permission to use the device that was previously created and whose data format and cooperative levels have been defined. As long as a device is acquired, DirectInput makes device data available to the application. Application code can change the characteristics of an unacquired device, but cannot obtain device data.

Device acquisition does not produce a permanent state; devices often have to be acquired many times during execution. For example, if the foreground cooperative level was selected, then the device is automatically unacquired when the application loses the foreground. By the same token, the mouse is automatically unacquired when the user clicks on a menu. Furthermore, except for some features of force-feedback devices, an application must unacquire a device before changing its properties.

Acquisition is necessary because DirectInput must inform the application when the flow of data from the device has been interrupted by the system or by another thread. For example, an application may need to know that the user has switched to another program by means of the Alt+Tab keystrokes. In these cases, the acquisition mechanism informs the application that input has been lost and allows it to recover from whatever may result.

Another reason for the acquisition mechanism is related to the fact that applications can change the properties of a device. If this change could take place at any time, then DirectInput would have to check the device properties before performing each data-fetch operation. By requiring that an application unacquire a device before changing its properties, DirectInput can make the assumption that device properties are unchanged if the device is currently acquired.

Most often, an application that moves to the background loses the acquired devices. Consequently, code must reacquire these devices when the foreground is regained. The WM_ACTIVATE message intercept provides a convenient location for performing this reacquisition. However, code must be careful to acquire the device at startup, usually as soon as the device has been initialized, since WM_ACTIVATE is not called at this time. Attempting to reacquire a device that is already acquired has no harmful effects. Redundant calls to the Acquire() function are ignored; therefore, a device can always be unacquired with a single call to the Unacquire() function. Although acquiring a device when it is already in the acquired state may seem like sloppy programming, in many cases it has no harmful effects, since execution time in this case is minimal. The Acquire() function's general form is as follows:

```
HRESULT Acquire();
```

The function has no parameters. The device acquired is the one making the call. For example:

```
LPDIRECTINPUTDEVICE  lpDIMouse;
     .
     .
     .
lpDIMouse->Acquire();
```

In this example, the call to the mouse device is through the interface pointer associated with the variable lpDIMouse. If the call succeeds, the return value is DI_OK or S_FALSE. S_FALSE indicates the device has already been acquired. The following error messages are returned if the call fails:

- DIERR_INVALIDPARAM
- DIERR_NOTINITIALIZED
- DIERR_OTHERAPPHASPRIO

How the returned value is handled by code depends on what information is important to the application. In the case of a redundant acquisition, the returned value S_FALSE may also be interpreted as successful. For example:

```
// Global variables
LPDIRECTINPUTDEVICE  lpDIMouse;
HRESULT              hRes;
   .
   .
   .
   hRes = lpDIMouse->Acquire();
     if(hRes != (DI_OK | S_FALSE))
        // Error handler goes here
```

The Unacquire() function is used to release access to the device. Its general form is as follows:

```
HRESULT Unacquire();
```

Here again, the function has no parameters. Its action is associated with the object making the call. For example:

```
LPDIRECTINPUTDEVICE  lpDIMouse;
    .
    .
    .
    lpDIMouse->Unacquire();
```

This call releases the mouse device whose interface pointer is associated with the variable lpDIMouse. If the call succeeds, the return value is DI_OK. The value DI_NOEFFECT is returned if the device was not in an acquired state. In most cases, code can ignore the value returned by the call to the Unacquire() function.

Getting and Setting Device Information

Applications often need information about input devices. Several DirectInput function returns related to this information are listed in Table 14-5. We have excluded functions that are directly related to force-feedback devices since they are not covered in this book.

TABLE 14-5 SOME DIRECTINPUT FUNCTIONS THAT RETURN DEVICE INFORMATION

Function	Purpose and Returned Data
`GetDeviceStatus()`	Retrieves the status of a device. Returns `DI_OK` if the device is attached.
`EnumObjects()`	Enumerates the device controls. This refers to buttons, axes, and other controls.
`GetCapabilities()`	Returns the device capabilities in the members of a `DIDEVCAPS` structure variable.
`GetDeviceData()`	Retrieves buffered data from a device.
`GetDeviceInfo()`	Returns other additional device information in the members of a `DIDEVICEINSTANCE` structure variable. Data items include the product and instance GUID, its friendly name, and the device title.
`GetDeviceState()`	Retrieves the current state of the device controls, such as buttons, wheels, and axes. This corresponds to immediate device data.
`GetObjectInfo()`	Retrieves information about a specific control. Information is returned in a structure of type `DIDEVICEOBJECTINFO`.
`GetProperty()`	Retrieves the behaviors of a device that can be changed by means of `SetProperty()`.

SetProperty()

The `SetProperty()` function is used to set properties that define the device behavior. These properties include input buffer size and axes mode. The function's general form is as follows:

```
HRESULT SetProperty(
                 REFGUID rguidProp,        // 1
                 LPCDIPROPHEADER pdiph     // 2
                );
```

The first parameter identifies the property to be set. This can be one of the predefined values, or a pointer to a GUID that identifies the property. Table 14-6 lists the predefined properties for an input device.

TABLE 14-6 PREDEFINED PROPERTIES FOR INPUT DEVICES

Property	Refers To
DIPROP_AUTOCENTER	Determines whether device controls are self-centering. This setting applies to the entire device, not to a particular control. For this reason, the dwHow member of the associated DIPROPDWORD structure must be DIPH_DEVICE. The dwData member can be one of the following values: DIPROPAUTOCENTER_OFF: The device should not automatically center when the user releases the device. DIPROPAUTOCENTER_ON: The device should automatically center when the user releases the device. For example, a joystick would engage the self-centering spring. Not all devices support the auto-center property.
DIPROP_AXISMODE	Sets the axis mode. The value being set is specified in the dwData member of the associated DIPROPDWORD structure. See Appendix A.
DIPROP_BUFFERSIZE	Sets the input-buffer size. The value being set must be specified in the dwData member of the associated DIPROPDWORD structure. See Appendix A.
DIPROP_CALIBRATIONMODE	Allows the application to specify whether DirectInput should retrieve calibrated or uncalibrated data from an axis. The default is calibrated data. The dwData member of the DIPROPDWORD structure may be one of the following values:
DIPROPCALIBRATIONMODE_COOKED	This is the default mode.
DIPROPCALIBRATIONMODE_RAW	

Property	Refers To
DIPROP_DEADZONE	Sets the value for the dead zone of a joystick, in the range 0 to 10,000. 0 indicates there is no dead zone. 5,000 indicates that the dead zone extends over 50 percent of the physical range. 10,000 indicates that the entire physical range of the axis is dead.
DIPROP_FFGAIN	Sets the gain for the device. This setting applies to the entire device. Unlike other properties, the gain can be set when the device is in an acquired state.
DIPROP_RANGE	Sets the range of values an object can possibly report. The minimum and maximum values are taken from the lMin and lMax members of the associated DIPROPRANGE structure (see Appendix A).
DIPROP_SATURATION	Sets the value for the saturation zones of a joystick, in the range 0 to 10,000.

The second parameter is the address of a structure variable of type DIPROP-HEADER, discussed in greater detail later in this section.

The call to SetProperty() returns DI_OK or DI_PROPNOEFFECT if it succeeds. If it fails, the function returns one of the following error values:

- DIERR_INVALIDPARAM
- DIERR_NOTINITIALIZED
- DIERR_OBJECTNOTFOUND
- DIERR_UNSUPPORTED

GetProperty()

GetProperty() is the data-retrieving counterpart of the SetProperty() function. Its general form is as follows:

```
HRESULT GetProperty(
                 REFGUID rguidProp,      // 1
                 LPDIPROPHEADER pdiph    // 2
                 );
```

The function parameters are identical to those of the SetProperty() function, previously described. The first parameter is the identifier of the property to be retrieved (see Table 14-6). The second parameter is the address of a structure of type DIPROPHEADER, discussed in the next section.

Device Property Structures

The structures used by the SetProperty() and GetProperty() functions require additional attention. Because DirectInput is designed to support devices that have not yet been developed, it cannot use standard data structures to define the device properties. The solution is to accept a user-defined structure that is suitable to whatever property needs to be defined.

The basic property-defining structure in DirectInput is DIPROPHEADER, which is passed as the second parameter in both the SetProperty() and GetProperty() functions. The DIPROPHEADER structure must be the first member of the user-defined property structure. It is also the first member of the two standard, predefined property structures named DIPROPWORD and DIPROPRANGE, described later. DIPROHEADER is defined as follows:

```
typedef struct DIPROPHEADER {
    DWORD    dwSize;
    DWORD    dwHeaderSize;
    DWORD    dwObj;
    DWORD    dwHow;
} DIPROPHEADER, *LPDIPROPHEADER;
typedef const DIPROPHEADER *LPCDIPROPHEADER;
```

The first structure member (dwSize) encodes the size of the enclosing structure. It must be initialized before the structure is used. The second member (dwHeaderSize) is the size of the DIPROPHEADER structure itself. It is usually initialized to sizeof(DIPROPHEADER). The third member (dwObj) identifies the control to which the property refers. If the entire device is involved, this member is set to zero. The fourth member (dwHow) specifies how the third member (dwObj) is to be interpreted. Table 14-7 lists the values that can be assigned to the dwHow member of DIPROPHEADER.

For devices that require minimal properties, there are two predefined structures that can be referenced in DIPROPHEADER: DIPROPDWORD defines a single doubleword data item, and DIPROPRANGE is used in case of a range defined by two values of type long. The structures are defined as follows:

```
typedef struct DIPROPDWORD {
    DIPROPHEADER     diph;
    DWORD            dwData;
} DIPROPDWORD, *LPDIPROPDWORD;
 typedef const DIPROPDWORD *LPCDIPROPDWORD;
```

TABLE 14-7 POSSIBLE VALUES OF THE DWHOW MEMBER OF THE DIPROHEADER STRUCTURE

Value	Meaning
DIPH_DEVICE	The dwObj member must be zero.
DIPH_BYOFFSET	The dwObj member is the offset into the current data format of the control whose property is being accessed.
DIPH_BYID	The dwObj member is the control's type/instance identifier. This identifier is returned in the dwType member of the DIDEVICEOBJECTINSTANCE structure returned from a previous call to the EnumObjects() function.

The first member (diph) is a DIPROPHEADER structure that must be initialized as shown in Table 14-8.

TABLE 14-8 INITIALIZATION OF THE DIPROPHEADER STRUCTURE FOR ACCESSING PROPERTIES OF DWORD TYPE

Member	Value
DwSize	sizeof(DIPROPDWORD)
DwHeaderSize	sizeof(DIPROPHEADER)
DwObj	If the dwHow member is DIPH_DEVICE, this member must be zero. If the dwHow member is DIPH_BYID, this member must be the identifier for the object whose property setting is referenced. If the dwHow member is DIPH_BYOFFSET, this member must be a data format offset for the object whose property setting is to be set or retrieved. For example, if the c_dfDIMouse data format is selected, it must be one of the DIIMOFS_* values.
DwHow	Specifies how the dwObj member should be interpreted. If dwObj is DIPROP_AXISMODE or DIPROP_BUFFERSIZE, dwHow should be DIPH_DEVICE.

The second structure member (dwData) is the property-specific value being set or retrieved. The following code fragment shows the initialization of the DIPROPDWORD structure used to obtain the buffer size of a device:

```
DIPROPDWORD       dipdw;
   .
   .
   .
dipdw.diph.dwSize       = sizeof(dipdw);
dipdw.diph.dwHeaderSize = sizeof(dipdw.diph);
dipdw.diph.dwObj        = 0;                    // No object
dipdw.diph.dwHow        = DIPH_DEVICE;
dipdw.dwData            = 0;                     // Storage for data
```

Once the structures are initialized, code can use the GetProperty() function to obtain the buffer size, as follows:

```
LPDIRECTINPUTDEVICE  lpDIMouse;
HRESULT              hRes;
   .
   .
   .
hRes = lpDIMouse->GetProperty(DIPRP_BUFFERSIZE,
                              &dipdw.diph);
    if(hRes != DI_OK)
       // Error handler goes here
```

The DIPROPRANGE structure contains the value range of a device control. This structure is used with the DIPROP_RANGE flag set in the GetProperty() and SetProperty() functions. The structure is defined as follows:

```
typedef struct DIPROPRANGE {
    DIPROPHEADER diph;
    LONG         lMin;
    LONG         lMax;
} DIPROPRANGE, *LPDIPROPRANGE;

typedef const DIPROPRANGE *LPCDIPROPRANGE;
```

The first structure member (diph) is a DIPROPHEADER structure that must be initialized as shown in Table 14-9.

Table 14-9 INITIALIZATION OF THE DIPROPRANGE STRUCTURE FOR ACCESSING A PROPERTY VALUE DEFINED AS A RANGE

Member	Value
`DwSize`	`sizeof(DIPROPRANGE)`
`DwHeaderSize`	`sizeof(DIPROPHEADER)`
`DwObj`	Identifier of the object whose range is being retrieved or set.
`DwHow`	How the `dwObj` member should be interpreted.
`Lmin`	The lower limit of the range, inclusive. If the range of the device is unrestricted, this value will be 5.
`Lmax`	The upper limit of the range, inclusive. If the range of the device is unrestricted, this value will be `DIPROPRANGE_NOMAX`.

The following code fragment shows the initialization of the property structure for setting the *x*-axis range of the joystick controller. The values defined for the range are -500 to 500.

```
DIPROPRANGE             diprg;
diprg.diph.dwSize        = sizeof(diprg);
diprg.diph.dwHeaderSize = sizeof(diprg.diph);
diprg.diph.dwObj         = DIJOFS_X;
diprg.diph.dwHow         = DIPH_BYOFFSET;
diprg.lMin               = -500;
diprg.lMax               = 500;
```

Once the structures are initialized, code can use the `SetProperty()` function to set the range of the joystick's *x*-axis control, as in the following code fragment.

```
LPDIRECTINPUTDEVICE  lpDIJoystick;
HRESULT              hRes;
   .
   .
   .
hRes = lpDIJoystick->SetProperty(DIPROP_RANGE, &diprg.diph);
     if(hRes != DI_OK)
         // Error handler goes here
```

One of the most important properties accessed by the SetProperty() and GetProperty() functions is the buffer size. This value determines the amount of data that the buffer can hold between calls to GetDeviceData(). If an application is not to read buffered data from a device, this value can be set to zero. The buffer size is defined in the dwData member of the DIPROPDWORD structure. If it is too large to be supported by the device, the largest possible buffer size is set. By retrieving the buffer-size property and comparing it to the original value, an application can determine if the requested buffer size was set. Applications that use standard input devices in buffered mode, such as the keyboard or the mouse, often need to set the DIPROP_BUFFERSIZE property only. This step cannot be avoided if buffered input is desired since the default buffer size is zero. The following code fragment shows how to set the buffer size to 32 elements for a standard mouse device:

```
DIPROPDWORD               dipdw;
LPDIRECTINPUTDEVICE       lpDIMouse;
HRESULT                   hRes;
   .
   .
   .
dipdw.diph.dwSize       = sizeof(dipdw);
dipdw.diph.dwHeaderSize = sizeof(dipdw.diph);
dipdw.diph.dwObj        = 0;                // No object
dipdwf.diph.dwHow       = DIPH_DEVICE;
dipdw.dwData            = 32;               // Buffer size
// Set the buffer size
  hRes = lpDIMouse->SetProperty(DIPROP_BUFFERSIZE, &dipdw.diph);
    if(hRes != DI_OK)
       // Error handler goes here
```

Obtaining Device Data

The main purpose of DirectInput is to access input device data directly, without having to wait for WM_KEYDOWN or WM_MOUSEMOUVE messages. In this section, we discuss the process of obtaining device data by means of DirectInput. The mechanisms used by DirectInput to obtain this data are different from the Windows message intercepts. In the first place, DirectInput recognizes two types of device data. One type, called *buffered data*, is based on storing user interaction with the input device in a dedicated buffer. The GetDeviceData() function can then be used to retrieve the data from the buffer. A second type of device data, called *immediate data*, relates to the current state of a device or control, such as whether a mouse button is down or up. This information is obtained by means of the GetDeviceState() function.

Both types, buffered and immediate data, are effective and often used simultaneously by applications. For example, a program that uses DirectInput to monitor mouse action may rely on buffered data to detect mouse movements and on immediate data to test for mouse-button action. By the same token, a keyboard handler may use buffered data for storing keystrokes and immediate data to see if a key is held down in order to produce a typematic burst or other action.

In addition to buffered and immediate data, DirectInput provides two different mechanisms for detecting input events. One is by polling the device, and the second one is by having DirectInput notify the application that an event has occurred. Both mechanisms, polling and event notification, are effective and have their spheres of application, although polling is more often used in graphics applications based on rendering loops.

Finally there is the matter of device axis coordinates that DirectInput can return as relative or absolute values. Relative values refer to the amount by which the coordinates have changed since the last call to `GetDeviceState()` or, in the case of buffered input, since the last item was put in the buffer. Absolute axis coordinates are a running total of all the relative coordinates returned by the system since the device was acquired. They serve to show the position of the axis in relation to a fixed point. By default, mouse axes are reported as relative coordinates and joystick axes as absolute coordinates. Code can use the `SetProperty()` function to change the default behavior.

Input Data Types

DirectInput supplies buffered and immediate data for each device. Buffered data is a record of events that is stored until an application retrieves it. Immediate data is a snapshot of the current state of a device or control. Buffered data is useful when the application needs to ascertain an input event such as a mouse click. Immediate data is useful to applications that respond to the state of a device, such as the position of a joystick.

Immediate data is obtained by means of the `GetDeviceState()` function. This function returns the state of a device; however, it provides no historical information about user action on the device or control. When using `GetDeviceState()`, there is no way of knowing what actions have occurred since the last time the function was called. For example, if the user has pressed the mouse button five times between successive calls to `GetDeviceState()`, the application cannot detect it. All that the function reports is that the mouse button is either down or up at the time of the call. The function's general form is as follows:

```
HRESULT GetDeviceState(
                    DWORD cbData,            // 1
                    LPVOID lpvData           // 2
                    );
```

The first parameter is the size, in bytes, of the buffer referenced in the second parameter. The second parameter is the address of a structure that receives the data. This format of the data has been previously established by a call to SetDataFormat(), as discussed earlier in this chapter.

If the call succeeds, the return value is DI_OK. If it fails, the return value is one of the following errors:

- DIERR_INPUTLOST
- DIERR_INVALIDPARAM
- DIERR_NOTACQUIRED
- DIERR_NOTINITIALIZED
- E_PENDING

Before an application can call the GetDeviceState() function, it must set the cooperative level, the data format, and acquire the input device. The structure passed to the GetDeviceState() call depends on the one defined for the particular device. The data structures for all four standard devices are shown in Table 14-10.

TABLE 14-10 DATA FORMATS AND STRUCTURES FOR STANDARD INPUT DEVICES

Device	Format	Structure
Mouse	c_dfDIMouse	DIMOUSESTATE
Keyboard	c_dfDIKeyboard	array of 256 bytes
Joystick type 1	c_dfDIJoystick	DIJOYSTATE
Joystick type 2	c_dfDIJoystick2	DIJOYSTATE2

For example, an application that used the c_dfDIMouse data format when calling the SetDataFormat() function must pass a structure variable of type DIMOUSESTATE when calling GetDeviceState().

When using buffered data, input events are stored in a dedicated buffer until the application retrieves them. Information about any user action on the device or control is placed in a structure variable of type DIDEVICEOBJECTDATA structure located in the buffer. Applications read the buffer by calling the GetDeviceData() function. The function's general form is as follows:

```
HRESULT GetDeviceData(
                    DWORD cbObjectData,          // 1
```

```
                    LPDIDEVICEOBJECTDATA rgdod,  // 2
                    LPDWORD pdwInOut,            // 3
                    DWORD dwFlags                // 4
                    );
```

The first parameter is the size, in bytes, of the DIDEVICEOBJECTDATA structure. The second parameter is an array of DIDEVICEOBJECTDATA structures that receive the buffered data. The third parameter is the number of elements in the array of the second parameter. On entry to the call, this parameter encodes the number of elements in the array pointed to by the second parameter. On exit from the call, the third parameter contains the number of elements actually obtained. The fourth parameter determines the manner in which the data is obtained. If this parameter is zero, then the read data is removed from the buffer. If this parameter is DIGDD_PEEK, then the read data is not removed. This provides a way to peek into the buffer without altering its contents.

If the call is a success, the return value is DI_OK or DI_BUFFEROVERFLOW. If the call fails, the return value is one of the following errors:

- DIERR_INPUTLOST
- DIERR_INVALIDPARAM
- DIERR_NOTACQUIRED
- DIERR_NOTBUFFERED
- DIERR_NOTINITIALIZED

The data structure DIDEVICEOBJECTDATA used by the GetDeviceData() function is defined as follows:

```
typedef struct DIDEVICEOBJECTDATA {
    DWORD dwOfs;                 // 1
    DWORD dwData;                // 2
    DWORD dwTimeStamp;           // 3
    DWORD dwSequence;            // 4
} DIDEVICEOBJECTDATA, *LPDIDEVICEOBJECTDATA;

typedef const DIDEVICEOBJECTDATA *LPCDIDEVICEOBJECTDATA;
```

The first structure member (dwOfs) is the offset of the object whose data is being reported into the current data format. In other words, it is the location of the data item. If the device is a mouse, keyboard, or joystick, the dwOfs member is one of the predefined constants for these devices (see Table 14-10). If the data format has been customized for a non-standard device, then the value is an offset relative to the custom data format.

The second member of the DIDEVICEOBJECTDATA structure (dwData) is the data obtained from the device. If the device is in relative axis mode, then the relative axis motion is stored. If the device is in absolute axis mode, then the absolute axis coordinate is stored. For button input, only the low byte of dwData is significant. The high bit of the low byte is set if the button was pressed. This bit is clear if the button was released. Applications can AND 0x80 with the dwData member to test for a button-up or button-down condition.

The third member (dwTimeStamp) is the tick count at which the input event is generated. The value is in milliseconds. The current system tick count can be obtained by calling the GetTickCount() function.

The fourth member (dwSequence) is the DirectInput sequence number for this event. All input events are assigned a sequence number in increasing order. This allows events from different devices to be sorted chronologically. Before an application can read buffered data using GetDeviceData() it must have set the data format, the buffer size, and acquired the device.

Event Notification and Polling

Applications can poll a device by regularly calling the functions GetDeviceState() or GetDeviceData(). In the first case, the state of the device is obtained; in the second case, the polling routine obtains the contents of the data buffer. Polling is typically used by applications that execute in real time, such as games and simulations that are based on rendering loops.

Some devices, including joysticks and other game controllers, or the controls on these devices, do not generate hardware interrupts. Therefore, they do not spontaneously produce input data. DirectInput provides a function named Poll(), which retrieves data from polled objects on a DirectInput device. The function has no effect if the device does not require polling; therefore, it is harmless to use it systematically. On the other hand, if a device that requires polling is not polled periodically, no new data is received. Applications can find out if a device requires polling by first setting the data format for the device, then calling the GetCapabilities() function and checking the DIDC_POLLEDDATAFORMAT flag in the DIDEVCAPS structure. Calling Poll() causes DirectInput to update the device state, generate input events (if buffered data is enabled), and set notification events (if notification is enabled). The function's general form is as follows:

```
HRESULT Poll()
```

If the call succeeds, the return value is DI_OK, or DI_NOEFFECT if the device does not require polling. If it fails, the return value is one of the following errors:

- DIERR_INPUTLOST
- DIERR_NOTACQUIRED
- DIERR_NOTINITIALIZED

Input processing based on event notification is suitable for applications that wait for user input before taking any action. For this reason, event notification is not suitable for most high-performance graphics programs. To use event notification, code sets up a thread synchronization object with the `CreateEvent()` function and then associates this event with a particular device by passing the device handle to the `SetEventNotification()`. The event is signaled by DirectInput whenever the state of the device changes. Applications receive notification of the event with a function such as `WaitForSingleObject()`, and then respond by checking the input buffer to find out the cause of the event.

Experimenting with DirectInput

The graphics programmer must often make sure that an application is compatible with several input devices, furnished by different vendors, and usually with different modes of operation and gadgetry. Sometimes these devices are of a new design or incorporate dissimilar features. To make sure that code is compatible with a particular input hardware, it is useful to be able to tinker with the device in question and to observe the values that its various components return during operation.

The Diquick Program

The DirectX 6 SDK contains an undocumented program, named Diquick, that is a useful tool for experimenting with input devices. The program is located in the folder `mssdk\samples\Multimedia\Dinput\bin`. No help or readme files are furnished with this application, but its use is intuitive and requires little explanation. The initial screen is shown in Figure 14-1.

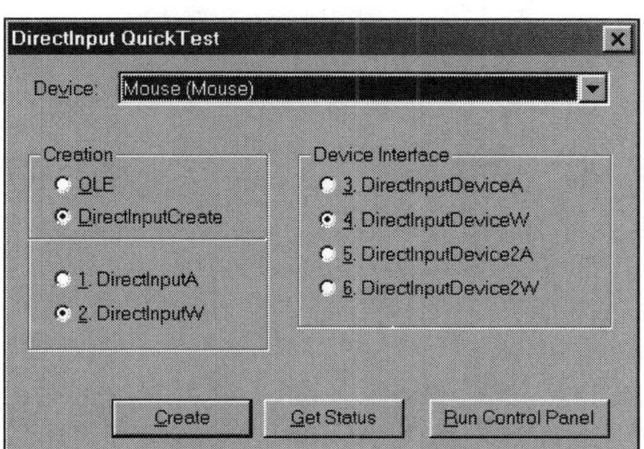

Figure 14-1: Screen snapshot of the Diquick program initial screen

The list box at the top of the program screen lists the various input devices that are supported by DirectDraw and that are found in the system. For experimenting with DirectInput, the box labeled Creation should have the `DirectInputCreate` radio button selected. The button designated DirectInputA refers to the ANSI version of the interface and the button labeled DirectInputW to the Unicode version. The Device interface box relates to the various updates of `DirectInputDevice`. Here again, the postfix letter A refers to the ANSI version, while the letter W refers to the Unicode version. Once you have selected the device with which you wish to experiment, pressing the Create button brings up the screen shown in Figure 14-2.

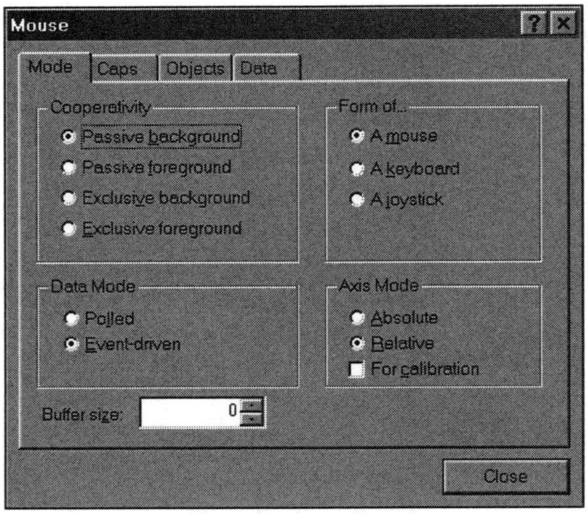

Figure 14-2: Screen snapshot of the Diquick program's second screen

The box labeled Cooperativity refers to the cooperative level modes discussed in this chapter. In this box, the word *passive* is used for the nonexclusive modes. You can select any of the four cooperative levels by means of radio buttons. The radio buttons in the box labeled Data Mode can be set for polled or event-driven operation. The scroll buttons on the box labeled Buffer size can be used to create an input buffer. The numbers generated by the scroll buttons are multiples of 32, but you can also enter a value from the keyboard. A value of 0 in the Buffer size box forces immediate data. The Axis Mode box allows you to select the relative or absolute mode for the axis coordinates. The checkbox labeled For calibration in the Axis Mode box is undocumented. The item selected in the box labeled "Form of" must correspond to the device selected in the initial screen.

After clicking the Caps tab, the Diquick program displays a screen that shows the device capabilities. The list box labeled Attribute contains most of the items of information returned by the `GetCapabilities()` function in the `DIDEVCAPS` structure. Figure 14-3 is a snapshot of the Caps tab screen of the Diquick program.

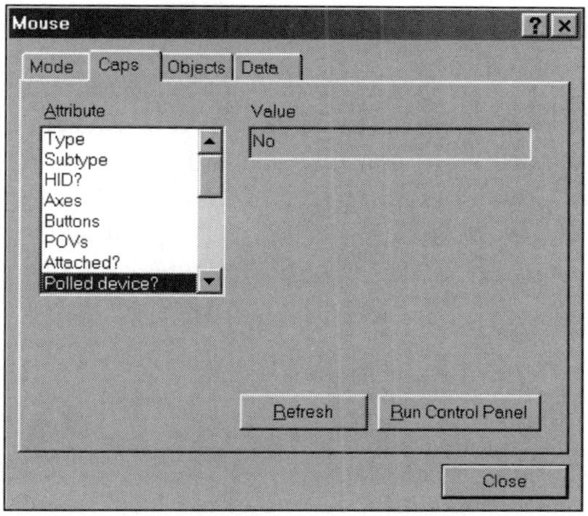

Figure 14-3: Screen snapshot of the Diquick program Caps tab screen

The Objects tab enumerates the axes, buttons, and point-of-view (POV) controllers on the device. Once you have selected one of these controls, pressing the Properties button produces a screen that contains detailed information about the control attributes and range, as well as its saturation and dead-zone values.

One of the most interesting screens produced by the Diquick program is the one activated by pressing the Data tab. In the buffered mode, the Data screen shows the information stored in the device buffer as the device is actuated. This is particularly useful in determining the values generated by activating device controls, especially when the technical documentation for the device is unavailable. Figure 14-4 is a snapshot of the Data tab screen.

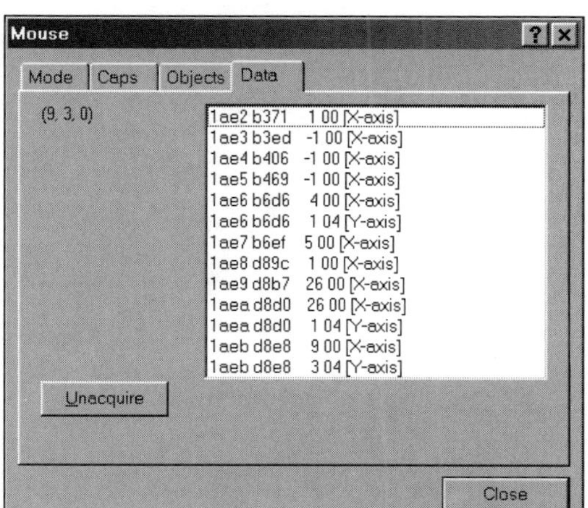

Figure 14-4: Screen snapshot of the Diquick program Data tab screen

The DI Mouse Demo Program

The book's CD-ROM contains a demonstration project for DirectInput programming called *DI Mouse Demo*. The program, which executes in DirectDraw exclusive mode, sets up the mouse for DirectInput operation and then reads the state of the left mouse button. If the button is down, the program zooms into the image. If the button is not down, the program zooms out. Although the code sets up the mouse device for both immediate- and buffered-mode operation, only the immediate mode is actually used.

Summary

In this chapter, we cover the fundamentals of DirectInput, one of the most important support services available in the DirectX 6 SDK. The discussion includes an overview of the DirectInput component of Direct X 6, preparatory operations necessary for using DirectInput, how to obtain device information and set up the device properties, and how to read device input data. We also mention the use of the Diquick demo program that is furnished with the DirectX 6 SDK and how this program can be useful in experimenting with input devices and in programming. We also present a demonstration program, named *DI Mouse Demo*, which is furnished in the book's SDK.

The next chapter covers graphics programming in a multi-monitor environment. The use of this most powerful feature requires both Windows 98 and DirectX 6. This new functionality is one of the most interesting characteristics of graphics PC programming that has been made available in recent years.

Chapter 15

Multiple Adapters and Monitors

IN THIS CHAPTER

- User and programmer perspectives regarding graphics programming in a multiple-monitor environment
- Windows and DirectX support for multi-monitor software
- Windows 98 multi-monitor API and programming
- DirectX 6 programming for multi-monitor applications
- Using multiple monitors for debugging DirectDraw programs that execute in exclusive mode

WINDOWS 98 AND NT 5 both support multiple monitors, while DirectX 6 enables programmers to develop DirectDraw applications that execute in this new and powerful environment. The technology enables you to install several video cards in the same machine, each one connected to its own monitor. The video systems can be different from each other in resolution and color depth. An application can span several monitors, or video output can be directed to any one monitor/adapter combination on the resulting virtual desktop.

In this chapter, we explore conventional Windows programming in a multi-monitor environment as well as DirectDraw programs that take advantage of this new functionality.

Graphics in a Multiple Monitor Environment

The idea of applications that output to multiple monitors is not new. Even in early PCs it was possible to implement a dual-monitor system by taking advantage of the fact that monochrome and color output were mapped to different areas in the video memory space. PC graphics software developers of that period often used a monochrome display for the debugger program, while graphics output was directed to a second monitor that executed the application code, usually in color. Applications that used this setup were also developed. The IBM XGA video adapter, introduced in 1990, could be programmed to support multiple monitors by manipulating the address decoding mechanism. Because XGA never achieved great popularity, its multi-monitor support features went mostly unnoticed.

Directing output to more than one monitor can be a powerful programming tool. For example, we can conceive an airline scheduling application in which one monitor displays the arrivals, another one displays the departures, and a third one is used for reservations and seating assignments. A computer-aided design (CAD) application could use multiple monitors to simultaneously display different views of the same object. A drawing program could use one monitor to display a clean image, while the drawing surface and tools are located on another monitor. A computer game could be designed to use three monitors in order to provide a panoramic view of the playing area, while a fourth one contains the game parameters, controls, and results. A digital image processing program could be coded to display the original image in one screen, the transformed image in another one, and use a third screen to specify the transformations that are to be performed. In any type of application, the possibilities are innumerable and captivating. A graphics development environment can be based on using the primary monitor for the programming tools, while another monitor shows the application. This setup makes possible the use of a conventional debugger in developing DirectX code, a topic discussed later in this chapter. In summary, it can be said that the development of programs that execute in multiple monitors creates a new graphics-programming paradigm for the PC.

Windows 98 is the first Windows version to provide support for multiple monitors. Microsoft has announced that this feature will also be available in Windows NT 5. The company makes available software stubs that enable the development of multi-monitor applications that run in systems that do not support this feature. We discuss their use in this chapter.

> **NOTE** At the time of this writing, the distribution version of Windows NT 5 has not yet been released. For this reason, we refer only to Windows 98 multi-monitor features and support. Information available at this time suggests that Windows NT 5 support for multiple monitors will be compatible with that in Windows 98.

The User's Perspective

In the discussion of multiple monitor environments, we must distinguish between the user's and the programmer's perspective. From the user's point of view, multiple monitors are a convenience, even when executing programs that are not specifically designed for this environment. For a long time, Windows' multitasking capabilities have enabled the simultaneous execution of several applications. However, as a result of the limited resolution of most systems, we are often forced to keep a single application in the foreground. The result is that not all information is visible at the same time. In this sense, multiple monitors do not add any new functionality to Windows, but do bring about a new "neatness" to the desktop. It is now possible to have a program on one monitor, a second application on another monitor, and perhaps a third or a fourth application in its own delimited space. The mouse moves seamlessly through the entire video space called the virtual desktop, and we can use the Windows clipboard to transfer data between programs.

The Programmer's Perspective

From a programmer's perspective, the introduction of multiple-monitor technology has many implications:

- New applications and revisions should now be coded to be *multi-monitor aware*. Some additional design and coding efforts may be necessary. These consist mostly of avoiding pitfalls that could make a program fail or misbehave in a machine equipped with more than one monitor.
- Multiple-monitor environments must be taken into account at application design time. The expansion of the Windows desktop that results from multiple monitors creates many new possibilities. The program designer cannot ignore this new environment.
- The programmer is also a user. Development environments that use multiple monitors can improve productivity considerably, particularly in developing graphics applications. One common possibility is to use one monitor for the development tools, such as Developer Studio, and a second one for application output. The result simulates a remote debugger system in which you have the code and the application output visible at the same time. This type of setup can be particularly valuable in developing DirectX applications.

Following are four reasons for using multiple monitors in applications that are immediately evident:

- To create a larger display area on the desktop
- To delimit application windows to a particular monitor
- To reproduce the same image on several monitors
- To create specialized display areas that are separate from the desktop

In this chapter, we explore some of these new possibilities.

Windows and DirectX Support

Multiple monitors are supported by Windows 98, and will also be supported by Windows NT 5 when it is released. Microsoft has stated that there will be minor differences in multi-monitor support in the two operating systems, but that applications designed for this technology will execute correctly in either one. DirectX 6 also supports multiple monitors and contains its own subset of new APIs. In addition, Microsoft makes available an include file that makes possible developing multi-monitor code that remains compatible with Windows 95 and NT 4. In this case, the multi-monitor features are bypassed and the code executes in the original environment.

Virtual Desktop

Multiple monitor display is based on the notion of a virtual desktop. On a single monitor system, the desktop is the size and shape of the monitor's display area. On a multi-monitor system, each monitor adds its video space to a continuous and seamless virtual desktop. One of the monitors of a multi-monitor setup is designated as the primary monitor. The Windows desktop, with its icons and toolbars, is displayed on this primary monitor. The coordinates of the upper-left corner of the primary monitor are always (0,0), while the coordinates of the lower-right corner of the primary monitor are determined by its resolution. The secondary monitors are connected to their own video cards and can be set to execute in any resolution or color depth available in the hardware. Both the resolution and the color depth can be different for each monitor in the virtual desktop.

The Display applet in the Windows Control Panel is used to set the resolution and color depth of each monitor on the virtual desktop. The screen area for each monitor can be adjusted within the limits supported by the video hardware. The position of the secondary monitors in relation to the primary monitor can also be changed. For example, one secondary monitor can be located to the right of the primary monitor and another one above it. The resulting virtual desktop is the combination of rectangular areas that correspond to each monitor, as shown in Figure 15-1.

In Figure 15-1, the virtual desktop is the polygon bound by the rectangular display of each monitor. The one requirement imposed by Windows is that the monitor areas must touch each other on the desktop. This is necessary to ensure the seamless operation of the mouse cursor when moving between the different rectangles of the virtual desktop. If this condition were not enforced, the mouse cursor could disappear from the screen.

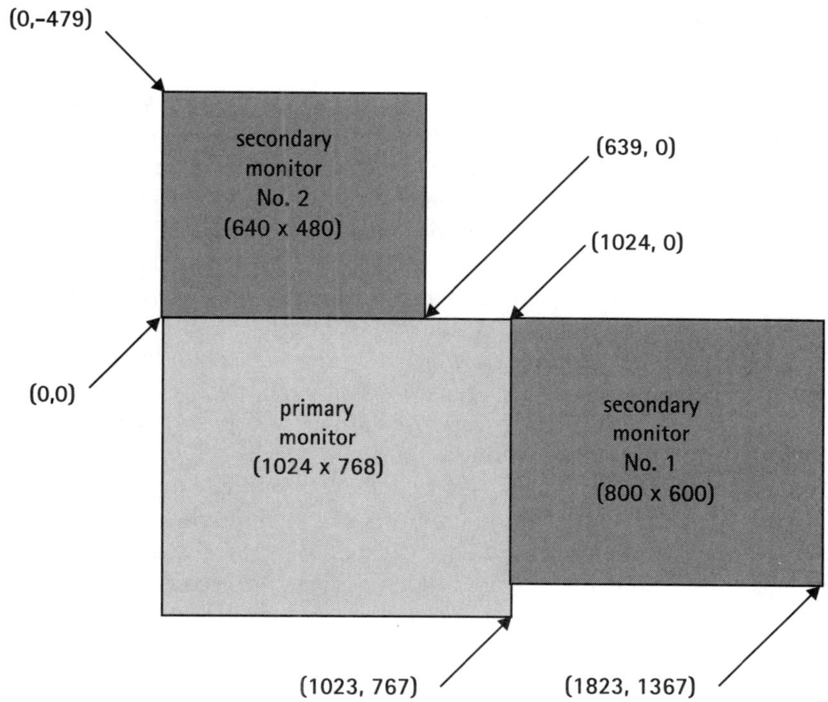

Figure 15-1: Three-monitor virtual desktop

The coordinates of any point in the virtual desktop are determined in terms of the origin, which is always the top-left corner of the primary monitor's rectangle, as well as by the position and resolution of the secondary monitors. In Figure 15-1, you can see that secondary monitor number 2, which is placed above the primary monitor, has negative coordinates on its *y*-axis. Secondary monitor number 1, which is to the right and at the same level as the primary monitor, has positive coordinates on both axes. Notice that the screen coordinates are based on the relative location of the secondary monitors in reference to the primary monitor. If the secondary monitor or monitors are to the right and below the primary monitor, then the *x* and *y* coordinates are all positive on the virtual desktop. However, the secondary monitors can be placed so that negative coordinates are necessary, as is the case with secondary monitor number 2 in Figure 15-1.

Installing and Configuring Multiple Monitors

Installing a multi-monitor system in Windows 98 or NT 5 consists simply of plugging in a video card that supports multiple monitors and configuring Windows for the resulting environment. Windows 98 documentation contains lists of adapters that support multiple monitor technology. Currently, the list includes virtually all major video cards on the PC market; however, it is still a good idea to check that the video hardware supports multiple-monitor operation before installing it.

You should start the installation process by making sure that the primary display is working correctly. The second card can then be inserted in a slot, the second monitor connected to its output, and Windows 98 restarted. You can determine which is the primary monitor by noticing which video card executes the Power-On Self Test (POST). To change to another primary display you must reverse the card order in the slots. When the secondary display is initialized correctly, Windows 98 displays a message on the attached monitor.

The next step is to configure Windows to operate with multiple monitors. To do this, double-click the Display icon in the Control Panel or right-click on the desktop and then select Properties from the shortcut menu. In the Display Properties dialog box, select the Settings tab. If both video systems were correctly installed and are supported by Windows 98 or NT 5, the Settings tab on the Display Properties dialog box shows two monitors, as in Figure 15-2.

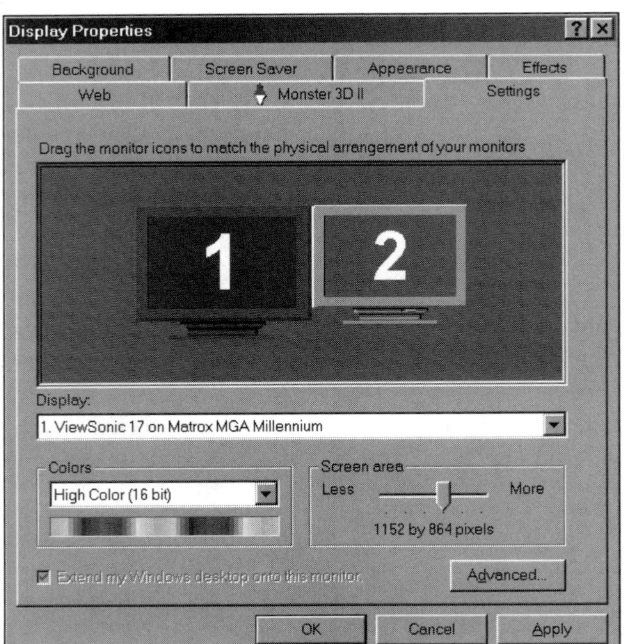

Figure 15-2: Typical display of the Settings tab in the Display Properties dialog box for a two-monitor system

The secondary monitor icon can now be selected and then dragged with the mouse to any position in relation to the primary monitor. The screen area slide control and the color depth list box are used to select the display properties for each monitor. As the screen area of each monitor is changed, Windows 98 updates the graphics to reflect the relative size of each monitor. When the secondary monitor is selected, a checkbox labeled "Extend my Windows desktop onto this monitor" is displayed. Click the checkbox to add the secondary monitor to the virtual desktop.

In Figure 15-2, the primary monitor has a resolution of 1152 by 864 pixels and the secondary monitor resolution is 1024 by 768. In this case, both monitors are set for 16-bit color depth. Once you have decided where to place the monitors and what resolution and color depths to use, click the Apply button to enable the settings. If everything has gone well, you can now start using the multi-monitor system.

Windows 98 follows these rules in displaying conventional programs in a multi-monitor environment:

- When a program is maximized, it is extended to fill the monitor in which it is located. If the program spans more than one monitor, it is maximized to the one in which it occupies the larger screen area.
- An application can be dragged into another monitor only when it is displayed in windowed mode. Maximized applications cannot be dragged to another monitor.
- An application executing in windowed mode can be expanded to cover more than one monitor.

Not all programs execute flawlessly in a multi-monitor system. One of the most common problems is that applications executing in the secondary monitor display menus on the primary monitor. Hopefully, these problems will be corrected in the new versions of these applications. Later in this chapter, we list some programming precautions that ensure that new programs are "multi-monitor aware."

Windows 98 Multi-monitormnAPI

Windows 98 includes several new APIs that support multiple-monitor programs. The new APIs are useful in developing applications that take advantage of the new display capabilities. Table 15-1 lists the multi-monitor APIs in Windows 98.

Each physical display device in a multi-monitor system is represented by a monitor handle, of type `HMONITOR`. Once a device has been assigned an `HMONITOR` value, it remains unchanged throughout its lifetime, even if changes are made to the corresponding display settings. A valid `HMONITOR` value is guaranteed to be non-`NULL`.

TABLE 15-1 MULTI-MONITOR API IN WINDOWS 98

Function	Action
`MonitorFromPoint()`	Determines the monitor that contains a specific screen point.
`MonitorFromRect()`	Determines the monitor that contains the largest portion of a rectangle.
`MonitorFromWindow()`	Determines the monitor that contains the majority of a window.
`GetMonitorInfo()`	Retrieves information for a monitor.
`ChangeDisplaySettingsEx()`	Version of the `ChangeDisplaySettings()` function that enables you to specify a device.
`EnumDisplayMonitors()`	Returns information about multiple video devices that an application may overlap. A monitor need not be part of the Windows virtual desktop.
`EnumDisplayDevices()`	Enables an application to determine the available devices on the host machine. Code can enumerate the devices and get a device context for any monitor supported by the system. This enables an application to work with a dedicated display device without sharing the screen with other applications.
`SystemParametersInfo()` `GetSystemMetrics()`	Windows 98 version of these APIs were updated to include support for multiple monitors.

Obtaining the Monitor Handle

Three multi-monitor APIs are used to obtain the handle to a specific monitor. The `MonitorFromPoint()` function obtains a handle to the display monitor that contains a specified screen point. The function's general form is as follows:

```
HMONITOR MonitorFromPoint(
                            POINT pt,      // 1
                            DWORD dwFlags  // 2
                          );
```

The first parameter is a `POINT` structure that determines the screen point of reference. The second parameter consists of flags that determine the function's return value if the point is not contained within any display monitor. Table 15-2 lists the predefined constants for this parameter.

TABLE 15-2 CONSTANTS FOR MONITORFROMPOINT() SECOND PARAMETER

Value	Return Value
MONITOR_DEFAULTTONEAREST	Returns the handle to the display monitor that is nearest to the point.
MONITOR_DEFAULTTONULL	Returns NULL.
MONITOR_DEFAULTTOPRIMARY	Returns the handle to the primary display monitor.

If the point is contained by a display monitor, the return value is an HMONITOR handle to that monitor. If not, the return value is determined by the flag used as the second parameter.

The MonitorFromRect() function obtains a handle to the display monitor that has the largest area of intersection with a specified rectangle. The function's general form is as follows:

```
HMONITOR MonitorFromRect(
                         LPCRECT lprc,      // 1
                         DWORD dwFlags      // 2
                        );
```

The first parameter is a pointer to a structure variable of type RECT that specifies the rectangle of reference. The second parameter, dwFlags, is one of the flags listed in Table 15-2.

If the rectangle defined in the first parameter intersects one or more display monitor rectangles, the return value is the HMONITOR handle to the display monitor that has the majority of the rectangle. If the rectangle does not intersect a display monitor, the return value depends on the flag set in the second parameter.

The MonitorFromWindow() function obtains a handle to the display monitor that has the largest area of intersection with the bounding rectangle of a specified window. The function's general form is as follows:

```
HMONITOR MonitorFromWindow(
                           HWND hwnd,         // 1
                           DWORD dwFlags      // 2
                           );
```

The first parameter is the handle to the window of reference. The second parameter is one of the flags listed in Table 15-2.

If the window specified in the first parameter intersects one or more display monitor rectangles, the return value is an `HMONITOR` handle to the display monitor that has the majority of the window. If the window does not intersect a display monitor, the return value depends on the flag used in the second parameter. If the window is currently minimized, `MonitorFromWindow()` uses the rectangle that the window occupied before it was minimized.

Enumerating Multiple Monitors

Applications executing in a multi-monitor environment often need to know which monitors intersect a particular region of the virtual screen. One possible use for this information is to develop an application that generates video output to more than one display. The `EnumDisplayMonitors()` function is used to obtain the handle to the device context for each monitor that intersects a predefined screen area. There are two well-defined reasons to call the `EnumDisplayMonitors()` function:

- An application wants to draw optimally into a device context that spans several display monitors that have different color depths.
- An application wants to obtain a handle for one or more monitors in a multi-monitor system.

A powerful and interesting feature of Windows multi-monitor support is that the individual monitors can execute at various resolutions and color depth. Consequently, the `EnumDisplayMonitors()` function returns a device context that matches the capabilities of the monitor. An application can use the resulting device context to optimally paint to this part of the virtual desktop. For example, a photo-editing program contains a display area that shows the photograph after being retouched. In this case, the application can use `EnumDisplayMonitors()` to make sure that this display area falls inside the monitor with the most adequate resolution and color depth. Then the code can render the image optimally to this area.

Note that applications can draw to a window that spans more than one display monitor with different color formats. In this case, Windows uses its standard algorithms to render the image. The `EnumDisplayMonitors()` function enables application code to customize output to a particular color depth, perhaps an improvement over the default results produced by Windows.

The `EnumDisplayMonitors()` function enumerates the display monitors contained in a region formed by the intersection of a specified rectangle and the visible part of a device context. The function calls an application-defined callback function once for each display monitor that intersects the region. The function's general form is as follows:

```
BOOL EnumDisplayMonitors (
                    HDC hdc,                      // 1
                    LPCRECT lprcClip,             // 2
                    MONITORENUMPROC lpfnEnum,     // 3
                    LPARAM dwData                 // 4
                    );
```

The first parameter is the handle to a display device context that defines the visible region of reference. If this parameter is NULL, the hdcMonitor parameter passed to the callback function is also NULL. In this case, the visible region of interest is the entire virtual desktop and all the displays that it contains.

The second parameter is a pointer to a structure of type RECT that specifies a clipping rectangle. The reference region is the intersection of the clipping rectangle with the visible region specified by the first parameter. If the first parameter (hdc) is non-NULL, the coordinates of the clipping rectangle are relative to the origin of the hdc. If hdc is NULL, the coordinates are the virtual screen coordinates. Applications can enter NULL in this parameter if they do not want to clip the region specified by the first parameter.

The third parameter is a pointer to an application-defined callback function. This function, which has the placeholder name MonitorEnumProc(), is discussed later in this section. The fourth parameter contains application-defined data that is passed directly to the callback function.

If the function succeeds, the return value is nonzero. If it fails, the return value is 0.

The first and the second parameters to EnumDisplayMonitors() can be combined to produce specific results. Table 15-3 lists the four possible combinations.

TABLE 15-3 COMBINATIONS OF THE FIRST AND SECOND PARAMETERS OF THE ENUMDISPLAYMONITORS() FUNCTION

Hdc	lprcClip	Behavior
NULL	NULL	Enumerates all display monitors. The callback function receives a NULL HDC.
NULL	Non-NULL	Enumerates all display monitors that intersect the clipping rectangle. The callback function receives a NULL HDC.
Non-NULL	NULL	Enumerates all display monitors that intersect the visible region of the device context. The callback function receives a handle to a DC for the specific display monitor.

Continued

TABLE 15-3 COMBINATIONS OF THE FIRST AND SECOND PARAMETERS OF THE ENUMDISPLAYMONITORS() FUNCTION *(Continued)*

Hdc	lprcClip	Behavior
Non-NULL	Non-NULL	Enumerates all display monitors that intersect the visible region of the device context and the clipping rectangle. The callback function receives a handle to a DC for the specific display monitor.

A MonitorEnumProc() function is an application-defined callback function that is called by EnumDisplayMonitors(). The function name can be defined by the application. The callback function is a pointer of type MONITORENUMPROC. The callback function's prototype is as follows:

```
BOOL CALLBACK MonitorEnumProc(
              HMONITOR hMonitor,      // 1
              HDC hdcMonitor,         // 2
              LPRECT lprcMonitor,     // 3
              LPARAM dwData           // 4
              );
```

When the callback function receives control, the first parameter is the handle to the display monitor being enumerated. Windows documentation states that this value is always non-NULL. The second parameter is the handle to a device context. The color attributes for the device context are those of the monitor identified by the first parameter. The clipping area of the device context is the intersection of the visible region of the device context, identified by the first parameter of EnumDisplayMonitors(), the rectangle pointed to by the second parameter of EnumDisplayMonitors(), and the display monitor rectangle. If the first parameter of EnumDisplayMonitors() is NULL, this parameter is also NULL.

The third parameter is a pointer to a structure of type RECT. If the second parameter is non-NULL, the rectangle is the intersection of the clipping area of the device context identified by the second parameter and the display monitor rectangle. If the second parameter is NULL, the rectangle returned in the third parameter is the display monitor rectangle.

Obtaining Monitor Information

Windows applications often need to obtain information about a particular monitor in the virtual desktop. The GetMonitorInfo() function provides several useful items of information about a display monitor. The function's general form is as follows:

```
BOOL GetMonitorInfo(
                    HMONITOR hMonitor,   // 1
                    LPMONITORINFO lpmi   // 2
                    );
```

The first parameter is the handle to the display monitor of reference. The second parameter is a pointer to a structure variable of type MONITORINFO, or MONITORINFOEX, in which monitor information is stored by the call. The difference between these structures is that the latter one includes a member string that contains a name for the display monitor. The MONITORINFOEX structure is defined as follows:

```
typedef struct tagMONITORINFOEX {
    DWORD  cbSize;
    RECT   rcMonitor;
    RECT   rcWork;
    DWORD  dwFlags;
    TCHAR  szDevice [CCHDEVICENAME]
} MONITORINFOEX, *LPMONITORINFOEX;
```

The cbSize member is the structure size, in bytes. This member must be set before calling GetMonitorInfo(), because it is the structure size that enables Windows to determine whether the caller is using a structure of type MONITORINFO or of type MONITORINFOEX. The rcMonitor member is a structure variable of type RECT that specifies the display monitor rectangle expressed in virtual screen coordinates. If the monitor is not the primary monitor, some of the rectangle's coordinates may be negative. The rcWork member is also a structure variable of type RECT. This member specifies the work area rectangle of the display monitor expressed in virtual screen coordinates. Here again, if the monitor is not the primary monitor, some of the rectangle's coordinates may be negative values. The dwFlags flags member represents the monitor attributes. At present, a single flag named MONITORINFOF_PRIMARY is defined. This flag identifies the primary display monitor. The szDevice member is a string name for the display monitor. Applications that have no use for the monitor's name can use the MONITORINFO structure type instead of MONITORINFOEX.

Enumerating Multiple Display Devices

Another function in the multi-monitor API is EnumDisplayDevices(). This function provides information about the display hardware installed in the system. Applications can use this function to detect the presence of a particular video card or to obtain a count of the number of installed video cards. The function's general form is as follows:

```
BOOL EnumDisplayDevices(
                        PVOID Unused,                        // 1
                        DWORD iDevNum,                       // 2
                        PDISPLAY_DEVICE lpDisplayDevice,     // 3
                        DWORD dwFlags                        // 4
                        );
```

The first parameter is not used and must be set to NULL. The second parameter is an index value that specifies the display device of interest. The operating system identifies each display device with a 0-based index value. For example, in a system with three displays these would be numbered 0, 1, and 2. Code can set this value to obtain data about a specific device. The third parameter is a pointer to a structure variable of type DISPLAY_DEVICE. This variable receives information about the display device. The fourth parameter consists of flags designed to define the function behavior. None of these flags are currently defined.

If the call succeeds, the return value is nonzero. The return value is 0 if the function fails. This fact can be used to call the function in a loop so as to obtain all devices in the system. In this case, the second parameter (iDevNum) is initially set to 0 and incremented during each loop iteration. When the function fails, iDevNum is one greater than the number of devices in the system.

Information about the device is contained in the structure variable of type DISPLAY_DEVICE passed in the second parameter to EnumDisplayDevices(). The structure is defined as follows:

```
typedef struct _DISPLAY_DEVICE {
    DWORD  cb;
    WCHAR  DeviceName[32];
    WCHAR  DeviceString[128];
    DWORD  StateFlags;
} DISPLAY_DEVICE, *PDISPLAY_DEVICE, *LPDISPLAY_DEVICE;
```

The cb member is the structure size in bytes. This member must be initialized prior to calling EnumDisplayDevices(). DeviceName is an array of char identifying the device name. DeviceString is another array of char containing the device context string. The StateFlags member is not currently defined.

When debugging code that uses the `DISPLAY_DEVICE` structure, it appears that the structure includes two undocumented members: a `DeviceID` member contains a device identification string and a `DeviceKey` member contains an identification code and a directory path. Some of the `StateFlags` have been implemented in the newer versions of the API. These elements of the `DISPLAY_DEVICE` structure have not yet been described in Microsoft documentation.

Multi-monitor Programming in Windows 98

It is easy to predict that sometime in the future, operating systems with multiple monitor support will become the norm, but at present this is not the case. Windows 95 and NT 4 still have a big share of the Windows market. Applications developed for the general market must take this fact into consideration and implement multiple monitor support in a way that does not preclude their execution in the older environments.

The Multimon.h Header File

Microsoft has addressed this problem and furnishes a header file named multimon.h that enables you to safely use the new multi-monitor API in any system. The file can be found in the DirectX 6 package and in the newer versions of the Microsoft Developer Network (MSDN) product. You can also find a copy of the multimon.h file in the *MM Info Demo* project directory on the book's CD-ROM. Applications that use multimon.h can copy the file to their development directory or to the system's header file path. In addition, the application code must define `COMPILE_MULTIMON_STUBS` before including multimon.h. If the header file is in the application's development directory, this can be accomplished as follows:

```
#define COMPILE_MULTIMON_STUBS
#include "multimon.h"
```

Microsoft documentation states that only one source file must contain the definition for `COMPILE_MULTIMON_STUBS`, otherwise link-time errors are produced.

Multimon.h contains definitions for the following multi-monitor functions described earlier in this chapter:

- `MonitorFromWindow()`

- `MonitorFromRect()`
- `MonitorFromPoint()`
- `GetMonitorInfo()`
- `EnumDisplayMonitors()`
- `EnumDisplayDevices()`

In addition, it also defines an update of the `GetSystemMetrics()` function which enables you to obtain the origin, width, and height of the virtual screen as well as the total number of monitors in the system.

Obtaining System Information

Applications that execute in a multi-monitor environment usually require information about the system configuration. The number of displays, the characteristics of the adapter hardware, the size of the virtual screen, and the coordinates of the individual monitors are among the most important data elements that are necessary. Several APIs can be used to obtain this and other information; `GetMonitorInfo()`, `EnumDisplayMonitors()`, `EnumDisplayDevices()`, and `GetSystemMetrics()` are the most useful.

Information about the virtual screen can be obtained by means of the new configuration settings added to the `GetSystemMetrics()` function. Table 15-4 lists the new constants returned by the call.

Table 15-4 GETSYSTEMMETRICS() NEW MULTI-MONITOR CONFIGURATION SETTINGS

Value	Meaning
SM_CMONITORS	Number of display monitors on the desktop.
SM_SAMEDISPLAYFORMAT	TRUE if all the display monitors have the same color format, FALSE otherwise. Two displays can have the same bit depth, but different color formats.
SM_XVIRTUALSCREEN	Left coordinate of the virtual screen.
SM_YVIRTUALSCREEN	Right coordinate of the virtual screen.
SM_CXVIRTUALSCREEN	Width, in pixels, of the virtual screen,
SM_CYVIRTUALSCREEN	Height, in pixels, of the virtual screen.

The index values SM_CXSCREEN and SM_CYSCREEN return the pixel width and height of the primary screen. Figure 15-3 shows the various values returned by GetSystemMetrics(). In this case we assume a virtual screen composed of three monitors.

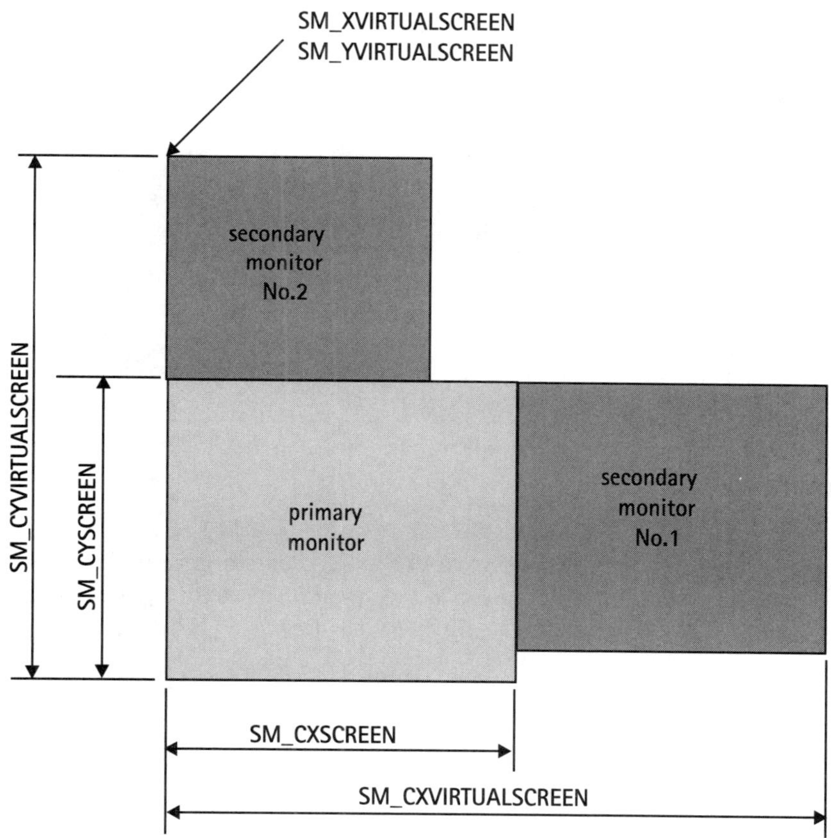

Figure 15-3: GetSystemMetrics() values in a virtual screen

The following code sample uses GetSystemMetrics() to obtain information about a multi-monitor system and stores the data in global variables for later reference:

```
// System metric variables
int             vsTop, vsLeft, vsRight, vsBottom;
int             smMonitors, smFormat;
   .
   .
   .
```

```
// Obtain system information
   vsTop = GetSystemMetrics(SM_YVIRTUALSCREEN);
   vsLeft = GetSystemMetrics(SM_XVIRTUALSCREEN);
   vsRight = GetSystemMetrics(SM_CXVIRTUALSCREEN);
   vsBottom = GetSystemMetrics(SM_CYVIRTUALSCREEN);
   smMonitors = GetSystemMetrics(SM_CMONITORS);
   smFormat = GetSystemMetrics(SM_SAMEDISPLAYFORMAT);
```

Figure 15-4 is a screen snapshot of the dump of the System Info menu command in the *MM Info Demo* project program.

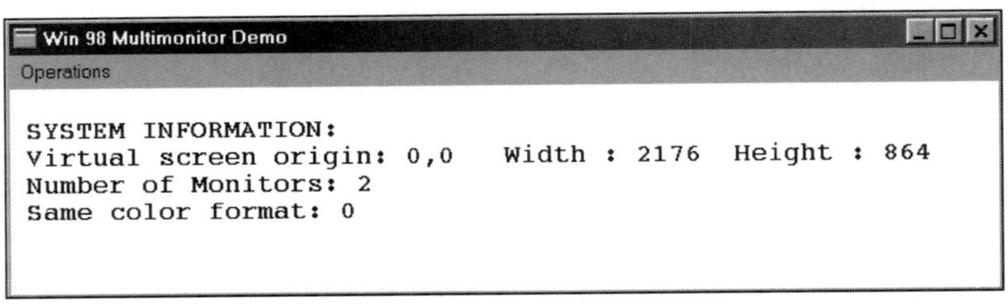

Figure 15-4: Screen snapshot of the System Info menu command in the MM Info Demo project program

The `EnumDisplayMonitors()` function can be used to obtain information about all the monitors in a region or all monitors in the system. The following code fragment shows the processing performed by the *MM Info Demo* project program:

```
// Monitor data
int             monCount = 0;  // Number of monitors
int             monData[9][4]; // Data arrays for 9 monitors
MONITORINFOEX   mi;
.
.
.
// Enumerate all monitors and store data
   EnumDisplayMonitors(NULL, NULL,
                       MonitorInfo,
                       0);
.
.
.
//**********************************
// Name: MonitorInfo
// Desc: Callback function for
```

```
//        EnumerateMonitorInfo()
//*******************************
BOOL CALLBACK MonitorInfo( HMONITOR hMon,
                           HDC hdc,
                           LPRECT rect,
                           LPARAM extra)
{
 mi.cbSize = sizeof(MONITORINFOEX);
 GetMonitorInfo(hMon, &mi);
 monData[monCount][0] = mi.rcMonitor.left;
 monData[monCount][1] = mi.rcMonitor.top;
 monData[monCount][2] = mi.rcMonitor.right;
 monData[monCount][3] = mi.rcMonitor.bottom;
 monCount++;            // Bump monitor counter
 return TRUE;
}
```

In the preceding code fragment we defined a two-dimensional array of type `int`, named `monData`, to hold four items of information for each of the nine possible monitors supported by Windows 98. The call to `EnumDisplayMonitors()` establishes the address of the callback function that receives control for each monitor enumerated. The information about each monitor is passed to the callback function in a `RECT` type variable that is encoded in the third parameter. The callback function, named `MonitorInfo()`, stores the four values passed in the RECT structure in the corresponding elements of the two-dimensional global array. The sample program later retrieves this information and displays it on the screen. Figure 15-5 is a screen snapshot of the Enumerate Monitors menu command in the *MM Info Demo* project program.

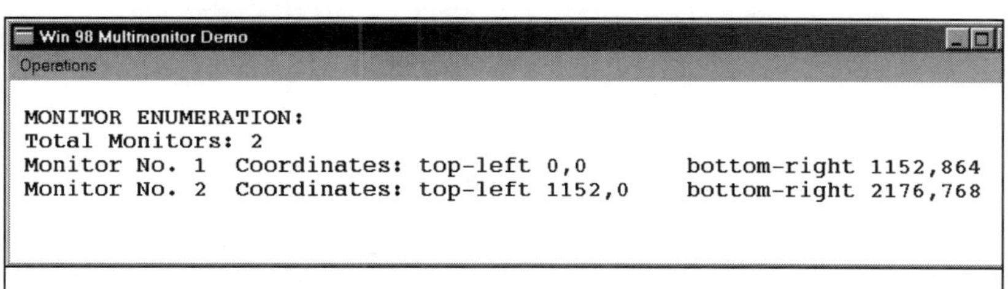

Figure 15-5: Screen snapshot of the Enumerate Monitors menu command in the MM Info Demo project program

Controlling Video Output

The first level of video output control in multi-monitor environments results from the fact that applications can use `EnumDisplayMonitors()` to obtain the handle to the device context corresponding to each monitor in the system. During each iteration, the callback function associated with the `EnumDisplayMonitors()` call passes the monitor-specific device context in the second parameter. This device context can then be used to paint pieces of windows that fall within a particular monitor. The technique makes possible the use of custom drawing algorithms that override the GDI default for specific areas.

In addition, an application can direct output to any monitor in a multi-monitor system. Because the application can determine the virtual screen and the individual monitors that form it, code can also calculate the coordinates of each monitor in the system. Note that programs that control output to individual monitors must usually make assumptions regarding the architecture of the video environment. In most cases, it would be fruitless to attempt to direct display to individual monitors if we have no prior knowledge of how many monitors are in the system or how they are placed in the virtual screen. In other words, output control to individual elements in the virtual screen normally implies some prior knowledge of the characteristics or the location of these elements.

Suppose there is an application designed for a two-monitor system in which the left-side monitor is to be used for program controls and the right-side one for the graphics image. In this case, code assumes that the monitors are placed side by side, and that the primary monitor is the one on the left. Given this minimal initial assumption, code may then allow considerable latitude about the resolution and the color depth of each monitor in the system, as well as to their specific placement. Figure 15-6 shows a virtual screen consisting of two monitors.

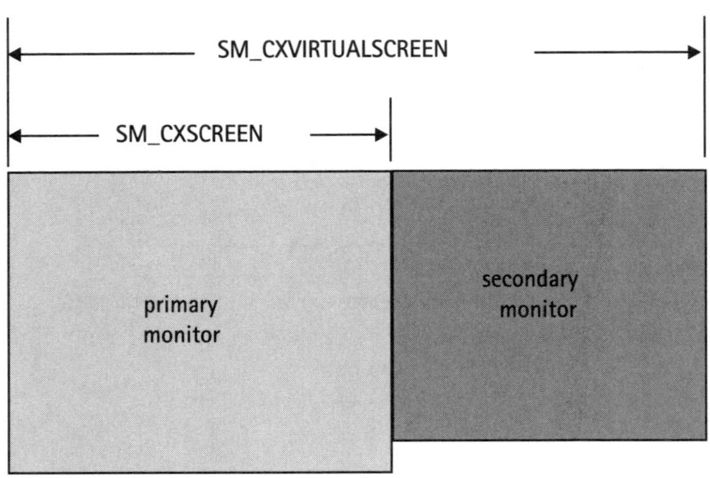

Figure 15-6: A dual-monitor virtual screen

In all cases, the coordinates of the primary monitor start at the origin. Therefore, it is safe to assume that a point at screen coordinates (0,0) is always in the primary monitor. The origin of the secondary monitor is returned in the first two members of the `RECT` type structure passed to the callback function during enumeration. If these values were stored at that time, code can now use them to find a position in any monitor on the virtual desktop. If you assume that there is a secondary monitor, and that it is placed to the right of the primary monitor, you can also use the values returned by `GetSystemMetrics()` to locate a coordinate pair in this second monitor, as shown in Figure 15-6.

The Change Display menu command in the project *MM Info Demo* enables you to move execution to a secondary monitor or to the primary monitor. In both cases, code uses the `MoveWindow()` function to move the program window to the corresponding monitor. When moving to the primary monitor, the coordinates of the top-left corner are assumed to be at (50,50). When moving to the secondary monitor, the coordinates of the origin are obtained from the array in which they were stored by the `EnumDisplayMonitors()` callback function. The following code fragment shows the processing in this case:

```
//********************************
//   Move to secondary monitor
//********************************
case ID_OP_SEC:
// Check for no secondary monitor
   if(monCount < 2)
   {
       MessageBox(hwnd,
                  "No secondary monitor",
                  "Multi-monitor Demo",
                   MB_OK);
       return 0;
    }
// Check for already in secondary monitor
   if(curMon == 2)
   {
       MessageBox(hwnd,
                   "Already in secondary monitor",
                   "Multi-monitor Demo",
                    MB_OK);
       return 0;
    }
    // Get current window dimensions
    GetWindowRect(hwnd, &winSize);
    MoveWindow(hwnd, monData[1][0]+50,
                monData[1][1]+50,
```

```
                winSize.right - winSize.left,
                winSize.bottom - winSize.top,
                1);
    curMon = 2;
 break;
```

The previous code first checks for a valid secondary monitor. If one is not found, a message box is displayed and execution ends. Then it makes certain that the program is not already displayed in the secondary monitor. If this test passes, the `GetWindowRect()` function is called to obtain the size of the current window. The resulting dimensions are passed to the `MoveWindow()` function that follows. This is necessary to ensure that the resulting window is the same size as the original one. The location of the window in the secondary monitor is based on adding 50 device units to the stored origin of the first secondary monitor found during the `EnumDisplayMonitors()` callback.

Programming for Multi-monitor Awareness

The existence of multi-monitor systems is a fact that must now be considered by all applications. Even programs that make no use of multiple monitors should make sure that they execute correctly in multi-monitor systems. Several programming practices may make applications misbehave in a multi-monitor system.

The most common practice is perhaps the manual centering of windows and dialog boxes. If you center a dialog box by using the `DS_CENTER` style, you let the operating system figure out on which monitor the dialog box is located and proceed accordingly. With regard to program windows, the main concern is centering in a different monitor from the one in which it is displayed. A possible source of problems relates to the fact that the `SM_CXSCREEN` and `SM_CYSCREEN` values returned by `GetSystemMetrics()` always refer to the primary monitor, while `SM_CXVIRTUALSCREEN` and `SM_CYVIRTUALSCREEN` refer to the virtual desktop. If an application is not running on the primary monitor, using `SM_CXSCREEN` and `SM_CYSCREEN` centers output on the wrong monitor. In any case, using `SM_CXVIRTUALSCREEN` and `SM_CYVIRTUALSCREEN` centers the window on the virtual screen, which may not be what you intended.

Microsoft has published a function for centering a window in a multiple-monitor environment. The source article is titled “How to Exploit Multiple Monitor Support in Memphis and Windows NT 5.0,” by David Cambell and is available in the MSDN 6.0 Library. Code listing is as follows:

```
void CenterWindowNew(HWND hWnd)
{
    HMONITOR hMonitor;
    MONITORINFO mi;
    RECT rcWnd;
```

```
    RECT rcMon;
          GetWindowRect(hWnd, &rcWnd);
    hMonitor = MonitorFromWindow(hWnd,
                             MONITOR_DEFAULTTONEAREST);
    mi.cbSize = sizeof(mi);
    GetMonitorInfo(hMonitor, &mi);
    rcMon = mi.rcMonitor;
 // Since we could no longer assume where the origin is, and
 // because we have to calculate the monitor dimensions the
 // equation is:
 rcWnd.left   = rcMon.left + ((rcMon.right  - rcMon.left) -
                             (rcWnd.right  - rcWnd.left)) / 2;
 rcWnd.top    = rcMon.top  + ((rcMon.bottom - rcMon.top)  -
                             (rcWnd.bottom - rcWnd.top)) / 2;
 // Note that if rcMon.left and rcMon.top were 0, this
 // simplifies to the above.
  SetWindowPos(hWnd, NULL, rcWnd.left, rcWnd.top,
               0, 0, SWP_NOSIZE | SWP_NOZORDER |
               SWP_NOACTIVATE);
}
```

The unconventional interpretation of negative coordinates can also create problems. Applications should not assume that negative coordinates indicate a window has wandered off the screen and must be repositioned. Neither can negative coordinates be used to hide a window. The same applies to coordinates that are greater than SM_CXSCREEN and SM_CYSCREEN.

Multi-monitor Programming in DirectX 6

The DirectDraw component of DirectX 6 supports multi-monitor architectures. Note that the use of this functionality requires an operating system that is multi-monitor enabled. DirectDraw applications can directly access the hardware on any display devices in multi-monitor systems and direct execution to any particular monitor on the virtual desktop. DirectDraw programs that execute in windowed mode access multi-monitor capabilities in the same manner as conventional Windows programs. This type of programming was described in previous sections. In the sections that follow, we discuss multi-monitor programming for DirectDraw applications that execute in exclusive, full-screen mode. The following topics relate to this theme:

- Enumerating multiple devices on systems with multiple monitors. The DirectDrawEnumerateEx() function is the DirectX counterpart to the

Windows 98/NT 5 `EnumerateDisplayMonitors()` and `EnumerateDisplayDevices()` functions discussed earlier in this chapter.

- Creating DirectDraw objects for each particular monitor in the system. This relates to the fact that each device in a multi-monitor system has its own GUID. The `DirectDrawCreate()` function can reference this GUID to create a specific object for the device. The resulting surfaces are also specific for the device in which they reside.
- DirectDraw exclusive-mode applications must have a single window that receives keyboard input, called the *focus window*. The notion of a device window is a new concept directly related to the DirectDraw object. In DirectDraw exclusive mode, multi-monitor applications must set both the focus and the device windows.

Enumerating Multiple Devices in DirectX

The `DirectDrawEnumerateEx()` function is used to enumerate the display devices in a multi-monitor system. The function calls an application-defined callback function, of type `DDEnumCallbackEx()` for each device found. This function is supported on Windows 98 and NT 5.0 operating systems. DirectDraw applications must reference Ddraw.lib and be compiled under DirectX 6.0 or later versions. The use of this function requires operating system and DirectX 6 support. Applications that use a previous version of DirectX or a single-monitor version of Windows fail when this call is made. The function's general form is as follows:

```
HRESULT WINAPI DirectDrawEnumerateEx(
                LPDDENUMCALLBACKEX lpCallback,  // 1
                LPVOID lpContext,               // 2
                DWORD  dwFlags                  // 3
                );
```

The first parameter is the address of a callback function, of type `DDEnumCallbackEx`. This function is called with a description of each enumerated DirectDraw-enabled HAL. The second parameter is the address of an application-defined value that is to be passed to the enumeration callback function each time it is called. The third parameter represents one or more flags that determine the enumeration scope. This parameter can be 0 or a combination of the flags listed in Table 15-5.

TABLE 15-5 ENUMERATION SCOPE FLAGS IN DIRECTDRAWENUMERATEEX()

Flag	Action
0	Enumerates the primary display only or a nondisplay device if one is installed.
DDENUM_ATTACHEDSECONDARYDEVICES	Enumerates the primary device and any display devices that are attached to the desktop.
DDENUM_DETACHEDSECONDARYDEVICES	Enumerates the primary device and any display devices that are not attached to the desktop.
DDENUM_NONDISPLAYDEVICES	Enumerates nondisplay devices such as 3-D accelerators that have no 2-D capabilities.

The function returns DD_OK if it succeeds and DDERR_INVALIDPARAMS if it fails.

This function is supported by DirectX 5 in machines running Windows 98. All other operating systems require DirectX 6. Applications that need to ensure compatibility with multiple versions of Windows and DirectX can retrieve the address of DirectDrawEnumerateEx() from the Ddraw.dll dynamic-link library by calling the GetProcAddress(). There are two versions of the DirectDrawEnumerateEx() function, one for ANSI and another one for the Unicode character set. The corresponding string names are DirectDrawEnumerateExA() for ANSI and DirectDraw EnumerateExW() for Unicode. If GetProcAddress() fails, then the installed version of the operating system does not support multiple monitors. The following code sample shows one possible approach:

```
LPDIRECTDRAWENUMERATEEX lpDDEnumEx;
HINSTANCE               h;
.
.
.
h = LoadLibrary("ddraw.dll);
if(!h)
    return DDInitFailed(hWnd, hRet,
           "DirectX not installed");
// Get ANSI version of function
lpDDEnumEx = (LPDIRECTDRAWENUMERATEEX)
             GetProcAddress(h,"DirectDrawEnumerateExA");
```

```
// GetProcAddress() returns NULL if it failed
// If it succeeded, use the pointer to call
// DirectDrawEnumerateEx()
if (lpDDEnumEx)
        lpDDEnumEx(Callback, NULL,
        DDENUM_ATTACHEDSECONDARYDEVICES |
        DDENUM_NONDISPLAYDEVICES
        );
else
    return DDInitFailed(hWnd, hRet,
           "Multiple monitors not supported");
```

Notice that the previous code fragment uses the `DDInitFailed()` function developed in Chapter 10 to exit in case of a terminal error. Also note that the sample code does not work for applications that link to Ddraw.dll at run time or at load time. Applications that assume that DirectX 6 is installed, and that the operating system supports multiple monitors, can call `DirectDrawEnumerateEx()` directly.

The callback function referenced in the first parameter of `DirectDrawEnumerateEx()` has the following prototype:

```
BOOL WINAPI DDEnumCallbackEx(
                   GUID FAR *lpGUID,               // 1
                   LPSTR     lpDriverDescription,  // 2
                   LPSTR     lpDriverName,         // 3
                   LPVOID    lpContext,            // 4
                   HMONITOR  hm                    // 5
                   );
```

The first parameter is the address of the globally unique identifier of the DirectDraw object. This parameter is later used by the `DirectDrawCreate()` to create an object that is specific to the enumerated display device. The second parameter is the address of a string that contains the driver description. The third parameter is the address of a string with the driver name. The fourth parameter is the address of an application-defined structure that is passed to the callback function each time it is called. The fifth parameter is the handle to the monitor associated with the enumerated DirectDraw object. If the DirectDraw object corresponds to the primary device, this parameter is `NULL`. The same applies when the enumerated DirectDraw object is a non-display device or a device not attached to the desktop.

The callback function returns nonzero to continue the enumeration and 0 to stop it. The pointer to the callback function is of type `LPDDENUMCALLBACKEX`. The following code fragment shows the processing of the `DirectDrawEnumerateEx()` function in the *MM Sprite Demo* project on the book's CD-ROM:

```
// The following statement determines the monitor used for
```

```
// DirectDraw output. Default (2) is second monitor in system.
// Change this statement and recompile program to force execution
// in another monitor
#define MONITOR_NUM 2
    .
    .
    .
// Multi-monitor data
GUID FAR*       lpGUIDMon2 = 0;
int             monCounter = 0;
int             monDesired = (int) MONITOR_NUM;
    .
    .
    .
//****************************************
//  Setup DirectDraw monitor enumeration
//****************************************
hRet = DirectDrawEnumerateEx(&EnumMonitors,
                             NULL,          // No data passed
                             DDENUM_ATTACHEDSECONDARYDEVICES);
  if (hRet != DD_OK)
     return DDInitFailed(hWnd, hRet,
                        "DirectDrawEnumerateEx() call failed");
  // Test for failure to find desired monitor
  if(monCounter != monDesired)
     return DDInitFailed(hWnd, hRet,
                        "Requested monitor not found");
   .
   .
   .
//*******************************************************
// Name: EnumMonitors
// Desc: Callback function for DirectDrawEnumerateEx()
//*******************************************************
BOOL WINAPI EnumMonitors(GUID FAR* lpGUID,
                   LPSTR lpDriverDescriptor,
                   LPSTR lpDriverName,
                   LPVOID lpContext,
                   HMONITOR hm)
{
   // hm is NULL if device is a primary monitor,
   // a non-display device, or a device not attached
   // to the desktop
   if(hm == NULL)
```

```
      return 1;      // Continue enumeration
   // At this point a monitor device has been located
   monCounter++;
   // Test to see if this is the desired one
   if(monCounter != monDesired)
      return 1;
   // At this point the desired monitor has been found
   // Create DirectDraw object using this monitor
      hRet = DirectDrawCreate (lpGUID,
                               &lpDD,
                               NULL);
   if(hRet == DDERR_INVALIDDIRECTDRAWGUID)
      return DDInitFailed(hWnd, hRet,
                          "InvalId DirectDraw GUID");

   if(hRet != DD_OK)
      return DDInitFailed(hWnd, hRet,
                          "DirectDrawCreate() call failed");

   return 0;          // Stop enumeration
}
```

NOTE: DirectDraw documentation states that the `HMONITOR` parameter to the `DirectDrawEnumerateEx()` callback function is `NULL` when the enumerated object is a primary device. This seems to imply that in a system with one primary and one secondary device, the first non-`NULL` value received in the callback function corresponds to the secondary monitor. However, this is not the case, because the function returns non-`NULL` for all devices in the system. Therefore, in a machine with a primary and a secondary device, two non-`NULL` values are passed to the callback function. The processing in the previous code fragment takes this into account.

Device-specific DirectDraw Object

An exclusive mode, DirectDraw application in a multiple monitor system can select the monitor on which it executes. This can be a convenient option if the program needs to pick the most adequate among several video systems, or if the application design requires a particular program module or thread to execute in a specific monitor. For example, a flight simulator program consists of two program modules: the first one contains the view from the cockpit window and the second one displays the airplane's instruments and controls. In this case, the program designers could require a host machine consisting of two monitors. The window view module executes on the top monitor, and the module that shows the flight instruments and controls is displayed on the bottom one.

The DirectDrawEnumerateEx() callback function listed in the previous section contains the following call to DirectDrawCreate():

```
// At this point the desired monitor has been found
// Create DirectDraw object using this monitor
   hRet = DirectDrawCreate (lpGUID,
                            &lpDD,
                            NULL);
```

In this case, the first parameter to DirectDrawCreate() is a pointer to the globally unique identifier for the enumerated monitor. The result of the call is that the DirectDraw object is specific for the display device. If the program is an exclusive mode application, it executes in the monitor of reference. This mechanism is used to create a DirectDraw program that executes full screen in any of the monitors on the virtual desktop.

Setting the Focus and Device Windows

The notion of a focus window refers to the window that receives keyboard input. The focus window has a highlighted title bar or dialog frame, as the case may be, if either one is present. The GetFocus() and SetFocus() functions are used to determine and change the window that owns the input focus. A DirectDraw application that executes in exclusive mode must have the input focus. If the application outputs to more than one monitor, a single window is the focus window.

A device window is defined as the visible application that DirectDraw uses for display. In a multi-monitor system there can be a device window for each display device in the machine. The concept is specific to DirectDraw programming: there are no device windows outside of DirectDraw. Each device that holds a full-screen DirectDraw surface must be represented by a DirectDraw object and a device window.

In DirectDraw applications that execute in a single monitor, the focus window is also the device window. In multi-monitor applications, however, the device window must be set for each monitor in the virtual desktop that is to be used by the program. When a device window is set, code must let the DirectDraw object know about the application's focus window. In a particular monitor, the focus window can also serve as the device window. In this case, other device windows are children of the focus window.

Applications set the focus window by calling the `SetCooperativeLevel()` function for each DirectDraw object. A newly defined flag, named `DSCL_SETFOCUSWINDOW`, is passed in this case, as in the following code fragment:

```
//Global variables
LPDIRECTDRAW4           lpDD4 = NULL;    // DirectDraw object
HWND                    hWnd;
HRESULT                 hRet;
    .
    .
    .
// Set focus windows
hRet = lpDD4->SetCooperativeLevel(hWnd, DDSCL_SETFOCUSWINDOW);
    if (hRet != DD_OK)
        return DDInitFailed(hWnd, hRet,
                            "Focus Window not set");
```

There are two ways to create a device window:

1. Create a window in the conventional manner and pass its handle to the `SetCooperativeLevel()` function. In this case, you use the flags `DDSCL_SETDEVICEWINDOW`, `DDSCL_FULLSCREEN`, and `DDSCL_EXCLUSIVE`. The result is a full-screen window with the device window set for the particular monitor. The window thus designated receives mouse messages. The window passed to `SetCooperativeLevel()` should be either the focus window (if it is on the same device) or a child of the focus window.
2. Let DirectDraw create the window. In this case, the application passes the focus window handle to `SetCooperativeLevel()` and uses the flags `DDSCL_CREATEDEVICEWINDOW`, `DDSCL_FULLSCREEN`, and `DDSCL_EXCLUSIVE`. The result is that DirectDraw creates a default device window that is a child of the focus window. With this method, the application does not receive any mouse messages for the window.

The following code fragment shows the first option for creating a device window. This is the most common approach:

```
// Set device windows and cooperative
hRet = lpDD4->SetCooperativeLevel(hWnd,
                 DDSCL_SETDEVICEWINDOW |
                 DDSCL_EXCLUSIVE |
                 DDSCL_FULLSCREEN);
   if (hRet != DD_OK)
      return DDInitFailed(hWnd, hRet,
                 "SetCooperativeLevel() call failed");
```

Although a focus window can be a device window, it is not possible to set a window as both the focus window and a device window with a single call to `SetCooperativeLevel()`. Code must first set it as the focus window, then as a device window. One exception is when the focus window and the device window are on the default device, typically the application window. The following code fragment shows the processing in this case:

```
hRet = lpDD4->SetCooperativeLevel(hWnd,
                  DDSCL_SETFOCUSWINDOW |
                  DDSCL_EXCLUSIVE |
                  DDSCL_FULLSCREEN |
                  DDSCL_CREATEDEVICEWINDOW);
   if (hRet != DD_OK)
      return DDInitFailed(hWnd, hRet,
                 "SetCooperativeLevel() call failed");
```

Notice that the `DDSCL_SETFOCUSWINDOW` and the `DDSCL_CREATEDEVICEWINDOW` flags must be entered in the order listed.

The MM Sprite Demo Project Program

The demonstration program in the *MM Sprite Demo* project folder on the book's CD-ROM is a version of the *DD Sprite Demo* program that executes in a multiple-monitor environment. The following comment is found at the beginning of the listing:

```
// The following statement determines the monitor used for
// DirectDraw output. The Default (2) is the second monitor.
// Change this statement and recompile program to force
// execution in another monitor
#define MONITOR_NUM 2
```

Code examines the value of the `MONITOR_NUM` constant to determine for which monitor the DirectDraw object is created. The program also serves to demonstrate the setup required for multi-monitor debugging, which we discuss in the following sections.

Debugging DirectDraw Applications

One of the problems associated with developing DirectDraw exclusive-mode applications is the difficulty in using conventional debuggers. Exclusive-mode applications take up the entire screen and temporarily disable the Windows multitasking features on which debuggers depend. A partial solution to this problem is to use debugging macros, such as `ASSERT`, that detect possible errors and notify the programmer. In the programs listed in this book we have used an even simpler solution: the `DDInitFailed()` function. This function, first described in Chapter 10, provides a way to display a screen message upon encountering a terminal error. But often neither of these schemes provides the necessary information for locating and correcting program errors.

A more satisfactory solution is remote debugging. In this case we use two networked computers: one runs the application code (the DirectDraw exclusive-mode program) and a second one runs the debugger. The result is that the debugger is visible and accessible at any time. Even when a program crashes, it is possible to examine the machine state. The one objection to remote debugging is that we must use two machines simultaneously and that the setup requires a network connection and protocol.

Multi-monitor Debugging

A simpler alternative to remote debugging is using a multi-monitor system to step through the code of a full-screen DirectDraw program. Typically, the primary monitor is used for the development environment and the secondary monitor for DirectDraw output. To enable multi-monitor debugging you must first select the DirectDraw page on the Windows Control Panel and change a registry setting through the DirectX property sheet. Once on the DirectDraw page, click Advanced Settings and select the Enable Multi-Monitor Debugging checkbox. This prevents DirectDraw from minimizing the application when it loses focus. The one limitation of this debugging method is that in Windows 98 it is not possible to step through code when a surface is locked.

Summary

In this chapter, we covered one of the most exciting features incorporated into Windows in recent years: support for multiple adapters and monitors. This new functionality adds a new dimension to Windows and to DirectX programming. Practically every type of program can make use of multiple monitors and applications can be designed to maximize this feature. The technology applies to conventional Windows 98 and NT 5 programs as well as to DirectDraw applications under DirectX 6. Furthermore, multiple monitors provide an effective environment for developing DirectX applications by making it possible to use one system for the development tools and the debugger and another one to execute the code being developed.

As a point of interest, Direct 3D and OpenGL hardware drivers do not support multi-monitor. If you are doing any 3-D graphics programming with DirectX, you can't use multi-monitor and get hardware acceleration. Hopefully, Microsoft will be able to fix this in future driver models.

Appendix A

Windows and DirectX Structures

This appendix contains the structures mentioned in the text. Structures are listed in alphabetical order.

```
BITMAP
   typedef struct tagBITMAP {  /* bm */
       int     bmType;
       int     bmWidth;
       int     bmHeight;
       int     bmWidthBytes;
       BYTE    bmPlanes;
       BYTE    bmBitsPixel;
       LPVOID  bmBits;
   };

BITMAPCOREHEADER
   typedef struct tagBITMAPCOREHEADER { // bmch
           DWORD   bcSize;
           WORD    bcWidth;
           WORD    bcHeight;
           WORD    bcPlanes;
           WORD    bcBitCount;
   } BITMAPCOREHEADER;

BITMAPCOREINFO
   typedef struct _BITMAPCOREINFO {    // bmci
           BITMAPCOREHEADER  bmciHeader;
           RGBTRIPLE         bmciColors[1];
   } BITMAPCOREINFO;

BITMAPFILEHEADER
   typedef struct tagBITMAPFILEHEADER { // bmfh
           WORD    bfType;
           DWORD   bfSize;
           WORD    bfReserved1;
           WORD      ;
```

```
        DWORD   bfOffBits;
    } BITMAPFILEHEADER;

BITMAPINFO
    typedef struct tagBITMAPINFO { // bmi
        BITMAPINFOHEADER bmiHeader;
        RGBQUAD          bmiColors[1];
    } BITMAPINFO;

BITMAPINFOHEADER
    typedef struct tagBITMAPINFOHEADER{ // bmih
        DWORD  biSize;
        LONG   biWidth;
        LONG   biHeight;
        WORD   biPlanes;
        WORD   biBitCount
        DWORD  biCompression;
        DWORD  biSizeImage;
        LONG   biXPelsPerMeter;
        LONG   biYPelsPerMeter;
        DWORD  biClrUsed;
        DWORD  biClrImportant;
    } BITMAPINFOHEADER;

CHOOSECOLOR
    typedef struct {    // cc
         DWORD        lStructSize;
         HWND         hwndOwner;
         HWND         hInstance;
         COLORREF     rgbResult;
         COLORREF*    lpCustColors;
         DWORD        Flags;
         LPARAM       lCustData;
         LPCCHOOKPROC lpfnHook;
         LPCTSTR      lpTemplateName;
    } CHOOSECOLOR;

COLORADJUSTMENT
    typedef struct  tagCOLORADJUSTMENT {    /* ca */
         WORD  caSize;
         WORD  caFlags;
         WORD  caIlluminantIndex;
         WORD  caRedGamma;
         WORD  caGreenGamma;
         WORD  caBlueGamma;
```

```
        WORD  caReferenceBlack;
        WORD  caReferenceWhite;
        SHORT caContrast;
        SHORT caBrightness;
        SHORT caColorfulness;
        SHORT caRedGreenTint;
    } COLORADJUSTMENT;
```

CREATESTRUCT

```
    typedef struct tagCREATESTRUCT { // cs
        LPVOID    lpCreateParams;
        HINSTANCE hInstance;
        HMENU     hMenu;
        HWND      hwndParent;
        int       cy;
        int       cx;
        int       y;
        int       x;
        LONG      style;
        LPCTSTR   lpszName;
        LPCTSTR   lpszClass;
        DWORD     dwExStyle;
    } CREATESTRUCT;
```

DDBLTFX

```
    typedef struct _DDBLTFX{
        DWORD  dwSize;
        DWORD  dwDDFX;
        DWORD  dwROP;
        DWORD  dwDDROP;
        DWORD  dwRotationAngle;
        DWORD  dwZBufferOpCode;
        DWORD  dwZBufferLow;
        DWORD  dwZBufferHigh;
        DWORD  dwZBufferBaseDest;
        DWORD  dwZDestConstBitDepth;
    union
    {
            DWORD                dwZDestConst;
            LPDIRECTDRAWSURFACE  lpDDSZBufferDest;
    };
        DWORD   dwZSrcConstBitDepth;
    union
    {
            DWORD                dwZSrcConst;
```

```
            LPDIRECTDRAWSURFACE  lpDDSZBufferSrc;

    };
        DWORD  dwAlphaEdgeBlendBitDepth;
        DWORD  dwAlphaEdgeBlend;
        DWORD  dwReserved;
        DWORD  dwAlphaDestConstBitDepth;
    union
    {
            DWORD                k;
            LPDIRECTDRAWSURFACE  lpDDSAlphaDest;
    };
        DWORD  dwAlphaSrcConstBitDepth;
    union
    {
            DWORD                dwAlphaSrcConst;
            LPDIRECTDRAWSURFACE  lpDDSAlphaSrc;
    };
    union
    {
            DWORD                 dwFillColor;
            DWORD                 dwFillDepth;

            LPDIRECTDRAWSURFACE  lpDDSPattern;
    };
    DDCOLORKEY  ddckDestColorkey;
    DDCOLORKEY  ddckSrcColorkey;
    } DDBLTFX,FAR* LPDDBLTFX;

DDCAPS
    typedef struct _DDCAPS{
        DWORD    dwSize;
        DWORD    dwCaps;
        DWORD    dwCaps2;
        DWORD    dwCKeyCaps;
        DWORD    dwFXCaps;
        DWORD    dwFXAlphaCaps;
        DWORD    dwPalCaps;
        DWORD    dwSVCaps;
        DWORD    dwAlphaBltConstBitDepths;
        DWORD    dwAlphaBltPixelBitDepths;
        DWORD    dwAlphaBltSurfaceBitDepths;
        DWORD    dwAlphaOverlayConstBitDepths;
        DWORD    dwAlphaOverlayPixelBitDepths;
        DWORD    dwAlphaOverlaySurfaceBitDepths;
```

```
        DWORD    dwZBufferBitDepths;

        DWORD    dwVidMemTotal;
        DWORD    dwVidMemFree;
        DWORD    dwMaxVisibleOverlays;
        DWORD    dwCurrVisibleOverlays;
        DWORD    dwNumFourCCCodes;
        DWORD    dwAlignBoundarySrc;
        DWORD    dwAlignSizeSrc;
        DWORD    dwAlignBoundaryDest;
        DWORD    dwAlignSizeDest;
        DWORD    dwAlignStrideAlign;
        DWORD    dwRops[DD_ROP_SPACE];
        DDSCAPS  ddsCaps;
        DWORD    dwMinOverlayStretch;
        DWORD    dwMaxOverlayStretch;
        DWORD    dwMinLiveVideoStretch;

        DWORD    dwMaxLiveVideoStretch;
        DWORD    dwMinHwCodecStretch;
        DWORD    dwMaxHwCodecStretch;
        DWORD    dwReserved1;
        DWORD    dwReserved2;
        DWORD    dwReserved3;
        DWORD    dwSVBCaps;
        DWORD    dwSVBCKeyCaps;
        DWORD    dwSVBFXCaps;
        DWORD    dwSVBRops[DD_ROP_SPACE];
        DWORD    dwVSBCaps;
        DWORD    dwVSBCKeyCaps;
        DWORD    dwVSBFXCaps;
        DWORD    dwVSBRops[DD_ROP_SPACE];
        DWORD    dwSSBCaps;
        DWORD    dwSSBCKeyCaps;

        DWORD    dwSSBCFXCaps;
        DWORD    dwSSBRops[DD_ROP_SPACE];
        DWORD    dwReserved4;
        DWORD    dwReserved5;
        DWORD    dwReserved6;
    } DDCAPS,FAR* LPDDCAPS;

DDCOLORKEY
    typedef struct _DDCOLORKEY{
        DWORD  dwColorSpaceLowValue;
```

```
        DWORD  dwColorSpaceHighValue;
    } DDCOLORKEY,FAR* LPDDCOLORKEY;

DDPIXELFORMAT
    typedef struct _DDPIXELFORMAT{
        DWORD  dwSize;
        DWORD  dwFlags;
        DWORD  dwFourCC;
    union
    {
            DWORD  dwRGBBitCount;
            DWORD  dwYUVBitCount;
            DWORD  dwZBufferBitDepth;
            DWORD  dwAlphaBitDepth;
    };
    union
    {
            DWORD  dwRBitMask;
            DWORD  dwYBitMask;
    };
    union
    {
            DWORD  dwGBitMask;
            DWORD  dwUBitMask;
    };
    union
    {
            DWORD  dwBBitMask;
            DWORD  dwVBitMask;
    };
    union
    {
            DWORD  dwRGBAlphaBitMask;

            DWORD  dwYUVAlphaBitMask;
    };
    } DDPIXELFORMAT, FAR* LPDDPIXELFORMAT;


DDSCAPS2
    typedef struct _DDSCAPS2 {
        DWORD    dwCaps;   // Surface capabilities
        DWORD    dwCaps2;  // More surface capabilities
        DWORD    dwCaps3;  // Not currently used
        DWORD    dwCaps4;  // .
```

```
} DDSCAPS2, FAR* LPDDSCAPS2;
```

DDSURFACEDESC2

```
typedef struct _DDSURFACEDESC2 {
    DWORD         dwSize;
    DWORD         dwFlags;
    DWORD         dwHeight;
    DWORD         dwWidth;
    union
    {
        LONG      lPitch;
        DWORD     dwLinearSize;
    } DUMMYUNIONNAMEN(1);
    DWORD         dwBackBufferCount;
    union
    {
        DWORD     dwMipMapCount;
        DWORD     dwRefreshRate;
    } DUMMYUNIONNAMEN(2);
    DWORD         dwAlphaBitDepth;
    DWORD         dwReserved;
    LPVOID        lpSurface;
    DDCOLORKEY    ddckCKDestOverlay;
    DDCOLORKEY    ddckCKDestBlt;
    DDCOLORKEY    ddckCKSrcOverlay;
    DDCOLORKEY    ddckCKSrcBlt;
    DDPIXELFORMAT ddpfPixelFormat;
    DDSCAPS2      ddsCaps;
    DWORD         dwTextureStage;
} DDSURFACEDESC2, FAR* LPDDSURFACEDESC2;
```

DIBSECTION

```
typedef struct tagDIBSECTION {
    BITMAP              dsBm;
    BITMAPINFOHEADER    dsBmih;
    DWORD               dsBitfields[3];
    HANDLE              dshSection;
    DWORD               dsOffset;
} DIBSECTION;
```

DIDATAFORMAT

```
typedef struct {
    DWORD dwSize;
    DWORD dwObjSize;
```

```
        DWORD dwFlags;
        DWORD dwDataSize;
        DWORD dwNumObjs;
        LPDIOBJECTDATAFORMAT rgodf;
    } DIDATAFORMAT;

DIDEVCAPS
    typedef struct {
        DWORD dwSize;
        DWORD dwDevType;
        DWORD dwFlags;
        DWORD dwAxes;
        DWORD dwButtons;
        DWORD dwPOVs;
    } DIDEVCAPS;

DIDEVICEINSTANCE
    typedef struct {
        DWORD dwSize;
        GUID  guidInstance;
        GUID  guidProduct;
        DWORD dwDevType;
        TCHAR tszInstanceName[MAX_PATH];
        TCHAR tszProductName[MAX_PATH];
    } DIDEVICEINSTANCE;

DIDEVICEOBJECTDATA
    typedef struct {
        DWORD dwOfs;
        DWORD dwData;
        DWORD dwTimeStamp;
        DWORD dwSequence;
    } DIDEVICEOBJECTDATA;

DIJOYSTATE
    typedef struct DIJOYSTATE {
        LONG    lX;
        LONG    lY;
        LONG    lZ;
        LONG    lRx;
        LONG    lRy;
        LONG    lRz;
        LONG    rglSlider[2];
        DWORD   rgdwPOV[4];
        BYTE    rgbButtons[32];
```

```
   } DIJOYSTATE, *LPDIJOYSTATE;

DIJOYSTATE2
   typedef struct DIJOYSTATE2 {
       LONG    lX;
       LONG    lY;
       LONG    lZ;
       LONG    lRx;
       LONG    lRy;
       LONG    lRz;
       LONG    rglSlider[2];
       DWORD   rgdwPOV[4];
       BYTE    rgbButtons[128];
       LONG    lVX;
       LONG    lVY;
       LONG    lVZ;
       LONG    lVRx;
       LONG    lVRy;
       LONG    lVRz;
       LONG    rglVSlider[2];
       LONG    lAX;
       LONG    lAY;
       LONG    lAZ;
       LONG    lARx;
       LONG    lARy;
       LONG    lARz;
       LONG    rglASlider[2];
       LONG    lFX;
       LONG    lFY;
       LONG    lFZ;
       LONG    lFRx;
       LONG    lFRy;
       LONG    lFRz;
       LONG    rglFSlider[2];
   } DIJOYSTATE2, *LPDIJOYSTATE2;

DIMOUSESTATE
   typedef struct {
       LONG lX;
       LONG lY;
       LONG lZ;
       BYTE rgbButtons[4];
   } DIMOUSESTATE;

DIPROPDWORD
```

```
   typedef struct {
       DIPROPHEADER     diph;
       DWORD            dwData;
   } DIPROPDWORD;

DIPROPHEADER
   typedef struct {
       DWORD    dwSize;
       DWORD    dwHeaderSize;
       DWORD    dwObj;
       DWORD    dwHow;
   } DIPROPHEADER;

DIPROPRANGE
   typedef struct {
       DIPROPHEADER diph;
       LONG         lMin;
       LONG         lMax;
   } DIPROPRANGE;

   DISPLAY_DEVICE
   typedef struct _DISPLAY_DEVICE {
       DWORD  cb;
       WCHAR  DeviceName[32];
       WCHAR  DeviceString[128];
       DWORD  StateFlags;
   } DISPLAY_DEVICE, *PDISPLAY_DEVICE, *LPDISPLAY_DEVICE;

DSETUP_CB_UPGRADEINFO
   typedef struct _DSETUP_CB_UPGRADEINFO
   {
       DWORD UpgradeFlags;
   } DSETUP_CB_UPGRADEINFO;

LOGBRUSH
   typedef struct tag LOGBRUSH { /* lb */
      UINT     lbStyle;
      COLORREF lbColor;
      LONG     lbHatch;
   } LOGBRUSH;

LOGPEN
   typedef struct tagLOGPEN {  /* lgpn */
       UINT     lopnStyle;
       POINT    lopnWidth;
```

```
        COLORREF lopnColor;
    } LOGPEN;

LV_KEYDOWN
    typedef struct tagLV_KEYDOWN {
        NMHDR hdr;
        WORD wVKey;
        UINT flags;
    } LV_KEYDOWN;

MONITORINFO
    typedef struct tagMONITORINFO {
        DWORD  cbSize;
        RECT   rcMonitor;
        RECT   rcWork;
        DWORD  dwFlags;
    } MONITORINFO, *LPMONITORINFO;

MONITORINFOEX
    typedef struct tagMONITORINFOEX {
        DWORD  cbSize;
        RECT   rcMonitor;
        RECT   rcWork;
        DWORD  dwFlags;
        TCHAR  szDevice[CCHDEVICENAME]
    } MONITORINFOEX, *LPMONITORINFOEX;

MSG
    typedef struct tagMSG {     // msg
        HWND   hwnd;
        UINT   message;
        WPARAM wParam;
        LPARAM lParam;
        DWORD  time;
        POINT  pt;
    } MSG;

NMHDR
    typedef struct tagNMHDR {
        HWND hwndFrom;
        UINT idFrom;
        UINT code;
    } NMHDR;

PAINTSTRUCT
```

```
typedef struct tagPAINTSTRUCT { // ps
    HDC  hdc;
    BOOL fErase;
    RECT rcPaint;
    BOOL fRestore;
    BOOL fIncUpdate;
    BYTE rgbReserved[32];
} PAINTSTRUCT;
```

POINT

```
typedef struct tagPOINT {
   LONG x;
   LONG y;
} POINT;
```

RECT

```
typedef struct tagRECT {
   LONG left;
   LONG top;
   LONG right;
   LONG bottom;
} RECT;
```

RGBQUAD

```
typedef struct tagRGBQUAD { // rgbq
    BYTE    rgbBlue;
    BYTE    rgbGreen;
    BYTE    rgbRed;
    BYTE    rgbReserved;
} RGBQUAD;
```

RGBTRIPLE

```
typedef struct tagRGBTRIPLE { // rgbt
    BYTE rgbtBlue;
    BYTE rgbtGreen;
    BYTE rgbtRed;
} RGBTRIPLE;
```

RGNDATA

```
typedef struct _RGNDATA { /* rgnd */
    RGNDATAHEADER rdh;
    char          Buffer[1];
} RGNDATA;
```

```
RGNDATAHEADER
   typedef struct _RGNDATAHEADER { // rgndh
       DWORD dwSize;
       DWORD iType;
       DWORD nCount;
       DWORD nRgnSize;
       RECT  rcBound;
   } RGNDATAHEADER;

SCROLLINFO
   typedef struct tagSCROLLINFO {  // si
       UINT cbSize;
       UINT fMask;
       int  nMin;
       int  nMax;
       UINT nPage;
       int  nPos;
       int  nTrackPos;
   }   SCROLLINFO;
   typedef SCROLLINFO FAR *LPSCROLLINFO;

SIZE
   typedef struct tagSIZE {
       int cx;
       int cy;
   } SIZE;

TBBUTTON
   typedef struct _TBBUTTON { \\ tbb
       int iBitmap;
       int idCommand;
       BYTE fsState;
       BYTE fsStyle;
       DWORD dwData;
       int iString;
   } TBBUTTON, NEAR* PTBBUTTON, FAR* LPTBBUTTON;
   typedef const TBBUTTON FAR* LPCTBBUTTON;

TEXTMETRICS
   typedef struct tagTEXTMETRIC {  /* tm */
       int  tmHeight;
       int  tmAscent;
       int  tmDescent;
       int  tmInternalLeading;
       int  tmExternalLeading;
```

```
        int  tmAveCharWidth;
        int  tmMaxCharWidth;
        int  tmWeight;
        BYTE tmItalic;
        BYTE tmUnderlined;
        BYTE tmStruckOut;
        BYTE tmFirstChar;
        BYTE tmLastChar;
        BYTE tmDefaultChar;
        BYTE tmBreakChar;
        BYTE tmPitchAndFamily;
        BYTE tmCharSet;
        int  tmOverhang;
        int  tmDigitizedAspectX;
        int  tmDigitizedAspectY;
    } TEXTMETRIC;

TOOLINFO
    typedef struct {  // ti
        UINT      cbSize;
        UINT      uFlags;
        HWND      hwnd;
        UINT      uId;
        RECT      rect;
        HINSTANCE hinst;
        LPTSTR     lpszText;
    } TOOLINFO, NEAR *PTOOLINFO, FAR *LPTOOLINFO;

WNDCLASSEX
    typedef struct _WNDCLASSEX {     // wc
        UINT    cbSize;
        UINT    style;
        WNDPROC lpfnWndProc;
        int     cbClsExtra;
        int     cbWndExtra;
        HANDLE  hInstance;
        HICON   hIcon;
        HCURSOR hCursor;
        HBRUSH  hbrBackground;
        LPCTSTR lpszMenuName;
        LPCTSTR lpszClassName;
        HICON   hIconSm;
    } WNDCLASSEX;
```

Appendix B

Ternary Raster Operation Codes

This appendix describes the ternary raster-operation codes used by the `BitBlt`, `PatBlt`, and `StretchBlt` functions. These codes determine how the GDI combines the bits in a source bitmap with the bits in the destination bitmap, taking into account a pattern determined by the brush currently selected in the device context.

The following abbreviations are used for the ternary operands and the Boolean functions:

D = destination bitmap

P = pattern (determined by current brush)

S = Source bitmap

& = bitwise AND

~ = bitwise NOT (inverse)

| = bitwise OR

^ = bitwise exclusive OR (XOR)

The most commonly used raster operations have been given special names in the Windows include file, *windows.h*. The symbolic names are also listed in Table 8-1. You should use these names whenever possible in your applications. The following table, taken from Developer Studio help files, lists all 256 ternary raster operations.

Raster Operation	ROP Code	Boolean Operation	Common Name
00	00000042	0	BLACKNESS
01	00010289	~(P|S|D)	-
02	00020C89	~(P|S)&D	-
03	000300AA	~(P|S)	-

Continued

<table>
<tr><th>Raster Operation</th><th>ROP Code</th><th>Boolean Operation</th><th>Common Name</th></tr>
<tr><td>04</td><td>00040C88</td><td>~(P|D)&S</td><td>-</td></tr>
<tr><td>05</td><td>000500A9</td><td>~(P|D)</td><td>-</td></tr>
<tr><td>06</td><td>00060865</td><td>~(|P~(S^D))</td><td>-</td></tr>
<tr><td>07</td><td>000702C5</td><td>~(P|(S&D))</td><td>-</td></tr>
<tr><td>08</td><td>00080F08</td><td>~P&S&D</td><td>-</td></tr>
<tr><td>09</td><td>00090245</td><td>~(P|(S^D))</td><td>-</td></tr>
<tr><td>0A</td><td>000A0329</td><td>~P&D</td><td>-</td></tr>
<tr><td>0B</td><td>000B0B2A</td><td>~P(|(S&~D))</td><td>-</td></tr>
<tr><td>0C</td><td>000C0324</td><td>~P&S</td><td>-</td></tr>
<tr><td>0D</td><td>000D0B25</td><td>~P|(~S&D))</td><td>-</td></tr>
<tr><td>0E</td><td>000E08A5</td><td>~P|~(S|D)</td><td>-</td></tr>
<tr><td>0F</td><td>000F0001</td><td>~P</td><td>-</td></tr>
<tr><td>10</td><td>00100C85</td><td>P&~(S|D)</td><td>-</td></tr>
<tr><td>11</td><td>001100A6</td><td>~(S|D)</td><td>NOTSRCERASE</td></tr>
<tr><td>12</td><td>00120868</td><td>~(S|~(P^D))</td><td>-</td></tr>
<tr><td>13</td><td>001302C8</td><td>~(S|(P&D))</td><td>-</td></tr>
<tr><td>14</td><td>00140869</td><td>~(D|~(P^S))</td><td>-</td></tr>
<tr><td>15</td><td>001502C9</td><td>~(D|(P&S))</td><td>-</td></tr>
<tr><td>16</td><td>00165CCA</td><td>P^(S^(D&~(P&S)))</td><td>-</td></tr>
<tr><td>17</td><td>00171D54</td><td>~(S^((S^P)&(S^D)))</td><td>-</td></tr>
<tr><td>18</td><td>00180D59</td><td>(P^S)&(P^D)</td><td>-</td></tr>
<tr><td>19</td><td>00191CC8</td><td>~(S^D&~(P&S)))</td><td>-</td></tr>
<tr><td>1A</td><td>001A06C5</td><td>P^(D|(S&P))</td><td>-</td></tr>
<tr><td>1B</td><td>001B0768</td><td>~(S^(D&(P^S)))</td><td>-</td></tr>
<tr><td>1C</td><td>001C06CA</td><td>P^(S|(P&D))</td><td>-</td></tr>
<tr><td>1D</td><td>001D0766</td><td>~(D^(S&(P^D)))</td><td>-</td></tr>
<tr><td>1E</td><td>001E01A5</td><td>P^(S|D)</td><td>-</td></tr>
</table>

<table>
<tr><th>Raster Operation</th><th>ROP Code</th><th>Boolean Operation</th><th>Common Name</th></tr>
<tr><td>1F</td><td>001F0385</td><td>~(P&(S|D))</td><td>-</td></tr>
<tr><td>20</td><td>00200F09</td><td>P&~S&D</td><td>-</td></tr>
<tr><td>21</td><td>00210248</td><td>~(S|(P^D))</td><td>-</td></tr>
<tr><td>22</td><td>00220326</td><td>~S&D</td><td>-</td></tr>
<tr><td>23</td><td>00230B24</td><td>~(S|(P&~D))</td><td>-</td></tr>
<tr><td>24</td><td>00240D55</td><td>(S^P)&(S^D)</td><td>-</td></tr>
<tr><td>25</td><td>00251CC5</td><td>~(P^(D&~(S&P)))</td><td>-</td></tr>
<tr><td>26</td><td>002606C8</td><td>S^(D|((P&S))</td><td>-</td></tr>
<tr><td>27</td><td>00271868</td><td>S^(D|~(P^S))</td><td>-</td></tr>
<tr><td>28</td><td>00280369</td><td>D&(P^S)</td><td>-</td></tr>
<tr><td>29</td><td>002916CA</td><td>~(P^(S^(D|(P&S))))</td><td>-</td></tr>
<tr><td>2A</td><td>002A0CC9</td><td>D&~(P&S)</td><td>-</td></tr>
<tr><td>2B</td><td>002B1D58</td><td>~(S^((S^P)&(P&D)))</td><td>-</td></tr>
<tr><td>2C</td><td>002C0784</td><td>S^(P&(S|D))</td><td>-</td></tr>
<tr><td>2D</td><td>002D060A</td><td>P^(S|~D)</td><td>-</td></tr>
<tr><td>2E</td><td>002E064A</td><td>P^(S|(P^D))</td><td>-</td></tr>
<tr><td>2F</td><td>002F0E2A</td><td>~(P&(S|~D))</td><td>-</td></tr>
<tr><td>30</td><td>0030032A</td><td>P&~S</td><td>-</td></tr>
<tr><td>31</td><td>00310B28</td><td>~(S|(~P&D))</td><td>-</td></tr>
<tr><td>32</td><td>00320688</td><td>S^(P|S|D)</td><td>-</td></tr>
<tr><td>33</td><td>00330008</td><td>~S</td><td>NOTSRCCOPY</td></tr>
<tr><td>34</td><td>003406C4</td><td>S^(P|(S&D))</td><td>-</td></tr>
<tr><td>35</td><td>00351864</td><td>S^(P|~(S^D))</td><td>-</td></tr>
<tr><td>36</td><td>003601A8</td><td>S^(P|D)</td><td>-</td></tr>
<tr><td>37</td><td>00370388</td><td>~(S&(P|D))</td><td>-</td></tr>
<tr><td>38</td><td>0038078A</td><td>P^(S&(P|D))</td><td>-</td></tr>
</table>

Continued

Raster Operation	ROP Code	Boolean Operation	Common Name
39	00390604	S^(P|~D)	-
3A	003A0644	S^(P^(S^D))	-
3B	003B0E24	~(S&(P|~D))	-
3C	003C004A	P^S	-
3D	003D18A4	S^(P|~(S|D))	-
3E	003E1B24	S^(P|(~S&D))	-
3F	003F00EA	~(P&S)	-
40	00400F0A	P&S&~D	-
41	00410249	~(D|(P^S))	-
42	00420D5D	(S^D)&(P^D)	-
43	00431CC4	~(S^(P&~(S&D)))	-
44	00440328	S&~D	SRCERASE
45	00450B29	~(D|(P&~S))	-
46	004606C6	D^(S|(P&D))	-
47	0047076A	~(P^(S&((P^D)))	-
48	00480368	S&(P^D)	-
49	004916C5	~(P^(D^(S|(P&D))))	-
4A	004A0789	D^(P&(S|D)	-
4B	004B0605	P^(~S|D)	-
4C	004C0CC8	S&~(P&D)	-
4D	004D1954	~(S^((P^S)|(S^D)))	-
4E	004E0645	P^(D|(P^S))	-
4F	004F0E25	~(P&(~S|D))	-
50	00500325	P&~D	-
51	00510B26	~(D|(~P&S))	-
52	005206C9	D^(P|(S&D))	-
53	00530764	~(S^(P&(S^D)))	-

Raster Operation	ROP Code	Boolean Operation	Common Name
54	005408A9	~(D|~(P|S))	-
55	00550009	~D	DSTINVERT
56	005601A9	D^(P|S)	-
57	00570389	~(D&(P|S))	-
58	00580785	P^(D&(P|S))	-
59	00590609	D^(P|~S)	-
5A	005A0049	P^D	PATINVERT
5B	005B18A9	D^(P|~(S|D))	-
5C	005C0649	D^(P|(S^D))	-
5D	005D0E29	~(D&(P|~S))	-
5E	005E1B29	D^(P|(S&~D))	-
5F	005F00E9	~(P&D)	-
60	00600365	P&(S^D)	-
61	006116C6	~(D^(S^(P|(S&D))))	-
62	00620786	D^(S&(P|D))	-
63	00630608	S^(~P|D)	-
64	00640788	S^(D&(P|S))	-
65	00650606	D^(~P|S)	-
66	00660046	S^D	SRCINVERT
67	006718A8	S^(D|~(P|S))	-
68	006858A6	~(D^(S^(P|~(S|D))))	-
69	00690145	~(P^(S^D))	-
6A	006A01E9	D^(P&S)	-
6B	006B178A	~(P^(S^(D&(S|P))))	-
6C	006C01E8	S^(P&D)	-
6D	006D1785	~(P^(D^(S&(P|D))))	-

Continued

Raster Operation	ROP Code	Boolean Operation	Common Name
6E	006E1E28	S^(D&(P|~S))	-
6F	006F0C65	~(P&~(S^D))	-
70	00700CC5	P&~(S&D)	-
71	00711D5C	~(S^((S^D)&(P^D)))	-
72	00720648	S^(D|(P^S))	-
73	00730E28	~(S&(~P|D))	-
74	00740646	D^(S|(P^D))	-
75	00750E26	~(D&(~P|S))	-
76	00761B28	S^(D|(P&~S))	-
77	007700E6	~(S&D)	-
78	007801E5	P^(S&D)	-
79	00791786	~(D^(S^(P&(S|D))))	-
7A	007A1E29	D^(P&(S|~D))	-
7B	007B0C68	~(S&~(P^D))	-
7C	007C1E24	S^(P&(~S|D))	-
7D	007D0C69	~(D&~(S^P))	-
7E	007E0955	(P^S)|(S^D)	-
7F	007F03C9	~(P&S&D)	-
80	008003E9	P&S&D	-
81	00810975	~((P^S)|(S^D))	-
82	00820C49	~(P^S)&D	-
83	00831E04	~(S^(P&(~S|D)))	-
84	00840C48	S&~(P^D)	-
85	00851E05	~(P^(D&(~P|S)))	-
86	008617A6	D^(S^(P&(S|D)))	-
87	008701C5	~(P^(S&D))	-
88	008800C6	S&D	SRCAND

Raster Operation	ROP Code	Boolean Operation	Common Name
89	00891B08	~(S^(D|(P&~S)))	-
8A	008A0E06	(~P|S)&D	-
8B	008B0666	~(D^(S|(P^D)))	-
8C	008C0E08	S&(~P|D)	-
8D	008D0668	~S(^(D|(P^S)))	-
8E	008E1D7C	S^((S^D)&(P^D))	-
8F	008F0CE5	~(P&~(S&D))	-
90	00900C45	P&~(S^D)	-
91	00911E08	~(S^(D&(P|~S)))	-
92	009217A9	D^(P^(S&(P|D)))	-
93	009301C4	~(S^(P&D))	-
94	009417AA	P^(S^(D&(P|S)))	-
95	009501C9	~(D^(P&S))	-
96	00960169	P^S^D	-
97	0097588A	P^(S^(D|~P|S)))	-
98	00981888	~(S^(D|~(P|S)))	-
99	00990066	~(S^D)	-
9A	009A0709	(P&~S)^D	-
9B	009B07A8	~(S^(D&(P|S)))	-
9C	009C0704	S^(P&~D)	-
9D	009D07A6	~(D^(S&(P|D)))	-
9E	009E16E6	(S^(P|(S&D)))^D	-
9F	009F0345	~(P&(S^D))	-
A0	00A000C9	P&D	-
A1	00A11B05	~(P^(D|(~P&S)))	-
A2	00A20E09	(P|~S)&D	-

Continued

Raster Operation	ROP Code	Boolean Operation	Common Name
A3	00A30669	~(D^(P|(S^D)))	-
A4	00A41885	~(P^(D|~(P|S)))	-
A5	00A50065	~(P^D)	-
A6	00A60706	(~P&S)^D	-
A7	00A707A5	~(P^(D&(P|S)))	-
A8	00A803A9	(P|S)&D	-
A9	00A90189	~((P|S)^D)	-
AA	00AA0029	D	-
AB	00AB0889	~(P|S)|D	-
AC	00AC0744	S^(P&(S^D))	-
AD	00AD06E9	~(D^(P|(S&D)))	-
AE	00AE0B06	(~P&S)|D	-
AF	00AF0229	~P|D	-
B0	00B00E05	P&(~S|D)	-
B1	00B10665	~(P^(D|(P^S)))	-
B2	00B21974	S^((P^S)|(S^D))	-
B3	00B30CE8	~(S&~(P&D))	-
B4	00B4070A	P^(S&~D)	-
B5	00B507A9	~(D^(P&(S|D)))	-
B6	00B616E9	D^(P^(D|(P&D)))	-
B7	00B70348	~(S&(P^D))	-
B8	00B8074A	P^(S&(P^D))	-
B9	00B906E6	~(D^(S|(P&D)))	-
BA	00BA0B09	(P&~S)|D	-
BB	00BB0226	~S|D	MERGEPAINT
BC	00BC1CE4	S^(P&~(S&D))	-
BD	00BD0D7D	~((P^D)&(S^D))	-

Raster Operation	ROP Code	Boolean Operation	Common Name
BE	00BE0269	(P^S)|D	-
BF	00BF08C9	~(P&S)|D	-
C0	00C000CA	P&S	MERGECOPY
C1	00C11B04	~(S^(P|(~S&D)))	-
C2	00C21884	~(S^(P|~(S|D)))	-
C3	00C3006A	~(P^S)	-
C4	00C40E04	S&(P|~D)	-
C5	00C50664	~(S^(P|(S^D)))	-
C6	00C60708	S^(~P&D)	-
C7	00C707AA	~(P^(S&(P|D)))	-
C8	00C803A8	S&(P|D)	-
C9	00C90184	~(S^(P|D))	-
CA	00CA0749	D^(P&(S^D))	-
CB	00CB06E4	~(S^(P|(S&D)))	-
CC	00CC0020	S	SRCCOPY
CD	00CD0888	S|~(P|D)	-
CE	00CE0B08	S|(~P&D)	-
CF	00CF0224	S|~P	-
D0	00D00E0A	~(^(S|(P^D)))	-
D1	00D1066A	P^(~S&D)	-
D2	00D20705	~(S^(P&(S|D)))	-
D3	00D307A4	S^((P^S)&(P^D))	-
D4	00D41D78	(~(D&~(P&S))	-
D5	00D50CE9	P^(S^(D|(P&S)))	-
D6	00D616EA	~(D&(P^S))	-
D7	00D70349	~(D&(P&S))	-

Continued

<table>
<tr><th>Raster Operation</th><th>ROP Code</th><th>Boolean Operation</th><th>Common Name</th></tr>
<tr><td>D8</td><td>00D80745</td><td>P^(D&(P^S))</td><td>-</td></tr>
<tr><td>D9</td><td>00D906E8</td><td>~(S^(D|(P&S)))</td><td>-</td></tr>
<tr><td>DA</td><td>00DA1CE9</td><td>D^(P&~(S&D))</td><td>-</td></tr>
<tr><td>DB</td><td>00DB0D75</td><td>~((P^S)&(S^D))</td><td>-</td></tr>
<tr><td>DC</td><td>00DC0B04</td><td>S|(P&~D)</td><td>-</td></tr>
<tr><td>DD</td><td>00DD0228</td><td>S|~D</td><td>-</td></tr>
<tr><td>DE</td><td>00DE0268</td><td>S|(P^D)</td><td>-</td></tr>
<tr><td>DF</td><td>00DF08C8</td><td>S|~(P&D)</td><td>-</td></tr>
<tr><td>E0</td><td>00E003A5</td><td>P&(D|S)</td><td>-</td></tr>
<tr><td>E1</td><td>00E10185</td><td>~(P^(S|D))</td><td>-</td></tr>
<tr><td>E2</td><td>00E20746</td><td>D^(S&(P^D))</td><td>-</td></tr>
<tr><td>E3</td><td>00E306EA</td><td>~(P^(S|(P&D)))</td><td>-</td></tr>
<tr><td>E4</td><td>00E40748</td><td>S^(D&(P^S))</td><td>-</td></tr>
<tr><td>E5</td><td>00E506E5</td><td>~(P^(D|(P&S)))</td><td>-</td></tr>
<tr><td>E6</td><td>00E61CE8</td><td>S^(D&~(P&S))</td><td>-</td></tr>
<tr><td>E7</td><td>00E70D79</td><td>~((P^S)&(P^D))</td><td>-</td></tr>
<tr><td>E8</td><td>00E81D74</td><td>S^((P^S)&*S^D))</td><td>-</td></tr>
<tr><td>E9</td><td>00E95CE6</td><td>~(D^(S^(P&~(S&D))))</td><td>-</td></tr>
<tr><td>EA</td><td>00EA02E9</td><td>(P&S)|D</td><td>-</td></tr>
<tr><td>EB</td><td>00EB0849</td><td>~(P^S)|D</td><td>-</td></tr>
<tr><td>EC</td><td>00EC02E8</td><td>S|(P&D)</td><td>-</td></tr>
<tr><td>ED</td><td>00ED0848</td><td>S|(~(P^D)</td><td>-</td></tr>
<tr><td>EE</td><td>00EE0086</td><td>S|D</td><td>SRCPAINT</td></tr>
<tr><td>EF</td><td>00EF0A08</td><td>~P|S|D</td><td>-</td></tr>
<tr><td>F0</td><td>00F00021</td><td>P</td><td>PATCOPY</td></tr>
<tr><td>F1</td><td>00F10885</td><td>P|(~(S|D)</td><td>-</td></tr>
<tr><td>F2</td><td>00F20B05</td><td>P|(~S&D)</td><td>-</td></tr>
</table>

Raster Operation	ROP Code	Boolean Operation	Common Name
F3	00F3022A	P|~S	-
F4	00F40B0A	P|(S&~D)	-
F5	00F50225	P|~D	-
F6	00F60265	P|(S^D)	-
F7	00F708C5	P|(~(S&D)	-
F8	00F802E5	P|(S&D)	-
F9	00F90845	P|~(S^D)	-
FA	00FA0089	P|D	-
FB	00FB0A09	P|~S|D	PATPAINT
FC	00FC008A	P|S	-
FD	00FD0A0A	P|S|~D	-
FE	00FE02A9	P|S|D	-
FF	00FF0062	1	WHITENESS

Appendix C

What's on the CD-ROM

This appendix describes the software contained in the book's CD-ROM. The software is located in two main-level folders:

- **WGP CODE** contains the book's sample programs and programming templates.
- **Dx6SDK** contains Micrsofts's DirectX 6.1 Software Development Kit.

Installation

No installation utility is provided for the sample programs contained in the WGP CODE folder. You can use Windows Explorer to copy the WGP CODE folder and all its subfolders to your hard drive, or to copy the individual chapter folders as needed.

Installation of the DirectX 6.1 Software Development Kit is done by the Setup program provided by Microsoft. To install the SDK, perform the following steps:

- Log on to the Dx6SDK directory on the book's CD-ROM.
- Double-click the icon for the Setup application program.
- Follow the instructions provided by the Setup program.

Sample Code Folder

The WGP CODE folder contains all the programs and projects discussed in the text. The project files are compatible with Microsoft Visual C++ version 5 and 6. The samples, project files, and templates are contained in subfolders with the chapter names in which they are first mentioned. The subfolders and their contents are as follows:

Chapter 02

Templates

Chapter 03

Do Nothing Demo

Hello Windows

Chapter 04

Private DC Demo

Text Demo No 1

Text Demo No 2

Text Demo No 3

Menu Demo

Keyboard Demo

Caret Demo

Chapter 05

Mouse Demo

Child Window Demo

Controls Demo

Dialog Box Demo

Resources

Toolbar Demo No 1

Toolbar Demo No 2

Tooltip Demo

Chapter 06

DC Info Demo

Pixel and Line Demo

Chapter 07

Filled Figure Demo

Chapter 08

Bitmap Demo

Chapter 09

DD Info Demo

Chapter 10

DD Template

DD Access Demo

Chapter 11

DD Bmap Demo

DD Template2

DD InWin Demo

Chapter 12

DD Animation Demo

DD Panning Demo

DD Zoom Demo

DD Sprite Demo

Chapter 13

DX Setup Demo

Chapter 14

DI Mouse Demo

Chapter 15

MM Info Demo

MM Sprite Demo

Index

B

C

D

M

Q

R

S

continued

T

continued

X

Y

Z

IDG BOOKS WORLDWIDE, INC.
END-USER LICENSE AGREEMENT

4. Restrictions on Use of Individual Programs. You must follow the individual requirements and restrictions detailed for each individual program in Appendix C of this Book. These limitations are also contained in the individual license agreements recorded on the Software Media. These limitations may include a requirement that after using the program for a specified period of time, the user must pay a registration fee or discontinue use. By opening the Software packet(s), you will be agreeing to abide by the licenses and restrictions for these individual programs that are detailed in Appendix Cand on the Software Media. None of the material on this Software Media or listed in this Book may ever be redistributed, in original or modified form, for commercial purposes.

5. Limited Warranty.

(a) IDGB warrants that the Software and Software Media are free from defects in materials and workmanship under normal use for a period of sixty (60) days from the date of purchase of this Book. If IDGB receives notification within the warranty period of defects in materials or workmanship, IDGB will replace the defective Software Media.

(b) IDGB AND THE AUTHORS OF THE BOOK DISCLAIM ALL OTHER WARRANTIES, EXPRESS OR IMPLIED, INCLUDING WITHOUT LIMITATION IMPLIED WARRANTIES OF MERCHANTABILITY AND FITNESS FOR A PARTICULAR PURPOSE, WITH RESPECT TO THE SOFTWARE, THE PROGRAMS, THE SOURCE CODE CONTAINED THEREIN, AND/OR THE TECHNIQUES DESCRIBED IN THIS BOOK. IDGB DOES NOT WARRANT THAT THE FUNCTIONS CONTAINED IN THE SOFTWARE WILL MEET YOUR REQUIREMENTS OR THAT THE OPERATION OF THE SOFTWARE WILL BE ERROR FREE.

(c) This limited warranty gives you specific legal rights, and you may have other rights that vary from jurisdiction to jurisdiction.

6. Remedies.

(a) IDGB's entire liability and your exclusive remedy for defects in materials and workmanship shall be limited to replacement of the Software Media, which may be returned to IDGB with a copy of your receipt at the following address: Software Media Fulfillment Department, Attn.: *Windows Graphics Programming*, IDG Books Worldwide, Inc., 7260 Shadeland Station, Ste. 100, Indianapolis, IN 46256, or call 1-800-762-2974. Please allow three to four weeks for delivery. This Limited Warranty is void if failure of the Software Media has resulted from accident, abuse, or misapplication. Any replacement Software Media will be warranted for the remainder of the original warranty period or thirty (30) days, whichever is longer.

(b) In no event shall IDGB or the authors be liable for any damages whatsoever (including without limitation damages for loss of business profits, business interruption, loss of business information, or any other pecuniary loss) arising from the use of or inability to use the Book or the Software, even if IDGB has been advised of the possibility of such damages.

(c) Because some jurisdictions do not allow the exclusion or limitation of liability for consequential or incidental damages, the above limitation or exclusion may not apply to you.

7. U.S. Government Restricted Rights. Use, duplication, or disclosure of the Software by the U.S. Government is subject to restrictions stated in paragraph (c)(1)(ii) of the Rights in Technical Data and Computer Software clause of DFARS 252.227-7013, and in subparagraphs (a) through (d) of the Commercial Computer – Restricted Rights clause at FAR 52.227-19, and in similar clauses in the NASA FAR supplement, when applicable.

8. General. This Agreement constitutes the entire understanding of the parties and revokes and supersedes all prior agreements, oral or written, between them and may not be modified or amended except in a writing signed by both parties hereto that specifically refers to this Agreement. This Agreement shall take precedence over any other documents that may be in conflict herewith. If any one or more provisions contained in this Agreement are held by any court or tribunal to be invalid, illegal, or otherwise unenforceable, each and every other provision shall remain in full force and effect.

CD-ROM Installation Instructions

The CD-ROM that accompanies this book contains the Microsoft DirectX 6.1 SDK as well as complete code examples from the book. For specific instructions on installing the SDK and the code examples, see Appendix C.

Microsoft Product Warranty and Support Disclaimer

The Microsoft program was reproduced by IDG Books Worldwide, Inc. under a special arrangement with Microsoft Corporation. For this reason, IDG Books Worldwide, Inc. is responsible for the product warranty and for support. If your CD-ROM is defective, please return it to IDG Books Worldwide, Inc. which will arrange for its replacement. PLEASE DO NOT RETURN IT TO MICROSOFT CORPORATION. Any product support will be provided, if at all, by IDG Books Worldwide, Inc. PLEASE DO NOT CONTACT MICROSOFT CORPORATION FOR PRODUCT SUPPORT. End users of this Microsoft program shall not be considered "registered owners" of a Microsoft product and therefore shall not be eligible for upgrades, promotions or other benefits available to "registered owners" of Microsoft products.